ROTE-METO COMPARATIVE DICTIONARY

ROTE-METO COMPARATIVE DICTIONARY

OWEN EDWARDS

PRESS

ASIA-PACIFIC LINGUISTICS

Published by ANU Press
The Australian National University
Acton ACT 2601, Australia
Email: anupress@anu.edu.au

Available to download for free at press.anu.edu.au

A catalogue record for this book is available from the National Library of Australia

ISBN (print): 9781760464561
ISBN (online): 9781760464578

WorldCat (print): 1268571904
WorldCat (online): 1268255637

DOI: 10.22459/RMCD.2021

Cover design and layout by ANU Press. Cover photograph by Kirsten Culhane.

Contents

Acknowledgements	vii
Abbreviations and symbols	ix
Speech varieties listed in the dictionary	xi
1. Introduction	1
1.1 Purpose	1
1.2 Limitations	1
1.3 Data sources	3
1.3.1 Rote	3
1.3.2 Meto	5
1.3.3 Other languages	7
1.4 Transcription	8
1.4.1 Jonker's transcription	8
1.4.2 Middelkoop's transcription	13
1.5 Structure of the dictionary	15
1.5.1 Out-comparisons	17
1.5.2 Multiple reflexes	18
1.5.3 Fields/parts of entries	20
1.5.4 Loan distributions	27
1.5.5 Finder lists	27
2. Language background	29
2.1 Introduction	29
2.2 Rote	30
2.3 Meto	32
2.4 Segmental phonologies	34
2.4.1 Rote	34
2.4.2 Meto	36
2.5 Meto morphophonemic processes	37
2.5.1 Metathesis	37
2.5.2 Consonant insertion	38
2.5.3 Diphthongisation and vowel assimilation	39

2.6 Morphology 40
2.6.1 Nominal suffix *-k/-ʔ* 41
2.6.2 Possessive morphology 42
2.6.3 Reduplication 43
2.6.4 Nominalisation 44
2.6.5 Verb agreement 45
2.6.6 Derivational verbal morphology 47
3. Historical background 49
3.1 Introduction 49
3.2 Sound correspondences 49
3.2.1 Initial and medial consonants 50
3.2.2 Final consonants 55
3.2.3 Vowels 55
3.3 Internal sub-grouping 57
3.3.1 Nuclear Rote (NRote) 61
3.3.2 Central East Rote and Meto (CERM) 62
3.3.3 West Rote-Meto (WRM) 64
3.3.4 Meto 64
3.4 Levels of reconstruction 69
3.5 Rote-Meto within Malayo-Polynesian 72
3.5.1 Sound changes between PMP and PRM 72
3.5.2 Sound change and language shift 74
3.5.3 Subgrouping within Malayo-Polynesian 76
4. Rote-Meto – English 87
5. English – Rote-Meto 405
6. Proto-Malayo-Polynesian – Proto-Rote-Meto 429
References 441

Acknowledgements

While this comparative dictionary is collated by only one author, much of the data was collected by many others.

I would like to thank all those who generously shared their unpublished lexical databases, listed in alphabetical order by surname of first author (see §1.3 for more information): Misriani Balle and Stuart Cameron (Helong); John Christensen (Kisar); João Cristo Rei and Mark Donohue (Galolen); Kirsten Culhane, Laurence Jumetan, and Yedida Ora (Amfo'an); James Fox (Termanu ritual language); Charles E. Grimes, Evelyn Cheng, Enna Adelaide Hayer-Pah, Jonathan Pandie, Neng Mulosing, and Johnny M. Banamtuan (Tii), Yustin Nako, Paulus Nako, Misriani Balle, and Johnny M. Banamtuan (Rikou), Thersia Tamelan (Dela), Catharina Williams-van Klinken (Fehan Tetun); as well as Albert Zacharias, Adika Getroida Balukh, Misriani Balle, and Johnny M. Banamtuan (Lole).

I would also like to thank my many consultants who provided me with data from their languages. It is with great regret that I do not have enough space to list all those who have generously shared knowledge of their languages. Nonetheless, I must mention the following people: Dominggus Atimeta (Timaus), Heronimus Bani (Kotos Amarasi), Toni Buraen and family (Ro'is Amarasi), Yulius Iu (Landu), Melianus Obhetan and family (Ro'is Amarasi), Yedida Ora (Kotos Amarasi), Pieter Sijoen (Oepao), Ferdis Tasae (Funai Helong), and Manuel Un Bria, Emerentiana Uduk, and Aloyisus Nurak (all Kusa-Manea).

I would further like to thank several scholars who have contributed in various ways.

Tom Hoogervorst consulted an earlier version of this dictionary and identified many forms that are ultimately loans. Malcolm Ross also read an earlier version of this dictionary and identified a number of forms that are inherited from a higher node, as well as a few connections between Proto-Rote-Meto reconstructions and Proto-Oceanic.

Antoinette Schapper first invited me to present on Rote-Meto at the international workshop on language contact and substrate in the languages of Wallacea and thus gave me the impetus to launch this project. She also suggested that the work be structured around Proto-Rote-Meto reconstructions with a clearer demarcation between Rote-Meto forms and out-comparisons. This has greatly improved the clarity of the work compared to early drafts.

Marian Klamer provided me with the job during which much data was added to this dictionary and many revisions were carried out. I am happy to say that this publication was supported by the VICI research project 'Reconstructing the past through languages of the present: the Lesser Sunda Islands', funded by the Netherlands Organisation for Scientific Research, project number 277-70-012.

Mark Donohue has greatly influenced my thinking on the history of Austronesian languages. He also invited me to the workshop in Kupang in July 2012 where I first encountered the languages and people of Timor.

I also need to thank Charles Grimes. Apart from his constant encouragement and support, I'm sure that this is a project that Chuck would have loved to have worked on himself, in some form or another. I am humbled by his generosity in allowing me to do this work.

Finally, the deficiencies that undoubtedly remain in this work are entirely my own responsibility and none of the people mentioned in these acknowledgements are responsible for them.

Abbreviations and symbols

*	reconstruction	(asterisk)
**	pseudo-reconstruction	(see §1.5.3.3)
=	clitic	(equals sign)
#	cognate set spread by borrowing	(hash)
-	productive affix	(hyphen)
º	borrowed word	(ordinal indicator)
/	historic compound; neither member independent	(slash)
~	reduplication	(tilde)
⁀	vowel sequence formed by diphthongisation	(tie; see §2.5.3)
_	historic compound; one member no longer independent	(underscore)
|	historic affix	(vertical bar)
CEMP	Central-Eastern Malayo-Polynesian	
CER	Central East Rote	(Nuclear Rote except Tii and Lole)
CERM	Central East Rote and Meto	
CMP	Central Malayo Polynesian	
dJ	de Josselin de Jong (1947)	
J	Jonker (1908)	
M	Middelkoop (1972)	
Mo	Morris (1984)	
nRM	Nuclear Rote-Meto	
nRote	Nuclear Rote	(Rote except Dela-Oenale and Dengka)
On	Onvlee (1984)	
PCEMP	Proto-Central-Eastern Malayo-Polynesian	
PCMP	Proto-Central Malayo-Polynesian	
PMeto	Proto-Meto	
PMP	Proto-Malayo-Polynesian	
PnMeto	Proto-Nuclear Meto	(Meto except Ro'is Amarasi)
POc	Proto Oceanic	

PnRote	Proto-Nuclear Rote	
PRM	Proto-Rote-Meto	
PWMP	Proto-Western Malayo-Polynesian	
PwRM	Proto-West Rote-Meto	
PwRote	Proto-West Rote	
UBB	Unit Bahasa dan Budaya	(Language and Culture Unit)
wRM	West Rote-Meto	
wRote	West Rote	(Dela-Oenale and Dengka)

Speech varieties listed in the dictionary

Rote-Meto speech varieties

Lect	Rote/Meto	ISO	Glottocode
Amanatun	Meto	aoz	aman1264
Amanuban	Meto	aoz	aman1264
Amanuban, South	Meto	aoz	aman1266
Amfo'an	Meto	aoz	amfo1237
Ba'a	Rote	llg	baaa1237
Baikeno	Meto	bkx	baik1238
Bilbaa	Rote	bpz	bilb1242
Bokai	Rote	twu	boka1251
Dela	Rote	row	dela1252
Dengka	Rote	dnk	deng1253
Fatule'u	Meto	aoz	amfo1237
Keka	Rote	twu	keka1234
Ketun	Meto	—	—
Kopas	Meto	—	—
Korbafo	Rote	twu	korb1237
Kotos Amarasi	Meto	aaz	koto1251
Kusa-Manea	Meto	aoz	kusa1252
Landu	Rote	rgu	land1257
Lole	Rote	llg	lole1239
Meto†	Meto	aoz	uabm1237
Miomafo	Meto	aoz	moll1242
Molo	Meto	aoz	moll1242
Oenale	Rote	row	oena1237
Oepao	Rote	rgu	oepa1237
Rikou	Rote	rgu	nucl1538
Ro'is Amarasi	Meto	aaz	rois1241
Termanu	Rote	twu	pada1259
Tii	Rote	txq	tiii1241
Timaus	Meto	—	—

† 'Meto' is used when a form is taken from Jonker (1908) who does not specify which variety of Meto his data is from.

Speech varieties (with at least four occurrences) in out-comparisons

Lect	Region	Sub-region	ISO	Glottocode
Alorese	Alor-Pantar	Alor and Pantar	aol	alor1247
Anakalang	Sumba	west Sumba	akg	anak1240
Asilulu	C. Maluku	Ambon Island	asl	asil1242
Bima	Sumbawa	East Sumbawa	bhp	bima1247
Bolok Helong	Timor	west Timor	heg	helo1244
Bugis	Sulawesi	south Sulawesi	bug	bugi1244
Buru	C. Maluku	Buru	mhs	buru1303
Central Lembata	Flores	Solor Islands	lvu	kali1300
Central Nage	Flores	central Flores	nxe	cent2355
Dadu'a	Timor	Atauro	—	dadu1237
Dhao	Timor	Dhao	nfa	dhao1237
East Tetun	Timor	east Timor	tet	east2473
Ende	Flores	central Flores	end	ende1246
Fehan Tetun	Timor	central Timor	tet	sout2898
Funai Helong	Timor	west Timor	heg	funa1237
Galolen	Timor	east Timor	gal	galo1243
Haruku	C. Maluku	Lease Islands	hrk	haru1244
Hawu	Timor	Sabu Island	hvn	sabu1255
Helong†	Timor	west Timor	heg	helo1243
Idate	Timor	east Timor	idt	idat1237
Ili'uun	S.W. Maluku	Wetar Island	ilu	iliu1237
Kaibobo	C. Maluku	west Seram	kzb	kaib1244
Kamarian	C. Maluku	west Seram	kzx	kama1362
Kambera	Sumba	east Sumba	xbr	nucl1521
Kemak	Timor	east Timor	kem	kema1243
Kisar	S.W. Maluku	Kisar Island	kje	kisa1266
Kodi	Sumba	west Sumba	kod	kodi1247
Komodo	Flores	west Flores	kvh	komo1261
Kupang Malay	Timor	west Timor	mkn	kupa1239
Lewa	Sumba	east Sumba	xbr	lewa1240
Makassar	Sulawesi	south Sulawesi	mak	maka1311
Mambae, Central	Timor	central Timor	mgm	—
Mambae, Northwest	Timor	central Timor	mgm	—
Mambae, South	Timor	central Timor	mgm	—
Mamboru	Sumba	west Sumba	mvd	mamb1305
Manggarai	Flores	west Flores	mqy	mang1405
Ngadha	Flores	central Flores	nxg	ngad1261
Roma	S.W. Maluku	Roma Island	rmm	roma1332
Semau Helong	Timor	Semau Island	heg	helo1245
Sika	Flores	east Flores	ski	sika1262
Tokodede	Timor	central Timor	tkd	tuku1254
Tugun	S.W. Maluku	Wetar Island	tzn	tugu1245
Waima'a	Timor	east Timor	wmh	waim1252
Welaun	Timor	central Timor	wlh	wela1235
Weyewa	Sumba	west Sumba	wew	weje1237

† 'Helong' is used when a form is taken from Jonker (1908) who does not specify which variety of Helong his data is from.

1

Introduction

1.1 Purpose

This comparative dictionary provides an initial bottom-up reconstruction of one low-level Austronesian subgroup of the linguistic area of Wallacea: the Rote-Meto subgroup. This work forms one part of the larger bottom-up reconstruction of languages in this region, which is needed to fully understand the history of these languages.

This dictionary contains 1,174 reconstructions to Proto-Rote-Meto (PRM) or one of its lower branches (Chapter 3) along with the reflexes in modern languages that support these reconstructions. Proto-Rote-Meto is the hypothesised shared common ancestor of the Rote languages and the Meto language/dialect cluster spoken on the western part of Timor (Chapter 2).

This dictionary is *not* a reconstruction of any putative node between Proto-Malayo-Polynesian (PMP) and Proto-Rote-Meto (PRM). Nodes between these two levels are debated (Blust 1993; Donohue and Grimes 2008; Blust 2009b). Although reconstructions from putative intermediate nodes such as Proto-Central-Eastern Malayo-Polynesian (PCEMP) or Proto-Central Malayo-Polynesian (PCMP) are sometimes included as etyma for PRM forms, this should not be taken as a claim that these nodes exist. I simply follow the labels given by others to their reconstructions without passing judgement on the validity of these labels. For the purposes of this comparative dictionary I am agnostic regarding the validity of Central-Eastern Malayo-Polynesian (CEMP) and Central Malayo-Polynesian (CMP). The most fruitful way of assessing the evidence for such intermediate nodes is to continue and expand the kind of bottom-up work carried out in this dictionary.

1.2 Limitations

The reconstruction of Proto-Rote-Meto in this dictionary has a number of limitations. There are a number of minor limitations imposed by the sources on which this dictionary is based, as discussed further in §1.3 and §1.4.

However, probably the most serious limitation on this dictionary is the availability of data. While we have a wealth of data on the Termanu variety of Rote due to the work of the Dutch linguist J. C. G. Jonker in the nineteenth and earlier twentieth centuries, we have comparatively far less data on other varieties of Rote and the Meto cluster. Based on my experience so far, I fully expect that, as more data become available, it will be possible to add more reconstructions to this dictionary, while some of the current reconstructions will need to be modified.

The kind of additional data that will probably be added to this dictionary can be illustrated with two examples of reconstructed bird terms. Firstly, there is PRM *sinaraʔe '*Todiramphus spp*. (kind of kingfisher)'. This is supported by Bilbaa *sulae* '*Todiramphus chloris*', Rikou *sirae* '*Todiramphus chloris*', Lole *sinlaʔe* 'kingfisher', Ro'is Amarasi *sanae* '*Todiramphus spp.*', Kotos Amarasi *saʔnaʔe|k* '*Todiramphus spp.*', and Amfo'an *senae-l* '*Todiramphus spp.*'. None of the data supporting this reconstruction occur in the works of Jonker. Apart from the Kotos Amarasi term, I collected all the other cognates only at the end of 2017.

Secondly, there is PRM *tadeŋgus 'kind of dove, possibly rose-crowned fruit-dove, *Ptilinopus regina*'. In this case Dengka *leŋgus* and Oenale *reŋgus* 'pigeon, dove' (Dutch *duif*) occur in Jonker (1908:772), but none of the other cognates do. These other cognates were also collected at the end of 2017: Ro'is Amarasi *kuum tre͡ukus* 'rose-crowned fruit-dove', Kusa-Manea *ra~rukis* 'wild doves', as well as Landu and Rikou *rekus* 'rose-crowned fruit-dove'.

Such examples indicate that, even though Jonker's works are, perhaps, the most detailed and voluminous works published on any language of eastern Indonesia, more data on the Rote-Meto languages will allow the identification of yet more cognate sets and associated reconstructions.

Some such cognate sets are probably present in Jonker's works and simply await the discovery of a Meto form to allow reconstruction to PRM. One such example is PRM *hida 'how many', which is reconstructed to PRM on the basis of the Rote reflexes combined with Kusa-Manea (Meto) *hian* 'how many' — a term not otherwise currently known in the Meto cluster.

There are also probably other cognate sets that are not represented in Jonker's works due to his focus on Termanu. One such example is *leu 'now, already', for which the Rote cognates (Bilbaa and Rikou *leu*) were collected during my own fieldwork.

The relative lack of available data on speech varieties apart from Termanu is partially mitigated by the fact that I am personally most familiar with the Meto cluster (particularly Kotos Amarasi). The language Jonker knew best is thus complemented by the one I know best. Nonetheless, I am quite certain that more detailed and comprehensive data on Rote languages apart from Termanu, as well as more data on the Meto cluster, will allow reconstruction of many more terms than are currently included in this dictionary.

1.3 Data sources

This dictionary is based on a number of different sources of data. This includes published sources, unpublished descriptions and dictionaries, as well as my own field notes. In this section I discuss the sources on which I have drawn, and the limitations associated with these sources. This includes detailed discussions of Jonker (1908), from which most of my Rote data is drawn, as well as Middelkoop (1972), from which most of my Molo (Meto) data is drawn. The transcriptions used by these works and the problems associated with them are discussed in §1.4.

Data from several languages is frequently cited without any explicit reference to the source from which such data comes. The languages for which this is the case and the sources from which data for them comes are given in Table 1.1 in alphabetical order. All data for these languages come from sources given here, unless otherwise cited. Sources for other languages are always indicated.

Table 1.1: Sources for languages when no source is specified

Language	Source	Notes
Amfo'an	Culhane, Jumetan and Ora (2018)	unpublished Toolbox file, 1,711 headwords, revision published as Grimes et al. (2021)
Dela (Rote)	Tamelan (2017)	unpublished Toolbox file, 1,911 headwords
Dhao	Grimes, Ranoh and Aplugi (2008)	
Ende	Aoki and Nakagawa (1993)	
Galolen	Cristo Rei and Donohue (2012)	unpublished spreadsheet, 1,128 headwords
Hawu	Grimes, Lado, Ly and Tari (2008)	
Helong, Funai	Edwards (2018b)	
Helong, Semau	Balle and Cameron (2014)	unpublished Toolbox file, 3,368 headwords
Helong, Bolok	Balle and Cameron (2014)	Semau is the main dialect of this source
Kemak	own field notes	archived with PARADISEC[1]
Kisar	Christensen (in progress)	unpublished Toolbox file, 2,518 headwords
Meto lects	own field notes	see §1.3.1.2
Rote lects	Jonker (1908)	abbreviated as 'J'
Sumba lects	Onvlee (1984)	includes Anakalang, Kodi, Lewa, Mamboru, and Weyewa
Tetun Fehan	van Klinken (1995)	unpublished Toolbox file, 3,444 headwords
Waima'a	Himmelmann et al. (2006)	archived Toolbox file, 3,890 headwords
Welaun	own field notes	on LexiRumah[2] and PARADISEC

1.3.1 Rote

In this section I discuss the sources of my data for the Rote languages. Four kinds of Rote data occur in this comparative dictionary: data from Jonker (1908), data from my own fieldwork, data from work by linguists associated with the Language and Culture Unit (UBB) in Kupang, and data from a draft ritual language dictionary by James Fox (Fox 2016b). See the front matter and §2.2 for a list of Rote language/dialects and corresponding ISO 693-3 codes and Glottocodes.

1 catalog.paradisec.org.au/collections/OE8.
2 lexirumah.model-ling.eu/languages/west2547-welaun.

1.3.1.1 Jonker (1908)

Jonker (1908) is the source for the vast bulk of my data on the Rote languages. Jonker (1908) is an 805-page 'Rote'-Dutch dictionary. Termanu is the primary variety around which this dictionary is organised. The main section of this dictionary is 672 pages long and lists Termanu headwords, often as underlying roots, with derivatives as sub-headings along with definitions and example sentences. Jonker also usually provides cognates/equivalents of the Termanu headwords in eight other Rote varieties: Korbafo, Bokai, Bilbaa, Rikou, Ba'a, Tii, Dengka and Oenale. He also occasionally gives cognates from Oepao and Keka.

The cognates from these varieties are listed after the Termanu headword and are not given full definitions. Additionally, the final 140 pages or so of Jonker's dictionary are devoted to 'Forms and words from the other dialects'. This section lists non-Termanu words that have already been given in the main body of the dictionary, as well as forms that are not given there. While some of the headwords in this second part have definitions and example sentences, many entries are simply cross-references to the Termanu form in the main body of the dictionary.

In the introduction, Jonker explains that the non-Termanu words were collected by means of the Termanu form (or a derivative) mostly in a sentence and combined with a Malay translation. The non-Termanu equivalents were then given in written form by various schoolteachers from Rote who were Jonker's consultants. He explicitly states that it should *not* be assumed that the non-Termanu words have the same shades of meaning as their Termanu cognate/equivalent and notes differences in meaning when he is aware of them.

This imposes one limitation on this comparative dictionary. The exact semantics of most words from varieties of Rote other than Termanu is unknown. When I do not give a definition for a particular Rote form, this is because Jonker does not specify any definition. In such cases, while we can assume that the semantics are similar to the Termanu form, we cannot assume that they are identical. A word from another Rote variety may well have additional meanings that are not present in the Termanu form and/or Termanu may have uses that another variety does not have.

Regarding the form of words from varieties other than Termanu, Jonker states that he has confidence in the accuracy of his data and he does not include words that he suspected were mistakes. Similarly, forms he judged to be dubious are given in brackets and/or with a question mark.

1.3.1.2 Other sources

Three other kinds of Rote data occur in this comparative dictionary: data from my own fieldwork, data from work by linguists associated with the Kupang based Language and Culture Unit (UBB), and data from Fox (2016b). These other sources are summarised in Table 1.2.

Table 1.2: Sources other than Jonker (1908) for Rote languages

Lect	Source	Notes
Dela	Tamelan (2017) Tamelan (2021)	Toolbox[3] file 1,911 headwords PhD thesis
Lole	Zacharias, Balukh Balle and Banamtuan (2014)	Toolbox file 2,688 headwords
Rikou	Nako, Nako, Balle and Banamtuan (2014)	Toolbox file 766 headwords
Tii	Grimes, Cheng, Hayer-Pah, Pandie, Mulosing and Banamtuan (2014)	Toolbox file 3,281 headwords
Bilbaa	own field notes	archived with PARADISEC
Landu	own field notes	archived with PARADISEC
Oepao	own field notes	archived with PARADISEC
Rikou	own field notes	archived with PARADISEC
Termanu	Fox (2016b)	draft ritual language dictionary

Note: PARADISEC can be found at catalog.paradisec.org.au/collections/OE9.

I carried out a week's worth of fieldwork at the beginning of November 2017 in eastern Rote on Bilbaa, Landu, Oepao and Rikou. The primary purpose of this trip was to gather preliminary data on Oepao and Landu, neither of which are well represented in Jonker (1908).[4] During this trip, I also worked through the Rikou forms that were then present in my comparative database, which Jonker gives as orthographically vowel initial to check whether they begin with an underlying glottal stop (see §1.4.1.1).

Another major source of Rote data comes from work carried out by linguists associated with the Kupang-based Language and Culture Unit (UBB). Particularly important is data on Dela collected and provided by Thersia Tamelan. This includes a draft Dela dictionary (Tamelan 2017), as well as her PhD thesis at The Australian National University (Tamelan 2021), which is a grammar of Dela. In addition to having lexical forms not found in Jonker (1908), Tamelan's work provides a clear, modern linguistic description of Dela, including information that cannot be easily extracted from Jonker's dense grammatical description of the Rote languages, focused on Termanu (Jonker 1915).[5] One example of the kind of information lacking in Jonker's work, but described in Tamelan's work, is the distinction between vowel initial and glottal stop initial words (§1.4.1.1).

1.3.2 Meto

Meto data mainly comes from two sources: Middelkoop (1972) and my own fieldwork. I also have data on Amfo'an compiled by Kirsten Culhane in the form of a toolbox file with 1,711 headwords (Culhane, Jumetan and Ora 2018), as well as Baikeno data provided by Charles E. Grimes. See the front matter and §2.3 for a list of varieties of Meto and corresponding ISO 693-3 codes and Glottocodes.

3 software.sil.org/toolbox/. Toolbox is software program for managing lexical and corpus data.

4 Particular thanks go to Pieter Sjioen and Yulius Iu who were my main consultants for Oepao and Landu respectively, as well as Paulus Nako who organised my trip and accompanied me on fieldwork in Rote.

5 Fox and Grimes (1995:611f) put it well regarding Jonker's works, stating: 'Neither Jonker's dictionary nor his grammar is, in any conventional sense, the study of a single language. Jonker used both of these works to advance comparative observations on an extensive array of other Austronesian languages. His desire to be comprehensive, exhaustive and at the same time comparative resulted in studies that present formidable obstacles to a simple comprehension of the basic structures of Rotinese [sic]'.

1.3.2.1 Middelkoop (1972)

One major source of Meto data is Middelkoop (1972), an unpublished draft 673-page Meto-Dutch dictionary, which was still under preparation when Middelkoop passed away. This dictionary is based on the Molo variety, though forms from other varieties of Meto are occasionally included.

Pieter Middelkoop was a missionary linguist posted to Timor in 1922, after which he began to learn Meto. The dictionary was initially compiled in card-file format, which Middelkoop states was mostly ready by about 1947. The copy that I possess is a photocopy onto (mostly) A4 pages of the typed version of these cards. This photocopy originally belonged to James Fox, who generously gave it to me when he rediscovered it when moving offices. I made a scan of the physical dictionary and had it OCR-ed to make it semi-searchable. References to pages of Middelkoop (1972) are to the pages of the PDF of this scanned copy.

Given that Middelkoop's dictionary is a draft, headwords usually have only a simple Dutch gloss and in many cases only an example sentence with translation occurs, from which the sense of a form can be worked out. There are also many handwritten corrections or emendations on parts of the dictionary. The transcription used in this dictionary is discussed in §1.4.2.

1.3.2.2 Fieldwork

My fieldwork on the Meto cluster has been focused on Amarasi, I have spent about eight months working on Kotos Amarasi (based in the *desa* of Nekmese') and, among other data, have compiled a lexical database of 2,509 headwords of which 2,110 are unique mono-morphemic roots. My work on Kotos Amarasi is the reason that many of the definitions for this language are more extensive than those of other varieties of Meto.

I have also conducted a month's worth of fieldwork on Ro'is Amarasi and 190 of the headwords in my Amarasi lexical database are marked as exclusively Ro'is and a further 234 Kotos Amarasi headwords given with non-identical cognate Ro'is variants. (Many Kotos and Ro'is Amarasi morphemes are also identical.) Ro'is Amarasi data is important from a comparative perspective as, according to the historical phonology, it forms a primary branch within the Meto cluster. All other Meto varieties, including Kotos Amarasi, form a single Nuclear Meto subgroup (§3.3.4).

In addition to all this Amarasi data, I have also collected data on the following varieties of Meto: Timaus (35 minutes of transcribed and translated texts and 72 minutes untranscribed texts, lexicon of 748 headwords), Kusa-Manea (4 hours of untranscribed texts, lexicon of 489 headwords), Amanuban (22 untranscribed texts, 8 wordlists), Ketun (1 transcribed text, 2 untranscribed texts, 3 wordlists), Kopas (1 transcribed text, 2 untranscribed texts, 5 wordlists), Fatule'u (2 wordlists), Amanatun (2 wordlists), Molo (2 wordlists) and Amfo'an (1 wordlist).

Finally, Jonker (1908) frequently provides forms from an unspecified variety of Meto in his etymological notes. When I include such forms, they are marked as *Meto* and a reference to Jonker (1908) is given. Jonker usually does not give definitions for these Meto forms.

1.3.3 Other languages

Forms from languages outside the Rote-Meto group are frequently given in the out-comparisons section of this comparative dictionary (§1.5.1). These are usually other languages from the greater Timor region, though data from languages of other regions are also occasionally given.

In most cases, a full citation for such data is given. The exceptions are languages for which data comes from electronic sources or unpublished sources: Dhao, Galolen, Hawu, Helong, Kemak, Kisar, Tetun Fehan, and Waima'a. The sources for these languages were given in Table 1.1.

Data from other languages are given full references, including page numbers. Languages that commonly occur in the out-comparisons that are drawn from published dictionaries are given in Table 1.3. Some of these sources are abbreviated in the references.

Table 1.3: Sources of other languages frequently cited

Language	Sources	Abbreviation
Bima	Ismail, Azis, Yakub, Taufih and Usman (1985), Jonker (1893)	—
East Tetun	Morris (1984)	Mo
Ili'uun	de Josselin de Jong (1947)	dJ
Kambera	Onvlee (1984)	On
Mambae	Grimes, Marçal and Fereira (2014), Fogaça (2017)	—
Sika	Pareira and Lewis (1998)	—

In addition to Kambera, Onvlee (1984) gives cognates/equivalents of his Kambera headwords for other languages of Sumba: Anakalang, Kodi, Lewa, Mamboru, and Weyewa. However, in a very similar way to Jonker (1908), these cognates/equivalents are usually given without any definition. When I cite such forms, I list them after the Kambera word without a definition. In such cases, these Sumba languages have the same reference as Kambera.

In addition to these sources, Jonker (1908) frequently gives putative cognates for his Termanu headwords from many other languages. Among these, the data for Meto, Helong, Ende, Hawu, Kambera and Bima come from his own work. Unfortunately, glosses are only given for languages other than Rote when they diverge significantly from that of the Rote forms.

Whenever possible I have sought independent verification for such cognates from other sources and give the form, definition and citation for such putative cognates according to these other sources. However, many terms from other languages remain known only from Jonker's etymological notes and thus must be given without definition. That Jonker does not include definitions for such forms indicates that their semantics are likely close to that of the Rote forms.

Jonker does not usually specify from which variety of Helong or Meto his data comes. Thus, when I give a form from one of these languages taken from Jonker (1908) I cannot usually specify the variety and each is given respectively as only 'Helong' or 'Meto'.

1.4 Transcription

PRM reconstructions and their reflexes are given in a phonemic transcription according to standard IPA conventions with the exception of the palatal approximant, which is transcribed <*y*> to avoid any confusion with the voiced palatal affricate <*ʤ*> [ʤ].

When the phonemic representation of a form is in doubt, it is enclosed in angled brackets < >. This is often the case for Molo forms taken from Middelkoop (1972), as discussed further in §1.4.2, as well as out-comparisons from Sumba taken from Onvlee (1984).

As discussed in §1.4.1.1, Jonker does not distinguish between vowel initial and glottal stop initial words in his works. Initial glottal stops in brackets (ʔ) are used to indicate that a word from one of the Rote languages may begin with a glottal stop, but that this has not been confirmed. Initial glottal stops without brackets in Dela, Oenale, Rikou, Oepao and Landu indicate that I have confirmation from other sources or my own fieldwork that this glottal stop is underlying.

A variety of different punctuation marks is used in these phonemic transcriptions to represent different kinds of morphology. These punctuation marks are summarised in the front matter and Table 1.4. Productive affixes are separated from their stem with the hyphen -. Reduplication is indicated by the tilde ~. Fossilised suffixes that are no longer productive are separated from the stem by a vertical bar |. Historic compounds for which neither member is known to exist as an independent word in the language are separated by a slash /. When one member of a (historic) compound does exist as an independent word, but the other does not, the two are separated by an underscore _.

Table 1.4: Punctuation representing morphological structure

Punctuation		Use
-	hyphen	productive affix
~	tilde	reduplication (including frozen reduplication)
|	vertical bar	fossilised affix
/	slash	historic compound; neither member independent
_	underscore	historic compound; one member no longer independent

1.4.1 Jonker's transcription

Jonker consistently represents the different contrastive sounds of the Rote languages, with the exception of initial glottal stops and some sequences of two identical vowels. Each of these is discussed in further detail in the next sections.

Jonker's representation of consonants (apart from the glottal stop) is mostly straightforward. Most consonant letters correspond to their modern IPA equivalents. The digraph <*ng*> represents the velar nasal [ŋ] and imploded stops are transcribed identically to plain voiced stops. Thus, for instance, Tii <*b*> = [ɓ] and <*d*> = [ɗ]. This is not a problem for comparative purposes as implosion is a non-contrastive feature of voiced stops in the Rote languages.

1.4.1.1 Glottal stop

Jonker consistently represents the glottal stop word medially and finally. Between two vowels the glottal stop is represented by a diaeresis on the second vowel; thus <V̈> = /ʔV/ Examples from Termanu are given in Table 1.5.

Table 1.5: Medial glottal stops in Termanu from Jonker (1908)

Medial glottal stop			**No medial glottal stop**		
Jonker	Phonemic	gloss	Jonker	Phonemic	gloss
<daï>	*daʔi*	'dirt on body'	*<dai>*	*dai*	'reach, arrive at'
<sòë>	*soʔe*	'coconut spoon'	*<sòe>*	*soe*	'disaster'
<leä>	*leʔa*	'fathom'	*<leak>*	*lea-k*	'cave'
<haö>	*haʔo*	'mineral lime'	*<hao>*	*hao*	'eat with hand'
<liü>	*liʔu*	'hit with stick'	*<iu>*	*iu*	'shark'

Apart from its use to represent a glottal stop, the diaeresis also represents a morpheme break between a reduplicant and its base when partial reduplication applies to a vowel initial word. Thus, for instance, Jonker (1908:10) transcribes Rikou *a~ana* [ʔa.ana] 'small', which has no underlying glottal stop as *<aäna>*.

Word finally the glottal stop is represented by a dot under the preceding vowel, thus: <Ṿ> = /Vʔ/. Final glottal stops occur most commonly in Korbafo, Bilbaa, Rikou, Dengka and Oenale, in which case they are usually suffixes. Examples from Dengka are given in Table 1.6.

Table 1.6: Final glottal stops in Dengka from Jonker (1908)

Final glottal stop			**No final glottal stop**		
Jonker	Phonemic	gloss	Jonker	Phonemic	gloss
<luị>	*lui-ʔ*	'bone'	*<lui>*	*lui*	'take off'
<atẹ>	*ate-ʔ*	'liver'	*<ate>*	*ate*	'slave'
<bunạ>	*buna-ʔ*	'flower'	*<bina>*	*bina*	'k.o. shellfish'
<kòlọ>	*kolo-ʔ*	'hole'	*<lòlo>*	*lolo*	'stretch out'
<seụ>	*seu-ʔ*	'Alstonia villosa'	*<seu>*	*seu*	'pick fruit'

Jonker states in the introduction to his dictionary that a final glottal stop in Bilbaa and Rikou was often not marked. Although regrettable, given that final glottal stops are almost always suffixes in these languages, this does not impact greatly on the application of the comparative method itself or the reconstruction of proto-forms in my comparative dictionary.

More worryingly, Jonker states that for Rikou (and to a lesser extent also Bokai) the difference between a sequence of two vowels without any intervening consonant and a sequence of two vowels with an intervening glottal stop was often not recorded. I have checked the Rikou forms against data from other sources (§1.3.1.2) wherever possible and the two nearly always agree; though in less than half a dozen cases, Jonker's form has a medial glottal stop where my other sources do not. All such cases are noted.

Jonker does not write word initial glottal stops. All Rote varieties for which modern phonetic and phonological data is available have a contrast between vowel initial and glottal stop initial roots. The contrast is neutralised phrase initially (including in isolation) due to an automatic process of phrase initial glottal stop insertion. The difference emerges phrase medially.

Thus, for instance, Rikou vowel initial *ura-ʔ* ‘scorpion’ and glottal stop initial *ʔuse-ʔ* ‘navel’ are both realised with an initial glottal stop in isolation: [ˈʔuraʔ] ‘scorpion’ and [ˈʔusɛʔ] ‘navel’. Phrase medially, however, ‘scorpion’ is vowel initial, as seen in the phrase *au ura=ka* [ˌʔauˈuraka] ‘my scorpion’, while ‘navel’ is glottal stop initial, as seen in *au ʔuse=ka* [ˌʔauˈʔusɛka] ‘my navel’.

Jonker does not distinguish between such words and writes both with an initial vowel. A selection of examples of Rikou vowel initial and glottal stop initial roots (based on my own fieldwork), along with their representation in Jonker, as well as their realisations initially and medially, is given in Table 1.7 to further illustrate.

Table 1.7: Initial glottal stops in Rikou

Jonker	*<inde>*	*<ea>*	*<apa>*	*<ofạ>*	*<usẹ>*
Phonemic	*ʔinde*	*ʔea*	*ʔapa*	*ʔofa-ʔ*	*ʔuse-ʔ*
Initial	[ˈʔindɛ]	[ˈʔea]	[ˈʔapa]	[ˈʔɔfaʔ]	[ˈʔusɛʔ]
Medial	*ria ʔinde=na*	*au ʔea=ka*	*ria ʔapa=na*	*au ʔofa=ka*	*ria ʔuse=na*
Phonetic	[ˌriaˈʔindɛna]	[ˌʔauˈʔɛaka]	[ˌriaˈʔapana]	[ˌʔauˈʔɔfaka]	[ˌriaˈʔusɛna]
Gloss	‘her/his spindle’	‘my turtle’	‘her/his buffalo’	‘my canoe’	‘her/his navel’
Jonker	*<ikọ>*	*<eị>*	*<ape>*	*<ò>*	*<urạ>*
Phonemic	*iko-ʔ*	*ei-ʔ*	*ape*	*oo*	*ura-ʔ*
Initial	[ˈʔikɔʔ]	[ˈʔeiʔ]	[ˈʔapɛ]	[ˈʔɔː]	[ˈʔuraʔ]
Medial	*ria iko=na*	*au ei=ka*	*ria ape=na*	*au oo=ka*	*ria ura=na*
Phonetic	[ˌriaˈikɔna]	[ˌʔauˈeika]	[ˌriaˈapena]	[ˌʔauˈɔːna]	[ˌriaˈurana]
Gloss	‘its tail’	‘my foot’	‘her/his saliva’	‘my bamboo’	‘her/his scorpion’

That Jonker does not transcribe initial glottal stops is a problem for comparative purposes, as an initial glottal stop is often a reflex of an earlier consonant. Fortunately, however, I have access to data for both Dela (Tamelan 2017) and Rikou (own field notes), which allows me to distinguish between most vowel initial and glottal stop initial roots for these languages. I have thus transcribed all underlying glottal stops for Rikou, as well as Dela and Oenale as befits their phonemic status.[6]

Initial glottal stops that are suspected to be underlying in other varieties of Rote are transcribed in brackets to indicate their unconfirmed status. Thus, for instance, for ‘buffalo’ Jonker gives Dengka and Oenale *<amba>* while Tamelan (2017) gives Dela *ʔamba*. I thus transcribe the Dela and Oenale forms as *ʔamba* and the Dengka form *(ʔ)amba* to indicate that Dengka probably has an initial, but unconfirmed, underlying initial glottal stop.

6 Dela and Oenale are nearly identical and can be treated to some extent as a single lect.

The status of some initial glottal stops in Dela and Rikou remains ambiguous. This is either because the form in Jonker (1908) is not present in Tamelan (2017) or was not known by my consultants. Additionally, a number of Rikou forms with an ambiguous glottal stop were added to my database after my fieldwork in Rote. Such ambiguous glottal stops are given in brackets (ʔ) in the same way as all unconfirmed initial glottal stops in the Rote languages.

Meto varieties also have a process of glottal stop insertion before vowel initial words. However, unlike the Rote languages this glottal stop insertion affects vowel initial words in all phrase positions — not just phrase initially. The relevance of this process in Meto for comparative purposes is discussed in §2.4.2.

1.4.1.2 Vowels

Jonker represents the five phonemic vowels of the Rote languages with and without various accents according to a combination of the placement of stress and phonetic vowel quality. His transcription of vowels is not phonemic, but is consistent. A summary of Jonker's transcription of vowels is given in Table 1.8. Observe in particular that some letters represent both single and double vowels.

Table 1.8: Jonker's transcription of vowels

Jonker	Phonetic	Phonemic	Use by Jonker
e	[e]	*e*	all environments
o	[o]	*o*	all environments
è	[ɛː]	*ee*	final/only vowel of word
	[ɛ]	*e*	elsewhere
ò	[ɔː]	*oo*	final/only vowel of word
	[ɔ]	*o*	elsewhere
i	[iː]	*ii*	only vowel of word
	[i]	*i*	elsewhere
a	[aː]	*aa*	only vowel of word
	[a]	*a*	elsewhere
u	[uː]	*uu*	only vowel of word
	[u]	*u*	elsewhere
í	[iː]	*ii*	final vowel of word
á	[aː]	*aa*	final vowel of word
ú	[uː]	*uu*	final vowel of word

Before this transcription is discussed in detail, several facts concerning the phonology of vowels in Termanu must be summarised. A fuller overview of Rote phonology is given in §2.4.

- Mid-vowels are lax [ɛ] and [ɔ] when stressed and before a syllable containing a mid-vowel.
- Mid-vowels are tense [e] and [o] before a syllable containing a high vowel.
- Content words contain at least two vowels.
- Nearly all vowel sequences occur, including double vowels /ii/, /ee/, /aa/, /oo/ and /uu/.

- Double vowels are realised as phonetically long vowels, i.e. /$V_{\alpha}V_{\alpha}$/ → [Vː].
- Stress is penultimate. Secondary stress is assigned to every second syllable to the left.

Given this knowledge of Rote phonology, the following generalisations account for Jonker's transcription. Jonker transcribes the lax allophones of the mid vowels [ɛ] and [ɔ] with a grave accent *<è>* and *<ò>* whenever these allophones are stressed. Unstressed lax vowels, as well as stressed tense allophones are transcribed as *<e>* and *<o>* without any accent.

Given that stress falls on the penultimate vowel of a word, a double vowel will always contain a vowel that is the locus of stress and the whole double vowel will thus bear stress (either primary or secondary). This — combined with the fact that the first vowel of a sequence of two mid vowels is by nature followed by another mid vowel — means that a double mid-vowel will always be lax. Thus, the double vowels /ee/ and /oo/ are always stressed lax [ɛː] and [ɔː].

Consequently, Jonker's *<è>* and *<ò>* represent double vowels /ee/ and /oo/ when they are the final or only orthographic vowel of a word. Jonker's *<è>* and *<ò>* do not represent double vowels when they are penultimate before another syllable or vowel. Examples of Jonker's transcription of the stressed lax allophones of the mid vowels in Termanu are given in Table 1.9.

Table 1.9: Stressed lax allophones of mid vowels

Jonker	Phonemic	Phonetic	gloss	Jonker	Phonemic	Phonetic	gloss
<nè>	*nee*	[ˈnɛː]	'six'	*<dène>*	*dene*	[ˈdɛnɛ]	'kapok'
<na-tanè>	*na-tanee*	[ˌnataˈnɛː]	'contain'	*<dèlo>*	*delo*	[ˈdɛlɔ]	'citrus'
<nò>	*noo*	[ˈnɔː]	'coconut'	*<bòle>*	*bole*	[ˈbɔlɛ]	'arenga palm'
<na-sakò>	*na-sa-koo*	[ˌnasaˈkɔː]	'sip'	*<bòö>*	*boʔo*	[ˈbɔʔɔ]	'cough'

For the non-mid vowels /i/, /a/, and /u/, Jonker transcribes a final double vowel with an acute accent, to indicate phonetic stress. Examples from Termanu include: *<nakapí>* = *na-ka-pii* 'tense', *<bitiná>* = *bitinaa* '*Kleinhovia hospita*', and *<na-tafú>* = *na-tafuu* 'inflated'.

In other situations, double /ii/, /aa/, and /uu/ are not distinguished orthographically from single vowels. However, given that Rote content words minimally contain two vowels, any content word that contains only a single orthographic vowel in Jonker (1908) must have a double vowel underlyingly. Termanu examples are given in Table 1.10. That such words do indeed contain a double vowel is confirmed by the fact that when they occur with a prefix or as final members of a compound, Jonker transcribes them with an acute accent, as shown in the right-hand side of Table 1.10.

Table 1.10: Double vowels in Termanu

Jonker	Phonemic	Phonetic	gloss	Jonker	Phonemic	Phonetic	gloss
<ki>	*kii*	[ˈkiː]	'left, north'	*<alu-kík>*	*alu kii-k*	[ˌaluˈkiːk]	'left shoulder'
<dak>	*daa-k*	[ˈdaːk]	'blood'	*<nadá>*	*na-daa*	[naˈdaː]	'bleed'
<huk>	*huu-k*	[ˈhuːk]	'trunk, source'	*<ai-húk>*	*ai huu-k*	[ˌʔaiˈhuːk]	'tree trunk'

In summary, Jonker's use of accents to mark stress, combined with the minimal divocalic word requirement, means that there are almost no cases in which it is unclear whether a particular orthographic vowel represents a single vowel or a sequence of two identical vowels.

The only words that remain ambiguous are functors with single <*i*>, <*a*> or <*u*>, such as <*ma*> 'and'. This is because functors can be monosyllabic in the Rote languages. In these cases, I have referred to other sources to determine whether such functors contain a single or double vowel. In the case of *ma* 'and', Tamelan (2017) gives Dela *ma* 'and' with a single vowel.

1.4.2 Middelkoop's transcription

The transcription used in Middelkoop (1972) is not phonemic and under-representation, particularly of the glottal stop and double vowels, is common. Middelkoop's orthography can be used to some extent by those who already know the language, but it cannot be used as a reliable, consistent representation of the phonological structures of Meto. The main issues with Middelkoop's transcription are summarised in the next sections.

- Double vowels /ii/, /ee/, /aa/, /oo/ and /uu/ are written with a single letter.
- The glottal stop is transcribed < ' > between two vowels.
- Word final < ' > indicates either doubling of the previous vowel or doubling of the previous vowel followed by a glottal stop; i.e. <V'> = /VV/ ~ /VVʔ/.
- Word finally and before consonants the glottal stop is usually not transcribed.
- The vowel sequences /ao/ and /au/ are both written <*au*>.
- The vowel sequence /ae/ appears to be written <*ai*> when non-final.
- Prefixes which are a single consonant are often written with a previous vowel final word.
- The final vowel of the pronouns *ina* 3SG, *sina* 3PL and *hita* 1PL.INCL is usually written with a following inflected verb.

Even with experience of working on Meto and having used Middelkoop (1972) for years, it is still sometimes unclear to me what the exact form of a particular word is. Such forms are indicated in this comparative dictionary with angle brackets < >. All words not given in angle brackets from Middelkoop (1972) have been re-transcribed according to their phonemic form.

Thus, Middelkoop's <*fule*> 'foam' is probably either *fuleʔ* or *ʔfuleʔ*, but I have no way of knowing whether the Molo form has an initial glottal stop or not; Kotos Amarasi has *ʔfuri-f*, indicating that an initial glottal stop might be present in the Molo form, while Kusa-Manea has *fa~fura-f* indicating that a glottal stop might not be present.

Similarly, the word for 'turtle' is given with the forms <*ke'*>, <*ke'a*>, <*ke*> and <*kel*> with no obvious way of knowing what the orthographic variation means. Indeed, there are probably variant forms of which the final two are certainly *kee* and *kee-l*, but whether <*ke'*> is *kee* or *keeʔ* is unclear and whether <*ke'a*> is *keʔa, kea, keaʔ*, *kee=aa* and/or *keeʔ=aa* is also unclear.

1.4.2.1 Glottal stop

The glottal stop phoneme /ʔ/ is usually only written when it occurs between two vowels. Between two vowels /ʔ/ is written with an apostrophe < ' >. An example is <*ma'eki*> = *maʔekiʔ* 'slippery'.

Word finally and before consonants the glottal stop is not usually written. Hence Middelkoop's <*mafena*> = *maʔfenaʔ* 'heavy' has two glottal stops in all known varieties of Meto, including my own Molo data collected on the basis of fieldwork.

Initial glottal stops before other consonants can sometimes be detected by the presence of variants with and without initial epenthetic /a/, which often occurs before consonant clusters. Thus, <*akalen*> and <*kale*> 'fraenulum' indicate a form with initial /ʔk/, probably *a-ʔkale-n* and *ʔkaleʔ*, respectively. However, such glottal stop detection is a very inexact science. Here my confidence that this word does indeed begin with a glottal stop comes mainly from my own Amarasi data where I have *ʔkare-f* 'palate'.

There are sporadic instances of the glottal stop being written < ' > when it is stem/root initial before another consonant, but this is rare and inconsistent. Sometimes it even appears to be written after the initial consonant, such as <*nak'ai*> = *na-ʔkai(ʔ)* 'hook (v.)'.

1.4.2.2 Double vowels

Like Rote, Meto has a minimum word requirement whereby every content word must contain at least two vowels, with double vowels realised phonetically as a single long vowel, e.g. *oo* → [ʔɔː] 'bamboo', *n-iit* → [niːt̪] 'sees'. The only words that can be exempt from this requirement are functors. But even for functors I found evidence that most also have a minimum of two vowels, at least historically.

Word final sequences of two identical vowels can be marked with the apostrophe < ' > in Middelkoop (1972). An example is < *o'* > = *oo* 'kind of bamboo'. But use of the apostrophe to represent double vowels is not a rule. Thus, for <*ne*> = *nee(ʔ)* 'six' there is no indication of the double vowel. Sometimes a word written with a final < ' > also ends in a glottal stop, such as in <*na'*> = *naaʔ* 'blood'. Word final < ' > indicates either doubling of the previous vowel or doubling of the previous vowel followed by a glottal stop, i.e. <V'> = /VV/ ~ /VVʔ/.

Before a consonant (other than glottal stop), sequences of two identical vowels are normally written with a single letter. Examples include <*bifel*> = *bifee-l* 'woman', <*hun*> = *huun* 'grass', <*lus*> = *luus* 'deer', and <*ek fui*> = *eek fui* 'kind of agave', and so on.[7]

1.4.2.3 Other vowel sequences

The vowel sequence /ao/ is written identically to /au/ as <*au*>. As an example, both *au* '1SG' and *ao-f* 'body' are given under a single <*au*> headword. Another example is <*nau*> = *nao* 'go'.

7 There are rare exceptions in which a double vowel is written with two letters such as <*eem*> '2PL come'.

When it is non-final the vowel sequence /ae/ appears to written as <*ai*>. Thus, Amarasi has *na-ʔaekaʔ* 'soak', which is cognate with the Molo forms <*naik*> *n-(ʔ)aek* and <*u aikat*> *u-ʔaeka-t* in Middelkoop (1972). Word finally Middelkoop writes /ae/ as <*aè*>. Two examples are <*saè*> = *sae* 'go up' and <*maè*> = *mae* 'ashamed'.

1.4.2.4 Morpheme boundaries

Verb agreement is usually obligatory in Meto, and one set of agreement prefixes consists of only a consonant: *ʔ-* 1SG, *m-* 2SG/2PL/1PL.EXCL, *n-* 3SG/3PL, *t-* 1PL.INCL (§2.6.5). When the agreement prefix *m-* occurs after any of its corresponding pronouns — *hoo* 2SG, *hii* 2PL or *hai* 1PL.EXCL — the prefix is often written as the final consonant of this pronoun. Examples include:

- <***hom** pau fe*> = *hoo **m-**pao feʔ* 'keep waiting for me'
- <***him** tok mitloe*> = *hii **m-**took mi-tloe* 'you sit parallel'
- <***haim** hek manu*> = *hai **m-**heek manu* 'we caught a chicken'

Consistent with the fact that Middelkoop (1972) does not usually write initial glottal stops, the 1SG prefix *ʔ-* is not usually written. Thus, <*au tebi kukis*> = *au ʔ-tebi kukis* 'I crumble bread'.

The 3SG, 3PL and 1PL.INCL pronouns are *in, sin* and *hit*, respectively. These pronouns have vowel final forms with are used before consonant clusters: *ina, sina* and *hita*, respectively. When these pronouns occur before an agreeing verb whose root begins with a consonant, the final vowel of these pronouns is written with the verb in Middelkoop (1972). Examples include:

- <***in a**nlo'*> = ***ina** n-looʔ* 's/he throws up' (p. 280)
- <***sin a**note hau neki fani*> = ***sina n-**ʔote hau n-eki fani* 'they cut a tree with an axe'
- <***hit a**tlaksaè talali noel*> = ***hita** t-laak sae ta-lali noe-l* 'we stepped over the river'

In such instances, a case can be made for writing these forms orthographically with the /a/ attached to the verb as this aids morpheme recognition. While this may be helpful for native speakers, it is unhelpful for identifying the underlying structures for the purposes of linguistic analysis and reconstruction.

Occasionally, enclitics are written attached to their host, but given the draft state of Middelkoop's dictionary these could just be typographical errors. One example is <*hom nau man**kit** ho feto*> = *hoo m-nao m-aan **=kiit** hoo fetoʔ* 'go and get your sister for us'.

1.5 Structure of the dictionary

This comparative dictionary is structured around reconstructions. Headwords are reconstructions to Proto-Rote-Meto, or to one of its sub-nodes (see §3.3). Headwords are arranged alphabetically with IPA symbols placed after their nearest equivalent.

Prenasalised stops are treated as separate letters. The complete order of all letters which occur in PRM reconstructions is as follows: *a, *b, *ɓ, *d, *ɗ, *ʤ, *e, *ə, *f, *h, *i, *k, *ʔ, *l, *m, *mb, *n, *nd, *ŋ, *ŋg, *o, *p, *r, *s, *t, *u, *w.

Each reconstruction is defined and a variety of other information is also given. Below each reconstruction are the forms in the Rote-Meto languages, which provide evidence for the reconstruction. A simple example entry is exemplified in Example 1.1.

Example 1.1: Simple PRM reconstruction

> ***ika** *Morph:* ***ika-k**. *PRM.* fish. *Etym:* *hikan. *Pattern:* k-10.
> **iʔa-k** *Termanu.* fish. (J:200)
> **iʔa-ʔ** *Korbafo.*
> **iʔa-k** *Bokai.*
> **ika-ʔ** *Bilbaa.*
> **ika-ʔ** *Landu.* fish. (own field notes)
> **ika-ʔ** *Rikou.*
> **ika-ʔ** *Oepao.* fish. (own field notes)
> **iʔa-k** *Ba'a.*
> **iʔa-k** *Tii.*
> **ia-ʔ** *Dengka.*
> **ʔuʔu_ia-ʔ** *Dela.* all kinds of fish. *[Form:* **ʔuʔu** is the normal word for 'fish' in Dela.*]*
> **ika|ʔ** *Ro'is Amarasi.* fish.
> **ika|ʔ** *Kotos Amarasi.* fish.
> **ika|ʔ** *Molo.* fish. (M:159)
> **ika|ʔ** *Kusa-Manea.* fish.
> ***Out-comparisons:***
> **ikan** *Semau Helong.* fish.
> **ikan** *East Tetun.* fish. (Mo:90)
> **iʔa** *Dhao.* fish.

Each entry is headed by a reconstruction in boldface, in this case ***ika**. Directly after the root is given any morphology with which this root occurred (§1.5.3.1); in this case, *ika took the nominal suffix *-k (§2.6.1). The level at which this reconstruction is made (§3.4) is given after this in italics, in this case Proto-Rote-Meto (PRM). This is followed by the reconstructed meaning ('fish'), which in turn is followed by any etymon at a higher level, usually PMP (§1.5.3.3). After the etymology, notes on any issues or problems with this reconstruction are given (§1.5.3.7).

Below the reconstruction are given its reflexes in the Rote-Meto languages. This begins with the varieties of Rote in the following order: Termanu, (Keka), Korbafo, Bokai, Bilbaa, (Landu), Rikou, (Oepao), Ba'a, (Lole), Tii, Dengka, Oenale and Dela.[8] Lects in brackets in this list are not always given, while forms from the other lects are given whenever they are known to be cognate.

8 The ordering in which the Rote languages are given is a compromise between geographic position and relatedness. Termanu is given first as this is the variety on which Jonker (1908) is based, followed by Korbafo, which is extremely similar. Bokai is given next with an eastwards progression from there to Bilbaa, Landu, Rikou and Oepao. After this Ba'a is given with a mostly westwards progression to Lole, Tii, Dengka, Oenale and Dela.

In line with the nature of Jonker (1908) (see §1.3.1), from which most Rote data comes, Termanu is often the only Rote variety defined. The definition is a free translation of Jonker's Dutch definition. When the source of a form does not come from Jonker (1908), it is usually glossed and the source is given. Thus, in the case of *ika 'fish' in Example 1.1 the Landu and Oepao forms *ika-ʔ* 'fish' come from my own field notes. When no definition is given for a variety of Rote, the definition must be assumed to be similar to that of Termanu. Thus, the Korbafo, Bokai, Bilbaa, Rikou, Ba'a, Tii and Dengka forms in Example 1.1 can be assumed to also mean 'fish'.

After the definition, any necessary notes are given on issues concerning this reflex. The final part of the entry for a reflex is the source of this form. In Example 1.1, Termanu *iʔa-k* comes from page 200 of Jonker (1908). When no alternate source is given for another Rote variety, it comes from the same page of Jonker (1908) as the Termanu form. The only exception is Dela, data for which always comes from Tamelan (2017). For more discussion on the sources on which this dictionary is based see §1.3.

After Rote, forms from different varieties of Meto are given. Often only a Kotos Amarasi and Molo form are given, as these are the varieties for which the most data is available. When other lects are given they are ordered roughly from east to west.[9] These entries follow the same model as the Rote entries except that glosses for all varieties are given.

1.5.1 Out-comparisons

The final part of an entry consists of putative cognates in languages outside of the Rote-Meto subgroup. These are preceded by *Out-comparisons* and further indented. These out-comparisons are forms from languages outside of the Rote-Meto group that are formally and semantically similar to the Rote-Meto languages. In most cases, these out-comparisons are from Austronesian languages in the greater Timor region, though occasionally out-comparisons from non-Austronesian or more distant languages are also given.

All languages that occur more than three times in the out-comparisons are listed in the front matter, along with their geographic location, ISO 693-3 codes, and Glottocodes (Hammarström et al. 2020). Equivalent information for languages that occur three or less times in the out-comparisons is included each time a form from that language occurs.

These out-comparisons have *not* been thoroughly vetted for whether they show regular sound correspondences with the PRM forms and thus cannot be taken unquestioningly as cognate. While it is likely that many of the out-comparisons are indeed cognate with the PRM forms, this cannot be assumed to be the case. A more thorough investigation of the sound correspondences may show that certain forms in certain lects are borrowings and not the result of shared inheritance.

9 The complete ordering of Meto lects is as follows: Ro'is Amarasi, Kotos Amarasi, Amanuban, Amanatun, Ketun, Kopas, Fatule'u, Molo, Amfo'an, Timaus, Baikeno, Kusa-Manea. With the exceptions of Ketun, Kopas and Timaus (which probably originate elsewhere), this is roughly east to west along the south coast, then east to west among remaining varieties, with Timaus after Amfo'an, from which it originated.

This is particularly the case for Helong out-comparisons. Helong and the Rote-Meto languages appear to have been in contact with one another since the time of PRM and have remained in contact ever since (see §3.3.4.2). It remains to be determined to what extent it may be possible to detect contact at different time depths between Helong and Rote-Meto.[10]

While I do give preliminary notes on what appear to be irregular sound correspondences between the PRM reconstruction and out-comparisons when I am aware of them, the nature of such irregularities remains to be properly investigated.

In general, I have searched fairly thoroughly for putative cognates in Tetun, Ili'uun, Helong and Kisar based on available sources. I have not made a thorough search for cognates in other regional languages, but have included similarities that I opportunistically stumbled upon.

When the out-comparison field contains forms that can be identified as loans from a Rote-Meto language, or a Rote-Meto entry can be identified as a loan from one of the out-comparisons, the form that is a loan is preceded by the degree sign ° and the source of the loan is given. An example is *ɗele 'Job's tears, Coix lachryma-jobi', from PMP *zəlay, which is inherited regularly in the Rote languages. Meto, however, has irregular *°sone*, which is probably a loan from Welaun *sole* (also from *zəlay). When all the forms under a single headword can be identified as loans, they are given in the Loan Distribution section (§1.5.4).

1.5.2 Multiple reflexes

In many cases, a language has more than one reflex of a single reconstruction; usually morphologically related forms. In such cases each form except the first is numbered sequentially, with these numbers corresponding to the equivalent numbered section of the definition. An example is given in Example 1.2.

Example 1.2: Multiple reflexes

> ***lasi₂** *Morph:* ***ma-lasi-k, *na-ma-lasi**. *PRM.* old, aged.
> **lasi-k (2) na-ma-lasi** *Termanu.* 1) old (especially of people and animals). 2) to be or become old, of people and animals. (J:283)
> **lasi-ʔ** *Korbafo.*
> **lasi-k** *Bokai.*
> **lasi-k** *Bilbaa.*
> **lasi-ʔ** *Rikou.*
> **lasi-k** *Ba'a.*
> **lasi-k** *Tii.*
> **lasi-ʔ** *Dengka.*
> **lasi-ʔ** *Oenale.*

10 As an additional complicating factor, it is not unlikely that Helong and the Rote-Meto languages both had contact with the same non-Austronesian language(s) and/or families that have since been lost due to shift to Helong and/or Rote-Meto. Again, it has not yet been determined to what extent it may be possible to detect which equivalents/cognates shared between Helong and the Rote-Meto languages are the result of mutual borrowing and/or borrowing from a third source.

m|nasi|ʔ *Ro'is Amarasi.* old, aged.
m|nasi|ʔ (2) na-m|mnasi *Kotos Amarasi.* 1) old, aged. 2) be or become old/aged.
m|nasi|ʔ *Molo.* old. (M:325)
m|nasi|ʔ (2) m|nasi-k *Kusa-Manea.* 1) old (e.g. of fruit). 2) old, aged (of people).

In this example, Termanu has two different forms. The definitions of these forms are given after the forms. Form (1) *lasi-k* means 'old (especially of people and animals)', and form (2) *na-ma-lasi* means 'be or become old, of people and animals'. When other varieties of Rote taken from Jonker (1908) also have multiple forms, these are given the same numbers as the parts of the Termanu entry to which they correspond.

Example 1.3: Example with multiple reflexes in all Rote varieties

***beli** *Rote.* price, bride price. *Etym:* *bəli 'buy, value, price; marriage prestations, bride price; purchase'.
beli (2) belis *Termanu.* 1) cost, price, value. 2) that which must be paid for a girl when taken for marriage, either paid with goods or money, the purchase price of a woman. (J:41)
beli (2) belis *Korbafo.*
beli (2) belis *Bokai.*
beli (2) belis *Bilbaa.*
beli (2) belis *Rikou.*
beli (2) belis *Ba'a.*
ɓeli (2) ɓelis *Tii.*
feli (2) felis *Dengka.*
feli (2) felis *Oenale.*
Out-comparisons:
foli-n *East Tetun.* price, cost, value; objects for barter. (Mo:35)
heli *Ili'uun.* property, valuable things. (dJ:117)
weli *Kisar.* buy.

Example 1.3 shows how the first form in all the Rote lects corresponds to Termanu *beli* 'cost, price, value' and the second form corresponds to Termanu *belis* 'bride-price'. Often it is only the Termanu entry that has multiple forms, as in Example 1.2. While equivalent numbered forms across the Rote lects are given the same numerals, such equivalency does not necessarily correspond to any forms among the Meto cluster.

I generally only give multiple reflexes of a single reconstruction when these additional forms contribute to understanding the history or development of the reconstruction. Thus, in Example 1.2, the Termanu and Meto forms attest that *lasi₂ probably had two forms in PRM: nominal *ma-lasi-k and verbal *na-ma-lasi.

In some cases multiple reflexes occur for a single language with no indication of a semantic difference. In such cases, the two forms are separated by a comma and receive a single gloss. Thus, for instance, two Molo reflexes of *mbeɗa 'put down' occur with no know semantic difference. They are given as **na-pela**, **na-bela** *Molo.* put down. (M:56, xxxix). Note also that in such cases the ordering of page numbers in the source follows the order in which the reflexes are given in this dictionary, rather than their actual ordering in the source — that is, *na-pela* occurs on page 56 of Middelkoop (1972) and *na-bela* occurs on page xxxix.

1.5.3 Fields/parts of entries

Apart from the forms and definitions, many entries have additional fields that give additional information on the entry. These fields include a morphology field marking any morphology with which the reconstruction occurred (§1.5.3.2), an etymology field indicating a higher level etymon (§1.5.3.3), a field for indicating doublets (§1.5.3.4), fields tracking irregular sound changes (§1.5.3.5), a field tracking patterns or correspondences among proto-phonemes that undergo unconditioned splits (§1.5.3.6), and four fields for different kinds of notes (§1.5.3.7).

1.5.3.1 Definitions and glosses

Glosses of reconstructions are always given, but glosses of the forms in daughter languages are not always given. All glosses of reconstructions are my own proposed semantics for the PRM form, but glosses for the reflexes in daughter languages follow verbatim the sources from which data is drawn (see §1.3). This includes not giving any gloss when no gloss is given in the source, as is usually the case for non-Termanu forms taken from Jonker (1908).[11] In such cases, we must assume that the meaning of the non-Termanu terms is similar to that of Termanu (see §1.1.1.1 for more discussion). Thus, most Rote forms are not glossed and the Termanu gloss can be taken as a proxy for the meaning.

The convention is to supply glosses as in the sources verbatim, including a lack of gloss, not to leave out glosses that are identical to the first language listed. Thus, nearly all data not drawn from Jonker (1908) is glossed. This is exemplified in Example 1.1 where the forms in Landu, Oepao, Dela, Meto and the out-comparisons are all glossed according to the sources from which they are drawn, even though theses glosses are usually identical. The forms without glosses are taken from Jonker (1908) where they listed as cognates of the Termanu headword.

In some cases, Jonker (1908) explicitly gives the meaning of one or more Rote forms as differing from their Termanu cognate. Likewise, word sets taken from the final section of his dictionary, which is devoted to 'Forms and words from the other dialects', often have no Termanu cognate. In this case, the gloss for the first language listed is given and the glosses for subsequent varieties of Rote in Jonker (1908) are not glossed and must be assumed to be equivalent to the language for which the gloss is given. When a cognate set is restricted to Dengka and Oenale the gloss is usually repeated for both forms.

The glossing of terms referring to biota follows the practice used elsewhere in the dictionary of citing glosses verbatim from the sources. Many biota terms only receive a vague definition in Jonker (1908), as 'kind of X', though they are often accompanied

11 The statements here also apply to terms from the Sumba languages taken from Onvlee (1984), in which case we must assume that the unglossed forms are similar to the Kambera forms. These statements also apply to some forms from Maluku, in which case the unglossed forms must be assumed to be similar to the first language listed.

by a description and/or their name in Kupang Malay, which can be used to identify the species referred to. Whenever a biota term is defined precisely in one source (often with a scientific name) and defined only vaguely in other sources, I usually assign the more precise definition to the reconstructed PRM form.

Some discussion of introduced species of biota is needed. There are a number of reconstructed terms in this dictionary that refer to recently introduced species of biota in daughter languages. When the sound correspondences of such terms are regular, this indicates that semantic shift has taken place. In an insightful article on the history of traditional agriculture, Fox (1991) has shown how newly introduced crops were assimilated to pre-existing categories in the Rote languages. Thus, for instance, based on a cursory examination of the present-day semantics, we could assign the meaning 'maize' to PRM *mbela. However, to quote Fox (1991:250):

> On Roti [sic], it is clear that maize when it was introduced was culturally assimilated to the category of 'sorghum'. It is also conceivable that at an earlier period when sorghum was introduced, it was assimilated to the category of Job's tears. Thus this category, *pela* [from PRM *mbela], may subsume three stages of an agricultural progression.

See the discussion in the entry for *mbela for more details on this particular form.

There is evidence that similar patterns of assimilation and subsequent semantic shift have occurred in many other cases with biota terms in the Rote-Meto languages. Thus, for instance, the usual designation of Kotos Amarasi *rinah*, a reflex of *ɗilah, is 'pomegranate', which is an introduced species in Timor. However, there is another term *riin fui* 'wild *rinah*' that refers to another fruit tree, probably Aegle marmelos, which appears to be native to the region.

In some cases, reflexes of a reconstructed term only refer to introduced species. Thus, for instance, all reflexes of *uas in daughter languages refer to 'jicama Pachyrhizus erosus', which is a tuber native to central America probably introduced into Southeast Asia during the 16th century. If the PRM form is valid, and did not spread by borrowing, this meaning cannot have been the original sense. Instead, *uas must have undergone semantic shift in all daughter languages. However, in the absence of further information as to what other tuber this term may have originally referred to, I have chosen to assign this meaning to the PRM term rather than a vague meaning such as 'kind of tuber'. I have done this on the assumption that any native designation was likely similar to the introduced term. Importantly, however, no conclusions as to the age of PRM should be drawn on the basis of terms that apparently refer to introduced biota in this dictionary.

1.5.3.2 Morphology

The reconstructed headwords are roots. Whenever there is evidence that such a root obligatorily took certain morphology in PRM — that is, the root probably did not occur as a bare stem — the form(s) in which it occurred are given in the morphology field. If the morphology field is filled, this means that I have no evidence that the reconstructed root occurred as a bare stem in PRM.

Thus, for instance, PRM *lasi 'old, aged' in Example 1.2 is given with the derivatives *ma-lasi-k and *na-ma-lasi. This means that all Rote-Meto reflexes are from either *ma-lasi-k or *na-ma-lasi. No modern-day language attests *lasi alone without morphology. Similarly, the PRM root *ŋgala '*Sesbania grandiflora*' is given with the derivative *ŋga~ŋgala. This means that all reflexes in the PRM languages are inherited from reduplicated *ŋga~ŋgala. There is no evidence that *ŋgala alone occurred at the level of PRM.

When the only reflexes for a reconstruction are morphologically complex, but there is no agreement on a single complex form for PRM, the morphology field is left empty. An example is PRM *ɓua 'gather', for which no modern language attests a bare root: Termanu has *na-ka-bua, bua~bua, bu~bua-k* and *be-bua* (among other derivatives), while varieties of Meto have *na-bua, na-k|bua?, bua?~bua?* and *n-bua*. Based on these reflexes we can probably posit that PRM had derivatives *na-ka-ɓua and *ɓua~ɓua, but we cannot posit that these derivatives were the only forms of this root that occurred in PRM. Thus, the morphology field is left blank for *ɓua.

When the reconstructed root itself is a reflex of a morphologically complex PMP term, this is not indicated in the headword. An example is PRM *mea 'red', which is a reflex of PMP *ma-iRaq, without any indication of the earlier *ma- prefix in the PRM headword.

When the root contains frozen morphology, which is not clearly inherited from a reconstructed morphologically complex form, this is indicated in the headword with the vertical bar, which is used for frozen morphology (§1.4). An example is the PRM root *natu|n 'hundred', which is a reflex of PMP *sa-ŋa-Ratus (via intermediate **ŋatus) with a final consonant *n of unclear origin, which is plausibly a suffix.

When a verb is reconstructed as taking agreement prefixes in PRM, the morphology field is filled by the third person form of the prefix, either *na- or *n-. An example is *faɗa 'say, tell' for which all reflexes take person agreement. Thus, I propose that this verb obligatorily took agreement in PRM and give *na-faɗa in the morphology field to indicate this.

As discussed further in §2.6.1, the Rote languages have a distinction between nouns that take the nominal suffix *-k/-?* in isolation and as the final member of an attributive phrase and nouns that are not eligible to take this suffix. This distinction is reconstructible to PRM. Thus, when the morphology field is filled by a form with final *-k, this means that I posit that this noun was eligible to take this suffix in the appropriate environments (not that it obligatorily occurred with this suffix in all environments). One example is *ika-k 'fish' in Example 1.1, for which I posit there was an NP final form *ika-k and an NP medial form *ika.

1.5.3.3 Etymology

The etymology field usually contains a reconstruction taken from the online Austronesian Comparative Dictionary (Blust and Trussel ongoing). This is the source of all reconstructions in the etymology field, unless otherwise indicated.

Most of these reconstructions are to Proto-Malayo-Polynesian (PMP). In a small number of cases no reconstruction at this level exists and I give a reconstruction from one of its putative daughter nodes: Proto-Western Malayo-Polynesian (PWMP), Proto-Central Eastern Malayo-Polynesian (PCEMP) and Proto-Central Malayo-Polynesian (PCMP). As discussed in §1.1, my use of these labels simply follows the use of others, in this case reflecting the labels given by Blust and Trussel (ongoing). For the purposes of this comparative dictionary, I am agnostic regarding all putative nodes between PMP and PRM, with the exception of Timor-Babar, for which evidence is presented in §3.5.3.1.

The transcription of PMP reconstructions follows the conventions of Blust and Trussel (ongoing), with the exception of PMP <e> [ə] which is transcribed <ə> to avoid confusion with *e [e], which occurs in putative sub-nodes of PMP, such as PCEMP.

Certain symbols within this transcription tradition are not standard IPA or have unexpected phonetic values. The symbols used for P(CE)MP reconstructions in this comparative dictionary, along with the phonetic values ascribed to them by Blust (2009a:547, 623) and Wolff (2010:31, 241) are given in Table 1.11.[12] Note particularly that the values of *z, *j, *r and *R may be unexpected.[13]

Table 1.11: Proto-Malayo-Polynesian consonants

P(CE)MP	*p	*t	*k	*q	*b	*d	*z		*j	*g	*m	*n	*ñ	*ŋ
Blust (2009a)	[p]	[t]	[k]	[q]	[b]	[d]	[dʒ]		[gʲ]	[g]	[m]	[n]	[ɲ]	[ŋ]
Wolff (2010)	[p]	[t]	[k]	[q]	[b]	[d]	[d̪ʲ]/[d̪͡ɹ]		[g]	—	[m]	[n]	[ɲ]	[ŋ]
P(CE)MP	*h	*s		*l	*r	*R	*w	*y	*i	*e	*ə	*a	*o	*u
Blust (2009a)	[h]	[s]/[ʃ]		[l]	[ɾ]	[r]	[w]	[j]	[i]	[e]	[ə]	[a]	[o]	[u]
Wolff (2010)	[h]	[t͡s̪]/[t̪͡θ]		[l]	—	[ʁ]	[w]	[j]	[i]	—	[ə]	[a]	—	[u]

Several kinds of additional information regarding reconstructions can also occur in entries. Firstly, when the reconstruction does not come from Blust and Trussel (ongoing), the source is given after the reconstruction. Secondly, when the PMP and PRM glosses are substantially different, the gloss ascribed to the PMP form is given in quotation marks after the PMP reconstruction. Often this means that semantic shift has occurred between PMP and PRM.

Thirdly, any comments on the reconstruction are given in brackets. This includes when the reconstruction is not to PMP, but at a putative lower level such as PWMP, PCEMP or PCMP. Other comments relate to problems that the PMP reconstruction presents, or give formally and semantically similar reconstructions that have also been made.

Apart from reconstructions to PMP, I also occasionally give putative forms marked with a double asterisk and assigned to 'pre-Rote-Meto', a level before PRM, which is left deliberately vague. Such pseudo-reconstructions are given when out-comparisons (§1.5.1) indicate that the PRM form is probably inherited from a higher node, but no

12 Wolff (2010) uses different symbols for several of his proto-phonemes, and he does not accept all the proto-phonemes posited by Blust. Reconstructions from Wolff (2010) and other sources are (re)transcribed according to the conventions used by Blust and Trussel (ongoing).

13 Blust (2009a) also reconstructs PMP *c [ʧ] and *D [ɖ], but these putative proto-phonemes do not occur in any of the reconstructions in this dictionary.

reconstruction has yet been made by another scholar. These pseudo-reconstructions should not be considered proper reconstructions, as we have only a preliminary understanding of the way in which the Rote-Meto languages relate to other language groups (§3.5) In the small number of cases in which I am confident of the level and form of my own reconstruction, I give it with a single asterisk and give *own reconstruction* as the source.

1.5.3.4 Doublets

When a form has an etymologically related counterpart, this counterpart is included preceded by *Doublet:*. In this comparative dictionary, a 'doublet' is only used for formally distinct reconstructions that are inherited from a single reconstructed etymon without being morphologically related. Thus, for instance, PRM *fai 'day, time' and *hoi 'dry in the sun' are both reflexes of PMP *waRi, but with different sound changes. Similarly, *mane 'man, male' and *mone 'man, male' are both from PMP *maRuqanay via slightly different pathways.

Formally and semantically similar reconstructions that may ultimately be cognate but cannot (yet) be identified as descending from a single etymon are not marked as doublets. Instead, such forms contain cross references to one another. This includes forms that are inherited from those given as doublets by Blust and Trussel (ongoing). An example of the latter is *lea-k 'cave' and *lua|t 'cave', which are inherited from PMP *liaŋ and *luaŋ, respectively.

1.5.3.5 Irregular sound changes

When the forms given do not show the expected correspondences (summarised in §3.2), this is recorded in one of three different fields. Based on our current understanding of the Rote-Meto languages, as well as our reconstruction of PMP, such comparisons require positing irregular sound changes (or irregular retention of certain sounds).

To allow the reader to quickly ascertain the strength of the reconstruction, the notes recording irregular sound changes are usually given in the entry for the reconstruction before all other notes. The only exception is when such notes are given for the out-comparisons, in which case they are given in the entry for the out-comparison.

Firstly, there is a field marked *'irr. from PMP'*. This field records irregular sound changes that must be posited to derive the reconstructed PRM form from a putative PMP etymon. Many such irregular sound changes only have one putative attestation.

Secondly, there is a field marked *'minority from PMP'*. This field records irregular sound changes between PMP and PRM that have multiple attestations. Thus, for instance, while the usual reflex of PMP *q is Ø in PRM, there are seven instances of PMP *q > PRM *h. These latter instances have the note: *[minority from PMP:* *q > *h*]*. See §3.5.1 for discussion of unconditioned splits between PMP and PRM.

The final field for irregular sound changes is marked *'Sporadic'*. This field records sporadic sound changes (both between PMP and PRM, and/or PRM and its daughters), such as consonant metathesis, as well as changes that are only partially complete in certain lects, such as the raising of final *a > *e* in West Rote and Meto (§3.2.3). When a sporadic sound change only affects one language, it is often given in the entry for that language.

Under a strict neo-grammarian view in which sound change is completely regular, all comparisons that involve irregular correspondences would need to be excluded from this comparative dictionary. This is not the approach I take. Instead, I include such comparisons when the form and semantics of two morphemes are so similar that I feel uncomfortable excluding them from the dictionary. Furthermore, the inclusion of such forms means that no potentially valuable information is excluded from the dictionary.

Unfortunately this is an inherently subjective exercise. How similar is similar enough? This is the main reason I explicitly list irregular sound changes. Others may wish to exclude comparisons they judge too dissimilar, or further evidence may show that the identification of a certain cognate set is erroneous in some way. This is also why I give irregular sound changes before most other notes. The problems with such reconstructions should be front and centre in order to allow them to be subject to proper scrutiny.[14]

A second reason for explicitly listing putative irregular sound changes is that they have the potential to advance our understanding of Austronesian comparative linguistics. It may be that a higher level reconstruction is currently in error, or it may be that irregularities similar to those in PRM are found in other languages and can be adduced as evidence for a higher node.

Despite the subjectivity of this criterion, in my experience most cases are actually quite clear-cut. Thus, consider PRM *naa-k 'brother of a woman' (from PMP *ñaRa) with the following reflexes: Rote *naa-k/naa-ʔ* and Meto *naʔo/nao-f* all 'brother of a woman'. I do not think any comparativist would attribute the formal and semantic similarity between these forms to chance. However, final *o* in Meto languages is not a regular reflex of *a. The reconstruction *naa-k thus requires irregular *a > *o* in Meto.

Similarly, consider PRM *ka-nduna-k 'nest' with the following reflexes: Oenale, Dengka *nduna-ʔ,* Rikou, Oepao *runu-ʔ*, Bokai, Bilbaa *lunu-ʔ*, other Rote *ndunu-k/ndunu-ʔ* 'nest', Ro'is Amarasi *kuna|ʔ*, other Meto *ʔ|kuna|ʔ* 'nest'. Again, these forms are almost certainly related but final *a > *u* in Rote languages is not regular and *nd > *k* in Ro'is Amarasi is also irregular (all other sound correspondences are regular). Thus, these irregular sound changes are flagged.

Whenever the posited irregular sound change can be motivated, such as PRM *ka-nduna-k > Termanu *ndunu-k* 'nest' where *a > *u* is probably sporadic vowel assimilation, such explanations are given in brackets after the irregular sound change. In this case the sound change is given as: '*[irr. from PRM:* *a > *u* in nRote (sporadic assimilation)*]*'. Particularly speculative or ad-hoc explanations are further followed by a question mark '?'.

14 I welcome correction on any reconstructions in this dictionary, as well as putative connections between my reconstructions and higher levels that can be shown to be false. I only ask that if others debunk reconstructions or connections when I have explicitly flagged them as involving irregular sound changes, that they extend me the generosity of stating that I acknowledge the problems with such reconstructions.

1.5.3.6 Patterns

The pattern field is used to show patterns of correspondences among the reflexes of PRM *k and *d. Each of these proto-phonemes shows unconditioned splits in which the reflexes are not completely random. Instead, there are patterns of regularity in the correspondences. Four patterns can be identified for initial *k, six for medial *k, and two for *d in all word positions. The correspondences for each pattern are summarised in Table 1.12 for a select number of daughter languages. The full correspondences are given in §3.2.

Table 1.12: Patterns for Proto-Rote-Meto *k and *d

PRM	*k-					*-k-						*d	
env.	#_	#_		#_	#_	V_V	V_V	V_V	V_V	V_V	V_V	all	all
pattern	k-1	k-2		k-3	k-4	k-5	k-6	k-7	k-8	k-9	k-10		d-2
Dela	*k*	*ʔ*		*ʔ*	*h*	*k*	*ʔ*	*k*	*ʔ/Ø*	*ʔ*	*ʔ/Ø*	*r*	*r*
Dengka	*k*	*ʔ*		*ʔ*	*h*	*k*	*ʔ*	*k*	*ʔ/Ø*	*ʔ*	*ʔ/Ø*	*l*	*l*
Tii	*k*	*k*		*k*	Ø	*k*	*k*	*ʔ*	*ʔ*	*ʔ*	*ʔ*	*ɗ*	*r*
Termanu	*k*	*k*		*k*	Ø	*k*	*k*	*ʔ*	*ʔ*	*ʔ*	*ʔ*	*d*	*l*
Bilbaa	*k*	*k*		*k*	Ø/*k*	*k*	*k*	*k*	*k*	*k*	*k*	*d*	*l*
Rikou	*k/ʔ/Ø*	*ʔ/Ø*		*ʔ*	Ø	*ʔ/k*	*ʔ/k*	*k/ʔ*	*ʔ/k*	*ʔ/k*	*k/ʔ*	*d*	r
		k-2a	k-2b										
Ro'is	*k*	*k*	*k*	*h*	*h*	*k*	*k/ʔ*	*ʔ*	Ø	*ʔ*	*k*	*n*	*r*
Kotos	*k*	*k*	*ʔ*	*h*	*h*	*k*	*k/ʔ*	*ʔ*	Ø	*ʔ*	*k*	*n*	*r*
Molo	*k*	*k*	*ʔ*	*h*	*h*	*k*	*k/ʔ*	*ʔ*	Ø	*ʔ*	*k*	*n*	*l*

Each of these patterns is tracked throughout this comparative dictionary in the field marked *Pattern*. Thus, for instance, a reconstruction with *k marked as '*Pattern:* k-1' indicates that this *k has reflexes according the k-1 pattern in Table 1.12, '*Pattern:* k-2' that it follows the k-2 pattern, and so on. When data from diagnostic languages is lacking, the possible patterns are given. Thus, k-2/3 indicates a *k, which could belong to either pattern k-2 or k-3.

Forms that mostly follow one of these patterns, but with one or two deviations in the reflexes, are marked with a prime symbol, with the deviations given afterwards. An example is *koro 'Rainbow Bee-eater' for which the reflexes follow pattern 1 with the exception of Meto which has *k > Ø rather than expected *k = *k*. Thus, this entry contains '*Pattern:* k-1′ (but *k > Ø in Meto; expect *k = *k*)'. Instances of *k or *d that do not follow any of these patterns are marked as k-irr. or d-irr. with the irregularities tracked in the *irr. from PRM* field, as discussed in §1.5.3.5.

1.5.3.7 Notes

Up to four different kinds of general notes are given for entries. Firstly, there is a field marked *Notes:*, which is used for all notes that do not clearly fit into any of the categories discussed. After this comes notes on irregular sound changes, discussed in more detail in §1.5.3.5.

After this is a note field flagged *Form*. This is used for notes on the form of an entry. Examples of the kinds of comments given here include giving the possible unmetathesised form(s) of a Meto word, which has only been attested metathesised, giving the gloss of part of a compound, or indicating regular sound changes that might not be immediately apparent. This field is also used for alternate forms from sources apart from the primary source used for a lect.

The note field flagged *History* is used for notes on the history of a form. This includes discussion of possible higher etyma for a PRM form, or comparisons with reconstructions that cannot straightforwardly be identified as the etymon for my reconstruction. Other miscellaneous notes on the history of a term are also given.

The note field flagged *Semantics* gives notes on the semantics of an entry. Examples of the kinds of notes given in this field include more detailed discussion of semantic shifts that certain comparisons involve, or indicating when a botanical term has only a vague gloss such as 'kind of tree' in my sources.

1.5.4 Loan distributions

In addition to the main part of this comparative dictionary, I have also included a number of loan distributions in the final part of the dictionary. That is, cognate sets that can be identified as being ultimately borrowed from another language. This section has the same organisation and structure as the main part of the dictionary, with the exception that the headwords in this section are preceded by a superscript hash # indicating that these headwords are not proper reconstructions, but rather generalisations across the forms in daughter languages.

This section does not include every instance of a loan in the Rote-Meto languages, but is focused on sets that might be mistaken for cognates shared by common inheritance. Some of the cognate sets in this section may have been borrowed at the level of PRM or one of its daughter nodes, though this seems unlikely for most sets.

1.5.5 Finder lists

Two finder lists are also included in this dictionary. Firstly, there is an English finder list. The glosses by which this finder list is organised include glosses for the reconstruction, and glosses for the reflexes in daughter languages which have undergone semantic shift.

Thus, for instance, PRM *ndelat is reconstructed with the meaning 'lightning', but the Meto cluster has forms that have undergone semantic shift to include 'gun' (e.g. Ro'is Amarasi *renet* 'gun', other Meto *kenat* 'gun'). Thus *ndelat is included in the finder list after both 'lightning' and 'gun'. Doing this allows the reader to look up the etymology of a particular word from one of the modern Rote-Meto languages based on its gloss. It also makes it easier for the reader to find potential PRM cognates that may have undergone similar semantic shift in related languages.

The finder list only gives glosses for PRM reconstructions or reflexes of them. Glosses for PMP forms that are the etymon of a PRM form are not given in the finder list. Thus for instance PMP *kuhkuh 'claw, talon, fingernail' has undergone semantic shift to PRM *kuku 'finger, toe' and no reflexes of this form attest the PMP semantics. As a result, 'fingernail' in the finder list does not point to PRM *kuku.

In addition to the English finder list, a finder list organised by reconstructions to a node higher than PRM is also given. This finder list gives the forms in the etymology field (§1.5.3.3) followed by the PRM reflex(es) and the gloss of the PRM reconstruction. Not all PRM reconstructions occur in this finder list, as not all are known to be inherited from a higher node.

2

Language background

2.1 Introduction

In this chapter I give an overview of the synchronic features of the Rote and Meto clusters, necessary for understanding the content of this dictionary. This includes an overview of the phonology (§2.4), morphophonemic processes (§2.5) and morphology (§2.6). The sources of data for this overview are the same as those for the body of the dictionary (§1.3).

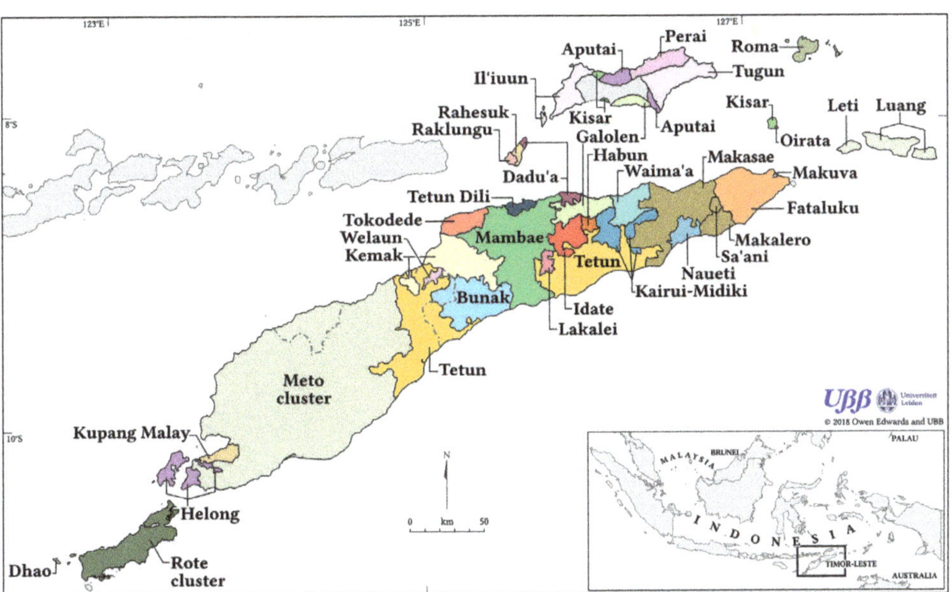

Map 2.1: Language groups of Timor
Source: Owen Edwards and UBB.

The Rote languages are spoken on the island of the same name immediately to the south-west of the island of Timor.[1] The Meto cluster is spoken in the western part of Timor including Oecusse, which is politically an enclave of Timor-Leste. The locations of the Rote and Meto clusters along with other languages of Timor are shown in Map 2.1. The location of languages in Timor-Leste is largely based on Williams-van Klinken and Williams (2015), who summarise census data.

2.2 Rote

The island of Rote is divided into 19 political units known in the anthropological literature as domains (*nusa-k* or *nusa-ʔ* in the languages of Rote), and many speakers claim that each domain has its own language (Fox 2016a:233). A map of the domains of Rote is given in Map 2.2. (The language of Dhao is not part of the Rote cluster.)

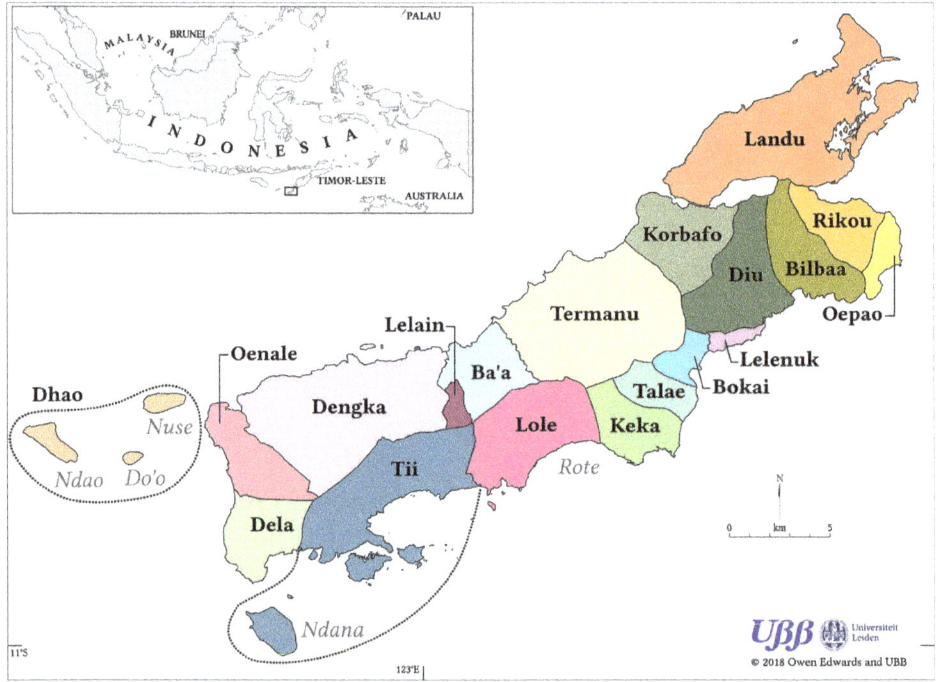

Map 2.2: Rote domains
Source: Owen Edwards and UBB.

The Rote cluster is a language/dialect chain like the Romance or West Germanic chains in Europe. Fox (2016a:233) summarises the complexity stating:

> Speakers in neighbouring domains are generally able to understand one another, but for speakers in domains separated from one another intelligibility is reduced. Domains at a distance from one another find mutual intelligibility difficult or impossible. Based on these criteria Rotenese [sic] consists of more than one language.

1 There are also pockets of Rote speakers on the Timor mainland. Such populations are due to migrations in historical times.

Given that we are dealing with a language/dialect chain, any classification that places an exact figure on the number of languages or dialects on Rote is necessarily somewhat arbitrary, depending on which criteria are privileged. Nonetheless, it is helpful to consider the classifications that have been made by various researchers. The different classifications are summarised in Table 2.1.

The earliest published classification of the speech varieties of Rote is that of Manafe (1889), a Rote speaker. Manafe (1889) identifies nine different Rote *lagu* (Malay 'song, tune, dialect'): (1) Oepao, Rikou and Landu; (2) Bilbaa, Diu and Lelenuk; (3) Korbafo; (4) Termanu, Keka and Talae; (5) Bokai; (6) Ba'a and Lole; (7) Dengka and Lelain; (8) Tii; (9) Dela and Oenale.

Jonker (1913) reviews the classification of Manafe (1889) and notes differences between varieties that Manafe grouped together as well as similarities between those he separated. One of the main points that arises from Jonker (1913) is that there is a sharper division between Dela-Oenale and Dengka in the west compared with the other Rote lects. This difference is found in morphology and lexicon, as well as the historical phonology, the latter which provides good evidence for a West Rote group separate from all other varieties of Rote (see §3.3).

The most recent classification is that of Fox (2016a) who to some extent follows the earlier classifications, though Fox groups related dialects together rather than differentiating them. Fox identifies six groupings: (1) Eastern dialect area: Rikou, Oepao and some of Landu; (2) East-Central dialect area: Bilbaa, Diu, Lelenuk, Korbafo and some of Landu; (3) Central dialect area: Termanu, Keka, Talae, Ba'a, Lelain and Bokai; (4) South-Western dialect area: Tii and Lole; (5) North-Western dialect area: Dengka; and (6) Western dialect area: Dela and Oenale.

Examining only the historical phonologies of the different speech varieties of Rote (see §3.2), we can identify 12 distinct varieties. (1) Dela and Oenale, (2) Dengka, (3) Tii, (4) Lole, (5) Ba'a, (6) Termanu and Keka, (7) Korbafo, (8) Bokai, (9) Bilbaa, (10) Rikou, (11) Landu[2] and (12) Oepao. Varieties in each of these 12 groupings currently appear to have undergone the same sound changes. No data is available from Lelain, Talae, Diu or Lelenuk to make a proper assessment of the sound changes in these varieties, though all classifications treat Talae with Termanu, as well as placing Diu and Lelenuk with Bilbaa.[3]

The different classifications of the Rote languages that have been made are summarised in Table 2.1, along with the names, ISO 693-3 codes, and Glottocodes (Hammarström et al. 2020) of each variety.

2 The population of Landu was decimated in 1756 by the Dutch. It was later resettled, partly from Rikou (Fox 2016a:236). During my fieldwork, Landu speakers reported that genuine/native Landu is spoken in the western/central villages (*desa*) of Sotimori, Bolatena and Nifuleu. Rikou is spoken in other areas.

3 Although Manafe (1889) appears to present data from Lelain, Talae, Diu and Lelenuk, such data always consist of a single form, which is labelled 'Dengka dan Lelain', 'Bilba, Diu dan Lĕlénuk' or 'Termanu, Keka dan Talaĕ' (where *dan* is Indonesian for 'and'). Similarly, he presents single forms for 'Baä dan Lålĕ', including in one instance when other sources show that Ba'a and Lole are different. Thus, Manafe (1889:641) gives Ba'a and Lole *<m 'Pui-kah lah> mpui-k=a laa* for 'a bird flies' while data from Jonker's works and Zacharias et al. (2014) never attest a voiceless prenasalised plosive in Lole. Instead, Zacharias et al. (2014) have *mbui-k* 'bird'. This indicates that in other cases the forms in Lelain, Talae, Diu and Lelenuk may differ from those presented in Manafe (1889).

Table 2.1: Classifications of Rote speech varieties

Lect	ISO	Glottocode	Sound changes	Manafe (1889)	Fox (2016a)		Lect
Dela	row	dela1252	1	1	1		Dela
Oenale	row	oena1237	1	1	1		Oenale
Dengka	dnk	deng1253	2	2	2		Dengka
Lelain	dnk	lela1245	2/5?	2	4		Lelain
Tii	txq	tiii1241	3	3	3		Tii
Lole	llg	lole1239	4	4	3		Lole
Ba'a	llg	baaa1237	5	4	4		Ba'a
Termanu	twu	pada1259	6	5	4		Termanu
Keka	twu	keka1234	6	5	4		Keka
Talae	twu	tala1297	6?	5	4		Talae
Bokai	twu	boka1251	7	6	4		Bokai
Korbafo	twu	korb1237	8	7	5		Korbafo
Bilbaa	bpz	bilb1242	9	8	5		Bilbaa
Diu	bpz	diuu1237	9?	8	5		Diu
Lelenuk	bpz	lele1271	9?	8	5		Lelenuk
Landu	rgu	land1257	10	9	5	6	Landu
Rikou	rgu	nucl1538	11	9	6		Rikou
Oepao	rgu	oepa1237	12	9	6		Oepao

2.3 Meto

Meto (a.k.a. Uab Meto, Dawan(ese), Timorese, or Atoni) is a language/dialect chain spoken in the western part of Timor.[4] Meto speakers usually identify their speech as a single language and call it *uab meto?, molok meto?, (uab) Timor*, or occasionally, to outsiders, *(bahasa) Dawan.* Speakers of Meto recognise more than a dozen named varieties. These varieties themselves have named dialects, with further differences being found between different villages and hamlets of a single dialect. A map of self-identified Meto varieties is given in Map 2.3.

While the Meto cluster is numerically and geographically larger than the Rote cluster,[5] it has less diversity in its segmental phonology. Based only on the historical phonologies of Meto (see §3.2), we can identify four different varieties, each of which is currently known to have undergone different sound changes: (1) Ro'is Amarasi, (2) Kotos Amarasi, Amabi and Kusa-Manea, (3) Amanuban and Amanatun, (4) all other varieties. Among

4 In earlier works I referred to this language cluster as Uab Meto. In many varieties *uab meto?* can be glossed as 'dry/ indigenous speech'. However, not all Meto speaking areas use *uab* for 'speech'. Thus, in Amfo'an 'speech' is *aguab*, in Timaus it is *molok* and in Baikeno *lasi* is used for 'language'. Use of Meto alone thus covers more varieties in an emic manner. It also matches the use of speakers in which *meto?* alone can refer to the language. Such use is seen in phrases like Kotos Amarasi *iin nahiin meto?* 'S/he knows (how to speak) Meto'.

5 Ethnologue (Eberhard et al. 2020) estimates 842,000 Meto speakers as opposed to 116,000 speakers for all Rote languages combined. Both these figures are probably underestimated.

other varieties, Amfo'an and Timaus can further be grouped together as, based on current knowledge, these are the only varieties that have developed consonant insertion after all vowel final roots (see §2.5.2).

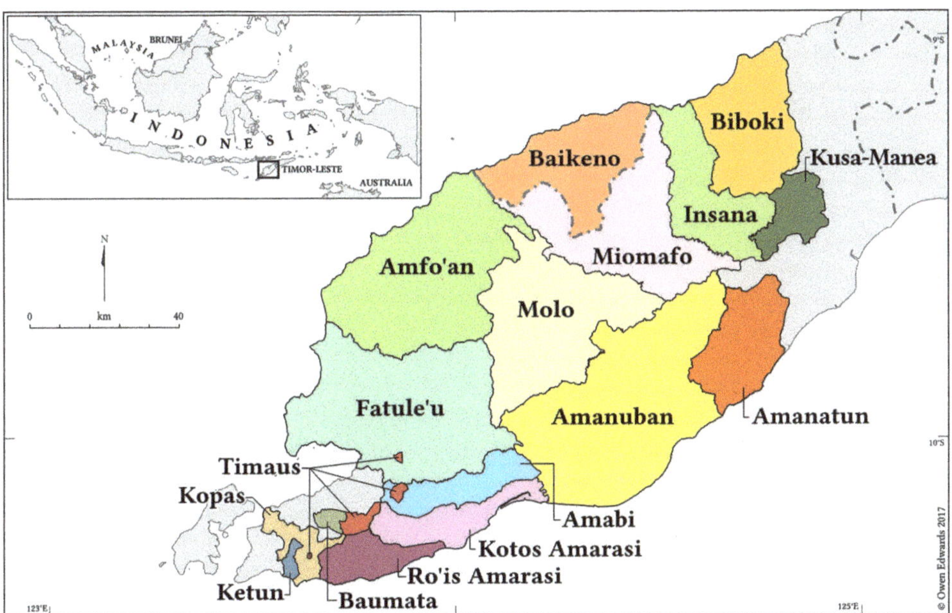

Map 2.3: Self-identified Meto varieties
Source: Owen Edwards.

While the historical sound changes within each of these groupings are mostly the same, there are many lexical and semantic differences between different varieties, as well as significant differences between different varieties in the forms and functions of the morphophonemic processes of metathesis, consonant insertion, vowel assimilation and diphthongisation. Differences in lexicon, semantics and morphophonemic processes are also found between individual hamlets or 'dialects' of the different varieties shown in Map 2.3.

The different varieties of Meto are listed in Table 2.2, along with ISO 693-3 codes, Glottocodes and their classification according to historical phonology. Not all varieties occur in Ethnologue (Eberhard et al. 2020) or Glottolog (Hammarström et al. 2020) and, of those that do, all except Kotos Amarasi, Ro'is Amarasi and Baikeno are listed as dialects/varieties of Meto.[6]

6 Amabi is lumped as part of a single 'Amfo'an-Fatule'u-Amabi' variety of Meto in both Ethnologue (Eberhard et al. 2020) and Glottolog (Hammarström et al. 2020). My consultants report that it is most similar to Kotos Amarasi, with occasional lexical and semantic differences.

Table 2.2: Varieties of Meto

Lect	ISO	Glottocode	Sound changes
Ro'is Amarasi	aaz	rois1241	1
Kotos Amarasi	aaz	koto1251	2
Amabi	aoz	amfo1237	2
Kusa-Manea	aoz	kusa1252	2
Amanuban	aoz	aman1265	3
Amanatun	aoz	aman1264	3
Molo	aoz	moll1242	4
Fatule'u	aoz	amfo1237	4
Miomafo	aoz	moll1242	4
Baikeno	bkx	baik1238	4
Insana	aoz	bibo1238	4
Biboki	aoz	bibo1238	4
Kopas	—	—	4
Ketun	—	—	4
Baumata	—	—	4
Amfo'an	aoz	amfo1237	5
Timaus	—	—	5

2.4 Segmental phonologies

In this section I describe the essential features of the segmental phonologies of the Rote-Meto languages. This is necessary to understand the historical sound changes that have occurred in these languages (§3.2).

2.4.1 Rote

The Rote languages have different consonant inventories. Consonants occur at four places: labial, coronal, velar and glottal with up to seven manners of articulation: voiceless plosive, prenasalised plosive, voiced plosive (often implosive), voiceless fricative, nasal, trill/tap and lateral.

Four voiceless stops /p t k ʔ/, two voiced stops /b d/ and three fricatives /f s h/ are present in all varieties.[7] Among other consonant series there is variation in which segments different varieties attest. Some varieties have two liquids /l r/, while others have only a single liquid /l/. Some varieties have only two nasals /m n/, while others have /ŋ/ in addition. Some varieties have a full series of prenasalised stops /mb nd ŋg/, while others have only a partial series or lack prenasalisation entirely.

7 In all Rote lects for which data is available, the voiceless coronal plosive /t/ is dental [t̪] while the voiced plosive /d/ or /ɗ/ is alveolar or even slightly retroflex.

There are also differences in the phonetic qualities of these consonants. In south-western lects including Dela-Oenale, Tii and Lole, voiced plosives are usually lightly imploded in all word positions. For these languages, imploded stops /ɓ/ and /ɗ/ can be treated as phonemes. Based on two Dengka recordings made available to me by Thersia Tamelan, it appears that Dengka /b/ is usually unimploded [b] while the apical voiced plosive is usually lightly imploded [ɗ].

In Termanu voiced plosives are reported as imploded only medially, thus /b/ → [ɓ] /V_V and /d/ → [ɗ] /V_V. During my fieldwork on Bilbaa, Landu and Oepao, I did not record implosion for /b/, but did occasionally record light implosion for intervocalic /d/, thus /b/ → [b] and /d/ → [d]~[ɗ] /V_V. The phonetics of voiced plosives in other Rote varieties are currently unknown. Regarding prenasalisation, in Ba'a the bilabial prenasalised stop is voiceless /mp/ while in other varieties it is voiced /mb/. The consonant inventories of the Rote lects are summarised in Table 2.3.

Table 2.3: Consonant inventories in Rote Languages

Dela-Oenale, Tii	*p*	*t*	*k*	*ʔ*	*mb*	*nd*	*ŋg*	*ɓ*	*ɗ*	*f*	*s*	*h*	*m*	*n*	*(ŋ)*†	*r*	*l*
Dengka	*p*	*t*	*k*	*ʔ*	*mb*	*nd*	*ŋg*	*b*	*ɗ*	*f*	*s*	*h*	*m*	*n*			*l*
Lole	*p*	*t*	*k*	*ʔ*	*mb*	*nd*	*ŋg*	*ɓ*	*ɗ*	*f*	*s*	*h*	*m*	*n*			*l*
Ba'a	*p*	*t*	*k*	*ʔ*	*mp*	*nd*	*ŋg*	*b*	*d*	*f*	*s*	*h*	*m*	*n*			*l*
Termanu, Korbafo	*p*	*t*	*k*	*ʔ*		*nd*	*ŋg*	*b*	*d*	*f*	*s*	*h*	*m*	*n*	*ŋ*		*l*
Bokai, Bilbaa	*p*	*t*	*k*	*ʔ*				*b*	*d*	*f*	*s*	*h*	*m*	*n*	*ŋ*		*l*
Rikou, Landu	*p*	*t*	*k*	*ʔ*		*nd*		*b*	*d*	*f*	*s*	*h*	*m*	*n*		*r*	*l*
Oepao	*p*	*t*	*k*	*ʔ*		*(nd)*‡		*b*	*d*	*f*	*s*	*h*	*m*	*n*		*r*	*l*

† In Dela the velar nasal /ŋ/ is a marginal phoneme only occurring in onomatopoeic words.

‡ In my Oepao data /nd/ occurs in Rikou borrowings and one possible native word.

All (known) varieties of Rote have five vowels /i e a o u/. For Termanu the mid-vowels are described as lax [ɛ] and [ɔ] in unstressed syllables, and when they bear stress followed by a syllable containing another mid vowel. Tense mid-high allophones [e] and [o] occur in stressed syllables followed by a syllable containing a high vowel. When the following syllable has /a/ as its nucleus there is apparently variation between tense [e]~[o] and lax [ɛ]~[ɔ] in Termanu (Jonker 1915:2f, Fox and Grimes 1995:614).

In Dela the low vowel /a/ is centralised to [ɐ] after stressed syllables and often further reduced towards schwa [ə] in antepenultimate syllables. The mid-vowels are mid-high [e] and [o] before a syllable containing a high vowel and mid-low [ɛ] and [ɔ] elsewhere. The high front vowel /i/ is [ɪ] in unstressed closed syllables while /u/ is slightly centralised to [ʊ] after stressed syllables (Tamelan 2021:22).

Content words contain at least two vowels. Some functors, such as the conjunction *ma* 'and', are monosyllabic. Stress falls on the penultimate vowel of a word with secondary stress assigned to every second syllable to the left. All vowel sequences occur with the exception of /uo/.[8] This includes double vowels (sequences of two identical vowels)

8 The vowel sequence /ie/ does occur in the Rote languages, but is rare. Based on current data it appears to only be found in Dela-Oenale, Dengka, Tii and Lole.

/ii/, /ee/, /aa/, /oo/ and /uu/. Such double vowels are realised phonetically as a single long vowel, i.e. [iː], [ɛː], [aː], [ɔː] and [uː]. Given the placement of stress, one member of a vowel sequence will always bear stress.

2.4.2 Meto

All (known) Meto varieties have 11 core consonants /p t k ʔ b f s h m n/ and either /r/ or /l/. A few varieties have both /r/ and /l/ and thus have 12 core consonants. To these core consonants most varieties of Meto add voiced obstruents /ʤ/ and /gw/, though some lack /gw/.

The obstruents /ʤ/ and /gw/ are restricted in distribution. They only occur under processes of consonant insertion (§2.5.2) that operate at clitic boundaries and/or word finally in different varieties of Meto, as well as between certain historic sequences of vowels. Both these obstruents are a result of glide fortition. These glides are still present in Amanuban which lacks these obstruents but has glides /y/ and /w/ in comparable environments.

All voiced obstruents are realised as plosives [b ʤ gw] or fricatives [β ʒ ɣw]. Fricative realisations are most common in unaffected speech, except after nasals, when the plosive realisations usually occur. The consonant inventories of several different varieties of Meto are summarised in Table 2.4 for comparison.

Table 2.4: Consonant inventories in Meto

Amarasi	*p*	*t*	*k*	*ʔ*	*b*	*ʤ*	*gw*	*f*	*s*	*h*	*m*	*n*	*r*	
Amanuban	*p*	*t*	*k*	*ʔ*	*b*	*y*	*w*	*f*	*s*	*h*	*m*	*n*		*l*
Amfo'an, Kopas	*p*	*t*	*k*	*ʔ*	*b*	*ʤ*	*gw*	*f*	*s*	*h*	*m*	*n*		*l*
Timaus	*p*	*t*	*k*	*ʔ*	*b*	*ʤ*	*gw*	*f*	*s*	*h*	*m*	*n*	*r*	*l*
Baikeno, Molo	*p*	*t*	*k*	*ʔ*	*b*	*ʤ*		*f*	*s*	*h*	*m*	*n*		*l*
Kusa-Manea	*p*	*t*	*k*	*ʔ*	*b*			*f*	*s*	*h*	*m*	*n*	*r*	*l*

Known Meto varieties have five vowels /i e a o u/. The mid vowels are usually phonetically mid-low [ɛ ɔ] but are raised to mid high [e o] in certain environments, particularly before high vowels. In some varieties of Meto this difference is becoming phonemic due to vowel assimilation after metathesis (§2.5.1). Thus, for instance, in Naitbelak Amfo'an *na-leko* → *na-leek* [naˈlɛːk] 'good' contrasts with *na-henu* → *naheen* [naˈheːn] at the surface level. As in the Rote languages, content words are minimally disyllabic, stress is penultimate, and double vowels /ii/, /ee/, /aa/, /oo/ and /uu/ are realised phonetically as a single long vowel.

Varieties of Meto have a process of glottal stop insertion whereby an automatic glottal stop is inserted before vowel initial words in all phrase positions. While there is a contrast between vowel initial roots and glottal stop initial roots, this contrast only surfaces after the addition of certain prefixes, e.g. Kotos Amarasi *n-ani* 'before' contrasts with *n-ʔani* 'head towards'. Because many Meto roots have never been attested with any prefixes, the status of many initial glottal stops is thus ambiguous. The issues surrounding initial glottal stops in one variety of Meto, Kotos Amarasi are discussed at length in Edwards (2017).

For the purposes of this dictionary, all words with an initial ambiguous glottal stop are transcribed as vowel initial, with the exception of words that have *k* in Ro'is Amarasi but initial glottal stop in other varieties of Meto (see Table 3.4).[9] One such example is the reflexes of *katefuan 'wasp' > Ro'is Amarasi *katfua|ʔ,* Kotos Amarasi, Molo *ʔatfuan,* Kusa-Manea *ʔaetfuan*, all 'kind of wasp'. Wherever evidence from prefixes is available for such words, it shows that their initial glottal stop is underlying and not an automatic insertion.

2.5 Meto morphophonemic processes

Meto has many complex morphophonemic processes including metathesis, multiple processes of vowel assimilation, consonant insertion, diphthongisation and epenthesis. All of these processes can co-occur to different extents depending on a number of semantic, phonological and syntactic factors. This results in a single word having a diversity of surface forms in a single variety and across different varieties of Meto. In this section I discuss only those processes that affect the presentation of words in this dictionary: metathesis, consonant insertion, vowel assimilation and diphthongisation.

2.5.1 Metathesis

All varieties of Meto have productive final CV → VC metathesis producing alternates such as Kotos Amarasi *fafi* → *faif* 'pig' or *neno* → *neon* 'sky, day'. Metathesis is a morphological process in Meto. In Kotos Amarasi it marks attributive modification in the noun phrase and resolution for verbs. Edwards (2020) provides a detailed description of metathesis in Kotos Amarasi.

When the final vowel of such words is /a/, it assimilates to the quality of the previous vowel after metathesis in most known varieties of Meto, except for Kusa-Manea. Thus, Kotos Amarasi *n-sena* → *n-seen* 'plant' and *nima* → *niim* 'five'. This results in surface minimal pairs such as Kotos *n-nene* → *n-neen* 'push' and *n-nena* → *n-neen* 'hear'. In Kusa-Manea such vowel assimilation does not occur, thus Kusa-Manea *n-sena* → *n-sean* 'plant' and *nima* → *niam* 'five'. Similarly, in Ro'is Amarasi assimilation of /a/ does not occur after metathesis when the medial consonant is /ʔ/, but does occur in all other situations. Thus, Kotos Amarasi *n-roʔa* → *n-rooʔ* 'vomit' but Ro'is Amarasi *n-roʔa* → *n-roaʔ* 'vomits'.

Many other processes of vowel assimilation also occur after metathesis to different extents in different varieties of Meto, but none are present in forms included in this dictionary. An overview of known instances of these processes is included in Edwards (2020:163–167).

Meto words are given in the unmetathesised form throughout this dictionary whenever these forms are known. When such data is lacking, I give the metathesised form with the putative unmetathesised form(s) given in the notes when it may be ambiguous.

9 All words with initial *k* in Ro'is Amarasi and *ʔ* in other varieties of Meto belong to the k-2b pattern for initial PRM *k. See §1.5.3.6 for discussion of patterns.

2.5.2 Consonant insertion

Most varieties of Meto have a process of consonant insertion that operates after vowel final words, before vowel initial enclitics, as well as phrase finally in some varieties. Consonant insertion has been described most fully for Amfo'an by Culhane (2018). Throughout this dictionary inserted consonants are separated from the stem by a hyphen. This means they are represented in the same way as suffixes.

Amfo'an, Timaus, Kopas, Fatule'u and Baikeno all have consonant insertion for certain nouns when phrase final, including in citation form. Consonant insertion also occurs with transitive verbs to mark a known third person object. Examples of consonant insertion in six different varieties of Meto are given in Table 2.5 to illustrate the following discussion.

Table 2.5: Phrase final consonant insertion

		Amfo'an	Timaus	Kopas T.†	Kopas U.	Fatule'u	Baikeno	Gloss
ai	→	*aidʒ*	*aar*	*aadʒ*	*aadʒ*	*aadʒ*	*aidʒ*	'fire'
tei	→	*teidʒ*	*teer*	*teedʒ*	*teedʒ*	*teedʒ*	*teidʒ*	'faeces'
oe	→	*oel*	*oel*	*oel*	*oel*	*oel*	*oel*	'water'
fee	→	*feel*	*feel*	*feel*	*feel*	*feel*	*feel*	'wife'
ao	→	*aog*	*aagw*	*aag*	*aagw*	*aob*	*aob*	'mineral lime'
meo	→	*meog*	*meegw*	*meeg*	*meegw*		*meob*	'cat'
hau	→	*haug*	*haadʒ*	*haag*	*haagw*	*haub*	*haub*	'tree, wood'
kiu	→	*kiug*	*kiidʒ*	*kiig*	*kiigw*	*kiub*	*kiub*	'tamarind'
uki	→	*ukidʒ*	*ukar*	—	—	—	—	'banana'
tani	→	*tanidʒ*	*tanar*	—	—	—	—	'rope'
ume	→	*umel*	*umal*	—	—	—	—	'house'
ane	→	*anel*	*anal*	—	—	—	—	'field rice'
neno	→	*nenog*	*nenugw*	—	—	—	—	'day, sky'
kolo	→	*kolog*	*kolugw*	—	—	—	—	'bird'
fatu	→	*fatug*	*fatidʒ*	—	—	—	—	'stone, rock'
feʔu	→	*feʔug*	*feʔidʒ*	—	—	—	—	'new'

† Kopas T. is from Tuale'u hamlet and Kopas U. is from Usapisonba'i hamlet. The difference between final [g] and final [gw] is distinctive and noticeable to native speakers.

In Amfo'an and Timaus final consonant insertion affects all vowel final nouns while in other varieties in which it is attested it only affects words that end in a vowel sequence VV#. Which consonant is inserted is conditioned by the quality of the final vowel. All varieties have insertion of /l/ after /e/ and most have insertion of /ʤ/ after /i/, with the exception of Timaus, which has insertion of /r/ after /i/. After /o/ and /u/ Amfo'an and Kopas have insertion of /gw/ (with /gw/ → [g] /_# in some varieties), Fatule'u and Baikeno have insertion of /b/, while Timaus has insertion of /ʤ/ after /u/ and /gw/ after /o/.

Furthermore, consonant insertion is often accompanied by assimilation or shift of the final vowel. When the root ends in a vowel sequence the final vowel undergoes complete assimilation in Kopas and Timaus with the exception of /e/, which does not assimilate.

In Fatule'u only /i/ assimilates after consonant insertion. In Timaus if the root ends in a consonant followed by a vowel (that is, CV#), the following vowel shifts occur: /i/→ /a/, /o/ → /u/, and /u/ → /i/.[10]

Phrase final consonant insertion similar to that in Baikeno occurs to a lesser extent in Molo, though for the varieties of Molo on which I have collected data it is not as consistent or regular and does not seem to have become phonological to the same extent as other Meto varieties with consonant insertion. In the variety of Molo represented by Middelkoop (1972), insertion of *l* occurs after *e* for some, but not all, words with a final vowel sequence.

In Middelkoop (1972) insertion of *l* also occurs for some words with final *a*. The three examples that are included in this comparative dictionary are *sikəh > **sia > *sia-l* 'lath', *fia > *fia-l* 'kind of wild tuber' and *huŋga > *uka-l* 'chop big branches'. Insertion of *l* after *a* is also attested in Fatule'u and Amfo'an, but in both varieties (and probably also in Molo) it does not appear to have exactly the same distributions and functions as consonant insertion in other varieties of Meto.

2.5.3 Diphthongisation and vowel assimilation

Ro'is Amarasi has two productive phonological processes that affect the citation forms of consonant final words: diphthongisation and assimilation of /a/. Both these processes affect words of the shape (C)VCVC# so long as the final consonant is not the glottal stop /ʔ/. Both processes are productive and affect vowel final words when their final syllable is closed by a following mono-consonantal enclitic or a word with an initial consonant cluster. See Edwards (2020:137f, 181) for more examples and discussion.

Firstly, the penultimate vowel of such words is diphthongised by addition of an off-glide of the same quality as the final vowel; that is, $V_{\alpha}CV_{\beta}C\# \rightarrow V_{\alpha}{}^{\frown}V_{\beta}CV_{\beta}C\#$. This process does not affect words that have /a/ as final vowel in varieties of Ro'is for which I have collected most data. Examples are given in Table 2.6 alongside their Kotos Amarasi cognates for comparison. Throughout this dictionary Ro'is Amarasi diphthongs that are a result of this process are transcribed with a tie-bar < ⁀ > to distinguish them that underlying vowel sequences.

Table 2.6: Ro'is Amarasi diphthongisation

Kotos	Ro'is	Gloss	Kotos	Ro'is	Gloss
tefis	*te͡ifik*	'roof'	*niis eno-f*	*niis e͡ono-f*	'incisors'
masik	*ma͡isik*	'salt'	*n-ʔator*	*n-ʔa͡otor*	'arrange'
toʔis	*to͡iʔis*	'trumpet'	*siʔu-f*	*si͡uʔu-f*	'elbow'
hunik	*hu͡inik*	'turmeric'	*esuk*	*e͡usuk*	'mortar'
anet	*a͡enet*	'needle'	*manus*	*ma͡unus*	'betel pepper'
rone-f	*ro͡ene-f*	'brain'	*ponu-f*	*po͡unu-f*	'body hair'†

10 To further complicate matters, the variety of Timaus spoken in Sanenu hamlet where most of my Timaus data was gathered has *e > a /C_#. Thus, Proto-Meto *ume > *uma* 'house' phrase medially and *uma-l* phrase finally. This change occurred after the development of consonant insertion in Timaus.

† Ro'is Amarasi *po͡unu-f* is 'body hair' and Kotos *ponu-f* is moustache.

Secondly, when the final vowel of (C)VCVC# words is /a/ (and the final consonant is not /ʔ/), this vowel usually assimilates to the quality of the penultimate vowel. Examples are given in Table 2.7. There is some variation in the application of this process and some words have been attested with and without variants with assimilation of final /a/. Assimilation of /a/ in final closed syllables also occurs in Timaus.

Table 2.7: Ro'is Amarasi assimilation of final /a/ /_C#

Kotos	Ro'is	Gloss
ʔnima-f	*nimi-f*	'arm, hand'
sbeta-f	*sbete-f*	'upper arm'
ekam	*erem, eram*	'wild pandanus'
na-tenab	*na-teneb*	'think'
okam	*okom, okam*	'gourd, melon'
oras	*oros*	'time'†
ruman	*rumun*	'empty'
utan	*utuk, utak*	'vegetables; pumpkin, squash'‡
surat	*surut*	'paper, book'#

† From Portuguese *horas* [ɔras] 'hours'.

‡ Kotos Amarasi *utan* means only 'vegetables'.

From Malay *surat* 'letter'.

Finally, Kotos Amarasi has historic assimilation of final /a/ in syllables preceded by a glottal stop and closed by a consonant other than a glottal stop; that is, V_αʔaC# → V_αʔV_αC#. Examples include Kotos Amarasi *keʔen,* other Meto *keʔan* 'room' and Kotos Amarasi *poʔon,* other Meto *poʔan* 'orchard'.

2.6 Morphology

In this section I provide an overview of the affixal morphology of the Rote-Meto languages. The purpose here is to present a succinct summary of the forms and usual semantic functions of morphology that occurs in this dictionary. This summary is based on Jonker (1915) and Tamelan (2021) for the Rote languages, as well as my own fieldwork for Meto. A more comprehensive description of Meto affixal morphology is Edwards (2020:439–458).

A summary of morphology is also needed as many forms included in this dictionary are only attested in morphologically complex forms with no putative mono-morphemic root attested. In most cases all such morphology is marked in the same way as productive morphology. Strings that can be confidently identified as an instance of frozen morphology are separated from the (historic) base by the vertical bar |, as discussed at the beginning of §1.4.

2.6.1 Nominal suffix *-k/-ʔ*

Many nouns in the Rote languages occur with the suffix *-k/-ʔ*. Tii, Lole, Ba'a, Keka, Termanu and Bokai have *-k*, while Dela-Oenale, Dengka, Korbafo, Bilbaa, Landu, Rikou and Oepao have *-ʔ*. The presence or absence of this suffix is partially lexically dependent. Nouns can be divided into two classes: those that are eligible to take this suffix, and those that never take this suffix (except after derivation with other nominalising morphology, see §2.6.4). Thus, for instance, Termanu *bafi* 'pig' and *manu* 'chicken' never occur with this suffix while *neʔe-k* 'ant' and *bau-k* 'bat' do take this suffix in appropriate environments. Nouns that are eligible to take this suffix in the Rote languages are given in this dictionary with this suffix.

One function of this suffix is to mark the end of the noun phrase. Thus, nouns modified by another noun do not take this suffix, with the final noun of an attributive phrase taking this suffix as long as it is a member of the class of eligible nouns. Examples of attributive phrases from Termanu extracted from Jonker (1908) are given in Table 2.8. Note also that there does not appear to be a grammatical basis for a noun/adjective distinction in the Rote languages.

Table 2.8: Termanu nominal *-k*

Noun			Modifier			Phrase	
lima-k	'arm/hand'	+	*kuʔu-k*	'finger/toe'	→	*lima kuʔu-k*	'finger'
lima-k	'arm/hand'	+	*dale-k*	'inside'	→	*lima dale-k*	'palm'
ei-k	'foot/leg'	+	*kuʔu-k*	'finger/toe'	→	*ei kuʔu-k*	'toe'
ei-k	'foot/leg'	+	*buʔu-k*	'joint'	→	*ei buʔu-k*	'ankle'
neʔe-k	'ant'	+	*ŋgeo-k*	'black'	→	*neʔe ŋgeo-k*	'black ant'
timi-k	'jaw'	+	*dui-k*	'bone'	→	*timi dui-k*	'jawbone'
beba-k	'leaf stalk'	+	*tula*	'gebang'	→	*beba tula*	'gebang palm leaf stalk'
iʔa-k	'fish'	+	*tasi*	'sea'	→	*iʔa tasi*	'ocean fish'

There also appear to be certain Termanu nouns that only take the suffix *-k* in isolation and do not take it when they are the final member of a phrase. Two examples are *meŋe* 'snake' + *maa-k* 'tongue' → *meŋe maa* 'snake tongue', and *kaa-k* 'fig tree' + *daa-k* 'blood' → *kaa daa* 'fig tree sap'. The extent to which there are similar nouns in other varieties of Rote is currently unknown.

When a noun that is eligible to take the suffix *-k* is modified by a non-nominal modifier, such as a quantifier, numeral or demonstrative, the suffix *-k* occurs on the head noun. One example is Termanu *bula-k* 'moon, month' + *telu* 'three' → *bula-k telu* 'three months'.

Tamelan (2021) identifies two main (non-derivational) functions for Dela nominal *-ʔ*. The first is as an attributive suffix with functions similar to Termanu *-k*. Like in Termanu, there are certain words that are eligible to occur with this suffix and certain words that are not. Those nouns that are eligible take this suffix in isolation and when they are the final member of an attributive phrase.

The second function is as a generic genitive in non-referential genitive constructions for nouns that are in a part–whole relationship with the possessor. In this second function the suffix *-ʔ* is not restricted to a subset of eligible nouns (as in the attributive use), but occurs on all nouns. Two examples are *noo oe-ʔ* 'water of a coconut' and *sapi tei-ʔ* 'faeces of a cow'. Neither *oe* 'water' nor *tei* 'faeces' occurs with *-ʔ* in isolation or as the final member of an attributive phrase.

The non-derivational uses of this suffix do not occur in Meto. However, Meto cognates of words that take the nominal suffix *-k/-ʔ* in Rote languages often have a final *k* or *ʔ*. These final consonants are probably not best analysed as suffixes in Meto, but as part of the root. When all Rote members of a cognate set are eligible to take *-k/-ʔ* and at least one variety of Meto has a final *k* or *ʔ*, I reconstruct the PRM noun as eligible to take *-k. This is indicated by the presence of this suffix in the morphology field (§1.5.3.1).

In some instances when PRM *-k has become a glottal stop in Meto, and Meto has a root final vowel sequence, perceptual metathesis (Blevins and Garrett 1998:510–522) of the glottal stop (from *-k) with the root final vowel has occurred; thus *$V_1V_2ʔ$ > $V_1ʔV_2$. Examples include PRM *beu-k 'new' > Amanuban *feu|ʔ* > Amarasi *feʔu*, and *doo-k 'leaf' > Amanuban *noo|ʔ* > Amarasi *noʔo* 'leaf'. Consistent with the origin of these glottal stops as affixes, they do not occur when such nouns take a productive suffix. Thus, Amarasi has *moen feu-f* 'son-in-law' and *noo-n* 'leaf-3SG.GEN'.

Finally, Kusa-Manea has a nominal suffix *-k,* the function and productivity of which is unclear. While it is possible that this suffix is a direct reflex of PRM *-k, this is not certain. Instead, this suffix may be borrowed from/influenced by Tetun *-k,* which occurs with a number of different nominal functions (van Klinken 1999:58ff). Examples include Kusa-Manea *fatu ~ fatu-k* 'stone, rock' (Tetun *fatu ~ fatuk*) and *noʔo-k* 'leaf' (but *noo-n* 'leaf-3GEN').

2.6.2 Possessive morphology

The Rote-Meto languages have productive possessive morphology that is attached to the possessed noun and agrees with the possessor in person and number. The Rote languages have enclitics and Meto has suffixes. The possessive paradigms of the Rote-Meto languages are given in Table 2.9.

Table 2.9: Rote-Meto possessive morphology

	1SG	2SG	3SG	1PL.INCL	1PL.EXCL/2PL	3PL	0
PRM	*ŋga	*ma	*na	*nda	*ma	*nda	
Dela	*=ŋga*	*=ma*	*=na*	*=na/=ta*	*=ma*	*=na*	
Oenale, Dengka, Tii	*=ŋga*	*=ma*	*=na*	*=na*	*=ma*	*=na*	
Termanu, Bilbaa, Bokai, Korbafo, Ba'a	*=ŋa*	*=ma*	*=na*	*=na*	*=ma*	*=na*	
Rikou	*=ka*	*=ma*	*=na*	*=na*	*=ma*	*=na*	
Ro'is	*-k*	*-m*	*-n*	*-r*	*-m*	*-r*	*-f*
Kotos Amarasi	*-k*	*-m*	*-n*	*-k*	*-m*	*-k*	*-f*
Amfo'an	*-k*	*-m*	*-n*	*-k*	*-m*	*-k*	*-f*
Kusa-Manea	*-k*	*-m*	*-n*	*-k*	*-m*	*-n*	*-f*

In Rote all possessed nouns take a genitive enclitic. These enclitics have four forms. In addition to the *=Ca* forms given in Table 2.9, these enclitics also have a reduced form with no final vowel, thus =C. When they attach to a consonant final stem the vowel /a/ is inserted between the stem and the enclitic. Thus, for example, the 3SG genitive enclitic has four forms: *=na* or *=n* with vowel final stems and *=ana* or *=an* with consonant final stems. The only Rote genitive enclitic that occurs in this dictionary is the 3SG enclitic, which occurs on a small number of terms given by Jonker (1908), as well as some Landu words collected during my fieldwork (§1.3.1.2).

The Meto languages have a paradigm of genitive suffixes. Unlike the Rote languages, only some nouns take genitive suffixes in Meto. Most such nouns are in a part–whole relationship with the possessor and typically include body parts or properties of the possessor. Furthermore, many nouns have only been attested with a genitive suffix. Such nouns are given in this dictionary with the suffix *-f*, which is used for unpossessed parts. Exceptions are a number of Ro'is Amarasi nouns that have only been attested with the 3SG suffix *-n*, as well as a number of Molo nouns that are only given by Middelkoop (1972) with either the 1SG suffix *-k* or 3SG suffix *-n*.

Some kin terms also occur with genitive suffixes in Meto. In Ro'is Amarasi the suffixes taken by kin terms are the same as those taken by other nouns, while in most other known varieties of Meto kin terms with 3SG possessors take the suffix *-f* while other possessors usually trigger no suffix.[11] In Kusa-Manea, kin terms do not appear to take any genitive suffixes, though this observation is based only on words elicited in isolation.

2.6.3 Reduplication

The Rote-Meto languages have two kinds of reduplication: partial reduplication and full reduplication. In the Rote languages partial reduplication copies the first (C)V syllable of a base and places it to the left of that base.[12] Termanu examples include *deʔa* 'say, speak' → *de~deʔa-k* 'that which is said', *bali* 'mix' → *ba~bali-k* 'mixture' and *n-inu* 'drink' → *ni~ninu-k* 'a drink'.

In all known varieties of Meto except Kusa-Manea, partial reduplication copies the first CVC syllable of a disyllabic CV(C)V(C) foot and places it to the left of this foot. If a root contains consonant clusters or has more than two syllables, the reduplicant is an infix. One productive use of syllable reduplication in Meto is as an intensive. Examples from Kotos Amarasi include: *koʔu* 'big' → ***koʔ**~koʔu* 'very big', *anaʔ* → ***an**~anaʔ* 'very small', *ʔroo* 'far' → ***ʔro**~roo* 'very far', *maʔfenaʔ* → *maʔ**fen**~fenaʔ* 'very heavy' and *paumakaʔ* 'near' → *pau**mak**~makaʔ* 'very near'.

11 The situation regarding kin terms and possessive suffixes in Meto is complex. Thus, in Kotos Amarasi third person plural possessors also occasionally trigger use of the suffix *-f* while in Koro'oto hamlet (where most of my Amarasi data was collected) all possessors optionally trigger use of the suffix *-f* with this suffix only not occurring for unpossessed kin terms, such as vocatives.

12 The base for reduplication in the Rote is identical to an underlying root in nearly all cases. The only exception is vowel initial verbs, which obligatorily occur with a consonantal prefix (§12.6.5) for which the third person form is the base for reduplication; e.g. the reduplicative base for √*-inu* 'drink' is *n-inu*.

The reduplicant in Kusa-Manea consists of the first consonant of the final foot and the default vowel /a/. Like other varieties of Meto, this reduplicant is placed to the immediate left of the foot; thus, $C_1V(C)V(C) \rightarrow C_1a{\sim}C_1V(C)V(C)$. This structure is the same as partial reduplication in Tetun (van Klinken 1999:44). Examples include the following: *neno* 'sun, day' → *na~neno-ʔ* 'bright, midday', *mii* 'urine' → *ma~mii-f* 'bladder', *mukə > **k|muʔa → *k|ma~muaʔ-r=aa* 'wild pigeon', and *na-ʔboniʔ* 'hang' → *ʔba~boniʔ* 'hanging'.

Full reduplication in Meto copies the entire root. Examples include *batuur* 'true' → *batuur~batuur* 'truly' and *neno* 'day' → *neno~neno* 'every day'. Full reduplication has the same structure in the Rote languages. Examples from Dela include *ume* 'house' → *ume~ume* 'various houses', *nduar* 'sleepy' → *nduar~nduar* 'very sleepy', and *na-mbeta* '3SG-painful' → *nambeta~nambeta* 'intensely painful' (Tamelan 2021:41).

Many forms in the Rote-Meto languages are only attested in a reduplicated form without any known base. Such frozen reduplication is not differentiated from productive reduplication in this dictionary. In both cases the reduplicant is separated from the base by a tilde '~'. Likely cases of frozen reduplication can be identified by the lack of any base without reduplication in their entry.

2.6.4 Nominalisation

The Rote languages have a handful of nominalising processes, which are attested in this dictionary. Firstly, partial reduplication combined with the nominal suffix *-k/-ʔ*, as seen in Termanu *deʔa* 'say, speak' → *de~deʔa-k* 'that which is said', *bali* 'mix' → *ba~bali-k* 'mixture', and *n-inu* 'drink' → *ni~ninu-k* 'a drink'. In Dengka and Dela-Oenale such reduplication combines with one of three suffixes: *-ʔ*, *-s* or *-t*. Examples from Dela include *ɓae* 'pay' → *ɓa~ɓae-ʔ* 'payment', *lemba* 'carry with a shoulder pole' → *le~lemba-t* 'shoulder pole', and *fitiʔ* 'fire slingshot' → *fi~fiti-s* 'fire with a slingshot'. In Dela, stems with a /t/ only take *-s* while other stems take any of the three suffixes.

Another Rote nominalising morpheme in this dictionary is the property prefix *ma-*. Examples from Termanu include *tane-k* 'sharp, pointy, sharpness' → *ma-tane* 'sharp', *dalu-k* 'long' → *ma-dalu* 'long, length', and *tobi* 'burn, scorch' → *ma-tobi-k* 'hot'. The prefix *ma-* is also a verbal prefix, in which case it forms stative verbs (§2.6.6).

The Meto cluster has half a dozen affixes that serve a nominalising function, given in Table 2.10. All except one of these affixes are circumfixes. A more complete discussion of the different functions of these affixes in Kotos Amarasi is given in Edwards (2020:439–458).

Table 2.10: Meto nominalisation morphology

Form			Gloss	Notes
		-t	result NMLZ	*-s* when root contains /t/
ʔa-	...	*-t*	actor NMLZ	*ka-*... *-t* in Ro'is Amarasi, suffix *-s* when root contains /t/
ʔ-	...	*-ʔ*	tool NMLZ	final *-ʔ* is an intervocalic infix for VV# final roots
ma-	...	*-ʔ*	property NMLZ	final *-ʔ* is an intervocalic infix for VV# final roots
m-	...	*-ʔ*	stative NMLZ	not fully productive, final *-ʔ* intervocalic infix for VV# final roots
Ca~	...	*-ʔ*	NMLZ	only known in Kusa-Manea, initial element is a reduplicant

2.6.5 Verb agreement

The Rote-Meto languages have productive verbal subject agreement prefixes. In all Rote-Meto languages there are two paradigms: a vocalic paradigm with prefixes of the shape CV-, and a consonantal paradigm in which the prefixes consist of a single consonant, which is the first consonant of the corresponding prefix in the vocalic paradigm. The vocalic and consonantal agreement prefixes are given in Table 2.11 and Table 2.12, respectively.[13]

Table 2.11: Vocalic agreement prefixes

	1SG	2SG	3SG	1PL.INCL	1PL.EXCL/2PL	3PL
PRM	*ku-	*mu-	*i-/*na-	*ta-	*mi-	*ra-
Dela, Oenale	*ʔu-*	*mu-*	*na-*	*ta-*	*mi-*	*ra-*
Dengka	*ʔu-*	*mu-*	*na-*	*ta-*	*mi-*	*la-*
Tii	*ʔa-*	*ma-*	*i-/na-*†	*ta-*	*ma-*	*ra-*
Lole	*ʔa-*	*ma-*	*ni-/i-/na-*†	*ta-*	*ma-*	*la-*
Termanu, Ba'a	*ʔa-*	*ma-*	*na-*	*ta-*	*ma-*	*la-*
Bilbaa, Bokai, Korbafo	*ka-*	*ma-*	*na-*	*ta-*	*ma-*	*la-*
Rikou, Oepao	*ʔa-*	*ma-*	*na-*	*ta-*	*ma-*	*ra-*
Ro'is Amarasi	*ku-*	*mu-*	*na-*	*ta-*	*mi-*	*na-*
Nuclear Meto	*ʔu-*	*mu-*	*na-*	*ta-*	*mi-*	*na-*

† Jonker (1915:411) has Tii 3SG *i-* and Lole 3SG *ni-*. Unit Bahasa and Budaya (2016:vi) and Zacharias et al. (2014) have Tii and Lole *na-*. For Lole, Adika Balukh (pers. comm. September 2020) reports that *i-* is still used regularly and is particularly associated with northeast regions. She reports that she may have heard *ni-* in the past, but is not confident. For Tii, Yanti Tunliu-Mooy (pers. comm. September 2020) recalls hearing *i-* more often in the past and associates this form with certain regions. The *na-* form is dominant.

Table 2.12: Consonantal Agreement prefixes

	1SG	2SG	3SG	1PL.INCL	1PL.EXCL/2PL	3PL
PRM	*k-	*m-	*n-	*t-	*m-	*r-
Bilbaa, Bokai, Korbafo	*k-*	*m-*	*n-*	*t-*	*m-*	*l-*
Dela, Oenale, Rikou, Tii	*ʔ-*	*m-*	*n-*	*t-*	*m-*	*r-*
Dengka, Lole, Termanu, Ba'a	*ʔ-*	*m-*	*n-*	*t-*	*m-*	*l-*
Ro'is Amarasi	*k-*#V *ʔ-*#C	*m-*	*n-*	*t-*	*m-*	*n-*
Nuclear Meto (all other Meto)	*ʔ-*	*m-*	*n-*	*t-*	*m-*	*n-*

Verbs that take agreement prefixes are usually cited throughout this comparative dictionary in the third person form. Tii and Lole verbs that take vocalic prefixes are usually cited with the third person prefix *na-*, except where Jonker (1908) gives only a form with *i-* or *ni-*.

In Meto nearly all verbs take agreement in most circumstances. One exception is Kusa-Manea, for which consonant initial verbs that take consonantal prefixes are often cited without any prefix. When this is the only form of a Kusa-Manea verb I have so far collected, I give this form as it is attested in my data without any prefix.

13 In addition to the prefixes given in Table 2.11, Tamelan (2021:129) also gives 0 person (a kind of obviative used when the subject is irrelevant or not in focus) *ne-* for Dela.

The 1SG consonantal prefix displays allomorphy in Meto. In all known varieties it is realised as Ø before another glottal stop; that is, *ʔ-ʔ* → *ʔ*. In Ro'is Amarasi it has the form *k-* before vowels and *ʔ-* before consonants other than glottal stop (where it is realised as Ø).

Which paradigm is used in Meto is partially determined by the phonotactic shape of the verb, partially determined by the semantics of the verb and partially lexically determined. The use of each paradigm is summarised in Table 2.13, with examples from Kotos Amarasi to illustrate. Roots that have more than two syllables, as well as vowel initial roots, take consonantal prefixes.[14] Roots that begin with a consonant cluster take the vocalic set. Consonant initial roots that consist of a single foot take either set with the choice lexically specified. Verbs that have both transitive and intransitive forms are an exception. Such verbs take the vocalic set when transitive and the consonantal set when intransitive.

Table 2.13: Meto agreement according to stem shapes

Stem Shape		Paradigm	Kotos Example	Gloss
(σ)σσσ	three or more syllables	consonantal	*n-ʔeus/fani*	'sneeze'
#CC	cluster initial disyllable	vocalic	*na-m|naha*	'hungry'
#V	vowel initial disyllable	consonantal	*n-inu*	'drink'
#C	consonant initial disyllable	75% consonantal†	*n-sae*	'go up'
		25% vocalic	*na-sai*	'flow'
#C	transitive	vocalic	*na-tama*	'make enter'
	intransitive	consonantal	*n-tama*	'enter'

† Percentages for Kotos Amarasi based on 836 verbs, of which 557 are consonant initial disyllables.

Like in Meto, there are a range of phonological, lexical and morphological factors that determine verb agreement in the Rote languages. However, unlike in Meto, there are many verbs that do not take any agreement prefix. My discussion in this section is based mainly on data from Dela, which is most clearly described (Tamelan 2021:129–138). The main conditioning factors determining verb agreement in the Rote languages are summarised in Table 2.14, illustrated with examples from Dela.

Table 2.14: Rote agreement according to stem shapes

Stem Shape		Paradigm	Dela Example	Gloss
#V	vowel initial	consonantal	*n-ala*	'get'
		vocalic	*na-iru*	'pregnant'
		none	*ale*	'chew'
#C	consonant initial	vocalic	*na-riu*	'bathe'
		none	*mae*	'ashamed'
N/V → V	derived verb	vocalic	*oe* → *na-oe*	'watery'
			mae → *na-mae-ʔ*	'make ashamed'
ma-	with stative *ma-*	none	*ma-lole*	'good'
CV-	with other prefix (§2.6.6)	vocalic	*na-sa-roi*	'lean'

14 Loan words in Meto also take prefixes drawn from the consonantal paradigm.

Derived verbs nearly always take vocalic prefixes. This includes verbs derived from a nominal base and verbs derived from another verb. For verbs derived from other verbs, agreement prefixes are used with causatives, such as in Dela *mae* 'ashamed' → *na-mae-ʔ* 'make ashamed' or reciprocals, such as Dela *ʔidu* 'kiss' → *na-ʔidu* 'kiss one another'.[15] Similarly, verbs that take any derivational CV- prefix (see §2.6.6) take vocalic prefixes, with the exception of verbs derived with the stative/inchoative prefix *ma-*, which do not take prefixes. All other verbs are divided into lexical classes. Vowel initial verbs are divided between verbs that take consonantal agreement prefixes, those that take vocalic agreement prefixes, and those that take no agreement prefixes. Consonant initial verbs are divided between those that take vocalic agreement prefixes, and those that do not take agreement prefixes.

Apart from the verbs that take agreement prefixes, there are also two verbs that have partially suppletive paradigms in some of the Rote-Meto languages. These are the reflexes of *emə 'come' and *eu 'go, to'. See the respective entries for each of these verbs for their declensions.

2.6.6 Derivational verbal morphology

There are two fully productive verbal derivational prefixes in the Rote languages and a number of unproductive or semi-productive prefixes. The most productive prefix in the Rote languages is *ma-*, which derives non-active verbs with a stative or process sense. In addition to productive prefixes, the Rote languages have a number of non-productive, or semi-productive, CV- prefixes that occur with verbs. Verbs that occur with these prefixes also take vocalic agreement prefixes. The semi-productive verb prefixes that can be identified in the Rote languages are given in Table 2.15, listed roughly in order of their productivity in Dela.

Table 2.15: Rote verb prefixes†

Dela, Oenale	*ʔV-*	*mV-*	*kV-*	*sV-*	*mbV-*	*lV-*	*tV-*	*fV-*	*pV-*	*ŋgV-*	*rV-*
Dengka	*ʔV-*	*mV-*	*kV-*	*sV-*	*mbV-*	*lV-*	*tV-*	*fV-*	*pV-*	*ŋgV-*	*lV-*
Tii	*kV-*	*mV-*	*kV-*	*sV-*	*mbV-*	*lV-*	*tV-*	*fV-*	*pV-*	*ŋgV-*	*rV-*
Ba'a	*ka-*	*ma-*	*ka-*	*sa-*	*mpa-*	*la-*	*ta-*	*fa-*	*pa-*	*ŋga-*	*la-*
Termanu, Bilbaa, Bokai, Korbafo	*ka-*	*ma-*	*ka-*	*sa-*	*pa-*	*la-*	*ta-*	*fa-*	*pa-*	*ŋa-*	*la-*
Rikou	Ø	*ma-*	Ø	*sa-*	*pa-*	*la-*	*ta-*	*fa-*	*pa-*	*ka-*	*ra-*

† The unspecified vowel in Dela, Oenale, Dengka and Tii assimilates to the quality of the vowel of the previous agreement prefix.

There are many verb roots in the Rote languages that always occur with one of these prefixes and do not occur without any verbal prefix. Thus, for instance, in Dela the verbs *na-ʔa-minaʔ* 'play' and *na-sa-pedoʔ* 'fold legs' always occur with these prefixes and the hypothetical roots √*minaʔ* and √*pedoʔ* do not occur independently.

15 The use of vocalic prefixes to derive verbs from a verbal base also occurs with vowel initial verbs that take consonantal prefixes, such as in *n-inu* 'drink' → *na-n-inu-ʔ* 'make drink'.

Apart from this, some of these prefixes have some use in deriving verbs from nouns or deriving alternate meanings from verbal stems. Tamelan (2021:139) describes the selection of these prefixes in Dela as partly semantically determined and partly lexically determined. The prefixes *ma-* and *mba-* tend to form stative or inchoative verbs, while *ʔa-* often derives process verbs from property nominals.[16] However, even among the more productive prefixes, any semantic properties are only tendencies and none are fully semantically determined.

All verbs that occur with a prefix usually also take an agreement prefix (§2.6.5). The vowel of the derivational prefix assimilates to the quality of the vowel of the agreement prefix. Examples from Dela are given in Table 2.16. Whether this assimilation occurs in the Nuclear Rote languages is mostly a moot point as the vowel of nearly all agreement prefixes in these languages is /a/. However, this assimilation does occur with Tii 3SG *i-* and Lole 3SG *ni-*. Examples include Tii *i-mi-nene*, and Lole *ni-mi-nene* 'hear' (see *nene), as well as lole *ni-fi-lende* 'remember' (see *farəndən).

Table 2.16: Assimilation of prefix vowel in Dela

	'play'	**'become smart'**	**'remember'**	**'reach'**	**'scatter'**
	-ʔV-minaʔ	*-mV-hine*	*-sV-neda*	*-mbV-nai*	*-lV-ono*
1SG	*ʔu-ʔu-minaʔ*	*ʔu-mu-hine*	*ʔu-su-neda*	*ʔu-mbu-nai*	*ʔu-lu-ono*
2SG	*mu-ʔu-minaʔ*	*mu-mu-hine*	*mu-su-neda*	*mu-mbu-nai*	*mu-lu-ono*
3SG	*na-ʔa-minaʔ*	*na-ma-hine*	*na-sa-neda*	*na-mba-nai*	*na-la-ono*
1PL.INCL	*ta-ʔa-minaʔ*	*ta-ma-hine*	*ta-sa-neda*	*ta-mba-nai*	*ta-la-ono*
1PL.EXCL/2PL	*mi-ʔi-minaʔ*	*mi-mi-hine*	*mi-si-neda*	*mi-mbi-nai*	*mi-li-ono*
3PL	*ra-ʔa-minaʔ*	*ra-ma-hine*	*ra-sa-neda*	*ra-mba-nai*	*ra-la-ono*
0	*ne-ʔe-minaʔ*	*ne-me-hine*	*ne-se-neda*	*ne-mbe-nai*	*ne-le-ono*

In several instances, the presence of one of these prefixes on a verb in the Rote languages is due to reanalysis of a historic antepenultimate syllable that was lost in one form but retained in another, leading to alternations with and without the prefix. Once example is PRM *salili 'armpit' for which Meto has *snini-f* 'armpit' and *na-snini* 'carry slung under the armpit' while Termanu has the noun *lili_bolo-k* 'armpit' (*bolo-k* = 'hole') and the verb *na-sa-lili* 'carry slung under the armpit'.

Apart from these prefixes, the only other Rote derivational verbal morphology that features in this dictionary is the applicative/transitive suffix *-k/-ʔ*. This suffix has the same form as the nominal *-k/-ʔ* suffix. That is, Tii, Lole, Ba'a, Keka, Termanu and Bokai have *-k*, while Dela-Oenale, Dengka, Korbafo, Bilbaa, Landu, Rikou and Oepao have *-ʔ*. Because verbs that take this suffix are derived, they also usually take agreement prefixes, as discussed in §2.6.5.

16 There are two formally similar prefixes in Dela: *ma-*, which productively derives non-active state or process verbs from nouns; and *mV-*, which is semi-productive. They can be distinguished, as verbs with fully productive *ma-* do not take agreement prefixes while those with semi-productive *mV-* always take vocalic agreement prefixes.

3

Historical background

3.1 Introduction

In this chapter I discuss the historical background of the Rote-Meto languages. This includes the sound correspondences (§3.2), the internal subgrouping of the Rote-Meto group (§3.3), and the way Rote-Meto fits into the Austronesian language family as a whole (§3.5).

Slightly earlier versions of the sound correspondences and internal subgrouping, along with detailed discussion, can be found in Edwards (2016, 2018a, 2018c). In this chapter I only discuss those parts of my analysis that have been revised since the appearance of these publications.

3.2 Sound correspondences

The reconstructed PRM phoneme inventory is given in Table 3.1. This is the same as the inventory posited in Edwards (2018a), with the addition of PRM *ʤ and *w for both of which evidence has since been adduced. Both these proto-phonemes are marginal, with only two attestations each.

Table 3.1: Proto-Rote-Meto phoneme inventory

	Consonants						Vowels		
	Labial	**Coronal**	**Palatal**	**Velar**	**Glottal**		**Front**	**Central**	**Back**
Voiceless plosive	*p	*t		*k	*ʔ	High	*i		*u
Voiced plosive	*b	*d	(*ʤ)			Mid	*e	*ə	*o
Implosive	*ɓ	*ɗ				Low		*a	
Prenasalised plosive	*mb	*nd		*ŋg					
Fricative	*f	*s			*h				
Nasal	*m	*n		*ŋ					
Rhotic		*r							
Lateral		*l							
Glide	(*w)								

The sound correspondences between PRM and its daughter languages are summarised in §3.2.1–§3.2.3, in a number of tables. Where there are multiple reflexes in a single language due to unconditioned splits, the more common reflex is given first. The number of attestations of each correspondence set is given in the second last row (*attestations*), while the final row (*irr. attestations*) shows the number of irregular correspondence sets that attest the reconstructed proto-phoneme. Most of these irregular correspondences have only one or two unexpected reflexes, which are noted in the *irr. from PRM* field (see §1.5.3.5) in the relevant entries.

Most of these correspondences have been discussed in full detail in Edwards (2018a), and I do not repeat that discussion in the following sections. Since the publication of that paper, however, my understanding of some correspondence sets is better developed, which has led to a number of minor adjustments. I discuss these adjustments in the following sections.

3.2.1 Initial and medial consonants

Table 3.2, Table 3.3 and Table 3.4 give the correspondences for consonants in intervocalic and foot initial position.[1] Discussion of word initial consonants in trisyllables can be found in Edwards (2018a:395f). PRM *k shows several unconditioned splits, with a number of different patterns identifiable. These splits are discussed in detail in Edwards (2018a:383–387), though that discussion is based on a slightly earlier understanding of the data.[2] Similarly, PRM *d shows a two-way unconditioned split, discussed further in §3.2.1.1.

Table 3.2: Proto-Rote-Meto voiceless plosive correspondences

Pattern			**k-1**	**k-2†**	**k-3**	**k-4**	**k-5**	**k-6**	**k-7**	**k-8**	**k-9**	**k-10**	
PRM	***p**	***t**	***k-‡**				***-k-#**						***ʔ**
Dela-Oenale	*p*	*t*	*k*	*ʔ*	*ʔ*	*h*	*k*	*ʔ*	*k*	*ʔ/Ø*	*ʔ*	*ʔ/Ø*	*ʔ/Ø*
Dengka	*p*	*t*	*k*	*ʔ*	*ʔ*	*h*	*k*	*ʔ*	*k*	*ʔ/Ø*	*ʔ*	*ʔ/Ø*	*ʔ/Ø*
Tii	*p*	*t*	*k*	*k*	*k*	Ø	*k*	*k*	*ʔ*	*ʔ*	*ʔ*	*ʔ*	*ʔ*
Lole	*p*	*t*	*k*	*k*	*k*	Ø	*k*	*k*	*ʔ*	*ʔ*	*ʔ*	*ʔ*	*ʔ*
Ba'a	*p/mp*	*t*	*k*	*k*	*k*	Ø	*k*	*k*	*ʔ*	*ʔ*	*ʔ*	*ʔ*	*ʔ*
Termanu	*p*	*t*	*k*	*k*	*k*	Ø	*k*	*k*	*ʔ*	*ʔ*	*ʔ*	*ʔ*	*ʔ*
Korbafo	*p*	*t*	*k*	*k*	*k*	*Ø/k*	*k*	*k*	*ʔ*	*ʔ*	*ʔ*	*ʔ*	*ʔ*
Bokai	*p*	*t*	*k*	*k*	*k*	*Ø/k*	*k*	*k*	*ʔ*	*ʔ*	*ʔ*	*ʔ*	*ʔ*
Bilbaa	*p*	*t*	*k*	*k*	*k*	*Ø/k*	*k*	*k*	*k*	*k*	*k*	*k*	Ø
Landu	*p*	*t*		*k/ʔ*	*ʔ*	Ø	*k*		k		*k*	*k*	*ʔ/Ø*
Rikou	*p*	*t*	*k/ʔ/Ø*	*ʔ/Ø*	*ʔ*	Ø	*ʔ/k*	*ʔ/k*	*k/ʔ*	*ʔ/k*	*ʔ/k*	*k/ʔ*	*ʔ/Ø*
Oepao	*p*	*t*	*k/ʔ/Ø*	*ʔ/Ø*	*ʔ*	Ø	ʔ/k	ʔ/k		ʔ/k		*k/ʔ*	*ʔ/Ø*

1 'Foot initial' is before the stressed syllable of the disyllabic foot. A quadrisyllabic reconstruction such as *baŋakuɗu 'Morinda citrifolia' has two foot initial consonants: *b and *k, respectively. Similarly, the foot initial consonant in a trisyllabic reconstruction such as *ɓalafo 'Mallotus philippensis' is the second consonant, in this case *l.

2 The patterns of PRM *k in Table 3.2 broadly match the discussion in Edwards (2018a:383ff), though with different labels. The cross-references between the labels in each work for initial *k- are as follows (label in this dictionary = label in Table 22 of Edwards 2018a:383): k-1 = set 2, k-2 = set 1, k-3 = set 3, k-4 = set 4. Set 5 in Edwards (2018a) is now considered irregular (marked k-irr). The patterns identified for medial *-k- in this dictionary are more fine-grained than those identified in Edwards (2018a). As a result, the two sets of patterns and their members do not exactly match. Cross-references that mostly hold for medial *-k- are as follows (label in this dictionary = label in Table 27 and Table 28 of Edwards 2018a:387): k-5 = set 1, k-8 = set 5, k-9 = set 3, k-10 = set 4.

Pattern			k-1	k-2†	k-3	k-4	k-5	k-6	k-7	k-8	k-9	k-10	
PRM	*p	*t	*k-‡				*-k-#						*ʔ
Proto-Meto	*p	*t	*k	*k	*h	*h	*k	*k/*ʔ	*ʔ	Ø	*ʔ	*k	*ʔ
Ro'is Amarasi	*p*	*t*	*k*	*k*	*h*	*h*	*k*	*k/ʔ*	*ʔ*	Ø	*ʔ*	*k*	*ʔ*
Kotos Amar.	*p*	*t*	*k*	*k/ʔ*	*h*	*h*	*k*	*k/ʔ*	*ʔ*	Ø	*ʔ*	*k*	*ʔ*
Amanuban	*p*	*t*	*k*	*k/ʔ*	*h*	*h*	*k*	*k/ʔ*	*ʔ*	Ø	*ʔ*	*k*	*ʔ*
Molo	*p*	*t*	*k*	*k/ʔ*	*h*	*h*	*k*	*k/ʔ*	*ʔ*	Ø	*ʔ*	*k*	*ʔ*
Kusa-Manea	*p*	*t*	*k*	*k/ʔ*	*h*	*h*	*k*	*k/ʔ*	*ʔ*	Ø	*ʔ*	*k*	*ʔ*
attestations	14	222	28	27	9	11	24	13	8	10	10	7	19
irr. attest.	5	17											7

† Pattern k-2 has two sub-patterns: 2a, in which Nuclear Meto (all Meto varieties except Ro'is Amarasi) has *k = *k*, and 2b in which Nuclear Meto has *k > *ʔ*.

‡ There are 36 reconstructions with initial *k- that are ambiguous between more than one pattern due to missing reflexes in diagnostic languages: eight are ambiguous between patterns 1 and 2a (k-1/2a), eight are ambiguous between patterns 1, 2 and 3 (k-1/2/3), and 20 are ambiguous between patterns 2 and 3 (k-2/3). There are also eight instances of initial *k- that are irregular and fit into no pattern.

There are 22 reconstructions with medial *-k- that are ambiguous between multiple patterns: seven are ambiguous between patterns 5 and 6 (k-5/6), nine are ambiguous between 8 and 9 (k-8/9), two are ambiguous between 7, 8, 9 and 10 (k-7/8/9/10), three are ambiguous between 6 and 9 (k-6/9), and one is ambiguous between 7 and 8 (k-7/8) There are also eight cases of medial *k which fit into no pattern.

Table 3.3: Proto-Rote-Meto voiced plosive correspondences

Pattern		d-1	d-2										
PRM	*b	*d		*ʤ	*ɓ	*ɗ		*mb	*nd			*ŋg	
environment							/*l,*rV_		#_	V_V	ə_	#_	V_V
Dela-Oenale	*f*	*r*	*r*	*r*	*ɓ*	*ɗ*	*ɗ*	*mb*	*nd*	*nd*	*nd/n*	*ŋg*	*ŋg*
Dengka	*f*	*l*	*l*	*l*	*b*	*ɗ*	*ɗ*	*mb*	*nd*	*nd*	*nd/n*	*ŋg*	*ŋg*
Tii	*ɓ*	*ɗ*	*r*	*ɗ*	*ɓ*	*ɗ*	*ɗ*	*mb*	*nd*	*nd*	*n/nd*	*ŋg*	*ŋg*
Lole	*ɓ*	*ɗ*	*l*	*ɗ*	*ɓ*	*ɗ*	*ɗ*	*mb*	*nd*	*nd*	*n/nd*	*ŋg*	*ŋg*
Ba'a	*b*	*d*	*l*	*d*	*b*	*d*	*d*	*mp*	*nd*	*n*	*n*	*ŋg*	*ŋg*
Termanu	*b*	*d*	*l*	*d*	*b*	*d*	*d*	*p*	*nd*	*n*	*n*	*ŋg*	*ŋ*
Korbafo	*b*	*d*	*l*	*d*	*b*	*d*	*d*	*p*	*nd*	*n*	*n*	*ŋg*	*ŋ*
Bokai	*b*	*d*	*l*	*d*	*b*	*d*	*d*	*p*	*l*	*n*	*n*	*ŋ*	*ŋ*
Bilbaa	*b*	*d*	*l*	*d*	*b*	*d*	*d*	*p*	*l*	*n*	*n*	*ŋ*	*ŋ*
Landu	*b*	*d*	*r*	*d*	*b*	*d*	*d*	*p*	*nd*	*nd*	*n*	*k*	*k*
Rikou	*b*	*d*	*r*	*d*	*b*	*d*	*d*	*p*	*r*	*nd*	*n*	*k*	*k*
Oepao	*b*	*d*	*r*	*d*	*b*	*d*	*d*	*p*	*r*	*r*	*n*	*k*	*k*
Proto-Meto	*f	*n	*d	*d	*b	*d	*n	*p	*r	*r	*r	*ŋ	*ŋ
Ro'is Amarasi	*f*	*n*	*r*	*r*	*b*	*r*	*n*	*p*	*r*	*r*	*r*	*k*	*k*
Kotos Amarasi	*f*	*n*	*r*	*r*	*b*	*r*	*n*	*p*	*k*	*k*	*k*	*k*	*k*
Amanuban	*f*	*n*	*l*	*l*	*b*	*l*	*n*	*p*	*k*	*k*	*k*	*k*	*k*
Molo	*f*	*n*†	*l*	*l*	*b*	*l*	*n*	*p*	*k*	*k*	*k*	*k*	*k*
Kusa-Manea	*f*	*n*	*r*	*r*	*b*	*r*	*n*	*p*	*k*	*k*	*k*	*k*	*k*
attestations	19	20	17	2	77	90	4	76	16	17	4	33	32
irr. attestations	18	2			5	5	1	4	7	3		5	2

† Molo and other varieties of North Meto have *n > *l* /*lV*_. See §3.3.4 for details.

Table 3.4: Proto-Rote-Meto fricative and sonorant correspondences

PRM	*f	*s	*h			*m	*n	*ŋ	*l	*r	*kl
environment			#_	V_V	a_a						
Dela-Oenale	*f*	*s*	*h*	Ø	Ø	*m*	*n*	*n*	*l*	*r*	*k*
Dengka	*f*	*s*	*h*	Ø	Ø	*m*	*n*	*n*	*l*	*l*	*k*
Tii	*f*	*s*	*h*	*ʔ*	Ø	*m*	*n*	*n*	*l*	*r*	*k*
Lole	*f*	*s*	*h*	*ʔ*	Ø	*m*	*n*	*n*	*l*	*l*	*k*
Ba'a	*f*	*s*	*h*	*ʔ*	Ø	*m*	*n*	*n*	*l*	*l*	*k*
Termanu	*f*	*s*	*h*	*ʔ*	Ø	*m*	*n*	*n*	*l*	*l*	*k*
Korbafo	*f*	*s*	*h*	*ʔ*	Ø	*m*	*n*	*n*	*l*	*l*	*k*
Bokai	*f*	*s*	*h*	*ʔ*	Ø	*m*	*n*	*n*	*l*	*l*	*k*
Bilbaa	*f*	*s*	*h*	Ø	Ø	*m*	*n*	*n*	*l*	*l*	*k*
Landu	*f*	*s*	*h*	Ø	Ø	*m*	*n*	*n*	*l*	*r*	
Rikou	*f*	*s*	*h*	Ø	Ø	*m*	*n*	*n*	*l*	*r*	*ʔ*
Oepao	*f*	*s*	*h*	Ø	Ø	*m*	*n*	*n*	*l*	*r*	
Proto-Meto	*f	*s	*h/Ø	*h/Ø	*h	*m	*n	*ŋ/*n	*n	*n	*kl
Ro'is Amarasi	*f*	*s*	*h/Ø*	*h/Ø*	*h*	*m*	*n*	*k/n*	*n*	*n*	*kr*
Kotos Amarasi	*f*	*s*	*h/Ø*	*h/Ø*	*h*	*m*	*n*	*k/n*	*n*	*n*	*kr*
Amanuban	*f*	*s*	*h/Ø*	*h/Ø*	*h*	*m*	*n*	*k/n*	*n*	*n*	*kl*
Molo	*f*	*s*	*h/Ø*	*h/Ø*	*h*	*m*	*n*‡	*k/n*	*n*	*n*	*kl*
Kusa-Manea	*f*	*s*	*h/Ø*	*h/Ø*	*h*	*m*	*n*	*k*	*n*	*n*	
attestations	110	183	49	23	6	124	155	10	214	99	3
irr. attestations	8	5	13	3	1	3	9	6	15	11	

† PRM *ŋ underwent a split in Proto-Meto between *ŋ and *n with subsequent Proto-Meto *ŋ > *k* and *n > *n*. See §3.3.4 for more details.

‡ Molo and other varieties of North Meto have *n > *l* //*lV*_. See §3.3.4 for details.

3.2.1.1 PRM *d

In Edwards (2018a) I identified two correspondence sets for PRM *r. In this dictionary I now reconstruct *d for the second of these sets. Thus, I identify two correspondence sets that attest PRM *d. On the basis of current evidence, I propose that these two correspondence sets are due to an unconditioned split of PRM *d. However, it may be that these correspondence sets attest different proto-phonemes. Throughout this dictionary the first set is not indicated, while the second set is marked as d-2 in the pattern field.

The first *d correspondence set has 19 unambiguous attestations at the level of PRM. It is retained as *ɗ* or *d* in the Nuclear Rote languages and has changed in West-Rote-Meto. The first step was *d > *r*, which is still the reflex in Dela-Oenale, followed by *r > *l* as retained in Dengka, with subsequent *l > *n* in Meto.

Of the 19 unambiguous PRM attestations of this set, 13 are word initial, and all except one are retentions of PMP *d.[3] There are only six word medial instances of this correspondence set, of which four trace back to PMP *j and one to PMP *z.[4]

3 The only instance of initial PRM *d-1 that is not a reflex of PMP *d is PRM *deŋe 'kapok tree', which is clearly connected with Helong *deŋen* 'kapok tree'. This may be a borrowing from pre-Helong into PRM, though borrowing in the opposite direction cannot currently be ruled out.

4 The only instance of medial PRM *d that does not come from PMP is that in *soda-k 'space'. This reconstruction has irregular medial *d > *ɗ* in West Rote, and an alternate reconstruction would be *soɗa-k with irregular *ɗ > (*d > *r > *l) > *n* in Meto.

The second *d correspondence set has 15 unambiguous PRM attestations. For this set *d changes in all languages. It is reflected as *r* in those languages that have this consonant (Dela-Oenale, Landu, Rikou, Oepao, Amarasi, and Kusa-Manea) with subsequent *r > *l* in other languages. This set is the one I conflated with PRM *r in Edwards (2018a), but the need to reconstruct Proto-Meto *d to account for the reflexes of this set in Meto (see Table 3.3 and §3.3.4) means that *d should also be reconstructed to PRM to avoid positing PRM *r > Proto-Meto *d — an unlikely sound change.

There are only four instances of this set that are known to be inherited from PMP: *daŋdaŋ > PRM *ɗada 'warm near a fire', *pandak > PRM *mbada-k 'short in height', *ŋadas > PRM *ŋgadas 'palate, gills', and *duyuŋ > PRM *dui 'dugong'. Of these, the first two attest an earlier nasal-stop cluster. This suggests that this second *d correspondence set may have been a nasal-obstruent combination/cluster in PRM. Given that a prenasalised plosive *nd is well supported by different correspondence sets, the best candidate if this analysis were taken would be PRM *nr.[5]

However, three of the four instances of the second set of PRM *d that can be traced back to PMP show additional irregularities: *daŋdaŋ > *ɗada has irregular initial *d > *ɗ (expect *d = *d), *pandak > *mbada-k has *p > *mb (expect *p > *h), and *ŋadas > *ŋgadas has minority *ŋ > *ŋg (against usual *ŋ > *n). Given these irregularities, I prefer to propose that these instances of PRM *d are also irregular rather than positing that they descend from another PRM sound. As suggested in Edwards (2018a:379), these irregularities may be attributable to these words not being normal inheritances in Meto and/or the Rote languages.

An alternate approach to positing a nasal-stop cluster or an unconditioned split would be to posit an extra PRM phoneme.[6] If this approach were taken, the most likely candidate is probably retroflex *ɖ as retroflex consonants are regionally attested. Kisar, to the east of Timor, has retroflex /ʈ/ (Christensen and Christensen 1992), while Dhao, spoken on the island of the same name just to the west of Rote, has /ɖ/. In Dhao /ɖ/ is a 'slightly retroflexed, lightly articulated alveolar affricate' (Grimes 2010:256), thus [ɖʐ] or [ḍẓ].

While further evidence, perhaps from other languages of the region, may lead me to reconstruct a nasal-stop cluster and/or an additional PRM proto-phoneme for the second PRM *d set, based on current evidence I attribute the two *d correspondence sets to an unconditioned split.

3.2.1.2 PRM *ʤ

One difference between the system proposed here and that in Edwards (2018a) is that I now reconstruct PRM *ʤ, though there are only two reconstructions I am confident attest this proto-phoneme: *fuʤə 'foam' (from PMP *bujəq) and *naʤa-k 'name'

5 If it is accepted that the second set attesting PRM *d was *nr, it may have even been the case that this was a separate prenasalised trill phoneme, as is attested in several languages of Oceania and indeed has been reconstructed for Proto-Oceanic (Lynch et al. 2002:64).

6 It is, of course, also possible that some instances of the second PRM *d correspondence set are from an earlier nasal-stop cluster and some are from another PRM phoneme and/or PRM *d.

(from PMP *ŋajan). The evidence for reconstructing medial *ʤ in these forms comes both from the distinct reflexes of the medial consonant and raising, or palatalisation, of the following vowel in some reflexes.

The first piece of evidence in favour of reconstructing *ʤ is its reflexes. The reflexes of *ʤ overlap with those of *d, *ɗ and *r, but are not identical to any. The reflexes of *ʤ, *d, *ɗ and *r in indicative languages are summarised in Table 3.3.

Table 3.5: Proto-Rote-Meto voiced coronal obstruent correspondences

West Rote	**PRM**	***ʤ**	***d**	***d**	***ɗ**	***r**
	Dela-Oenale	*r*	*r*	*r*	*ɗ*	*r*
	Dengka	*l*	*l*	*l*	*ɗ*	*l*
Nuclear Rote	Tii	*ɗ*	*ɗ*	*r*	*ɗ*	*r*
	Lole	*ɗ*	*ɗ*	*l*	*ɗ*	*l*
	Termanu	*d*	*d*	*l*	*d*	*l*
	Rikou	*d*	*d*	*r*	*d*	*r*
Meto	Amarasi	*r*	*n*	*r*	*r*	*n*
	Molo	*l*	*n*	*l*	*l*	*n*

While the reflexes of *ʤ and *d are the same in the Rote languages, they are different in Meto. Similarly, while the reflexes of *ʤ and *ɗ are the same in Nuclear Rote and Meto, they are different in West Rote. In no case can the reflexes of *ʤ be conflated with those of another proto-phoneme. This indicates that *ʤ was distinct from other proto-phonemes in PRM.

The second piece of evidence in favour of PRM *ʤ is that it often triggers raising of a following vowel. Regarding *fuʤə 'foam', the normal reflex of final *ə in Dela-Oenale, Dengka and Meto for other words is *a*. However, reflexes of *fuʤə 'foam' in all these languages except the Kusa-Manea variety of Meto have final *e*: Dela-Oenale *na-fu~fure,* Dengka *na-fu~fule,* Kotos Amarasi *ʔ|furi-f* (from intermediate **ʔ|fure), Molo *<fule>*, but Kusa-Manea *fa~fura-f* 'foam'.[7]

A similar, though not identical, situation holds regarding reflexes of *naʤa-k 'name'. This reconstruction only has direct reflexes in the Rote languages:[8] Dengka *nala-ʔ*, Dela-Oenale *nara-ʔ*, Tii, Lole *naɗe-k*, other Rote *nade-k* or *nade-ʔ* 'name'. In this case final *a > *a* is expected in all languages, but Rote languages apart from Dela-Oenale and Dengka have unexpected *a > *e*.

The unexpected vowel changes in each of PRM *fuʤə 'foam' and *naʤa-k 'name' can be explained as cases of sporadic raising of final *a > *e* after a palatal consonant — a case of assimilation. This change is also attested in several PRM forms inherited from PMP: *añam > *ane 'braid', *suja > *sure-k 'caltrop, sword', and *utaña > *tane ~ *tana 'ask'.

7 The normal reflex of PMP *ə before *q in PRM is *e. Thus, *bujəq > *fuʤə also requires irregular *ə = *ə. Kusa-Manea with final /a/ provides the evidence for PRM *ə, as final Kusa-Manea *a* is a regular reflex of either final *ə or *a.

8 Meto *kana-f* 'name, clan' is a borrowing from Helong *ŋala* 'name, clan' (also ultimately from PMP *ŋajan). The evidence for the Meto form being a borrowing from Helong comes both from irregular initial *ŋ > *k* and the identical semantic expansion from 'name' to include 'clan'.

The main difference between palatalisation in these forms and that in *fudʒə 'foam' and *nadʒa-k 'name' is that for these two latter reconstructions palatalisation of the vowel and subsequent de-palatalisation of the consonant occurred after the break-up of PRM.

Reconstruction of medial *dʒ in *fudʒə 'foam' and *nadʒa-k 'name' thus accounts for both the medial consonants and provides an explanation for otherwise unexpected final mid-high vowels in some languages. More complete discussion of these forms can be found in the relevant entries for these reconstructions.

3.2.1.3 PRM *w

Another difference between the proto-phonemes posited here and in Edwards (2018a) is the addition of the glide *w. Only two forms have been identified with this proto-phoneme: *wani 'honey bee' and *wadi 'younger sibling'.

3.2.2 Final consonants

Eight consonants can be reconstructed in word final position in PRM: *t, *k, *m, *n, *r, *h, *ʔ and *s. Of these consonants, *t and *s in particular may be analysable as nominalising suffixes for some forms in the daughter languages, and thus also in PRM. In general, Dela-Oenale, Dengka and Meto preserve word final consonants in the most forms, while they are usually lost in other languages. The correspondence sets attesting word final consonants in PRM are given in Table 3.6.

Table 3.6: Proto-Rote-Meto word final consonant correspondences

PRM	***t**	***k**	***m**	***n**	***r**	***h**	***ʔ**	***s**
Dela-Oenale	*t/Ø*	Ø/k	Ø	Ø/*n*	*r*	Ø	Ø/*ʔ*	*s/Ø*
Dengka	*t/Ø*	Ø	Ø	Ø/*n*	Ø/*l*	Ø	Ø	*s/Ø*
Ba'a, Tii, Lole	Ø	Ø	Ø	Ø/*n*	Ø	Ø	Ø	*s/Ø*
Termanu	Ø	Ø	Ø	Ø/*n*	Ø	Ø	Ø	*s/Ø*
Korbafo, Bokai, Bilbaa	Ø	Ø	Ø	Ø	Ø	Ø	Ø	Ø
Rikou, Oepao	Ø	Ø	Ø	Ø	Ø	Ø	Ø	*s/Ø*
Proto-Meto	*t/Ø	*k/*ʔ	*m	*n	Ø/*n	*h	*ʔ	*s
Meto	*t/Ø*	*k/ʔ*	*m*	*n*	Ø/*n*	*h*	*ʔ*	*s*
regular attestations	26	6	12	19	9	6	3	40
irregular attestations		3	1	5	1			7

3.2.3 Vowels

Table 3.7 gives the sound correspondences for vowels and glides in the PRM languages in penultimate and final syllables. Vowels in antepenultimate and pre-antepenultimate position are often deleted in daughter languages due to the preference among the Rote-Meto languages for disyllabic words.

Table 3.7: Proto-Rote-Meto vowel correspondences (penultimate and final syllables)

PRM	*i	*e	*a	*a	*a	*ə	*ə	*o	*u	*wa
environment				/_#	/_#	/σ̲σ#	/σσ̲#			
Dela-Oenale	*i*	*e*	*a*	*a*	*a/e*	*e/o*	*a/e*	*o*	*u*	*o*
Dengka	*i*	*e*	*a*	*a*	*a/e*	*e/o*	*a/e*	*o*	*u*	*o*
Tii	*i*	*e*	*a*	*a*	*a*	*e/o*	*e*	*o*	*u*	*fa*
Lole	*i*	*e*	*a*	*a*	*a*	*e/o*	*e*	*o*	*u*	*fa*
Ba'a	*i*	*e*	*a*	*a*	*a*	*e/o*	*e*	*o*	*u*	*fa*
Termanu	*i*	*e*	*a*	*a*	*a*	*e/o*	*e*	*o*	*u*	*fa*
Korbafo	*i*	*e*	*a*	*a*	*a*	*e/o*	*e*	*o*	*u*	*fa*
Bokai	*i*	*e*	*a*	*a*	*a*	*e/o*	*e*	*o*	*u*	*fa*
Bilbaa	*i*	*e*	*a*	*a*	*a*	*e/o*	*e*	*o*	*u*	*fa*
Landu	*i*	*e*	*a*	*a*	*a*	*e/o*	*e*	*o*	*u*	*fa*
Rikou	*i*	*e*	*a*	*a*	*a*	*e/o*	*e*	*o*	*u*	*fa*
Oepao	*i*	*e*	*a*	*a*	*a*	*e/o*	*e*	*o*	*u*	*fa*
Proto-Meto	*i	*e	*a	*a	*e	*e	*a	*o	*u	*o
Ro'is Amarasi	*i*	*e*	*a*	*a*	*e*	*e*	*a*	*o*	*u*	*o*
Kotos Amarasi	*i*	*e*	*a*	*a*	*e*	*e*	*a*	*o*	*u*	*o*
Amanuban	*i*	*e*	*a*	*a*	*e*	*e*	*a*	*o*	*u*	*o*
Molo	*i*	*e*	*a*	*a*	*e*	*e*	*a*	*o*	*u*	*o*
Kusa-Manea	*i*	*e*	*a*	*a*	*e*	*e*	*a*	*o*	*u*	*o*
attestations	372	371	384	229	28	10	33	295	494	2
irr. attestations	20	20	14	21	4	2	10	8	19	

While PRM *ə is well-supported on the basis of the bottom-up evidence in final syllables, there is much less support for it in penultimate syllables, with only 12 putative cases identified. Firstly, there are five words in which PRM *ə undergoes a split between *e* and *o* in daughter languages: *ɗəma 'drown', *səru 'meet', *səu 'Alstonia villosa', *təlo 'egg' and *ɗəmbə 'dip'.

Secondly, there are five words that have *ə > *e* in all daughter languages. Nonetheless, penultimate schwa can be detected as several Rote languages undergo otherwise unexpected *nd > *n* for the consonant following schwa (see Table 3.3). These five words are: *əndi 'bring', *farəndən 'thoughts', *həndi 'finish', *kənda 'close' and *lənde 'still (water)'.

Apart from these 10 words, I have also reconstructed initial schwa in the root forms of *əmə 'come' and *əu 'go'. The initial vowel of these verbs shows irregularities in the 1SG, 2SG and 1PL/1PL.EXCL verb forms, which appear to be a result of loss and/or coalescence of the initial vowel with the historic vowel of the agreement prefixes (§2.6.5). The 3SG, 3PL and 1PL.INCL forms of these verbs have regular *ə > *e* in most daughter languages.

As discussed in §3.5.1.2, PMP *ə usually became *e in PRM, and we can propose that the change of *ə > *e* in penultimate syllables was a change in progress that was not completed until after the break-up of the proto-language. It is likely that there were many more instances of penultimate schwa in PRM than can be reconstructed on the basis of bottom-up evidence from the modern-day languages.

3.3 Internal sub-grouping

The internal sub-grouping of the Rote-Meto languages is complex, with several overlapping and conflicting sets of sound changes. On the basis of shared sound changes, three subgroups can be identified within Rote-Meto: West Rote-Meto (Dela-Oenale, Dengka, and Meto), Nuclear Rote (all other Rote languages) and Central East Rote and Meto (Meto and all Rote languages except Dela-Oenale, Dengka, Tii and Lole). The sound changes that would define each subgroup are summarised in Table 3.8.

Table 3.8: Subgrouping within Rote-Meto

West Rote-Meto	Nuclear Rote	Central East Rote and Meto
*b > *f*	*ə > *e* /σσ̲#	*mb > *mp* > *p*
*d > *r*	*wa > *fa*	*nd > *r*
*ə > *a* /σσ̲#	*d/ɗ/dʒ > *ɗ* ~ *d*	*ŋg > *ŋ* > *k*
*a > *a, e* /_#		
*k > *k, h* /#_		
*wa > *o*		

Meto shares a number of sound changes with both West Rote and Central East Rote. As discussed in Edwards (2018a), I propose that this is because it has shared a period of common development with each. However, it is likely that the period of common development Meto shared with each group was not of the same kind. While Meto and West-Rote probably descend from a single ancestral language, Meto and East-Rote appear to descend from a common ancestral speech community comprised of two languages: pre-Central East Rote and pre-Meto. Thus, while West Rote-Meto is a 'classic' subgroup in which the defining sound changes arose once in a language ancestral to all daughters, the Central East Rote and Meto grouping is a result of contact and convergence between its members.

My current hypothesis is that the first split was between West Rote-Meto and Nuclear Rote. After this initial split, pre-Meto split from West Rote and entered into a period of intense contact with Central East Rote, which resulted in common development. During the initial period of this contact, pre-Meto and pre-Central East Rote were probably mutually intelligible.

Two different visual representations of the relationships of the Rote-Meto languages are given as a simplified tree diagram in Figure 3.1 and a wave diagram in Figure 3.2. As discussed in Edwards (2018a), I do not think these models are incompatible. Changes can diffuse between proto-languages and can thus be used to define the descendants of such a proto-language. Instead, each model captures and emphasises different aspects of the social history of the Rote-Meto languages. A complete tree diagram of the Rote-Meto languages is shown in Figure 3.3.

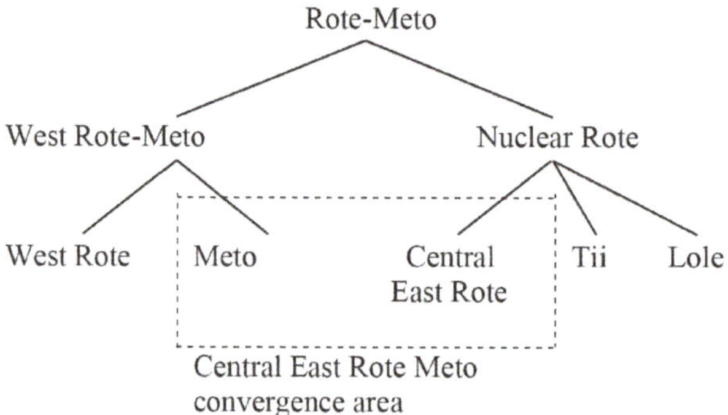

Figure 3.1: Simplified Rote-Meto family tree

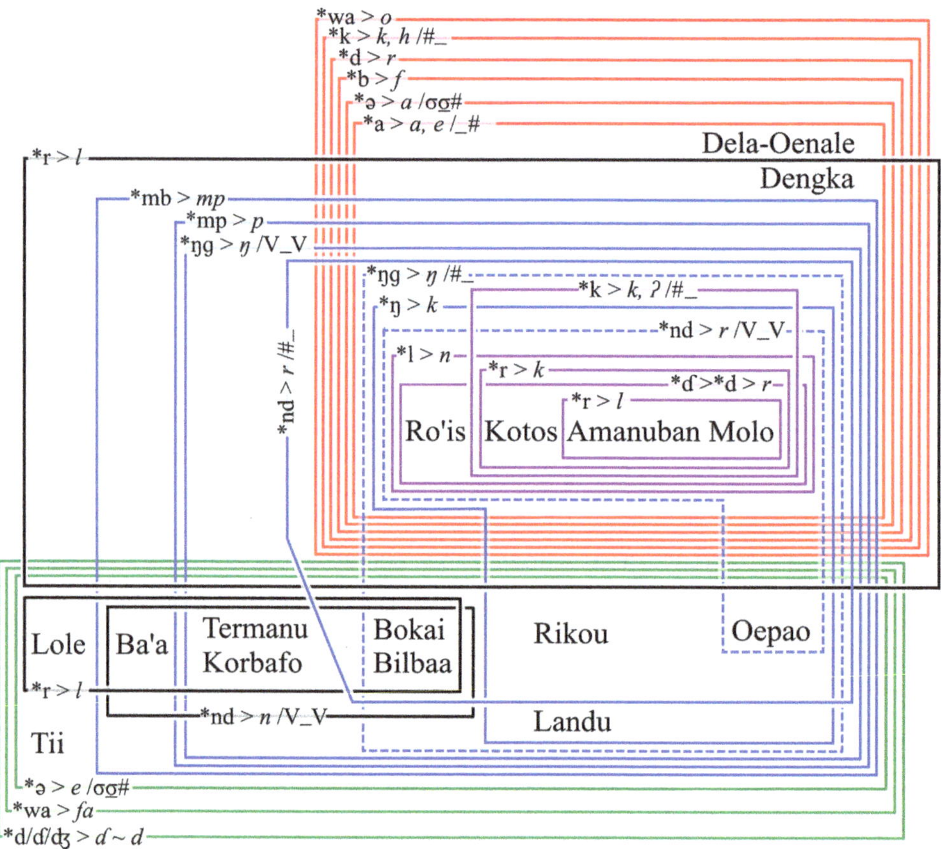

Figure 3.2: Rote-Meto wave diagram

Figure 3.2 is a wave diagram showing the main sound changes that affect individual languages. Red lines are for changes that define West Rote-Meto, blue lines are those shared between Central East Rote and Meto (dashed lines are used only to indicate more clearly which isoglosses affect which languages), green lines indicate Nuclear Rote, and purple lines are for the changes that affect only Meto. Black lines are used for other changes.

When one change occurred before another, it is overlayed before the secondary change. Thus, for instance, *mb > *mp* in Central East Rote and Meto occurred before *mp > *p* in these languages. Likewise, *r > *l* happened after *nd > *r* /#_ in Bokai and Bilbaa.[9] In other cases the order in which the lines are placed is essentially arbitrary, with visual clarity being the main consideration.

The wave diagram in Figure 3.2 shows visually that the sound changes that are shared between Meto and central East Rote languages (represented by blue lines) fully encircle the Meto languages but only encircle some of the Rote languages, and do so in a more unordered fashion. This indicates that the direction of influence was mostly from Meto. Additional evidence for this probably comes from the fact that the change of *ŋ > *k* must have occurred after the change of *k > *k, ʔ* /#_, which only affects some varieties of Meto. Thus. *ŋ > *k* must have spread between these languages *after* the break-up of Proto-Meto. This is discussed in more detail in §3.3.4.

A complete tree diagram showing the proposed internal structure of the Rote-Meto languages is given in Figure 3.3, along with sound changes that define each node. Due to the complexity involved, changes that likely spread by diffusion are only represented for the Rote languages. Of these changes, it is likely that diffusion happened between proto-languages in some cases. Thus, for instance *nd > *n* /V_V and *r > *l* may have arisen once in Proto-Central Rote, from which they then spread into Proto-Bokai-Bilbaa, or vice versa.

9 The change *r > *l* is shown twice in Figure 3.5 as it occurred at different times in relation to *nd > *r* /#_ in different languages. In Bokai and Bilbaa *nd > *r* /#_ occurred before *r > *l*, thus resulting in a merger of *nd/*r > *l* word initially. In Meto, on the other hand, *r > *l* occurred before *nd > *r* and these proto-phonemes did not merge.

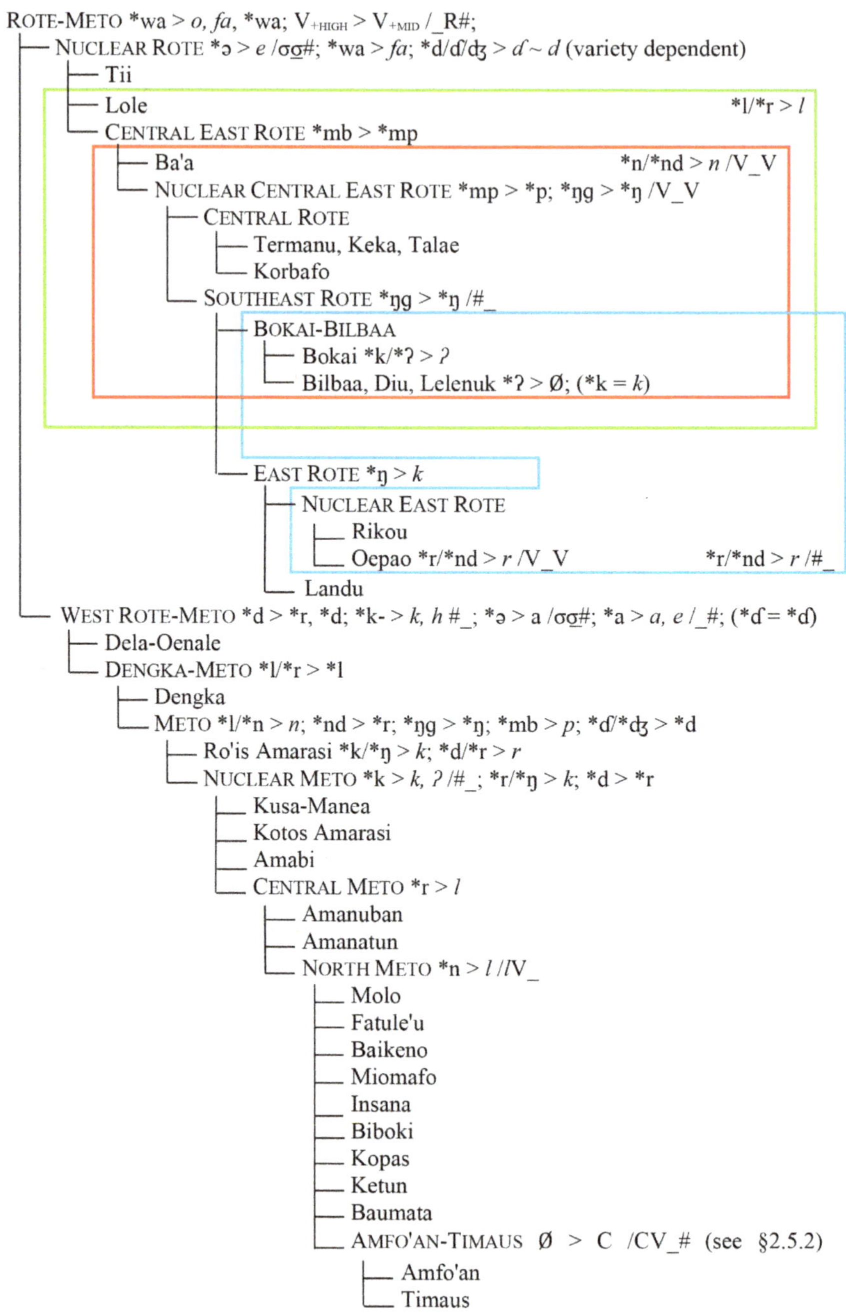

Figure 3.3: Rote-Meto family tree

There are no sound changes that affect all of the Rote languages to the exclusion of Meto. That is, there is no 'Rote' subgroup. The only changes shared between all the languages of Rote that are not found in Meto are shared phonological irregularities in specific lexical items. There are nine lexically specific shared irregularities that unambiguously affect only the Rote languages:[10]

- *u > *o* in *bua-k > *boa-k/-ʔ, ɓoa-k/-ʔ* 'fruit'
- *u > *o* in *lua > *loa-k/-ʔ* 'open, wide'
- *i > *e* in *hiri > *here, hele* 'choose'
- *u > *a* in *tufu > *tufa* 'punch'
- *ə > *o* in *səru > *na-so~soru, na-so~solu* 'meet'
- *m > *mb in *simo > *simbo, simpo, sipo* 'receive'
- *t > *d/ɗ* in *tui > *dui-k/-ʔ, ɗui-k, ɗui* 'stripe'
- *h > Ø in *halu-k > *alu-k/-ʔ* 'pestle'
- *h > Ø in *haru-k > *aru-k/-ʔ, alu-k/-ʔ* 'shoulder'

While these shared irregularities do show that the Rote languages have undergone some common development apart from Meto, the evidence for splitting the Rote languages into a West Rote and Central East Rote subgroup (each of which has shared a period of common development with Meto) is much stronger as both these branches are supported both by shared sound changes *and* shared irregularities in specific lexical items.

3.3.1 Nuclear Rote (NRote)

There are three sound changes shared between the Nuclear Rote languages; *w > *f* (attested in only two lexical items), *ə > *e* in final syllables, and merger of *d/*ɗ/*ʤ > *ɗ* ~ *d* (see §2.4.1 for the realisation of the voiced alveolar plosive in the Rote languages). There are also at least 10 lexically specific innovations which support Nuclear Rote. These are the changes:

- *ii > *oe in *ka-mii > *moe 'urine'
- *ə > *o in *səu > *sou 'Alstonia villosa'
- *ə > *o in *təlo-k > *tolo-k 'egg'
- *a > *e in *naʤa-k > *nade-k 'name'
- *a > *u in *ka-nduna-k > *ndunu-k
- *au > *eu in *taun > *teu-k 'year'
- *s > Ø in *mbusu-k > *mbuu-k 'thigh'
- *k > *ŋg in *ka-kelas > *ŋgelas 'winter melon'
- *t > *d in *tahi > *dahi 'winnow'
- vowel metathesis in *midu > *mudi 'spit'

10 The lexically specific irregularities in these sections include only those that can confidently be assigned to a specific subgroup, often on the basis of external evidence. For instance, I posit irregular *r > *l* in Nuclear Rote for *saraa 'shine, sunbeam'. An alternate hypothesis would be to reconstruct *salaa with irregular *l > *r* in Oenale. Ambiguous cases such as this are excluded from my discussion.

In addition to the phonological evidence and these lexically specifically phonological irregularities, evidence for Nuclear Rote also comes from the forms of the vocalic agreement prefixes (see Table 2.15) as all Nuclear Rote languages have changed the vowels of these prefix to /a/. Specifically, PRM 1SG *ku- > Proto-Nuclear Rote *ka- > Bilbaa *ka-*, other Nuclear Rote *ʔa-*, and PRM 1PL.EXCL/2PL *mi- and 2SG *mu- > Proto-Nuclear Rote *ma- = all Nuclear Rote 1PL.EXCL/2PL/2SG *ma-*. Within Nuclear Rote, we can identify a number of subgroups on the basis of changes affecting prenasalised plosives, as discussed further in the next section.

3.3.2 Central East Rote and Meto (CERM)

The Central East Rote and Meto grouping contains Meto and all members of Nuclear Rote except Tii and Lole. While this group reflects a period of shared development between members, it probably does not reflect descent from a single common ancestor, but rather descent from a common ancestral speech community of closely related languages. The languages that belong to this group share the changes affecting the prenasalised plosives, with these changes diffusing between these languages after Meto had split from Proto West Rote-Meto.

The changes affecting the bilabial and velar prenasalised plosives each follow a single pathway, which is carried out to different extents in different languages. The bilabial prenasalised plosive undergoes *mb > *mp* > *p*, while the velar prenasalised plosive undergoes *ŋg > *ŋ* > *k*. All members of Central East Rote-Meto share *mb > *mp*, with voiceless prenasalised *mp* retained in Ba'a. All other Central East Rote-Meto languages share *mp > *p* and medial *-ŋg- > *ŋ*. All these languages except Termanu and Korbafo further share initial *ŋg- > *ŋ*. A tree showing these changes is given in Figure 3.4.

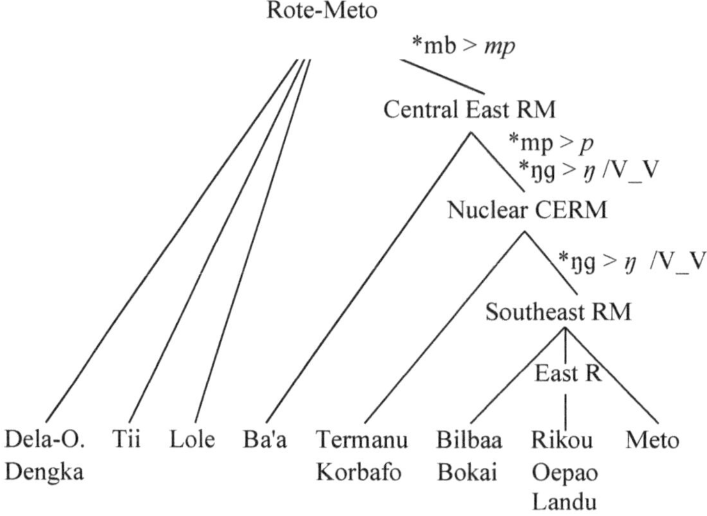

Figure 3.4: Rote-Meto bilabial and velar prenasalised plosives

The velar nasal *ŋ (from earlier *ŋg) further changes into *k* in Rikou, Oepao, Landu and all Meto lects. However, as discussed further in §3.3.4, this change must have been completed after Meto had split from this group and after the break-up of Proto-Meto.

The changes affecting *nd are more complex, with more than one pathway of change. *nd is retained unchanged in Landu and is unchanged word initially in Ba'a, Termanu and Korbafo. Ba'a, Termanu, Korbafo, Bokai and Bilbaa have medial *nd > *n*. Medial *nd is unchanged in Rikou.

The other reflexes of *nd in Central East Rote-Meto can be derived from intermediate *r. Rikou has initial *nd > *r*, Bokai and Bilbaa have initial *nd > *r > *l*, and Oepao and Meto have *nd > *r in all word positions with all varieties of Meto apart from Ro'is Amarasi subsequently having *r > *k*. The reflexes of PRM *nd are summarised:

- *nd = *nd* #_ Ba'a, Termanu, Korbafo, Bokai, Bilbaa, Landu
- *nd = *nd* V_V Rikou, Landu
- *nd > *n* V_V Ba'a, Termanu, Korbafo, Bokai, Bilbaa
- *nd > *r* > *l* #_ Bokai, Bilbaa
- *nd > *r* #_ Rikou, Oepao, Ro'is Amarasi
- *nd > *r* V_V Oepao, Ro'is Amarasi
- *nd > *r* > *k* #_, V_V Nuclear Meto (Meto apart from Ro'is Amarasi)

The main difficulty these changes provide with regards to subgrouping concerns the position of Bokai and Bilbaa. The change of medial *nd > *n* groups these languages with those to their west (Termanu and Korbafo), while the change of initial *nd > *r* > *l* groups them with the languages to the east (Rikou and Oepao).

On the basis of current evidence there is no principled reason to privilege either of these changes in defining which languages Bokai and Bilbaa subgroup with. For this reason, I have privileged the evidence from other sound changes in representing the relationship of Bokai and Bilbaa to other languages in the tree diagrams in Figure 3.3 and Figure 3.4. This has resulted in a Southeast Rote subgroup in which Bokai and Bilbaa are placed with East Rote (Rikou, Oepao and Landu) on the basis of *ŋg > *ŋ /#_.

Nonetheless, while the changes of *nd > *n* /V_V and initial *nd > *r* > *l* are contradictory in determining with which languages Bokai and Bilbaa subgroup, the fact that they are both shared by Bokai and Bilbaa is evidence for placing these languages in a single subgroup. Similarly, shared *nd > *n* in Termanu and Korbafo provides evidence for placing these languages in a single subgroup. The historical phonologies of Termanu and Korbafo are almost identical, with the exception of some of the reflexes of *k (Table 3.2) and word final consonants (Table 3.6). There are also morphological differences between Termanu and Korbafo (see §2.6). The changes affecting *k, word final consonants, and the morphology of Korbafo are the same as in Bokai and Bilbaa.

While the Central East Rote and Meto grouping, along with several internal subgroups, is well defined on the basis of the changes affecting the prenasalised plosives, there are no phonological irregularities in specific lexical items which unambiguously only occur in these languages.

3.3.3 West Rote-Meto (WRM)

The West Rote-Meto subgroup is well supported by six shared sound changes: *b > *f*, *d/*ʤ > *r*, *ə > a /σσ̲#, *a > *a, e* /_#, *k > *k, h* /#_, and *wa > *o*. However, with the exception of *d/*ʤ > *r* and *wa > *o*, none of these sound changes is complete in Dela-Oenale and Dengka. That is, there are forms that have undergone these sound changes in Meto while cognates in West Rote have not.

This probably indicates that (the speech community of what was to become) Meto was the centre of diffusion with changes originating there and spreading into West Rote. Additionally, it probably indicates that Proto-West Rote-Meto was not a single language for long enough for pre-Meto to exert the pressure needed for these sound changes to be completed in Dela-Oenale and Dengka. In concrete terms, this probably indicates that speakers of what was to become Meto were more socially influential during the development of Proto-West Rote-Meto and that they were exerting influence for a relatively short period of time before leaving the speech community.

In addition to the sound changes that are shared between West Rote-Meto, there are also at least seven irregularities in specific lexical items which are exclusively shared by West Rote-Meto:

- *e > *i in *henuh > *inuh 'beads'
- *b > *mb in *boo > *mboo 'herd (v.)'
- *a > *o in *fuloat > *fuloot '*Sterculia urceolata*'
- *ee > *oe in *lee > *loe 'river'
- *ei > *eʔa in *bei > *feʔa 'still'
- *man > *nam in *maneu > *nameu 'bright'
- *h > Ø in
  - *hade > *are 'rice plant'
  - *hatahori > *atahori 'person'
  - *hedu-k > *eru-ʔ 'gall bladder'
  - *henuh > *inuh 'beads'
  - *hendam > *endam 'pandanus'

3.3.4 Meto

The main defining sound change of Meto as a distinct subgroup is *l > *n* in nearly all forms. This change also affected PRM *d and *r as these had already merged with *l in the pre-Meto period. Despite this change, there are half a dozen or so forms in which PRM *l appears to have been retained as *l in Proto-Meto. Thus, we must posit that this consonant was present, at least marginally, in Proto-Meto. Forms that retain *l unchanged may represent borrowings into Proto-Meto after *l > *n* and/or borrowings after the break-up of Proto-Meto.[11] The Proto-Meto consonant inventory is given in Table 3.9. The velar nasal *ŋ may have become *g by the time of Proto-Meto. This is discussed in §3.3.4.1 below. Proto-Meto also had five vowels: *i, *e, *a, *o and *u.

Table 3.9: Proto-Meto consonant inventory

	Labial	Coronal	Velar	Glottal
Voiceless stops	*p	*t	*k	*ʔ
Voiced stops	*b	*d		
Fricatives	*f	*s		*h
Nasals	*m	*n	*ŋ	
Rhotic		*r		
Lateral		(*l)		

Within Meto there is a primary split between Ro'is Amarasi and all other Meto varieties (Nuclear Meto). Nuclear Meto is defined by initial *k > *k, ʔ* followed by Proto-Meto *r (from PRM *nd) > *k*. While Meto shares PRM *ŋg > *ŋ > *k* with Landu, Rikou and Oepao (East Rote), no instances of PRM *ŋg become *ʔ* in Nuclear Meto. Thus, the change of *ŋ > *k* probably occurred in Meto after the change of Nuclear Meto initial *k > *k, ʔ* and thus after the split between Ro'is Amarasi and Nuclear Meto.

PRM *ŋ split into Proto-Meto *ŋ and *n. For some cognate sets we can only reconstruct Proto-Meto *ŋ, while for others there is variation. Some Meto varieties have *k* (< *ŋ) and some varieties have *n*. There is also occasional variation within a single variety. This indicates that such words themselves had variants in Proto-Meto. An example of such a word is PRM *riŋin 'cold', which is reflected as *mainikin* or *<maniki>* in most varieties of Meto, but with the variant *<mainini>* in Amanuban. This points to Proto-Meto *ma|niŋin ~ *ma|ninin. Similarly, PRM *nuŋa 'Cordia species' is reflected in Molo as *nun/baʔi, nuk/baʔi, kuk/baʔi,* which probably attests Proto Meto *nun/baʔi ~ *nuŋ/baʔi ~ *ŋuŋ/baʔi.

While Kusa-Manea shares *k > *k, ʔ* /#_ and *r > *k* with Nuclear Meto, it also has a number of conservative features where most other known varieties of Nuclear Meto have innovated. On the basis of these innovations, we can place these other varieties of Meto together, leaving Kusa-Manea as a primary branch of Nuclear Meto. The retentions and innovations which separate Kusa-Manea from most other known varieties of Meto are given as follows:

- retention of final /a/ after metathesis (§2.5.1)
  - other known Nuclear Meto varieties have assimilation of /a/
- optional retention of initial *n = *n* in *nuɗu > *nuru-f, ruru-f* 'lips'
  - other known Nuclear Meto varieties have assimilation; *ruru-f, lulu-f* 'lips'

11 Proto-Meto *l > *r* in Amarasi and *l = *l* in all other varieties of Meto for which data is available. (No clear unambiguous reflexes of Proto-Meto *l have so far been identified in Kusa-Manea.) The forms for which I posit Proto-Meto *l are: *ɓolo$_1$ 'hole', *hela 'pull', *laa$_2$ 'hut', *laɓa 'wind (v.)', *lasa 'underlay', *lole$_1$ 'kind of tuber', as well as three forms with initial *kl: *klaha 'coals', *klou 'bow (and arrow)' and *kleet 'mock'. Finally, there is Proto-Meto *kalusa 'fingernail', which has no known cognates in the Rote languages.

- retention of PRM *hida > *hian* 'how many'
  - other known Meto varieties have *fauk* 'how many' (see *ɓaʔu)
- retention of final *m in PMP *ma-qitəm > *metom* 'black'
  - other known Meto varieties have *m > *n*; *metan* 'black'
- retention of initial *e in PwRM *ela > *n-ʔean* 'run, flee'
  - other known Meto varieties have *e > *ae*; *n-aena* 'run, flee'
- retention of semantics for *hanas > *manas* 'hot'
  - other known Meto varieties have *manas* 'sun'
- retention of semantics 'sun' for *ledo > *neno* 'sun, day, sky'
  - other known Meto varieties have *neno* 'day, sky'[12]

Ro'is Amarasi groups with known varieties of Meto, and groups apart from Kusa-Manea, for most of these features, except retention of *n = *n* in *nuɗu > *nuru-f* 'lips' and retention of /a/ after metathesis in forms with a medial glottal stop. Nuclear Meto shares sound changes with Kusa-Manea, but other innovations with Ro'is Amarasi. The relationship between Ro'is Amarasi, Kusa-Manea and other varieties of Meto is represented with a simplified wave diagram in Figure 3.5.

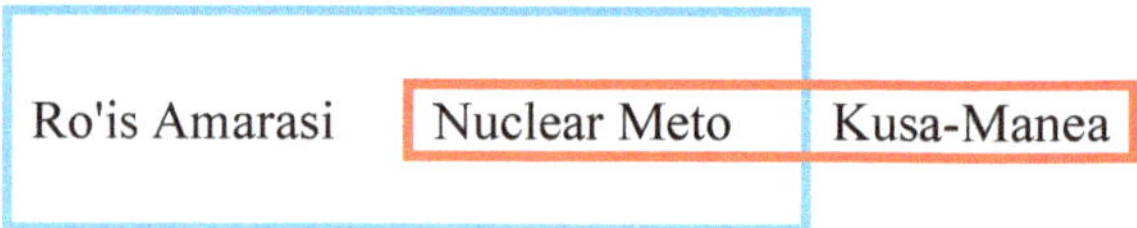

Figure 3.5. Simplified Meto wave diagram

Proto-Meto *d (usually from PRM *ɗ, though some instances are from PRM *d or *ʤ — see §3.2.1.1 and §3.2.1.2) undergoes changes in all varieties of Meto. Ro'is Amarasi, Kotos Amarasi, Amabi and Kusa-Manea all have *d > *r* while all other known Meto varieties have *d > *r > *l*. However, we must reconstruct Proto-Meto *d for this correspondence set rather than *r, as reconstruction of *r would falsely predict that it merges with Proto-Meto *r (from PRM *nd) as *k* in Nuclear Meto. Thus, we must posit that *d > *r spread between Nuclear Meto and Ro'is Amarasi after the breakup of Proto-Meto; Proto-Meto *d > Proto-Nuclear Meto *r.

Within Nuclear Meto the change of (*d >) *r > *l* defines a Central Meto subgroup that excludes Kotos Amarasi, Amabi and Kusa-Manea. Within Central Meto we can further identify a North Meto subgroup on the basis of *n > *l* // V_V. North Meto contains all members of Central Meto except Amanuban and Amanatun. Examples of this *n > *l* sound change include PRM *ɗalan 'path, way' > Proto-Meto *danan > Kotos Amarasi *ranan* > Amanuban > *lanan* > Molo *lalan*, and PRM *ɗilah '*Aegle marmelos*' > Proto-Meto *dinah > Kotos Amarasi *rinah* > Amanuban *linah* > Molo *lilah*.

12 The meaning 'sun' is retained in certain set phrases for *neno* in Nuclear Meto, such as the terms for 'east' and 'west'. See the notes on *ledo.

3.3.4.1 Contact with languages of central Timor

There is evidence for a period of pre-historic contact between Meto and languages of the Central Timor subgroup: Welaun, Kemak, Tokodede and Mambae (see Edwards (2019) for the evidence for this subgroup). This contact almost certainly occurred before the northwards spread of Tetun, which now separates these groups.

Firstly, there are a number of words that are shared between Meto and Central Timor languages that have no (regular) cognates in the Rote languages and are almost certainly due to borrowing, though it is not always possible to determine whether these words were borrowed from Central Timor into Meto or vice versa. Examples of likely loans between Meto and Central Timor languages.

- Meto *sone* 'Job's tears' from Welaun *sole* 'corn, maize'. Weluan *sole* is regular from PMP *zəlay 'Job's tears'. Semantic shift to 'maize' probably occurred in Welaun after it was borrowed into Meto.
- Meto *mneas* 'hulled rice', Kemak *mreas* 'hulled rice'. Both forms are irregular from PMP *bəRas. While irregular retention of *R and metathesis of *əR > *Rə is common throughout Timor — pointing to widespread borrowing — Meto and Kemak are the only two languages known to also have irregular *b > *m* thus indicating a specific case of borrowing between these languages.
- Amarasi, Kusa-Manea *babaʔ* 'paternal aunt, maternal uncle', Kemak, Welaun *baba* 'maternal uncle' (Rote languages have *toʔo* 'maternal uncle').
- Meto *kase* 'foreigner', Kemak *kase* 'foreigner' (probably borrowed from Meto).
- Ro'is Amarasi *akaʔtaʔe*, Kotos Amarasi *ataʔraʔe*, Molo *ataʔlaʔe* 'praying mantis', Welaun *astatae* 'praying mantis'.
- Ro'is Amarasi *kupu* 'fog', Kotos Amarasi *kupu* 'water vapour', Tokodede *api kupu* 'smoke' (Tokodede *api* = 'fire').
- Amarasi *naiʔbesi*, Amfo'an *beʔi-ʤ*, Kusa-Manea *beʔi* 'crocodile', Welaun (Oele'u hamlet) *naʔibein*, Welaun (Mahein hamlet) *bei liurai* 'crocodile'.
- Amarasi *na-ʔbaʔe* 'play', Welaun *baʔan* 'play'.

In addition to such likely borrowings, denasalisation of *ŋ > *g is one of the defining sound changes of Central Timor as a subgroup. Welaun and some varieties of Mambae further have *ŋ > *g > *k*. Given the lexical evidence for contact between Meto and Central Timor, it is likely that denasalisation of *ŋ in both groups also spread by contact between these languages, though parallel development also could have taken place.

There are three language groups that have denasalisation of *ŋ in Timor: East Rote (Landu, Rikou and Oepao), Meto and Central Timor. Furthermore, we have evidence of a genetic relationship between East Rote and Meto and a contact relationship between Meto and Central Timor, but no evidence for any kind of relationship between East Rote and Central Timor.

Thus, if *ŋ > *k* spread by contact in this region, positing East Rote as the ultimate source of *ŋ > *k* would require positing that Central Timor acquired this change via influence from Meto. On the other hand, positing that *ŋ > *k* spread from Meto into East Rote leaves open the possibility that the ultimate origin of this change was either with Meto or with Central Timor. On the balance of probabilities then, it seems more likely that East Rote acquired *ŋ > *k* from Meto rather than vice versa. Additional support for the idea that *ŋ > *k* had a westwards spread from Meto into East Rote comes from the fact that the most eastern variety of Meto, Kusa-Manea, only has Proto-Meto *ŋ > *k*, while the most western variety, Ro'is Amarasi, has the most instances of Proto-Meto *ŋ > *n*. This is expected if *ŋ > *k* spread westwards from the east.[13]

Given that Central Timor has *ŋ > *g (with subsequent *g > *k* in some languages), this provides circumstantial evidence that Meto *ŋ > *k* also went through an intermediate *g stage. If this was the case, we could propose *ŋ > *g had occurred by Proto-Meto and that *g > *k* occurred after the split between Ro'is Amarasi and Nuclear Meto. Similarly, *r > *k* (which occurred in Nuclear Meto) is cross-linguistically extremely rare, while *r > *g is more common. Thus, it could be that the merger of *r/*ŋ > *k* in Nuclear Meto went through an intermediate *g stage at some point.

In addition to contact with languages of the Central Timor subgroup, there is also evidence for prehistoric contact between Meto and Tetun. Five terms that are probably shared between Tetun and Meto due to borrowing are given below. Each of these terms would have undergone irregular sound changes in Tetun, but regular sound changes in Meto. Thus, they were probably borrowed from Meto into Tetun. Note that these five terms are not only found in varieties of Tetun spoken in central Timor (Foho Tetun and Fehan Tetun), but also in East Tetun that is currently separated from Meto by the speakers of Bunak (non-Austronesian) and Mambae (Central Timor).

- Tetun *feto* 'woman' from Meto *feto* 'man's sister, woman'
- Tetun *naʔi(n)* 'lord; male honorific' from Meto *naʔi-f* 'grandfather', *naiʔ* 'Mr'
- Tetun *koto* 'variety of bean' from Meto *kotoʔ, koto* 'hyacinth bean, Lablab purpureus'
- Tetun *kunus* 'capsicum', from Meto; Ro'is Amarasi, Kusa-Manea *kunus* 'chilli', other Meto *ʔunus* 'chilli'
- Tetun *naʔi bei* 'respectful name for the crocodile' from Meto; Amarasi *naiʔbesi*, Amfo'an *beʔi-ʤ*, Kusa-Manea *beʔi* 'crocodile'

In addition to terms that were borrowed from Meto into Tetun, there are also a number of terms that are probably shared by borrowing but for which the direction of borrowing cannot be determined as neither language has undergone distinctive sound changes. One example is Tetun *bukae* 'provisions for a trip, food taken on a journey', Molo *bukae-l* 'provisions', *n-bukae* 'eat', Amarasi *n-bukae* 'eat, drink, dine'. There are also several forms that are probably loans into Meto from Tetun. One example is Tetun *fukar* 'season, spice', Kotos Amarasi *fukar* 'herbs, spices, seasonings', Molo *fukal* 'seasonings'.

Finally, Kusa-Manea has been in more intense contact with Tetun than other varieties of Meto. Kusa-Manea is spoken in territory that was historically part of the Tetun kingdom of Wehali and Kusa-Manea speakers are nearly universally multilingual and also speak

13 Two examples of Ro'is Amarasi *ŋ > *n* where other Meto varieties have *ŋ > k are PRM *ŋilu > *niu* 'tamarind' and PMeto *ŋinu > *na-ninu* 'spit'.

Tetun. Tetun is also the language used by them in traditional ceremonies. Unsurprisingly, there are many loans from Tetun into Kusa-Manea across all semantic spheres, including functors such as *mos* 'to, also' or *tan* 'because, therefore'.

3.3.4.2 Contact with Helong

Meto has been in extensive contact with Helong since prehistoric times and this contact is still ongoing. At present, Meto is dominant and the nature of contact is overwhelmingly from Meto into Helong. However, in prehistoric times the relationship appears to have been more equal and many borrowings can be identified that are from Helong into Meto.

Examples of likely borrowings from Helong into Meto include Helong *ŋala* 'name, tribe, clan, people group' (regular from PMP *ŋajan) → Meto *kana-f* 'name, clan', Helong *blapas* 'side' → Meto *bnapa-f* 'side' (initial *bl* is common in Helong, but *bn* is rare in Meto), Helong *nale-n* 'daughter-in-law' → Meto *nane-f* 'daughter-in-law, opposite sex sibling's daughter' (Rote languages have compounds of *feto* 'female' and *feu-k* 'new'), Helong *el* 'like, similar; to, towards' → Ro'is Amarasi *en* 'like, similar; to, towards', Nuclear Meto *on* 'like, similar' (Rote languages have *leo* 'like, similar').

However, this is not to say that the direction of prehistoric borrowing was exclusively from Helong into Meto. Many loans in the other direction can also be identified, including PRM *hatahori 'person' > Pre-Meto **atoli → Helong *atuli* 'person' > Proto-Meto *atoni 'man, person', and PRM *sarakaen 'sand' > Pre-Meto **slaen → Funai Helong *slaen*, Semau Helong *hlaen* 'sand' > Proto-Meto *snaen 'sand'. The fact that many of these borrowings involve items of basic vocabulary points to long-term intense contact between Helong and Meto involving extensive bilingualism. This contact continues today, with the difference that Meto is the dominant language.

Apart from contact between Helong and Meto, there is also evidence that Proto-Rote-Meto was in contact with Proto-Helong. There are a little over 100 vocabulary items in this comparative dictionary, for which cognates are only known in Rote-Meto and Helong. Many of these cognates sets show regular sound changes in both groups, thus indicating borrowing at an early stage. In addition to this vocabulary, the change of *w > *f is partly shared between Rote-Meto and Helong. (See §3.5.3.2 for more discussion of this change.)

3.4 Levels of reconstruction

Reconstructions in this dictionary are assigned to one of 10 levels according to the language varieties in which their reflexes occur. These levels are summarised in Table 3.10, along with the number of reconstructions made to each level. Of these levels, the first six are all proto-languages, which can be identified on the basis of exclusively shared innovations, while the final four are groupings that have a shared common history but do not necessarily descend from a single unitary proto language below the level of PRM or, in the case of Central East Rote, below the level of PnRote (§3.3).

Table 3.10: Reconstructive levels†

Abbreviation	Level	Must include at least one of	No.
PRM	Proto-Rote-Meto	West Rote, Nuclear Rote, and Meto	664
PwRM	Proto-West Rote-Meto	West Rote, and Meto	37
PMeto	Proto-Meto	Meto	39
PnMeto	Proto-Nuclear Meto	Nuclear Meto	22
PnRote	Proto-Nuclear Rote	Nuclear Rote	23
PwRote	Proto-West Rote	West Rote	3
Rote	Rote	West Rote, and Nuclear Rote	264
nRM	Nuclear Rote-Meto	Nuclear Rote, and Meto	50
CERM	Central East Rote-Meto	Central East Rote, Meto	45
CER	Central East Rote	Central East Rote	27

† West Rote includes Dela, Oenale and Dengka. Nuclear Rote includes all other Rote lects. Nuclear Meto includes all varieties of Meto except Ro'is Amarasi. Central East Rote includes all Nuclear Rote except Tii and Lole.

There are two factors which determine to which level a reconstruction is assigned. Firstly, when cognate forms with (mostly) regular sound correspondences are identified, a reconstruction is made to the appropriate level according to the lects that attest the cognate forms. Thus, for instance, *ɓole 'arenga palm, Arenga pinnata' is reconstructed to PRM on the basis of cognates in West Rote languages, Nuclear Rote and Meto.

Secondly, when a Rote-Meto cognate set has likely cognates in other Austronesian languages, a reconstruction is made to the highest level justified by the Rote-Meto evidence. This is accompanied by any P(CE)MP reconstruction in the etymology field for terms that have been reconstructed to P(CE)MP) and/or the external cognates in the out-comparison section (§1.5.1). Thus, for instance, PRM *laŋga 'head' has cognates in Helong, Kisar, Tokodede and Kemak, which are all included in the out-comparisons section (§1.5.1). Similarly, PRM *ate 'liver' has numerous cognates in Austronesian languages and its PMP etymon *qatay is given in the etymology field (§1.5.3.3).

A reconstruction to any of the levels lower than PRM has three logical explanations:

- the reconstruction is an innovation at that level
- the reconstruction is inherited from PRM, but cognates are unknown (perhaps due to loss) in all daughter languages of a particular branch
- the cognate set is ultimately a loan.

While we can never, in principle, definitively decide which of these three explanations explains any particular lower level reconstruction (or any reconstruction at any level for that matter), there are certain situations in which one explanation is more likely than another.

When a reconstruction is made on the basis of internal Rote-Meto evidence and is assigned to Rote, Nuclear Rote-Meto or Central East Rote-Meto, the second explanation is most likely: the terms are probably inherited from PRM, but cognates are not known in the languages that do not belong to these groups. Innovation is unlikely as none of these groups are descended from unitary proto-languages (see §3.3), though we cannot rule out innovation in one branch with borrowing into the other branch (a combination of the first and third explanations).

Similarly, when a reconstruction is made to a level below PRM on the basis of evidence external to Rote-Meto, and these cognates are widely distributed, the second explanation is probably most likely: the form was present in PRM, but is unknown or lost in daughter languages from a particular branch. Thus, for instance, Proto-Meto *metam 'black' is a reflex of PMP *ma-qitəm. While it cannot technically be reconstructed to PRM on the basis of the internal evidence, it was almost certainly present in PRM but has been lost without known trace in all the modern Rote languages. Likewise, Proto-Meto *k|teom 'sea-urchin' has cognates in Flores and other languages of Timor. There is no reason to suppose that borrowing accounts for *all* these cognate forms (though it might account for some), thus unless the Proto-Meto term itself is a borrowing after the breakup of Proto-Meto, it is likely that Proto-Meto *k|teom is a reflex of an earlier PRM etymon, which has been lost in the Rote languages.

On the other hand, when a lower level reconstruction is made for which external cognates have only a limited range, we cannot yet decide between any of the explanations, though the second explanation (loss in all daughter languages of a particular branch) usually seems unlikely. Thus, for instance, Proto-Meto *domi 'love, like' has cognates in Tetun and languages of central Timor. It could be a Proto-Meto innovation that was then borrowed by these other languages, or it could have been borrowed by (Proto)-Meto.

When I am fairly confident that a particular cognate set is due to borrowing into the Rote-Meto languages, the cognate set is included in the loan distribution section of the dictionary (see §1.5.3.6 for more discussion of this section) usually with discussion of the evidence as to why this set is identified as a loan. When the evidence is ambiguous, it is included in the main section, again often with discussion as to the possibility that this term is a borrowing.

The cognate sets that are most ambiguous between explanation one (innovation at a lower level) and explanation two (PRM innovation with loss in daughter languages) are those that are made to a lower level only on the basis of Rote-Meto internal evidence. Thus, for instance, Proto-West Rote-Meto *ɓatus 'sea-snail' is reconstructed on the basis of Dengka *ɓa~ɓatu-ʔ* 'sea-snail', Ro'is Amarasi *k|ba͡utus*, and Kotos Amarasi *k|batus* 'sea-snail, oyster'. At present, this term has no other known cognates. It may be a West Rote-Meto innovation, it may have been present in PRM but lost in the other Rote languages, or further work may reveal cognates in other languages of Rote or other regional languages.

To summarise, I assign reconstructions to one of 10 levels as is appropriate according to the internal Rote-Meto evidence. Reconstructions assigned to Rote, Nuclear Rote-Meto or Central East Rote-Meto were probably present in PRM, but cognates are unknown (perhaps due to complete loss) in West Rote or Meto. Similarly, when external cognates of lower level reconstructions are widely distributed, borrowing into Rote-Meto is unlikely.

3.5 Rote-Meto within Malayo-Polynesian

In this section I discuss the way in which Rote-Meto fits within Malayo-Polynesian. This includes discussion of the sound correspondences between PMP and PRM (§3.5.1), the probable role of language shift from non-Austronesian languages (§3.5.2) and the position of Rote-Meto within Malayo-Polynesian (§3.5.3).

3.5.1 Sound changes between PMP and PRM

Edwards (2018c) provides a detailed discussion of most aspects of the top-down history of the Rote-Meto languages, though that paper is based on an earlier and smaller database, as well as an earlier understanding of the sound changes. In this section I summarise the latest understanding of the sound changes that have occurred between PMP and PRM. This includes the changes affecting consonants (§3.5.1.1), vowels and glides (§3.5.1.2) and word final consonants (§3.5.1.3). Two different kinds of sound correspondences between PMP and PRM can be identified: those that are mostly regular and those which involve unconditioned splits.

3.5.1.1 Initial and medial consonants

The PMP consonants that have regular reflexes in PRM are summarised in Table 3.11, along with the number of attestations of each correspondence set. PMP *t, *k, *m, *n, *s and *l are usually retained unchanged in PRM. PMP *h > Ø and *ñ > *n. The correspondences shown in Table 3.11 represent more than 95 per cent of cases for each PMP consonant, with the exception of *k = *k which is retained unchanged in 82 per cent of cases (68/83).[14]

Table 3.11: Regular P(CE)MP to PRM consonant correspondences

PMP	*t	*k	*m	*n	*ñ	*h	*s	*l
PRM	*t	*k	*m	*n	*n	Ø	*s	*l
No.	117	72	59	55	8	36	60	97

Other PMP consonants undergo unconditioned splits in PRM. The main reflexes are summarised in Table 3.12 and Table 3.13, along with the number of times each reflex is attested. Correspondences with only a single attestation, as well as those that constitute less than 10 per cent of all cases, are not included.

Table 3.12: P(CE)MP to PRM consonant correspondences with unconditioned splits: Part 1

env.					/#_				/V_V			/#_			/V_V	
PMP	*p		*q		*b-				*-b-			*d-			*-d-	
PRM	*h	*p	Ø	*h	*f	*b	*ɓ	*mb	*f	*ɓ	*mb	*d	*ɗ	*r	*r	*ɗ
No.	39	6	45	8	36	29	25	14	24	5	3	16	7	4	16	3

14 The other reflexes of PMP *k are as follows: six instances of *k > Ø, four of *k > *ʔ, three of *k > *h and two of *k > *ŋg. None of these constitute more than 10 per cent of the reflexes of PMP *k.

Table 3.13: P(CE)MP to PRM consonant correspondences with unconditioned splits: Part 2

PMP	*z			*j				*g		*ŋ			*R		*r	
PRM	*ɗ	*nd	*d	*ɗ	*d	*r	*ʤ	*ŋg	*k	*n	*ŋ	*ŋg	Ø	r	Ø	r
No.	7	2	2	7	4	3	2	6	6	21	8	4	42	9	3	9

The reflexes of PMP nasal-plosive clusters in PRM are given in Table 3.14. Of these, bilabial nasal-plosive clusters merge as PRM *mb, while others have a split between a PRM prenasalised plosive or plain plosive.

Table 3.14: P(CE)MP nasal-plosive clusters

PMP	*mb/*mp	*nd/*ŋd		*nt		*ŋk	
PRM	*mb	*nd	*d	*t	*nd	*ŋg	*k
No.	8	3	2	4	3	3	2

3.5.1.2 Vowels and glides

The reflexes of PMP vowels are given in Table 3.15 and the reflexes of vowel-glide sequences are given in Table 3.16. Of these, PMP *ə undergoes an unconditioned split word finally, *u undergoes a split before PMP *R and the vowel-glide sequences *wa and *ya each undergo unconditioned splits (see §3.5.3.2 for more discussion of the reflexes of *wa and vowels before final *R). Other reflexes are mostly regular. As in previous tables, correspondences with only a single attestation and those which constitute less than 10 per cent of instances are not included.

Table 3.15: P(CE)MP to PRM vowel correspondences

env.		/_R#	/#σ̲σ	/#σσ̲			/_q#			/_R#	
PMP	*i	*i	*ə	*ə			*ə	*a	*u	*u	
PRM	*i	*e	*e	*ə	*e	*a	*e	*a	*u	*u	*o
No.	180	3	64	22	14	7	5	328	247	7	7

Table 3.16: P(CE)MP to PRM vowel-vowel and vowel-glide correspondences

PMP	*wa			*wi/*iw	*au/*aw	*ya		*ay/*ai	*uy/*yu
PRM	*o	*fa	*wa	*i	*o	*e	*a	*e	*i
No.	9	3	2	7	25	4	2	22	7

3.5.1.3 Final consonants

Most final PMP consonant are lost in PRM, though in some cases *p, *t, *s, *m, *n, *ŋ and *k have been retained. Among all the Rote-Meto languages, Meto is the most conservative in retaining final consonants. Table 3.17 summarises the extent to which final consonants have been lost or retained in reconstructions in PRM. In addition to these retentions, there is one example each of final *q > *h (*buaq > *mbuah 'betel nut') and *R > *h (*niuR > *noh 'coconut').

Table 3.17: Retention and loss of final consonants

PMP	*p		*t		*k			*s		*m			*n			*ŋ	
PRM	*s	Ø	*t	Ø	*k	*h	Ø	*s	Ø	*m	*n	Ø	*n	*m	Ø	*n	Ø
No.	4	5	7	27	2	1	36	11	14	4	1	11	10	1	38	1	22
Retention rate	40%		21%		7%			48%		31%			22%			4%	

The change of *p > *s is unusual and requires further discussion. The four forms with this change are *qudip > *horis 'alive, living', *ma-qudip > *moris 'live, be alive', *malip > *malis 'laugh, smile' and *qatip > *atis 'breast beam of a loom'. All these forms have *i as the final vowel, and this appears to be a conditioning environment. The usual reflex of PMP *p in PRM is *h, and final *p > *s in these forms is probably assimilation of earlier **h to the place of the previous palatal vowel. The complete pathway may have been *p > **h > **ç > *s.

For most of these forms the Rote-Meto languages have multiple reflexes, some of which have loss of the final consonant and some of which have retention of *s = *s*. Thus, for instance, Meto has *malis > *n-manis* 'laugh at (transitive)' and *malis > *n-mani* 'laugh, smile (intransitive)', similarly Termanu has *moris > *moli* 'live, be alive', *molis* 'life! health! (said to a child who sneezes)'. Because of such variation, it would be plausible to analyse the final /s/ in forms in which it is retained as a reflex of a suffix. While there *is* a suffix *-s* in the Rote-Meto languages, this is a nominalising suffix and thus probably cannot account for final *s in forms such as Meto *n-manis* 'laugh at (transitive)'.

Further support for identifying *p > (**h) > *s as a sound change in these forms rather than positing that the final /s/ is a historic suffix comes from external witnesses. Putative cases of *p > *s* /i_# have been identified in several other languages of the region, none of which are known to have a suffix *-s*. Additionally, all languages with this change are members of the Timor-Babar subgroup to which Rote-Meto belongs (see §3.5.3), which is defined by *p > *h. Thus, the proposed assimilation of **h > *s /i_# may have occurred at the level of Proto-Timor-Babar. Forms for which the change of final *p > *s* /i_# have been identified in other languages are as follows:

- *qudip > Semau Helong *nulis* 'life' (*nuli* 'live', *kuli?* 'alive'), Fehan Tetun *horis* 'living', East Tetun *houris* 'alive, with life'
- *ma-qudip > Fehan Tetun *moris* 'live, be alive', East Tetun *moris* ~ *mouris* 'live, be alive, exist, be born'
- *qatip > Helong, Fehan Tetun *atis* 'breast beam of a loom', East Tetun *atis* 'fine cloth, or cloth still on the loom; a part of the loom', Galolen *atis* 'weåving loom'

3.5.2 Sound change and language shift

The correspondences between PMP and PRM raise two problems that require explanation. Firstly, there are a large number of unconditioned splits between PMP and PRM. PMP *b, *d, *j, *g and *ŋ have all undergone unconditioned splits with each of the PRM reflexes relatively well attested, even if one reflex is a majority. Similarly, *p, *q and *z also show unconditioned splits, though for these correspondences one reflex clearly predominates. Among the vowels and glides there are fewer splits. Nonetheless, word final PMP *ə has undergone a split between PRM *e and *ə, while *wa has undergone a three-way split.

Secondly, several PRM proto-phonemes are not particularly well represented in inheritances from PMP. The prenasalised plosives do not have a robust and consistent source in PMP. In particular, *nd has no robust PMP source and initial *ŋg is mostly unexpected based on inheritance from PMP. Only about a third of prenasalised plosives have a PMP source, and furthermore — as discussed in Edwards (2018a:398f) — PMP forms that develop a prenasalised plosive in PRM often show additional irregularities. Similarly, the mid-vowel *o is mostly unexpected based on inheritance from PMP.

The two main issues that are not accounted for by inheritance from PMP are the large number of splits between PMP and PRM, as well as the fact that the PRM phoneme inventory has been restructured when compared with its PMP source. In this section I propose a tentative scenario that may go some way towards partly explaining these two issues. I do not think that this scenario provides a complete explanation and it is almost certainly an over-simplification of a much more complex process. With those disclaimers in mind, I present it as a starting point for understanding the history of PRM and other languages in this region.

PRM is partly a result of large-scale language shift from at least one non-Austronesian language to the incoming Austronesian language, which was to become PRM. The large number of unconditioned splits between PMP and PRM is due to adaptation of the new Austronesian phonological system to the pre-Austronesian phonological system. The 'Austronesian' system probably contrasted plain voiced plosives *b *d *g with voiceless plosives *p *t *k, as is reconstructed for PMP, while the 'non-Austronesian' system probably contrasted three series of plosives: voiceless *p *t *k, prenasalised *mb *nd *ŋg, and imploded *ɓ *ɗ, as is areally common in this region.

The way the incoming Austronesian phonological system may have been transformed by speakers of the pre-Austronesian languages can be illustrated with the labial obstruents. The Austronesian language probably had a single bilabial obstruent /b/ with both plosive [b] and fricative [β] realisations. The fricative realisation was probably most common intervocalically while there was some variation word initially. That is, the Austronesian language had /b/ → [β] /V_V, /b/ → [b]~[β] /#_.[15]

The pre-Austronesian language(s), on the other hand, contrasted three labial obstruents: /ɓ/, /mb/ and /f/. As speakers of this language began to acquire the new Austronesian language, the fricative realisation [β] of /b/ may have been interpreted as /f/, while the plosive realisation was interpreted as either /ɓ/ or /mb/. As language contact intensified and the non-Austronesian speakers became more fluent in the new Austronesian language, they may have acquired /b/ 'correctly' as /b/, thus leading to the PRM system with *b, *ɓ, *mb and *f.

15 Modern-day varieties of Meto similarly have plosive and fricative realisations of voiced stops (§2.4.2).

As previously stated, the scenario sketched in the previous three paragraphs is highly tentative and is almost certainly a simplification. As currently presented, language shift is treated as a unitary event that affected an entire population at a single time. This is a gross over-simplification. Instead, different speakers would have acquired the new Austronesian language with different degrees of proficiency and at different times.

Thus, for instance, as discussed in Edwards (2018a:398f), forms with PMP *b > PRM *mb often show additional irregularities. If we envisage a scenario in which the new Austronesian language was learnt at first by only a minority of the non-Austronesian speaking population, forms with PMP *b > PRM *mb may represent the first layer of vocabulary acquired by the Austronesian learners before they were fully proficient. These forms may have then spread to non-Austronesian speakers who were not otherwise learning the Austronesian language. Forms with PMP *b > PRM *ɓ do not usually show additional irregularities and these may represent forms that were acquired later when more of the non-Austronesian-speaking population was learning the Austronesian language, while forms with PMP *b = PRM *b may have been the most recent acquisitions perhaps being brought into PRM by bilingual children.

Furthermore, this scenario treats every sound change that has occurred between PMP and PRM as due to contact. This was almost certainly not the case. It is likely that there was a mix of changes due to contact and changes due to 'natural' causes. Thus, for instance, the shift of *β > *f could also quite easily have come about without contact as intervocalic devoicing of fricatives is not uncommon.

While this represents one step towards a more realistic picture, I must emphasise that this scenario remains too simplistic. Many different variables remain unaccounted for. What about the possibility that different Austronesian learners had different accents (e.g. some with *b > *mb, other with *b > *ɓ)? What effect would the children of the Austronesian learners have had on the formation of PRM? What could have been the effects of borrowing between the Austronesian and non-Austronesian languages? What about the effects of acquisition of the non-Austronesian language by Austronesian speakers? What about the possibility of multiple language shift events, such as one at the level of Proto-Timor-Babar and another at the level of PRM?

There is a significant mismatch between the data revealed by a bottom-up reconstruction and that expected by simple 'normal' top-down inheritance from PMP. This mismatch demands explanation. Language shift with substrate transference of non-Austronesian features is almost certainly part of the explanation.

3.5.3 Subgrouping within Malayo-Polynesian

In this section I discuss the position of the Rote-Meto family within the Austronesian language family and its relationships with other nearby languages. Rote-Meto can be placed in a larger Timor-Babar family, which includes most, but not all, the Austronesian languages of Timor and Southwest Maluku. Rote-Meto is justified as a separate subgroup within Timor-Babar on the basis of two shared phonological innovations.

3.5.3.1 Timor-Babar

Within the greater Timor region, languages belonging to two families are spoken: Austronesian languages; and Timor-Alor-Pantar languages, which are non-Austronesian, or 'Papuan'. In addition, there are also Austronesian-based contact creoles in the region that do not fit normal genetic classification.

Among the Austronesian languages of this region, four primary branches of (CE)MP can be identified on the basis of shared sound changes from PMP, one of which is Timor-Babar, within which Rote-Meto is located. The other branches of (CE)MP within the greater Timor region are Bima-Lembata, Central Timor and Tanimbar-Bomberai. Other branches of (CE)MP that are coordinate with these branches are found in other parts of eastern Indonesian.

The Bimba-Lembata subgroup contains the languages of Bima, Sumba, Flores and the Solor archipelago, as well as Hawu and Dhao, the last of which is spoken just to the west of Rote. The Central Timor subgroup contains four languages of central Timor: Welaun, Kemak, Tokodede and Mambae. The Tanimbar-Bomberai subgroup contains Yamdena and Fordata of the Tanimbar Islands, as well as Kei and several languages of the Bomberai Peninsula of New Guinea. The Timor-Babar subgroup contains all other Austronesian languages of this region extending from Rote to Wetar and across to Selaru in the east.

The distribution of the different language families in the greater Timor, along with their member languages, is shown in Map 3.1. A tree showing the higher order subgroups in the region along with primary subgroups of Timor-Babar is given in Figure 3.6. As discussed in §1.1 and §1.5.3.3, for the purposes of this dictionary I am agnostic regarding the putative intermediate nodes of CEMP and CMP.

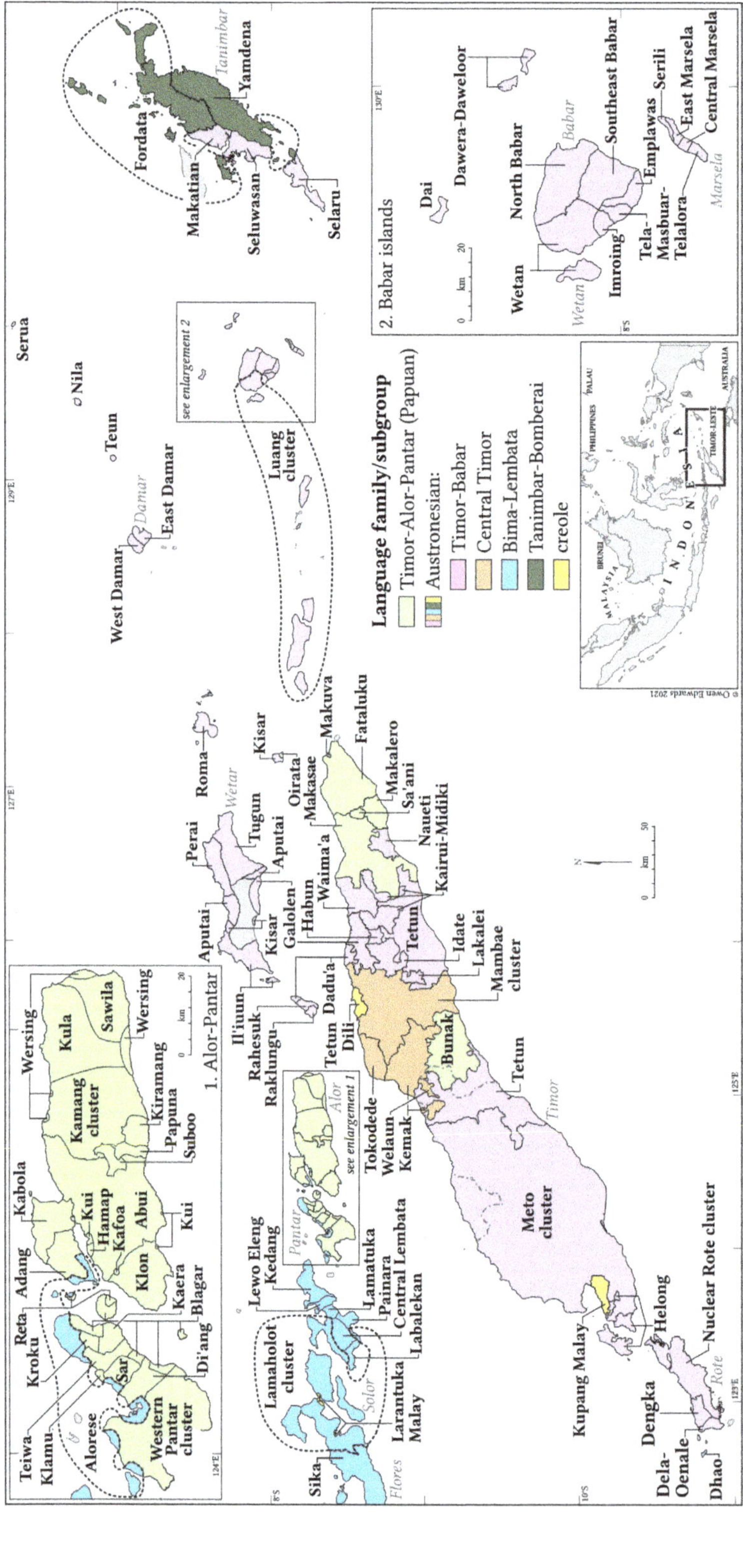

Map 3.1: Languages and language families of the greater Timor region

Source: Owen Edwards.

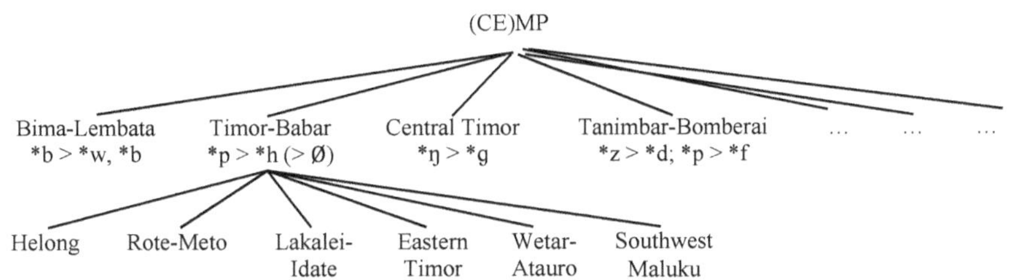

Figure 3.6: Timor-Babar and Rote-Meto within Malayo-Polynesian

It is beyond the scope of the present work to justify the proposed classification shown in Figure 3.6. In this section I only discuss the evidence for Timor-Babar as a valid subgroup of (CE)MP, and the evidence for Rote-Meto as a valid subgroup within Timor-Babar. Evidence for Bima-Lembata has been presented by Fricke (2019:229ff), Central Timor by Edwards (2019:42ff) and evidence for Tanimbar-Bomberai (under different names) is presented in Mills (1991) and Blust (1993:276f).

The Timor-Babar subgroup is supported by reflexes of PMP *p as *h* or Ø, with several languages showing a split of *p > *h,* Ø. To account for this, we can posit *p > *h in Proto-Timor-Babar with subsequent *h > Ø where relevant. The change *p > *h* is cross-linguistically well attested. However, within the geographical context of the greater Timor region, this sound change *does* set Timor-Babar apart. The Bima-Lembata and Central Timor subgroups retain *p = *p (Fricke 2019:176f; Edwards 2019:43f) and the Tanimbar-Bomberai subgroup has *p > *f (Mills 1991:243). Given that *p > *f > *h is a natural sequence of changes, it may be possible at a higher level to link Timor-Babar with Tanimbar-Bomberai on the basis of shared *p > *f. However, even if this is done, Timor-Babar would still be a valid subgroup on the basis of shared *f > *h. Reflexes of word initial *ma-p must be treated separately to those of *p as most Timor-Babar languages have *ma-p > *p* or *ma-p > *b*, probably as a result of an intermediate nasal-stop cluster stage, either **mp and/or **mb.

Examples of *p > *h,* Ø in most languages of the Timor-Babar subgroup are given in Table 3.18 to illustrate this defining sound change. Languages are grouped according to their likely subgroup within Timor-Babar. Non-cognate forms with the same gloss as the PMP reconstructions are given in brackets, to indicate potential lexical replacement.

Table 3.18: Reflexes of *p in Timor-Babar

Gloss	'four'	'seven'	'how much'	'banana'	'fire'	'thin'
PMP	*əpat	*pitu	*pija	*punti	*hapuy	*ma-nipis
Proto Timor-Babar	*haat	*hitu	*hija	*hundi	*ahi	*manihis
ROTE-METO						
PRM	*haa	*hitu	*hiɗa	*hundi	*ahi	*nihis
HELONG						
Funai Helong	*aat*	*itu*	*ila*	*(bua)*	*ai*	*mnihis*
Semau Helong	*aat*	*itu*	*ila*	*(bua)*	*ai*	*nihis*

Gloss	'four'	'seven'	'how much'	'banana'	'fire'	'thin'
EASTERN TIMOR						
East Tetun	*haat*	*hitu*	*hira*	*hudi*	*ahi*	*mihis*
Fehan Tetun	*haat*	*hitu*	*hira*	*hudi*	*haʔi*†	*niʔis*
Habun	*haʔa*	*hitu*	*hira*	*(muku)*	*ahi*	
Waima'a	*kai-haa*	*kai-hitu*	*kai-hire*	*hudi*	*(daha)*	*nihi*
Midiki	*kai-haa*	*kai-hitu*	*kai-hira*	*hudi*	*(yaha)*	
LAKALEI-IDATE						
Lakalei	*aat*	*hitu*	*ila*		*wai*	
Idate	*aat*	*hitu*	*yila*	*(muʔu)*	*wai*	*mihis*
WETAR-ATAURO						
Galolen	*ih-aat*	*i-hitu*	*i-hila*	*(muʔu)*	*i-morin*	*miis*
Tugun	*f-aat*	*faʔ-itu*	*faʔ-ira*	*(muu)*	*ai-moriŋ*	*miis*
Perai	*aak*	*itu*	*faʔ-ira*	*(muu)*	*ai-moriŋ*	*miis*
Aputai	*aak*	*itu*	*faʔ-ira*	*(muu)*	*ai-moriŋ*	*miis*
Dadu'a	*waʔ-itu*	*w-aak*	*waʔ-ira*	*(muu)*	*ai-mori*	*miih*
Raklungu	*ha-itu*	*h-aaʔ*	*ha-iraʔ*	*(muʔu)*	*a-mori*	
Rahesuk	*heʔ-itu*	*h-aat*	*heʔ-ira*	*(muʔu)*	*i-mori*	*ne-mniis*
SOUTHWEST MALUKU						
Makuva‡				*utu*	*a-ke*	
Selaru	*ena-at*	*itw*	*(enai)*	*(kwe)*	*ay*	*mani~nias*
East Damar	*wo-atu*	*wo-itu*	*wi*	*(wu)*	*ai*	*na-mnihu*
Roma	*woʔ-atta*	*woʔ-itu*	*woʔ-ira*	*(wui)*	*ai*	*mnihana*
Kisar	*woʔ-akka*	*woʔ-iku*	*wo-ira*	*(muʔu)*	*ai*	*na-mnisa*
Luang	*wog-atə*	*wo-itu*	*wo-irə*	*udi*	*ai*	*mnihə*
Serua	*natu*	*itu*	*ira*	*(wia)*	*ai*	*ni-mnisu*
Teun	*natu*	*yitu*	*yiru*	*(fiwa)*	*wai*	*ni-mnis~nisu*
Nila	*watu*	*itu*	*ira*	*(hia)*	*wai*	*n-nisu*
West Damar	*wi-oto*	*wi-iti*	*wo-ire*	*(us-o)*#	*os-o*#	*miŋidoi*
Dawera	*aty*	*ity*	*irei*	*(urus)*	*(am)*	*me-lid~lid*
Dai	*at*	*ity*	*ire*	*(diamny-on)*	*(amʔ-on)*	*me-mnit*
North Babar	*ato*	*iti*	*ire*	*ud wia*	*(ami-ai)*	*ne-mnido*
Central Marsela	*fi-ak*	*wo-ie*	*fi-era*	*ut*	*ei-ei*	*ne-mni~nit*
East Marsela	*wu-a*	*wo-ik*	*fi-era*	*ut*	*ui*	*le-mni~nit*
Serili	*boʔ-a*	*boʔ-ot*	*(nomia)*	*ut*	*ui-e*	*me-li~lit*
Southeast Babar	*wo-ax*	*wo-ixy*	*(nomya)*	*uty*	*ui*	*(pilpil)*
Emplawas	*wi-ek*	*wo-ik*	*vi-era*	*uti-e*	*ui-e*	*(piliti)*
Tela-Masbuar	*wi-eky*	*wo-iky*	*wo-iri*	*uti-e*	*ui-e*	*ne-minitə*

† Initial /h/ in East Tetun *haʔi* 'fire' is an insertion before a glottal stop.

‡ Additional Makuva forms that show *p > *h*, Ø are *paŋdan > *hene* 'pandanus', *pusəj > *hutre* 'navel', and *nipay > *ne* 'snake'.

West Damar *os-o* 'fire' has regular *i > *s* /_-V and comes thus from *hapuy > *ahi > **oi. Despite the superficial similarity between PMP *punti and West Damar *us-o* 'banana', this latter form is from earlier **ui, which is cognate with Roma *wui*, and East Damar *wu*. These forms are not inherited from *punti.

Examples of the reflexes of PMP *p in illustrative languages of other subgroups of (CE)MP neighbouring Timor-Babar are given in Table 3.19 to show that they do not share *p > *h*, Ø. PMP *p is retained as *p* in most forms in Bima-Lembata, and Central Timor. While some languages have subsequent changes, *p must be reconstructed for each of these subgroups. The only exception is Central Timor *pitu > *hitu* 'seven', which may represent later borrowing in daughter languages from Tetun. (Note also that all Welaun forms except *hoat* 'four' are identical to Fehan Tetun forms from which they may be borrowed.) Tanimbar-Bomberai languages usually have *p > *f*, with subsequent sporadic *f > Ø in Yamdena.

Table 3.19: Reflexes of *p in subgroups neighbouring Rote-Meto

*Gloss	'four'	'seven'	'how much'	'banana'	'fire'	'thin'
PMP	*əpat	*pitu	*pija	*punti	*hapuy	*ma-nipis
Bima-Lembata	*əpat	*pitu	*pida	*punti	*api	*manipis
Bima	*upa*	*pidu*	*pila*	*(kalo)*	*afi*	*nipi*
Manggarai	*paat*	*pitu*	*pisa*	*punti*†	*api*	*mipis*
Sika	*(hutu)*	*pitu*	*pira*	*(muʔu)*	*api*	*(blelər)*
Lewotobi Lamaholot	*paa*	*pito*	*pira*	*(muko)*	*ape*	*mənipi*
Kedang	*apaʔ*	*pitu*	*pie*	*(muʔu)*	*api*	*mipi*
Central Lembata	*paat*	*pito*	*pira*	*(muku)*	*ape*	*mipiv*
Kambera	*pat-u*	*pihu*	*piraŋ*	*(kaluu)*	*epi*	*manipa*
Hawu	*əpa*	*pidu*	*pəri*	*(muʔu)*	*ai*	*menii*
Dhao	*əpa*	*pid͡ʑu*	*pəri*	*(muu)*	*ai*	*manii*
Central Timor	*pəat	*hitu	*pija		*api	
Welaun	*hoat*	*hitu*	*hira*	*hudi*	*haʔi*	*niʔis*
Kemak	*paat*	*hitu*	*pila*	*(muu)*	*api*	*(diren)*
Tokodede	*paat*	*(hoho ruu)*	*piil*		*api*	*(lihire)*
Northwest Mambae	*paat*	*(hoho rua)*	*ar-piil*	*(muuk-a)*	*aep-a*	*(hilire)*
Central Mambae	*faat*	*hitu*	*ar-fiil*	*(muu-a)*	*aif-a*	*(mihis)*‡
South Mambae	*paat*	*(liim nai rua)*	*piil*	*(muu)*	*aap*	*(hilire)*
Tanimbar-Bomberai	*faat	*fitu	*fija	*fundi	*afuy	*manifis
Yamdena	*fat*	*itw*	*fir*	*fundi*	*au*	*manisik*
Fordata	*(i)faʔat*	*(i)fitu*	*ifira*	*(muʔu)*	*yafu*	*masnifit*
Kei	*faak*	*fit*	*n-fir*	*(muk)*	*yaf*	*manifin*
Sekar	*fat*	*(buteras)*	*firas*	*fudi*	*yafi*	*(bair)*

† The Pacar dialect of Manggarai has *punti* 'banana'. Other Manggarai varieties have *muku* 'banana'.

‡ Central Mambae *mihis* 'thin' is probably a borrowing from East Tetun *mihis* 'thin'.

In Edwards (2018c) I adduced the change *ŋ/*n > *n* as evidence for Timor-Babar. However, since publication of that paper a closer examination of a wider range of data has shown that this cannot be cited in support of Timor-Babar. While PMP *ŋ usually undergoes change in most Timor-Babar languages, it is retained unchanged in Helong (e.g. *ŋajan > *ŋala* 'name', *haŋin > *aŋin* 'wind') and languages of South Atauro (e.g. Raklungu *ŋajan > *ŋai* 'name' and *haŋin > *aŋi* 'wind'). Some languages of Southwest Maluku also have different outcomes of *ŋ compared with *n (Mills 2010:284ff). Similarly, in Rote-Meto PMP *ŋ undergoes a three-way split between *n, *ŋg and *ŋ (§3.5.1.1).

Apart from the change of *p > *h*, Ø, the Timor-Babar languages usually share *ñ > *n, *h > Ø and *q > Ø, though there are reflexes of *q in some languages in some forms that indicate that a reflex of it probably needs to be reconstructed in some forms for Proto-Timor-Babar. Most Timor-Babar languages also have medial *d > *r*. All of these changes are extremely common among all Austronesian languages and have negligible subgrouping value. Apart from these four changes, the proto-phonology of Timor-Babar appears to be the same as that reconstructed for P(CE)MP.

3.5.3.2 Rote-Meto within Timor-Babar

Within Timor-Babar, there is phonological evidence that Rote-Meto forms a distinct subgroup. The main defining change of Rote-Meto is *wa > *o*. There are 15 examples of PMP *wa in the current database, of which nine show *wa > *o*. Six of these examples are given in Table 3.20 alongside cognates in representative languages from other subgroups of Timor-Babar. Discussion follows.

Table 3.20: Reflexes of *wa in Timor-Babar

Gloss	'water'	'root'	'dry in sun'	'right'	'nine'	'spouse'
PMP	*wahiR	*wakaR	*(pa)-waRi	*kawanan	*siwa	*qasawa
PRM	*oe	*oka-k	*hoi	*kona	*sio	*sao
Funai Helong	*ui*	*(kbakat)*	*huiʔ*	*kanan*	*sipa*	*safa*
Semau Helong	*ui*	*(klaput)*	*huiʔ*	*kanan*	*sipa*	*sapa*
Fehan Tetun	*wee, ue*	*(abut)*	*ha-wai*	*kwana*	*siwi*	*fetosawa*†
East Tetun	*bee, uee*	*(abut)*	*ha-bai, ha-uai*	*kuana*	*sia*	
Waima'a	*wai*	*(ʔkaka)*	*ʔwai*	*wali wana*	*siwe*	
Lakalei	*weer*	*(rabut)*		*(kloon)*	*sia*	
Idate	*weer*	*(raput)*	*a-wari*	*(he kaer)*	*sia*	
Galolen	*wee*	*(amut)*	*(reʔa)*	*mawana*	*i-sia*	
Ili'uun	*eer*	*akar*	*(rese)*	*wana*	*ha-sia*	
Raklungu	*(irai)*	*aʔa*	*(krari)*		*ha-sia*	*saa*
Kisar	*oir*	*aʔarn*	*(loilere)*	*malanna*	*wo-hii*	*hoo*
Luang	*gerə*	*gaʔrə*	*gari*	*malgana*	*wo-siewa*	
S.E. Babar	*wey*	*(wia)*	*(mo-yare)*		*wu-si*	
Dawera	*wee*	*(woi-el-ol)*	*mewael*		*siuw*‡	*daw-ei*

† Fehan Tetun *fetosawa* is glossed as 'sister (of a man)'.

‡ Dawera *siuw* 'nine' has irregular *s = *s* (expect *s > *d*, as in *sawa > *daw-ei* 'husband').

The three forms not shown in Table 3.20 that also have *wa > *o* are: *sawa 'python' > *kai/sao 'green viper' (see under *sao2), PWMP *qambawaŋ > *mbao 'mango', and *hawak 'waist, back of waist' > *ao 'body'. Of the seven forms that do not have *wa > *o* three have *w > *f*, two have *w = *w*, one has *w > Ø, and one has *wa > *u*. These seven forms are:

- *wa > *f
  - *walu > *falu 'eight'
  - *waRi > *fai 'day, time'
  - *bayawak > *ɓaiafa 'monitor lizard'
- *w = *w
  - *huaji > **waji > *waɗi 'same-sex younger sibling'
  - *wani = *wani 'bee'
- other
  - *kali-wati > *kalati 'earthworm'
  - *lawaq > *ɓo/lau 'spider'

Although some other Timor-Babar languages also have *wa > *o* in some forms, there is no reason to suppose that this is due to a period of common development shared between Rote-Meto and these languages. Thus, Kisar also has *wa > *o* in two forms in which this change occurs in Rote-Meto: *wahiR > *oir* 'water' and *qasawa > *hoo* 'marry'. However, cognates in other languages of Southwest Maluku show that this sound change occurred in Kisar after the break-up of Proto-Southwest Maluku.[16] It thus cannot be assigned to a single common ancestor of Rote-Meto and Southwest Maluku.

Likewise, Wetar-Atauro languages have *wa > *o* in reflexes of *sawa 'python', which is also seen in PRM *kai/sao 'green viper'. The available reflexes are Galolen, Ili'uun, Tugun, Aputai *sao* and Perai *soo* 'snake'. However, this is the only change among reflexes of *w which is the same in Rote-Meto and Wetar-Atauro. It is best viewed as a case of parallel development.

Helong has *wa > *u* in *wahiR > *ui* 'water' and *pa-waRi > *huiʔ* 'dry in sun'. Helong does not allow sequences of a mid vowel followed by a high vowel, and thus both these forms could be from intermediate **oi and **hoiʔ respectively, though they could also be from intermediate **ue or **hueʔ. Thus, in these two forms Helong may share *wa > *o with Rote-Meto. However, *pa-waRi > *huiʔ* 'dry in sun' has irregular *R > Ø instead of regular *R > *l* and is thus probably a borrowing from a Rote-Meto language. Thus, at best, there is one form in which Rote-Meto and Helong may share *wa > *o; reflexes of *wahiR 'water', and in this case Helong *ui* may be from earlier **ue, in which case it would not show *wa > *o*.[17]

The usual reflex of *w in other Helong forms is *w > *f* in Funai Helong and *w > *f > *p* in Semau Helong. A form in addition to those shown in Table 3.20 in which this sound change occurs is *hawak 'waist, back of waist' > Funai Helong *afaʔ* 'body, self', Semau Helong *apa* 'body, self', both of which are in contrast to Rote-Meto *ao 'body' with *wa > *o*.

16 Roma also has *wa > *o* in *wahiR > *ori* 'water'.

17 The only other reflex of *ahi currently known in Helong is *bahi 'female, woman, wife; female of animals', which is reflected in the first syllable of Semau Helong *bihata* ~ *behata*, Funai Helong *bihata* 'woman, female'. There are also two reflexes of *aqi: *taqi > Semau and Funai Helong *tai* 'faeces', and *baqi 'grandmother' > Semau Helong *bee* 'mother-in-law'.

As discussed above, three forms have *wa > *fa in PRM: *walu > *falu 'eight', *waRi > *fai 'time, day' and *bayawak > *ɓaiafa 'monitor lizard'. In addition, both forms in which *wa is retained unchanged in PRM have *wa > *fa in Nuclear Rote: PRM *wani > Nuclear Rote *fani 'bee' (West Rote-Meto *oni) and *huaji > **waji > PRM *waɗi > Nuclear Rote *faɗi 'same-sex younger sibling' (West Rote-Meto *oɗi). Of the five forms that show *wa > *fa in at least some Rote-Meto languages, three are known to occur in Helong in which they have regular *w > *f: *walu > Funai Helong *falu* 'eight', Semau Helong *palu* 'eight', *huaji > **waji > Funai Helong *falin*, Semau Helong *palin* 'same-sex younger sibling' and *wani > Semau Helong *pani* 'bee'.

The best explanation of most of this data is that *wa > *o* was a change in progress in Proto-Rote-Meto. At the same time, *w > *f was probably taking place in Proto-Helong. The two proto-languages then came into contact and the change of *w > *f* spread by contact from Proto-Helong into Proto-Rote-Meto and/or Proto Nuclear Rote and affected instances of *wa, which had not yet undergone *wa > *o*.

The change *wa > *o* can be posited as a sound change that defines Rote-Meto. While we cannot posit *wa > *o* in all forms, *wa > *o* took place in 9/15 forms for which *wa has been reconstructed to PMP. Of all changes of *wa > *o* in PRM, only the change of *wa > *o* in *wahiR > *oe 'water' is potentially shared with Helong and in this case Helong *ui* 'water' may be from earlier **ue, in which case it would not show *wa > *o*. In addition to the nine instances of PMP *wa > *o* there is at least one other likely instance of **wa > *o* in a form that has not yet been reconstructed to PMP. This is *osi 'garden in a village', which has cognates in Maluku with initial /wa/. (See the entry *osi for details.)

An additional sound change that provides evidence that Rote-Meto is a valid subgroup within Timor-Babar is sporadic lowering of high vowels to mid before *R. Six examples of this change are shown Table 3.21 along with examples from representative languages other languages of Timor. (No cognates of *qənuR 'animal path, trail' are yet known in other languages of Timor.)

Table 3.21: Reflexes of *uR and *iR /_# in Timor-Babar

Gloss	'tail'	'egg'	'calcium'	'grain head'	'water'	'trail'
PMP	*ikuR	*qatəluR	*qapuR	*buliR	*wahiR	*qənuR
PRM	*iko-k	*təlo-k	*aho	*mbule-k	*oe	*eno
TIMOR-BABAR						
Helong	*iku-n*	*tilu-n*	*ao*	*bulin*	*ui*	
East Tetun	*iku-n*	*tolu-n*	*ahu*	*fulin*	*uee, bee*	
Waimaha	*iku*	*thelu*	*au*	*wulin*	*wai*	
Lakalei	*hiʔon*	*manu telor*	*aur*		*weer*	
Idate	*(y)iʔan*	*manu telor*	*waʔur*		*weer*	
Galolen	*iʔun*	*manu telun*	*aur*	*hulin*	*wee*	
Ili'uun	*iku*	*telu*	*aʔur*	*hulin*	*eer*	
Raklungu	*iʔuʔ*	*manuʔ teluʔ*	*auʔ*		*(irai)*	
Kisar	*iʔur-n*	*kerru-n*	*aur*	*wurna*	*oir*	
Luang	*liʔiru*	*ternu*	*auru*	*wurani*	*gerə*	
Southeast Babar	*iy*	*kely*	*uir*		*wey*	

Gloss	'tail'	'egg'	'calcium'	'grain head'	'water'	'trail'
CENTRAL TIMOR						
Welaun	*hiʔu-n*	*man tolu-n*	*(haul)*†	*fulin*	*wee*	
Kemak	*hiʔo-n*	*telo-n*	*(rapo)*	*hulen*	*bia, bea*	
Tokodede	*iko*	*manu telo*	*(rapo)*		*ee*	
South Mambae	*io*	*maun telo*	*(gau)*		*eer*	

† While both Welaun *haul* and South Mambae *gau* 'calcium, mineral lime' are ultimately from *qapuR, neither are regular and both are probably borrowed from an unidentified intermediate source. Kemak and Tokodede *rapo* 'calcium, mineral lime' are either from *dapuR 'hearth' with semantic shift via intermediate 'ash in hearth' > 'ash' (also attested in Meto, see PRM *raho) or are irregular from *dabuk reconstructed to PMP by Wolff (2010:778).

The two forms not shown in Table 3.21 with this lowering are *bibiR > *ɓife 'lip' and *dapuR > *raho 'three stone hearth'. Thus, there are eight forms that have lowering of mid vowels before *R. Apart from these eight forms there are six forms in which a high vowel is retained as high before *R. These six forms are listed:[18]

- *muRmuR > *mumu 'gargle, rinse the mouth'
- *tuquR > *tuu 'dry'
- *busuR > *ɓusu 'bow for cleaning cotton'
- *kuluR > Proto-Meto *kunu 'breadfruit'
- *qizuR > *midu 'saliva, spit out', Proto-Meto *ŋinu 'spit out'
- *qusiR > *usi 'pursue'

The penultimate vowel of all these forms is high. While this provides a conditioning environment for why the final vowel was not lowered in these forms, there are also three forms with a penultimate high vowel that *do* have lowering of final mid vowels (*bibiR > *ɓife 'lip', *buliR > *mbule-k 'grainhead', and *ikuR > *iko-k 'tail').

Within Timor-Babar, Lakalei and Idate also have vowel lowering before *R in reflexes of *qatəluR 'egg' and *ikuR 'tail' but do not have it in reflexes of *qapuR. No other Timor-Babar languages have lowering of final high vowels, with the possible exception of Helong *qapuR > *ao* 'calcium, mineral lime', which is identical to Meto *ao* 'calcium, mineral lime' and may be a loan. While we could subgroup Lakalei-Idate and Rote-Meto together on the basis of lowering of high vowels to mid, this would currently rest on only two forms.

All languages of the Central Timor subgroup also have lowering of high vowels to mid before final *R, with the exception of Welaun. Indeed, Lakalei and Idate may have acquired such vowel lowering due to influence from Mambae, with which they are in contact. Vowel lowering before *R is a regional feature of west and central Timor. Nonetheless, even if vowel lowering before *R in Rote-Meto is due to contact with Central Timor, the fact that it had occurred in a lexically specific subset of words by the time of Proto-Rote-Meto can thus be taken as supporting evidence for Rote-Meto as a subgroup.

18 An additional form which may show lowering of *u > *o /_R# is *niuR > *noh. However, this form has *u > *o* in most languages of the region.

Other sound changes shared between all members of Rote-Meto are common throughout the region. The change of *R > Ø is found in most languages of the Timor mainland.[19] The change of *ə > *e* in penultimate syllables is found in all other Timor-Babar languages except Tetun and Habun, which have *ə > *o*. The other changes that occur in Rote-Meto are *q > Ø, *h*; *h > Ø, and medial *-d- > *r. Some of these changes had probably occurred by the level of Proto-Timor-Babar and in any case are extremely widespread among Austronesian languages and are of negligible subgrouping value.

In summary, within the greater Timor region, there is phonological evidence for a Timor-Babar subgroup on the basis of shared *p > *h,* Ø. This subgroup contains all the Austronesian languages of Timor and Southwest Maluku, except for the languages that belong to the Central Timor subgroup (Welaun, Kemak, Tokodede and Mambae). Rote-Meto can in turn be identified as a valid member of Timor-Babar on the basis of shared *wa > *o and lowering of high vowels before *R, though neither of these changes take place in all Proto-Roto-Meto forms.

19 The only languages of the Timor mainland that do not have *R > Ø are Helong (*R > *l*), Lakelei-Idate (*R = *r*), Mambae (*R > Ø, *r*) and Makuva (*R = *r*).

4

Rote-Meto – English

A - a

***aa** *PRM.* the; marker of definiteness.

=a *Termanu.* singular form of the definite article. (J:1)

=a *Landu.* nominal article. Frequently occurs on nouns in the citation form. *[Form:* Stress remains on the penultimate syllable of the host. In citation form the enclitic is often non-syllabic, e.g. **ani=a** ['ʔanie̯] 'the wind'.*]* (own field notes)

=a *Dela.* the, a (known referent).

=aa *Ro'is Amarasi.* zero person nominal determiner. *Usage:* Frequently occurs with nouns in the citation form during wordlist-style elicitation. *[Form:* This enclitic surfaces as =**ia**, =**ea** or =**oa** after nouns after stems of a certain phonological shape, thus confirming that this enclitic has two underlying vowels. An example is **atoniʔ** 'man, person' + =**aa** → **atoonʔ=ia**.*]*

=aa *Kotos Amarasi.* zero person nominal determiner which occurs on nouns that are both given/accessible (in the sense of Chafe 1994) and definite. Cannot occur on referents which have the pragmatic function of focus (= 'The semantic component of a pragmatically structured proposition whereby the assertion differs from the presupposition' (Lambrecht 1994:213)). *Usage:* In Kotos Amarasi from Nekmese' village (where the bulk of my data comes from) =**aa** is used less frequently than in other varieties of Meto. Instead, the first person nominal determiner =**ii** is most frequent, followed by third person =**ee**.

=aa *Kusa-Manea.* zero person nominal determiner. *Usage:* Only post-nominal determiner currently known in Kusa-Manea. Nouns are almost always cited with this determiner.

***aem** *PRM.* tame, domesticated. *Etym:* *qayam 'domesticated animal' (PWMP).

ae-k *Termanu.* native, own; the opposite of foreign, belonging to the house, the opposite of running around in the wild; cultivated, the opposite of growing in the wild (of a plant). (J:3)

ae-ʔ *Korbafo.*

ae-k *Bokai.*

ae-ʔ *Bilbaa.*

ae-ʔ *Rikou.*

ae-k *Ba'a.*

ae-k *Tii.*

ae-ʔ *Dengka.*

ae-ʔ *Oenale.*

aem *Kotos Amarasi.* tame.

aem *Molo.* tame. (M:4)

Out-comparisons:

baeŋ *Helong. [irr. from PMP: Ø > b]* (J:3)

***afa** *CER.* insipid. *[History:* Blust and Trussel (ongoing) connect the Rote form with PMP *qambaR (a doublet of *tabaR) but this requires irr. *mb > *f*. Similarly any connection with *tabaR would require irr. *t > Ø.*]*

afa~afa *Termanu.* without odour or taste; insipid. (J:3)

Out-comparisons:

<kàba> *Kambera.* insipid, tasteless. (On:73)

<kòba> *Kodi. [Note:* also in Mangili, Lewa, Anakalang, Mamboru, and Weyewa*]*

***afi** *PRM.* yesterday. *See:* ***beni, *esak**. *Etym:* *Rabiqi 'late afternoon, evening; evening meal; yesterday'.

afi-k=a *Ba'a.* yesterday. (J:676)

afi-k *Tii.*

afis *Dengka.*

afis *Oenale.*
afis *Dela.* yesterday.
afi naa *Ro'is Amarasi.* yesterday, the other day.
afi naa *Kotos Amarasi.* yesterday.
afi, aif neno *Molo.* lately, recently. (M:5)
Out-comparisons:
slahin *Funai Helong.* yesterday.
lahin *Semau Helong.* yesterday.
klahin *Bolok Helong.* yesterday.

***afu** *PRM.* ash, dust. *Etym:* *qabu 'ash, hearth, cinder, powder, dust; grey'.
afu *Termanu.* ash, dust. (J:4)
afu *Korbafo.*
afu *Bokai.*
afu *Bilbaa.*
afu *Rikou.*
afu *Ba'a.*
afu *Tii.*
afu *Dengka.*
afu *Oenale.*
afu *Dela.* dust.
afu *Ro'is Amarasi.* ground, earth.
afu *Kotos Amarasi.* soil, ground, floor. *[Note:* **skukuʔ** = 'dust'*]*
afu *Molo.* dust, ground. (M:6)
afu, auf *Kusa-Manea.* ash, dust.
Out-comparisons:
ahu *Semau Helong.* ash, dust.
apu uban *Kemak.* ashes. *[irr. from PMP:* *b > *p]*
apu *Kisar.* ashes. *[irr. from PMP:* *b > *p]*

***ahi1** *PRM.* tread out. *[Sporadic:* Ø > *h* /#_Vʔ in Ba'a*]*
a~aʔi *Termanu.* tread on, trample, tread out. (J:6)
a~aʔi *Bokai.*
a~ai *Bilbaa.*
a~ai *Rikou.* trample on, tread on. (J:6; own field notes)
ha~haʔi *Ba'a.*
a~aʔi *Tii.*
ai *Dengka.*
ai *Oenale.*
<ume ahi> *Molo.* the house where the field rice is trodden out of its stalk. *[Note:* Jonker (1908:6) gives 'Amarasi' **ahi.***]* (M:7)

***ahi2** *PRM.* fire. *Etym:* *hapuy. *[Sporadic:* Ø > *h* /#_Vʔ in Termanu, Korbafo, Bokai, Ba'a and Lole*]*
haʔi *Termanu.* fire. (J:155)
haʔi *Korbafo.*
haʔi *Bokai.*
ai *Bilbaa.*
ai *Rikou.*
haʔi *Ba'a.*
haʔi *Lole.* (Zacharias et al. 2014)
aʔi *Tii.*
ai *Dengka.*
ai *Oenale.*
ai *Dela.* fire.
ai *Ro'is Amarasi.* fire.
ai *Kotos Amarasi.* fire.
ai *Molo.* fire. (M:7)
ai *Kusa-Manea.* fire.
Out-comparisons:
ai *Semau Helong.* fire.
haʔi *Fehan Tetun.* flame, fire. (Mo:48)
ahi *East Tetun.* fire. (Mo:1)
ai *Kisar.* fire.
ai *Ili'uun.* fire. (dJ:111)

***aho** *PRM.* mineral lime, calcium. *Etym:* *qapuR. *[Sporadic:* *u > *o /_*R#, Ø > *h* /#_Vʔ in Termanu, Korbafo, Bokai, Ba'a and Lole*]*
haʔo *Termanu.* mineral lime. (J:162)
haʔo *Korbafo.*
haʔo *Bokai.*
ao *Bilbaa.*
ao *Rikou.*
haʔo *Ba'a.*
haʔo *Lole.* (Zacharias et al. 2014)
aʔo *Tii.*
ao *Dengka.*
ao *Oenale.*
ao *Dela.* lime paste.
ao *Ro'is Amarasi.* mineral lime.
ao *Kotos Amarasi.* mineral lime.
ao *Molo.* mineral lime, chalk. (M:34)

ao *Kusa-Manea.* mineral lime.

Out-comparisons:

°**ao** *Semau Helong.* chalk, lime. *Borrowed from:* either Rote or Meto, as shown by irr. final *u > *o*.

ahu *Fehan Tetun.* lime. *[irr. from PMP:* *p > *h* /V_V (expect *ʔ*, perhaps actually a reflex of *qabu 'ash, dust')*]*

ahu *East Tetun.* lime, calcium. (Mo:2)

aʔur *Ili'uun.* lime. (dJ:113)

haul *Welaun.* mineral lime. *[irr. from PMP:* *q > *h*; *R > *l] [History:* The irregular correspondences indicate that this is a loan from an intermediate source, but no likely donor language has been identified. The closest match is Bunak **hau**, which also has initial *h* but this Bunak form too is ultimately a loan from an unidentified Austronesian source.*]*

aur *Lakalei.* mineral lime. *[Note:* language of east Timor ISO 639-3 [lka]*]* (Klamer 2002)

***ahu** *CER.* dew. *See:* ***aŋgum**. *Etym:* *hapun.

aʔu(s) *Termanu.* dew. *Usage:* poetic. *[Note:* The non-poetic word for 'dew' is **dinis**.*]* (J:17)

***ala** *Morph:* ***n-ala**. *PRM.* get, fetch, take; converts verbs into an accomplishment carried out with purposeful intent (Jacob and Grimes 2011). *Etym:* *ala[q/p].

n-ala *Termanu.* he (she) gets, takes. (J:374)

n-ala *Korbafo.*

n-ala *Bokai.*

n-ala *Bilbaa.*

n-ala *Rikou.*

n-ala *Ba'a.*

n-ala *Tii.*

n-ala *Dengka.*

n-ala *Oenale.*

n-ala (2) n-ala-ʔ *Dela.* 1) take, get; accomplishment, purposeful action, toward speaker. 2) can, able.

n-ana *Ro'is Amarasi.* get; converts verbs into an accomplishment carried out with purposeful intent.

n-ana *Kotos Amarasi.* get; converts verbs into an accomplishment carried out with purposeful intent.

n-ana *Molo.* get, buy. (M:21)

***ama** *Morph:* ***ama-k**. *PRM.* father. *Etym:* *ama.

ama-k *Termanu.* father. (J:9)

ama-ʔ *Korbafo.*

ama-k *Bokai.*

ama-k *Bilbaa.*

ama-ʔ *Rikou.*

ama-k *Ba'a.*

ama-k *Tii.*

ama-ʔ *Dengka.*

ama-ʔ *Oenale.*

ama-ʔ *Dela.* father, father's brother (paternal uncle).

amaʔ *Ro'is Amarasi.* father.

amaʔ, ama-f *Kotos Amarasi.* father.

ama-f *Molo.* father. (M:20)

amaʔ *Kusa-Manea.* father.

***anak** *PRM.* child, son/daughter, small. *Etym:* *anak.

ana-k (2) ana-k (3) na-ana (4) na-ana-k *Termanu.* 1) child in respect to its parents, the young of an animal. *[Form:* usually without **-k** as the second member of an expression.*]* 2) be small, small, as a specific word both predicative and attributive. *[Form:* usually used in the form with a final **-k**.*]* 3) have a child, adopt or consider someone as a child; have sprouts (of a plant). 4) call someone a child, address someone as 'child'. (J:10)

ana-ʔ (2) ana(-ʔ) *Korbafo.*

ana-k (2) ana(-k) *Bokai.*

ana-ʔ (2) ana(-ʔ) *Bilbaa.*

ana=na *Landu.* son, daughter. (own field notes)
ana-ʔ (2) a~ana *Rikou.*
ana-k (2) ana(-k) *Ba'a.*
ana-k (2) ana(-k) *Tii.*
ana-ʔ (2) ana(-ʔ) *Dengka.*
ana-ʔ (2) ana(-ʔ) *Oenale.*
anak (2) ana-ʔ *Dela.* 1) child. 2) small.
ana|ʔ *Ro'is Amarasi.* son/daughter; small, baby (animal). *[Form:* Unlike other varieties of Meto, Ro'is is only known to have a single form.*]*
anah (2) ana|ʔ (3) n-ʔana *Kotos Amarasi.* 1) son/daughter, nephew/niece from a same-sex sibling. 2) small, baby (animal). 3) address as 'child'; produce a sapling (said of plants).
anah (2) ana|ʔ *Molo.* 1) child. 2) diminutive, young. (M:21f)
anah (2) ana|ʔ *Kusa-Manea.* 1) child. 2) small.

***ane** *nRM.* braid. *Etym:* *añam. *[irr. from PRM:* *e > *i* in Kusa-Manea and Molo verbal form; *Ø > *n* /#_ in Ba'a and Tii*] [Sporadic:* *a > *e /*C+palatal_*]*
ane *Termanu.* braid something. (J:12)
ane *Korbafo.*
ane *Bilbaa.*
ane *Rikou.*
nane *Ba'a.* (J:736)
n͡ane *Tii.* (J:736)
a͡ene|t *Ro'is Amarasi.* needle. *[Form:* Final *-t* is a productive nominaliser. The hypothetical independent root ***ane** is not attested in Meto.*]*
ane|t *Kotos Amarasi.* needle.
n-ani (2) ane|t *Molo.* 1) braid. 2) needle. (M:23)
ani|t *Kusa-Manea.* needle.

***anin** *PRM.* wind. *Etym:* *haŋin.
ani(n) *Termanu.* wind. (J:13)
ani *Korbafo.*
anin *Bokai.*
ani *Bilbaa.*
ani *Rikou.*
anin *Ba'a.*
anin *Tii.*
anin *Dengka.*
anin *Oenale.*
anin (2) na-la-ani *Dela.* 1) wind. 2) windy.
ainn *Ro'is Amarasi.* wind.
anin *Kotos Amarasi.* wind.
anin *Molo.* wind. (M:23)
anin *Kusa-Manea.* wind.
Out-comparisons:
aŋin *Semau Helong.* wind, breeze.
anin *East Tetun.* wind, current of air. (Mo:4)

***aŋgum** *CERM.* dew.
a~aŋu-k *Bokai.* mist, fog. (J:677f)
a~aŋu-ʔ *Bilbaa.*
a~aku-ʔ *Rikou.*
akum *Fatule'u.* dew.
akum *Molo.* evening dew. (M:17)

***ao** *Morph:* ***ao-k**. *PRM.* body. *Etym:* *hawak 'waist, back of the waist'.
ao-k *Termanu.* body. (J:13)
ao-ʔ *Korbafo.*
ao-k *Bokai.*
ao-ʔ *Bilbaa.*
ao-ʔ *Rikou.*
ao-k *Ba'a.*
ao-k *Tii.*
ao-ʔ *Dengka.*
ao-ʔ *Oenale.*
ao-ʔ *Dela.* body, self, reflexive pronoun.
ao-n *Ro'is Amarasi.* body.
ao-f *Kotos Amarasi.* body.
ao-f *Molo.* body. (M:34)
Out-comparisons:
afa *Funai Helong.* body, self. (J:13)
apa *Semau Helong.* body, self.

***arum** *PMeto.* cuscus. *See:* ***ʔ|mauka|ʔ**. *[Note:* Schapper (2011:264) gives Meto **urem** without indicating which variety it is from. If this form is not an error, it attests additional complications in the cognate sets I have included here.*]* *[irr. from PRM:* *a > *u* in all Meto except Kusa-Manea*]* *[Form:* Penultimate *a has been reconstructed instead of *u as *a > *u* can be motivated as a case of sporadic assimilation to the quality of the following vowel. The alternate hypothesis, *u > *a* in Kusa-Manea, would be phonetically unmotivated.*]* *[History:* Although PMeto *r is regular from PRM *nd, connecting this reconstruction with PCEMP *mansər requires positing far too many irregularities for me to make this connection.*]*

urum *Ro'is Amarasi.* cuscus.

ukum *Kotos Amarasi.* cuscus.

ukum *Amanuban, South.* cuscus.

ukum *Amfo'an.* cuscus.

akum *Kusa-Manea.* cuscus.

***aso** *CER.* fetch water, scoop up water. *Etym:* *qasu. *[irr. from PMP:* *u > *o*]*

aso *Termanu.* scoop water out of a river or water source with one's hand. (J:15)

***asu** *CERM.* dog. *Etym:* *asu.

asu *Termanu.* dog. *Usage:* poetic. *[Note:* The non-poetic word for 'dog' is **busa**.*]* (J:16)

asu *Ro'is Amarasi.* dog.

asu *Kotos Amarasi.* dog.

asu *Molo.* dog. (M:30)

asu *Kusa-Manea.* dog.

Out-comparisons:

asu *Semau Helong.* cow. *[Note:* **ŋoot** = 'dog'.*]*

aus *Mambae, South.* dog. (Fogaça 2017:233)

asu *East Tetun.* dog. (Mo:23)

asu *Galolen.* dog.

ahu *Kisar.* dog.

***ata1** *PRM.* above, up, on top. *Etym:* *atas 'high, tall'.

ata *Termanu.* the heavens, the top (of); above, on top of. *Usage:* possibly poetic. (Fox 2016b:2)

ata *Dengka.* above, up. (J:678)

ata *Oenale.* above, up. (J:678)

ata-ʔ *Dela.* above, upper, on, on top.

ata *Kotos Amarasi.* up, top. *Usage:* Most often occurs in the phrase **ata nee** 'up there' and rarely in other constructions with the meaning 'top'.

***ata2** *Rote.* first person plural possessive pronoun; our. *Etym:* *ata.

ata *Termanu.* non-emphatic form of the first person plural inclusive pronoun **ita**. (J:16)

ata *Ba'a.*

ata *Dengka.*

ata *Oenale.*

***ata3** *PRM.* slave. *Doublet:* ***hatahori**. *Etym:* *qaRta 'negrito, black person' (The semantics across a wide range of MP languages point to the original meaning being 'black/Negrito person', which, depending on the race of the speakers, was applied either to themselves or a subjugated population (Mahdi 1994:464ff).). *[Sporadic:* *a > *e* / _# in wRM*]*

ata *Termanu.* slave. (J:16)

ata *Korbafo.*

ata *Bokai.*

ata *Bilbaa.*

ata *Rikou.*

ata *Ba'a.*

ata *Tii.*

ate *Dengka.*

ate *Oenale.*

ate *Dela.* servant, slave.

ate *Kotos Amarasi.* servant, slave.

ate *Molo.* slave. (M:32)

Out-comparisons:

ata (2) at (3) hutu ata *Semau Helong.* 1) underling, slave. 2) counter (classifier) for people. 3) citizen. *[Note:* **hutun** = 'society, populace, citizens, common people'.*]*

ata *East Tetun.* slave, servant; shepherd, herdsman. (Mo:5)

aka, ake *Kisar.* slave.

***ate** *Morph:* ***ate-k**. *PRM.* liver. *Etym:* *qatay 'liver; seat of the emotions, inner self'.
  ate-k *Termanu.* liver, also heart of person or animal in the physical (non-metaphorical) sense. (J:16)
  ate-ʔ *Korbafo.*
  ate-k *Bokai.*
  ate-ʔ *Bilbaa.*
  ate=na *Landu.* liver. (own field notes)
  ate-ʔ *Rikou.*
  ate-k *Ba'a.*
  ate-k *Tii.*
  ate-ʔ *Dengka.*
  ate-ʔ *Oenale.*
  a͜te-ʔ *Dela.* liver.
  aete-f *Ro'is Amarasi.* liver.
  ate-f *Kotos Amarasi.* liver. *[Semantics:* Only refers to the physical organ, the seat of emotions is **neka-f**.*]*
  ate-f *Molo.* liver. (M:32)
  ate-f *Kusa-Manea.* liver.
  Out-comparisons:
    faten *Funai Helong.* liver. *[irr. from PMP: Ø > (*w) > f* in Helong (also seen in Sika **vaten**)*]*
    paten *Semau Helong.* liver.
    ate-n *East Tetun.* liver. (Mo:5)
    akin *Kisar.* liver.

***atis** *CERM.* breast beam of a loom consisting of two wooden bars. *Etym:* *qatip 'breast beam of a back loom'. *[Form:* expected *p > *s* / _# (§3.5.1.3).*]*
  atis *Termanu.* the part of the loom which the weaver holds in front of themself. (J:16)
  atis *Molo.* piece of weaving equipment. (M:32)
  Out-comparisons:
    atis *Helong.* (J:16)
    atis *East Tetun.* fine cloth, or cloth still on the loom; a part of the loom. (Mo:5)

***atu** *PRM.* charcoal, soot.
  atu-k (2) hade atu-k *Termanu.* 1) soot, the black part of a lamp or candle, what remains of burnt grass. 2) the fine dust that flies up at the stamping out of the field rice. (J:16)
  (2) hade atu-ʔ *Korbafo.*
  ai_atu-ʔ (2) hade_atu-ʔ *Rikou.* 1) that which is left over after burning something. 2) dust from rice. (own field notes)
  (2) hade_atu-ʔ *Ba'a.*
  (2) haɗe_atu-ʔ *Dengka.*
  ai atu *Ro'is Amarasi.* charcoal.
  atu *Kotos Amarasi.* charcoal.
  atu *Molo.* charcoal. (M:33)
  atu *Kusa-Manea.* charcoal.

***au** *PRM.* first person singular pronoun; I, me. *Etym:* *aku. *[irr. from PMP:* *k > Ø*]*
  au *Termanu.* first person singular pronoun. (J:16)
  au *Korbafo.*
  au *Bokai.*
  au *Bilbaa.*
  au *Landu.* first person singular pronoun. (own field notes)
  au *Rikou.*
  au *Ba'a.*
  au *Tii.*
  au *Dengka.*
  au *Oenale.*
  au *Dela.* first person singular pronoun.
  au *Ro'is Amarasi.* first person singular nominative pronoun.
  au (2) kau *Kotos Amarasi.* 1) first person singular nominative pronoun. 2) first person singular accusative pronoun.
  au *Molo.* first person singular nominative pronoun. (M:34)
  au *Kusa-Manea.* first person singular nominative pronoun.

***auee** *CER.* exclamation of joy or sorrow. *Etym:* *qaué (PCEMP).
  au-é, awé (2) au~au *Termanu.* 1) cry of joy, also of pain, e.g. while mourning for the dead. (J:17) 2) shout, shout constantly. (J:16)

B - b

***baa** *Morph:* ***baa-k**. *Rote.* lung. *Etym:* *baRaq.
baa-k (2) ba/deʔe-k *Termanu.* 1) lungs of people and animals. (J:18) 2) heart of people and animals. (J:19)
baa-ʔ *Korbafo.*
baa-k *Bokai.*
baa-ʔ *Bilbaa.*
baa-ʔ *Rikou.*
baa-k *Ba'a.*
ɓaa-k *Tii.*
faa-ʔ *Dengka.*
faa-ʔ *Oenale.*
Out-comparisons:
afaak *Fehan Tetun.* lungs.

***baba|ʔ** *PMeto.* parent's opposite sex sibling.
baba-f *Ro'is Amarasi.* parent's opposite sex sibling, spouse's parent.
baba-f *Kotos Amarasi.* parent's opposite sex sibling, spouse's parent.
aam babaʔ *Molo.* father-in-law. (M:39)
babaʔ *Kusa-Manea.* parent's opposite sex sibling, spouse's parent.
Out-comparisons:
baba *Kemak.* maternal uncle. *Usage:* Kutubaba and Leosibe dialects.
baba *Welaun.* maternal uncle.
baba *Ende.* father, father's brother, mother's sister's husband, male third cousin on the father and grandfather's side (FFBSS).

***badoe** *Morph:* ***na-badoe**. *PRM.* grope, touch. *Pattern:* d-2. *[irr. from PRM:* vowel metathesis in Meto *oe > *eo*; *b = *b* in Meto*]*
na-fa-loe *Termanu.* grope, touch. (J:321)
na-fa-loe *Korbafo.*
na-fa-loe *Bokai.*
na-fa-loe *Bilbaa.*
na-fa-roe *Rikou.*
na-fa-loe *Ba'a.*
na-fa-roe *Tii.*
na-fa-loe *Dengka.*
na-fa-roe *Oenale.*
na-breo *Kotos Amarasi.* grope around.
na-bleo *Molo.* gropes. *[Form:* Middelkoop (1972:265) also gives **lefo** 'grope' and Amfo'an **anleok** 'grope' (p.359) which may be connected.*]* (M:73)

***bafi** *PRM.* pig. *Etym:* *babuy.
bafi *Termanu.* pig. (J:22)
bafi *Korbafo.*
bafi *Bokai.*
bafi *Bilbaa.*
bafi *Rikou.*
bafi *Ba'a.*
ɓafi *Tii.*
fafi *Dengka.*
fafi *Oenale.*
fafi *Ro'is Amarasi.* pig.
fafi *Kotos Amarasi.* pig.
fafi *Molo.* pig. (M:107)
fafi *Kusa-Manea.* pig.
Out-comparisons:
bahi *Semau Helong.* pig.
fahi *East Tetun.* pig, swine. (Mo:31)
haeh *Mambae, South.* pig, swine. (Grimes et al. 2014b:20)
wawi *Kisar.* pig.
hahi *Dhao.* pig.
vavi *Hawu.* pig.

***bafo** *PRM.* upper surface, top, above. *Etym:* *ba(w)baw. *[irr. from PRM:* *o > *a* in Termanu, Bokai and Kusa-Manea*]*
bafa-k *Termanu.* the top layer of a liquid substance. (J:21)
bafo-ʔ *Korbafo.*
bafa-k *Bokai.*
bafo-ʔ *Bilbaa.*

bafo-ʔ *Rikou.*
bafo-k *Ba'a.*
ɓafo-k *Tii.*
fafo-ʔ *Dengka.*
fafo-ʔ *Oenale.*
fafo *Ro'is Amarasi.* above.
fafo *Kotos Amarasi.* above, on top of.
fafo-n *Molo.* upper, or top part of something. (M:108)
faaf *Kusa-Manea.* above, on top.
Out-comparisons:
wawan(ne) *Kisar.* top.

***bali1** *PRM.* again, go back, return. *Etym:* *baliw2 'return'. *[irr. from PRM:* *l > Ø in Termanu, Bilbaa, Rikou, Dengka, and Dela*] [Semantics:* Collapse/interference from reflexes of ***bali2** < *balik. It is not always clear which forms are reflexes of which reconstruction. I have grouped them by likely semantics.*]*
bai *Termanu.* again, once more. **ana mai bai** he comes back (J:22)
bai *Bilbaa.*
bai *Rikou.*
Bali *Ba'a.*
ɓali *Tii.*
Fai *Dengka.*
fali *Oenale.*
fai *Dela.* again.
n-fani *Ro'is Amarasi.* again, go back, return.
n-fani *Kotos Amarasi.* again, go back, return.
n-fani *Molo.* go back. (M:110)
fain *Kusa-Manea.* go back, return.
Out-comparisons:
palit (2) pait *Semau Helong.* 1) return, go home; again, once more. 2) again, once more. *[irr. from PMP:* *b > *p* (perhaps through intermediate *f); *l > Ø in second sense. Both irregular changes possibly point to borrowing from a Rote language*]*
fali *East Tetun.* again, another time. (Mo:31)
fali *Fehan Tetun.* in turn.
vari (2) vəri *Hawu.* 1) return, go home; again, repeatedly; times. 2) anymore.

***bali2** *PRM.* turn back, turn around. *Etym:* *balik 'reverse, turn around'. *[irr. from PRM:* *b = *b* in Meto*] [Semantics:* Collapse/interference from reflexes of ***bali1** < *baliw2. It is not always clear which forms are reflexes of which reconstruction. I have grouped them by likely semantics.*]*
fali (2) na-sa-fali *Termanu.* 1) turn back; turning back, back. (J:122f) 2) turn something around, reverse. (J:123)
fali (2) na-sa-fali *Korbafo.*
fali (2) na-sa-fali *Bokai.*
fali (2) na-sa-fali *Bilbaa.*
fali (2) na-sa-fali *Rikou.*
fali (2) na-sa-fali *Ba'a.*
fali (2) na-sa-fali *Tii.*
fali (2) na-sa-bali, na-sa-fali *Dengka.* 1) turn back; turning back, back. (J:122f) 2) reverse, translate. (J:680,123)
fali (2) na-sa-ɓali, na-sa-fali *Oenale.* 1) turn back; turning back, back. (J:122f) 2) reverse, translate. (J:680,123)
ɓaliʔ *Dela.* return, again.
n-bani *Ro'is Amarasi.* let it be.
n-bani (2) na-ʔ-bani-ʔ (3) na-banit *Kotos Amarasi.* 1) let, turn, work. 2) turn something/someone around. 3) turn something/someone around, translate. *[Note:* Amarasi also has **n-bani** 'work' that may be related.*]*
na-bani *Amfo'an.* turn.
Out-comparisons:
bali *Semau Helong.* turn, back. Contrary to the momentum of what has been happening or assumptions.

balik *Fehan Tetun.* soon, at (future time).

ɓale *Hawu.* return, go home.

***balu1** *PRM.* mourn the dead. *Etym:* *baluq (Blust and Trussel (ongoing) state: 'Jonker (1908) points out that the Korbaffo [sic] dialect of Rotinese has **fali** "mourn the dead", **falu** "orphan, widow", and he gives this as evidence that … Termanu **falu** "mourn the dead" and **falu** "orphan, widow" are distinct words.' I agree that this is evidence they are distinct words.). *[irr. from PRM:* *u > *i* in Korbafo*]*

falu *Termanu.* mourn for the deceased. (J:124)

fali *Korbafo. [History:* Jonker (1908:124) considers this to be a different (non-cognate) word.*]* (J:124,694)

falu *Bokai.*

falu *Ba'a.*

(falu ?) *Tii.*

falu *Dengka.*

(falu ?) *Oenale.*

<banu> *Molo.* mourning atmosphere, mourning taboo, widow. (M:49)

***balu2** *PRM.* widow(er). *Etym:* *balu. *[irr. from PRM:* *b = *b* in Meto*]*

falu *Termanu.* widow, widower. (J:124)

falu *Korbafo.*

falu *Bokai.*

falu *Bilbaa.*

falu *Rikou.*

falu *Ba'a.*

falu *Tii.*

falu *Dengka.*

falu *Oenale.*

banuʔ *Kotos Amarasi.* widow, widower.

<banu> *Molo.* mourning atmosphere, mourning taboo, widow. (M:49)

Out-comparisons:

bebalu *Semau Helong.* widow, widower.

faluk *East Tetun.* widowed, deprived. (Mo:31)

ɓalu *Hawu.* widow, widower.

wal~walum *Kisar.* widow. *[irr. from PMP:* *Ø > *m]*

***balu3** *CER.* cover, envelop. *Doublet:* ***mbalu**. *Etym:* *balun 'bind, bundle, wrap in cloth; death shroud; cloth(ing)'.

balu *Termanu.* cover, envelop. (J:28)

balu *Korbafo.*

balu *Bilbaa.*

balu *Rikou.*

balu *Ba'a.*

Out-comparisons:

falun *East Tetun.* packet, parcel, bundle; *v.* wrap up, bag up. (Mo:31)

***baŋakuɗu** *PRM.* Indian mulberry. Morinda citrifolia. *Etym:* *baŋkudu 'tree with white fruit and roots that yields a useful dye: Morinda citrifolia' (PWMP). *Pattern:* k-2b. *[minority from PMP:* *d > *ɗ (expect *r); *ŋ = *ŋ*] [irr. from PRM:* *b > *m* in Rote; *b = *b* in Meto; *ŋ > *r* in Kusa-Manea*] [Form:* The addition of the antepenultimate vowel occurred to bring this form into line with the disyllabic CVCV foot structure of PRM. Landu, Rikou and Dengka have added *a*. (This vowel is also possibly attested by Kotos Amarasi **bakʔuruʔ** and Molo <**bakulu**> with CV → VC metathesis of earlier initial **baka with subsequent reduction of the double vowel.) Other languages have added *u* which can be derived from *a via sporadic assimilation to the following vowel. Initial irregular *b > *m* in Rote is also paralleled in Malay *mengkudu* and could be sporadic assimilation to the following nasal and/or due to borrowing from a source different to the source of the Meto forms. The first *r* in the Kusa-Manea form is currently unexplained.*] [History:* A likely loan spread after the break-up of PRM connected with the spread of weaving and textile dyeing.*]*

manukudu *Termanu.* kind of tree, the *bengkudu* [OE = Morinda citrifolia], also the red dye which can be extracted from it. (J:347)
manukudu *Korbafo.*
manukudu *Bokai.*
manukudu *Bilbaa.*
manaʔudu-ʔ *Landu.* Indian Mulberry. Morinda citrifolia. (own field notes)
manaʔudu *Rikou.*
manukudu *Ba'a.*
manukuɗu *Tii.*
manaʔuɗu *Dengka.*
manuʔuɗu *Oenale.*
kuruʔ *Ro'is Amarasi.*
ʔbakʔuruʔ *Kotos Amarasi.* Indian Mulberry. Morinda citrifolia.
<bakulu>, <baukulu> *Molo.* kind of tree, dye is made from the bark of the roots. Morinda tinctora. (M:46)
baurʔuruʔ *Kusa-Manea.* kind of plant mixed with **nohob** (kind of plant) to make a red dye.
Out-comparisons:
kudu, pkudu *Helong.* (J:347)

***batu** *PRM.* stone, rock. *Etym:* *batu. *[irr. from PRM:* *b > ɓ in second Dela form*]*
batu *Termanu.* stone or rock. (J:33)
batu *Korbafo.*
batu *Bokai.*
batu *Bilbaa.*
batu *Rikou.*
batu *Ba'a.*
ɓatu *Tii.*
fatu *Dengka.*
fatu *Oenale.*
fatu (2) tua ɓatu-ʔ *Dela.* 1) stone, rock. 2) solid sugar. *[Form:* **tua-ʔ** = 'lontar palm'.*]*
fatu *Ro'is Amarasi.* rock, stone.
fatu *Kotos Amarasi.* rock, stone.
fatu *Molo.* stone. (M:112)
fatu, fatu-k *Kusa-Manea.* rock, stone.
Out-comparisons:
batu *Semau Helong.* rock, stone.
fatu(k) *East Tetun.* stone, rock. (Mo:32)
waku *Kisar.* rock; classifier for animals.

***bau** *PRM.* small shore tree, sea hibiscus. Hibiscus tiliaceus. *Etym:* *baRu. *[irr. from PRM:* *b = *b*/*ɓ* in wRote*]*
bau *Termanu.* Sea Hibiscus. (J:33)
bau *Korbafo.*
bau *Bokai.*
bau *Bilbaa.*
bau *Rikou.*
bau *Ba'a.*
ɓau *Tii.*
bau *Dengka.*
ɓau *Oenale.*
fau *Molo.* kind of tree, Sea Hibiscus. Hibiscus tiliaceus. (M:112)
Out-comparisons:
bau *Helong.* Sea Hibiscus. *[irr. from PMP:* *R > Ø (expect *l*)*]* (J:33)
kfau *Fehan Tetun.* type of tree, whose new shoots are used to bathe a newborn baby.
(k)fau(k) *East Tetun.* tree with stringy bark for making strong rope. Hibiscus tiliaceus. (Mo:32,106)
hau *Ili'uun.* hibiscus tree. (dJ:117)

bei** *PRM.* still, yet. *[irr. from PRM:* glottal stop insertion and final vowel in wRM attesting PwRM ***feʔa]*
bei *Termanu.* still, yet. (J:38)
bei *Korbafo.*
bei *Bokai.*
bei *Bilbaa.*
bei *Rikou.*
bei *Ba'a.*
ɓei *Tii.*
feʔa *Dengka.*
feʔe *Oenale.*
feʔ *Ro'is Amarasi.* still, yet.
feʔe, feʔ *Kotos Amarasi.* still, yet.
feʔa *Molo.* still, yet. (M:113)
Out-comparisons:
bii *Semau Helong.* still, yet.

be, bei *Fehan Tetun.* also.

be *East Tetun.* particle (not translatable). (Mo:12)

***belas** *PRM.* machete. *Etym:* *belas (Blust and Trussel (ongoing) reconstruct this form to PCMP. While reconstruction to a lower level, such as Proto-Timor-Babar, may be justified, this form is not (currently) known to occur outside greater Timor and reconstruction to PCMP is unlikely to be supported unless more cognates are forthcoming.). *[irr. from PRM:* *b = *b* in most Meto but not Ro'is and Kusa-Manea*]*

felas *Termanu.* machete. (J:130)

fela-ʔ *Korbafo.*

felaʔ *Bokai.*

fela-ʔ *Bilbaa.*

felas *Rikou.*

felas *Ba'a.*

felas *Tii.*

felas *Dengka.*

felas *Oenale.*

fenas, fenes *Ro'is Amarasi.* machete.

benas *Kotos Amarasi.*

benas *Molo.* machete. (M:57)

fenas *Kusa-Manea.* machete.

Out-comparisons:

helaʔ *Semau Helong.* machete. *[Form:* Jonker (1908:130) gives Helong <**khela**>.*]*

vela *Hawu.* machete.

hela *Dhao.* machete.

<kabela> *Kambera.* machete. (On:123)

wela *Komodo.* machete. (Verheijen 1982:134)

wehla *Luang.* machete. *[Note:* language of southwest Maluku ISO 639-3 [lex].*]* (Taber 1993:428)

kawela, ŋgawela *Pamona.* machete, iron. *[Note:* language of central Sulawesi ISO 639-3 [pmf].*]* (Adriani 1928:268)

***beli** *Rote.* price, bride price. *Etym:* *bəli 'buy, value, price; marriage prestations, bride price; purchase'.

beli (2) belis *Termanu.* 1) cost, price, value. 2) that which must be paid for a girl when taken for marriage, either paid with goods or money, the purchase price of a woman. (J:41)

beli (2) belis *Korbafo.*

beli (2) belis *Bokai.*

beli (2) belis *Bilbaa.*

beli (2) belis *Rikou.*

beli (2) belis *Ba'a.*

ɓeli (2) ɓelis *Tii.*

feli (2) felis *Dengka.*

feli (2) felis *Oenale.*

Out-comparisons:

foli-n *East Tetun.* price, cost, value; objects for barter. (Mo:35)

heli *Ili'uun.* property, valuable things. (dJ:117)

weli *Kisar.* buy.

***beni** *PRM.* last night. *See:* ***afi, *esak**. *Etym:* *bəRŋi 'night'. *[irr. from PRM:* *e > *i* in nRM (sporadic assimilation to *i?); *i > *a*/Ø in nRote (antepenultimate vowel reduction)*] [Form:* Obligatorily compounded with reflexes of ***esak** in Rote.*]*

bina_esa-k (2) (ndee) bina_esa-k=a *Termanu.* 1) day after tomorrow. 2) day before yesterday. (J:50)

bina_esa-ʔ (2) bina_esak=a *Korbafo.*

bina_esa-k (2) bina_esa-k=a *Bokai.*

bin/esa-ʔ (2) bin/esak=a *Bilbaa.*

bina_esa-ʔ (2) bina_esa-ʔ=a *Rikou.*

bina_esa-k (2) bina_esa-k=a *Ba'a.*

ɓin/esa-k *Tii.*

feni_esa-ʔ *Dengka.*

feni_esa-ʔ *Oenale.*

afiin, afiin=ii *Ro'is Amarasi.* yesterday, a few days ago. *[Form:* Initial *a* is probably due to influence from **afi naa** 'yesterday' (see ***afi**).*]*

fini (2) afina (3) nmeu_n-fini (4) n-fini *Kotos Amarasi.* 1) last night. 2) yesterday. 3) early in the morning. 4) go past, pass. *Usage:* fourth sense poetic.

fini (2) fini fai (3) n-fini *Molo.* 1) recently. 2) yesterday evening. 3) goes past. (M:119)

Out-comparisons:

biŋin (2) biŋin_tai *Semau Helong.* 1) day. *[Semantics:* Used with numbers to indicate a future day; e.g. **biŋin dua** 'in two days', **biŋin aat** 'in four days'.*]* 2) midnight.

***berat** *PRM.* heavy, hard work, weight. *Etym:* *bəRəqat 'weight, heaviness, weightiness; difficult; pregnant'. *[minority from PMP:* *R = *r (fairly widespread in the region for this term)*]* *[irr. from PRM:* *b = *b*/*ɓ* in wRote*]*

bela-k (2) bela-k (3) ma-bela *Termanu.* 1) heavy, heaviness, weight. 2) hard work (in general), corvée (in particular). (J:40) 3) heavy, (usually used attributively, except in a few expressions **mabela** does not tend to be used predicatively in equative clauses or before **hiik** 'very'). (J:41)

bela-k (2) bela-k (3) ma-bela *Bokai.*

bela-ʔ (2) bela-ʔ (3) ma-bela *Bilbaa.*

bera-ʔ (2) bera-ʔ (3) ma-bera *Rikou.*

bela-k (2) bela-k (3) ma-bela *Ba'a.*

ɓera-k (2) ɓera-k (3) ma-ɓera *Tii.*

bela-ʔ (2) belat (3) ma-bela, ma~ma-bela-ʔ *Dengka.*

ɓera-ʔ (2) ɓerat (3) ma-ɓela, ma~ma-ɓera-ʔ *Oenale.*

maʔ|fena|ʔ *Ro'is Amarasi.* heavy.

maʔ|fena|ʔ *Kotos Amarasi.* heavy, weight.

maʔ|fena|ʔ *Molo.* heavy. (M:296)

Out-comparisons:

werek *Kisar.* heavy.

***betə** *Morph:* ***betə-k**. *Rote.* foxtail millet. *Etym:* *bətəŋ 'millet species, probably foxtail millet Setaria italica'.

bete-k *Termanu.* millet, both the grain and the fruit. (J:47)

bete-ʔ *Korbafo.*

bete-k *Bokai.*

bete-ʔ *Bilbaa.*

bete-ʔ *Rikou.*

bete-k *Ba'a.*

ɓete-k *Tii.*

feta-ʔ *Dengka.*

feta-ʔ *Oenale.*

Out-comparisons:

botoʔ *Semau Helong.* foxtail millet. *[irr. from PMP:* *ə > *o* (expect *e*)*]*

heten *Ili'uun.* millet. (dJ:117)

***beu1** *Morph:* ***beu-k**. *PRM.* new. *Etym:* *baqəRu 'new, fresh; recent(ly)'. *[Sporadic:* *VV-k > *VVʔ > VʔV in most Meto (perceptual metathesis).*]*

beu-k *Termanu.* new. (J:47)

beu-ʔ *Korbafo.*

beu-k *Bokai.*

beu-ʔ *Bilbaa.*

beu-ʔ *Rikou.*

beu-k *Ba'a.*

ɓeu-k *Tii.*

feu-ʔ *Dengka.*

feu-ʔ *Oenale.*

feʔu *Ro'is Amarasi.* new.

feʔu *Kotos Amarasi.* new.

feu|ʔ *Amanuban/Amanatun.* new.

feʔu *Molo.* new. (M:117)

feʔu-k *Kusa-Manea.* new.

Out-comparisons:

balu *Semau Helong.* new.

foun *East Tetun.* new, recent. (Mo:36)

woru *Kisar.* new.

***beu2** *PRM.* bogo tree. Garuga Floribuna. *Etym:* *bəRus 'tree Acalypha amentacea' (Blust and Trussel (ongoing) reconstruct *bəRus to proto-Philippine.). *[Semantics:* vague Rote semantics.*]*

beu *Termanu.* kind of tree. (J:47)

beu *Korbafo.*

beu *Bokai.*

beu *Bilbaa.*

beu *Rikou.* designates three trees: the kedondong, a tree similar to the kedondong, and the same tree which Amarasi **feu** designates. Spondias dulcis; Garuga floribuna. (J:47; own field notes)

beu *Ba'a.*

ɓeu *Tii.*

feu *Dengka.*

feu *Oenale.*

feu *Kotos Amarasi.* Bogo tree, a kind of tree the leaves of which are fed to cows. Garuga floribuna.

feu *Molo.* kind of tree. Garuga floribuna. (M:117)

Out-comparisons:

bilu *Helong.* (J:47)

kfeu *Fehan Tetun.* type of tree. Goats like to eat the flowers.

kfeu (2) feu *East Tetun.* 1) tree with good dark timber. Garuga floribunda. (Mo:106) 2) tree with medicinal bark. (Mo:33)

***biae** *PMeto.* buffalo. *[Form:* Amarasi, Amfo'an, and Molo have consonant insertion to break up *VVV. Ro'is Amarasi has antepenultimate vowel deletion after consonant insertion. Other varieties have vowel deletion to avoid a sequence of three vowels.*]* *[Semantics:* The original meaning was 'buffalo' with later semantic shift to 'cow' in many varieties as cows supplanted buffalo as the dominant kind of cattle.*]*

bʤae (2) bʤae meetn *Ro'is Amarasi.* 1) cow. *[Form:* antepenultimate vowel deletion from earlier ***biʤae.***]* 2) buffalo. *Lit:* 'black cow'.

biʤae (2) biʤae metan *Kotos Amarasi.* 1) cow. 2) buffalo. *Lit:* 'black cow'.

bie, bia *Amanuban, South.* cow.

biʤae-l (2) biʤae metan *Amfo'an.* 1) cow. 2) buffalo. *Lit:* 'black cow'.

biʤae-l *Kopas.* cow.

bia, biʤae-l *Molo.* buffalo. (M:64, 66)

bea (2) bea ma~metoʔ (3) bea ʔbakaʔ *Kusa-Manea.* 1) cow, cattle. 2) buffalo. *Lit:* 'dry/indigenous cow'. 3) cow (specifically not buffalo). *Borrowed from:* **ʔbakaʔ** from Portuguese *vaca* 'cow'.

***bibi** *CER.* pinch. *Doublet:* ***ɓiti, *fiti3.** *Etym:* *bitbit 'pull at body part; hold something dangling from the fingers'. *[irr. from PRM:* *b > *mp* in Ba'a*]*

fiʔ pou=na *Bilbaa.* holds her sarong tightly with her fingertips as she walks. *[Note:* Under the Termanu sub-entry **fiʔi-k.***]* (J:135)

bifiʔ *Rikou.* pinch with the finger and thumb. (J:49,682)

mpimpik mpou=na *Ba'a.* holds her sarong tightly with her fingertips as she walks. *[Note:* Under the Termanu sub-entry **fiʔi-k.***]* (J:135)

ɓifik *Lole.* pinch. (J:682)

***bini** *PRM.* seed for replanting. *Etym:* *binəhiq 'seed rice, rice set aside for the next planting'.

bini *Termanu.* seed, seed for sowing. (J:50)

bini *Korbafo.*

bini *Bokai.*

bini *Bilbaa.*

bini *Rikou.*

bini *Ba'a.*

ɓini *Tii.*

fini *Dengka.*

fini *Oenale.*

fini *Ro'is Amarasi.* seed.
fini *Kotos Amarasi.* seed for replanting.
fini *Molo.* seed. (M:119)
Out-comparisons:
bini *Semau Helong.* seed, grain seed.
fini *East Tetun.* seed (grain for sowing). (Mo:34)
wini *Kisar.* seed.

***biti1** *PRM.* calf of leg. *Etym:* *bitiəs 'lower leg (below the knee); calf of the leg'. *[irr. from PRM:* *t > *k* in Kusa-Manea*]*
biti_boa-k *Termanu.* calf of leg. (J:51)
biti_boa-ʔ *Korbafo.*
biti_boa-k *Bokai.*
biti_boa-k *Bilbaa.*
biti_boa-ʔ *Rikou.*
biti_boa-k *Ba'a.*
ɓiti_ɓoa-k *Tii.*
fiti_isi *Dengka.*
fiti_ɓoa-ʔ *Oenale.*
fiti-n *Ro'is Amarasi.* calf (of leg).
fiti-f *Kotos Amarasi.* calf (of leg).
fiti-k *Molo.* calf. (M:121)
fiki-f *Kusa-Manea.* calf of leg.
Out-comparisons:
pitis_boa *Helong.* calf (of leg). (J:51)

***biti2** *Rote.* jerk, jump up. *Doublet:* ***fiti1**. *Etym:* *bitik 'snare, noose trap; spring up suddenly, jerk up (as a fishing line or noose trap)'. *[irr. from PRM:* *b > *p* in Meto*]*
na-ka-biti *Termanu.* suddenly jump up, like a shrimp. (J:51)
pitil, pitir *Meto.* fish with a fishing rod. (J:137)
Out-comparisons:
pitin *Semau Helong.* leap. *[irr. from PMP:* *b > *p]*

***biti3** *PRM.* slingshot. *[irr. from PRM:* *i > *e* in Meto*]*
fi~fiti-k *Termanu.* kind of weapon made from bamboo with pebbles for ammunition. (J:137)
fi~fiti-ʔ *Bilbaa.*
fi~fiti-ʔ *Rikou.*
fi~fiti-ʔ *Dengka.*
ɓi~ɓitis *Oenale.*
fi~fitis (2) fitiʔ *Dela.* 1) slingshot. 2) slingshot, pulled.
k|feiti-s *Ro'is Amarasi.* slingshot.
na-k|feti (2) k|feti-s *Kotos Amarasi.* 1) fire a slingshot. 2) slingshot.
fa~fetiʔ *Kusa-Manea.* slingshot.
Out-comparisons:
fiti *Alorese.* shoot with a slingshot. *Usage:* Pandai village. (Moro 2016)

***boaʔ** *PMeto.* ten. *[Note:* While Helong has a cognate, positing this as a simple case of borrowing between Helong and Meto is problematic. If Helong was the donor, this would not explain the form **boaʔ** used with twenty and above in Ro'is. Similarly, if Meto was the donor it would not explain the *k* in the Helong form. One possible explanation is that the final *ʔ* in Meto is from an earlier *k and that this is an early borrowing from pre-Meto into Helong before *k > *ʔ* occurred in Meto.*] [History:* Middelkoop (1950:48) connects the Meto forms with Meto **bua** 'gather' (see ***ɓua**) and this is possible.*]*
boʔ=ees (2) boaʔ nua *Ro'is Amarasi.* 1) ten. 2) twenty. *[Semantics:* Multiples of ten from twenty upwards use **boaʔ**.*]*
boʔ *Kotos Amarasi.* ten, multiples of ten (e.g. **boʔ**=es 'ten', **boʔ=nua** 'twenty').
boʔ=ees *Molo.* ten. (M:76)
boʔ=eas *Kusa-Manea.* ten.
Out-comparisons:
buk *Semau Helong.* multiples of ten; e.g. **buk dua** 'twenty', **buk tilu** 'thirty', etc. *[Note:* **hŋulu** = 'ten'; e.g. **hŋul esa** 'eleven', **hŋul dua** 'twelve', etc.*]*

***boo1** *PRM.* drive forward, herd. *[irr. from PRM:* *b > *mb in wRM; *b > (*f) > *h* in Ba'a*] [Form:* Jonker (1908:138) suggests this is an onomatopoeic word from a sound made by herders.*]*
foo *Termanu.* drive, drive forward. (J:138)
foo *Korbafo.*
foo *Bokai.*
foo *Bilbaa.*
foo *Rikou.*
hoo *Ba'a.*
foo *Tii.*
mboo *Oenale.*
na-poʔo *Kotos Amarasi.* herd.
<npo'> *Molo.* herds. (M:442)
Out-comparisons:
poa *Semau Helong.* chase out, shoo, hunt, herd.

***boo2** *Morph:* ***boo-k, *na-boo**. *PRM.* smell (good or bad), odour. *Etym:* *bahuq 'odour, stench'.
boo-k (2) na-boo (3) ma-boo-k *Termanu.* 1) the air of something, smell, odour, stink. 2) smell, have an aroma. 3) have a smell, odour, as an individual word especially: stinking, smell bad. (J:51)
boo-ʔ *Korbafo.*
boo-k *Bokai.*
boo-ʔ *Bilbaa.*
boo-ʔ *Rikou.*
boo-k *Ba'a.*
ɓoo-k *Tii.*
foo-ʔ *Dengka.*
foo-ʔ *Oenale.*
na-foo *Ro'is Amarasi.* stink.
na-foo (2) foo meni (3) foo punuʔ *Kotos Amarasi.* 1) stink. 2) fragrant smell. 3) rotten smell.
na-foo *Molo.* stink. (M:124)
na-foo *Kusa-Manea.* stink.

***bua** *Morph:* ***bua-k**. *PRM.* fruit. *Doublet:* ***mbuah**. *Etym:* *buaq 'fruit; areca palm and nut …'. *[irr. from PRM:* *u > *o* in Rote*] [Sporadic:* *b = *b*/*ɓ* in wRote*]*
boa-k *Termanu.* fruit; mainly used as a separate word to refer to the fruit of a tree already mentioned. (J:52)
boa-ʔ *Korbafo.*
boa-k *Bokai.*
boa-ʔ *Bilbaa.*
boa=na *Landu.* fruit. (own field notes)
boa-ʔ *Rikou.*
boa-k *Ba'a.*
ɓoa-k *Lole.* fruit. (Zacharias et al. 2014)
ɓoa-k *Tii.*
boa-ʔ *Dengka.*
ɓoa-ʔ *Oenale.*
ɓoa-ʔ *Dela.* fruit.
fua|ʔ *Ro'is Amarasi.* fruit.
fua|ʔ *Kotos Amarasi.* fruit.
<fua> *Molo.* fruit. (M:129)
fua|ʔ *Kusa-Manea.* fruit.
Out-comparisons:
bua *Semau Helong.* banana.
fuan *East Tetun.* fruit (plants and trees **ai fuan**); heart (of persons or living things). (Mo:36)
hua *Mambae, South.* a) fruit. b) counter (e.g. classifier). (Grimes et al. 2014b:22)

***bufu** *PRM.* fish trap. *Etym:* *bubu 'conical bamboo basket trap for fish'. *[irr. from PRM:* *b = *b* in Meto; *u > *o* in Meto*]*
bufu (2) teʔek bufu *Termanu.* 1) fish trap. 2) set a fish trap. (J:62)
bufu *Korbafo.*
bufu *Bokai.*
bufu *Bilbaa.*
bufu *Rikou.*
bufu *Ba'a.*
ɓufu *Tii.*
fufu *Dengka.*
fufu *Oenale.*
bofu *Meto.* (J:62)
Out-comparisons:
buhu *Helong.* (J:62)

***bulan** *PRM.* moon, month. *Etym:* *bulan.
bula-k *Termanu.* moon, month. (J:63)
bula-ʔ *Korbafo.*

bula-k *Bokai.*
bula-ʔ *Bilbaa.*
bula-ʔ *Rikou.*
bula-k *Ba'a.*
ɓula-k *Tii.*
fula-ʔ *Dengka.*
fulan *Oenale.*
funun, fuunn *Ro'is Amarasi.* moon, month.
funan *Kotos Amarasi.* moon, month.
funan *Molo.* moon. (M:132)
funan *Kusa-Manea.* moon.
Out-comparisons:
bulan *Semau Helong.* moon.
fulan *East Tetun.* moon; lunar month, the period between the new moons. (Mo:37)
wollo *Kisar.* moon, month.

***bulu** *Morph:* ***bulu-k**. *PRM.* body hair; fur; feather. *Etym:* *bulu.
bulu-k *Termanu.* hair, feather(s). *[Semantics:* Both **laŋa_bulu-k** and **laŋa_doo-k** (literally 'head leaf') are given for 'head hair'.*]* (J:63)
bulu-ʔ *Korbafo.*
bulu-k *Bokai.*
bulu-ʔ *Bilbaa.*
bulu-ʔ *Landu.* body hair. (own field notes)
bulu-ʔ *Rikou.*
bulu-k *Ba'a.*
ɓulu-k *Tii.*
fulu-ʔ *Dengka.*
fulu-ʔ *Oenale.*
funu-f *Ro'is Amarasi.* body hair. *[Note:* **naak_buʔu** = 'head hair'.*]*
funu|ʔ *Kotos Amarasi.* hair (including head hair, though 'head hair' is usually specified in a compound as **ʔnaak funu-f**).
<funu> *Molo.* body hair. (M:133)
Out-comparisons:
bulu *Semau Helong.* hair.
wulla *Kisar.* fur, feathers, hair.

***buni** *PRM.* ringworm. Tinea imbricata. *Etym:* *buqəni. *[irr. from PRM:* *b > *h* in Meto; *i > *e* in Meto; *b = *b/ɓ* in wRote*]*
bu~buni *Termanu.* ringworm, kind of skin disease. (J:65)
bu~buni *Korbafo.*
bu~buni *Bokai.*
buni *Bilbaa.*
bu~buni *Rikou.*
bu~buni *Ba'a.*
ɓuni *Lole.* ringworm. (Zacharias et al. 2014)
ɓu~ɓuni *Tii.*
buni *Dengka.*
ɓuni *Oenale.*
hune *Kotos Amarasi.* ringworm.
hune ʔhonis *Molo.* kind of ringworm. (M:156)
Out-comparisons:
buna *Helong.* (J:65)
wuni *Kisar.* ringworm.
vuni *Hawu.* (J:65)

***buu** *PRM.* blow, blowpipe. *Doublet:* ***fuu**. *Etym:* *buu (PCEMP). *[irr. from PRM:* *b > *p* in wRote; *b = *b* /V_V in some Meto*]*
na-ta-fuu *Termanu.* inflated, blown up. (J:143)
na-ta-fuu *Korbafo.*
na-ta-fuu *Bokai.*
na-ta-fuu *Rikou.*
na-ta-fuu *Ba'a.*
na-ta-fuu *Tii.*
na-sa-puu *Dengka.*
na-sa-puu *Oenale.*
sfuut *Kotos Amarasi.* blowpipe, darts.
sbuut *Amanuban.* blowpipe made from a kind of bamboo that is also used to make flutes. (M:457)
na-sbuu, na-sfuu *Molo.* someone blows a dart from a blowpipe. *[Note:* The form <**tfo'**> 'kind of reed, cat's-tail, Thypha latifolia' may be related.*]* (M:479)
Out-comparisons:
hahuuk *East Tetun.* blowpipe, a long length of bamboo used for blowing darts (to hunt birds and sometimes small animals). (Mo:48)

Ɓ - ɓ

***ɓaat** *PRM.* crossbeam. *Etym:* *baRat. *[minority from PMP:* *b > *ɓ*]*

na-ta-baa *Termanu.* across (lying, etc.). (J:17)

na-ta-ba~baa *Dengka.* lying down, of objects. (J:678)

oʔolaʔa na-ta-ɓa~ɓaa *Oenale.* speech is obstructed or blocked. (J:678)

t|baa-t *Ro'is Amarasi.* something which lies across or in between two other things.

t|baa-t *Kotos Amarasi.* large thick beam that is supported by the **nii ainaf** ('mother post' = main supporting post) in a house. 'Each of the four 'mother posts' has a curved fork at the top, and they support two large beams termed **atbaat** which must run parallel to the centre-line of the house. Lying above and across them are beams called **kranit** that are each the same length and that number 8, 12, 16, or 24, depending upon house size. The rafters, **nesaʔ**, lie above and across these, parallel to the **atbaat**, and usually number the same as the **kranit**'. (Cunningham 1964:37, 43)

<na-baat> (2) <na-kbata> *Molo.* 1) closes with planks. 2) lays across. **a-moe lele na-kbata lalan neki hau uuʔ ees** someone who makes a garden lays a tree across the path (as a barrier) *[Form:* Medial *t* in **na-kbata** may be a retention of the final consonant with reanalysis of **baat as the metathesised form of **bata.*]* (M:51)

***ɓafa₁** *Morph:* ***ɓafa-k**. *Rote.* valley. *Etym:* *babaq 'lower surface, bottom; short, low; below, beneath, under'. *[minority from PMP:* *b > *ɓ*]*

bafa-k *Termanu.* valley, space between the mountains. (J:21)

bafa-ʔ *Korbafo.*

bafa-k *Bokai.*

ba~bafa-ʔ *Bilbaa.*

bafa-ʔ *Rikou.*

bafa-k *Ba'a.*

ɓafa-k *Tii.*

bafa-ʔ *Dengka.*

ɓafa-ʔ *Oenale.*

***ɓafa₂** *Morph:* ***ɓafa-k**. *Rote.* mouth, opening. *See:* ***fefa**. *Etym:* *baqbaq 'mouth, opening; speak, say' (Reconstructed with the doublet *bəqbəq. Both forms are attested in the Timor region.). *[minority from PMP:* *b > *ɓ*]*

bafa-k *Termanu.* mouth of a person or animal, beak of a bird, mouth of a river, opening of a water course.

bafa-ʔ *Korbafo.*

bafa-k *Bokai.*

bafa-ʔ *Bilbaa.*

bafa-ʔ *Landu.* mouth. (own field notes)

bafa-ʔ *Rikou.*

bafa-k *Ba'a.*

ɓafa-k *Tii.*

bafa-ʔ *Dengka.*

ɓafa-ʔ *Oenale.*

ɓafa-ʔ *Dela.* mouth.

Out-comparisons:

baha *Semau Helong.* mouth.

waban *Habun.* mouth. *[Note:* language of east Timor ISO 639-3 [hbu]*]* (Dawson 2014)

kahan *Ili'uun.* mouth (of man or animal). *[irr. from PMP:* *b > (*Ø) > *k* (compare *paŋdan > **keʧan**, *pusəj > **kusan**, and *hutək > **gutan**)*]* (dJ:119)

***ɓaiafa** *PRM.* monitor lizard. Varanus species. *Etym:* *bayawak (PWMP). *[minority from PMP:* *b > *ɓ*]*

baʔiafa *Termanu.* monitor lizard. *[History:* Jonker attributes the irregular glottal stop to the word becoming associated with that for 'grandfather'; **baʔi.***]* (J:23)

baʔiafa *Korbafo.*

baʔiafa *Bokai.*

baiafa *Bilbaa.*

baiafa-ʔ *Landu.* monitor lizard. (own field notes)

baiafa *Rikou.*

baiafa *Dengka.*

ɓaiafa *Oenale.*

bairafa *Timaus.* lizard. *[Form:* regular (*y) > *ʤ > *r.]*

baiafa, baiʤafa *Meto.* (J:23)

***ɓakos** *PRM.* barn owl. *Pattern:* k-8′ (*k = *k* in Korbafo, Tii, and Oenale; expect *ʔ*).

kolo_baʔo-k *Termanu.* kind of bird called *koro baʔok* in Kupang. (J:248)

kolo_bako-ʔ *Korbafo.*

kolo_baʔo-k *Bokai.*

kolo_bako-ʔ *Bilbaa.*

koro_bako-ʔ *Rikou.*

kolo_baʔo-k *Ba'a.*

koro_ɓako-k *Tii.*

kolo_baʔo-ʔ *Dengka.*

koro_ɓako-ʔ *Oenale.*

baos *Ro'is Amarasi.* barn owl.

baos *Kotos Amarasi.* barn owl.

Out-comparisons:

baos *Semau Helong.* evil spirit, ghost, apparition.

***ɓaʔi** *Rote.* grandfather. *Etym:* *baki (Reconstructed to PAN based only on Formosan reflexes.). *[minority from PMP:* *b > *ɓ*]*

baʔi *Termanu.* grandfather, also used in conjunction with proper names for all old men. (J:22)

baʔi *Korbafo.*

baʔi *Bokai.*

bai *Bilbaa.*

baʔi=na *Landu.* grandfather. (own field notes)

baʔi *Rikou.*

baʔi *Ba'a.*

ɓaʔi *Tii.*

baʔi *Dengka.*

ɓaʔi *Oenale.*

ɓaʔi *Dela.* grandfather.

Out-comparisons:

baki *Semau Helong.* mother's brother.

***ɓaʔu** *CERM.* several, many.

baʔu *Termanu.* many, great in number. (J:33)

baʔu *Korbafo.*

baʔu *Bokai.*

bau *Bilbaa.*

bau bea *Landu.* how many? (own field notes)

bau bea *Oepao.* how many? (own field notes)

baʔu|k *Kotos Amarasi.* several, many. *[Form:* Two forms with initial *f* are probably related: **mfaun** = 'many', and **fauk** = 'how many?, several'.*]*

<baʔu> *Molo.* great, many. (M:52)

Out-comparisons:

bakun *Semau Helong.* how many, several.

waʔu *Waima'a.* many.

***ɓalafo** *Morph:* ***ɓalafo-k.** *PRM.* kamala tree. Mallotus philippensis. *[Semantics:* vague Rote semantics*]*

kai_lafo-k *Termanu.* kind of tree. (J:216)

kai_lafo-ʔ *Korbafo.*

kai_lafo-k *Bokai.*

kai_lafo-ʔ *Bilbaa.*

ai_lafo-ʔ *Rikou.* (J:33; own field notes)

ai_lafo-k *Ba'a.*

hau_lafo-ʔ *Dengka.*

bnafu|ʔ, bnafo|ʔ *Kotos Amarasi.* Kamala tree. Mallotus philippensis.

<nafu>, <banafo>, <benafo> *Molo.* kind of tree. Mallotus philippensis. (M:341)

***ɓali** *Rote.* mix, add something to something else. *Etym:* *balik (PCMP. Blust and Trussel (ongoing) only give Yamdena and Fordata **valik** 'mixture of liquid and dry substances' and the Rote forms as evidence for this reconstruction.). *[minority from PMP:* *b > *ɓ*]*

bali (2) ba~bali-k *Termanu.* 1) mix, add something to something else. (J:27) 2) mixture, mixing, all mixed up. (J:28)

bali *Korbafo.*

bali *Bokai.*

bali *Bilbaa.*

bali *Rikou.*

bali *Ba'a.*

ɓali *Tii.*

bali *Dengka.*

ɓali *Oenale.*

***ɓanafi** *PRM.* sea cucumber. *[irr. from PRM:* *n > *r* in Meto*]*

nafi *Termanu.* sea cucumber. (J:373)

nafi *Korbafo.*

nafi *Bokai.*

nafi *Bilbaa.*

nafi *Landu.* sea cucumber. (own field notes)

nafi *Rikou.*

nafi *Ba'a.*

nafi *Tii.*

nafi *Dengka.*

nafi *Oenale.*

brafi *Ro'is Amarasi.* sea cucumber.

brafi *Kotos Amarasi.* sea cucumber.

Out-comparisons:

nahe *Semau Helong.* sea cucumber. *[Note:* Jonker (1908:373) gives Helong **hnahe**.*]*

banahi *East Tetun.* round edible shellfish. (Mo:10)

<kanewi> *Kambera.* sea cucumber. (On:164)

<kanawi> *Kodi.* edible sea cucumber. (On:543)

<nawi> *Sika.* kind of blue fat fish without a shell. (Calon 1891:334)

***ɓandae** *PRM.* hover, hang over. *[irr. from PRM:* *nd > *d* in Bilbaa; *nd > *d > *r*/*l* in Meto*]*

ndae *Termanu.* hang something over somewhere. (J:412)

ndae *Korbafo.*

lae *Bokai.*

dae *Bilbaa.*

rae *Rikou.*

ndae *Ba'a.*

ndae *Tii.*

ndae *Dengka.*

ndae *Oenale.*

na-brae *Kotos Amarasi.* hover.

na-blae *Molo.* it stays hanging from the hair (in a tree); it floats away. (M:72)

***ɓaraka** *Rote.* box. *Pattern:* k-6. *[Form:* This could be a loan but no likely donor language has yet been identified.*]*

balaka *Termanu.* box or suitcase made from wood or iron. (J:26)

balaka *Korbafo.*

balaka *Bokai.*

balaka *Bilbaa.*

baraʔa *Rikou.*

balaka *Ba'a.*

ɓaraka *Tii.*

balaʔa *Dengka.*

ɓaraʔa *Oenale.*

Out-comparisons:

baraka *Hawu.* box. (J:26)

barakaŋ *Sika.* wooden box for betel-vine. (Pareira and Lewis 1998:12)

***ɓasoko** *PRM.* slant, sway, dance. *Pattern:* k-7' (*k = *k* in Tii; expect *k > *ʔ*) for sense 1, *k-6 for sense 2, *k-irr for senses 3 and 4. *[irr. from PRM:* *k > Ø /V_V in Rote for senses 3 and 4.*]*

na-soʔo (2) soko~soko, soʔo~soʔo (3) soo (4) so~soo bapa=a *Termanu.* 1) slant, sloping. (J:563) 2) very slanted. (J:557, 563) 3) swinging, swaying, wobbling, like a drunken man, etc. (J:550) 4) dancing to the sound of the drum, including both men and women, each gender according to their way. (J:550)

na-soʔo (2) — (3) soo (4) so~soo *Korbafo.*

na-soʔo (2) soko~soko (3) soo (4) so~soo *Bokai.*

soʔo *Rikou.*

na-soʔo (2) — (3) soo (4) so~soo *Ba'a.*

na-soko (2) soko~soko *Tii.*

soko (2) soko~soko (3) — (4) ili_ so~soo *Dengka.*

soko (2) soko~soko (3) — (4) so~soo *Oenale.*

na-bsoʔo *Kotos Amarasi.* dance, sway (jocular).

na-sboʔo *Amanuban.* dance.

na-bsoʔo *Molo.* one dances. (M:85)

***ɓate** *Morph:* ***ka-ɓate**. *PRM.* edible grub. *Etym:* *qabatəd 'sago grub'. *[irr. from PMP:* *ə > *e (expect *ə > *a* in wRM, possibly *ə > *a > *e* in wRM)*]* *[minority from PMP:* *b > *ɓ*]*

ba~bate *Termanu.* kind of fat grub or worm, called *ular babate* in Kupang Malay, it occurs in the **bubuni** tree. These grubs are used as medicine to heal thrush in children. (J:32)

ba~bate *Korbafo.*

ba~bate *Bokai.*

ba~bate *Bilbaa.*

ba~bate *Rikou.*

ɓa~ɓate *Tii.*

ɓuni_ɓate *Oenale.*

ɓuni_ɓate-ʔ *Dela.* kind of maggot usually found at the **ɓu~ɓuni** tree.

k|bate|ʔ *Kotos Amarasi.* kind of edible grub that eats rotten wood, reported to turn into a cicada.

k|bate|ʔ *Molo.* grub that lives in a certain tree (Indonesian *tengguli*, Meto **nikis** = <u>*Cassia fistula*</u>), it is as long as a thumb, yellowish and very fat. When cooked in a pan its fat drips out and is used as medicine against thrush. This grub makes itself a chrysalis and turns into a moth/butterfly. (M:189)

ka|bata|ʔ *Timaus.* kind of edible grub which eats rotten wood. *[Form:* regular final *e > *a.]*

k|ba~bate *Kusa-Manea.* kind of edible grub.

***ɓati** *CERM.* distribute.

baʔe_ba~bati *Termanu.* distribute. (J:32f)

bati *Bokai.*

bati *Bilbaa.*

bati *Rikou.*

n-bati *Ro'is Amarasi.* distribute, share, divide.

n-bati (2) n-batis *Kotos Amarasi.* 1) distribute, share, divide. 2) separate.

n-bati *Molo.* distribute. (M:51)

bati *Kusa-Manea.* share, divide.

Out-comparisons:

batiŋ *Semau Helong.* divide, give.

ɸaka-ɸati *Maori.* cause to disperse. *[Note:* language of New Zealand ISO 639-3 [mri].*]* (Tregear 1891:615)

***ɓatus** *Morph:* ***ka-ɓatus**. *PwRM.* sea snail.

ba~batu-ʔ *Dengka.* shellfish. (J:681)

k|ba͡utus *Ro'is Amarasi.* sea-snails; oysters.

k|batus *Kotos Amarasi.* sea-snails; oysters.

***ɓau** *Morph:* ***ka-ɓau-k**. *PRM.* bat, flying fox. *[Sporadic:* *VV-k > *VVʔ > VʔV in Meto (perceptual metathesis); consonant metathesis *kb > *bk* in Amarasi.*]*

bau-k *Termanu.* bat. (J:33)

bau-ʔ *Korbafo.*

bau-k *Bokai.*

bau-ʔ *Bilbaa.*

bau-ʔ *Landu.* bat. (own field notes)

bau-ʔ *Rikou.*

bau-k *Ba'a.*

ɓau-k *Tii.*

bau-ʔ *Dengka.*
ɓau-ʔ *Oenale.*
ɓau-ʔ *Dela.* bat.
bkaʔu *Ro'is Amarasi.* bat, flying fox.
bkaʔu *Kotos Amarasi.* bat, flying fox.
k|baʔu *Kopas.* bat, flying fox.
ʔ|baʔu *Molo.* bat. (M:52)
ʔ|baʔu *Kusa-Manea.* bat, flying fox.
Out-comparisons:
khau *Funai Helong.* bat, flying fox.
fau *Semau Helong.* bat, flying fox. *[Note:* Jonker (1908:33) gives Helong **kfau**.*]*
hau *Bolok Helong.* bat, flying fox.
kabau *Kupang Malay.* bat.

***ɓeɓa** *Morph:* ***ka-ɓeɓa-k**. *PRM.* palm leaf stems or stalks (the middle bit without the leaves). *Etym:* *papaq 'frond of a palm'. *[irr. from PMP:* *p > *ɓ; *a > *e*]*
beba-k *Termanu.* palm leaf stalks. *[Note:* Jonker lists **beba** as the headword with the note that **beba-k** occurs in compounds. The examples have the bare form as the first member of the compound and the suffixed form phrase finally.*]* (J:36)
beba *Korbafo.*
beba *Bokai.*
beba *Bilbaa.*
beba *Rikou.*
beba *Ba'a.*
ɓeɓa *Tii.*
beba *Dengka.*
ɓeɓa *Oenale.*
ʔ|beba|ʔ *Kotos Amarasi.* palm leaf stems, typically used to make walls for houses or fences.
<beba> *Molo.* gebang palm. (M:53)
Out-comparisons:
hepaŋ *Semau Helong.* gebang stem.
beba|k *East Tetun.* stalk or stem of a palm frond, used for building walls of houses and panels in fences. (Mo:12)
əpa *Dhao.* stem (of leaf).
əpa *Hawu.* stem (of leaf). *[Note:* Jonker (1908:36) gives Hawu **pipa**.*]*

***ɓee** *PRM.* where. *[Note:* Possibly combines two cognate sets: ***mee** and ***ɓee**, though the formal and semantic similarity leads me to present them together.*] [irr. from PRM:* *ɓ > *m* in Meto (also Ili'uun); *e > *a* in Bilbaa, Landu, Rikou, and Oepao*]*
bee *Termanu.* where? wherever (with a preposition); how, what, whatever. (J:35)
bee *Korbafo.*
bee *Bokai.*
bea *Bilbaa.*
bea *Landu.* who, where, how. (own field notes)
(u)bea *Rikou.*
bea *Oepao.* who, where, how. (own field notes)
bee *Ba'a.*
ɓee *Tii.*
bee *Dengka.*
ɓee *Oenale.*
ɓee *Dela.* where.
mee *Ro'is Amarasi.* where.
mee *Kotos Amarasi.* where.
mee *Molo.* where. (M:317)
mee *Kusa-Manea.* where.
Out-comparisons:
la mee *Ili'uun.* which, where; also used as a general interrogative particle. (dJ:128)
ɓee *Bima.* where. (Ismail et al. 1985:14)

***ɓei** *PRM.* grandmother. *Etym:* *baqi. *[minority from PMP:* *b > *ɓ*] [Sporadic:* *VV-k > *VVʔ > VʔV in Meto (perceptual metathesis).*]*
bei *Termanu.* grandmother, also used to address older women or before the name of older women. (J:37)
bei *Korbafo.*
bei *Bokai.*
bei *Bilbaa.*
bei *Rikou.*

bei *Ba'a.*
ɓei *Tii.*
bei *Dengka.*
ɓei *Oenale.*
ɓei *Dela.* grandmother.
beʔi *Ro'is Amarasi.* grandmother.
bei-f, beʔi *Kotos Amarasi.* grandmother.
beʔi (2) bai-f *Molo.* 1) mother-in-law. (M:54) 2) mother-in-law. (M:41)
beʔi *Kusa-Manea.* grandmother.
Out-comparisons:
bee (2) been *Semau Helong.* 1) mother's brother's wife. 2) mother-in-law.
bei-n *East Tetun.* grandparent, ancestor. (Mo:12)

***ɓeis** *PRM.* crocodile. *See:* ***foe₂**. *[irr. from PRM:* *VVs > VsV in many varieties of Meto*] [Form:* As noted by Jonker (1908:38) some of the irregular correspondences (especially forms with *a* and *ʔ*) probably arose because the crocodile is addressed as **baʔi** 'grandfather'.*] [History:* Possibly connected with PMP *buqaya, though the vowel correspondences and final consonant are difficult to account for. *buqaya is regularly inherited in Nuclear Rote as ***foe**.*]*
beis *Termanu.* crocodile. (J:38)
bei *Korbafo.*
bei *Bokai.*
bai *Bilbaa.*
bais *Rikou.*
baʔis *Oepao.* crocodile. (own field notes)
baʔis *Ba'a.*
ɓei *Tii.*
bei *Dengka.*
ɓaʔi *Oenale.*
ɓaʔi *Dela.* crocodile.
naiʔ_besi *Ro'is Amarasi.* crocodile. *[Form:* Initial **naiʔ** from **naʔi** 'grandfather'.*]*
naiʔ_besi *Kotos Amarasi.* crocodile.
besi_mnasiʔ *Amanuban.* crocodile. *[Form:* **mnasiʔ** = 'old'.*]*
besi_mnasiʔ *Molo.* crocodile. (M:61)
beʔi-ʤ *Amfo'an.* crocodile.
naiʔ_bais *Amfo'an.* name of an Amfo'an clan
na/basa-r, na/besi_nasiʔ *Timaus.* crocodile.
beʔi *Kusa-Manea.* crocodile.
Out-comparisons:
°naʔi_bei *East Tetun.* respectful name for the crocodile. (Mo:145)
°naʔibein *Welaun.* crocodile. *Usage:* Oele'u village.
bei liurai *Welaun.* crocodile. *Usage:* Mahein village.

***ɓeki** *Morph:* ***na-ɓeki**. *PRM.* strong, capable. *Pattern:* k-9′ (*k > Ø in Rikou; expect *ʔ* or *k*).
na-beʔi *Termanu.* strong, can, is able to. (J:38)
na-beʔi *Korbafo.*
na-beki *Bilbaa.*
na-bei *Rikou.*
na-beʔi *Ba'a.*
na-ɓeʔi *Tii.*
na-beʔi *Dengka.*
na-ɓeʔi *Oenale.*
na-beʔi *Ro'is Amarasi.* strong, capable, able, can.
na-beʔi *Kotos Amarasi.* strong, capable, able, can.
na-beʔi *Molo.* strong, able, can. (M:54)
na-beiʔ *Kusa-Manea.* able, possible.
Out-comparisons:
biki *Bolok Helong.* power, exceptional strength.
biit *East Tetun.* force, strength. *[irr. from PRM:* *k = Ø correspondence*]* (Mo:14)
bik *Wersing.* strong. *[Note:* non-Austronesian language of Alor ISO 639-3 [kvw].*]* (Schapper 2017:263)
biˈki *Sawila.* strong. *[Note:* non-Austronesian language of Alor ISO 639-3 [swt].*]* (Schapper 2017:263)

***ɓeko** *CERM.* sway, shake. *Pattern:* k-5/6.
beko *Termanu.* shake from behind. (J:39)
na-beko *Kotos Amarasi.* sway, shake.
na-beko *Molo.* shake. (M:55)
Out-comparisons:
beko (2) heko *Semau Helong.* 1) shake, move, sway. 2) shake.

***ɓeku** *Rote.* bent over. *Etym:* *bəŋkuq 'bend, curve'. *Pattern:* k-6′ (*k > Ø in Rikou, expect *ʔ* or *k*). *[minority from PMP:* *b > *ɓ; *ŋk > *k*]*
beku_tee *Termanu.* hanging bent over like an ear of rice or a broken branch. (J:39)
beku_tee *Korbafo.*
beku_tee *Bokai.*
(beu_tee ?) *Rikou.*
beku_tee *Ba'a.*
ɓeku_tee *Tii.*
beʔu_tee *Dengka.*
ɓeʔu_tee *Oenale.*
ɓeʔu_tee *Dela.* bow (in respect).

***ɓeʔe** *PRM.* stay awake.
beʔe *Termanu.* watch, remain awake. (J:37)
beʔe *Ba'a.*
ɓeʔe *Tii.*
beʔe *Dengka.*
ɓeʔe *Oenale.*
ɓeʔe *Dela.* stay up late.
n-beʔe *Kotos Amarasi.* stay awake. Normally implies someone has died, and one is staying awake overnight with the family of the deceased in the presence of the corpse.
n-beʔe *Amfo'an.* be aware.
n-beʔa *Molo.* watch. (M:53)
beʔan *Kusa-Manea.* stay up overnight.
Out-comparisons:
beke *Hawu.* (J:37)

***ɓela** *PRM.* spread out, flat. *Doublet:* ***fela**. *Etym:* *bəkəlaj 'spread out, unroll (mats, etc.), open out, unfold (as the hand); wide' (Blust and Trussel (ongoing) reconstruct PEMP *bolaj and the Rote-Meto forms provide evidence for PCEMP *bəlaj.). *[minority from PMP:* *b > *ɓ*]*
bela (2) be~bela-k *Termanu.* 1) spread out as a mat, cover something with something that is spread out. (J:39) 2) flat. (J:40)
bela (2) be~bela-ʔ *Korbafo.*
bela (2) be~bela-k *Bokai.*
bela (2) be~bela-ʔ *Bilbaa.*
bela (2) be~bela-ʔ *Rikou.*
bela (2) be~bela-k *Ba'a.*
ɓela (2) ɓe~ɓela-k *Tii.*
bela (2) be~bela-ʔ *Dengka.*
ɓela (2) ɓe~ɓela-ʔ *Oenale.*
ɓela (2) ɓe~ɓela-ʔ *Dela.* 1) unfold or place on the ground. 2) flat, smooth.
na-ʔbena *Kotos Amarasi.* spread out (e.g. mat, blanket).
na-ʔbena *Molo.* spreads something out. (M:57)
Out-comparisons:
bela *Semau Helong.* open eyes.
belar *East Tetun.* level, flat, even, broad; *v.* to spread, to strew, multiply. *[irr. from PMP:* *ə > *e* (expect *o*)*]* (Mo:13)
hele *Ili'uun.* unfold, open, spread out. (dJ:117)
bəla *Hawu.* spread out, expanse, open by separating.

***ɓesa** *Morph:* ***ɓesa-k**. *PRM.* reonja tree. Vachellia leucophloea.
kai/besa-k *Termanu.* kind of tree the bark of which is used to colour sails and nets brown, deer like to eat the leaves of this tree. Vachellia leucophloea. (J:215, Heyne 1950:713, lxxii)
kai/besa-k *Bokai.*
kai_besa-ʔ *Bilbaa.*
ai_besa-ʔ *Rikou.*
kai/besa-k *Ba'a.*
ai_ɓesa-k *Tii.*
hau_besa-ʔ *Dengka.*

ɓesa-ʔ *Oenale.*
besa|k *Kotos Amarasi.* kind of tree with branches like the white leadtree (= Leucaena leucocephala).
besa|k *Molo.* name of a screen tree. Acacia leucophloea. (M:60)
Out-comparisons:
besa|ʔ *Semau Helong.* kind of thorn tree.

***ɓeta** *Rote.* cut vegetation. *Etym:* *bəntas 'hack a passage through vegetation, blaze a trail'. *[minority from PMP:* *b > *ɓ*]*
beta ai *Termanu.* cut a tree, cut off branches, prune. (J:46)
beta *Korbafo.*
beta *Bokai.*
beta *Bilbaa.*
beta *Rikou.*
beta *Ba'a.*
ɓeta *Tii.*
beta *Dengka.*
ɓeta *Oenale.*

***ɓetə** *Morph:* ***na-ka-ɓetə**. *PRM.* tense, tight. *Etym:* *bəntəŋ 'extended, stretched taut, put under tension'. *[minority from PMP:* *b > *ɓ*]* *[Form:* The unmetathesised form has not yet been attested in Meto. It could be ***kbeta** or ***kbete**.*]*
na-ka-bete *Termanu.* tense, tight. (J:46)
na-ka-bete *Korbafo.*
na-ka-bete *Bokai.*
na-ka-bete *Bilbaa.*
na-bete *Rikou.*
na-ka-bete *Ba'a.*
na-ka-ɓete *Tii.*
na-ʔa-beta *Dengka.*
na-ʔa-ɓeta *Oenale.*
na-k|beet *Kotos Amarasi.* stiff, tight.
na-k|beet *Molo.* tight, braced. (M:189)

***ɓetu** *Morph:* ***na-ka-ɓetu**. *PRM.* bent, folded. *Doublet:* ***fedu**. *Etym:* *bəntuk 'curve'. *[minority from PMP:* *b > *ɓ*]*
na-ka-betu *Termanu.* flexible (mainly said of fingers); bent in, bent through; crooked; stick up crookedly. (J:47)
betu *Dengka.*
na-k|betu *Molo.* folded. *[History:* Middelkoop (1972:63) also gives **na-kfetu**, and **na-kfeti** as variants meaning 'jumps or bounces back' which may be connected.*]* (M:63)
Out-comparisons:
(s)beton *Helong.* (J:128)

***ɓia** *PRM.* split. *Etym:* *biqak. *[Note:* The irregularities in the Meto forms indicate that they may not be cognate with the Rote forms.*]* *[minority from PMP:* *b > *ɓ*]* *[irr. from PRM:* *ɓ > *p* in Meto; *i > *e* in Meto*]* *[Sporadic:* glottal stop insertion in Meto*]*
bia *Termanu.* split. (J:48)
bia *Korbafo.*
bia *Bokai.*
bia *Bilbaa.*
bia *Rikou.*
bia *Ba'a.*
ɓia *Tii.*
bia *Dengka.*
ɓia *Oenale.*
n-peʔa *Ro'is Amarasi.* break.
n-peʔe *Kotos Amarasi.* break, crack.
n-peeʔ (2) peʔas *Molo.* 1) broken through. 2) fissure or split in the ground. (M:428)
Out-comparisons:
mbiʔa (2) ɓiʔa *Bima.* 1) piece, broken off from glass and earthenware, etc. in the meaning of Malay *pecah*. (Jonker 1893:55) 2) break something. (Jonker 1893:9, Ismail et al. 1985:15)
mbiʔa (2) piʔa *Ende.* 1) broken. 2) blow, hit, break.

***ɓiɓi** *Morph:* ***ka-ɓiɓi**. *PRM.* goat. *[irr. from PRM:* *ɓ > *ʔ* in Termanu, Korbafo, Bokai, and Ba'a*]* *[Semantics:* onomatopoeia*]*

biʔi_hii-k, biʔi_ae-k (2) biʔi_lopo *Termanu.* 1) goat, buck. 2) ram, sheep. (J:49)
biʔi *Korbafo.*
biʔi *Bokai.*
bibi *Bilbaa.*
bibi *Rikou.*
biʔi *Ba'a.*
ɓiɓi *Tii.*
bibi *Dengka.*
ɓiɓi *Oenale.*
ɓiɓi *Dela.* sheep, goat.
ʔ|bibi *Kotos Amarasi.* goat.
ʔ|bibi *Molo.* goat. (M:65)
ʔ|bibi *Kusa-Manea.* goat.
Out-comparisons:
bibi *East Tetun.* goat. (Mo:14)
pipi *Ili'uun.* goat. (dJ:133)
biub *Mambae, South.* goat. (Grimes et al. 2014b:14)
pipi *Kisar.* goat.
kahiɓi *Dhao.* goat.

***ɓife** *Rote.* lip. *Etym:* *bibiR 'lower lip'. *[minority from PMP:* *b > *ɓ*]* *[Sporadic:* *i > *e /_*R#*]* *[Form:* Assimilations of *ɓ > *d* in the first sense are due to this term being compounded with reflexes of ***doo-k** 'leaf', compare ***ndiki** > **diʔi_doo-k** and ***ndake_doo-k** > **daʔe_doo-k**.*]*
difa_doo-k (2) bifa-k (3) na-bifa ule-k *Termanu.* 1) lips (of people and animals). (J:86) 2) the cut off edge of a leaf. 3) shape the earth to follow the edge of a pot. (J:49)
bife_doo-ʔ (2) bifa-ʔ *Korbafo.*
difa_doo-k *Bokai.*
bife_doo-ʔ *Bilbaa.*
bifi_doo-ʔ *Landu.* lips. (own field notes)
bifi_doo-ʔ *Rikou.*
bifi_doo-ʔ *Oepao.* (own field notes)
difi_doo-k (2) bifa-k *Ba'a.*
ɓifi_ɗoo-k (2) ɓifa-k *Tii.*
ɓife *Dela.* side of, edge.

***ɓina** *Rote.* kind of volute shell. *Etym:* *biŋaq. *[minority from PMP:* *b > *ɓ*]*
bina *Termanu.* kind of shellfish; the shell or a part of the shell of this shellfish is used to rest the **ine** (spindle) on. (J:49)
bina *Korbafo.*
bina *Bokai.*
bina *Bilbaa.*
bina *Rikou.*
bina *Ba'a.*
ɓina *Tii.*
bina *Dengka.*
Out-comparisons:
biŋan *Helong.* (J:49)

***ɓisu** *PRM.* ulcer, pimple. *Etym:* *bisul 'boil, abscess'. *[minority from PMP:* *b > *ɓ*]*
bisu *Termanu.* ulcer, pimple; have an ulcer or wound. (J:50)
bisu *Korbafo.*
bisu *Bokai.*
bisu *Bilbaa.*
bisu *Rikou.*
bisu *Ba'a.*
ɓisu *Tii.*
bisu *Dengka.*
ɓisu *Oenale.*
ɓisu *Dela.* wound.
bisu *Kotos Amarasi.* kind of wound, pustule.
na-bisu *Molo.* pimply. (M:71)
Out-comparisons:
fisur, fisul *East Tetun.* abscess, boil. (Mo:34)
vihu *Hawu.* (J:50)

***ɓiti** *PRM.* pinch. *Doublet:* ***bifi**, ***fiti**3. *Etym:* *bitbit 'pull at body part; hold something dangling from the fingers'. *[minority from PMP:* *b > *ɓ*]* *[irr. from PRM:* *t > *ʔ* /V_V in Rote*]* *[Form:* The Meto forms meaning 'scorpion' are mostly from ***ka-ɓiti** with the nominal ***ka-** prefix.*]*
biʔi *Termanu.* pinch with the finger and thumb. (J:49)
ɓiʔi *Tii.*
biʔi *Dengka.*
k|biti *Ro'is Amarasi.* scorpion.

k|biti *Kotos Amarasi.* scorpion.
<biti> (2) ka|biti *Molo.* 1) give a little pinch. (M:71) 2) scorpion. (M:166)
biti *Kusa-Manea.* scorpion. *Usage:* Upper Manulea village.
ka|biti *Kusa-Manea.* scorpion. *Usage:* Uabau' village.
Out-comparisons:
bitin *Semau Helong.* flick something (especially rock or marble).

***ɓitinaa** *PRM.* guest tree. Kleinhovia hospita.
bitinaa *Termanu.* kind of tree. Kleinhovia hospita. (J:51, Heyne 1950:1064, lxxv)
bitinaa *Korbafo.*
bitinaa *Bilbaa.*
bitinaa *Ba'a.*
ɓitinaa *Tii.*
betinaa *Dengka.*
ɓetinaa *Oenale.*
<bitna> *Molo.* kind of tree which becomes green quickly. Kleinhovia hospita. (M:72)

***ɓoho** *PRM.* cough.
boʔo *Termanu.* cough. (J:58)
boʔo *Korbafo.*
boʔo *Bokai.*
boo *Bilbaa.*
boo *Landu.* cough. (own field notes)
boo *Rikou.* *[Note:* Jonker (1908) gives the Rikou form as **boʔo** and marks it as dubious. If this form is accurate, it would be only one of two forms with medial *h > *ʔ* in Rikou, the other being ***kahu** > **kaʔu**).*]* (own field notes)
bo~boo-s *Oepao.* cough. *[Form:* nominalisation*]*
boʔo *Ba'a.*
ɓoʔo *Tii.*
boo *Dengka.*
ɓoo *Oenale.*
ɓoo *Dela.* cough.
n-boho *Ro'is Amarasi.* cough.
n-boho *Kotos Amarasi.* cough.
<boho> *Molo.* cough. (M:77)
ba~booh *Kusa-Manea.* cough.

***ɓoki** *Morph:* ***ka-ɓoki-k**. *PRM.* hollowed out coconut shell used as a container. *Pattern:* k-9.
bo~boʔi-k *Termanu.* whole hollowed out coconut shell with an opening used to contain sugar sap. (J:54)
bo~boʔi *Korbafo.*
bo~boʔi-k *Bokai.*
bo~boki *Bilbaa.*
bo~boki *Rikou.*
bo~boʔi-k *Ba'a.*
ɓo~ɓoʔi-k *Tii.*
bo~boʔi *Dengka.*
ɓo~ɓoʔi *Oenale.*
a-ʔ|boʔi *Meto.* (J:54)
Out-comparisons:
buki *Helong.* (J:54)

***ɓo/lau** *Rote.* spider. *Doublet:* ***k|naba|ʔ**. *Etym:* *lawaq 'spider; spider web' (Possibly a chance similarity.). *[irr. from PMP:* *wa > *u in Rote*] [Form:* source of initial ***bo** unknown*]*
bolau *Termanu.* spider. (J:55)
bolau *Korbafo.*
bolau *Bokai.*
bolau *Bilbaa.*
bolau *Landu.* spider. (own field notes)
bolau *Rikou.*
bolau *Ba'a.*
ɓolau *Tii.*
bolau *Dengka.*
ɓolau *Oenale.*
Out-comparisons:
lailaon *Helong.* *[irr. from PMP:* *wa > *o* (expect *pa*)*]* (J:55)

***ɓole** *PRM.* areng palm. Arenga pinnata.
bole *Termanu.* areng palm, called *gemuti* in Kupang. (J:56)
bole *Korbafo.*
bole *Bokai.*
bole *Bilbaa.*
bole *Rikou.*
bole *Ba'a.*
ɓole *Tii.*

bole *Dengka.*
ɓole *Oenale.*
bone *Kotos Amarasi.* areng palm. Arenga pinnata.
bone *Molo.* areng palm. Arenga pinnata. (M:82)
bone *Kusa-Manea.* areng palm. Arenga pinnata.
Out-comparisons:
°**bone** *Fehan Tetun.* type of tree which is as tall as a sago palm. *Borrowed from:* Meto, as shown by irr. *l > *n*.

***ɓolo**1 *Morph:* ***ɓolo-k**. *PRM.* hole. *[irr. from PRM:* *l > *r*/*l* in Meto*]*
bolo-k *Termanu.* hole, cavity, hollow, pit. (J:56f)
bolo-ʔ *Korbafo.*
bolo-k *Bokai.*
bolo-ʔ *Bilbaa.*
bolo-ʔ *Rikou.*
bolo-k *Ba'a.*
ɓolo-k *Tii.*
na-boor, n-boor *Kotos Amarasi.* make a hole.
bola|ʔ *Meto.* (J:57)
Out-comparisons:
boloʔ *Funai Helong.* hole.
bolo *Semau Helong.* hole.

***ɓolo**2 *PwRM.* scabies, smallpox.
ɓo~ɓolo *Oenale.* have scabies. (J:683)
bono *Kotos Amarasi.* smallpox.
bono *Molo.* smallpox. (M:83)
Out-comparisons:
bobolo *Helong.* smallpox. (J:683)

***ɓona** *Morph:* ***ɓona-k**. *CERM.* fragrant pandanus.
bona-k *Termanu.* fragrant pandanus. (J:57)
bona-k *Bokai.*
bona-k *Ba'a.*
bona|k, bono|k *Ro'is Amarasi.* fragrant pandanus.
bona|k *Kotos Amarasi.* fragrant pandanus.
bona|ʔ *Amfo'an.* fragrant pandanus.
bona|k *Molo.* fragrant pandanus. (M:82)
boan|k=aa *Kusa-Manea.* fragrant pandanus.
Out-comparisons:
bonak *Kupang Malay.* pandanus.

***ɓone** *CERM.* circle dance.
bo~bone *Termanu.* kind of circle dance, only performed by men. (J:57)
n-bone (2) bone-t *Molo.* 1) sings in a choir dance. 2) choir dance in a large circle, singing in a choir dance. (M:82)

***ɓoni** *nRM.* hang, depend on.
tai_boni *Termanu.* hang out for something = desire something, demand something. (J:588)
tai_boni *Korbafo.*
tai_boni *Bokai.*
tai_boni *Bilbaa.*
tai_boni *Rikou.*
tai_boni *Ba'a.*
tai_ɓoni *Tii.*
na-ʔboniʔ *Kotos Amarasi.* depending on.
<na-boni> *Molo.* it depends on something. (M:83)
ta-ʔboniʔ *Kusa-Manea.* hang.

***ɓoŋgo**1 *PRM.* round, bulbous.
bo~boŋo-k *Termanu.* round. (J:58)
bo~boŋo-ʔ *Korbafo.*
bo~boŋo-k *Bokai.*
bo~boŋo-ʔ *Bilbaa.*
bo~boko-ʔ *Rikou.*
bo~boŋgo-k *Ba'a.*
ɓo~ɓoŋgo-k *Tii.*
bo~boŋgo-ʔ *Dengka.*
ɓo~ɓoŋgo-ʔ *Oenale.*
ɓo~ɓoŋgo-ʔ *Dela.* round.
siim tai_boko *Kotos Amarasi.* kind of large katydid with a large belly. *[Form:* **simah** = 'katydid', **tai-f** = 'belly'.*]*
Out-comparisons:
bukas *Semau Helong.* round. *[irr. from PRM:* *u = *o*; final *o = *a*; *ŋg = *k]*

bokur *East Tetun.* fat, fatty, well fed; *n.* fat, tallow, grease. (Mo:16)

boku *Waima'a.* fat, round.

<kabunggulu> *Kambera.* squat of stature, short and round. *[Note:* also in Mangili and Lewa.*]* (On:126)

<kaḅugulu> *Anakalang.*

<kawonggila> *Mamboru.*

<kamunggila> *Weyewa.*

***ɓoŋgo2** *Morph:* ***ka-ɓoŋgo**. *PRM.* gourd, pumpkin, squash.

boŋo *Termanu.* calabash, called *bongko* in Kupang, which is hollowed out and used for the storage of liquids. (J:57f)

boŋo *Korbafo.*

boŋo *Bokai.*

boŋo *Bilbaa.*

boko *Rikou.*

boŋgo *Ba'a.*

ɓoŋgo *Tii.*

boŋgo_meluʔ *Dengka.*

ɓoŋgo *Oenale.*

boko *Ro'is Amarasi.* kind of vegetable the skin of which is used as a water container. *[Note:* **uut boʔo** = 'pumpkin blossom' may be related with irr. *ŋg > (*k) > *ʔ.]*

ʔ|boko *Kotos Amarasi.* pumpkin, squash.

ʔ|boko (2) atoni na-k|boko *Molo.* 1) pumpkin. 2) bald-headed man (used for a Christian, who has had his hair cut off). (M:79)

Out-comparisons:

boŋo *Helong.* (J:58)

boko *Fehan Tetun.* type of chilli, so named as the fruits are fat.

ɓoŋgo *Ende.* vessel made of gourd.

***ɓoto1** *Morph:* ***na-ka-ɓoto**. *CERM.* whisper, mutter.

na-ka-bo~boto-ʔ *Bilbaa.* whisper. (J:684)

na-bo~boto-ʔ *Rikou.*

na-ʔboto *Kotos Amarasi.* remind.

<bot~boto> *Meto.* mutter. (J:684)

Out-comparisons:

hakbotuk *East Tetun.* whisper, speak in a secret and low voice, to mutter to oneself. (Mo:51)

***ɓoto2** *PRM.* Indian beech tree. *Millettia pinnata*. *[Semantics:* Scientific identification given on the basis of the Molo reflex and the Termanu example sentence. 'While the oil and residue of the plant [*Millettia pinnata*] are toxic and will induce nausea and vomiting if ingested, the fruits and sprouts, along with the seeds, are used in many traditional remedies.' ('Millettia pinnata', *Wikipedia.* en.wikipedia.org/wiki/Millettia_pinnata. Accessed 17 September 2020).*]*

bo~boto *Termanu.* plant kind. **see naʔa boboto=a boa-na naa see mate** whoever eats the fruit of the **bo~boto** will die (J:59)

ɓo~ɓoto *Dela.* kind of tree.

botoʔ *Kotos Amarasi.* cluster fig tree; Indian fig tree; goolar fig. *Ficus racemosa*. *[Semantics:* Scientific identification from Meijer-Drees (1950:4).*]*

<boto'is> *Molo.* kind of tree. *Millettia pinnata*. (M:85)

***ɓoto3** *PRM.* fontanelle. *[Form:* The second element of the Rote forms is a reflex of ***lii** < *liqəR.*]*

boto_lii-k *Termanu.* neck. (J:59)

boto_lii-ʔ *Korbafo.*

boto_lii-k *Bokai.*

boto_lii-ʔ *Bilbaa.*

bo/lii-ʔ *Landu.* neck. (own field notes)

bo/lii-ʔ *Rikou.*

bo/lii-ʔ *Oepao.* neck. (own field notes)

boto_lii-k *Ba'a.*

ɓoto_lii-k *Tii.*

ɓoto_lii-ʔ *Oenale.*

boto-n *Ro'is Amarasi.* fontanelle.

boto-f *Kotos Amarasi.* fontanelle (the pulsating part of a baby's head).
boto-f *Kusa-Manea.* head.
Out-comparisons:
ba~boto-n *East Tetun.* fontanel [sic], the gap between the bones in the skull of young children. (Mo:7)

***ɓua** *PRM.* gather. *[Sporadic:* *a > *e* /_# in wRote*]*
na-ka-bua (2) bua~bua (3) bu~bua-k (4) bebua *Termanu.* 1) gathering, coming together, accumulating. 2) together, gathered, in piles. 3) being together, that which is together, heap, herd, swarm, clod, clump. 4) together in piles. (J:60)
na-ka-bua *Korbafo.*
na-ka-bua *Bokai.*
na-ka-bua *Bilbaa.*
na-bua *Rikou.*
na-ka-ɓua *Tii.*
na-ʔa-bue *Dengka.*
na-ʔa-ɓue *Oenale.*
na-bua *Ro'is Amarasi.* gather.
na-bua (2) na-k|buaʔ, na-ʔ|buaʔ (3) buaʔ~buaʔ *Kotos Amarasi.* 1) gather together (intransitive). 2) gather (transitive). 3) together. *[Note:* **kboʔes** 'clump' may be related with final *a > *e*, vowel height harmony, lowering *u > *o*, and addition of various affixes.*]*
na-bua (2) <atoni> na-k|buaʔ (3) buaʔ~buaʔ (4) <anbua nakan> *Molo.* 1) coming together. 2) man with his hair tied together in as opposed to a Christian who cuts his hair off. 3) close together. 4) makes a hair roll. (M:85)
ta-bua *Kusa-Manea.* gather.
Out-comparisons:
°nakbua (2) °buan *Semau Helong.* 1) gather. 2) gather, collect, group, cluster. *Borrowed from:* Rote or Meto, as indicated by the irregular lack of any reflex for pre-RM *k which is evidenced by the Tetun form below (*k > *ʔ* is attested in Tetun).
fuʔa|k *East Tetun.* group of things or animals very close together. (Mo:36)

***ɓuas** *Rote.* thing, equipment.
buas *Termanu.* equipment. (J:61)
bua-ʔ *Korbafo.*
bua-ʔ *Bokai.*
bua-ʔ *Bilbaa.*
buas *Rikou.*
buas *Ba'a.*
ɓuas *Tii.*
buas *Dengka.*
ɓuas *Oenale.*
ɓuas *Dela.* generic clothes.
Out-comparisons:
buat *East Tetun.* thing, object. (Mo:18)

***ɓuɓu** *PRM.* bubbling, boiling. *Etym:* *bukbuk1. *[minority from PMP:* *b > *ɓ (both initially and medially)*]*
na-sa-bubu *Termanu.* bubbling up, boiling up of water. (J:61f)
bubu *Bokai.*
bubu *Bilbaa.*
bubu *Dengka.*
na-sa-ɓuɓu *Oenale.*
n-bubu *Molo.* boils, trembles. (M:87)
Out-comparisons:
bubu *East Tetun.* swell. (Mo:18)
bubu *Hawu.* boil over, overflow; anger.

***ɓuə** *Morph:* ***ɓuə-k**. *nRM.* head hair, frizzy haired. *Etym:* *buhək 'head hair'. *[minority from PMP:* *b > *ɓ*] [irr. from PRM:* *ə > *u* in Ro'is Amarasi*] [Sporadic:* *VV-k > *VVʔ > VʔV in Ro'is Amarasi (perceptual metathesis)*]*
laŋa_bue-k *Bokai.* frizzy haired. (J:684)
laka doo bue-ʔ *Rikou.* frizzy haired. (own field notes)

(laŋga) ɓue-k *Tii.* frizzy haired. (J:684)
naak_buʔu *Ro'is Amarasi.* head hair.
bu/ratu *Kotos Amarasi.* frizzy (of hair). *[Form:* Neither element of this (probable) historic compound is known to be attested independently.*]*
Out-comparisons:
fuhuk *Fehan Tetun.* hair of the head.
fuuk *East Tetun.* hair of the head. (Mo:38)

***ɓuit** *PRM.* rear, backside. *Etym:* *buRit 'hind part, rear, back'. *[minority from PMP:* *b > *ɓ*] [irr. from PRM:* *i > *a* in Molo; *i > *u* in Kotos Amarasi (sense 1)*] [Sporadic:* *VV-k > *VVʔ > VʔV in some Meto (perceptual metathesis)*]*
bui-k (2) tane_bui *Termanu.* 1) rear. (J:62) 2) kind of black ant with an acutely painful sting. *Lit:* 'sharp rear'. (J:817)
bui-ʔ (2) tane_bui *Korbafo.*
bui-k (2) tane_bui *Bokai.*
bui-ʔ (2) tene_bui *Bilbaa.*
bui-ʔ (2) tande_bui *Rikou.*
(2) tane_bui *Ba'a.*
ɓui-k *Tii.*
na-ʔa-ɓuit *Dela.* go last, from behind.
(2) kas/buʔi *Ro'is Amarasi.* 2) ant.
ʔ|buʔu-f (2) sa/buit *Kotos Amarasi.* 1) buttocks, anus. 2) ant. *[Form:* I have an (unconfirmed) variant **buʔi** for the first sense in my dictionary. This would be a regular reflex.*]*
<bu'an> *Molo.* posterior. (M:86)
(2) as/bui|k *Kusa-Manea.* 2) ant.
Out-comparisons:
hui *Dhao.* stern of boat.
vui *Hawu.* stern, rear.

***ɓuku** *Morph:* ***ɓuku-k**. *PRM.* node, joint. *Etym:* *buku 'node (as in bamboo or sugarcane); joint; knuckle; knot in wood; knot in string or rope'. *Pattern:* k-7. *[minority from PMP:* *b > *ɓ*]*
buʔu-k *Termanu.* protuberance, joint. (J:66)
buʔu-ʔ *Korbafo.*
buʔu-k *Bokai.*
buku-ʔ *Bilbaa.*
buku-ʔ *Rikou.*
buʔu-k *Ba'a.*
ɓuʔu-k *Tii.*
buku-ʔ *Dengka.*
ɓuku-ʔ *Oenale.*
buʔu-f *Ro'is Amarasi.* joints.
buʔu-f *Kotos Amarasi.* joints; knuckles, wrist, ankle, etc.
Out-comparisons:
buku-n *Semau Helong.* joint, knot, knee.
fuku-n *East Tetun.* knot (of trees, ropes, etc.); knuckle, joint (of limbs). (Mo:37)

***ɓula** *Rote.* open one's eyes wide. *Etym:* *bulat 'open the eyes wide, stare with round eyes'. *[minority from PMP:* *b > *ɓ*]*
na-ka-bu~bula (2) bula~bula (mata deʔe-n-) *Termanu.* 1) he opens his eyes wide. 2) his eyes are wide open. (J:63)
na-ka-bu~bula *Korbafo.*
na-ka-bu~bula *Bokai.*
na-ka-bu~bula *Bilbaa.*
na-bu~bula *Rikou.*
na-ka-bu~bula-k *Ba'a.*
na-ka-ɓu~ɓula-k *Tii.*
na-ta-bu~bula-ʔ *Dengka.*
na-ʔa-ɓu~ɓula-ʔ *Oenale.*
Out-comparisons:
<kabula> *Kambera.* with the eyes wide open. (On:125)

***ɓuna** *Morph:* ***ɓuna-k**. *PRM.* flower, blossom. *Doublet:* **#ɓuŋga**. *Etym:* *buŋa. *[minority from PMP:* *b > *ɓ*] [irr. from PRM:* *u > *o* in Meto*]*
buna-k *Termanu.* flower, blossom. (J:64)
buna-ʔ *Korbafo.*
buna-k *Bokai.*
buna-ʔ *Bilbaa.*

buna=na *Landu.* flower. (own field notes)
buna-ʔ *Rikou.*
buna-k *Ba'a.*
ɓuna-k *Tii.*
buna-ʔ *Dengka.*
ɓuna-ʔ *Oenale.*
fu/bona|ʔ *Ro'is Amarasi.* ornamental flower.
fu/bona|ʔ, fua_bona|ʔ *Kotos Amarasi.* ornamental flower. *[Form:* first element from **fuaʔ** = 'fruit'.*]*
Out-comparisons:
buŋaʔ *Semau Helong.* flower.
funan *East Tetun.* flower, bloom. (Mo:37)

***ɓuni** *PRM.* Cassia tree, kinds of legume trees.
bu~buni_hedu (2) bu~buni doo lutu *Termanu.* 1) kind of tree with hard wood the leaves of which can be used as medicine for ringworm. 2) kind of tree with small leaves the bark of which can be used as a substitute for betel nut. *Lit:* 'slender leaved **bubuni'**. *[Semantics:* Heyne (1950:741, lxxvi) gives <**boeboeni sèla**> as *Cassia fistula.]* (J:65)
bu~buni_hedu *Korbafo.*
bu~buni_hedu *Bilbaa.*
bu~buni_lama (2) bu~buni lutu (3) bu~buni sela-ʔ *Rikou.* 1) kind of tree the bark of which can be used as a substitute for betel nut. 2) kind of tree with white flowers. 3) kind of tree with yellow flowers. (own field notes)
bu~buni_hedu *Ba'a.*
ɓuni, ɓu~ɓuni_mali *Tii.*
bu~buni_meluʔ *Dengka.*
ɓuni_meruʔ *Oenale.*
ɓu~ɓuni *Dela.* kind of tree.
buni *Kotos Amarasi.* kind of tree the bark of which can be used as a substitute for betel nut.
buni *Molo.* kind of tree. Cassia javanica; Cassia siamea. (M:90)
Out-comparisons:
vuni *Hawu.* (J:65)

***ɓunda** *Rote.* fat bellied. *Etym:* *buntər 'distended, inflated (of the belly)' (Blust and Trussel (ongoing) give a host of semantically and formally similar reconstructions some of which they posit as doublets and some of which they mark as 'disjuncts': *buntəR 'round', *bə(n)tur 'glutted, sated; swollen (of the belly)', *bə(n)tuR 'glutted, sated; swollen (of the belly)', *buntuʔ 'bloated, swollen (of the belly)', *buntuD 'swollen, distended, of the belly', *buntuR 'bloated, swollen', and *bu(n)tu 'bloated'. It seems extremely likely that several of these forms are spurious and we are dealing with cases of irregular sound change. Manggarai and Rembong forms are given as evidence for multiple reconstructions and are the only witnesses from Wallacea.). *[irr. from PMP:* *ə > *a (expect *ə > *e* in nRote)*] [minority from PMP:* *b > *ɓ; *nt > *nd (expect *t)*]*
buna_tei-k (2) iʔa_buna-k *Termanu.* 1) have a fat belly, get a fat belly (only said of children). 2) a kind of fish which inflates itself like a ball at the slightest touch. (J:64)
buna_tei-ʔ *Korbafo.*
buna_tei-ʔ *Bilbaa.*
bunda_tei-ʔ *Rikou.*
ɓunda_tei-k *Tii.*
bunda~bunda *Dengka.* stuffed. *[Semantics:* Jonker gives a cross reference to Termanu **lamu~lamu** which is glossed as 'very stuffed, of the belly'. Thus, it seems likely that the usual reference of the Dengka form was also to the belly.*]* (J:684)

***ɓusa** *Rote.* dog. *[History:* possibly connected with PWMP *musaŋ 'civet' or Dutch *poes* [pu:s] 'cat'.*]*
busa *Termanu.* dog. (J:65)

busa *Korbafo.*
busa *Bokai.*
busa *Bilbaa.*
busa *Landu.* dog. (own field notes)
busa *Rikou.*
busa *Ba'a.*
ɓusa *Tii.*
busa *Dengka.*
ɓusa *Oenale.*
ɓusa *Dela.* dog.
Out-comparisons:
busa *East Tetun.* cat. (Mo:19)
busa *Kemak.* cat.
busan *Lamaholot, Ile Mandiri.* cat. *Usage:* Lewoingu dialect. *[Note:* language of east Flores ISO 639-3 [slp].*]* (Nishiyama and Kelen 2007:90)

***ɓusu** *Rote.* bow for cleaning cotton. *Etym:* *busuR 'hunting bow'. *[minority from PMP:* *b > *ɓ*]*
busu (2) bu~busu-k *Termanu.* 1) clean cotton with a bow. 2) cleaning; the bow used to clean cotton. (J:65)
busu *Korbafo.*
busu *Bokai.*
busu *Bilbaa.*
busu *Rikou.*
busu *Ba'a.*
ɓusu *Tii.*
busu (2) bu~busu-t *Dengka.*
(2) ɓu~ɓusu-t *Oenale.*
Out-comparisons:
fusu *East Tetun.* an arched comb used for carding cotton. (Mo:38)

D - d

***daa** *Morph:* ***daa-k**. *PRM.* blood. *Etym:* *daRaq.
daa-k *Termanu.* blood, sap. (J:66)
daa-ʔ *Korbafo.*
daa-k *Bokai.*
daa-ʔ *Bilbaa.*
daa-ʔ *Landu.* blood. (own field notes)
daa-ʔ *Rikou.*
daa-k *Ba'a.*
ɗaa-k *Tii.*
laa-ʔ *Dengka.*
raa-ʔ *Oenale.*
naa|ʔ *Ro'is Amarasi.* blood.
naa|ʔ *Kotos Amarasi.* blood.
naa|ʔ *Molo.* blood. (M:338)
naa|ʔ *Kusa-Manea.* blood.
Out-comparisons:
dala *Semau Helong.* blood.
raa-n *East Tetun.* blood. (Mo:159)
laa-t *Welaun.* blood.
rara *Kisar.* blood.
rara(n) *Ili'uun.* blood. (dJ:135)

***dae** *PRM.* soil, land, earth. *Etym:* *daRəq 'soil, probably clay'. *[irr. from PRM:* *e > *i* in Meto with additional subsequent irregularities in the Meto vowels*] [Form:* regular *ə > *e* /_q#.*]*
dae *Termanu.* soil, land, earth. (J:68)
dae *Korbafo.*
dae *Bokai.*
dae *Bilbaa.*
dae *Rikou.*
dae *Ba'a.*
ɗae *Tii.*
lae *Dengka.*
rae *Oenale.*
nain (2) nai raʔe *Kotos Amarasi.* 1) ground. 2) clay. *Usage:* **nain** occurs in place names and phrases, such as **nai mutiʔ** 'white ground'. (The normal word for ground in Amarasi is **afu**.). *[History:* The second element of **nai raʔe** 'clay' could also be an irregular reflex of ***dae**.*]*

nain *Amanuban/Amanatun.* ground.
naidʒan *Amfo'an.* earth.
naidʒan *Molo.* earth. *[Form:* Insertion of medial *dʒ* is unexpected. It probably came about via a pathway such as **nain > **naiyin > **naiyan.*]* (M:342)
naidʒaan *Baikeno.* earth. (Charles E. Grimes pers. comm.)
nian *Kusa-Manea.* earth. *[Form:* This form is derivable from intermediate **naian with subsequent reduction of the initial vowel sequence.*]*
Out-comparisons:
dale *Semau Helong.* ground.
rai *East Tetun.* earth, soil, ground; land estate, kingdom; the world. (Mo:158)
°**rai** *Kisar.* king. *Borrowed from:* perhaps Tetun, as shown by irr. *R > Ø instead of expected *R > *r* combined with the semantic shift.
ra(ra), rare *Ili'uun.* land, ground, especially in contrast to sea, water. (dJ:134)

***daem** *nRM.* termites.
(ʔ)ana/dae *Termanu.* termites. (J:12)
hana/dae *Korbafo.*
(ʔ)ana/dae *Bokai.*
(ʔ)ana/dae *Bilbaa.*
ʔana/dae *Rikou.* *[Form:* My consultants gave **ʔandae**.*]*
(ʔ)ana/dae *Ba'a.*
(ʔ)ana/ɗae *Tii.*
naem *Ro'is Amarasi.* termites.
naem *Kotos Amarasi.* termites.
<name> *Molo.* flying white ants. *[Form:* Molo may have unmetathesised an original CVVC root.*]* (M:347)
na~naem=aa *Kusa-Manea.* termites.
Out-comparisons:
°**naen** *Semau Helong.* termite. *Borrowed from:* probably Amarasi (shown by irr. *d = *n* correspondence).

***dai** *PMeto.* rooster comb or wattle. *[irr. from PRM:* *i > *e* in Ro'is*]*
took rae-n (2) iuk rae-n *Ro'is Amarasi.* 1) rooster wattle (the bit which hangs down). 2) the long tail feathers of a rooster.
fo/lai-n *Amanuban.* rooster wattle. *[Form:* **nai-n** = 'chicken/rooster comb'.*]*
Out-comparisons:
manu lain *East Tetun.* the long tail feathers of a rooster. (Mo:124)

***daki** *PRM.* body dirt. *Etym:* *daki 'dirt on skin; dandruff; tartar on teeth'. *Pattern:* k-irr. *[irr. from PRM:* *d > *r* in Meto (expect *n*); *k > *h* /V_V in Meto*]*
daʔi *Termanu.* dirt on the body. (J:71)
daʔi *Korbafo.*
daʔi *Bokai.*
da~daki *Bilbaa.*
daʔi *Rikou.*
daʔi *Ba'a.*
ɗaʔi *Tii.*
rai *Oenale.*
rahi *Kotos Amarasi.* body filth.
lahi *Molo.* skin filth. (M:256)
Out-comparisons:
dakin *Semau Helong.*
raʔi *Hawu.* filth, dirt, body filth.

***dalə** *Morph:* ***dalə-k**. *PRM.* in, inside, feelings. *Etym:* *daləm 'in, area within, inner part of something; between; below, under; deep; mind, feelings, liver (fig.)'.
dale-k *Termanu.* a) inside. b) the interior of a person, the heart, the mind. (J:72)
dale-ʔ *Korbafo.*
dale-k *Bokai.*
dale-ʔ *Bilbaa.*
dale=na *Landu.* seat of emotions. (own field notes)
dale-ʔ *Rikou.*
dale-k *Ba'a.*
ɗale-k *Tii.*
lala-ʔ *Dengka.*
rala-ʔ *Oenale.*

nana|ʔ *Ro'is Amarasi.* inside. *[Note:* **nere-f** = 'seat of emotions'.*]*

nana-f *Kotos Amarasi.* inside, in. *[Note:* **neka-f** = 'seat of emotions'.*]*

<nana> *Molo.* inner, inside. (M:425)

naan *Kusa-Manea.* inside.

Out-comparisons:

dale *Semau Helong.* inside; seat of emotions, lower, ground.

laran *East Tetun.* the interior, the inside part. *[Sporadic:* consonant metathesis *lVr > *rVl]* (Mo:127)

raram (2) rorom *Kisar.* 1) inside. 2) down into earth or into seas, depth.

ɗara *Hawu.* 1) inside. 2) character, seat of emotions, heart, thoughts.

***damei** *PRM.* lick. *Pattern:* d-2. *[irr. from PRM:* *ei > *i* in Meto; *ei > *oi* in Rikou (possibly sporadic assimilation to previous *m)] [Form:* The Galolen and Dadu'a forms are similar to the RM forms, but it is unclear what vowels or medial consonant a higher level reconstruction might have.*] [History:* Ross and Osmond (2016a:268) reconstruct POc *d(r)am^{w}i(s) 'lick (intr.)'.*]*

na-la-mei (2) mei~mei *Termanu.* 1) lick. 2) the tongue of the snake constantly goes in and out, as in licking motion. (J:354)

na-la-mei *Korbafo.*

na-la-mei *Bokai.*

na-la-moi *Bilbaa.*

na-ra-moi, na-la-moi *Rikou.*

na-la-mei *Ba'a.*

na-ra-mei *Tii.*

na-la-mei *Dengka.*

na-ra-mei *Oenale.*

n-rami *Kotos Amarasi.* lick.

lami *Molo.* lick. *[Note:* Jonker (1908:354) gives Meto **lame**.*]* (M:261)

Out-comparisons:

rema *Galolen.* lick, flatter.

rabi *Dadu'a.* lick. (Penn 2006:103)

***daru** *Morph:* ***daru-k, *ma-daru**. *CER.* long, length. *Doublet:* ***naru**. *Etym:* *adaduq.

dalu-k (2) ma-dalu *Termanu.* 1) long. 2) long, length. (J:74)

dalu-ʔ *Korbafo.*

dalu-k *Bokai.*

dalu-ʔ *Bilbaa.*

daru-ʔ *Rikou.*

dalu-k *Ba'a.*

***dei** *Morph:* ***dei-k**. *Rote.* forehead. *Etym:* *daqih.

de~dei-k *Termanu.* forehead. (J:81)

de~dei-ʔ *Korbafo.*

de~dei-k *Bokai.*

de~dei-ʔ *Bilbaa.*

de~dei-ʔ *Rikou.*

lee-ʔ *Dengka.*

ree-ʔ *Oenale.*

Out-comparisons:

ree-n *East Tetun.* forehead, brow. (Mo:160)

***deki** *CER.* kiss. *Pattern:* d-1/2, k-7/8/9/10. *[Note:* Jonker (1908:81) gives Loura (ISO 693-3 [lur]) **diki** as possibly cognate, but I have been unable to locate this form anywhere.*] [irr. from PRM:* *i > *a* in Meto (possibly influence from **neka-f** 'feelings')*] [Form:* The lack of reflexes in wRote and Meto means that the initial consonant is ambiguous between *d and *ɗ. I have tentatively reconstructed *d on the basis of the Helong reflex as this may attest borrowing from Meto or wRote in which *d > *r had taken place. The other out-comparisons provide conflicting evidence for PRM *d and *ɗ. Fehan Tetun would be consistent with PRM *ɗ but East Tetun would be consistent with PRM *d.*]*

deʔi *Termanu.* kiss. (J:81)

deʔi *Korbafo.*

deʔi *Bokai.*

deki *Bilbaa.*
deʔi *Rikou.*
Out-comparisons:
liki *Semau Helong.* kiss, sniff. *[irr. from PRM:* *d = *l* /#_ correspondence*]*
deʔi *Fehan Tetun.* kiss. *[irr. from PRM:* *d = *d* correspondence (expect *r*)*]*
rei *East Tetun.* kiss. (Mo:160)
riʔi *Sika.* kiss. (Pareira and Lewis 1998:174)

***deku** *PnMeto.* strike, knock. *Pattern:* k-5/6.
n-reku *Kotos Amarasi.* strike (e.g. clock).
n-leku *Molo.* knocks. (M:266)
reuk *Kusa-Manea.* hit, knock.
Out-comparisons:
diku *Semau Helong.* hit, pound, punish, flail, whip, beat.
deku *East Tetun.* give light blows, tap, knock. (Mo:23)

***deŋe** *PRM.* kapok tree.
dene *Termanu.* kapok, kapok tree. (J:84)
dene *Korbafo.*
dene *Bokai.*
dene *Bilbaa.*
dene *Rikou.*
dene *Ba'a.*
ɗene *Tii.*
lene *Dengka.*
rene *Oenale.*
neke *Ro'is Amarasi.* kapok tree.
neke *Kotos Amarasi.* kapok tree.
neke *Molo.* kapok tree. (M:361)
Out-comparisons:
deŋen *Semau Helong.* kapok. *[Note:* Jonker (1908:84) gives Helong **kdeŋen/deŋen**.*]*
°**neke** *Fehan Tetun.* kapok. *Borrowed from:* Meto **neke** (shown by irr. *d = *n* correspondence).
riŋi *Bima.* kapok. (Jonker 1893:86)

***deras** *Morph:* ***ka-deras**. *PRM.* tree. Erythrina species. *Etym:* *dəpdəp (Blust and Trussel (ongoing) reconstruct doublets *dəpdəp and *dapdap. The Termanu form appears as evidence for both, though the vowels are not regular from either. They would be regular from (unreconstructed) ***dədap** (final *ə > *e* in Termanu, but *a > *a*).). *[irr. from PMP:* Ø > *s; *ə > *a /_(C)#*] [irr. from PRM:* *a > *e* in Amarasi; *d > *l* in Oenale (possibly sporadic dissimilation from earlier *rVr)*]*
delas *Termanu.* the dedap, or shadow-tree, varieties thereof. (J:82)
dela-ʔ *Korbafo.*
dela-k *Bokai.*
dela-ʔ *Bilbaa.*
deras *Rikou.*
delas *Ba'a.*
ɗeras *Tii.*
lelas *Dengka.*
relas *Oenale.*
ʔ|nenes *Kotos Amarasi.* kind of large tree.
<nenas> *Molo.* kind of tree. Erythrina species. (M:362)
Out-comparisons:
kdela *Helong.* (J:82)

***dete** *PMeto.* Blackboard tree. Alstonia scholaris. *Etym:* *ditaq. *[irr. from PMP:* *i > *e*] [minority from PMP:* *d = *d (expect *d > *r > *l > *n)*] [Sporadic:* *a > *e* /_# in Meto*] [Form:* The PMeto forms are probably cognate with the Tetun form, and both could be derived from earlier **ɗətəq which would require irregular PMP *d > *ɗ and *i > *ə. However, unless the Waima'a form is a borrowing from Tetun, it indicates that Tetun *o* is from earlier *o (*ə > *e* in Waima'a). Despite the phonological problems in explaining the Meto, Tetun and Waima'a forms, they are too similar (and furthermore too similar to PMP *ditaq) to be ignored.*]*

rete *Ro'is Amarasi.* Blackboard tree; a kind of evergreen tree. Alstonia scholaris.
rete *Kotos Amarasi.* Blackboard tree; a kind of evergreen tree. Alstonia scholaris.
lete *Molo.* kind of tree. Alstonia scholaris. (M:271)
Out-comparisons:
(k)doti *East Tetun.* tree whose bark is used as an antifebrile; the bark has two varieties, one white and the other black. Alstonia scholaris. *[Note:* **ai henak** is given as having the same meaning.*]* *[History:* Morris (1984:119) gives **kroti** 'a tree with a very straight trunk' with the same scientific name. Van Klinken (1995) identifies **kroti** as 'a tall thin palm with feathery leaves. Is used to make **balok**, **papan**, **ai riin** (house posts)'.*]* (Mo:27, 104)
doti-buto, doti *Waima'a.* devil tree. Alstonia scholaris.

***dii1** *Morph:* ***na-mba-dii**. *Rote.* stand. *Doublet:* ***dii2**. *Etym:* *diRi. *[irr. from PRM:* *i > *e* in nRote (sporadic medial lowering before *R ?)*]*
na-pa-dei-ʔ (2) na-pa-de-dei *Termanu.* 1) stand, stand still, remain standing. 2) stand something up. (J:80f)
na-pa-dei-ʔ (2) na-pa-de~dei-ʔ *Korbafo.*
na-pa-dei-k (2) na-pa-de~dei *Bokai.*
na-pa-dei-ʔ (2) na-pa-de~dei *Bilbaa.*
na-pa-dei-ʔ (2) na-pa-de~dei *Rikou.*
na-pa-dei-ʔ *Oepao.*
na-mpa-dei-k (2) na-mpa-de~dei *Ba'a.*
na-mba-ɗei-k (2) na-mba-ɗe~ɗei *Tii.*
na-mba-lii-ʔ *Dengka.*
na-mba-rii-ʔ *Oenale.*
Out-comparisons:
dili *Semau Helong.* stand.
harii *East Tetun.* stand upright, straight, erect, or raised. (Mo:78)

***dii2** *PRM.* house post. *Doublet:* ***dii1**. *Etym:* *hadiRi.
dii *Termanu.* pole, stile pillar. (J:86)
dii *Korbafo.*
dii *Bokai.*
dii *Bilbaa.*
dii *Rikou.*
dii *Ba'a.*
ɗii *Tii.*
lii *Dengka.*
rii *Oenale.*
nii *Kotos Amarasi.* pole, post, pillar.
nii *Molo.* pole, mast. (M:367)
Out-comparisons:
hdiin *Semau Helong.* *[irr. from PMP:* *R > Ø (expect *l*)*]*
rii(n) *East Tetun.* column, pillar, post, pier, or stake. (Mo:161)
gerii *Hawu.* pole, post.
agarii *Dhao.* pole, post.

***diʔu** *PMeto.* chase, chase away. *[History:* Given that Kemak has both /r/ and /l/, the Kemak form is most likely a borrowing from a variety of Meto in which PMeto *d > *r > *l.]*
n-riʔu *Ro'is Amarasi.* chase out, expel.
n-riʔu *Kotos Amarasi.* chase out, expel.
n-liʔu *Molo.* chase. (M:279)
Out-comparisons:
liʔu *Kemak.* chase.

***dindi** *PRM.* wall made of dried palm leaf stems. *Etym:* *diŋdiŋ 'wall of a house; partition off'. *[irr. from PRM:* *d > *l* in Lole (expect *d*)*]*
dini *Termanu.* wall, side (of a house) made of **bebak** ['palm leaf stems'], verb **dini uma**, provide a house with a wall. (J:88)

dindi *Rikou.* wall. (own field notes)
diri *Oepao.* wall. (own field notes)
lindi *Lole.* wall. (Zacharias et al. 2014)
li~lindi *Dengka.* (J:88)
ri~rindi *Dela.* palm wall.
ʔ|niki-t (2) <na-niki> *Molo.* 1) wall of a house. 2) protects. (M:369)
na~niki *Kusa-Manea.* edge.
Out-comparisons:
didin *East Tetun.* wall of house, both internal and external. (Mo:25)

***diu** *Morph:* ***na-diu**. *PRM.* bathe. *Etym:* *diRus.
na-diu *Termanu.* bathe. (J:90)
na-diu *Korbafo.*
na-diu *Bokai.*
na-diu *Bilbaa.*
na-diu *Rikou.*
na-diu *Ba'a.*
na-ɗiu *Tii.*
na-liu *Dengka.*
na-riu *Oenale.*
na-niu *Ro'is Amarasi.* bathe.
na-niu *Kotos Amarasi.* bathe.
na-niu *Kusa-Manea.* wash, bathe.
Out-comparisons:
diu *Semau Helong.* bathe, wash. *[irr. from PMP:* *R > Ø (expect *l*)*]*
hariis *East Tetun.* bathe, take a bath. (Mo:78)

***domi** *PMeto.* love, like. *[History:* Ross and Osmond (2016b:545) reconstruct POc *drom-i (from PMP *dəmdəm) 'think, worry; love, be sorry for, long for', but the similarity between this form and the PMeto form may be chance.*]*
n-romi *Ro'is Amarasi.* like, want to.
n-romi *Kotos Amarasi.* like, want to.
n-lomi *Molo.* like. (M:285)
Out-comparisons:
hadomi *East Tetun.* love, give love, have an affection for. (Mo:43)
domi *Waima'a.* love.
domi *Mambae, South.* love. (Fogaça 2017:267)
adomi *Welaun.* love, like. (da Silva 2012:113)

***doo** *Morph:* ***doo-k**. *PRM.* leaf. *Etym:* *dahun. *[Sporadic:* *VV-k > *VVʔ > VʔV in Amarasi (perceptual metathesis)*]*
doo-k *Termanu.* leaf. (J:92)
doo-ʔ *Korbafo.*
doo-k *Bokai.*
doo-ʔ *Bilbaa.*
doo=na *Landu.* leaf. (own field notes)
doo-ʔ *Rikou.*
doo-k *Ba'a.*
ɗoo-k *Tii.*
loo-ʔ *Dengka.*
roo-ʔ *Oenale.*
noʔo *Ro'is Amarasi.* leaf.
noʔo, noo-f *Kotos Amarasi.* leaf.
nooʔ *Molo.* leaves of trees. (M:375)
noʔo-k, noo-n *Kusa-Manea.* leaf.
Out-comparisons:
roon *Ili'uun.* leaf. (dJ:136)

***dua** *PRM.* two. *Etym:* *duha.
dua *Termanu.* two, both. (J:103)
dua *Korbafo.*
dua *Bokai.*
dua *Bilbaa.*
dua *Rikou.*
dua *Ba'a.*
ɗua *Tii.*
lua *Dengka.*
rua *Oenale.*
nua *Ro'is Amarasi.*
nua *Kotos Amarasi.*
nuga *Amfo'an.* two. *[Form:* Medial consonants in Amfo'an and Baikeno are a result of fortition of a medial phonetic glide.*]*
nua *Molo.* two. (M:388)
nuban *Baikeno.* two. (Charles E. Grimes pers. comm.)
nua *Kusa-Manea.* two.

Out-comparisons:
dua *Semau Helong.* two.
rua *East Tetun.* two. (Mo:162)
woroʔo *Kisar.* two.

***dui1** *Morph:* ***dui-k.** *PRM.* bone. *Etym:* *duRi 'thorn, splinter, fish bone' (Helong retains the meaning 'thorn'.).
dui-k *Termanu.* bone. (J:106)
dui-ʔ *Korbafo.*
dui-k *Bokai.*
dui-ʔ *Bilbaa.*
dui-ʔ *Landu.* bone. (own field notes)
dui-ʔ *Rikou.*
dui-k *Ba'a.*
ɗui-k *Tii.*
lui-ʔ *Dengka.*
rui-ʔ *Oenale.*
nui-f *Ro'is Amarasi.* bone.
nui-f *Kotos Amarasi.* bone.
nui-f *Amanuban.* bone.
nui-f *Molo.* bone. (M:390)
nui-f *Kusa-Manea.* bone.
Out-comparisons:
duliʔ *Semau Helong.* thorn.
rui-n *East Tetun.* bone, bones of the skeleton. (Mo:162)
lui-t *Welaun.* bone.
ruri (2) rurna *Kisar.* 1) thorn. 2) bones.
rurin *Ili'uun.* bone. (dJ:136)

***dui2** *Rote.* dugong. *Etym:* *duyuŋ (Blust and Trussel (ongoing) posit PCEMP *ruyuŋ, but initial *r cannot regularly account for the PRM form or Helong **duiŋ**.). *Pattern:* d-2.
lui-k *Termanu.* sea cow. (J:332)
lui-ʔ *Korbafo.*
lui-k *Bokai.*
lui-ʔ *Bilbaa.*
rui-ʔ *Rikou.*
lui-k *Ba'a.*
rui-k *Tii.*
lui-ʔ *Dengka.*
rui-ʔ *Oenale.*
lui *Meto.* (J:332)
Out-comparisons:
duiŋ *Helong.* (J:332)

***duman** *PRM.* some. *Pattern:* d-2. *[Note:* Jonker (1908) gives **ruma** as being found in Seram and Ambon, but I have been unable to track down his source.*]*
luma *Termanu.* portion, some, a few. (J:333)
luma *Korbafo.*
luma *Bokai.*
luma *Bilbaa.*
ruma *Rikou.*
luma *Ba'a.*
ruma *Tii.*
luma *Dengka.*
ruma *Oenale.*
rumun *Ro'is Amarasi.* empty.
ruman (2) ruum *Kotos Amarasi.* 1) empty. 2) plain, 'emptily', without anything extra. *[Note:* Jonker (1908:333) glosses Meto **luum, ruum** as 'just, plainly'.*]*
luman *Molo.* empty. (M:292)
ruman *Kusa-Manea.* empty, blank.
Out-comparisons:
ruman *Fehan Tetun.* some.
ruma *East Tetun.* some, any, several, few. (Mo:162)

***dupi** *PnMeto.* wall. *Etym:* **dumbi (pre-Meto).
krupit, rupit *Kotos Amarasi.* wall.
klupit, lupit, klipi, klipit *Molo.* wall (of a house). (M:218, 369)
Out-comparisons:
rupi *Kisar.* wall, make walls of the house, plaster walls(?).

Ɗ - ɗ

***ɗada** *PRM.* warm near a fire. *Etym:* *daŋdaŋ 'warm oneself or something near a fire; heat or dry near a fire'. *Pattern:* d-2. *[minority from PMP:* *d > *ɗ (expect *d)*]*

dala (2) dala haʔi *Termanu.* 1) roast. 2) warm oneself by a fire, warm up, like a woman after childbirth. (J:72)

dala *Korbafo.*

dala *Bokai.*

dala *Bilbaa.*

dara *Rikou.*

dala *Ba'a.*

ɗara *Tii.*

ɗala *Dengka.*

ɗara *Oenale.*

n-rara *Ro'is Amarasi.* warm oneself by a fire.

n-rara *Kotos Amarasi.* warm oneself by a fire.

malalaʔ *Amfo'an.* hot.

n-lala *Molo.* roast, warm oneself. (M:259)

Out-comparisons:

eʔ-rara (2) eʔ-rara-n *Buru.* 1) warm over fire. 2) heat, fever. (Grimes and Grimes 2020:245)

***ɗade** *PRM.* basil. *Pattern:* d-2. *[irr. from PRM:* *a > *e* in Meto; *d > *r* in Amarasi*]* *[Sporadic:* antepenultimate vowel reduction in most Rote.*]*

dala_dae, dale_dae *Termanu.* basil. (J:72)

dali_dai *Bokai.*

dara_dae *Rikou.*

dala_dai *Ba'a.*

ɗara_ɗae *Tii.*

ɗale_mbake *Dengka.*

ɗare_ɗae *Oenale.*

ɗare *Dela.* basil.

to/rere *Ro'is Amarasi.* basil. *[Form:* The source of initial **to** is currently unknown.*]*

to/rere *Kotos Amarasi.* basil.

to/lene, to/nene *Molo.* kind of mint. (M:569)

to/nena-l *Timaus.* basil. *[Form:* regular *a > *e* word finally.*]*

***ɗafu₁** *Morph:* ***ka-ɗafu**. *PRM.* useless, waste. *[Form:* Helong indicates earlier medial *b.*]*

ka|dafu-k (2) na-ka-da~dafu *Termanu.* 1) garbage, dry garbage. 2) make dirty. (J:70)

ka|dafu-ʔ *Korbafo.*

ka|dafu-k *Bokai.*

ka|dafu-ʔ *Bilbaa.*

ka|dafu-ʔ *Rikou.*

ka|dafu-k *Ba'a.*

ka|ɗafu-k *Tii.*

ka|ɗafu-ʔ *Dengka.*

ka|ɗafu-ʔ *Oenale.*

k|rafun *Kotos Amarasi.* useless.

<ma(k)lafu> *Molo.* dust, riddle. (M:255)

Out-comparisons:

dabun *Semau Helong.* not enough.

(k)rahuk *East Tetun.* brittle, fragile. (Mo:158)

***ɗafu₂** *Morph:* ***ɗafu~ɗafu**. *PRM.* chaotic, random.

dafu~dafu *Termanu.* indifferent, wrong. (J:69)

dafu~dafu *Korbafo.*

dafu~dafu *Bokai.*

dafu~dafu *Bilbaa.*

dafu~dafu *Rikou.*

dafu~dafu *Ba'a.*

ɗafu~ɗafu *Tii.*

ɗafu~ɗafu *Dengka.*

ɗafu~ɗafu *Oenale.*

rafuʔ~rafuʔ *Kotos Amarasi.* without cause, reason, or purpose, or thought as to the consequences, usually resulting in chaos for someone.

lafuʔ~lafuʔ *Molo.* in a wild manner. (M:255)

Out-comparisons:

da~dahut, dahut~dahut *Semau Helong.* messy, chaotic, commotion, uproar, tumult.

rahuk (2) rahun (3) rahu~rahun *East Tetun.* 1) rain in large scattered drops. 2) powder, small fragments, small pieces. 3) small things, little objects. (Mo:158)

***ɗai1** *Morph:* ***na-ɗai**. *PRM.* store, put inside.

na-dai *Termanu.* put something in somewhere, store. (J:71)

na-dai *Korbafo.*

na-dai *Bokai.*

na-dai *Bilbaa.*

na-dai *Rikou.*

na-dai *Ba'a.*

na-ɗai *Tii.*

na-ɗai *Dengka.*

na-ɗai *Oenale.*

na-ɗai *Dela.* fill (bottle).

na-rai *Kotos Amarasi.* put inside, fill.

na-lai *Meto.* (J:71)

Out-comparisons:

rai *East Tetun.* put down, retain, remain, keep, to guard. (Mo:158)

rai *Waima'a.* put, lay.

***ɗai2** *Rote.* reach, arrive at.

dai *Termanu.* reach, arrive at. (J:70)

dai *Korbafo.*

dai *Bokai.*

dai *Bilbaa.*

dai *Rikou.*

dai *Ba'a.*

ɗai *Tii.*

ɗai *Dengka.*

ɗai *Oenale.*

Out-comparisons:

ɗai *Hawu.* arrive, until, the point that. *[Form:* **ɗae** = singular.*]*

***ɗalan** *PRM.* path. *Etym:* *zalan.

dala-k *Termanu.* course. *[Semantics:* In Termanu the meaning is restricted to 'course'; in other Rote varieties the meaning is broader.*]* (J:72)

dala-ʔ *Korbafo.* course, way.

dala-k *Bokai.*

dala-ʔ *Bilbaa.*

dala-ʔ *Rikou.*

dala-k *Ba'a.*

ɗala-k *Tii.*

ɗala-ʔ *Dengka.*

ɗala-ʔ *Oenale.*

ɗala-ʔ *Dela.* way, path, road.

ranan *Ro'is Amarasi.* way, path, road.

ranan *Kotos Amarasi.* way, path, road.

lanan *Amanuban.* way. (M:259)

lalan *Molo.* way. *[Form:* regular *n > *l* /lC_.*]* (M:259)

ranan *Kusa-Manea.* way, path, road.

Out-comparisons:

lalan *Semau Helong.* road, trail, path.

dalan *East Tetun.* road, track, path. (Mo:22)

saal *Mambae, South.* road, path, way. (Grimes et al. 2014b:39)

salan *Galolen.* road, path, way.

ʄara *Dhao.* path, trail, road, way.

kalla *Kisar.* road, path, street.

sala(n) *Ili'uun.* road, path, way. (dJ:136)

ruʄara *Hawu.* way, path, road.

***ɗama** *PRM.* resin, gum, plaster. *Etym:* *damaR 'resin or gum exuded by certain trees, notably of the genera <u>Shorea</u> and <u>Hopea</u>; resinous torch; resinous tree'. *[minority from PMP:* *d > *ɗ (expect *d)*]* *[Sporadic:* *a > *e* /_# in Meto.*]* *[History:* If this is a borrowing (from Malay *damar* or similar), then it is an early borrowing as final *a > *e* in Meto does not otherwise occur in loans.*]*

dama *Termanu.* a) gum, resin. b) **dama ofa-k** tar a boat. From that, more generally: cover with; also: work with mortar, or concrete masonry: **dama uma**, plaster a house; **dama lates**, make a grave with mortar; **late na-na-dama-k**, a plastered grave or a grave made with mortar. (J:74)
dama *Korbafo.*
dama *Bokai.*
dama *Bilbaa.*
dama *Rikou.*
dama *Ba'a.*
ɗama *Tii.*
ɗama *Dengka.*
ɗama *Oenale.*
ɗama *Dela.* build concrete wall.
rameʔ (2) n-rame *Kotos Amarasi.* 1) concrete wall, safety, security. 2) plaster, build concrete wall. *[Semantics:* The semantic expansion to include 'concrete' is obviously recent.*]*
Out-comparisons:
°**dame** *Helong.* tar, plaster, cover. *Borrowed from:* Meto before *ɗ > *r* (shown by final *a = *e* correspondence). (J:74)

***ɗano** *Rote.* lake. *Etym:* *danaw. *[minority from PMP:* *d > *ɗ (expect *d)*] [History:* possibly a borrowing from Malay *danau* or similar.*]*
dano *Termanu.* lake, pool. (J:75)
dano *Korbafo.*
dano *Bokai.*
dano *Bilbaa.*
dano *Rikou.*
dano *Ba'a.*
ɗano *Tii.*
ɗano *Dengka.*
ɗano *Oenale.*

***ɗaŋga**1 *PRM.* step over. *[History:* possibly connected with PMP *laŋkaq.*]*
daŋa *Termanu.* softly tiptoe, step over. **<ana danga seli-n>** he steps over him (J:75)
daŋa *Korbafo.*
daŋa *Bokai.*
daŋa *Bilbaa.*
daka *Rikou.*
daŋga *Ba'a.*
ɗaŋga *Tii.*
ɗaŋga *Dengka.*
ɗaŋga *Oenale.*
n-raka, n-rakan *Kotos Amarasi.* step over, cross, stride.
n-laka *Molo.* steps over. (M:256)

***ɗaŋga**2 *PwRM.* hand span. *Etym:* *zaŋkal (PWMP. Blust and Trussel (ongoing) also reconstruct PMP *zaŋan 'hand span'.).
ɗaŋga *Dengka.* span. (J:621,686)
n-raka (2) raka-t *Kotos Amarasi.* 1) measure with hand span. 2) hand span.
hae-n laka-n (2) <nima-n> laka-n *Molo.* 1) step of foot. 2) span of hand. (M:256)
Out-comparisons:
daŋa *Semau Helong.* span of hand, inch. *[Note:* Jonker (1908:621) gives Helong **sdaŋa**.*]*

***ɗasi** *nRM.* discussion, speech.
dasi (2) dasi-k *Termanu.* 1) singing of birds; used in combination with **soda** [OE = 'sing']. Also (though less common in Termanu): say, tell (frequently with this meaning in poems). 2) song (also of people), speech, word. *Usage:* mainly poetic. (J:76)
ɗasi *Tii.* discuss, speak. (Grimes et al. 2014a)
rasi *Ro'is Amarasi.* matter, affair, issue.
rasi *Kotos Amarasi.* matter (non-physical), affair, issue.
lasi *Molo.* case, ritual, story, lawsuit. (M:263)
rasi *Kusa-Manea.* language, speech.
Out-comparisons:
dasi *Semau Helong.* language, matter, thing, dispute, litigation, affairs.

***ɗee** *PRM.* subordinating particle.
dee *Termanu.* and, and then, and therefore. (J:76)
dee *Korbafo.*
dee *Bokai.*
dee *Bilbaa.*
dee *Rikou.*
dee *Ba'a.*
ɗee *Tii.*
ɗee *Dengka.*
ɗee *Oenale.*
ɗe *Dela.* then, thus, so.
heʔ *Ro'is Amarasi.* RELATIVISER. *[irr. from PRM:* *r > *h]*
reʔ *Kotos Amarasi.* a) general purpose relativiser, including time ('when') and location ('where'). b) marker of an NP that is already a known referent.
leʔ *Molo.* which. (M:264)
on roʔ *Kusa-Manea.* like, similar to. *Usage:* In Amarasi **on** and **on reʔ** (when the following NP is a topic) are used to mean 'like'. Kusa-Manea **roʔ** has not yet been attested without preceding **on**. *[irr. from PRM:* *e > *o]*
Out-comparisons:
ʄe *Hawu.* then, while. Realis, indicating actual action or result.

***ɗeha** *Rote.* speak.
deʔa (2) de~deʔa-k *Termanu.* 1) say, speak. 2) that which is said, saying, word, language, report; therefore: matter. (J:79)
deʔa (2) de~deʔa-ʔ *Korbafo.*
deʔa (2) de~deʔa-k *Bokai.*
dea (2) de~dea-ʔ *Bilbaa.*
de~dea *Landu.* speak. (own field notes)
dea (2) de~dea-ʔ *Rikou.*
deʔa (2) de~deʔa-k *Ba'a.*
ɗeʔa (2) ɗe~ɗeʔa-k *Tii.*
(2) ɗe~ɗea-t *Dengka.*
(2) ɗe~ɗea-t *Oenale.*
Out-comparisons:
dehet (2) nahdehe *Semau Helong.* 1) story, news, language. 2) talk, tell a story. *[irr. from PRM:* *a = *e* correspondence*]*
deʔan *Fehan Tetun.* speak angrily; speak abusively (e.g. 'you're a dog').
dehan *East Tetun.* speak. (Mo:23)

***ɗeke** *Morph:* ***ɗeke-k**. *Rote.* kernel, pip of fruit. *Pattern:* k-7.
deʔe-k *Termanu.* kernel, pip of fruit. (J:80)
deʔe-ʔ *Korbafo.*
deʔe-k *Bokai.*
deke-ʔ *Bilbaa.*
deke-ʔ *Rikou.*
deʔe-k *Ba'a.*
ɗeʔe-k *Tii.*
ɗeke-ʔ *Dengka.*
ɗeke-ʔ *Oenale.*
Out-comparisons:
ai tahan dikin *East Tetun.* bud, shoot, sprout. *[Form:* Jonker (1908:80) gives Tetun Dili **dikin** = 'eye, knot of a plant'.*]* (Mo:2)

***ɗeʔu** *PwRM.* sacred, awe inspiring, awful, bad.
ɗeʔu *Dengka.* cattle plague. (J:688)
reʔu (2) reʔuf (3) n-reʔu *Kotos Amarasi.* 1) sacred, holy, awe-inspiring. 2) bad, evil. 3) broken.
leʔu *Molo.* magic. (M:272)
na-mreuʔ *Kusa-Manea.* broken.

***ɗele** *PRM.* Job's tears. <u>*Coix lachryma-jobi*</u>. *Etym:* *zəlay.
dele *Termanu.* kind of millet, which is a staple food in eastern Rote. (J:82)
dele *Korbafo.*
dele *Bokai.*
dele *Bilbaa.*
dele *Rikou.*
dele *Ba'a.*
ɗele *Tii.*
ɗele *Dengka.*
ɗele *Oenale.*

°**sone** *Ro'is Amarasi.* Job's tears. *Borrowed from:* Welaun (or extinct related language) **sole** before *l > *n* in Meto. For Welaun *z > *s* and *ə > *o* are both regular.
°**sone** *Kotos Amarasi.* Job's tears.
°**sone** *Molo.* kind of grain. (M:513)
Out-comparisons:
sele *Kemak.* corn, maize.
sole (2) sole fatun *Welaun.* 1) corn, maize. 2) Job's tears. *[Note:* **fatun** = 'stone'.*]* *[Semantics:* It is likely that the original designation was 'Job's tears' and that maize was assimilated as a kind of Job's tears. With increased importance of corn at the expense of Job's tears, the core semantic meaning also shifted. See the discussion under ***mbela**.*]*
sela *Mambae, Northwest.* corn, maize. (Fogaça 2017:236)
°**tsele** *Fataluku.* corn, maize. *Borrowed from:* an Austronesian language. *[Note:* non-Austronesian language of east Timor ISO 639-3 [ddg].*]* (Heston 2015:84)
***ɗeli** *CERM.* tendril, vine.
deli *Termanu.* kind of climbing plant with bean shaped fruit, small oval leaves, and blue flowers with white calyx. (J:83)
uut k|reni|ʔ *Ro'is Amarasi.* pumpkin tendril.
k|reni|ʔ *Kotos Amarasi.* tendril (particularly of a pumpkin).
***ɗene** *nRM.* field, garden. *[irr. from PRM:* *ɗ > *r* ~ *l* in Rikou and Bilbaa for the second sense*]*
na-dene *Termanu.* give a field (etc.) to others in return for the cost of wages. (J:84)
na-dene *Korbafo.*
na-dene *Bokai.*
na-dene (2) lene *Bilbaa.* 2) wet rice field. (J:721)
na-dene (2) rene *Rikou.* 2) wet rice field. (J:721)
na-dene *Ba'a.*
na-ɗene *Tii.*
rene *Ro'is Amarasi.* field.
rene *Kotos Amarasi.* field.
lene *Amanuban.* field. (M:267)
lele-l *Amfo'an.* field. *[Form:* regular *n > *l* /lC_.*]*
lele *Molo.* garden. *[Form:* regular *n > *l* /lC_.*]* (M:267)
rene *Kusa-Manea.* field.
***ɗenu** *Morph:* ***na-ɗenu**. *PRM.* order, command.
na-denu *Termanu.* send someone; command. (J:84)
na-denu *Korbafo.*
na-denu *Bokai.*
na-denu *Bilbaa.*
na-denu *Rikou.*
na-denu *Ba'a.*
na-ɗenu *Tii.*
ɗenu *Dengka.*
ɗenu *Oenale.*
n-renu *Kotos Amarasi.* order, command.
n-lenu *Amanuban.* commands. (M:268)
n-lelu *Molo.* commands. *[Form:* regular *n > *l* /lC_.*]* (M:268)
reun *Kusa-Manea.* order, command.
Out-comparisons:
donu *Welaun.* order, command.
***ɗere** *Rote.* beat a drum.
dele labu *Termanu.* beat the drum quickly, beat the ruffle, ruffle up. (J:82)
dele *Korbafo.*
dele *Bilbaa.* beat.
dere *Rikou.*
de~dele *Ba'a.*
ɗere *Tii.*
ɗele *Dengka.* beat.
ɗere *Oenale.*

Out-comparisons:
dele *Helong.* beat. (J:82)
dere *East Tetun.* give repeated blows with a hitting implement. (Mo:24)
ɗere *Hawu.* (J:82)

***ɗero** *Morph:* ***ka-ɗero**. *PRM.* citrus. *[History:* Ultimately connected with Malay *jeruk* [ʤeruʔ] or a related form, but *l > *n* in Meto indicates this was an early borrowing.*]*
delo *Termanu.* all kinds of citrus trees and fruit. (J:83)
delo *Korbafo.*
delo *Bokai.*
dero *Bilbaa.*
dero munde *Landu.* (own field notes)
delo *Ba'a.*
ɗelo *Tii.*
ɗelo-ʔ *Dengka.*
ɗero *Oenale.*
reno|ʔ *Ro'is Amarasi.* sweet orange.
ʔ|reno|ʔ *Kotos Amarasi.* sweet orange.
<lelo> *Molo.* orange (fruit). Citrus species. (M:268)
ʔ|lelo|ʔ *Timaus.* citrus.
reno|ʔ *Kusa-Manea.* citrus.
Out-comparisons:
derok *East Tetun.* orange fruit. (Mo:24)

***ɗeta** *Rote.* dip, dunk.
deta *Termanu.* dip. (J:85)
deta *Korbafo.*
deta *Bokai.*
deta *Bilbaa.*
deta *Rikou.*
deta *Ba'a.*
ɗeta *Tii.*
ɗetaʔ *Dengka.*
ɗeta *Oenale.*
Out-comparisons:
ketəɗa *Hawu. [irr. from PRM:* consonant metathesis*]* (J:85)
<dàtalu> *Kambera.* momentarily touch. *[Note:* also in Mangili, Lewa, and Anakalang.*]* (On:33)
<dàtala> *Mamboru.*
<dètala> *Weyewa.*

***ɗeu** *Rote.* make a fire, strike up a fire with a fire lighter.
deu *Termanu.* make a fire, strike up a fire with a fire lighter. (J:85)
deu *Korbafo.*
deu *Bokai.*
deu *Bilbaa.*
deu *Rikou.*
deu *Ba'a.*
ɗeu *Tii.*
ɗeu *Dengka.*
ɗeu *Oenale.*
Out-comparisons:
ɗeu *Hawu.* (J:85)

***ɗəma** *PRM.* deep. *[irr. from PRM:* *ɗ > *r* in Dela (expect *d*); *ə > *o* in Dela*]*
ma-dema (2) na-ma-dema (3) dema-k (4) na-dema *Termanu.* 1) high, deep. 2) be or become high or deep. 3) high, height, deep, depth. 4) make high or deep. (J:83)
ma-dema *Korbafo.*
ma-dema *Bokai.*
ma-dema *Bilbaa.*
ma-dema *Rikou.*
ma-dema *Ba'a.*
ma-ɗema *Lole.* tall, high, deep. (Zacharias et al. 2014)
ma-ɗema *Tii.*
ma-ɗema *Dengka.*
roma-ʔ *Dela.* deep.
n-rema *Kotos Amarasi.* drown.
n-lema *Molo.* drown. (M:268)
Out-comparisons:
merəma *Hawu.* deep.
ɹəma *Ende.* deep.
ləmaŋ *Sika.* deep or far-away place. *[irr. from PRM:* *ɗ = *l* correspondence*]* (Pareira and Lewis 1998:12)
ləma *Ngadha.* deep. (Djawanai 1995:Part 4, 1)

***ɗəmbə** *PRM.* dip into. *[irr. from PRM:* *ə > *o* in Rote*]*
dope *Termanu.* dip. (J:101)
dope *Korbafo.*

dope *Bokai.*
dope *Rikou.*
dompe *Ba'a.*
ɗombe *Tii.*
ɗombo *Dela.* dip, swim.
na-repaʔ *Kotos Amarasi.* dip.
<n-lepe> *Molo.* dip, dunk. (M:270)
Out-comparisons:
dopon *Semau Helong.* dip.

***ɗii1** *Morph:* ***ka-ɗii**. *PwRM.* left (side). *Doublet:* ***kii**. *Etym:* *di-wiRi (combination of ***di** 'locative case marker' and ***wiRi** 'left side or direction'.).
ɗii *Dengka.* left, north. (J:688)
ɗii-ʔ *Oenale.* left, north. (J:688)
ʔ|rii *Kotos Amarasi.* left.
ʔ|lii *Molo.* left. (M:273)
Out-comparisons:
kliu *Semau Helong. [irr. from PRM:* *ɗ = *l* correspondence*]*
mariri *Kisar.* left.

***ɗii2** *PRM.* whinny. *[Semantics: onomatopoeia.]*
na-ka-dii *Termanu.* make the sound *dii*, whinny of a horse. (J:86)
na-ka-dii *Korbafo.*
na-ka-dii *Bokai.*
na-ka-dii *Bilbaa.*
na-dii *Rikou.*
na-ka-dii *Ba'a.*
na-ka-ɗii *Tii.*
na-ʔa-ɗii *Dengka.*
na-ʔa-ɗii *Oenale.*
eku_lii, euk_rii *Meto.* whinny. (J:86)

***ɗiki** *PRM.* small. *Etym:* *dikit 'little, few, small in amount'. *Pattern:* k-7. *[minority from PMP:* *d > *ɗ (expect *d)*] [irr. from PRM:* *ɗ > *h* in Dengka*]*
ka-diʔi *Termanu.* be(come) small. (J:86)
ka-diʔi *Korbafo.*
ka-diʔi *Ba'a.*
ka-ɗiʔi *Tii.*
ana_hiki-ʔ *Dengka.* small. (J:677)
ana_ɗiki-ʔ *Oenale.* small. (J:677)
ana_ɗiki-ʔ (2) ana_hiki-ʔ *Dela.* 1) small child. 2) small.
riʔi|t (2) riʔ/anaʔ (3) riʔ/feto (4) riʔ/mone *Kotos Amarasi.* 1) younger sibling. 2) child. 3) girl. 4) boy.
liʔa|t (2) liʔ/mone (3) liʔ/feto *Molo.* 1) young man. 2) boy. 3) girl. (M:273)
Out-comparisons:
kiʔik *East Tetun.* small or little in size. *[irr. from PMP:* *d > *k]* (Mo:107)
iki *Hawu.* tiny, small.
ʕiki *Dhao.* tiny, small.

***ɗila1** *Morph:* ***ɗila-k**. *CER.* wing. *See:* ***liɗa**.
dila-ʔ *Landu.* (own field notes)
dila-ʔ *Rikou.*
dila-ʔ *Oepao.* (own field notes)
Out-comparisons:
kdilaʔ, klilaʔ *Funai Helong.* wing.
dilaʔ *Semau Helong.* wing.
dila/paan *Kemak.* wing. *Usage:* Leosibe dialect.

***ɗila2** *Rote.* shine, glitter. *Etym:* *dilap 'sparkle, shine'. *[minority from PMP:* *d > *ɗ*]*
na-ŋa-dila (2) dila~dila *Termanu.* 1) shine, glitter. 2) shine, glitter. (J:87)
na-ŋa-dila *Korbafo.*
na-ŋa-dila *Bokai.*
na-ŋa-dila *Bilbaa.*
na-ka-dila *Rikou.*
na-ŋga-dila *Ba'a.*
na-ŋga-ɗilak *Tii.*
na-ʔa-ɗilaʔ *Dengka.*

***ɗilah** *PRM.* bael, wood apple. Aegle marmelos. *[Semantics:* The designation was almost certainly a native tree, probably the bael/wood apple (Aegle marmelos), which has fruit similar to the pomegranate. The pomegranate was then classified as a sub-type of this tree and eventually took over the meaning entirely.*]*

dila-k (2) dila dae loo-k *Termanu.* 1) kind of wild pomegranate tree. 2) the normal pomegranate. (J:87)
dila-ʔ *Korbafo.*
dila-k *Bokai.*
dila(-ʔ) *Bilbaa. [Form:* final **-ʔ** given with a question mark.*]*
dila(-ʔ) *Rikou. [Form:* final **-ʔ** given with a question mark.*]*
dila boi-k *Ba'a.*
ɗila-k *Tii.*
ɗila *Dengka.*
ɗila *Oenale.*
rinah *Ro'is Amarasi.* kind of tree with a fruit like a pomegranate.
rinah (2) riin fui *Kotos Amarasi.* 1) pomegranate. 2) kind of tree with a fruit like a pomegranate which grows in the wild.
liin hau (2) liin kase *Amanuban.* 1) kind of tree the fruit of which has a gelatinous fluid. Aegle marmelos. 2) kind of pomegranate. (M:275)
lilah (2) liil kase, lila kase *Molo.* 1) kind of tree whose fruit has gelatinous fluid. Aegle marmelos. 2) kind of pomegranate. Punica granatum. *[Form:* regular *n > *l* / lC_.*]* (M:275)
rinah *Kusa-Manea.* pomegranate.

Out-comparisons:

dila *Fehan Tetun.* pomegranate, pawpaw.
ai dila (2) ai dila tukun, ai dila fatuk *East Tetun.* 1) pawpaw tree and fruit. (Mo:2) 2) tree known as the quince tree of Timor, bearing hard orange coloured fruit. (Mo:25)
kai dile wai *Waima'a.* bael fruit. Aegle marmelos.
<diliméné> *Kisar.* pomegranate. Punica granatum. (Heyne 1950:1158, lxxxv)
dila *Kemak.* papaya, paw-paw.
dila *Welaun.* papaya, paw-paw.
dila *Mambae, Northwest.* papaya. (Fogaça 2017:235)

***ɗio** *Morph:* ***ɗio-t**. *PRM.* crushed grain.
di~dio-k (2) dio-k *Termanu.* 1) grit of grains. 2) kind of rash on the face with (the appearance of) the grit of granules. (J:89)
di~dio-ʔ (2) dio-ʔ *Korbafo.*
kadio-k (2) dio-k *Bokai.*
kadio-ʔ (2) dio-ʔ *Bilbaa.*
(2) dio-ʔ *Rikou.*
di~dio-k (2) dio-k *Ba'a.*
ɗi~ɗio-k (2) ɗio-k *Tii.*
ɗi~ɗio-ʔ (2) ɗio-t *Dengka.*
ɗi~ɗio-ʔ (2) ɗio-t *Oenale.*
reo|t *Kotos Amarasi.* crushed grains (typically corn or rice). *[Sporadic:* vowel height harmony *i > *e* /_o.*]*
lio|t *Amanatun.* crushed rice grains. (M:278)
leo|t *Molo.* fine grains of crushed rice or maize. (M:270)

***ɗitə** *PRM.* gum, resin, glue, sticky, stick to. *[irr. from PRM:* *ə > *a* in Ba'a*] [Sporadic:* *ə > *e* /σ_# in wRote (perhaps *ə > *a > *e* /_#).*] [History:* Blust and Trussel (ongoing) reconstruct PAN *ditəq 'sticky substance' on the basis of the Termanu reflex and Amis **ditaʔ** 'a lump of clay for making pottery; clay; a type of soil'. Unless more evidence is forthcoming, I do not find this reconstruction convincing. They also reconstruct PMP *litəq 'sap of a tree or plant' on the basis of much better evidence, though this reconstruction cannot account regularly for the forms given here.*]*
di~dite (2) na-ka-dite *Termanu.* 1) plant gum, bird lime. 2) be sticky, stick to. (J:89)
di~dite *Korbafo.*
di~dite *Bokai.*
di~dite *Bilbaa.*
di~dita *Ba'a.*
ɗi~ɗite *Tii.*
ɗite *Dengka.*

ɗite *Oenale.*
n-rita (2) a-rita-s *Kotos Amarasi.* 1) frozen, coagulated (can be said of blood or liquid). 2) thick (e.g. of milk).
n-liit (2) <lit> *Molo.* 1) sticks to, cures (milk). 2) glue, adhesive. (M:278)
Out-comparisons:
°litas *Semau Helong.* thick. **Eta unit ta litas son nam nakin tia.** When the sugar is thick, take it off the heat. *Borrowed from:* Meto **rita-s** (shown by irr. *ɗ = *l* correspondence and final *s*).
ritan (2) ha-ritan *East Tetun.* 1) resin, gum. (Mo:161) 2) glue, stick together with glue, gum or resin. *[irr. from PRM:* *ɗ = *r* correspondence*]* (Mo:78)
krite *Waima'a.* sticky.

***ɗoa** *PRM.* burp, belch. *[Sporadic:* glottal stop insertion in Meto.*]*
doa *Termanu.* have an eructation, burp. (J:92)
doa *Korbafo.*
doa *Bokai.*
doa *Bilbaa.*
doa *Rikou.*
doa *Ba'a.*
ɗoa *Tii.*
ɗoa *Dengka.*
ɗoa *Oenale.*
ɗoa *Dela.* burp.
n-roʔa *Ro'is Amarasi.* vomit.
n-roʔa *Kotos Amarasi.* vomit.
n-looʔ *Molo.* throws up. (M:280)
roaʔ *Kusa-Manea.* vomit.
Out-comparisons:
deaŋ *Semau Helong.* burp, belch. *[irr. from PRM:* *o = *e* correspondence*]*

***ɗoɗo** *PRM.* kill by stabbing. *Etym:* *dodok 'pierce, stab' (PCMP). *[minority from PMP:* *d > *ɗ /#_; *d > *ɗ /V_V*]*
dodo *Termanu.* slit the throat, slaughter. (J:94)
dodo *Korbafo.*
dodo *Bokai.*
dodo *Ba'a.*
ɗoɗo *Tii.*
ɗoɗo *Dengka.*
n-roro *Ro'is Amarasi.* kill.
n-roro *Kotos Amarasi.* kill by stabbing. *[Semantics:* Does not refer exclusively to slitting the throat.*]*
n-lolo *Molo.* slaughters. (M:284)
roor *Kusa-Manea.* kill.
Out-comparisons:
dodo *Semau Helong.* technique of multiple stabbing of carotid artery (for goat).

***ɗoi** *PRM.* carry on shoulder with pole.
na-la-doi *Termanu.* carry something on a pole so that the load hangs from one end of the pole above one's back. (J:95)
na-la-doi *Korbafo.*
na-ŋa-doi *Bokai.*
na-ka-doi *Rikou.*
doi *Ba'a.*
na-la-ɗoi *Tii.*
na-ŋga-ɗoi *Dengka.*
ɗoi *Oenale.*
n-roi *Kotos Amarasi.* carry on shoulder with pole.
n-loi *Molo.* carries a pole on his shoulder. (M:282)
roi *Kusa-Manea.* carry.
Out-comparisons:
dui, ɗui *Dhao.* carry on shoulder, carry with a pole.
ɗui *Hawu.* carry on shoulder.
ɗoi *Keo.* carry something with stick on shoulder. *[Note:* language of central Flores ISO 639-3 [xxk].*]* (Baird 2002:547)

***ɗoka** *Morph:* ***ɗoka_daləa-k**. *Rote.* knee cavity. *Pattern:* k-5. *[History:* Perhaps related to PMP *dəkuk 'bow, bend downward', though this requires irr. *d > *ɗ and *ə > *o.*]*

doka_dale(-k) *Termanu.* knee cavity. (J:96)

loka_dale-ʔ *Korbafo.*

doka_dale-k *Bokai.*

doka_dale-k *Ba'a.*

ɗoka_ɗale-k *Tii.*

ɗoka_rala-ʔ *Oenale. [Form:* This form is given as 'resp. **ɗoka_ɗale-ʔ**' but the word for 'inside' in Oenale is **rala-ʔ**.*]*

Out-comparisons:

kerəki *Hawu.* (J:96)

<karoka> *Kambera.* cavity, bend. *[Note:* also in Mangili, Lewa, and Anakalang.*]* (On:188)

<kaleka> *Mamboru.*

***ɗoki** *Morph:* ***ɗo~ɗoki**. *Rote.* desire. *Pattern:* k-5′ (*k > Ø in Rikou; expect *ʔ* or *k*, and *k > *ʔ* in Dengka; expect *k = *k*).

do~doki *Termanu.* desire or crave something. (J:97)

do~doki *Korbafo.*

do~doki *Bokai.*

do~doi, (do~doʔi ?) *Rikou.*

do~doki *Ba'a.*

ɗo~ɗoki *Tii.*

ɗo~ɗoʔi *Dengka.*

ɗo~ɗoki *Oenale.*

Out-comparisons:

ɗuki *Hawu.* (J:97)

***ɗoʔi** *PRM.* prise out, lever out.

doʔi *Termanu.* picks out, e.g. to lever something up with a stick like a lever. (J:96)

doʔi *Korbafo.*

doʔi *Rikou.*

doʔi *Ba'a.*

ɗoʔi *Tii.*

ɗoʔi *Dengka.*

ɗoʔi *Oenale.*

n-roʔe *Kotos Amarasi.* pick out, pick seeds from a piece of fruit. *[Sporadic:* vowel height harmony *i > *e* /oC_.*]*

loʔi *Molo.* churns the ground up. (M:282)

roʔi *Kusa-Manea.* dig out.

Out-comparisons:

tuki *Semau Helong.* dig out, peck, adze. *[irr. from PRM:* *ɗ = *t* correspondence*]*

<ruki> *Kambera.* take out. (On:449)

<rauku> *Lewa.*

<rauki> *Anakalang.*

dokit *Sika.* dig out. (Pareira and Lewis 1998:40)

***ɗole** *Morph:* ***ɗole-k**. *nRM.* brains, marrow.

do~dole-k (2) laŋa do~dole-k (3) mata do~dole-k (4) na-do~dole *Termanu.* 1) anything like grease, therefore brains. 2) marrow from bones. 3) eye grease, dirt from the eyes. 4) have brains or marrow. (J:98)

do~dole-ʔ *Korbafo.*

do~dole-k *Bokai.*

do~dole-ʔ *Bilbaa.*

do~dole-ʔ *Rikou.*

do~dole-k *Ba'a.*

ɗo͡~ɗole-k *Tii.*

roene-f *Ro'is Amarasi.* brain.

rone-f (2) maat roneʔ *Kotos Amarasi.* 1) brain. 2) rheum, eye gunk.

lone-f *Amanuban/Amanatun.* brains. (M:283)

lole-f *Molo.* brains. *[Form:* regular *n > *l* /lC_.*]* (M:283)

rone-f *Kusa-Manea.* brain.

Out-comparisons:

dole-n *East Tetun.* marrow (of bones). (Mo:26)

ɗole *Hawu.* marrow. (J:98)

***ɗolu** *PRM.* draw water, lower, fish with a rod.

dolu *Termanu.* a) draw water by tying the dipper onto a rope and lower it down into the well by means of a rope; also: lower on a rope. c) well (n.). b) fish, fish with a rod. (J:99)

dolu *Korbafo.*

dolu *Bokai.*

dolu *Bilbaa.*

dolu *Rikou.*

dolu *Ba'a.*

ɗolu *Tii.*

ɗolu *Dengka.* fish, fish with a rod. *[Semantics:* Only the final Termanu sense is recorded as being present in Dengka and Oenale.*]* (J:99)

ɗolu *Oenale.* fish, fish with a rod. (J:99)

<lolu> (2) an-lolu *Molo.* 1) hook, anchor of ship. 2) taken with a harvesting hook. (M:284)

Out-comparisons:

ɗulu *Hawu.* enter deeply, pierce downward.

<dúlungu> *Kambera.* hang down, dangle. *[Note:* also in Mangili.*]* (On:41)

<dolungu> *Lewa.*

<ḍaulungu> *Anakalang.*

<padulungu> *Mamboru.*

<dòluna> *Weyewa.*

<dalungo> *Kodi.*

***ɗombe** *Rote.* knife. *See:* **#kopi**.

dope *Termanu.* knife. (J:101)

dope *Korbafo.*

dope *Bokai.*

dope *Bilbaa.*

dope *Rikou.*

dompe *Ba'a.*

ɗombe *Tii.*

ɗombe *Dengka.*

ɗombe *Oenale.*

Out-comparisons:

supi *Sika.* knife. (Pareira and Lewis 1998:187)

ʄobe *Hawu.* knife. (J:101)

***ɗoo** *Morph:* ***ka-ɗoo**. *PRM.* far, distant. *Etym:* *zauq.

doo-k *Termanu.* long of distance, far, long of time. (J:90)

doo-ʔ *Korbafo.*

doo-k *Bokai.*

doo-ʔ *Bilbaa.*

doo-ʔ *Rikou.*

doo-k *Ba'a.*

ɗoo-k *Tii.*

ɗoo-ʔ *Dengka.*

ɗoo-ʔ *Oenale.*

na-ʔ|roo *Ro'is Amarasi.* far.

na-ʔ|roo *Kotos Amarasi.* far.

na-k|loo-g *Amfo'an.* far. (own field notes)

ʔ|loo *Molo.* far. (M:280)

roo *Kusa-Manea.* far.

Out-comparisons:

(k)dook (2) dodook *East Tetun.* 1) far, distant, remote. (Mo:27, 104) 2) go further away. (Mo:26)

soo *Galolen.* far.

koʔu *Kisar.* far.

soo *Ili'uun.* far. (dJ:137)

kaʄəu *Dhao.* far.

ʄəu *Hawu.* far.

***ɗosa** *Rote.* vinegar.

dosa (2) na-ka-do~dosa *Termanu.* 1) vinegar. 2) make sour. (J:102)

dosa *Korbafo.*

dosa *Bokai.*

dosa *Ba'a.*

ɗosa *Tii.*

ɗosa *Dengka.*

ɗosa *Oenale.*

Out-comparisons:

ei do kedoha *Hawu. [Form:* **ei** = 'water', **do** = 'relativiser'.*]* (J:102)

***ɗoto** *Morph:* ***na-ka-ɗoto**. *PRM.* thunder, make a loud noise.

na-ka-doto (2) doto~doto *Termanu.* 1) make noise, cause a din. 2) make a din. (J:102)

na-ka-doto *Korbafo.*

na-ka-doto *Bokai.*

na-ka-doto *Bilbaa.*

na-doto *Rikou.*

na-ka-doto *Ba'a.*
na-ka-ɗoto *Tii.*
na-ʔa-ɗoto *Dengka.*
na-ʔa-ɗoto *Oenale.*
na-ʔ|roto (2) ʔ|roto-s *Kotos Amarasi.* 1) rumbling, thundering. 2) thunder.
na-ʔ|loto *Molo.* it thunders. (M:287)
na-ʔroot *Kusa-Manea.* noisy.
Out-comparisons:
loto *Semau Helong.* rumble, grumble. *[irr. from PRM:* *ɗ = *l* correspondence*]*
ɗoro *Hawu.* thunder. *[irr. from PRM:* *t = *r* correspondence (expect *d*)*]*

***ɗuɗi** *PRM.* stoop, bow.
dudi *Termanu.* crouch down to go through or into somewhere, creep out or into somewhere, like a chick under or out of their mother's wing, or as a thief through the trees. (J:105)
dudi *Korbafo.*
dudi *Bokai.*
dudi *Bilbaa.*
dudi *Rikou.*
dudi *Ba'a.*
ɗuɗi *Tii.*
ɗuɗi *Dengka.*
ɗuɗi *Oenale.*
na-ʔruriʔ *Ro'is Amarasi.* bend down, bow.
na-ʔruriʔ *Kotos Amarasi.* bow (in respect).
<na-luli> *Molo.* bows. (M:291)

***ɗuɗu** *Rote.* tinder, oakum.
dudu *Termanu.* tinder; also oakum used to plug up a vessel, and from that everything which is used to plug things up, e.g. putty. (J:105)
dudu *Korbafo.*
dudu *Bokai.*
dudu *Bilbaa.*
dudu *Rikou.*
dudu *Ba'a.*
ɗuɗu *Tii.*
ɗuɗu *Dengka.*
ɗuɗu *Oenale.*
Out-comparisons:
dudu *Semau Helong.*
duduk *East Tetun.* tinder, made from the velvety exterior of **tua naa**, a palm tree. (Mo:28)
dudu *Sika.* tinder from an areng palm used to make a fire. (Pareira and Lewis 1998:42)
ɗuɗu *Ende.* stuff for catching a fire, made of sugar palm.
<kadudu> *Kambera.* tinder (from the areng palm). (On:130)
nduru *Bima.* tinder. (Jonker 1893:65)
ʤuʔʤuʔ (2) anʤuʔʤuʔ *Makassar.* 1) coconut husk with rags twisted into a wick. 2) set on fire. (Cense 1979:190)

***ɗula** *PRM.* engrave, tattoo, pattern.
dula (2) dula-k *Termanu.* 1) making drawings, figures or patterns on sarongs and sheets, etc. 2) drawing, pattern, design on a scarf, sarong, etc. (J:106)
dula *Korbafo.*
dula *Bokai.*
dula *Bilbaa.*
dula *Rikou.*
dula *Ba'a.*
ɗula *Tii.*
ɗula *Dengka.*
ɗula *Oenale.*
ɗula-ʔ *Dela.* pattern.
runu-t *Ro'is Amarasi.* plan, scheme, event.
n-runa (2) runa-t *Kotos Amarasi.* 1) carve, chisel, inscribe. 2a) cloth pattern, tattoo, branding. 2b) plan, scheme, event.
luna (2) luna-t *Amanuban/ Amanatun.* 1) engrave. (M:291) 2) tattooed figure, also pattern in cloth and carved figures in bamboo or bone. (M:291, 293)

lula (2) lula-t *Molo.* 1) engrave. (M:291) 2) tattooed figure, also pattern in cloth and carved figures in bamboo or bone. *[Form:* regular *n > *l* /lC_.*]* (M:291, 293)

ruan *Kusa-Manea.* tattoo, writing.

Out-comparisons:

dula (2) hdulat *Semau Helong.* 1) write. 2) picture, illustration, portrait, image, sculpture, carving; colour, characteristic.

***ɗuŋgu** *Rote.* insert.

duŋu *Termanu.* insert somewhere, prod with something. (J:107)

duŋu *Korbafo.*

duŋu *Bokai.*

duŋu *Bilbaa.*

duku *Rikou.*

duŋgu *Ba'a.*

ɗuŋgu *Tii.*

ɗuŋgu *Dengka.*

ɗuŋgu *Oenale.*

Out-comparisons:

duŋun *Helong.* (J:107)

E - e

***eɗa** *PRM.* ladder, stairs. *Etym:* *haRəzan 'notched log ladder'. *[Sporadic: Ø > ʔ /#_ in Dela-Oenale.]*

eda-k (2) heda_huu-k *Termanu.* 1) stairs, ladder. (J:108) 2) ladder. *[irr. from PRM: Ø > h* in sense 2 probably influenced by following **huu-k***]*. (J:167)

eda (2) heda_huu-ʔ *Korbafo.*

eda-k *Bokai.*

(2) heda_huu-k *Bilbaa.*

eda *Rikou.*

eda-k (2) heda_huu-k *Ba'a.*

eɗa-k (2) heɗa_huu-ʔ *Tii.*

(ʔ)e~(ʔ)eɗa-ʔ (2) (ʔ)e~(ʔ)eɗa_huu-ʔ *Dengka.*

ʔe~ʔeɗa-ʔ *Oenale.*

ʔe~ʔeɗa-ʔ *Dela.* ladder.

era|ʔ, era|k *Kotos Amarasi.* steps, ladder.

ela|k *Molo.* ladder. (M:98)

Out-comparisons:

elan *Semau Helong.* ladder.

oda(n) *East Tetun.* stairs, staircase. (Mo:156)

rokon *Kisar.* ladder.

***ee** *PwRM.* 3SG.ACC. *[History:* Possibly connected with PRM ***ia** 'this, here' (from PMP *ia), though this is retained with a demonstrative meaning in all branches of Rote-Meto.*]*

ee, nee *Dengka.* shortened form of Dengka and Oenale **eni** = Termanu **n, ana** (3SG) as direct object or subject suffix ... sometimes also **nee**. (J:691)

ee, nee *Oenale.*

ee *Dela.* 3SG.ACC.

=ee (2) =nee *Kotos Amarasi.* 1) 3SG.OBJ, 3DET. 2) 3SG.OBJ. *Usage:* Occurs with the verb **n-ok** 'with, accompany' and occasionally with **n-fee** 'give'.

***ei** *Morph:* ***ei-k**. *Rote.* foot, leg. *Doublet:* ***hae**. *Etym:* *qaqay. *[irr. from PMP:* *ay > *i; *a > *e (sporadic assimilation)*]*

ei-k *Termanu.* foot, leg of a person, paw of an animal. (J:109)

ei-ʔ *Korbafo.*

ei-k *Bokai.*

ei-ʔ *Bilbaa.*

ei-ʔ *Landu.* leg. (own field notes)

ei-ʔ *Rikou.*

ei-k *Ba'a.*

ei-k *Tii.*

ei-ʔ *Dengka.*

ei-ʔ *Oenale.*

ei-ʔ *Dela.* foot/leg.

Out-comparisons:

ii-n *Funai Helong.* foot/leg.

ii-n *Semau Helong.* foot.

ai-n *East Tetun.* leg, foot. (Mo:3)

ai-n *Habun.* leg/foot. *[Note:* language of east Timor ISO 639-3 [hbu].*]* (Dawson 2014)

wei-r *Idate.* leg/foot. *[History:* This form may be from *waqay, but initial [w] also occurs on at least two other words where it is unexpected: *qahəlu > **walu** 'pestle' and *hapuy > **wai** 'fire.*]* (Dawson 2014)

ee-n *Galolen.* foot/leg. *Usage:* Talur (Wetar Island) dialect. (Hinton 2000:104)

ee *Dadu'a.* foot/leg. (Penn 2006:93)

ei-n *Kisar.* foot/leg.

ai-t *Welaun.* leg, foot.

***eki** *Rote.* shout, cry out. *Etym:* *əkit 'squeak, shriek' (Blust and Trussel (ongoing) give the Termanu form as evidence for both *əkit and the 'disjunct' *ə(ŋ)kik. The Termanu form is their only eastern evidence for *ə(ŋ) kik.). *Pattern:* k-5. *[Sporadic:* Ø > *h* /#_Vʔ in Rikou.*]*

eki *Termanu.* shout, cry out loudly. (J:110)

eki *Korbafo.*

eki *Bokai.*

eki *Bilbaa.*

heʔi *Rikou.*

eki *Tii.* shout, make a racket. (J:700)

eki *Oenale.*

***eko** *Rote.* shake, sift. *Pattern:* k-5/6′ (Dengka *ʔ* Dela *k* correspondence, expect either *k* in both for pattern 5, or *ʔ* in both for pattern 6).

(ʔ)e~(ʔ)eko *Termanu.* sift the rice through the horizontal sift by rotating and shaking. (J:110f)

(ʔ)eko *Korbafo.*

(ʔ)eko *Bokai.*

(ʔ)eko *Bilbaa.*

ʔeʔo *Rikou.* (J:110f; own field notes)

(ʔ)eko *Ba'a.*

(ʔ)eko *Tii.*

eʔo *Dengka.*

eko *Dela.*

Out-comparisons:

keko *Semau Helong.* sift.

keku *East Tetun.* shake, wag. (Mo:105)

kerifi-kerəgu *Hawu.* tremble, shake. *[Note:* Jonker (1908:111) gives **herego**, **kereko**, **keko**.*]*

ekok *Sika.* sift rice round and round. (Pareira and Lewis 1998:45)

***ekut** *PRM.* palm fibres, woven ring from palm fibres. *Pattern:* k-6. *[irr. from PRM:* *u > *e* in Rote*]* *[Form:* I have reconstructed final *u rather than *e as irr. *u > *e* in Rote can be motivated as an instance of sporadic vowel assimilation, while alternate *e > *u* in Meto would be unmotivated.*]*

eke-k (2) eke_naa-k *Termanu.* 1) kind of ring braided from rattan or palm stems to put a hot pot or pan on, also something similar that is placed on the head to carry a load, a kind of braided ring around the opening of a popper. (J:110) 2) the outermost hard part of a young gebang palm (called **tula pato**), which is processed (called **dusi**) and separated from the useless inner part (called **tula tei-k**) and used to make a kind of rope or string called **tali_eke/ naa-k** (in Kupang called *tali heknaak*), which is used to make various things (**lapik**). (J:110)

eke-ʔ (2) eke_naa-ʔ *Korbafo.*

eke-k (2) eke_naa-k *Bokai.*

eke-ʔ (2) heke/na-ʔ *Bilbaa.*

eke-ʔ (2) ? henaa-ʔ *Rikou.*

eke-k (2) heke/naa-k *Ba'a.*

eke-k (2) aki/naa-k *Tii.* *[irr. from PRM:* *e > *a*; *e > *i* for second form*]*

eʔe-t *Dengka.*

eʔe-t *Oenale.*

eku|t *Kotos Amarasi.* base of a cooking pot on the ground.

eku|t *Molo.* braided ring of twigs used a support for a pot carried on the head. (M:98)

Out-comparisons:

eket *Helong.* (J:110)

ekat *East Tetun.* fibres of the palm Piassava. (Mo:29)

***ela1** *PRM.* already, marker of perfective aspect. *[irr. from PRM:* *l > *n* in wRote; *Ø > *h* in Ro'is Amarasi*]*

la *Termanu.* an enclitic which attaches to the end of verbs to exclude something else; it can sometimes be represented with 'but, only'. (J:260)

ela *Rikou.* so that. (Nako et al. 2014)

ena, ela, la *Tii.* already, PRF. (Grimes et al. 2014a)

ena, en, na *Dengka.* already. (J:692)

ena *Oenale.* already. (J:692)

ena *Dela.* already. With active non-punctual verbs can either indicate that the situation (seen as a whole) is completed or that a particular stage of the situation, such as the beginning of the situation, is completed. With punctual verbs it indicates that the situation is completed.

=hena *Ro'is Amarasi.* perfective aspect.

=ena *Kotos Amarasi.* perfective aspect.

=een *Molo.* perfective suffix. *[Form:* metathesised form of =**ena**.*]* (M:101)

Out-comparisons:

ela *Semau Helong.* like that.

ele, le *Dhao.* already, PRF.

əla *Hawu.* already, PRF, has, completed.

***ela2** *PwRM.* run, flee. *[Sporadic:* diphthongisation *e > *ae* in most Meto.*]*

n-ela *Dengka.* he flees. (J:736)

n-ela *Oenale.* he flees. (J:736)

n-ela-ʔ *Dela.* run.

n-aena *Ro'is Amarasi.* run.

n-aena *Kotos Amarasi.* run, evade, flee.

n-aen *Molo.* run away, flee. (M:10)

n-ʔean *Kusa-Manea.* run. *[irr. from PRM: Ø > ʔ] [Form:* metathesised form of (currently unattested) ***n-ʔena**.*]*

***ele** *nRM.* yonder, there. *[irr. from PRM:* *e > Ø in Amarasi*]*

ele *Termanu.* yonder, points at something that is further off than **naa**. (J:113)

ele *Korbafo.*

ele *Bokai.*

ele *Bilbaa.*

ele *Rikou.*

ele *Ba'a.*

ele *Tii.*

nee *Kotos Amarasi.* 3DEM, 3rd person demonstrative.

Out-comparisons:

nee, əne *Hawu.* that, there, then. *Usage:* Seba dialect. *[irr. from PRM:* *l = *n* correspondence*]*

***elus** *PRM.* rainbow.

elus *Termanu.* rainbow. (J:113)

elu-ʔ *Korbafo.*

elu-ʔ *Bokai.*

elu-ʔ *Bilbaa.*

elus *Rikou.*

elus *Ba'a.*

elus *Tii.*

elus *Dengka.*

elus *Oenale.*

e͡lus *Dela.* rainbow.

eunus *Ro'is Amarasi.* rainbow.

enus *Kotos Amarasi.* rainbow.

enus *Molo.* rainbow. (M:102)

euns=aa *Kusa-Manea.* rainbow.

***ena** *Rote.* property, possession. *[Sporadic:* Ø > ʔ /#_ in Dela-Oenale.*]*

ena-na (2) na-ena *Ba'a.* 1) his property. 2) possess.

ena *Tii.*

(ʔ)ena *Dengka.*
ʔena *Oenale.*
ʔena (2) ma-ʔena-ʔ *Dela.* 1) have, own. 2) possess, have, rich.
Out-comparisons:
nena *Semau Helong.* share, portion, own.

***eni** *PwRM.* third person.
eni *Dengka.* = **ndia** (3SG) as personal pronoun. (J:693)
eni *Oenale.*
eni *Dela.* 3SG.ACC.
=eni *Kotos Amarasi.* PL, DEF.PL.

***eno** *Morph:* ***eno-k**. *nRM.* way, path. *Etym:* *qənuR 'animal path, trail'. *[Sporadic:* *u > *o /_*R#.*]*
eno-k (2) na-eno *Termanu.* 1) way, path, road. *Usage:* in Termanu, **eno** is the more common word and **dala-k** the more unusual (Fox 2016b:11). 2) serve as a path. (J:114)
eno-ʔ *Korbafo.*
eno-k *Bokai.*
eno-ʔ *Bilbaa.*
eno-ʔ *Rikou.*
eno-k *Tii.*
eno|ʔ (2) eno_sneer *Kotos Amarasi.* 1) door. 2) window.
eno|ʔ *Molo.* door. *[Form:* Middelkoop gives a parallelism with **lalan** 'way'; **enoʔ ma lalan**. This probably attests older semantics.*]* (M:101)
Out-comparisons:
enon *Helong.* path. (J:114)

***endən** *PRM.* soak. *See:* ***lende**. *Etym:* *(R)ədəm (Blust and Trussel (ongoing) reconstruct *ədəm with 'disjunct' *Rədəm. Blust and Trussel (ongoing) give Termanu **ene** and Mongondow **onop** as evidence for *əñəp 'sunken, submerged'. This connection is spurious as the other Rote reflexes all point to medial *nd.). *[irr. from PMP:* *d > *nd*]* *[minority from PMP:* *ə > *e /_# in second Oenale form (expect *ə > *a*, possibly *ə > *a > *e*)*]* *[Sporadic:* diphthongisation *ə > (*e) > *ae* in Meto; Ø > *ʔ* /#_ in Dela-Oenale.*]* *[Form:* The nasal-stop cluster reconstructed for PRM is also supported by Malay **rəndam**.*]*
ene (2) oe ma-na|ene-k *Termanu.* 1) soak something, have something soak, make soak. 2) still-standing water. *[Form:* This form probably has consonant metathesis from earlier ***na-ma-ene-k**.*]* (J:114)
ene *Korbafo.*
ene *Bokai.*
ene (2) oe=a ene *Bilbaa.* 2) standing still, said of water. (J:692)
enden *Landu.* soak. (own field notes)
ende *Rikou.*
ere *Oepao.* (own field notes)
ene *Ba'a.*
ende *Lole.* submerge. (Zacharias et al. 2014)
ende *Tii.*
(ʔ)enda *Dengka.*
ʔenda (2) ende~ende *Oenale.* 2) standing still, said of water. (J:692)
ʔenda *Dela.* soak.
na-ʔaeraʔ *Ro'is Amarasi.* soak. *[Form:* automatic glottal stop insertion between CV- prefix and #V-initial stem.*]*
na-ʔaekaʔ *Kotos Amarasi.* soak.
<n-aika> *Molo.* soak. (M:9)
Out-comparisons:
neneŋ *Semau Helong.* soak.

***esa** *PRM.* one. *Etym:* *əsa.
esa *Termanu.* one. (J:115)
esa *Korbafo.*
esa *Bokai.*
esa *Bilbaa.*
esa *Rikou.*
esa *Ba'a.*
esa *Tii.*
esa *Dengka.*
esa *Oenale.*

esa, es, sa (2) ka-esan *Dela.* 1) one. 2) first.
=esa *Ro'is Amarasi.* one.
=esa *Kotos Amarasi.* one.
=ees *Molo.* one. *[Form:* metathesised form of =**esa**.*]* (M:103)
eas (2) =ees *Kusa-Manea.* 1) one. 2) one (enclitic). *[Form:* The second form apparently shows assimilation of final *a* after metathesis, which is not normally expected in Kusa-Manea.*]*
Out-comparisons:
esa *Semau Helong.* one.

***esak** *PRM.* day after tomorrow. *See:* ***afi**, ***beni**. *[Form:* Final *k has been reanalysed in most Rote forms as the nominal suffix *-**k**.*]*
bina_esa-k (2) (ndee) bina_ esa-k=a *Termanu.* 1) day after tomorrow. 2) day before yesterday. (J:50)
bina_esa-ʔ (2) bina_esak=a *Korbafo.*
bina_esa-k (2) bina_esa-k=a *Bokai.*
bin/esa-ʔ (2) bin/esak=a *Bilbaa.*
bina_esa-ʔ (2) bina_esa-ʔ=a *Rikou.*
bina_esa-k (2) bina_esa-k=a *Ba'a.*
ɓin/esa-k *Tii.*
feni_esa-ʔ *Dengka.*
feni_esa-ʔ *Oenale.*
esah *Kotos Amarasi.* day after the day after tomorrow, two days from now.
<anesa> *Molo.* day after tomorrow. (M:103)

***eti** *PRM.* come by, go by. *[irr. from PRM:* *t > *ʔ* /V_V in Termanu*]*
n-eʔi *Termanu.* go, (often translated with 'come'). (J:387)
n-eti *Ba'a.* he goes. (J:737)
n-eti *Tii.* go. (Grimes et al. 2014a)
eti *Dengka.* go. (J:737)
n-eti *Dela.* indicates motion away from the speaker and motion towards the addressee.
n-eiti *Kotos Amarasi.* go, come.
eti *Molo.* come round. **au ʔ-eti** I'll come to you (M:105)

***eto** *Morph:* ***eto-ʔ**. *PwRote.* bran. *See:* ***taa2**. *[Sporadic:* Ø > *ʔ* /#_ in Dela-Oenale.*]* *[History:* Possibly related to PMP *qəta, though this is retained as **taa-ʔ** in wRote.*]*
(ʔ)eto-ʔ *Dengka.* bran. (J:694)
ʔeto-ʔ *Oenale.* bran. (J:694)
ʔeto-ʔ *Dela.*
Out-comparisons:
əto *Hawu.* (J:694)

***etu1** *PRM.* catfish. *[irr. from PRM:* *t > *ʔ* in Keka*]*
etu *Termanu.* kind of small poisonous fish. (J:116)
eʔu *Keka.* *[Note:* The form **eʔu** is noted as also occurring in other (unspecified) varieties.*]* (J:694)
etu *Korbafo.*
etu *Bokai.*
etu *Bilbaa.*
etu *Rikou.*
etu *Ba'a.*
etu *Tii.*
etu *Dengka.*
etu *Oenale.*
etu *Dela.* catfish.
iik etu *Ro'is Amarasi.* catfish.
Out-comparisons:
<naétu> *Hawu.* (J:116)

***etu2** *PMeto.* therefore, that is why. *[History:* The Meto and Tetun forms are likely borrowings, but the direction of borrowing is unclear.*]*
etu naa *Ro'is Amarasi.* that is why, because of that.
etun *Kotos Amarasi.* that is why, because of that.
etun *Amanuban.* therefore. (M:105)
Out-comparisons:
etuk *East Tetun.* therefore, for that reason. (Mo:30)

Ə - ə

***əmə** *Morph:* 1SG ***kumə,** 2SG ***mumə,** 3SG ***nemə,** 2PL/1PL.EXCL ***mimə,** 1PL.INCL ***temə,** 3PL ***remə**. *PRM.* come. *See:* ***mai**. *[irr. from PRM:* *ə > *a* /_# in Lole and Tii; initial *m > Ø in 2SG form in Lole, Tii, and wRM; initial *m > Ø in 2PL/1PL.EXCL form in wRM*] [Form:* With the exception of Tii and Lole, all the Nuclear Rote languages have a vowel initial root **-eme** which takes the expected consonantal agreement prefixes (see §2.6.5). The other languages all have irregular inflections none of which I can explain adequately at this stage. While I propose a possible account for these irregular forms here, I am not completely satisfied with it, as it requires positing several ad-hoc changes. Firstly, I have reconstructed irregular inflections to PRM as it seems simpler to posit regularisation of the paradigm between PRM and some daughter languages than to posit creation of irregular forms from an originally regular paradigm. Secondly, I propose that this root took vocalic prefixes for all forms at a stage prior to PRM and that the root was originally disyllabic **əmə. Thus, I propose pre-RM 1SG **ku-əmə, 2SG **mu-əmə, 3SG **na-əmə, 2PL/1PL.EXCL **mi-əmə, 1PL.INCL **ta-əmə, 3PL **ra-əmə. The 3SG, 3PL, and 1PL.INCL forms all show **aə > *e which is supported by four other forms (*ma-əsa > ***mesa** 'alone', *ma-qəti > ***meti** 'low tide', *baqəRu > **baəRu > ***beu** 'new', and *haRəzan > *aəzan > ***eɗa** 'ladder'), though there are also three forms that attest *aə > *a (*ma-həmis > **maəmis > ***mamis** 'insipid', *mahəyaq > ***mae₂** 'shy', *qahəlu > **qaəlu > ***halu** 'pestle'). Thus, I propose, as illustrated with the 3SG form, pre-RM **na-əmə > PRM ***nemə**. The Nuclear Rote languages (apart from Tii and Lole) then reanalysed 3SG ***nemə**, 3PL **remə**, and 1PL.INCL ***temə** as containing a root ***-emə** and a consonantal prefix. They then regularised the paradigm by using this root and a consonantal prefix for all persons. The PRM 1SG, 2SG, and 2PL/1PL.EXCL forms are a result of **ə > Ø in the inflected forms. This follows the normal pattern for trisyllables with medial schwa and initial *i or *u, though there are only three putative examples: *binəhiq > ***bini** 'seed', *buqəni > ***buni** 'ringworm', and perhaps *quhənap > ***unə** 'scale'. Thus, the complete pathway for the 2PL/1PL.EXCL form in wRM, Tii, and Lole was probably: pre-RM **mi-əmə > PRM ***mimə** > **mima**. wRM further has loss of initial *m in both this form and the 2SG form, while Tii and Lole only have loss of *m in the 2SG form. Thus, **mu-əmə > PRM ***mumə** > **(ʔ)uma**. The only explanation I can offer for initial *u* in Tii and Lole 3SG **numa** and 3PL **ruma/luma** is that this is due to the initial vowel of the 1SG/2SG form **(ʔ)uma** exerting paradigmatic pressure. While this goes against cross-linguistic norms where we expect the more common 3SG form to be the one to exert paradigmatic pressure, it finds some support from the fact that in the inflection of ***əu** 'go' in Ro'is Amarasi it is also the 1SG/2SG stem that has spread to other parts of the paradigm. Regarding the vowels of the Meto forms, apart from the Amarasi and Amfo'an forms, other known varieties of Meto show irregular vowel developments in the metathesised 1SG/2SG and 2PL/1PL.EXCL forms. These changes have three sequenced stages: (1) vowel breaking, as seen in Fatule'u 1SG/2SG **uum > **aum** and 2PL/1PL.EXCL **iim > **aim**, (2) partial assimilation, as seen in Amanatun 1SG/2SG **aum > **oum**, and (3) complete assimilation, as seen in Baikeno 2PL/1PL.EXCL **aim > **eim > **eem**. The unmetathesised forms of the 1SG/2SG and 2PL/1PL. EXCL forms in these varieties of Meto are unknown, and I cannot confidently predict what they might be.*]* *[History:* The final syllable of ***əmə** is possibly related to *ma(R)i with irregular *ai > *ə, but note that *ma(R)i is regularly reflected as **mai** in the Nuclear Rote languages.*]*

-eme *Termanu.* can sometimes mean 'come from or come out' but usually 'from' or 'out of'. *Morph:* 1SG **(ʔ)-eme,** 2SG **m-eme,** 3SG **n-eme,** 2PL/1PL.EXCL **m-eme,** 1PL.INCL **t-eme,** 3PL **l-eme**. (J:387)

-eme *Korbafo. Morph:* 1SG **k-eme,** 2SG **m-eme,** 3SG **n-eme,** 2PL/1PL. EXCL **m-eme,** 1PL.INCL **t-eme,** 3PL **l-eme**.

-eme *Bokai. Morph:* 1SG **k-eme,** 2SG **m-eme,** 3SG **n-eme,** 2PL/1PL. EXCL **m-eme,** 1PL.INCL **t-eme,** 3PL **l-eme**.

-eme *Bilbaa. Morph:* 1SG **k-eme,** 2SG **m-eme,** 3SG **n-eme,** 2PL/1PL. EXCL **m-eme,** 1PL.INCL **t-eme,** 3PL **l-eme**.

-eme *Rikou. Morph:* 1SG **(ʔ)-eme,** 2SG **m-eme,** 3SG **n-eme,** 2PL/1PL. EXCL **m-eme,** 1PL.INCL **m-eme,** 3PL **r-eme**.

-eme *Ba'a. Morph:* 1SG **(ʔ)-eme,** 2SG **m-eme,** 3SG **n-eme,** 2PL/1PL. EXCL **m-eme,** 1PL.INCL **t-eme,** 3PL **l-eme**.

-Vma *Lole. Morph:* 1SG/2SG **(ʔ)uma,** 3SG **numa,** 2PL/1PL.EXCL **mima,** 1PL.INCL (no form given), 3PL **luma**. *[Form:* Zacharias et al. (2014) gives only Lole **neme** 'from, of'.*]* (J:739)

-Vma *Tii. Morph:* 1SG/2SG **(ʔ)uma,** 3SG **numa,** 2PL/1PL.EXCL **mima,** 1PL.INCL (no form given), 3PL **ruma**. *[Form:* Grimes et al. (2014a) gives singular **numa** and plural **ruma**. A search of the Tii Bible indicates that **ruma** is used with third person plural subjects and **numa** with all other persons, including other plural persons.*]* (J:739)

-Vma *Dengka.* come. *Morph:* 1SG/2SG **(ʔ)uma,** 3SG **nema,** 2PL/1PL.EXCL, **(ʔ)ima,** 1PL. INCL **tema,** 3PL **lema**. (J:736)

-Vma *Oenale.* come. *Morph:* 1SG/2SG **ʔuma,** 3SG **nema,** 2PL/1PL.EXCL **ʔima,** 1PL.INCL **tema,** 3PL **rema**. (J:736)

-Vma *Dela.* come. *Morph:* 1SG/2SG **ʔuma,** 3SG **nema,** 2PL/1PL.EXCL **ʔima,** 1PL.INCL **tema,** 3PL **rema**.

-Vma *Ro'is Amarasi.* come. *Morph:* 1SG **kuma,** 2SG **uma,** 3SG **nema,** 2PL/1PL.EXCL **ima,** 1PL.INCL **tema,** 3PL **nema-n**.

-Vma *Kotos Amarasi.* come. *Morph:* 1SG/2SG **uma,** 3SG **nema,** 2PL/1PL.EXCL **ima,** 1PL.INCL **tema,** 3PL **nema-n**.

-Vma *Amanatun.* come. *Morph:* 1SG/2SG **oum,** 3SG **neem**.

-Vma *Amfo'an.* come. *Morph:* 1SG/2SG **uma,** 3SG **nema,** 2PL/1PL.EXCL **ima,** 1PL.INCL **tema,** 3PL **nema-n**.

-Vma *Fatule'u.* come. *Morph:* 1SG/2SG **aum,** 3SG **neem,** 2PL/1PL.EXCL **aim,** 1PL.INCL **teem,** 3PL **nema-n**.

-Vma *Baikeno.* come. *Morph:* 1SG/2SG **oum,** 3SG **neem,** 2PL/1PL.EXCL **eem** or **aim,** 1PL.INCL **teem,** 3PL **nema-n**. (Charles E. Grimes pers. comm.)

-Vma *Kusa-Manea.* come. *Morph:* 1SG/2SG **oom,** 3SG **neam,** 2PL/1PL.EXCL **eem,** 1PL.INCL **team,** 3PL **nema-n**. *[Form:* Although at first sight the 1SG/2SG form **oom** and 1PL/2PL.EXCL form **eem** seem to show the third stage of development (full assimilation of earlier diphthong) as discussed above, this is not straightforward as in Kusa-Manea /a/ does not undergo assimilation after metathesis. Thus, I would predict that these forms are reflexes of earlier **uam and **iam rather than **uum and **iim.*]*

***əndi** *Morph:* ***n-əndi**. *PRM.* bring, take. *[Form:* *nd > *n* /ə_ in Tii and Rikou.*]* *[History:* Blust and Trussel (ongoing) ACD give a Minangkabau and Ngadha cognate as 'noise'.*]*

n-eni *Termanu.* brings. (J:388)
n-eni *Korbafo.*
n-eni *Bokai.*
n-eni *Bilbaa.*
n-eni *Rikou.*
n-eni *Oepao.* (own field notes)
n-eni *Ba'a.*
n-eni *Tii.*
n-endi *Dengka.*
n-endi *Oenale.*
n-endi *Dela.* bring; use, with.
n-eri *Ro'is Amarasi.* bring, take.
n-eki *Kotos Amarasi.* bring, take, use.
n-eki *Molo.* brings. (M:99)

Out-comparisons:

nini *Semau Helong.* use, with, using.
hodi *East Tetun.* bring; *prep.* with (an instrument). (Mo:87)
odi *Galolen.* bring, carry, take. *[irr. from PMP:* *ə > *o* (expect *e*)*]*
oid *Mambae, South.* take, bring, use. *[irr. from PMP:* *ə > *o* (expect *e*)*]* (Grimes et al. 2014b:36)
n-ot̪i *Kisar.* bring. *[irr. from PMP:* *ə > *o* (expect *e*)*]*
n-əti *Dhao.* carry, bring.
məndi *Ende.* bring, carry.
n-əti *Sika.* bring, carry. *[Form:* **n-əti** 3SG-bring, **m-əti** 2SG/1PL.EXCL-bring.*]* (Pareira and Lewis 1998:136)
<ngàndi> *Kambera.* bring. *[Note:* also in Kodi.*]* (On:342)
<ngidi> *Anakalang.*
<ngindi> *Weyewa.* *[Note:* also in Mamboru.*]*
nenti *Bima.* hold, hold in the hand, e.g. a staff. (Jonker 1893:60)
ənti *Sumbawa.* *[Note:* language of Sumbawa ISO 639-3 [smw].*]* (J:389)

***əu** *Morph:* 1SG ***kuu,** 2SG ***muu,** 3SG ***neu,** 1PL.INCL ***teu,** 2PL/1PL.EXCL ***miu,** 3PL ***reu**. *PRM.* go; dative marker: to, for. *[irr. from PRM:* *u > *i* in wRM (for 2PL/1PL.EXCL **mii**)*]* *[Form:* The inflection shows several irregularities which are not dissimilar to those seen in the inflection of ***əmə** 'come, from'. As with that stem, I propose that these irregularities are due to this stem taking vocalic prefixes at a stage prior to PRM with subsequent loss of the root initial vowel in some cases. Similarly, for the 3SG, 3PL, and 1PL.INCL inclusive forms I propose **aə > *e* (e.g. **na-əu > **n-eu**). I have reconstructed the 1SG and 2SG forms with irregular double *uu as this is attested in all branches. Similarly, I have reconstructed the 2PL/1PL.EXCL form as ***miu** as this best explains the Tii, Lole, and West Rote forms. West Rote further shows irregular assimilation of the final vowel of the 2PL/1PL.EXCL form. Other varieties of Rote have regularised the 2PL/1PL.EXCL slot of the paradigm with the stem **-eu**. Similarly, known varieties of Nuclear Meto have regularised the entire paradigm by using the stem **-eu** for all persons. In Ro'is Amarasi, on the other hand, the original 1SG/2SG stem **-uu** has spread at the expense of **-eu**, which is only retained in the third person in my data.*]*

-eu *Termanu.* go. *Morph:* 1SG **(ʔ)uu,** 2SG **muu,** 3SG **n-eu,** 1PL.INCL **t-eu,** 2PL/1PL.EXCL **m-eu,** 3PL **l-eu.** (J:392f)

-eu *Korbafo. Morph:* 1SG **kuu,** 2SG **muu,** 3SG **n-eu,** 1PL.INCL **t-eu,** 2PL/1PL.EXCL **m-eu,** 3PL **l-eu.**

-eu *Bokai. Morph:* 1SG **kuu,** 2SG **muu,** 3SG **n-eu,** 1PL.INCL **t-eu,** 2PL/1PL.EXCL **m-eu,** 3PL **l-eu.**

-eu *Bilbaa. Morph:* 1SG **kuu,** 2SG **muu,** 3SG **n-eu,** 1PL.INCL **t-eu,** 2PL/1PL.EXCL **m-eu,** 3PL **l-eu.**

-eu *Rikou. Morph:* 1SG **(ʔ)uu,** 2SG **muu,** 3SG **n-eu,** 1PL.INCL **t-eu,** 2PL/1PL.EXCL **m-eu,** 3PL **r-eu.**

-eu *Ba'a. Morph:* 1SG **(ʔ)uu,** 2SG **muu,** 3SG **n-eu,** 1PL.INCL **t-eu,** 2PL/1PL.EXCL **m-eu,** 3PL **l-eu.**

-Vu *Lole. Morph:* 1SG **(ʔ)uu,** 2SG **muu,** 3SG **n-eu,** 2PL/1PL.EXCL **miu.** *[Note:* **miu** is given by Jonker (1908:733). The other forms are from Zacharias et al. (2014). The 1PL.INCL and 3PL forms are missing from both sources.*]* (Zacharias et al. 2014; Jonker 1908:733)

-Vu *Tii. Morph:* 1SG **(ʔ)uu,** 2SG **muu,** 3SG **neu,** 1PL.INCL **teu,** 2PL/1PL.EXCL **miu,** 3PL **reu.** *[Form:* Jonker (1908:393) implies that the Tii 2PL/1PL.EXCL form is the same as the Termanu form, but does not explicitly list it. Grimes et al. (2014a) only has **miu** for the 2PL/1PL.EXCL form. This is also the form used throughout the Tii Bible translation.*]*

-eu/-uu/-ii *Dengka. Morph:* 1SG **(ʔ) uu,** 2SG **muu,** 3SG **neu,** 1PL.INCL **teu,** 2PL/1PL.EXCL **mii,** 3PL **leu.**

-eu/-uu/-ii *Oenale. Morph:* 1SG **ʔuu,** 2SG **muu,** 3SG **neu,** 1PL.INCL **teu,** 2PL/1PL.EXCL **mii,** 3PL **reu.**

-eu/-uu/-ii *Dela.* go, to. *Morph:* 1SG **ʔuu,** 2SG **muu,** 3SG **neu,** 1PL.INCL **teu,** 2PL/1PL.EXCL **mii,** 3PL **reu.**

-uu/-eu *Ro'is Amarasi.* 3SG-DATIVE. *Morph:* 1SG **kuu,** 2SG **muu,** 3SG/3PL **nuu/n-eu,** 1PL.INCL **tuu.** *[Form:* The 2PL/1PL.INCL form is not currently known. Both **nuu** and **neu** are attested for the third person, though **neu** is about twice as common in my current database.*]*

n-eu *Kotos Amarasi.* DATIVE. *[Form:* All persons have the root **-eu**.*]*

n-eu *Amanuban.* DATIVE, ALLATIVE.

F - f

***fa** *PRM.* little, just, NEG.
fa *Termanu.* a little. In phrases that contain a negative **fa** also often means 'a little', but is mostly meaningless (like Meto **fa**). (J:117)
fa *Korbafo.*
fa *Bokai.*
fa *Bilbaa.*
fa *Ba'a.*
fa *Tii.*
fa *Dengka.*
faa *Dela.* some.
ka=...=fa *Kotos Amarasi.* negator. *[Semantics:* Kotos Amarasi has a two part negator with the element =**fa** occurring after the negated predicate. Prescriptive norms dictate that =**fa** is always present, but in natural data it is occasionally omitted.*]*
fa *Molo.* still, not. (M:106)
Out-comparisons:
ve *Hawu.* just, only, mitigative; must, command. Particle used with manipulative verbs to indicate direct command or imperative.
<-wa> *Kambera.* modal particle after an imperative, request or proposal. (On:519)

***faa** *Rote.* current; flows, streams, overflows. *Etym:* *bahaq 'flood; to overflow, be in flood'.
faa *Termanu.* current; flowing, streaming, overflowing. (J:116)
faa *Korbafo.*
faa *Bokai.*
faa *Bilbaa.*
faa *Rikou.*
faa *Ba'a.*
faa *Tii.*
faa *Dengka.*
fa~faa *Oenale.*
Out-comparisons:
baa *Semau Helong.* flow, spread.
əi-vaa *Hawu.* overflowing. (J:116)

***faat** *PRM.* rainy season, southwest monsoon. *Etym:* *habaRat 'southwest monsoon'.
oe faa-k, fai oe faa-k (2) ani faa-k *Termanu.* 1) the rainy season, the west monsoon. (J:454) 2) in Termanu mostly sea wind, in the other varieties also west wind. (J:118)
oe faa-ʔ (2) ani faa-ʔ *Korbafo.* *[Form:* Jonker gives Korbafo, Bilbaa, Rikou <**òe-fá**> without a final glottal stop for the first form, but this probably a typographical error given that it is included for the second form and Termanu is clearly given as <**Òe-fák**> **oe faa-k** with the nominal suffix **-k**.*]*
oe faa-k (2) ani faa-k *Bokai.*
oe faa-ʔ (2) ani faa-ʔ *Bilbaa.*
oe faa-ʔ (2) ani faa-ʔ *Rikou.*
oe faa-k (2) ani faa-k *Ba'a.*
oe faa-k (2) ani faa-k *Tii.*
oe faat (2) ani faat *Dengka.*
oe faat (2) ani faat *Oenale.*
oe_faat *Meto.* (J:454)
Out-comparisons:
oe_haat (2) haat *Semau Helong.* 1) rainy season. 2) west monsoon. *[Note:* Jonker (1908:454) gives **ui haat** which has the normal Helong word for 'water', **ui**.*]* *[irr. from PMP:* *R > Ø (expect *l*)*]*

***fado** *PnMeto.* pierce.
faro *Kotos Amarasi.* ear-ring, nose ring.
falo, faol noniʔ (2) n-falo (3) n-falo bia (4) n-falon *Molo.* 1) silver earring. 2) wear or put on earrings. 3) put a rope through the nostrils of a buffalo. *[Form:* **bia** = cow, buffalo.*]* 4) stabs. (M:109)

Out-comparisons:

fadu *Fehan Tetun.* introduce, insert (key, etc.). **fadu karau inur** put a piece of wood through a buffalo's nose (to stop it suckling) (Mo:30)

***faɗa** *Morph:* ***na-faɗa**. *PRM.* say, speak, tell, inform. *Etym:* *bajaq 'know, understand; ask, inquire'. *[Note:* The putative Meto reflexes may be chance resemblances. The semantic match is not great and they have an unexplained final consonant.*] [Sporadic:* *a > *e* / _# in wRM.*]*

na-fada *Termanu.* speak, say, inform, enumerate. (J:118)

na-fada *Korbafo.*

na-fada *Bokai.*

na-fada *Bilbaa.*

na-fada *Rikou.*

na-fada *Ba'a.*

na-faɗa, i-faɗa *Tii.* (J:118,705)

na-faɗe *Dengka.*

na-faɗe *Oenale.*

na-faɗe *Dela.* tells.

n-fareʔ (2) uab fareʔ *Kotos Amarasi.* 1) ridicule, scoff at. *Usage:* collocates with **n-mani** 'laugh'. 2) round about talk, oblique speech.

n-falek *Molo.* care about, care for. **au ka ʔ-falek fa in uab** I don't care about what s/he said (M:109)

***fae** *Morph:* ***fae-k**. *CER.* kind of large lizard.

ŋgolo/fae-k *Termanu.* kind of lizard. (J:446)

ŋgolo/fae-ʔ *Korbafo.*

Out-comparisons:

lafaek *East Tetun.* crocodile, and some large lizards. (Mo:123)

***fai** *PRM.* day, time. *Doublet:* ***hoi**. *Etym:* *waRi 'day, sun'.

fai *Termanu.* day, in the sense of time in general. (J:120f)

fai *Korbafo.*

fai *Bokai.*

fai *Bilbaa.*

fai *Rikou.*

fai *Ba'a.*

fai *Tii.*

fai *Dengka.*

fai *Oenale.*

fai *Ro'is Amarasi.* night.

fai *Kotos Amarasi.* night.

fai *Molo.* night. (M:108)

fai *Kusa-Manea.* night.

Out-comparisons:

wain *Foho Tetun.* day. *Usage:* archaic. *[Note:* variety of Tetun spoken in the northern part of the Tetun-speaking area of central Timor ISO 693-3 [tet].*]* (van Klinken 1995)

bai(n) (2) bai-bain, uai-uain (3) bai(n)_hira, uai_hira(k) *East Tetun.* 1) day. 2) often, continually. (Mo:8) 3) when, how long, since when. (Mo:8, 191)

***faka1** *Rote.* split in half. *Doublet:* ***faka2**, ***paha**. *Etym:* *bakaq 'spread apart, split'. *Pattern:* k-8/9.

faʔa *Termanu.* split something cut through. (J:118)

faʔa *Korbafo.*

faka *Bilbaa.*

faʔa *Rikou.*

faʔa *Ba'a.*

faʔa *Tii.*

faʔa *Dengka.*

faʔa *Oenale.*

Out-comparisons:

bəka *Hawu.* divide, split.

***faka2** *Morph:* ***faka-k**. *Rote.* split in ground, crack in ground. *Doublet:* ***faka1**, ***paha**. *Etym:* *bakaq 'spread apart, split'. *Pattern:* k-5.

faka-k *Termanu.* split, crack in the ground. (J:122)

faka-ʔ *Korbafo.*

faka-k *Bokai.*

faka-ʔ *Bilbaa.*

faka-ʔ *Rikou.*

faka-k *Ba'a.*

faka-k *Tii.*

faka-ʔ *Dengka.*
fa~faka-ʔ *Oenale.*
***fake** *PRM.* petai tree; kind of tree with pods. Parkia speciosa. *Pattern:* k-8′ (*k > Ø in Bilbaa; expect *k = *k*).
fa~faʔe *Termanu.* kind of hard flat round fruit, which is called *fafake* in Kupang Malay, children play with it. (J:120)
fa~faʔe *Korbafo.*
fa~faʔe *Bokai.*
fa~fae *Bilbaa.*
fa~fake *Rikou.*
fa~faʔe *Ba'a.*
fa~faʔe *Tii.*
fa~faʔe *Dengka.*
fa~faʔe *Oenale.*
fae *Kotos Amarasi.* kind of wild legume tree.
fae *Molo.* kind of liana, the fruits of which are cooked as bush-pods, the sap of which foams up. The sap or decoction is used as an anthelminthic [OE = kills parasitic worms] agent and is lain on bruises and cramps, a paste of the leaves heals unclean wounds. Curanga amara. (M:106)
Out-comparisons:
kbaki *Helong.* (J:120)
fae matan metan *East Tetun.* tree whose berries are used as glue by goldsmiths. (Mo:30)
<kawaka> *Kambera.* kind of creeper, or climbing plant on the riverbank; the fruit has the shape of long beans, the sap serves as an adhesive to seal a crack in a pot. (On:199)
***fakur** *PRM.* pull out. *Pattern:* k-10. *[irr. from PRM:* *u > *i* in Meto*]*
faʔu *Termanu.* pull out (e.g. grass). (J:126)
faʔu *Korbafo.*
faku *Bilbaa.* (J:122)
faʔu *Rikou.*
faʔu *Tii.*
na-ʔa-fa~faʔu *Dengka.*
na-ʔa-fa~faʔur *Oenale.*
n-faki *Kotos Amarasi.* draw (a weapon).
n-faki *Molo.* pull, draw (sword). (M:109)
***fali** *Rote.* help, stand with. *Etym:* *baliw1 'dual division, moiety = cluster (a) answer, oppose, opposite side or part; partner, friend, enemy'.
fali *Termanu.* help, stand with. (J:122)
fali *Korbafo.*
fali *Bokai.*
fali *Bilbaa.*
fali *Rikou.*
fali *Ba'a.*
fali *Tii.*
fali *Dengka.*
fali *Oenale.*
***falu** *PRM.* eight. *Etym:* *walu. *[irr. from PRM:* *u > *a* in Ro'is Amarasi*]*
falu *Termanu.* eight. (J:124)
falu *Korbafo.*
falu *Bokai.*
falu *Bilbaa.*
falu *Rikou.*
falu *Ba'a.*
falu *Tii.*
falu *Dengka.*
falu *Oenale.*
fana *Ro'is Amarasi.* eight.
fanu *Kotos Amarasi.* eight.
fanu *Molo.* eight. (M:111)
Out-comparisons:
falu *Funai Helong.* eight.
palu *Semau Helong.* eight.
walu *Fehan Tetun.* eight.
ualu *East Tetun.* eight. (Mo:192)
balu *Kemak.* eight.
***fandi** *PRM.* cut. *Etym:* **panti (pre-RM). *[Note:* Jonker (1908:125) also gives 'Bul.' **wanti** 'chop down', **pati** 'chop'. I have been unable to figure out which language/dialect 'Bul.' refers to.*] [irr. from PRM:* *nd > *n* in Meto*]*
fani *Termanu.* incising, cutting. (J:125)

fani *Korbafo.*
fani *Bokai.*
fani *Ba'a.*
fandi *Dengka.*
fani *Kotos Amarasi.* axe.
fani *Molo.* axe. (M:110)
Out-comparisons:
fani *Waima'a.* hook.
fati (2) manti *Bima.* 1) chop, chop down, e.g. a tree. (Jonker 1893:21) 2) chop, e.g. wood. (Jonker 1893:50)

***fandu** *Morph:* ***fandu-k**. *PRM.* dry season.
fanu-k *Termanu.* the dry season. (J:125)
fanu-ʔ *Korbafo.*
fanu-k *Bokai.*
fanu-ʔ *Bilbaa.*
fai fandu-ʔ *Landu.* drought. (own field notes)
fandu-ʔ *Rikou.*
faru-ʔ *Oepao.* (J:x)
fanu-k *Ba'a.*
fandu-k *Tii.*
fandu-ʔ *Dengka.*
fandu-ʔ *Oenale.*
faur/nais *Ro'is Amarasi.* dry season.
fauk/nais *Kotos Amarasi.* dry season, drought.
fauk/ʔais *Ketun.* dry season, drought. *Usage:* Bone village.
fauk/nais *Molo.* dry season. (M:288)
fak/nais *Kusa-Manea.* dry season, drought.
Out-comparisons:
vəru vadu *Hawu.* dry season, hot season. *[Form:* **vəru** = 'month, moon'.*]*
<wandu> *Kambera.* dry season. (On:525)
<wadu> *Anakalang.*

***fanduun** *PRM.* star. *Etym:* *bituqən. *[irr. from PMP:* *ə > *u (sporadic assimilation); *t > *nd (Several other languages show a medial *nt* cluster, such as Sikule **bintun** 'star' (Kähler 1959:17, Barrier Islands ISO 693-3 [skh]), or Pazeh **bintun** (Blust 1999:361, Taiwan, ISO 693-3 uun), and it is likely that PRM *nd developed from earlier *nt.)*]* *[Sporadic:* consonant metathesis *fk > *kf* in some Meto.*]* *[Form:* The change *i > *a is due to the general reduction of ante-penultimate syllables seen also, for instance in reflexes of *sumaŋəd > ***sumanə**. *nd follows the pattern for word initial *nd in Rote.*]*
nduu-k *Termanu.* star. (J:425)
nduu-ʔ *Korbafo.*
luu-k *Bokai.*
luu-ʔ *Bilbaa.*
fanduu-ʔ *Landu.* (own field notes)
ruu-ʔ *Rikou.*
ruu-ʔ *Oepao.* (own field notes)
nduu-k *Ba'a.*
nduu-k *Lole.* star. (Zacharias et al. 2014)
nduu-k *Tii.*
nduu-ʔ *Dengka.*
nduu-ʔ *Oenale.*
fruun *Ro'is Amarasi.* stars.
kfuun *Kotos Amarasi.* stars. *[Form:* The final *n* has been reanalysed by at least some speakers as the plural enclitic/suffix.*]*
kfuun, fkuun *Molo.* star. (M:204)
fkuun *Kusa-Manea.* stars.
Out-comparisons:
bduun *Funai Helong.* star.
duun *Semau Helong.* star.
fitu(n) *East Tetun.* star. (Mo:15)
hiut *Mambae, South.* star. (Grimes et al. 2014b:22)
tuu *Ili'uun.* star. (dJ:140)

***faŋga** *Morph:* ***faŋga-k**. *Rote.* nail.
faŋa-k *Termanu.* finger or toe nail. (J:124)
faŋa-ʔ *Korbafo.*
faŋa-k *Bokai.*
faŋa-ʔ *Bilbaa.*
faka-ʔ *Rikou.*
faŋga-k *Ba'a.*

faŋga-k *Lole.* nail. (Zacharias et al. 2014)
faŋga-k *Tii.*
faŋga-ʔ *Dengka.*
faŋga-ʔ *Oenale.*
Out-comparisons:
waŋa-n *Buru.* digit, limb, strip, finger, slat; counter for cylindrical shaped things. (Grimes and Grimes 2020:994)

***farəndən** *nRM.* thoughts, mind, feelings, hope. *[irr. from PRM:* *r > (*l) > *n* in Korbafo*]* *[Sporadic:* consonant metathesis *rVnd > *ndVr in Termanu, Ba'a, and Korbafo.*]* *[Form:* *nd > *n* /ə_ in Rikou and Oepao.*]* *[Semantics:* It is questionable whether the required semantic shift from 'think, be mindful' in Rote to 'hope' in Meto is a likely one.*]*
na-fa-ndele *Termanu.* think about something, be mindful, remember. (J:417)
na-fa-ndene *Korbafo.*
na-fa-lene *Bokai.*
na-fa-lene *Bilbaa.*
na-fa-rene *Rikou.*
na-fa-re~rene *Oepao.* remember. (own field notes)
na-fa-ndele *Ba'a.*
ni-fi-lende *Lole.* remember. (J:721)
na-fa-rende *Tii.* remember. (Grimes et al. 2014a)
(2) nere-f (4) ma-nere-t *Ro'is Amarasi.* 2) seat of emotions. 4) love (n.). *[Form:* **ma-** = productive reciprocal prefix.*]*
na-fneka, na-fnekan (2) neka-f (3) n-neka (4) ma-neka-t *Kotos Amarasi.* 1) hope, trust, have assurance. 2) seat of emotions; feelings, mind, thoughts. cannot be equated with any physical organ in the body. 3) love, nose kiss. 4) love (n.).
na-fnekan (2) neka-n (3) n-ma-neka (4) ma-neka-t *Molo.* 1) hopes. (M:122) 2) character, nature. 3) give one another a nose kiss, love one another. 4) beloved, dear. (M:360)

***fase** *PRM.* wash (clothes). *Etym:* *basəq 'wet; wash clothes'. *[Sporadic:* consonant metathesis *fVs > *sVf* in all instances except Amfo'an and Timaus.*]* *[Form:* regular *ə > *e* /_q#.*]*
safe *Termanu.* wash, clean with water. (J:511)
safe *Korbafo.*
safe *Bokai.*
safe *Bilbaa.*
safe *Rikou.*
safe *Ba'a.*
safe *Tii.*
safe *Dengka.*
safe *Oenale.*
n-safe *Ro'is Amarasi.* wash (clothes).
n-safe *Kotos Amarasi.* wash (clothes).
safe *Molo.* undergo cleaning. leaves of the **safe** plant would be used with water to clean clothes. (M:111, 465)
n-fase *Amfo'an.* wash. *[Form:* Middelkoop (1972:111) gives Amfo'an **fasel**.*]*
n-fasa *Timaus.* wash. *[Form:* regular final *e > *a.]*
Out-comparisons:
base *Semau Helong.* wash clean.
fasi, fase *East Tetun.* wash. (Mo:32)
ɓahe *Hawu.* wash.
wase *Ili'uun.* wash (objects). (dJ:141)

***fata** *Rote.* female. *Etym:* **bata (pre-RM. Blust (1993:277) reconstructs ***bat-bata** 'woman' as evidence for a Yamdena-North Bomberai subgroup and also notes cognates in Ili'uun and Wetan (Luang cluster).).
tua_fata *Tii.* female lontar palm. (J:695)

Out-comparisons:

bataʔ (2) bi/hata *Funai Helong.* 1) sister of man. 2) woman, female. *[Form:* initial syllable of **bihata** from PMP *bahi (see ***fee**$_1$).*]*

bata (2) bi/hata, be/hata *Semau Helong.* 1) sister, opposite sex sibling (male speaking). 2) female, woman.

babata *Galolen.* woman.

wawata *Dadu'a.* woman, wife, female. (Penn 2006:111)

hahata *Ili'uun.* female (of human beings), woman. (dJ:116)

fafata *Tugun.* woman. (Hinton 2000:125)

awatwata *Wetan.* woman. *[Note:* language of southwest Maluku, member of Luang language/ dialect cluster ISO 639-3 [lex].*]* (de Josselin de Jong 1987)

pata *Roma.* woman. *[irr. from PRM:* *b = *p* correspondence (expect *b = *w*)*]* (Taber 1993:426)

***fati** *Morph:* ***na-fa~fati**. *Rote.* feed, give a drink to.

na-fa~fati *Termanu.* give a drink to a child. (J:126)

na-fa~fati *Korbafo.*

na-fa~fati *Bokai.*

na-fa~fati *Bilbaa.*

na-fa~fati *Rikou.*

na-fa~fati *Ba'a.*

na-fa~fati *Tii.*

na-ʔa-fa~fati *Dengka.*

na-ʔa-fa~fati *Oenale.*

Out-comparisons:

vati *Hawu.* feed, maintain animals.

***faun** *Morph:* ***ma-faun**. *PwRM.* thick.

fau-ʔ *Dengka.* thick. (J:695)

fau-ʔ *Oenale.* thick. (J:695)

fau-ʔ (2) na-ma-fau *Dela.* 1) thick. 2) be thick (e.g. skin).

ma|faun *Ro'is Amarasi.* thick.

ma|faun *Kotos Amarasi.* thick.

n-ma|fau-b *Molo.* it has many layers, thick. (M:113)

Out-comparisons:

ba~bakun *Semau Helong.* thick, dense.

***feɗu** *Rote.* bent through. *Doublet:* ***ɓetu**. *Etym:* *bəntuk. *[irr. from PMP:* *nt > *ɗ*]*

fedu (2) fe~fedu *Termanu.* 1) bent through. 2) be flexible. (J:128)

fedu *Korbafo.*

fedu *Bokai.*

fedu *Bilbaa.*

fedu *Rikou.*

fedu *Ba'a.*

feɗu *Tii.*

feɗu *Dengka.*

feɗu *Oenale.*

***fee**$_1$ *PMeto.* wife, woman. *Etym:* *bahi 'female, woman, wife; female of animals'. *[History:* The forms **fenai** 'wife of an important person' and Kusa-Manea **fa/nai** 'woman' are historically compounds of ***fee** 'wife' + ***laʔi** 'male, grandfather, king'. Despite the superficial similarity, they are not from PMP *b<in>ahi.*]*

fee (2) bi/fee *Ro'is Amarasi.* 1) wife. 2) woman. *[Form:* **bi** is used before female names in Meto.*]*

fee (2) fe/nai (3) bi/fee *Kotos Amarasi.* 1) wife. 2) wife of an important person. *[Form:* **nai** in **fenai** is probably connected with **naʔi-f** 'grandfather'.*]* 3) woman.

fee (2) fe/nai *Amanuban.* 1) wife. 2) woman. *Usage:* Kualiin village.

fee (2) fe/nai (3) bi/fee-l *Molo.* 1) wife. (M:113) 2) wife of a chief. (M:113) 3) woman. (M:66)

fee (2) fa/nai *Kusa-Manea.* 1) wife. 2) woman.

Out-comparisons:

bi/hata *Funai Helong.* woman. *[Form:* second element **hata** from ****bata** (see ***fata**).*]*

bi/hata, be/hata *Semau Helong.* female, woman.
fee-n *East Tetun.* wife. (Mo:33)

***fee2** *PRM.* give. *Etym:* *bəRay.
fee *Termanu.* give, give gift. (J:127)
fee *Korbafo.*
fee *Bokai.*
fee *Bilbaa.*
fee *Rikou.*
fee *Ba'a.*
fee *Tii.*
fee *Dengka.*
fee *Oenale.*
n-fee *Ro'is Amarasi.* give.
n-fee *Kotos Amarasi.* give.
fee *Molo.* give. (M:113)
fee *Kusa-Manea.* give.
Out-comparisons:
bele *Semau Helong.* give.
foo *East Tetun.* give, grant, deliver. (Mo:35)
vie *Hawu.* give, present.

***fefa** *Morph:* ***fefa-f**. *PMeto.* mouth (internal). *See:* ***ɓafa2**. *Etym:* *bəqbəq 'mouth, opening; speak, say' (Reconstructed with the doublet *baqbaq. Both forms are attested in the Timor region.). *[irr. from PMP:* *ə > *a /_q# (expect *e)*]*
fefe-f *Ro'is Amarasi.* mouth.
fefa-f *Kotos Amarasi.* mouth (internal).
fefa-f *Molo.* mouth. (M:113)
Out-comparisons:
foha-t *Welaun.* voice.

***fei** *PRM.* open. *Etym:* *bəriq 'split, tear open'. *[irr. from PMP:* *r > Ø (expect *r)*]*
fei *Termanu.* open. (J:130)
fei *Korbafo.*
fei *Bokai.*
fei *Bilbaa.*
fei *Rikou.*
fei *Ba'a.*
fei *Tii.*
fei *Dengka.*
fei *Oenale.*
n-fei *Kotos Amarasi.* open.
fai, fei *Amanuban/Amanatun.* (M:108)

***fekə** *Rote.* separate, other. *Doublet:* ***feka**. *Etym:* *bəkaq 'split, crack open'. *Pattern:* k-8. *[irr. from PMP:* *aq > *ə (expect *a)*]*
feʔe (2) feʔe-k *Termanu.* 1) separate oneself out from, individuate oneself, be alone. 2) other. (J:128)
feʔe (2) feʔe-ʔ *Korbafo.*
feʔe *Bokai.*
feke *Bilbaa.*
feke (2) feke-ʔ *Rikou.*
feʔe (2) feʔe-k *Ba'a.*
feʔe (2) feʔe-k *Tii.*
fea (2) fea-ʔ *Dengka.*
fea (2) fea-ʔ *Oenale.*
Out-comparisons:
weke *Kisar.* split.
bəka (2) bəke *Hawu.* 1) divide, split (pl.). 2) divide, split (sg.).

***feku** *PRM.* flute. *Pattern:* k-5.
feku *Termanu.* kind of flute from wood or bamboo with two holes at each end, used to whistle at animals. (J:130)
feku *Korbafo.*
feku *Bokai.*
feku *Bilbaa.*
feku-k *Ba'a.*
feku *Tii.*
feku *Oenale.*
feku *Kotos Amarasi.* flute.
n-feku *Amfo'an.* blow.
feku *Molo.* flute. (M:114)
feku *Kusa-Manea.* trumpet.
Out-comparisons:
heko *Ende.* flute. *[Form:* Jonker (1908:130) gives Ende **feko**.*]*

***fela1** *PwRM.* get up, rise.
fela *Dengka.* get up. (J:695)
fela *Oenale.* get up. (J:695)
n-fena *Ro'is Amarasi.* get up.
n-fena *Kotos Amarasi.* get up.
n-fena *Molo.* gets up. (M:115)

***fela**2 *Morph:* ***na-fe~fela**. *CER.* spread out, flat. *Doublet:* ***ɓela**. *Etym:* *bəkəlaj 'spread out, unroll (mats, etc.), open out, unfold (as the hand); wide' (Blust and Trussel (ongoing) reconstruct PEMP *bolaj and there is also evidence for PCEMP *bəlaj.).

na-fe~fela *Termanu.* spread out, said of plants; also to cover a large expanse, said of a landslide. (J:130)

na-fe~fela *Korbafo.*

na-fe~fela *Bokai.*

na-fe~fela *Bilbaa.*

na-fe~fela *Rikou.*

la-sa-fe~fela *Ba'a.*

Out-comparisons:

felar *East Tetun.* unfold, open. *[irr. from PMP:* *ə > *e* (expect *o)]* (Mo:33)

***felu** *Morph:* ***fe~felu-k**. *CER.* bend. *Doublet:* ***helu, *fenu**. *Etym:* *bəluk.

fe~felu-k *Termanu.* trap used to catch birds, the snare is attached to a bent piece of wood. (J:131)

***femba** *Rote.* hit in general, especially with a stick. *[irr. from PRM:* *f > *h* in wRote*] [History:* Blust and Trussel (ongoing) reconstruct a number of similar terms the first or second syllable of which could be reconciled with this PRM reconstruction, but in no case can both syllables be regularly reconciled with ***femba**. Similar reconstructed terms include PAN *pəkpək, PMP *tambak, *tambək, and *sambak.*]*

fepa *Termanu.* hit in general, especially with a stick or something like that. (J:133)

fepa *Korbafo.*

fepa *Bokai.*

fepa *Bilbaa.*

fepa *Rikou.*

fempa *Ba'a.*

femba *Lole.* beat, hit. (Zacharias et al. 2014)

femba *Tii.*

hemba *Dengka.*

hemba *Oenale.*

hemba *Dela.* hit with a wooden stick.

Out-comparisons:

vəbe (2) dede vəbe *Hawu.* 1) beat, smash; as in waves against a boat. 2) hit, pound; Repeatedly. By hand, or with something else, most commonly with a stick. *Usage:* Raijua dialect.

***fenu** *PRM.* bend. *Doublet:* ***helu, *felu**. *Etym:* *bəluk. *[irr. from PMP:* *l > *n*] [irr. from PRM:* *f > *p* in Meto*]*

fenu (2) fe~felu-k *Termanu.* 1) bend. (J:131) 2) trap used to catch birds, the snare is attached to a bent piece of wood.

fenu *Korbafo.*

fenu *Bokai.*

fenu *Bilbaa.*

fenu *Rikou.*

fenu *Ba'a.*

fenu *Tii.*

fenu *Dengka.*

fenu *Oenale.*

penu *Kotos Amarasi.* crooked, twisted.

n-penu *Molo.* crooked, bent. *[Note:* Jonker (1908:131) gives **fenu** as a Meto variant.*]* (M:433)

***fera**1 *Morph:* ***na-fera**. *PMeto.* decide, break. *[Form:* Probably from earlier **fenda.*]*

na-fera (2) na-t|fer~fera *Ro'is Amarasi.* 1) decide. 2) broken up, stop-start.

na-feka *Kotos Amarasi.* decide.

n-feek (2) na-t|feek *Molo.* 1) breaks. 2) broken off. (M:114)

***fera**2 *Rote.* landslide, ravine. *See:* ***ndefa**. *Etym:* **fəran (pre-RM). *[irr. from PRM:* *f > *h* in Oepao, Bilbaa and Korbafo (also Tetun)*] [Form:* Interference/collapse with ***ndefa**, which is likely related with consonant metathesis.*]*

fela (2) (fe~)fela-k *Termanu.* 1) landslide, but only said about the ground (not stones). **dae=a fela** the ground has collapsed/there has been a landslide *[Semantics:* Sense one is a verbal form.*]* 2) ravine. (J:130)

hela (2) hela-ʔ *Korbafo.*

fela (2) fela-k *Bokai.*

hela *Bilbaa.*

hera *Oepao.* landslide into a space. (own field notes)

fela (2) fela-k *Ba'a.*

fera (2) fera-k, re~refa-k *Tii.* *[Form:* Jonker actually gives Tii **feraʔ** but this is surely a typographical error.*]*

(fe~)fera-ʔ *Oenale.*

Out-comparisons:

horun *Fehan Tetun.* cliff.

rai hourun, horun *East Tetun.* precipice, chasm. *[irr. from PRM:* *a = *u* correspondence*]* (Mo:88)

werne *Kisar.* cliff.

***feto** *Morph:* ***feto-k**. *PRM.* man's sister, female. *Etym:* *bətaw 'sister (man speaking)'. *[irr. from PRM:* *t > *ʔ* /V_V for third and fourth uses in Termanu*]*

feto-k (2) tua feto (3) feʔo (4) ana feʔo-k *Termanu.* 1) sister of a man. 2) the female, that is, the fruit-bearing lontar palm. (J:134) 3) sister, used to address a sister, young girl, or young woman. Also used as a friendly word when speaking about her. (J:132f) 4) daughter, girl, young daughter.

feto-ʔ (2) tua feto *Korbafo.*

feto-k (2) tua feto *Bokai.*

feto-ʔ (2) tua feto *Bilbaa.*

feto-ʔ (2) tua feto *Rikou.*

feto-k (2) tua feto *Ba'a.*

feto-k *Tii.*

feto-ʔ (2) tua feto *Dengka.*

feto-ʔ (2) tua feto *Oenale.*

feto|ʔ (2) feto *Ro'is Amarasi.* 1) sister (of man). 2) female, feminine.

feto-f (2) feto *Kotos Amarasi.* 1) sister (of man). 2) female, feminine.

<feto> *Molo.* sister. (M:117)

feto|ʔ *Kusa-Manea.* sister.

Out-comparisons:

bata *Semau Helong.* sister (male speaking).

°feto (2) °feto-n *East Tetun.* 1) woman. 2) sister, cousin. *Borrowed from:* Meto **feto** (shown by irr. *ə = *e* correspondence, expect *o*). (Mo:33)

***fetu** *Morph:* ***ka-fetu**. *CERM.* trap, snare.

fe~fetu-k *Termanu.* kind of trap (like **hi~hiʔi-k**), which is placed on the ground. (J:134)

na-k|fetu (2) k|fetu-s *Kotos Amarasi.* 1) set a **kfetus** trap. 2) snare trap for catching wild chickens made by bending part of a tree down to the ground so that when a chicken steps on it, it flips out.

na-k|fetu *Molo.* sprung back into its original position. (M:203)

***feu** *Morph:* ***feu-k**. *PRM.* in-law. *Doublet:* ***beu₁**. *Etym:* *baqəRu 'new, fresh; recent(ly)'. *[Form:* PMP *b > *f (rather than *b = *b as in the doublet ***beu₁** may have been due to this term always occurring as the second member of a compound and thus intervocalic.*]* *[Semantics:* Only used in the phrases for 'daughter-in-law' and 'son-in-law'. The semantic association between 'new' and 'in-law' is connected with the fact that from someone who has just married into a family is the newest member of that kin group.*]*

mane_feu-k (2) feto_feu-k *Termanu.* 1) son-in-law. 2) daughter-in-law. (J:134)

mana/feu-ʔ *Korbafo.* child-in-law (ambiguous between male and female).
mana/feu-k *Bokai.* child-in-law (ambiguous between male and female).
mana/feu-ʔ *Bilbaa.* child-in-law (ambiguous between male and female).
mana/feu-ʔ (2) feto/feu-ʔ *Rikou.*
mone_feu-k (2) feto_feu-k *Ba'a.*
mone_feu-k (2) feto_feu-k *Tii.*
mone_feu-s (2) feto_feu-s *Dengka.*
mone_feu-s (2) feto_feu-s *Oenale.*
moen feʔu, moen feu-f *Kotos Amarasi.* son-in-law, opposite sex sibling's son.
moen feʔu *Molo.* son-in-law. (M:117)
Out-comparisons:
°manhiu *Funai Helong.* son-in-law, opposite sex sibling's son. *Borrowed from:* either Rote or Meto, as shown by irr. *R > Ø compared with regular *maRuqanay > **blanen** 'brother of woman' and **balu** 'new'.
mane foun (2) feto foun *East Tetun.* 1) son-in-law, nephew. 2) daughter-in-law, niece. (Mo:36)

***fia** *PRM.* wild taro, elephant's ear or itching taro. <u>Alocasia</u> species. *Etym:* *biRaq.
fia *Termanu.* yam. *Usage:* poetic. (Fox 1991:256)
fia *Dengka.* kind of aquatic plant. (J:696)
fia-l *Molo.* kind of wild tuber. (M:118)
Out-comparisons:
fia *East Tetun.* variety of yam, edible but care must be taken in cooking otherwise it will irritate the mouth and tongue to cause swelling (a member of the *Arum* family). (Mo:34)

***fiti₁** *Rote.* jerk up, flip upwards with great force. *Doublet:* ***biti₂**. *Etym:* *bitik 'snare, noose trap; spring up suddenly, jerk up (as a fishing line or noose trap)'.
fiti-k (2) na-ka-fi~fiti-k (3) ma-ka-fi~fiti-k, ma-ka-fi~fiti ana-k (4) fiti *Termanu.* 1) go upwards with great strength, or go back to one end. **ai=a fiti-k** one end of the piece of wood goes upwards because someone stood on the other end (or it did this because after someone bent it they released the other end). 2) go as high up as possible. 3) the outermost point. 4) come up with a jerk, like a fishing rod. (J:137)
fiti-ʔ *Korbafo.*
fiti-k *Bokai.*
fiti-ʔ *Rikou.*
fiti-k *Ba'a.*
fiti-k *Tii.*
fiti-ʔ *Dengka.*
fiti-ʔ *Oenale.*

***fiti₂** *Rote.* kick. *Etym:* *bintiq 'calf-kicking contest'.
fiti *Termanu.* kick, give a kick, stick the leg out sideways (also of a horse). (J:137)
fiti *Korbafo.*
fiti *Bokai.*
fiti *Bilbaa.*
fiti *Rikou.*
fiti *Ba'a.*
fiti *Tii.*
fiti *Dengka.*

***fiti₃** *CERM.* carry something hanging from the hand. *Doublet:* ***bifi, *ɓiti**. *Etym:* *bitbit 'pull at body part; hold something dangling from the fingers'. *[irr. from PRM:* *t > ʔ in Rote and Kusa-Manea*] [Form:* The parallel irregular sound change in both Rote and Kusa-Manea suggests a doublet at the level of PRM; ***fiti** and ***fiʔi**.*]*

fiʔi *Termanu.* pinch with the tip of the fingers or fingernails. From that: hold fast with the tips of the fingers. (J:135)
fiʔi *Korbafo.*
fiʔi *Ba'a.*
fiʔi *Tii.*
n-fiti *Kotos Amarasi.* carry an item hanging below the waist, typically hanging from a rope or strap.
n-fiti *Molo.* one carries something hanging from a rope. (M:121)
fiiʔ *Kusa-Manea.* carry an item hanging below the waist. *[irr. from PRM:* *t > *ʔ] [Form:* metathesised form of (currently unattested) ***fiʔi**.*]*
Out-comparisons:
biʔit (2) fiʔit *East Tetun.* 1) lift by the fingers. (Mo:14) 2) remove with the points of the fingers, to lift up suspended in the paw or claw. *Usage:* Luka village. (Mo:34)
tiwi *Bima.* carry something hanging from the hand. *[Sporadic:* consonant metathesis *wVt > *tVw.]* (Jonker 1893:105)

***foe1** *PRM.* white spots. *[irr. from PRM:* *f > *p* in Amarasi (also Funai Helong)*] [History:* The Funai Helong and Amarasi forms are probably borrowings as both have irr. *f > *p*. Both forms may come from Bolok Helong or Semau Helong that has undergone a *f > *p* sound change.*]*
foe-k *Termanu.* white (albino) spot or spots on the hand or foot of a person, or on other places on an animal. (J:139)
foe *Korbafo.*
foe-k *Bokai.*
foe *Bilbaa.*
foe *Rikou.*
(muti/)foe-k *Ba'a.*
muti/foe-k *Tii.*
foe *Dengka.*
foe *Oenale.*
pe/muti(-s) *Kotos Amarasi.* tinea.
mut/foe, met/foe *Meto.* (J:139)
Out-comparisons:
poemuti *Funai Helong.* tinea.

***foe2** *CER.* crocodile. *See:* ***ɓeis**. *Etym:* *buqaya. *[Form:* Through the pathway *buqaya > **buaya > **boya > **boe > ***foe** in which all the intermediate steps are regular.*]*
foe *Landu.* crocodile. (own field notes)
foe *Ba'a.* crocodile. *[Note:* This form is given with a note that this form occurs in other dialects, but which other varieties are not specified.*]* (J:697)
Out-comparisons:
voe *Hawu.* (J:697)

***foe3** *PRM.* move, struggle.
foe *Termanu.* get up in a metaphorical sense. **tasi=a foe** the sea is turbulent (J:139)
foe *Korbafo.*
foe *Bokai.*
foe *Bilbaa.*
foe *Rikou.*
foe *Ba'a.*
foe *Tii.*
foe *Dengka.*
foe *Oenale.*
n-foe *Kotos Amarasi.* move around a lot, struggle hard.
n-foe *Molo.* severe (disease). (M:124)

***foʔa** *Rote.* get up, wake up.
foʔa *Termanu.* get up. (J:138)
foʔa *Korbafo.*
foʔa *Bokai.*
foa *Bilbaa.*
foa *Landu.* get up. (own field notes)
foʔa *Rikou. [Form:* Nako et al. (2014) gives **foa**.*]*
foʔa *Ba'a.*
foʔa *Tii.*
foa *Dengka.* sally forth.
foa *Oenale.* sally forth.
Out-comparisons:
buka *Semau Helong.* wake up, awaken.

***foʔi** *PRM.* lever (v.), turn. *[irr. from PRM:* *ʔ > Ø in Termanu, Korbafo, Bokai, and Ba'a*]*
foi *Termanu.* tilt by means of a lever, or with a crowbar or machete, which one sticks in the ground and then raises earth. (J:139f)
foi *Korbafo.*
foi *Bokai.*
foi *Bilbaa.*
foi *Rikou.*
foi *Ba'a.*
foi *Tii.*
foʔi *Dengka.*
foʔi *Oenale.*
n-foʔi, n-foʔe *Kotos Amarasi.* lever.
<an-foi> (2) ʔ-foʔi *Molo.* 1) turns (e.g. ground). 2) key. (M:125)
Out-comparisons:
fokit *East Tetun.* pull along abruptly, jerk along. (Mo:35)
vuki *Hawu.* tilt with a lever, grub around (in dirt). (J:139)

***foo** *Morph:* ***kai_foo-k**. *PRM.* moringa tree. Moringa oleifera. *[Sporadic:* *VV-k > *VVʔ > VʔV in Meto (perceptual metathesis).*]* *[Form:* initial ***kai** probably from ***kaiu** 'tree, plant, wood'.*]*
kai/foo-k, ka/foo-k *Termanu.* moringa tree, the fruits of the moringa tree. (J:215)
kai/foo-ʔ *Korbafo.*
kai/foo-k *Bokai.*
kai_foo-ʔ *Bilbaa.*
ai/foo-ʔ *Rikou.*
kai/foo-k *Ba'a.*
kai/foo-k *Tii.*
ai/foo-ʔ *Dengka.*
ai/foo-ʔ *Oenale.*
ai/foo-ʔ *Dela.* moringa.
uut hau_ʔ|foʔo *Ro'is Amarasi.* moringa leaves.
uta_ʔ|foʔo *Kotos Amarasi.* moringa leaves. *[Form:* **utan** = 'vegetable'.*]*
<hau_fo'> *Molo.* moringa tree. Moringa oleifera. (M:124)
Out-comparisons:
°uut hau fooʔ *Funai Helong.* moringa leaves. *Borrowed from:* Ro'is Amarasi (shown by first two elements).
ut_poo *Semau Helong.* moringa leaves.

***fora** *PRM.* grate, scour.
fola *Termanu.* scour, scrub, file, e.g. the fingers. (J:141)
fola *Korbafo.*
fola *Bokai.*
fola *Bilbaa.*
fora *Rikou.*
fola *Ba'a.*
fora *Tii.*
fola *Dengka.*
fora *Oenale.*
n-fona (2) ʔ-fona-ʔ *Kotos Amarasi.* 1) grate, rasp. 2) grater.
n-fona (2) ʔ-fona-ʔ *Molo.* 1) sharpen (knife). 2) rasp, grater. (M:127)
Out-comparisons:
hola *Semau Helong.* sharpen sword or knife.
pəla *Hawu. [irr. from PRM: p =* *f; *ə =* *o*]* (J:141)

***foti** *PRM.* race back and forth.
foti *Termanu.* a) run or jump back and forth, e.g. deer in the wood. b) dance, dance of men, also perform the king's dance. c) horses running and jumping, do a dance, which takes place on the occasion of a **kuus** party. (J:142)
foti *Korbafo.*
foti *Bokai.*
foti *Bilbaa.*
foti *Rikou.*
foti *Ba'a.*
foti *Tii.*
foti *Dengka.*
foti *Oenale.*
n-foti *Kotos Amarasi.* back and forth.
n-foti *Molo.* racing, dances. (M:128)

***fua1** *Rote.* carry a burden, load. *Etym:* *buhat 'stand up, arise, emerge, begin, carry; cargo; take something; take a wife'.

fua *Termanu.* lay on something, load, have as a burden, carry. (J:143)

fua *Korbafo.*

fua *Bokai.*

fua *Bilbaa.*

fua *Rikou.*

fua *Ba'a.*

fua *Tii.*

fua *Dengka.*

fua *Oenale.*

***fua2** *PMeto.* traditional religion, traditional beliefs. *[History:* No entry for **fua** or a similar form with a similar meaning has been found in Morris (1984), this term is probably thus a loan from Meto into Fehan Tetun.*]*

fuan (2) fua-t *Ro'is Amarasi.* 1) traditional worship/religion. 2) objects or matters associated with traditional religion.

n-fua (2) fua-t *Kotos Amarasi.* 1) traditional worship/religion. 2) objects or matters associated with traditional religion.

n-fua *Molo.* sacrifice, used in the meaning of **anʔonen** = 'calls upon, invokes'. (M:129)

n-fua (2) uma ʔ-fuʔa *Timaus.* 1) worship. 2) house of traditional religion.

Out-comparisons:

ai_fuan, afuan *Fehan Tetun.* divination. *[Semantics:* Therik (2004:122) gives **afuan** as 'spear divination'.*]*

***fuɗi** *PRM.* persuade.

fu~fudi *Termanu.* cajole, entice, seduce. (J:145)

fu~fudi *Korbafo.*

fu~fudi *Bokai.*

fu~fudi *Rikou.*

fu~fudi *Ba'a.*

fu~fuɗi *Tii.*

fu~fuɗi *Dengka.*

fu~fuɗi *Oenale.*

n-furi *Kotos Amarasi.* persuade, beg, coax.

n-fuli (2) <fuli> *Molo.* 1) persuade. 2) bait. (M:132)

***fuʤə** *PRM.* foam, foaming. *Etym:* *bujəq 'foam, bubbles, lather, scum, froth; to foam, to bubble; foam at the mouth; fond of talking; type of white bead' (Blust and Trussel (ongoing) provide the third Termanu form as evidence for PCEMP *budeq 'sponge' and the first two forms for PMP *bujəq. However, the retention of PCEMP *d as *d* in Termanu would be irregular and the complete semantics of **tasi_fude**, which includes 'foam', shows that this third form is also from PMP *bujəq. PCEMP *budeq is probably spurious.). *[irr. from PMP:* *ə = *ə /_q# (expect *e)*]* *[minority from PMP:* *j > *ʤ (expect *ɗ)*]* *[Sporadic:* *ə > *e* /C+palatal_ in all except Kusa-Manea.*]* *[Form:* The correspondences for the medial consonant are not the same as either *d or *ɗ. Reconstructing medial *ʤ has the potential to both explain these (otherwise) irregular correspondences, as well as explaining the final vowel correspondences. We can propose that regular final *ə > *a took place in wRM, followed by sporadic raising of *a > *e* under the influence of preceding palatal *ʤ, followed by the change of *ʤ > *d > *r* > *l*. This raising has not taken place in Kusa-Manea, thus indicating that two forms ***fude** (from ***fuʤe** with raising of final *a > *e*) and ***fuda** (from ***fuʤa** without raising of the final vowel) probably existed in PMeto.*]*

na-fu~fude (2) fude-k (3) tasi_ fude *Termanu.* 1) foaming. 2) foam. (J:145) 3) sea foam, also: sponge. (J:144)

na-fu~fude *Korbafo.*
na-fu~fude *Bokai.*
na-fu~fude *Bilbaa.*
na-fu~fude *Rikou.*
na-fu~fude *Ba'a.*
na-fu~fuɗe *Tii.*
na-fu~fule *Dengka.*
na-fu~fure *Oenale.*
fure-ʔ *Dela.* foam.
fu͡iri-f *Ro'is Amarasi.* foam.
ʔ|furi|ʔ, ʔ|furi-f *Kotos Amarasi.* bubble, foam. *[Sporadic:* vowel height harmony *e > *i* /uC_ in Amarasi.*]*
<fule> (2) <na-fule> *Molo.* 1) foam. 2) it foams. (M:132)
ʔ|fula|ʔ, ʔ|fula-f (2) na-ʔ|fula|ʔ *Timaus.* 1) foam. 2) foaming. *[Form:* regular final *e > *a.]*
fa~fura-f *Kusa-Manea.* foam.
Out-comparisons:
budat [ˈbʊrɐt] *Funai Helong.* foam.
bulat *Semau Helong.* foam, froth.
furin *East Tetun.* foam (of water), froth (of mouth). (Mo:38)
nawuri *Kisar.* froth, foam at mouth.

***fue** *PRM.* legumes, beans. *Etym:* *buay (Helong, Tetun, Kemak, and Tagalog attest PMP *buday or *bujay.). *[Sporadic:* vowel height harmony *u > *o* /_e in some Meto.*]*
fu~fue *Termanu.* generic name of beans and legumes. (J:146)
fu~fue *Korbafo.*
fu~fue *Bokai.*
fu~fue *Bilbaa.*
fu~fue *Rikou.*
fu~fue *Ba'a.*
fu~fue *Tii.*
fu~fue *Dengka.* mung beans, green grams. (J:146)
fu~fue *Oenale.*
foe *Ro'is Amarasi.* mung beans, green grams.
foe *Kotos Amarasi.* mung beans, green grams.
fue, fua *Amanuban.* beans.
foe-l *Fatule'u.* beans (generic).
fue *Molo.* legumes (generic). (M:130)
fa~foa *Kusa-Manea.* beans. *[Form:* regular *e > *a* /V_# in Upper Manulea.*]*
Out-comparisons:
bula *Semau Helong.* bean, nut. *[irr. from PMP:* *ay > *a]*
fore *East Tetun.* bean, plants with pods and edible seeds. (Mo:35)
hure *Kemak.* mung bean, green gram.
bue *Sika.* mung bean, green gram. (Pareira and Lewis 1998:28)
mbue *Ende.* bean, pea.
wue *Manggarai.* kind of small bean. Phaeseolu ?angularis. (Verheijen 1967:768)
keɓui *Hawu.* (J:146)
kaɓoe (2) ɓuwe *Bima.* 1) mung bean. (Ismail et al. 1985:48) 2) kind of long bean. (Jonker 1893:12)
buwe *Bugis.* long beans. (Masse 2013:96)
tambue *Pamona.* kind of edible bean of which the leaves are also eaten. Phaseolus species. *[Note:* language of central Sulawesi ISO 639-3 [pmf].*]* (Adriani 1928:796)
bulai *Tagalog.* *[Note:* language of the Philippines ISO 639-3 [tgl].*]* (J:146)

***fufu₁** *PMeto.* peak of the skull, ridgepole of house. *Doublet:* ***fumbu**. *Etym:* *bubuŋ 'fontanelle; crown of the head; ridge of the roof; ridge of a mountain, peak; deck of a boat; cover the ridgepole with thatch'.
fufu-n *Ro'is Amarasi.* peak of the skull.
fufu-f *Kotos Amarasi.* peak of the skull, ridgepole of house.

fufu-f *Molo.* skull, crown, top of head. (M:130)

Out-comparisons:

fuhur *East Tetun.* fontanelle. (Mo:35)

*__fufu__$_2$ *Morph:* __*ka-fufu-k__. *PRM.* weevil. *Etym:* *bukbuk$_3$ 'weevil that infests wood, bamboo, and rice; dust produced by the boring of this insect'.

fufu-k *Termanu.* rice worm, woodworm, rotten. (J:146)

fufu-ʔ *Korbafo.*

fufu-k *Bokai.*

fufu-ʔ *Bilbaa.*

fufu-ʔ *Rikou.*

fufu-k *Ba'a.*

fufu-k *Tii.*

fufu-ʔ *Dengka.*

fufu-ʔ *Oenale.*

ʔ|fufu|ʔ *Kotos Amarasi.* weevil.

<fufuk> *Molo.* black beetle with a boring snout, with which it drills holes in corn, rice and wood. (M:130)

Out-comparisons:

hupu *Semau Helong.* black corn beetle. *[irr. from PMP:* *b > *h* /#_; *b > *p* /V_V (possibly with consonant metathesis from earlier **puhu, but initial *b > *p* would still be irregular)*]*

fuhuk *East Tetun.* weevil that eats grain. (Mo:36)

vuɓu *Hawu. [Form:* Jonker's entry is ambiguous between <b> [b] and <ḅ> [ɓ].*]* (J:146)

*__fui__$_1$ *nRM.* pour water on, douse (as a fire). *Etym:* *buqi (PCEMP).

fui *Termanu.* pour on, douse. (J:146)

fui *Korbafo.*

fui *Bokai.*

fui *Bilbaa.*

fui *Rikou.*

fui *Ba'a.*

fui *Tii.*

n-fui *Kotos Amarasi.* pour on, sprinkle on.

Out-comparisons:

fui *East Tetun.* pour liquids, pour out, empty, pour water upon, water, irrigate. (Mo:37)

*__fui__$_2$ *PRM.* wild. *Etym:* *bukij 'mountain; forested inland mountain areas'. *[irr. from PMP:* *k > Ø*] [History:* The loss of the medial consonant in *bukij (even in languages that otherwise retain *k) is common in the greater Timor area, as is the semantic shift to 'wild'. That the same semantic shift is accompanied by the same irregular sound change in a number of languages indicates these forms have spread by contact.*]*

fui-k *Termanu.* the opposite of **ae-k** [OE = tame], wild in the expression. (J:146)

fui-ʔ *Korbafo.*

fui-k *Bokai.*

fui-ʔ *Bilbaa.*

fui-ʔ *Rikou.*

fui-k *Ba'a.*

fui-k *Tii.*

fui-ʔ *Dengka.*

fui-ʔ *Oenale.*

fui *Ro'is Amarasi.* wild.

fui *Kotos Amarasi.* wild.

fui *Molo.* wild. (M:131)

Out-comparisons:

huin *Semau Helong.* wild, untamed.

fuik *East Tetun.* wild, savage, untamed. (Mo:37)

hui *Ili'uun.* forest, used only in connection with beings living in the forest, e.g. **hahi hui**, 'wild boar'. (dJ:118)

hui *Dhao.* wild.

*__fui__$_3$ *Morph:* __*na-fui__. *Rote.* wash (hands). *Etym:* *buRiq.

na-fui oe *Termanu.* wash the hands. (J:146)

na-fui oe *Korbafo.*

na-fui oe *Bokai.*

na-fui oe *Bilbaa.*

na-fui oe *Rikou.*

na-fui oe *Ba'a.*
na-fui oe *Tii.*
(na-fui oe ?) *Oenale.*
°n-boe *Kotos Amarasi.* wash. *Borrowed from:* probably Helong, but there are phonological irregularities no matter whether we posit borrowing from Helong into Meto or vice-versa. I tentatively identify Helong as the source language as it usually preserves initial *b = *b*.
°an-boe hae-n *Molo.* washes one's feet. (M:78)
Out-comparisons:
boe *Semau Helong.* wash. *[irr. from PMP:* *R > Ø (expect *l*), vowel lowering*]*

***fuka** *Rote.* dig or work the ground around a plant. *Doublet:* ***huka**. *Etym:* *buka 'open, uncover, expose' (Blust and Trussel (ongoing) reconstruct PCEMP *buqal 'levered up; uprooted' on the basis of Rembong **boal** 'levered up', Termanu **fuʔa**, Tetun **fuʔa** 'pull out roots and dirt together' and Maori **hua** 'lever; raise with a lever; steer, paddle'. Bilbaa **fu~fuka** with medial *k* shows that any connection between putative *buqal and the Rote forms is spurious. Likewise, medial *ʔ* in Tetun attests earlier *k not *q.). *Pattern:* k-8/9. *[Semantics:* While the sound changes from PMP *buka are regular, I am not completely confident that the required semantic shift is justified.*]*
(fu)~fuʔa *Termanu.* a) dig or work the ground around a plant. b) also used for: fertilisation of the ground. (J:144)
fu~fuʔa *Korbafo.*
fu~fuʔa *Bokai.*
fu~fuka *Bilbaa.*
fu~fuʔa *Rikou.*
fu~fuʔa *Ba'a.*
fu~fuʔa *Tii.*
fu~fuʔa *Dengka.*
Out-comparisons:
boka (2) voka *Hawu.* 1) open, undo, reveal, confess, begin; dismantle, tear apart. 2) work open the ground, work with a spade. (J:144)

***fula** *Rote.* white. *Etym:* *bula[n/R] 'unnaturally white, albino'.
fula (2) fula-k *Termanu.* 1) be(come) white. 2) white. (J:146f)
fula *Korbafo.*
fula *Bokai.*
fula *Bilbaa.*
fula *Rikou.*
fula *Ba'a.*
fula *Tii.*
fula *Dengka.*
fula *Oenale.*
fula-ʔ *Dela.* silver, white (used for skin colour and colour of leaves that are drying up).

***fulə** *nRM.* wrap around.
fule *Termanu.* twist around. **meŋe a fule manu** the snake wraps itself around the chicken (J:147)
fule *Korbafo.*
fule *Bokai.*
fule *Bilbaa.*
fule *Rikou.*
fule *Ba'a.*
(fule ?) *Tii.*
n-funa *Kotos Amarasi.* go around, wrap around.
n-fuun *Molo.* go throughout. *[Form:* metathesised form of **n-funa**.*]* (M:132)

***fuli** *Rote.* cowrie shell. <u>*Cypraea mauritiana*</u>. *Etym:* *buliq.
fuli *Termanu.* a) kind of shell. b) shells or pieces of lead used to weight a net. (J:147)
fuli *Korbafo.*
fuli *Bokai.*
fuli *Bilbaa.*
fuli *Rikou.*
ful *Ba'a.*
fuli *Tii.*

meo_fuli (2) fuli *Dengka.* 1) kind of shell. 2) shells or pieces of lead used to weight a net. (J:147)

ndai_fuli (2) fuli *Oenale.* 1) kind of shell. 2) shells or pieces of lead used to weight a net. (J:147)

Out-comparisons:

vovuri (2) vuri *Hawu.* (J:147)

***fuloat** *PRM.* kind of tropical chestnut tree. Sterculia urceolata. *[irr. from PRM:* *a > *o* in wRM, glottal stop insertion in Meto*]*

faloa *Termanu.* kind of tree. Sterculia urceolata. *[Semantics:* Scientific identification comes from Middelkoop (1972:123) who has Molo '<**flolo**> = kind of tree; Sterculia urceolata Smith; Rote **faloa**'.*]* (J:124)

faloa *Korbafo.*

faloa *Bokai.*

faloa *Bilbaa.*

faloa *Rikou.*

faloa *Ba'a.*

faloa *Tii.*

fuloo *Dengka.*

fuloo *Oenale.*

filoo *Dela.* kind of tree.

fnoʔot *Kotos Amarasi.* kind of tropical chestnut tree. Sterculia urceolata.

***fumbu** *Morph:* ***ka-fumbu-k**. *PRM.* crown of the head, ridgepole, peak. *Doublet:* ***fufu**. *Etym:* *bubuŋ 'fontanelle; crown of the head; ridge of the roof; ridge of a mountain, peak; deck of a boat; cover the ridgepole with thatch'. *[irr. from PMP:* *b > *mb*] [irr. from PRM:* *f > *p* in Meto (sporadic assimilation?); *f > *h* in Oenale*]*

fupu-k (2) na-fupu *Termanu.* 1) crown of the head. 2) be hot. (J:149)

fupu-ʔ (2) na-fupu *Korbafo.*

fupu-k (2) na-fupu *Bokai.*

fupu-ʔ (2) na-fupu *Bilbaa.*

fupu-ʔ (2) na-fupu *Rikou.*

(2) na-fumpu *Ba'a.*

(2) na-fumbu *Tii.*

humbu-ʔ *Oenale.*

maans=ii na-ʔ|pupu *Ro'is Amarasi.* midday, noon. *[Form:* **maans**=ii = 'sun'*] [Semantics:* Literally '(when) the sun peaks'.*]*

maans=ee na-ʔ|pupu (2) ʔ|pupu-n *Kotos Amarasi.* 1) midday, noon. 2) house ridge.

<ume pupu-n> *Molo.* ridge of a house. (M:457)

Out-comparisons:

muhuŋ *Semau Helong.* peak, ridge cap.

bβəŋu *Dhao.* ridgepole.

***funi1** *PRM.* hide, conceal. *Etym:* *buni.

funi (2) na-funi *Termanu.* 1) hide oneself. 2) hide something. (J:148)

funi (2) na-funi *Korbafo.*

funi (2) na-funi *Bokai.*

funi (2) na-funi *Bilbaa.*

funi (2) na-funi *Rikou.*

funi (2) na-funi *Ba'a.*

funi (2) na-funi *Tii.*

(2) na-ʔa-funi *Dengka.*

na-ʔa-funi-ʔ (2) ma-ʔa-funi-ʔ *Dela.* 1) hide something from someone. 2) hidden.

<na-funi> *Molo.* hides something. *[Note:* Middelkoop identifies this as a loan from Rote, though the reason for this is not clear.*]* (M:133)

Out-comparisons:

huni *Semau Helong.* hide.

hakfunin *Fehan Tetun.* hide or conceal oneself. (Mo:54)

***funi2** *Rote.* placenta, afterbirth. *Etym:* *tabuni. *[irr. from PRM:* *f > *h* in wRote*]*

funi-k *Termanu.* after birth, placenta. (J:148)

funi-ʔ *Korbafo.*

funi-k *Bokai.*

funi *Landu.* afterbirth, placenta. (own field notes)

funi-k *Ba'a.*

funi-k *Tii.*
huni-ʔ *Dengka.*
huni-ʔ *Oenale.*

***funu** *PnMeto.* betel-pepper. *Etym:* *burun 'inferior kind of betel nut' (Blust and Trussel (ongoing) reconstruct this on the basis of cognates in Mongondow, Pamona, and Tetun. They note it may be a chance resemblance.).
funu *Amanuban.* betel-vine fruit. *Usage:* Kusi village.
Out-comparisons:
furu *East Tetun.* creeper with leaves similar to the betel-pepper. (Mo:38)
huru roon *Galolen.* betel. *Usage:* Talur dialect. (Hinton 2000:120)
buru *Welaun.* betel-vine fruit.
huru *Kemak.* betel-vine fruit.

***fura** *Rote.* trim lontar palm leaves. *[irr. from PRM:* *a > *i* in wRote*]*
fula so~soŋa (2) fu~fula-k *Termanu.* 1) cut off the edge of young lontar palm leaves. 2) cutting off; the tool for cutting off: a leaf vein folded in half against which one holds a knife. (J:147)
fula *Korbafo.*
fula *Bokai.*
fula *Bilbaa.*
fura *Rikou.*
fula *Ba'a.*
fura *Tii.*
fuli *Dengka.*
furi *Oenale.*
Out-comparisons:
hula *Helong.* (J:147)

***futu** *PRM.* bundle up, tie, bind. *Doublet:* ***mbutu**. *Etym:* *butu 'group, crowd, flock, school, bunch, cluster' (PCEMP).
futu-s *Termanu.* yarn tied in bundles for weaving. (J:149)
futu-ʔ *Korbafo.*
futu-k *Bokai.*
futu-ʔ *Bilbaa.*
futu-s *Rikou.*
futu-s *Ba'a.*
futu-s *Oenale.*
n-futu *Ro'is Amarasi.* tie together.
n-futu (2) ʔ-futu-ʔ (3) na-ʔ-futu-ʔ *Kotos Amarasi.* 1) bind. 2) band, sash. 3) wear a sash.
n-futu (2) ʔ-futu-ʔ (3) ʔ-futu-ʔ (4) futu-s *Molo.* 1) bind. 2) girdle. 3) wears a girdle. 4) bound thread ready to be dyed. (M:133)
Out-comparisons:
butu *Semau Helong.* tie, tie up.
futu *East Tetun.* tie into a bundle, bundle up. (Mo:38)
futu (2) fuut *Mambae, South.* 1) gather, come together. 2) accompany, together with. (Grimes et al. 2014b:19)
wuku *Kisar.* tie.

***fuu** *PRM.* blow. *Doublet:* ***sabuu**. *Etym:* *buu (PCEMP. Blust and Trussel (ongoing) provide the Termanu form as evidence for both PCEMP *buu and PMP *qəmbus 'blow hard; snort, pant'. The connection between *qəmbus and **fuu** is spurious. (The expected regular reflex would be *epu.) The Termanu form is, furthermore, their only eastern evidence for positing *qəmbus at PMP rather than PWMP.).
fuu *Termanu.* blow, blow with the mouth. (J:143)
fuu *Korbafo.*
fuu *Bokai.*
fuu *Bilbaa.*
fuu *Rikou.*
fuu *Ba'a.*
fuu *Tii.*
fuu *Dengka.*
fuu *Oenale.*
n-fuu *Kotos Amarasi.* blow.
n-fuu (2) ʔ-fuʔu *Molo.* 1) blows (e.g. wind). 2) harmonica. (M:128)
Out-comparisons:
huu *Semau Helong.* blow.
huu *East Tetun.* blow on. (Mo:89)

H - h

***ha** *Morph:* ***na-ha**. *PRM.* eat. *Etym:* *kaən. *[irr. from PMP:* *k > *h (expect *k = *k)*]* *[Form:* This is one of the few monosyllabic roots reconstructed to PRM. Similarly, it is the only monosyllabic verb root in the Rote-Meto languages. *h develops as though it were a medial consonant in all daughters, thus providing evidence that this root obligatorily took vocalic agreement prefixes in PRM. The verbal inflection is irregular (and historically more conservative) in the Nuclear Rote languages with the prefixes having vowels other than /a/. (The segmentation in the entries below follows their historical analysis for these languages.) The wRM forms are regular for a verb that takes vocalic prefixes (see §2.6.5).*]*

- **-ʔa** *Termanu.* eats. *Morph:* 1SG **(ʔ)u-ʔa,** 2SG **mu-ʔa,** 3SG **na-ʔa,** 2PL/1PL.EXCL **mi-ʔa,** 1PL.INCL **ta-ʔa,** 3PL **la-ʔa**. (J:368)
- **-ʔa** *Korbafo.* *Morph:* 1SG **ku-ʔa,** 2SG **mu-ʔa,** 3SG **na-ʔa,** 2PL/1PL.EXCL **mi-ʔa,** 1PL.INCL **ta-ʔa,** 3PL **la-ʔa**.
- **-ʔa** *Bokai.* *Morph:* 1SG **ku-ʔa,** 2SG **mu-ʔa,** 3SG **na-ʔa,** 2PL/1PL.EXCL **mi-ʔa,** 1PL.INCL **ta-ʔa,** 3PL **la-ʔa**.
- **-a** *Bilbaa.* *Morph:* 1SG **ku-a,** 2SG **mu-a,** 3SG **na-a,** 2PL/1PL.EXCL **mi-a,** 1PL.INCL **ta-a,** 3PL **la-a**.
- **-a** *Landu.* eat. *Morph:* 3SG **na-a**. *[Note:* Forms for other persons are currently unknown.*]* (own field notes)
- **-a** *Rikou.* *Morph:* 1SG **(ʔ)u-a,** 2SG **mu-a,** 3SG **na-a,** 2PL/1PL.EXCL **mi-a,** 1PL.INCL **ta-a,** 3PL **ra-a**.
- **-a** *Oepao.* eat. *Morph:* 3SG **na-a,** 1PL.INCL **ta-a**. *[Note:* Forms for other persons are currently unknown, but are probably the same as Rikou.*]* (own field notes)
- **-ʔa** *Ba'a.* *Morph:* 1SG **(ʔ)u-ʔa,** 2SG **mu-ʔa,** 3SG **na-ʔa,** 2PL/1PL.EXCL **mi-ʔa,** 1PL.INCL **ta-ʔa,** 3PL **la-ʔa**.
- **-ʔa** *Lole.* *Morph:* 1SG **(ʔ)u-ʔa,** 2SG **mu-ʔa,** 3SG **na-ʔa,** 2PL/1PL.EXCL **mi-ʔa,** 1PL.INCL **ta-ʔa,** 3PL **la-ʔa**.
- **-ʔa** *Tii.* *Morph:* 1SG **(ʔ)u-ʔa,** 2SG **mu-ʔa,** 3SG **na-ʔa,** 2PL/1PL.EXCL **mi-ʔa,** 1PL.INCL **ta-ʔa,** 3PL **ra-ʔa**.
- **-a** *Dengka.* *Morph:* 1SG **(ʔ)u-a,** 2SG **mu-a,** 3SG **na-a,** 2PL/1PL.EXCL **mi-a,** 1PL.INCL **ta-a,** 3PL **la-a**.
- **-a** *Oenale.* *Morph:* 1SG **ʔu-a,** 2SG **mu-a,** 3SG **na-a,** 2PL/1PL.EXCL **mi-a,** 1PL.INCL **ta-a,** 3PL **ra-a**.
- **-a** *Dela.* eat. *Morph:* 1SG **ʔu-a,** 2SG **mu-a,** 3SG **na-a,** 2PL/1PL.EXCL **mi-a,** 1PL.INCL **ta-a,** 3PL **ra-a**.
- **-ha** *Ro'is Amarasi.* eat (soft food). *Morph:* 1SG **ku-ha,** 2SG **mu-ah,** 3SG **na-ah,** 2PL/1PL.EXCL **mi-ah,** 1PL.INCL **ta-ah**. *[Form:* Not all forms have been attested unmetathesised, but 1SG **ku-ha**, 3SG **na-ha**, and 3PL **na-ha-n** (the last two in Kotos below) indicate that metathesis is fully productive with this verb.*]*
- **-ha** *Kotos Amarasi.* eat (soft food). *Morph:* 1SG **ʔu-ah,** 2SG **mu-ah,** 3SG **na-ha,** 2PL/1PL.EXCL **mi-ah,** 1PL.INCL **ta-ah,** 3PL **na-ha-n**.
- **-ha** *Molo.* eat. *Morph:* 3SG **na-ha**. (M:51)

-ah *Kusa-Manea.* eat. *Morph:* 1PL.INCL **ta-ah**. *[Form:* metathesised form of **ta-ha**.*]*
Out-comparisons:
kaa *Semau Helong.* eat.
haa *East Tetun.* eat. (Mo:101)
-ʔon, -ʔan *Kisar.* eat. *Morph:* 1SG **oʔon,** 2SG/2PL/1PL.EXCL **moʔon,** 3SG **naʔan,** 1PL.INCL **kaʔan,** 3PL **raʔan**.

***haa1** *CER.* lontar thorn.
beba_haa-k *Termanu.* the edge of the branching thorn of the **beba**; also in **paŋa_haa-k**. (J:150)
Out-comparisons:
haa *Semau Helong.* lontar stem.

***haa2** *PRM.* four. *Etym:* *əpat. *[irr. from PMP:* *ə > Ø with doubling of the final vowel to create a disyllable*] [Form:* External witnesses suggest earlier **paat. The Welaun correspondence indicates #VC > #CV metathesis of *əpat > **pəat.*]*
haa *Termanu.* four. (J:150)
haa *Korbafo.*
haa *Bokai.*
haa *Bilbaa.*
haa *Rikou.*
haa *Ba'a.*
haa *Tii.*
haa *Dengka.*
haa *Oenale.*
haa *Ro'is Amarasi.* four.
haa *Kotos Amarasi.* four.
haa|ʔ *Molo.* four. (M:134)
Out-comparisons:
aat *Semau Helong.* four.
haat *East Tetun.* four. (Mo:39)
paat *Kemak.* four.
hoat *Welaun.* four.
faat *Mambae, South.* four. (Grimes et al. 2014:17)
ihaat *Galolen.* four.
woʔakka *Kisar.* four.

***habu** *PnMeto.* cloud, fog. *Etym:* *kabut 'fog, haze, mist; indistinct, blurry'. *[Note:* Reconstructed with initial *h (not *k) as this is a Proto-Nuclear Meto form. Thus, I am proposing PRM *k > Proto-Nuclear Meto *h in this form.*] [minority from PMP:* *b (> *ɓ) = *b /V_V (expect *f)*] [Form:* If this form were ***kaɓu** in PRM it would exemplify pattern k-3/4 for initial *k.*]*
habu *Kusa-Manea.* cloud, fog.

***hade** *PRM.* rice in the field; rice plant. *Etym:* *pajay. *[minority from PMP:* *j > *d (expect *ɗ)*] [Sporadic:* *h > Ø in wRM.*]*
hade *Termanu.* rice, the plant and the crop, the grains as long as they have not yet been husked. (J:151)
hade *Korbafo.*
hade *Bokai.*
hade *Bilbaa.*
hade *Rikou.*
hade *Ba'a.*
haɗe *Tii.*
ale *Dengka.*
are *Oenale.*
are *Dela.* rice plant.
aan/ʔoe|k *Ro'is Amarasi.* wet rice field. *[Form:* The final element is from **oe** 'water' with **k** presumably from nominal suffix ***-k**.*]*
ain/ʔoe|k *Kotos Amarasi.* wet rice field.
ane *Amanuban/Amanatun.* field rice.
ane (2) aan/ʔoe|k *Molo.* 1) paddy rice. 2) wet rice field. (M:22)
ane (2) aen/oa|k *Kusa-Manea.* 1) field rice. 2) wet rice field. *[Form:* no medial glottal stop.*]*
Out-comparisons:
ale *Semau Helong.* field rice.
hare *East Tetun.* rice (plant and unhusked grain). (Mo:77)
are *Dhao.* rice on stalk; grain plant.
are *Hawu.* rice on stalk; grain plant.

***hae** *PRM.* breathe.
hae (2) hae, hai *Termanu.* 1) breathe. 2) rest, stop. (J:152)
hae (2) hae, hai *Korbafo.*

hae (2) hae, hai *Bokai.*
hae (2) hae, hai *Bilbaa.*
hae (2) hae, hai *Rikou.*
hae (2) hae, hai *Ba'a.*
hae (2) hae, hai *Tii.*
hae (2) hae, hai *Dengka.*
hae (2) hae, hai *Oenale.*
n-hae *Kotos Amarasi.* physically tired, exhausted.
Out-comparisons:
kae, hkae *Semau Helong.* tire, weary. *[irr. from PRM:* *h = *(h)* *k* correspondence*]*
a~ae, ae *Dhao.* breath, stop.

***haeǀʔ** *PMeto.* foot/leg. *Doublet:* ***ei**. *Etym:* *kakay (Wolff 2010:862) (Reconstructed with the doublets *waqay and *qaqay.). *[Note:* Reconstructed with initial *h (not *k) as this is a Proto-Meto form. Thus, I am proposing PRM *k > PMeto *h in this form.*] [Sporadic:* *VV-k > *VVʔ > VʔV in Amarasi (perceptual metathesis).*] [Form:* If this form is regular from *kakay it exemplifies pattern k-3/4 for initial *k and pattern k-8 for medial *k).*]*
hae-f *Ro'is Amarasi.* foot/leg.
haʔe, hae-f *Kotos Amarasi.* foot/leg.
hae-k *Molo.* leg. (M:134)
Out-comparisons:
kae_ʃəla *Hawu.* foot, leg.

***hai1** *Morph:* ***hai-k**. *Rote.* container woven from lontar leaves. *Etym:* **pai (pre-RM).
hai-k *Termanu.* bucket woven from lontar leaves. (J:154)
hai-ʔ *Korbafo.*
hai-k *Bokai.*
hai-k *Bilbaa.*
hai-ʔ *Rikou.*
hai-k *Ba'a.*
hai-k *Tii.*
hai-ʔ *Dengka.*
hai-ʔ *Oenale.*
Out-comparisons:
pai *Semau Helong.* basket.
fai *Bolok Helong.* basket.
pai *Hawu.* plate (woven from lontar leaves).

***hai2** *PRM.* stingray. *Etym:* *paRih 'skate, stingray (generic); a constellation'.
hai *Termanu.* (sting)ray. (J:153)
hai *Korbafo.*
hai *Bokai.*
hai *Bilbaa.*
hai *Rikou.*
hai *Ba'a.*
hai *Tii.*
hai *Dengka.*
hai *Oenale.*
haiǀf *Meto.* (J:153)
Out-comparisons:
ai *Helong.* *[irr. from PMP:* *R > Ø (expect *l*)*]* (J:153)

***ha(ʔ)i** *Rote.* take.
hai (2) hai (3) hai (4) hai (5) hai (6) haʔi *Termanu.* 1) dismiss. 2) take out in certain expressions. 3) bring in the expressions **ala hai oe=a leo dae neu** 'someone brings the water to the lower regions' and **manakolu-la hai soo** 'the harvesters have brought (the ears of corn) to the big mat'. 4) decamp, leave, in the expression **ala hai leo dea leu** 'they leave, they go to the field to stay there temporarily during the harvest season'. 5) as a separate word usually **haik** e.g. **hai(k) ndai, (bufu)** 'pull up a scoop-net (or a trap), take something out of the water'. 6) take, fetch, take away. (J:153f)
hai (2) haʔi (3) hai (4) hai (5) hai (6) haʔi *Korbafo.*
(2) hai (3) haʔi (4) hai (5) hai (6) haʔi *Bokai.*
hai (3) hai (4) hai (5) hai (6) hai *Bilbaa.*
(2) hai (3) hai (4) hai (5) hai (6) (hai ?) *Rikou.*
hai (2) hai (3) haʔi (4) hai (5) hai (6) haʔi *Ba'a.*

hai (2) hai (3) haʔi (4) hai (5) hai (6) haʔi *Tii.*
hai (2) haʔi (3) haʔi (4) hai (6) haʔi *Dengka.*
hai (3) hai (4) hai (6) haʔi *Oenale.*
Out-comparisons:
əgo *Hawu.* take. *[Note:* Jonker (1908:154) gives **agi** 'take out', which may be from Malay *angkit.]*
ahi *Bima.* take something out of somewhere, take away. (Jonker 1893:1)

***halu** *Morph:* ***halu-k**. *PRM.* pestle. *Etym:* *qahəlu. *[minority from PMP:* *q > *h*] [irr. from PRM:* *h > Ø in Rote*]*
alu-k *Termanu.* pestle. (J:8)
alu-ʔ *Korbafo.*
alu-k *Bokai.*
alu-ʔ *Bilbaa.*
alu-ʔ *Rikou.*
alu-k *Ba'a.*
alu-k *Tii.*
alu-ʔ *Dengka.*
alu-ʔ *Oenale.*
alu̯-ʔ *Dela.* pounder.
ha͡unu|k *Ro'is Amarasi.* pestle.
hanu|k *Kotos Amarasi.* pestle.
hanu *Amanuban/Amanatun.* pestle.
hanu *Kopas.* pestle.
hanu *Kusa-Manea.* pestle.
Out-comparisons:
alu *Semau Helong.* pestle, pounder.
alu(k) *East Tetun.* pestle for grinding grain. (Mo:3)

***hambu** *PRM.* overtake, catch up with. *[History:* Blust and Trussel (ongoing) reconstruct Proto-Philippine *qabut 'reach, overtake, catch up with'.*]*
hapu *Termanu.* overtake. (J:162)
hapu *Korbafo.*
hapu *Bokai.*
hapu *Bilbaa.*
hapu *Rikou.*
hampu *Ba'a.*
hambu *Tii.*
hambu *Dengka.*
hambu *Oenale.*
n-hapu *Molo.* overtakes, finds. *[Note:* Jonker (1908:162) specifies **hapu** as being from Taebenu.*]* (M:140)
Out-comparisons:
hapu *Semau Helong.* get, obtain, able.
abβu *Dhao.* get, find, receive; able, can, be able to; exist, be, there are.
abu (2) abo *Hawu.* 1) get, find, encounter (pl.). 2) get, find, encounter (sg.).

***hanas** *Morph:* ***ma-hanas, *na-hana**. *PRM.* warm, hot. *Etym:* *panas.
hanas (2) na-ma-hana (3) na-hana *Termanu.* 1) hot, warm of water and everything which can be heated up, also of the body; warmth. 2) be warm, such as water or the body. 3) warm up. (J:158f)
hana-ʔ *Korbafo.*
hana-k *Bokai.*
hana-ʔ *Bilbaa.*
hanas *Rikou.*
hanas *Ba'a.*
hanas *Tii.*
hanas *Dengka.*
hanas *Oenale.*
m|anas *Ro'is Amarasi.* sun.
m|anas (2) na-hana (3) k|hanas *Kotos Amarasi.* 1) sun, midday. 2) cook. 3) drought.
m|anas (2) na-hana *Molo.* 1) sun. 2) cooks. (M:304)
m|anas *Kusa-Manea.* hot. *[Semantics:* **maputuʔ** is also 'hot'. The semantic difference between **manas** and **maputuʔ** is currently unclear.*]*
Out-comparisons:
manas *East Tetun.* hot, warm, burning; pungent, caustic, hot to the taste; *n.* heat. (Mo:138)
manha *Kisar.* hot.

***hani**1 *Rote.* bait, feed (animals). *Etym:* *paniŋ 'bait; fodder; to feed animals'.
hani-k *Termanu.* bait, bait for fishing. (J:161)
hani-ʔ *Korbafo.*
hani-k *Bokai.*
hani-ʔ *Bilbaa.*
hani-ʔ *Rikou.*
hani-k *Ba'a.*
hani-k *Tii.*
hani-ʔ *Dengka.*
ha~hani-ʔ *Oenale.*
hani *Dela.* feed animals.
Out-comparisons:
hani *Semau Helong.* feed the chickens.
ani *Hawu.* bait, chicken-feed. (J:161)
<pàni> (2) <pàningu> *Kambera.* 1) feed especially for chickens. 2) bait. (On:398)
pəniŋ *Sika.* give food to chickens. (Pareira and Lewis 1998:158)

***hani**2 *Morph:* ***hani-k**. *PnRote.* kind of shell, turtle shell. *Etym:* **napi (pre-RM). *[Sporadic:* consonant metathesis *nVp > *pVn > *hVn.*]*
hani-k (2) kea hani-k (3) poe hani-k *Termanu.* 1) kind of shell. 2) the shell of a turtle. 3) the shell/shuck of a shrimp. (J:161)
hani-ʔ *Korbafo.*
hani-k *Bokai.*
hani-ʔ *Rikou.*
hani-k *Ba'a.*
(hani-k ?) *Tii.*
Out-comparisons:
<nepi> *Kambera.* scale. (On:317)
<napi> *Anakalang. [Note:* also in Mamboru, Weyewa, and Kodi.*]*
<napu> *Lewa.*

***hano** *Morph:* ***ka-hano**. *PRM.* fungus infection which produces light patches on the skin: Tinea flava or Pityriasis. *Etym:* *panaw.
ha~hano *Termanu.* spots of a lighter colour on the skin. (J:161)
ha~hano *Korbafo.*
ha~hano *Bokai.*
ha~hano *Bilbaa.*
ha~hano *Rikou.*
ha~hano *Ba'a.*
ha~hano *Tii.*
hano *Dengka.*
hano *Oenale.*
ʔ|hano *Kotos Amarasi.* tinea.
<hano> *Molo.* rash on the face. (M:139)
Out-comparisons:
ano *Helong.* (J:161)

***haŋga** *PwRote.* hand span. *See:* ***teŋga**. *Etym:* **paŋga (pre-RM).
haŋga *Dengka.* span. (J:699)
haŋga *Oenale.* span. (J:699)
Out-comparisons:
<ăga> *Hawu.* (J:621)
<pangga> *Kambera.* span (from thumb to middle-finger), to measure that distance. (On:400)
paga *Sika.* span. (Pareira and Lewis 1998:155)

***hao** *PRM.* feed. *Etym:* **pao (pre-RM).
hao *Termanu.* eat with the hand, put a bite (of food) in one's mouth. (J:161)
hao *Korbafo.*
hao *Bokai.*
hao *Bilbaa.*
hao *Rikou.*
hao *Ba'a.*
hao *Tii.*
hao *Dengka.*
hao *Oenale.*
n-hao *Ro'is Amarasi.* feed.
n-hao *Kotos Amarasi.* feed.
Out-comparisons:
pao *Bima.* mouthful, make mouthfuls, place into the mouth. (Jonker 1893:79)

***hapi** *PRM.* pinch, clamp. *Doublet:* ***kaɓi**. *Etym:* *kapit 'pinch, press between; fasten thatch together with slats in roofing a house'. *[irr. from PMP:* *k > *h*] [minority from PMP:* *p = *p*] [irr. from PRM:* *h > *h*, Ø in Oenale*]*

hapi *Keka.* pinch. (J:699)

hapi *Ba'a.*

na-ka-hapi *Tii.*

hapi *Dengka.*

hapi (2) api *Oenale.* 1) pinch. (J:699) 2) clamps. (J:678)

n-hapi *Kotos Amarasi.* clasp, entreaty.

n-hapi *Molo.* cuts through the skin with a clamp. (M:134)

***hara** *Morph:* ***hara-k**. *PRM.* voice, sound.

hala-k *Termanu.* voice, noise of a person or animal. (J:156)

hala-ʔ *Korbafo.*

hala-k *Bokai.*

hala-ʔ *Bilbaa.*

hara-ʔ *Rikou.*

hala-k *Ba'a.*

hara-k *Tii.*

hala-ʔ *Dengka.*

hara-ʔ *Oenale.*

hana-f (2) na-hana *Ro'is Amarasi.* 1) voice. 2) make a sound.

hana-f (2) na-hana *Kotos Amarasi.* 1) voice, sound, news. 2) make a sound, hum, resound (like a bell).

hana-f (2) na-haan *Molo.* 1) sound. 2) resound. (M:138)

Out-comparisons:

bhala, khala *Funai Helong.* voice, sound.

fala *Semau Helong.* taste; voice, sound.

hala *Bolok Helong.* voice, sound.

***haru** *Morph:* ***haru-k**. *PRM.* shoulder. *[irr. from PRM:* *h > Ø in Rote*]*

alu-k *Termanu.* shoulder of people and animals. (J:8)

alu-ʔ *Korbafo.*

alu-k *Bokai.*

alu-ʔ *Bilbaa.*

aru-ʔ *Landu.* shoulder. (own field notes)

aru-ʔ *Rikou.*

alu-k *Ba'a.*

aru-k *Tii.*

alu-ʔ *Dengka.*

aru-ʔ *Oenale.*

ar͡u-ʔ *Dela.* shoulder.

ha͡unu-f *Ro'is Amarasi.* shoulder.

hanu-f *Kotos Amarasi.* shoulder.

hanu-k *Amfo'an.* shoulder.

hanu-f *Kusa-Manea.* shoulder.

Out-comparisons:

adu *Semau Helong.* shoulder.

***hatahori** *PRM.* man, person. *Doublet:* ***ata**. *Etym:* *qaRta + *qudip 'person + living' (Charles Grimes pers. comm.). *[Note:* Osmond and Ross (2016b:47) reconstruct POc *[qa]ta-maquri 'living person' noting it '... spans a large piece of Oceania, but it has few reflexes and may reflect parallel innovations'. Kemak has **atamoas** 'human being', which is similarly a compound of a reflex of *qaRta with **moas** 'living'.*] [minority from PMP:* *q > *h; *q > *h*] [Sporadic:* *h > Ø in wRM.*] [Form:* Loss of medial *h in Meto is probably due to historic antepenultimate vowel reduction with subsequent simplification of the resulting consonant cluster; e.g. ***hatahori** > **ataholi > **atholi > pre-Meto **atoli > Proto-Meto ***atoni**.*]*

hataholi *Termanu.* person. (J:164f)

hataholi *Korbafo.*

hataholi *Bokai.*

hataholi *Ba'a.*

hataholi *Lole.* (Zacharias et al. 2014)

hatahori *Tii.*

atahori *Oenale.*

atahori *Dela.* person.

atoni|ʔ *Ro'is Amarasi.* man, person.

atoni|ʔ *Kotos Amarasi.* man, person. *[Semantics:* By default this term refers to males, but can be used more generally to refer to 'person'.*]*

atoni-ʤ *Amfo'an.* man, person.

<atoni> *Molo.* human, man. (M:34)
atoin *Kusa-Manea.* person.
Out-comparisons:
°atuli *Semau Helong.* person, people. *Borrowed from:* Meto before *l > *n*.
***hauk** *PRM.* soothe.
na-ka-ha~hau-k (2) hau-k *Termanu.* 1) calm down, soothe, e.g. a crying child. 2) quieten down, stop crying (e.g. like a small child). (J:166)
na-ka-ha~hauʔ *Korbafo.*
na-ka-ha~hau-k *Bokai.*
na-ha~hau-ʔ *Rikou.*
na-ka-ha~hau-k *Ba'a.*
na-ka-ha~hau-k *Tii.*
na-ʔa-ha~hau-ʔ *Oenale.*
(na-)hauk *Meto.* stop crying. (J:166)
***hedu** *Morph:* ***hedu-k**. *PRM.* gall bladder, bitter. *Etym:* *qapəju 'gall, gall bladder, bile'. *[minority from PMP:* *j > *d (expect *ɗ)*]* *[Sporadic:* *h > Ø in wRM.*]* *[Form:* PwRM ***meru** can be reconstructed. It is from earlier **ma-hedu.*]*
hedu-k (2) ma-ka-hedu-k *Termanu.* 1) gallbladder. 2) bitter. (J:169)
hedu-ʔ (2) ma-ka-hedu-ʔ *Korbafo.*
hedu-k (2) ma-ka-hedu-k *Bokai.*
hedu-ʔ *Bilbaa.*
hedu=na *Landu.* gallbladder. (own field notes)
hedu-ʔ (2) ma-hedu-ʔ *Rikou.*
hedu-k (2) ma-ka-hedu-k *Ba'a.*
heɗu-k (2) ma-ka-heɗu-k *Lole.* (Zacharias et al. 2014)
heɗu-k *Tii.*
elu-ʔ (2) m|elu *Dengka.*
eru-ʔ (2) m|eru *Oenale.*
eru-ʔ (2) m|eru *Dela.* 1) gallbladder. 2) bitter.
e͡unu-f *Ro'is Amarasi.* gallbladder.
enu-f (2) m|enu|ʔ *Kotos Amarasi.* 1) gallbladder. 2) bitter.
<enu> (2) m|enu|ʔ *Molo.* 1) gall bladder. (M:102) 2) bitter. (M:319)
enu-f (2) m|enu|ʔ *Kusa-Manea.* 1) gallbladder. 2) bitter.
Out-comparisons:
ilu-n *Semau Helong.* gall bladder.
horun *Fehan Tetun.* gall, if you vomit till vomit is blue, this stuff comes from the **horun**.
naʔan hourun *East Tetun.* bile. (Mo:88)
ʔeru~ʔeru-n *Kisar.* gallbladder.
***heɗis** *Rote.* sick, pain. *Doublet:* ***meras**. *Etym:* *hapəjis 'smarting, stinging pain'.
hedis (2) na-ma-hedi *Termanu.* 1) pain, sickness, painful. 2) be or become sick. (J:168)
hedi-ʔ *Korbafo.*
hedi-k *Bokai.*
hedi-ʔ *Bilbaa.*
(2) na-ma-hedi *Landu.* s/he's sick. (own field notes)
hedis *Rikou.*
hedis *Ba'a.*
heɗis *Tii.*
heɗis *Dengka.*
heɗis *Oenale.*
heɗis (2) na-ma-heɗi-ʔ *Dela.* 1) illness, sickness. 2) be sick.
Out-comparisons:
ili *Semau Helong.* sick, pain.
***hee₁** *CERM.* lobster.
poe_hee-k *Termanu.* kind of big lobster. (J:166)
poe_hee-ʔ *Korbafo.*
poe_hee-ʔ *Bilbaa.*
kpoe_hee oo *Ro'is Amarasi.* lobster.
poe_hee *Kotos Amarasi.* lobster.
Out-comparisons:
eeŋ *Semau Helong.* lobster, crayfish.
***hee₂** *Rote.* press out. *Etym:* *pəRəq 'squeeze out juice, wring out water'. *[irr. from PRM:* Ø > ʔ ~ Ø in Termanu and Bokai*]* *[Form:* regular *ə > *e* / _q#.

Forms with medial *ʔ* are perhaps due to influence from ***keʔe** and/or reflexes of PMP *gəmgəm.*]*

heʔe, hee *Termanu.* press, press out. (J:169)

hee *Korbafo.*

heʔe, hee *Bokai.*

hee *Bilbaa.*

hee *Rikou.*

hee *Ba'a.*

hee *Tii.* *[Form:* A putative alternate form **heʔe** is given with question mark.*]*

hee, ee *Dengka.*

hee *Oenale.*

Out-comparisons:

hele *Helong.* (J:169)

***hela** *nRM.* pull. *[irr. from PRM:* *l > *r/l* in Meto*]*

hela *Termanu.* pull, drag, drag along. (J:170)

hela *Korbafo.*

hela *Bokai.*

hela *Bilbaa.*

hela *Rikou.*

hela *Ba'a.*

hela *Tii.*

n-hera *Kotos Amarasi.* pull.

n-hela *Molo.* pulls. (M:144)

Out-comparisons:

pela *Semau Helong.* pull.

***helu** *Rote.* bend. *Doublet:* ***fenu, *felu.** *Etym:* *bəluk. *[irr. from PMP:* *b > *h*]*

helu *Termanu.* bend something, bent back to the point of breaking. (J:172)

helu *Korbafo.*

helu *Bokai.*

helu *Bilbaa.*

helu *Rikou.*

helu *Ba'a.*

helu *Tii.*

helu *Dengka.*

helu *Oenale.*

Out-comparisons:

hilu *Semau Helong.* curve, bend. *[irr. from PMP:* *b > *h* /#_ (possibly a loan from Rote)*]*

***hena** *PRM.* hope.

na-ma-hena (2) dale=na hena~hena *Termanu.* 1) hope, wish, expect, trust. 2) her/his heart is full of hope, s/he is full of hope. (J:173)

na-ma-hena *Korbafo.*

na-ma-hena *Bokai.*

na-ma-hena *Bilbaa.*

na-ma-hena *Rikou.*

na-ma-hena *Ba'a.*

na-ma-hena *Tii.*

na-ma-hena *Dengka.*

na-ma-hena *Oenale.*

na-mhena *Meto.* (J:173)

Out-comparisons:

°namhena *Semau Helong. Borrowed from:* Meto. (J:173)

***hene** *PRM.* climb. *Etym:* *panahik. *[Sporadic:* antepenultimate *a > **ə > *e.*]*

hene *Termanu.* in the other varieties of Rote still means ‘climb’ but in Termanu only in the phrase **hene (noo): ‘climb a coconut tree to pick the fruit’. Also in metaphorical senses: climb = ‘increase, grow’**. (J:174)

hene *Bokai.*

hene *Bilbaa.*

hene *Rikou.*

hene *Ba'a.*

hene *Tii.*

hene *Oenale.*

***henu** *CERM.* full. *Etym:* *pənuq.

henu-k *Termanu.* full. (J:176)

henu-ʔ *Korbafo.*

henu-k *Bokai.*

henu-ʔ *Bilbaa.*

henu-ʔ *Rikou.*

henu-k *Ba'a.*

na-henu *Ro'is Amarasi.* be full, fill up.

na-henu *Kotos Amarasi.* be full, fill up.

<henu> *Molo.* full. (M:145)

na-heun *Kusa-Manea.* fill, full.

Out-comparisons:

inu *Semau Helong.* full.

benu *Kemak.* full.

penu *Kisar.* full.

***henuh** *PRM.* beads. *Etym:* **penuk (pre-RM). *[Sporadic:* *h > Ø in wRM; vowel height harmony *e > *i* /_Cu in wRM*]* *[Form:* Blust and Trussel (ongoing) reconstruct PMP *hinuq, and PAN *SiNuq. The eastern correspondences point to **penuk, and it may be that we have to reconstruct a doublet to P(CE)MP. If so, the wRM reflexes could reflect PMP *hinuq (but with irregular final *q > *h* as retained by Meto), while the other Rote reflexes reflect **penuk.*]*

henu *Termanu.* bead, beads. (J:176)

henu *Korbafo.*

henu *Bokai.*

henu *Bilbaa.*

henu *Rikou.*

henu *Ba'a.*

henu *Tii.*

inu *Dengka.*

inu *Oenale.*

inu *Dela.* beads.

inuh *Kotos Amarasi.* beads.

inuh *Molo.* bead. (M:161)

inuh *Kusa-Manea.* necklace, beads.

Out-comparisons:

henu *East Tetun.* wear on the neck, anything worn on the neck. (Mo:85)

enu *Ili'uun.* bead. (dJ:114)

pinu (2) pinu e-wadun *Buru.* 1) carry with strap over shoulder (e.g. hunting pouch). 2) necklace. *[Form:* **wadun** = 'nape of neck'.*]* (Grimes and Grimes 2020:745)

penu *Ende.* hang on the neck.

***hendam** *PRM.* wild pandanus. *Etym:* *paŋdan 'pandanus'. *[irr. from PMP:* *a > *e; *n > *m*]* *[Sporadic:* *h > Ø in wRM; Ø > *ʔ* /#_ in Dela-Oenale.*]* *[Form:* The initial *ʔ* in Dela-Oenale may point to an earlier initial **k. Additional evidence for this comes from Ili'uun **keʧan**. The source of this initial **k could be the nominal prefix ***ka-**.*]*

hena-k *Termanu.* pandanus, also: pineapple. (J:174)

hena-k *Bokai.*

hena-ʔ *Bilbaa.*

henda-ʔ *Landu.* pandanus. (own field notes)

henda-ʔ *Rikou.*

hera-ʔ *Oepao.* (own field notes)

hena-k *Ba'a.*

henda-k *Lole.* (Zacharias et al. 2014)

henda-k *Tii.*

(ʔ)enda-ʔ *Dengka.*

ʔenda-ʔ *Oenale.*

ʔenda-ʔ *Dela.* pandanus.

eram, erem *Ro'is Amarasi.* wild pandanus.

ekam *Kotos Amarasi.* wild pandanus.

ekam *Molo.* pandanus. (M:99)

ekam *Kusa-Manea.* wild pandanus. *Usage:* Upper Manulea village.

ekom *Kusa-Manea.* wild pandanus. *Usage:* Uabau' village. *[Sporadic:* *a > *o* /_m (compare PMP *maqitəm > PMeto ***metam** > **metom** 'black').*]*

Out-comparisons:

edan *Semau Helong.* pandanus.

keʧan *Ili'uun.* pandanus. *[irr. from PMP:* *p > (*Ø) > *k* (compare *pusəj > **kusan**, *hutək > **gutan**, and *baqbaq > **kahan**)*]* (dJ:121)

***heŋge** *PRM.* hang (rope/cord), tie. *[History:* possibly connected with PMP *hikət.*]*

heŋe *Termanu.* tie (general). (J:174)

heŋe *Korbafo.*

heŋe *Bilbaa.*

heke *Rikou.*

heŋge *Ba'a.*

heŋge *Tii.*

heŋge *Dengka.*

na-ʔ|heke (2) ʔ-heke-ʔ *Kotos Amarasi.* 1) hang/suspend around the neck. 2) necklace.
na-ʔ|heke *Molo.* garland with a cord. (M:143)
Out-comparisons:
eki *Kisar.* living beings that hang from something, e.g. bat hanging from branch, people hanging from a branch.

***heŋgu** *PRM.* eat something hard. *Etym:* *pagut 'snap at with the mouth' (Blust and Trussel (ongoing) note regarding their reconstruction: 'The semantics of this comparison leave something to be desired.' They also reconstruct the root *-gut 'gnaw'.). *[irr. from PMP:* *a > *e*] [Sporadic:* *h > Ø in Meto.*]*
heŋu *Termanu.* nibble on something hard; bite a piece of something with the teeth. (J:175)
heŋu *Korbafo.*
heŋu *Bokai.*
heŋu *Bilbaa.*
heku *Rikou.*
heŋgu *Ba'a.*
heŋgu *Tii.*
heŋgu *Dengka.*
heŋgu *Oenale.*
n-eku *Kotos Amarasi.* eat; implies eating something hard such as sugar, coconut, bread, cake.
n-eku *Molo.* eats. (M:98)
Out-comparisons:
<pànggitu> *Kambera.* chew on. *[Form:* The final vowels in the forms from languages of Sumba is epenthetic.*]* (On:401)
<pànggutu> *Lewa.*
<pàgutu> *Anakalang.*
<pangguta> *Mamboru.*

***heo** *Morph:* ***he~heo**. *Rote.* move.
he~heo-k *Termanu.* he turns himself, rotates himself. (J:178)
he~heo-ʔ *Korbafo.*
he~heo-k *Bokai.*
he~heo-ʔ *Rikou.*
he~heo-k *Ba'a.*
he~heo-k *Tii.*
he~heo-ʔ *Dengka.*
he~heo-ʔ *Oenale.*
Out-comparisons:
he~heon *Semau Helong.* move.

***hesu** *PnRote.* fart. *Etym:* **pəsu (pre-RM). *[irr. from PRM:* *h > Ø in Central East Rote*]*
esu *Termanu.* fart, wind. (J:116)
esu *Korbafo.*
esu *Bokai.*
esu *Bilbaa.*
esu *Rikou.*
esu *Ba'a.*
hesu *Tii.*
Out-comparisons:
nisu *Semau Helong.* fart.
hosu, housu *East Tetun.* expel flatus through the anus, break wind, fart. (Mo:88)
pəhu *Hawu.*
<kapíhu> *Kambera.* wind, flatulence, pass wind. (On:165)
<kapísu> *Anakalang.*
<kapàsu> *Mamboru.*
<pou> *Weyewa.*
<pàsu> *Kodi.*
potʃu *Bima.* wind, pass wind. (Jonker 1893:82)

***həndi** *Rote.* finish, finished. *Etym:* *qəti 'stop, end, finish, complete; finished, used up'. *[irr. from PMP:* *t > *nd (also in Helong)*] [minority from PMP:* *q > *h*] [Form:* *nd > *n* /ə_ in Tii and Rikou.*]*
heni *Termanu.* out or gone, disappeared or drained away. (J:175)
heni *Korbafo.*
heni *Bokai.*
heni *Bilbaa.*
heni *Rikou.*
heni *Ba'a.*
heni *Tii.*
hendi *Dengka.*
hendi *Oenale.*
Out-comparisons:
hidi *Semau Helong.* finish, end.

***hia** *PRM.* want. *Etym:* *pian 'want, desire, wish or long for'. *[irr. from PRM:* *a > *i* in Rote; *ia > (*e) > *a* in Kusa-Manea*] [Form:* Medial *ia is required to account for *e* in Amarasi.*]*

hii *Termanu.* want, be inclined to, desire, wish, consent. (J:179)

hii *Korbafo.*

hii *Bokai.*

hii *Bilbaa.*

hii *Rikou.*

hii *Ba'a.*

hii *Tii.*

hii *Dengka.*

hii *Oenale.*

hii *Dela.* like.

he *Kotos Amarasi.* irrealis marker; want, will. *[Note:* **hena** and **henatiʔ** appear to have the same functions.*]*

ha *Kusa-Manea.* irrealis marker.

***hida** *PRM.* how much, how many. *Doublet:* ***hiɗa**. *Etym:* *pija 'interrogative of quantity: how much?, how many?; adjective of indefinite quantity: some, several, a few'. *[minority from PMP:* *j > *d (expect *ɗ)*]*

hida *Termanu.* how much/many? (J:182)

hida *Korbafo.*

hida *Bokai.*

hida *Bilbaa.*

hida *Rikou.*

hida *Ba'a.*

hiɗa *Lole.*

hiɗa *Tii.*

hira *Oenale.*

hira *Dela.* several, how many, some, how much.

hian *Kusa-Manea.* how much/many? *[Form:* metathesised form of (currently unattested) ***hina**.*]*

Out-comparisons:

ila *Semau Helong.* how many?, several.

hira *East Tetun.* how much, how many? (Mo:86)

***hiɗa** *PwRote.* few, reduce. *Doublet:* ***hida**. *Etym:* *pija 'interrogative of quantity: how much?, how many?; adjective of indefinite quantity: some, several, a few'. *[irr. from PRM:* *h > Ø in Dengka*]*

iɗa-ʔ (2) na-ma-iɗa *Dengka.* 1) few. 2) reduce. (J:705)

na-ma-hiɗa *Oenale.* reduce. (J:702)

hiɗa(k) *Dela.* few.

***hine** *PwRM.* know. *[Sporadic:* vowel height harmony *e > *i* /iC_ in some Meto*]*

na-hine *Dengka.* know. (J:702)

na-hine *Oenale.* know. (J:702)

na-hini *Ro'is Amarasi.* know.

na-hini, na-hine (2) ma-hine-ʔ *Kotos Amarasi.* 1) know. *Usage:* The form **na-hini** is much more common than **na-hine**. 2) knowledge, wisdom.

na-hiin (2) <hine-n> *Molo.* 1) knows. 2) knowledge. (M:148)

na-hini *Kusa-Manea.* know.

***hiri** *PRM.* choose, select; to pick out. *Etym:* *piliq. *[irr. from PMP:* *l > *r*] [irr. from PRM:* *i > *e* in Rote*] [Sporadic:* *h > Ø in Meto; diphthongisation in Meto: *i > *ai.]*

hele *Termanu.* choose, select. (J:170)

hele *Korbafo.*

hele *Bokai.*

hele *Bilbaa.*

here *Rikou.*

hele *Ba'a.*

here *Tii.*

hele *Dengka.*

here *Oenale.*

<anaini> *Molo.* one chooses stones in a row for the sequence, in which one tells a story or investigates a matter. (M:11)

Out-comparisons:

huli *Semau Helong.* choose, select, appoint, pick; select out from a bunch. *[irr. from PMP:* *i > *u]*

hili *East Tetun.* pick up from the ground; to arrange. (Mo:86)
piɗi *Hawu.* choose, select, appoint, set aside.

***hitu** *PRM.* seven. *Etym:* *pitu.
hitu *Termanu.* seven. (J:185)
hitu *Korbafo.*
hitu *Bokai.*
hitu *Bilbaa.*
hitu *Rikou.*
hitu *Ba'a.*
hitu *Tii.*
hitu *Dengka.*
hitu *Oenale.*
hitu *Ro'is Amarasi.* seven.
hitu *Kotos Amarasi.* seven.
hitu *Molo.* seven. (M:149)
hiut *Kusa-Manea.* seven.
Out-comparisons:
itu *Semau Helong.* seven.
hitu *East Tetun.* seven (7). (Mo:86)
itu *Kemak.* seven.
(haʔ)itu *Ili'uun.* seven. (dJ:119)

***hoi** *PRM.* dry in the sun. *Doublet:* ***fai**. *Etym:* *waRi 'day, sun'. *[irr. from PMP:* Ø > *h*]* *[Sporadic:* vowel height harmony *i > *e* /o_ in Amarasi.*]* *[Form:* Tetun provides evidence that the unexpected initial *h* in the reflexes could be retention of a causative prefix; e.g. **pa-waRi.*]*
hoi *Termanu.* expose something to the heat of the sun, dry something in the sun. (J:186)
hoi *Korbafo.*
hoi *Bokai.*
hoi *Bilbaa.*
hoi *Rikou.*
hoi *Ba'a.*
hoi *Tii.*
hoi *Dengka.*
hoi *Oenale.*
n-hoe *Ro'is Amarasi.* dry in the sun.
n-hoe *Kotos Amarasi.* dry in the sun.
n-hoi *Molo.* dry in the sun, scorch. (M:151)
hoi *Kusa-Manea.* dry in sun.
Out-comparisons:
°huiʔ *Semau Helong.* dry in sun. *Borrowed from:* Meto (shown by irr. *R > Ø, expect *R > *l*). *[Form:* regular Helong mid-vowel raising before/after a high vowel *o > *u* / _i.*]*
hawai *Fehan Tetun.* dry by placing in the sun.
habai, hauai *East Tetun.* expose in the sun, dry in the sun. (Mo:39, 83)
noe *Hawu.* dry in sun.

***hoka** *PRM.* call up, invite. *Pattern:* k-5.
hoka *Termanu.* call up, convene for public work. (J:187)
hoka *Korbafo.*
hoka *Bokai.*
hoka *Bilbaa.*
hoʔa *Rikou.*
hoka *Ba'a.*
hoka *Tii.*
hoka *Dengka.*
hoka *Oenale.*
n-hoka *Ro'is Amarasi.* call up.
n-hoka *Kotos Amarasi.* invite, call up.
<hoka> *Molo.* invite, first announcement of an invitation. (M:151)
Out-comparisons:
hoka *Helong.* (J:187)

***holas** *PRM.* naked. *[Sporadic:* *h > Ø in Meto.*]*
ma-ka-hola-k (2) hola~hola, tao hola (3) na-ka-hola *Termanu.* 1) naked, someone who is usually naked. 2) naked, be unclothed. 3) bare; bare oneself, mainly unknowingly while asleep. (J:188)
ma-ka-hola-ʔ *Korbafo.*
ma-ka-hola-k *Bokai.*
(2) hola~hola *Bilbaa.*
ma-ka-hola-k *Ba'a.*
hola *Lole.* naked. (Zacharias et al. 2014)
ma-ka-hola-k *Tii.*

ma-ʔa-hola-ʔ (2) hola~hola *Dengka.*
ma-ʔa-hola-ʔ (2) hola~hola *Oenale.*
monos *Ro'is Amarasi.* naked.
mutiʔ_monas (2) n-ʔafaʔ_monas *Kotos Amarasi.* 1) openly. 2) stark naked. *[Form:* **n-ʔafaʔ** = 'clean, shaved, naked'.*]*
n-monas (2) <amonak> *Molo.* 1) be naked. (M:xxxiii, 88) 2) naked. (M:129)
Out-comparisons:
keʔula *Hawu. [irr. from PRM:* *l = *r* correspondence; *o = *u* correspondence*]* (J:188)
holar *Sika.* naked. (Pareira and Lewis 1998:78)

***holu1** *PRM.* hug, embrace. *Etym:* *pəluk 'bend, curve'. *[irr. from PMP:* *ə > *o*] [irr. from PRM:* *l > Ø in Meto; *u > *o* in Meto*]*
holu *Termanu.* hug, embrace. (J:190)
holu *Korbafo.*
holu *Bokai.*
holu *Bilbaa.*
holu *Rikou.*
holu *Ba'a.*
holu *Lole.*
holu *Tii.*
holu *Dengka.*
holu *Oenale.*
holu *Dela.* hug.
n-hoo *Kotos Amarasi.* hug, embrace, put one's arm around.
n-hoo *Molo.* hug. (M:149)

***holu2** *Rote.* help, assist. *[History:* Possibly connected with PMP *tuluŋ and/or Malay *tolong*, though this would require irregular *t > *h.*]*
holu *Termanu.* help, assist. (J:190)
holu *Korbafo.*
holu *Bokai.*
holu *Bilbaa.*
holu *Ba'a.*
(holu ?) *Tii.*
holu *Dengka.*
Out-comparisons:
huluŋ *Semau Helong.* help, assist. *[Form:* regular Helong mid-vowel raising before/after a high vowel *o > *u* / _u.*]*

***horis** *PRM.* life, living. *Doublet:* ***mori**. *Etym:* *qudip 'live'. *[irr. from PMP:* *u > *o*] [minority from PMP:* *q > *h*] [Form:* expected *p > *s* / _# (§3.5.1.3).*]*
holis *Keka.* living. (J:703)
horis *Oenale.* living. (J:703)
ka-hoînis (2) na-honiʔ *Ro'is Amarasi.* 1) living one. 2) give birth to.
ʔ|honis (2) na-honis (3) na-honiʔ (4) honiʔ (5) a-mahoni-t *Kotos Amarasi.* 1) life. 2) give birth to. 3) be born. 4) genetic (of relation). 5) parent, clan elders.
<honi> (2) oe ʔhonis (3) na-honiʔ (4) au mahoni-k *Molo.* 1) live. 2) spring that never dries up. 3) bears (child). 4) my parent. (M:152)
Out-comparisons:
nulis (2) nuli *Semau Helong.* 1) life. 2) live.
horis *Fehan Tetun.* living.
houris *East Tetun.* alive, with life. (Mo:188)
ʔori~ʔori *Kisar.* life, foliage.

***hosu** *PRM.* loosen. *[Form:* The Rote forms with initial *m* probably come from earlier **ma-hosu.*] [History:* Jonker (1908:496) also gives Termanu, Korbafo, Bokai, Bilbaa, and Rikou **posu** 'loosen, come off, slip', which is probably related and points to earlier **posu. This term is related to a network of formally and semantically similar terms including Termanu, Korbafo, Bokai **podu** 'slip, slip off, loosen' (Jonker 1908:489), Termanu, Korbafo, Bokai, Ba'a **odu** 'pull on, put on, pull something on, put something on' (Jonker 1908:452), and all Rote **olu**

'pull on, put on' (Jonker 1908:457), Termanu, Korbafo, Bokai, Bilbaa, Tii **kosu** 'remove skin, loosening of the skin'. Among these terms, the first could have reinforced irregular retention of pre-RM *p = *p* in **posu**.*]*

m|osu *Termanu.* be loose. (J:362)

m|osu *Korbafo.*

m|osu *Bokai.*

m|osu *Bilbaa.*

m|osu *Rikou.*

m|osu *Ba'a.*

m|osu *Tii.*

m|osu *Dengka.*

m|osu *Oenale.*

n-osu *Kotos Amarasi.* pull out.

n-osu (2) n-hosu (3) na-t|hosu *Molo.* 1) draws (sword). (M:408) 2) draws (sword). (M:154) 3) come loose. (M:154)

***hotu** *PRM.* burn. *See:* ***mbutu** 'hot, burning'. *[Sporadic:* *h > Ø in Meto*]*

hotu *Termanu.* burning, set on fire. (J:191)

hotu *Korbafo.*

hotu *Bokai.*

hotu *Bilbaa.*

hotu *Rikou.*

hotu *Ba'a.*

hotu *Tii.*

hotu *Dengka.*

hotu *Oenale.*

n-otu *Ro'is Amarasi.* burn.

n-otu *Kotos Amarasi.* burn.

n-otu (2) maʔ-otu-ʔ *Molo.* 1) burns. 2) hot. (M:409)

n-out *Kusa-Manea.* burn.

Out-comparisons:

otot *Semau Helong.* hot.

hotu *Waima'a.* firewood.

***huka** *Rote.* open. *Doublet:* ***fuka**. *Etym:* *buka 'open, uncover, expose'. *Pattern:* k-6. *[irr. from PMP:* *b > *h*]*

huka *Termanu.* open. (J:195)

huka *Korbafo.*

huka *Bokai.*

huka *Bilbaa.*

huka *Ba'a.*

huka *Tii.*

huʔa *Dengka.*

huʔa *Oenale.*

Out-comparisons:

boka *Semau Helong.* open. *[irr. from PMP:* *u > *o]*

***huʔe** *PnMeto.* eucalyptus. *Etym:* **pue (pre-Meto). *[History:* Several Alor-Pantar languages have likely cognates of this form, e.g. Kabola has **puʔ**.*]*

huʔe-l *Amfo'an.* eucalyptus tree.

huʔe *Molo.* eucalyptus. *Eucalyptus alba*. *[Form:* Other varieties of Meto are known to have **hoʔe**.*]* (M:154)

Out-comparisons:

poe *Kemak.* eucalyptus.

oe *Welaun.* eucalyptus.

***hulu** *PRM.* first, in front. *Doublet:* ***ulu**. *Etym:* *qulu 'head; top part; leader, chief; headwaters; handle of a bladed implement; prow of a boat; first, first-born'. *[minority from PMP:* *q > *h*]* *[irr. from PRM:* *h > Ø in Rikou*]*

na-ka-hulu-k *Termanu.* be in front, first, be the first. (J:196)

na-ka-hulu-k *Bokai.*

na-ulu *Rikou.* first. (own field notes)

na-ka-hulu-k *Ba'a.*

na-ka-hulu-k *Tii.*

na-ʔa-hulu-ʔ *Dengka.*

na-ʔa-hulu-ʔ *Oenale.*

na-hunu *Ro'is Amarasi.* go first, be first.

na-hunu *Kotos Amarasi.* go first, be first, at first.

na-hunu *Molo.* go in front of. (M:156)

***humək** *PRM.* smile, be joyful. *[Sporadic:* *ə > *e* /σ_# in wRote (perhaps *ə > *a > *e* /_#).*]*

hume *Termanu.* smile. (J:197)

hume *Korbafo.*

hume *Bokai.*

hume *Bilbaa.*

hume *Rikou.*

hume *Ba'a.*

hume *Tii.*

hume~hume, humel *Dengka.*
humek *Oenale.*
humek *Dela.* smile.
humu-f (2) humaʔ *Ro'is Amarasi.* 1) face. 2) kind, type.
huma-f (2) humaʔ (3) na-huma (4) n-humaʔ_moe *Kotos Amarasi.* 1) face. 2) kind, type. 3) beautiful. 4) smile, be joyful, be glad.
huma-n (2) n-humaʔ_moe *Molo.* 1) his form, his face. 2) smiles, chuckles. (M:156)
humuʔ *Kusa-Manea.* face.

***hundi** *PRM.* banana. *Etym:* *punti. *[minority from PMP:* *nt > *nd (expect *t)*] [Sporadic:* *h > Ø in Meto.*]*
huni *Termanu.* banana. (J:197)
huni *Korbafo.*
huni *Bokai.*
huni *Bilbaa.*
hundi *Landu.* (own field notes)
hundi *Rikou.*
huri *Oepao.* (own field notes)
huni *Ba'a.*
hundi *Tii.*
hundi *Dengka.*
hundi *Oenale.*
uri *Ro'is Amarasi.* banana.
uki *Kotos Amarasi.* banana.
uki *Molo.* banana. (M:663)
uki *Kusa-Manea.* banana.
Out-comparisons:
hudi *East Tetun.* banana. (Mo:88)

***huŋga** *PRM.* chop with force, chop big branches. *Etym:* *pu(ŋ)kaq 'break off'. *[Sporadic:* *h > Ø in Meto.*]*
huŋa *Termanu.* chop with an axe or machete firmly held with both hands. (J:197)
huka *Rikou.*
huŋga *Ba'a.*
huŋga *Tii.*
huŋga *Oenale.*
uka-l *Molo.* chop big branches. *[Form:* insertion of /l/ after /a/ to mark a third person object.*]* (M:585)
Out-comparisons:
<púnggu> *Kambera.* chop, chop down, fell. *[Note:* also in Mangili.*]* (On:423)
<ponggu> *Mamboru. [Note:* also in Lewa.*]*
<pogu> *Anakalang.*
<ponggo> *Kodi. [Note:* also in Weyewa.*]*
poŋgo *Bima.* chop, chop with an axe, split or cut with an axe. (Ismail et al. 1986:121)

***husə** *Morph:* ***husə-k**. *PRM.* navel. *Etym:* *pusəj 'navel, umbilicus; mid-point or centre of something'. *[irr. from PRM:* *h > *ʔ* in most Rote*] [Sporadic:* *h > Ø in Meto.*] [Form:* The initial *ʔ* in wRote possibly from earlier *k, also attested by Ili'uun **kusan**. These forms are perhaps via intermediate ***ka-husə-k**.*]*
(ʔ)use-k *Termanu.* navel. (J:671)
(ʔ)use-ʔ *Korbafo.*
(ʔ)use-k *Bokai.*
(ʔ)use-ʔ *Bilbaa.*
ʔuse-ʔ *Rikou.*
(ʔ)use-k *Ba'a.*
huse-k *Lole.* (Zacharias et al. 2014)
huse-k *Tii.*
(ʔ)usa-ʔ *Dengka.*
ʔusa-ʔ *Oenale.*
ʔusa-ʔ *Dela.* belly button, navel.
usu-f *Ro'is Amarasi.* navel, belly button.
usa-f *Kotos Amarasi.* navel, belly button; shoot, sprout, off-shoot.
<usa> *Molo.* navel. (M:591)
usa-f *Kusa-Manea.* navel.
Out-comparisons:
husar, husor *East Tetun.* umbilicus, navel. (Mo:89)
huso *Waima'a.* navel.
ohor-ne *Kisar.* navel.
kusan *Ili'uun.* navel. *[irr. from PMP:* *p > (*Ø) > *k* (compare *paŋdan > **keʧan**, *hutək > **gutan**, and *baqbaq > **kahan**)*]* (dJ:122)

əhu *Hawu.* navel.

***huti** *CERM.* provoke, incite. *[Form:* There is also a variant ***huhi** found outside wRote, e.g. Termanu **na-ka-hu~huʔi-k**, Bilbaa **na-ka-hu~hui-ʔ** and others (Jonker 1908:195).*]*

huti, na-ka-hu~huti-k *Termanu.* provoke. **na-ka-hu~huti-k au nonook=a busa** he provokes me like I was a dog (J:198)

<n-huit(a)> *Molo.* incite. **a|n-huit asu** incites a dog (M:154)

***hutu** *Morph:* ***na-hutu**. *nRM.* rub, smear.

na-hutu (2) na-la-hu~hutu *Termanu.* 1) rub, rub in, besmear oneself or one another. 2) pulverise by rubbing. (J:199)

na-hutu (2) na-la-hu~hutu *Korbafo.*

na-hutu (2) na-la-hu~hutu *Bokai.*

na-hutu (2) na-la-hu~hutu *Bilbaa.*

na-hutu (2) na-la-hu~hutu *Rikou.*

(2) na-la-hu~hutu *Ba'a.*

na-hutu (2) na-la-hu~hutu *Tii.*

n-huta *Kotos Amarasi.* rubs, smears (e.g. oil).

n-huut *Molo.* smears (e.g. blood). (M:157)

***huu** *Morph:* ***huu, *huu-k, *ma-huu-k**. *PRM.* base of a tree; cause; source, origin; beginning. *Etym:* *puqun 'base of a tree; cause; source, origin; beginning; foot of a hill or mountain; first wife; model or example (to be copied); expression for the mother's brother'. *[Sporadic:* *h > Ø in Meto; *VV-k > *VVʔ > VʔV in Meto (perceptual metathesis).*]*

huu-k (2) huu (3) ma-huu-k (4) na-ta-huu, mete/huu-n *Termanu.* 1) trunk of a tree. 2) cause reason. 3) having a trunk. 4) starting from, from. (J:193f)

huu-ʔ (2) huu *Korbafo.*

huu-k (2) huu *Bokai.*

huu-ʔ (2) huu *Bilbaa.*

huu-ʔ (2) huu *Rikou.*

huu-k (2) huu *Ba'a.*

huu-k (2) huu *Tii.*

huu-ʔ (2) huu *Dengka.*

huu-ʔ (2) huu *Oenale.*

uu-f *Ro'is Amarasi.* source, tree trunk.

uʔu (2) uu-f (3) maʔ-uʔu (4) naʔ-uu-b=oo-n *Kotos Amarasi.* 1) tree counter. 2) source, beginning. 3) based on. 4) go back to; finds its source in. *Lit:* '3-base-TR=REFL-3SG.GEN'.

uu|ʔ (2) uu-f *Molo.* 1) tree counter. 2) trunks. (M:583)

Out-comparisons:

uun *Semau Helong.* bamboo.

huun *East Tetun.* base, foot, bottom, the lower part of flank; the beginning, the source; the trunk of any tree. (Mo:89)

I - i

***ia** *PRM.* this, here. *Etym:* *ia 'demonstrative pronoun and adverb: this, here; that, there'.

ia *Termanu.* this, here. (J:199)

ia *Korbafo.*

ia *Bokai.*

ia *Bilbaa.*

ia *Rikou.*

ia *Ba'a.*

ia *Tii.*

ia *Dengka.*

ia *Oenale.*

ia *Dela.* this, here.

ai *Ro'is Amarasi.* here, this.

ia (2) =ii *Kotos Amarasi.* 1) here, this. 2) 1DET, definiteness marker for things (physically or metaphorically) near the speaker.

ii *Amanuban.* here.
iin, ii *Fatule'u.* here.
ii *Molo.* this. (M:158)
ii *Amfo'an.* here.
ain, iin *Timaus.* here.
ia *Kusa-Manea.* here.
Out-comparisons:
ia *Semau Helong.* here.

***iɗu** *Rote.* nose, kiss. *Etym:* *ijuŋ 'nose'. *[Sporadic:* Ø > *ʔ* /#_ in Dela-Oenale.*]*
idu_ai-k (2) pana_idu *Termanu.* 1) back of the nose. 2) nostrils. (J:200)
idu-ʔ *Bilbaa.* nose. (own field notes)
idu-ʔ *Landu.* nose. (own field notes)
idu-ʔ *Rikou.* nose. (own field notes)
idu-ʔ *Oepao.* nose. (own field notes)
idu *Ba'a.* kiss. *[Note:* In Timor 'kissing' is to rub noses.*]* (J:705)
iɗu-k *Lole.* nose. (Zacharias et al. 2014)
iɗu-k (2) iɗu *Tii.* 1) nose. 2) kiss. (J:705)
(ʔ)iɗu *Dengka.* kiss. (J:705)
ʔiɗu *Oenale.* kiss. (J:705)
ʔiɗu *Dela.* kiss.
Out-comparisons:
ilu *Semau Helong.* nose.
ilu-r *Kemak.* nose. *Usage:* Lemia, Atsabe, Saneri, and Diirbati dialects.
ilug-aaŋ *Kemak.* nose. *Usage:* Kutubaba dialect.
iliguur *Kemak.* nose. *Usage:* Leolima dialect. *[Form:* The correct morphological analysis of this form is unclear. It could be **ilig-uur** or **iliguu-r**. Either way, *g* is a retention of PMP *ŋ.*]*
iluk-aat *Welaun.* nose.

***ifa** *PRM.* lap. *Etym:* *riba. *[irr. from PMP:* *r > Ø (expect *r)*] [Sporadic:* diphthongisation *i > *ai* in Meto; Ø > *ʔ* /#_ in Dela-Oenale.*]*
ifa (2) ifa-k *Termanu.* 1) hold in the lap. 2) lap. (J:200)
ifa *Korbafo.*
ifa *Bokai.*
ifa *Bilbaa.*
ifa *Rikou.*
ifa *Ba'a.*
ifa *Tii.*
(ʔ)ifa *Dengka.*
ʔifa *Oenale.*
(2) ʔifa-ʔ *Dela.*
na-ʔaifa|ʔ *Ro'is Amarasi.* carry in the lap. *Usage:* poetic, only currently known in the parallelism **na-skau** =ma_na-ʔaifaʔ metaphor 'cares for people' where **na-skau** = 'hold in the arms, hug'. *[Form:* automatic glottal stop insertion between CV- prefix and #V-initial stem.*]*
ifa-n (2) aifa-f (3) n-aifan (4) a-fafa-t =ma a-mn-aifa-t *Molo.* 1) intestinal fat. (M:158) 2) lap. 3) held in the lap (said of a child who has the same character as its mother). 4) the one who cares and holds (us) in his lap. (M:9)
Out-comparisons:
iha *Semau Helong.* lap.

***iha** *PnRote.* sister-in-law. *Etym:* *hipaR 'sibling-in-law (probably of the same sex only)'. *[irr. from PRM:* *h > *ʔ* /V_V in wRote (expect Ø); *Ø > *h* in Tii and Lole*] [Sporadic:* Ø > *h* /#_Vʔ in Termanu, Korbafo, Bokai, Ba'a and Lole.*] [History:* The irregularities in wRote, Tii, and Lole indicate that this term is a borrowing in these lects.*]*
hiʔa *Termanu.* sister-in-law, used mutually by sisters. (J:182)
hiʔa *Korbafo.*
hiʔa *Bokai.*
ia *Bilbaa.*
ia *Rikou.* (own field notes)
hiʔa *Ba'a.*
hiʔa *Lole.* sister-in-law (male speaking). (Zacharias et al. 2014)
hiʔa *Tii.*

hiʔa *Dengka.*
hiʔa *Oenale.*
Out-comparisons:
iha *Semau Helong.* cousin, in-law.

***ika** *Morph:* ***ika-k**. *PRM.* fish. *Etym:* *hikan. *Pattern:* k-10.
iʔa-k *Termanu.* fish. (J:200)
iʔa-ʔ *Korbafo.*
iʔa-k *Bokai.*
ika-ʔ *Bilbaa.*
ika-ʔ *Landu.* fish. (own field notes)
ika-ʔ *Rikou.*
ika-ʔ *Oepao.* fish. (own field notes)
iʔa-k *Ba'a.*
iʔa-k *Tii.*
ia-ʔ *Dengka.*
ʔuʔu_ia-ʔ *Dela.* all kinds of fish. *[Form:* **ʔuʔu** *is the normal word for 'fish' in Dela.]*
ika|ʔ *Ro'is Amarasi.* fish.
ika|ʔ *Kotos Amarasi.* fish.
ika|ʔ *Molo.* fish. (M:159)
ika|ʔ *Kusa-Manea.* fish.
Out-comparisons:
ikan *Semau Helong.* fish.
ikan *East Tetun.* fish. (Mo:90)
iʔa *Dhao.* fish.

***ikə** *Rote.* snare, noose. *Etym:* *hikət 'tie, bind, attach to by tying'. *Pattern:* k-6′ (*k > Ø in Bilbaa, *k > *ʔ* in Ba'a; expect *k = *k* in both). *[irr. from PRM:* *ə > *a* in Termanu, Korbafo, Ba'a, and Tii*] [Sporadic:* Ø > *h* /#_Vʔ in Bilbaa, Rikou and Ba'a.*] [Form:* *ə > (*e) > *i* in Bilbaa can be explained by the prohibition against the vowel sequences *ie* and *uo.] [History:* Rote ***iʔi-k** 'kind of liana suitable for tying' may also be from PMP *hikət. Reflexes of Rote ***iʔi-k** are as follows: Termanu, Bokai, Tii, **iʔi-k** Korbafo, Rikou, Dengka **iʔi-ʔ**, Bilbaa **ii-ʔ**, and Ba'a **hiʔi-k**.*]*
ika (2) i~ika-k, ika-k *Termanu.* 1) snare with a noose attached to a stick. 2) snare, noose, which is tied to a stick and used to catch wild animals (and chickens, etc.). (J:200f)
ika (2) i~ika-ʔ *Korbafo.*
ike (2) i~ike-k *Bokai.*
na-ka-hi~hii (3) hi~hii *Bilbaa.*
hiʔe (2) hi~hiʔe *Rikou.*
(2) hi~hiʔa-k *Ba'a. [Note:* Jonker (1908:200) gives the Ba'a equivalent of Termanu **ika** as **ike**, but on page 705 he indicates that this is not certain.*]*
ike (2) i~ike-k, ike-k *Tii.*
(ʔ)iʔa (2) (ʔ)iʔa-t *Dengka.*
ʔiʔa (2) ʔi~ʔiʔa-t *Oenale.*
ʔiʔa *Dela.*

***iko** *Morph:* ***iko-k**. *PRM.* tail. *Etym:* *ikuR. *Pattern:* k-5. *[Sporadic:* *u > *o /_*R#.*]*
iko-k *Termanu.* tail of a four-footed animal or of a fish. (J:201)
iko-ʔ *Korbafo.*
iko-k *Bokai.*
iko-ʔ *Bilbaa.*
iko=na *Landu.* tail. (own field notes)
iko-ʔ *Rikou.*
iko-k *Ba'a.*
iko-k *Tii.*
iko-ʔ *Dengka.*
iko-ʔ *Oenale.*
i͡ko-ʔ *Dela.* tail.
iuku-f *Ro'is Amarasi.* tail.
iku-f *Kotos Amarasi.* tail. *[Sporadic:* vowel height harmony *o > *u* /iC_ in Amarasi and Kusa-Manea.*]*
iko-f *Molo.* tail. (M:159)
iku-f *Kusa-Manea.* tail.
Out-comparisons:
ikun *Semau Helong.* tail.
iku-n *East Tetun.* tail, buttocks; final. (Mo:90)
hiʔon *Kemak.* tail.

***ila** *Rote.* mole, freckle, birthmark. *Etym:* *qila 'any natural mark on human skin: birthmark, freckle, mole'.

i~ila *Termanu.* spots on the skin or the body, including: **i~ila ŋgeok** [OE = 'black spot'] freckles, and **i~ila pilas** [OE = 'red/brown spot'] birthmark. (J:201)
i~ila *Korbafo.*
i~ila *Bokai.*
ila *Bilbaa.*
ila *Rikou. [Form:* My consultants gave vowel initial **i~ila**.*]*
ila *Ba'a.*
ila *Tii.*
ila *Dengka.*
ila *Oenale.*
ila *Dela.* mole.

***imun** *PMeto.* kind of biting flying insect; midge, mosquito.
imun *Ro'is Amarasi.* kind of small white mosquito whose bite is worse than a normal mosquito.
imun *Kotos Amarasi.* kind of small white mosquito whose bite is worse than a normal mosquito.
<imu> *Molo.* flies. (M:160)
Out-comparisons:
əmu *Central Nage.* mosquito with a horizontally striped black-and-white body. (Forth 2016:332)
xəmu, səmu, əmu *Ngadha.* mosquito. *[History:* The variant forms suggest Proto-Central Flores *kləmu, as discussed by Elias (2018:84, 115). Thus the similarity between the Meto forms and Central Flores forms may be due to chance.*]* (Arndt 1961)

***ina** *Morph:* ***ina-k**. *PRM.* mother, mother's sister. *Etym:* *ina. *[Sporadic:* diphthongisation *i > *ai* in Meto.*]*
ina-k *Termanu.* woman, a female human being; mother. (J:202f)
ina-ʔ *Korbafo.*
ina-k *Bokai.*
ina-k *Bilbaa.*
ina-ʔ *Landu.* woman. (own field notes)
ina-ʔ *Rikou.*
ina-k *Ba'a.*
ina-k *Tii.*
ina-ʔ *Dengka.*
ina-ʔ *Oenale.*
ina-ʔ (2) ina-n *Dela.* 1) female human. 2) mother.
inaʔ *Ro'is Amarasi.* mother.
aina-f, ainaʔ *Kotos Amarasi.* mother.
ainaʔ, oin *Molo.* mother. (M:88)
ena-f *Baikeno.* mother. (Charles E. Grimes pers. comm.)
eneʔ *Kusa-Manea.* mother.
Out-comparisons:
ina *Semau Helong.* mother.
ina-n (2) inan *East Tetun.* 1) mother, maternal aunt. 2) female (animals). (Mo:90)
ina *Hawu.* mother, mother's older sister (maternal aunt), father's brother's wife.

***inu** *Morph:* ***n-inu**. *PRM.* drink. *Etym:* *inum.
n-inu *Termanu.* drinks. (J:397)
n-inu *Korbafo.*
n-inu *Bokai.*
n-inu *Bilbaa.*
n-inu *Rikou.*
n-inu *Ba'a.*
n-inu *Tii.*
n-inu *Dengka.*
n-inu *Oenale.*
n-inu *Dela.* drink.
n-inu *Ro'is Amarasi.* drink.
n-inu *Kotos Amarasi.* drink.
n-inu *Molo.* drink. (M:160)
Out-comparisons:
n-inu *Semau Helong.* drink.

***inus** *CER.* certain kind of bird called *burung angin* in Kupang Malay.
inus *Termanu.* kind of bird called *burung angin* (wind bird) in Kupang. (J:205)
inu-ʔ *Korbafo.*
inu-k *Bokai.*
inu-ʔ *Bilbaa.*
inus *Ba'a.*

Out-comparisons:
maun_inus *Helong.* (J:205)

***iŋgu** *PRM.* country, land.
iŋu *Termanu.* in the proper sense means 'country, place', but also used in the game of **te~teŋa-k** (Malay *congkak*), in which the holes which belong to one side are called **iŋu** (those holes that belong to the opposite side are called **iŋu feʔe-k**, 'foreign land'). (J:204)
iŋu *Korbafo.*
iŋu *Bokai.*
iŋu *Bilbaa.*
iku *Rikou.*
iŋgu *Ba'a.*
iŋgu *Tii.*
iŋgu *Dengka.*
iŋgu *Oenale.*
iŋgu *Dela.*
iku *Kotos Amarasi.* place of rest in the centre of the fields for the spirits of the rice and corn. 'The new seeds, which are called **peen iku** [corn *iku*] and **maak iku** [rice *iku*], are made with a ritual in the field. There are no restrictions as to which seeds from home should be planted. A planting of **peen iku** is placed in the middle of the field, and the same affair occurs with rice seed which is called **maak iku**. They place a border (**nakat**) around it using a sign (**ʔsoko**) made from a coconut which has been drained of water. This mark is meant to inform people that the crop of corn and rice in the middle of the field is like a house of rest for the spirit of the corn and the spirit of the rice. This marker is called **iku**. The **iku** is intended to be a house of rest for the spirits of the rice and corn which come from all four corners of the globe.' (Heronimus Bani, unpublished typescript).

Out-comparisons:
iŋu *Funai Helong.* village, island.
iŋu *Semau Helong.* village. *[Semantics:* Jonker (1908:204) gives the meaning of Helong **iŋu** as 'country, village'.*]*

***isa₁** *PRM.* tie together. *[Note:* Those languages with only one form given use it for both the Termanu senses unless otherwise indicated.*] [irr. from PRM:* *a > *e* in several lects and senses*] [Sporadic:* diphthongisation *i > *ai* in Meto.*]*
isa (2) ise (3) ise-k *Termanu.* 1) tie something so that it stays hanging. 2) tie something with a rope, tie a rope around something so that it can be picked up or hung up. (J:205) 3) the loop, or the part of a rope, by which something is picked up or hung. *[Semantics:* Some Rote varieties have different forms for each of these senses, and some varieties have only one form which covers both senses.*]* (J:206)
isa (2) ise *Korbafo.*
ise *Bokai.*
isi (2) (ise) *Bilbaa.*
ise *Rikou.*
isa (2) isa *Ba'a.*
ise *Tii.*
(ʔ)isa *Dengka.*
ʔisa *Oenale.*
ʔisa *Dela.* tie with a rope, tie something so that it hangs.
na-ʔaisa *Kotos Amarasi.* tie something so that there is a handle which hangs out. *[Form:* automatic glottal stop insertion between CV-prefix and #V-initial stem.*]*
aisa-t *Molo.* four or eight corn cobs tied/hung together in pairs. (M:11)
aisi-t *Timaus.* tied bundle. *[Form:* regular assimilation of *a in final closed syllables.*]*

***isa₂** *Morph:* ***n-isa**. *PRM.* utterly, the final point.

n-isa *Termanu.* s/he kills. (J:398)
n-isa *Korbafo.*
n-isa *Bokai.*
n-isa *Bilbaa.*
n-isa *Rikou.*
n-isa *Ba'a.*
n-isa *Tii.*
n-isa *Dengka.*
n-isa *Oenale.*
n-isa *Kotos Amarasi.* completely, totally, the logical end point; win.
n-isa *Molo.* death; wins. (M:161)
Out-comparisons:
isi *Semau Helong.* too, very.

***isi** *Morph:* ***isi-k**. *Rote.* contents, fruit flesh. *Etym:* *isiʔ 'flesh (of humans, animals, fruits, tubers); reside; blade of a knife; inhabitants, residents'.
isi=na, isi-k *Termanu.* contents of something; flesh, muscles; the contents as the main part of something. (J:206)
isi=na *Korbafo.*
isi=na *Bokai.*
isi=na *Bilbaa.*
isi=na *Rikou.*
isi=na *Ba'a.*
isi=na *Tii.*
isi-ʔ *Dengka.*
isi=na *Oenale.*
isi-ʔ *Dela.* flesh, contents.
Out-comparisons:
isi-n *Semau Helong.* contents.
isi-n *East Tetun.* the body or torso; the product, the internal part, the contents, the useful part, a layer; a keen cutting edge of a knife, etc. (Mo:91)

***ita** *Morph:* ***n-ita**. *PRM.* see; try, attempt. *Etym:* *kita2. *[irr. from PMP:* *k > Ø /#_*]*
n-ita (2) n-ita-k *Termanu.* 1) sees. 2) mainly used in more metaphorical senses including those where 'see' = attempt. (J:398f)
n-ita *Korbafo.*
n-ita *Bokai.*
n-ita *Bilbaa.*
n-ita *Rikou.*
n-ita *Ba'a.*
n-ita *Tii.*
n-ita *Dengka.*
n-ita *Oenale.*
n-ita (2) n-ita-ʔ *Dela.* 1) see. 2) suppose.
n-ita *Ro'is Amarasi.* see; try.
n-ita *Kotos Amarasi.* see, look at; try, see if.
n-ita *Molo.* see. (M:239)
iat *Kusa-Manea.* see.
Out-comparisons:
n-eta *Semau Helong.* see.

***iu** *PRM.* shark. *Etym:* *qihu.
iu *Termanu.* shark. (J:207)
iu *Korbafo.*
iu *Bokai.*
iu *Bilbaa.*
iu *Rikou.*
iu *Ba'a.*
iu *Tii.*
iu *Dengka.*
iu *Oenale.*
iu *Dela.* shark.
iu *Ro'is Amarasi.* shark.
iik_iu *Kotos Amarasi.* shark.
iu *Molo.* shark. (M:163)
Out-comparisons:
iu *Semau Helong.* shark.
uu *Fehan Tetun.* shark, some long thin sea animal, about 1–2 m long, 5' wide. It is claimed that it also lives in the **wee knuuk** (underground water), along with crocodile. *[irr. from PMP:* *i > *u] [Form:* East Tetun has **uud** 'large whale' (Morris 1984:76), and if this is cognate with Fehan Tetun **uu**, it would indicate that these forms are not from PMP *qihu.*]*

K - k

***kaa1** *Rote.* bite. *Etym:* *kaRat. *Pattern:* k-1/2/3.
- **kaa** *Termanu.* take something between the teeth, bite off, bite, also said of snakes and birds. (J:208)
- **kaa** *Korbafo.*
- **kaa** *Bokai.*
- **kaa** *Bilbaa.*
- **ʔaanan** *Landu.* bite. *[Form:* The correct morphological analysis of this form is unclear.*]* (own field notes)
- **ʔaa** *Rikou.*
- **ʔaa** *Oepao.* bite. (own field notes)
- **kaa** *Ba'a.*
- **kaa** *Dela.* bite.

***kaa2** *PRM.* crow (the bird). *Pattern:* k-1. *[History:* Blust and Trussel (ongoing) reconstruct ***wakwak** which may be cognate.*]* *[Semantics:* onomatopoeia.*]*
- **kaa** *Termanu.* crow (the bird). (J:208)
- **kaa** *Korbafo.*
- **kaa** *Bokai.*
- **kaa** *Bilbaa.*
- **kaa** *Rikou.*
- **kaa** *Ba'a.*
- **kaa** *Tii.*
- **kaaʔ** *Dengka.*
- **kaaʔ** *Oenale.*
- **koor_kaaʔ** *Ro'is Amarasi.* crow.
- **koor_kaaʔ metan** *Kotos Amarasi.* crow.
- **kool_kaaʔ** *Molo.* crow. (M:164)
- ***Out-comparisons:***
  - **kakalo** *Semau Helong.* crow.
  - **kaoa** *East Tetun.* crow (bird). (Mo:101)

***ka|benu** *PMeto.* fly. *Doublet:* ***mbena**. *Etym:* *bəRŋaw (Blust and Trussel (ongoing) reconstruct both *bəRŋaw and *baŋaw.). *[irr. from PMP:* *aw > *u (expect *o)*]* *[minority from PMP:* *b > (*ɓ) > *b*]*
- **kbenu** *Ro'is Amarasi.* fly.
- **kbenu** *Kotos Amarasi.* fly.
- **akbenu** *Kusa-Manea.* fly.

***kaɓi** *PRM.* clamp. *Doublet:* ***hapi**. *Etym:* *kapit 'pinch, press between; fasten thatch together with slats in roofing a house'. *Pattern:* k-3. *[irr. from PMP:* *p > *ɓ*]*
- **kabi** *Termanu.* clamp, squeeze with pliers, press with a press. (J:209)
- **kabi** *Korbafo.*
- **kabi** *Bokai.*
- **kabi** *Bilbaa.*
- **ʔabi** *Rikou.*
- **kabi** *Ba'a.*
- **kaɓi** *Tii.*
- **(ʔ)abi** *Dengka.*
- **ʔaɓi** *Oenale.*
- **ʔaɓi** *Dela.* squeeze the lontar palm flowers with a squeezer made of the rib of a lontar palm leaf.
- **<abi> (2) n-habi (3) <kiba habi>** *Molo.* 1) clamp. (M:3) 2) clamping. (M:134) 3) kind of ant which bites. (M:134)
- **n-ʔaib** *Kusa-Manea.* pinch, clamp.
- ***Out-comparisons:***
  - **habit** *East Tetun.* squeeze between two things, put in a splint. (Mo:40)

***kaɗe** *Morph:* ***kaɗe-k**. *Rote.* charcoal. *Etym:* *qajəŋ. *Pattern:* k-1' (*k > *ʔ* in Ba'a, expect *k = *k*). *[minority from PMP:* *ə > *e /_# (expect *ə > *a* in wRote, possibly *ə > *a > *e*)*]* *[Sporadic:* *a > *e /*C+palatal_.*]* *[Form:* The initial *k may be from the PRM nominal prefix *ka-.*]*
- **(haʔi) kade-k** *Termanu.* charcoal. (J:211)
- **kade-k** *Bokai.*
- **kade-ʔ** *Bilbaa.*
- **ʔade-ʔ** *Rikou.*
- **(ʔ)ade-k** *Ba'a.*
- **kaɗe-k** *Tii.*
- **kaɗe-ʔ** *Dengka.*
- **kaɗe-ʔ** *Dela.* burned.

Out-comparisons:
aleŋ *Semau Helong.* charcoal.
arne *Kisar.* charcoal. (Rinnooy 1886:169)

***kae** *PRM.* cockatoo. *Pattern:* k-1. *[History:* Clark (2011:321) reconstructs Proto Papuan Tip *wakeke ~ *kakawe which may be cognate.*] [Semantics:* onomatopoeia.*]*
ka~kae *Termanu.* cockatoo. (J:211)
ka~kae *Korbafo.*
ka~kae *Bokai.*
ka~kae *Bilbaa.*
ka~kae *Rikou.*
ka~kae *Dengka.*
koor kae *Ro'is Amarasi.* Yellow Crested Cockatoo.
koor kae mutiʔ *Kotos Amarasi.* Yellow Crested Cockatoo.
kool kae, kae mutiʔ *Molo.* cockatoo. (M:167)
Out-comparisons:
ka~kae, ka~kai *East Tetun.* cockatoo (bird). (Mo:96)

***kahi1** *PRM.* pull towards oneself. *Pattern:* k-2b.
kaʔi *Termanu.* pull towards oneself. (J:214)
kaʔi *Korbafo.*
(ʔ)ai *Rikou. [Form:* Whether the initial glottal stop is underlying or epenthetic is not clear. I could not elicit this form from my consultants.*]*
kaʔi *Ba'a.*
kaʔi *Tii.*
(ʔ)ai *Dengka.*
ʔai *Oenale.*
ʔai *Dela.*
n-ʔai *Kotos Amarasi.* push down.
n-ʔai (2) na-ʔai-b=on (3) na-ʔai-b-aʔ *Molo.* 1) pushes down. 2) withdraws. 3) moves someone sideways. (M:8)
Out-comparisons:
kahi *Helong.* (J:214)

***kahi2** *Rote.* count. *Pattern:* k-2/3.
kaʔi *Termanu.* count, calculate. (J:214)
kaʔi *Korbafo.*
kaʔi *Ba'a.*
kaʔi *Tii.*
(ʔ)a~(ʔ)ai *Oenale.*
Out-comparisons:
kahi, kasi *Semau Helong.* count, one, a.

***kahin** *PRM.* stop, prevent. *Pattern:* k-2a. *[irr. from PRM:* *k > *ŋ* in Bilbaa*]*
kaʔi *Termanu.* stop, prevent. (J:214)
kaʔi *Bokai.*
na-sa-ŋai *Bilbaa.*
ʔai *Rikou. [Form:* My consultants gave **na-sa-ʔai**.*]*
kaʔi *Ba'a.*
kaʔi *Tii.*
(ʔ)ai *Dengka.*
ʔai *Oenale.*
ʔai *Dela.* rebuke.
na-kain-aʔ *Kotos Amarasi.* forbid.
Out-comparisons:
kaiŋ *Semau Helong.* prohibit, forbid.
hakahik *East Tetun.* prohibit, prevent, retain, hold, to not allow the action of any practice. (Mo:49)

***kahu** *Rote.* kind of fish. *Pattern:* k-1. *[irr. from PRM:* *h > *ʔ* in Rikou (expect *h > Ø)*] [Semantics:* vague semantics weaken reconstruction.*]*
kaʔu *Termanu.* kind of ocean fish. (J:224)
kaʔu *Korbafo.*
kaʔu *Bokai.*
kau *Bilbaa.*
kaʔu *Rikou.*
kaʔu *Ba'a.*
kaʔu *Tii.*
kau *Dengka.*
kau *Oenale.*
Out-comparisons:
khau *Helong.* (J:224)

***kai1** *Rote.* stiff, awkward. *Pattern:* k-2/3.

na-ma-kai (2) bala/kai-k *Termanu.* 1) have a stiff or tired feeling, like someone who has been sitting for, lying on one side or carrying something for a long time, often combined with **sota**. (J:214) 2) stiff, hard, strong, powerful. (J:26)

na-ma-kai (2) bala/kai-ʔ *Korbafo.*

na-ma-kai (2) bala/kai-k *Bokai.*

na-ma-kai (2) bala/kai-ʔ *Bilbaa.*

na-ma-ʔai (2) bara/ai-ʔ *Rikou.*

na-ma-kai (2) bala/kai-k *Ba'a.*

na-ma-kai (2) ɓara/kai-k *Tii.*

(2) balaʔai-ʔ *Dengka.*

Out-comparisons:

kalkait (2) kain *Semau Helong.* 1) stiff, awkward. 2) tighten. *[Note:* Jonker (1908:213) gives Helong **balakaik** and **bkain**.*]*

kai *Ili'uun.* fixed, stiff, hard, taut, stuck fast; avaricious. (dJ:120)

***kai$_2$** *PRM.* hook. *Etym:* *kawit. *Pattern:* k-1.

kai *Termanu.* hook, be hooked. (J:212)

kai *Korbafo.*

kai *Bokai.*

kai *Bilbaa.*

ʔai (2) ʔa~ʔai *Rikou.* 1) hook, be hooked. (J:212) 2) hook which is affixed to one's waist from which buckets can be hung while ascending a lontar palm. (own field notes)

kai *Ba'a.*

kai *Tii.*

kai *Dengka.*

kai *Oenale.*

ʔ-kaʔi *Kotos Amarasi.* kind of hook with a sharp angle, these used to be put on the saddle of a horse and people would hang goods from them for transportation. *[Note:* **tanu** = 'fish-hook'.*]*

<nak'ai> *Molo.* fetches towards oneself with a hook. (M:169)

Out-comparisons:

kait *Semau Helong.* fish hook.

***kai/ou** *PRM.* Casuarina tree. Casuarina species. *Etym:* *qaRuhu 'shore tree Casuarina equisetifolia'. *Pattern:* k-2b′ (*k > *ʔ* in Tii, expect *k = *k*). *[irr. from PMP:* *a > *o (sporadic assimilation)*] [Sporadic:* *k > *ʔ* /#_ in Tii.*] [Form:* initial ***kai** probably from ***kaiu** 'tree, plant, wood'.*]*

kai/ou *Termanu.* the *cemara* tree (in Kupang *pohon kasuwari[s]*). (J:216f)

kai/ou *Korbafo.*

kai/ou *Bokai.*

kai_ou *Bilbaa.*

kai/ou *Landu.* Casuarina tree. (own field notes)

(ʔ)ai/ou *Rikou.*

kai/ou *Ba'a.*

(ʔ)ai/ou *Tii.*

(ʔ)ai/ou *Dengka.*

(ʔ)ai/ou *Oenale.*

kaiʤoʔo *Ro'is Amarasi.* Casuarina.

ʔaiʤoʔo *Kotos Amarasi.* Casuarina tree. *[Form:* expected epenthetic consonant in *VVV Final *ʔo* disappears when modified. This also occurs for **naisoʔo** 'onion'.*]*

ʔaioo, ʔaiyoo *Amanuban, South.* Casuarina.

ʔuʤau *Kopas.* Casuarina tree. *Usage:* Usapisonba'i village.

ʔaiʤoo *Kopas.* Casuarina tree. *Usage:* Bone village.

ʔaʤau *Molo.* Casuarina. Casuarina junghuhniana. *[Form:* Middelkoop (1972:4) transcribes this <**adjau**>. Meijer Drees (1950) gives the Molo form as <**adjáo**>.*]* (M:4, Meijer Drees 1950:1)

ʔaiʤau *Amfo'an.* Casuarina tree.

ʔaroo-gw *Timaus.* Casuarina tree. *Usage:* Sanenu village.

ʔuroʔ *Timaus.* Casuarina tree. *Usage:* Oekona' village.

ʔaioo *Kusa-Manea.* Casuarina tree.
Out-comparisons:
ka/keu *Fehan Tetun.* Casuarina tree (e.g. found at the beach and near the river).
ka/keu *East Tetun.* Casuarina tree. (Mo:97)
kʔau *Waima'a.* Casuarina. Casuarina junghuhniana.
gou *Kemak.* Casuarina tree.
ai hou *Welaun.* Casuarina tree.
<kajú> *Kambera.* kind of Casuarina tree. Casuarina junghuhniana. *[Note:* Another name for a (possibly different) kind of Casuarina tree is <**kajiu**> for which Lewa has **kadiu**, indicating that Kambera *ʤ* may be from palatalisation of earlier *d and that this term is not cognate.*] [Form:* <j> = [ʤ]*]* (On:137)

***kais** *Morph:* ***ma-kais**. *PRM.* sour. *Pattern:* k-3.
ma-keis (2) ma-kei *Termanu.* 1) sour. 2) become sour, has become sour. (J:228)
ma-kei-ʔ *Korbafo.*
ma-kei-ʔ *Bokai.*
ma-kei-ʔ *Bilbaa.*
ma-ʔeis *Rikou.*
ma-keis *Ba'a.*
ma-keis *Tii.*
ma-ʔeis *Dengka.*
ma-ʔeis *Oenale.*
ma-ʔei *Dela.* sour.
<ma|hai> *Molo.* sour. (M:297)

***kaiu** *PRM.* tree, plant; wood. *Etym:* *kahiw. *Pattern:* k-4. *[Note:* Several names of specific trees in Rote lects begin with a (fossilised) reflex of ***kaiu**. These reflexes of ***kaiu** are not always identical to the reflexes given here.*]*
ai *Termanu.* tree, stem, wood. (J:5)
ai *Korbafo.*
ai *Bokai.*
kai *Bilbaa.*
ai *Landu.* tree, wood. (own field notes)
ai *Rikou.*
ai *Ba'a.*
ai *Tii.*
hau *Dengka.*
hau *Oenale.*
hau *Ro'is Amarasi.* wood, tree.
hau *Kotos Amarasi.* wood, tree.
hau *Molo.* tree, plant, wood. (M:141)
hau *Kusa-Manea.* tree, wood.
Out-comparisons:
kai *Semau Helong.* wood, tree.
ai *East Tetun.* tree, bush, shrub, plant, vegetable; stick, wood, timber, firewood. (Mo:2)
kau *Habun.* tree. *[Note:* language of east Timor ISO 639-3 [hbu].*]* (Dawson 2014)
ai *Kemak.* plant, wood.
au *Kisar.* wood.
aʃu *Hawu.* tree, wood.
aʃu *Dhao.* tree, wood.

***kai/usu** *Rote.* ribs. *Etym:* *Rusuk. *Pattern:* k-2/3. *[irr. from PRM:* *Ø > *h* in Tii*] [Form:* Source of initial ***kai** unclear, Jonker connects it with the prefix **ka-**.*]*
kai/usu-k *Termanu.* rib(s). (J:217)
kai/usu-ʔ *Korbafo.*
kai/usu-k *Bokai.*
(ʔ)ai/usu-ʔ *Rikou.*
kai/usu-k *Ba'a.*
kai/husu-k *Tii.*
(ʔ)ai/usu-ʔ *Dengka.*
ʔai/usu-ʔ *Oenale.*
ʔai/usu-ʔ *Dela.* ribs.
Out-comparisons:
rusan *Kisar.* ribs.

***kaka** *Morph:* ***kaka-k**. *Rote.* elder sibling of the same sex. *Etym:* *kaka. *Pattern:* initial k-2/3′, medial k-8′. *[Form:* The alternate Dengka form with initial *k* is not regular under pattern k-2/3, similarly medial *k* in the alternate Dengka and Tii forms is not regular under pattern k-8.

These irregularities may be due to borrowing, though the nearest Rote form with medial *k* is Bilbaa which does not neighbour either Tii or Dengka. If a borrowing hypothesis is taken to explain these irregularities Malay *kakak* would be the most likely source.*]*

kaʔa-k *Termanu.* older brother or sister, used by brothers for brothers and sisters for sisters. (J:209)

kaʔa-ʔ *Korbafo.*

kaʔa-k *Bokai.*

kaka-ʔ *Bilbaa.*

ʔaʔa=na *Landu.* older sibling. (own field notes)

ʔaʔa *Rikou.*

kaʔa-k *Ba'a.*

kaʔa *Lole.* older sibling (same sex). (Zacharias et al. 2014)

kaka-k, kaʔa *Tii. [Form:* Jonker (1908:209) gives **kaka-k**, Grimes et al. (2014a) gives **kaʔa**.*]*

kaka-ʔ, ʔaʔa *Dengka. [Note:* Jonker (1908:209) gives the putative Dengka form **ʔaʔa** with the note: 'also surely Dengka'.*]*

ʔaʔa *Oenale.*

ʔaʔa *Dela.* older sibling.

Out-comparisons:

kaka *Semau Helong.* older sibling.

kaka *Kisar.* older relatives.

aʔa *Hawu.* elder sibling same sex.

***kalati** *Rote.* earthworm. *Etym:* *kali-wati. *Pattern:* k-1/2/3. *[irr. from PMP:* *w > Ø*] [irr. from PRM:* Ø > *n* in Landu*] [Sporadic:* antepenultimate syllable loss in wRote.*]*

kalati-k (2) kelati dae *Termanu.* 1) worm, both earthworm and intestinal worm. 2) earthworm. (J:219)

kalati-ʔ *Korbafo.*

kalati-k *Bokai.*

kalati-ʔ *Bilbaa.*

kalnati *Landu.* earthworm. (own field notes)

kalati-ʔ *Rikou.*

sikalati-k *Ba'a.*

sikalati-k *Tii.*

la~lati-ʔ *Dengka.*

la~lati-ʔ *Oenale.*

Out-comparisons:

blatiʔ *Semau Helong.* worm, earthworm, roundworm. *[Form:* Probably from the alternate PMP form *bulati.*]*

(k)la~latik *East Tetun.* earthworm, intestinal worm. (Mo:108)

***kali** *PRM.* dig. *Etym:* *kali. *Pattern:* k-3.

kali *Termanu.* dig, excavate. (J:219)

kali *Korbafo.*

kali *Bokai.*

kali *Bilbaa.*

ʔali *Rikou.*

kali *Ba'a.*

kali *Tii.*

(ʔ)ali *Dengka.*

ʔali *Oenale.*

ʔali *Dela.* dig.

n-hani *Ro'is Amarasi.* dig.

n-hani *Kotos Amarasi.* dig.

n-hani *Molo.* dig. (M:139)

Out-comparisons:

kali *Semau Helong.* dig.

***kalusa** *PMeto.* fingernail, toenail, claw. *Etym:* **kilusa (pre-Meto). *Pattern:* k-1/2a. *[irr. from PRM:* *l > *l* ~ *n* in Kualiin Amanuban*] [Form:* I have posited an original trisyllable as most varieties of Meto show regular *l > *n*, unlike PRM *kl which is reflected as *kl* or *kr*. However, the alternate form in Kualiin Amanuban, **klusa-n**, points to early reduction of the antepenultimate syllable. Thus, ***kalusa** may have had the alternate form ***klusa** in PMeto.*]*

tnusu-f *Ro'is Amarasi.* fingernail, toenail, claw.

knusa-f *Kotos Amarasi.* fingernail, toenail, claw. *[Note:* An alternate form for 'nail' is **ʔtusa-f**, though **knusa-f** seems more common.*]*

knusa-f *Amanuban.* fingernail, toenail, claw.

klusa-n, knusat *Amanuban.* fingernail, toenail, claw. *Usage:* Kualiin village.

Out-comparisons:

kalusun, klusun *Ili'uun.* nail, claw. (dJ:120)

kilusu *Tugun.* fingernail. (Hinton 2000:124)

***kame** *Rote.* knead. *Doublet:* ***keʔe, *keme, *kumu₂, *ŋgumu**. *Etym:* *gəmgəm. *Pattern:* k-2/3. *[minority from PMP:* *ə > *a /#C_; *ə > *e /_#*]*

kame (2) ka~kame *Termanu.* 1) knead. 2) knead repeatedly. (J:220)

kame *Korbafo.*

kame *Bokai.*

kame *Bilbaa.*

keme *Rikou.*

kame *Ba'a.*

kame *Tii.*

(ʔ)ame *Dengka.*

(ʔ)ame *Oenale.*

***ka(m)i** *PRM.* we, first person plural exclusive pronoun. *Etym:* *kami. *Pattern:* k-4. *[Form:* Lynch et al. (2002) state that POc *kami 'sometimes occurred as *kai'. Reflexes of putative *kai also occur outside of the Oceanic subgroup. In the Bungku-Tolaki subgroup, for example, Mead (1998:154) gives 18 isolects with **kami**, **mami** and 11 isolects with **kai**, **mai**. The Moronene language has both **ikami** and **ikai** as free pronouns. Likewise, Moronene has genitive **-mami**/**-mai** and absolutive **-kami**/**-kai**). (In Moronene the forms without medial *m* are optionally used when certain enclitics attach to the pronoun.) Another area in which forms without medial *m* are known to occur is in the Barrier Islands where Enggano has **ʔai** and Mentawai has **kai**. Based on such forms, it seems possible to reconstruct the reduced variant *kai to PMP. Among the RM languages most nRote languages show only reflexes of *kami, while wRM, Ba'a, Tii and Lole have reflexes of *kai.*]*

ami *Termanu.* 1PL.EXCL. (J:10)

ami *Korbafo.*

ami *Bokai.*

ami *Bilbaa.*

ami *Landu.* (own field notes)

ami *Rikou.*

ai *Ba'a.*

ai *Lole.* (Zacharias et al. 2014)

ai *Tii.*

hai *Dengka.*

hai *Oenale.*

hai *Ro'is Amarasi.* 1PL.EXCL.

hai (2) =kai *Kotos Amarasi.* 1) 1PL. EXCL.NOM. 2) 1PL.EXCL.ACC.

hai *Molo.* 1PL.EXCL. (M:135)

Out-comparisons:

kami *Semau Helong.* 1PL.EXCL.

ami *East Tetun.* we, 1PL.EXCL. (Mo:4)

***kamiri** *Rote.* candlenut tree: Aleurites moluccana. *Etym:* *kamiri (This reconstruction is not without its problems and reflexes may have been distributed by Malay, though Blust and Trussel (ongoing) note '[Malay borrowing] is much harder to argue for Hanunóo, since the term is unknown in many Philippine languages that have borrowed much more heavily from Malay'.) *Pattern:* k-1. *[irr. from PRM:* *ri > *ʔa* in Termanu, Bokai, and Ba'a; *k > *ŋg* in Oenale*] [Semantics:* The reflexes in eastern Timor point to earlier **kamiRi.*]*

kamiʔa *Termanu.* candlenut. (J:220)

kamiʔa *Bokai.*

kamili *Bilbaa.*

(kamia ?) *Rikou.*

kamiʔa *Ba'a.*

kamiri *Tii.*

kamili *Dengka.*

ŋgamiri *Oenale.*

Out-comparisons:

kamii(n), kmii *East Tetun.* tree with oily fruit, the candlenut. Aleurites Moluccana. (Mo:100)

mii *Galolen.* candlenut.

***kambe** *PRM.* saliva, spittle. *Etym:* *kambeR (own reconstruction) (PCMP). *Pattern:* k-4. *[irr. from PRM:* *e > *u* in Dela*]* *[Form:* I have tentatively reconstructed final *e (rather than *ə) as this best explains the forms in Rote-Meto, Ili'uun and central Maluku. However, it seems unlikely that *e can account for the Central Timor forms or the alternate Tetun form **kaban**.*]* *[History:* May be connected with PMP *ibəR 'saliva in the mouth; drool; desire, crave, lust for'.*]*

ape *Termanu.* saliva, spittle. (J:14)

ape *Korbafo.*

ape *Bokai.*

ape *Bilbaa.*

ape=na *Landu.* saliva. (own field notes)

ape *Rikou.*

ape *Oepao.* (own field notes)

ampe *Ba'a.*

ambe *Tii.*

hambu oe-ʔ *Dela.* saliva.

hape *Ro'is Amarasi.* saliva.

hape *Kotos Amarasi.* saliva, spit.

hape *Molo.* saliva. (M:139)

hape *Kusa-Manea.* saliva.

Out-comparisons:

kapen *Semau Helong.* saliva, spittle.

kaba-n, kabe-n, kabuee-n *East Tetun.* saliva, slobber (of animals). *[Form:* **uee** = water*]* (Mo:91)

ape(n) *Ili'uun.* cheek, throat. *[Note:* de Josselin de Jong (1947:112) also gives **apore(n)**, **apure(n)** 'spittle' which is probably also related.*]* (dJ:112)

apar *Kisar.* spittle.

aba *Mambae, South.* saliva, spittle. (Grimes et al. 2014b:9)

aba-r *Kemak.* saliva, spittle.

aba-t been *Welaun.* saliva, spittle.

aper *Kamarian.* mucus. (van Ekris 1864:76)

apel *Haruku.* *[Note:* also in some varieties of Kaibobo.*]* (van Ekris 1864:76)

apel *Nusa Laut.* mucus, snot. *[Note:* language of Lease Islands, central Maluku ISO 639-3 [nul].*]* (van Hoëvell 1877:105)

***kambu** *PwRM.* belly, uterus. *Etym:* *kambu 'lower stomach, bladder'. *Pattern:* k-2b.

(ʔ)ambu-ʔ *Dengka.* stomach. (J:678)

ʔambu-ʔ *Oenale.* belly. (J:678)

ʔambu-ʔ *Dela.* belly, stomach.

na-kapuʔ *Ro'is Amarasi.* pregnant.

ʔapu-f (2) na-ʔapuʔ *Kotos Amarasi.* 1) womb. 2) pregnant.

ʔapu-f *Amfo'an.* side. (M:27)

ʔapu-f (2) <na-apu> *Molo.* 1) uterus in general; a kind of little basket. 2) pregnant. (M:27)

na-ʔaup *Kusa-Manea.* pregnant.

Out-comparisons:

kabu-n *East Tetun.* stomach, abdomen (of humans). (Mo:93)

kapun *Ili'uun.* belly. (dJ:120)

ʔapun *Kisar.* pregnant.

***kandi** *PwRM.* whetstone. *Pattern:* k-2b.

(ʔ)andi *Dengka.* whetstone. (J:678)

ʔandi *Oenale.* whetstone. (J:678)

ʔandi *Dela.* whetstone.

kari *Ro'is Amarasi.* whetstone.

ʔaki *Kotos Amarasi.* whetstone.

ʔaki *Molo.* whetstone. (M:14)

Out-comparisons:

kadi *East Tetun.* sharpen to a keen edge (any cutting instrument). (Mo:94)

katʃi *Ili'uun.* whetstone, grind. (dJ:120)

at̪i *Kisar.* sharpen.

***kao** *PRM.* scrape, scratch. *Etym:* *kaRaw (Blust and Trussel (ongoing) reconstruct many forms of a similar shape which mean ‘scrape, scratch’: PMP *kaRus, PMP *gadus, PMP *garut, PWMP *kaus, PWMP *kərud, PWMP *kərus, PMP *kaRud, PAN *karut, PWMP *aRud, PWMP *karus. Of these, the RM reflexes would be regular from *kaRaw.). *Pattern:* k-1/2a. *[irr. from PMP:* *u > *o*] [irr. from PRM:* *k > *ŋg* in Dengka*]*

kao *Termanu.* scrape the hands together. (J:221)

kao *Korbafo.*

kao *Ba'a.*

kao *Tii.*

ŋgao *Dengka.* scrape, scratch. (J:743)

n-kao *Kotos Amarasi.* scratch.

kao *Meto.* scratch. (J:221)

Out-comparisons:

kau *Hawu.* (J:221)

<kau> *Kambera.* scratch. (On:197)

<kaü> *Weyewa.*

<kayo> *Kodi.*

***kara** *Morph:* ***kara-k**. *nRM.* chest. *Etym:* **karas (pre-RM). *Pattern:* k-2b.

kala-ʔ *Bilbaa.* breast. (J:708)

ara-ʔ *Rikou.* chest. *[Form:* Jonker (1908:708) gives <arậ> = **araaʔ**, my consultants gave **ara-ʔ**.*]*

ara-ʔ *Oepao.* chest. (own field notes)

kala-k *Lole.* chest. (Zacharias et al. 2014)

kara-k *Tii.* breast. (J:708)

kan/sao-f *Ro'is Amarasi.* chest.

ʔan/sao-f *Kotos Amarasi.* pit of the stomach, solar plexus, ‘heart’ in the metaphorical sense. *Usage:* Occurs in parallelisms with **neka-f** ‘feelings’.

ʔan/sao-n *Molo.* feelings, chest. (M:145, 360)

ʔa/sao-f *Kusa-Manea.* chest.

Out-comparisons:

kalas *Funai Helong.* chest.

karas *East Tetun.* breast, the outer front part of the chest; a half fathom, measured from the tips of the outstretched fingers to the middle of the chest. (Mo:101)

kakara *Dhao.* chest, breast.

***karu** *Morph:* ***ka~karu**. *Rote.* scrape, rasp; scratch. *Etym:* *karut (Blust and Trussel (ongoing) reconstruct many forms of a similar shape which mean ‘scrape, scratch’: PMP *gadus, PMP *garut, PWMP *kaus, PAN *kaRus, PWMP *kərud, PWMP *kərus, PMP *kaRud, PWMP *aRud, PWMP *karus. Of these, the RM reflexes would be most regular from *karut or *gadus.). *Pattern:* k-1/2/3′ (Dengka *ʔ* Oenale *k* correspondence; expect both to have either *ʔ* for pattern 2/3, or *k* for pattern 1).

ka~kalu *Termanu.* scratch. (J:220)

ka~kalu *Korbafo.*

ka~kalu *Bokai.*

ka~kalu *Bilbaa.*

(ʔ)a~(ʔ)aru *Rikou.*

ka~kalu *Ba'a.*

ka~karu *Tii.*

(ʔ)a~(ʔ)alu *Dengka.*

ka~karu *Oenale.*

Out-comparisons:

kalo *Semau Helong.* scratch.

haruk *Kisar.* scratch.

***kase** *PMeto.* foreigner, foreign. *Pattern:* k-1/2a. *[History:* This is probably a borrowing from Meto into Kemak. Waima'a has raising of final *a > o in open syllables, from which final *u* could further be derived. Similarly, Meto has sporadic raising of *a > *e* in final open syllables. Kemak, however, does not have such sound changes thus suggesting pre-Meto **kasa with *a > *e* in Meto and subsequent borrowing into Kemak.*] [Semantics:* It could be that the original meaning was ‘person’. This meaning occurs in the Meto phrase **kase ʔnaek** literally 'great foreigner' (Amarasi **kaes koʔu**) which is used poetically to refer to any highly honoured dignitary, including members of the Atoni ethnolinguistic group.*]*

kase *Ro'is Amarasi.* foreign, foreigner.

kase *Kotos Amarasi.* foreign, foreigner.

kase *Molo.* foreigner from overseas. (M:182)

kase *Kusa-Manea.* foreign, foreigner.

Out-comparisons:

wasa-kasu *Waima'a.* enemy.

kase *Kemak.* foreigner.

***katefuan** *CERM.* wasp, hornet. *Etym:* *tabuqan 'yellow-jacket wasp'. *Pattern:* k-2b. *[irr. from PRM:* *a > *e* in Termanu and Landu*] [Sporadic:* consonant metathesis *kVt > *tVk* in Termanu and Landu.*] [Form:* The source of initial ***kate** is unclear, but reflexes of ***kate-** occur with at least two other biting insect terms (see the note for the Termanu reflex). Jonker connects it with Termanu **kete** 'itch', (probably from PMP *gatəl) and this is possible.*]*

teke/fua-k *Termanu.* kind of wasp. *[Form:* Initial **teke** occurs with at least two other biting insect terms, **tekefia-k** 'tick', **tekemela-k** 'bedbug' (from *qatiməla). It also occurs with **tekelaba-k** 'house gecko'.*]* (J:614)

tekefua-ʔ *Landu.* wasp. (own field notes)

katfua|ʔ *Ro'is Amarasi.* kind of stinging/biting wasp. *[Form:* From intermediate **kaetfua with regular CV > VC metathesis of the first element of a compound.*]*

ʔatfuan *Kotos Amarasi.* kind of stinging/biting wasp.

ʔatfuan *Molo.* wasp. (M:32)

ʔaetfuan *Kusa-Manea.* kind of stinging or biting wasp.

Out-comparisons:

tohan *Semau Helong.* wasp. *[irr. from PMP:* *a > *o* (perhaps via intermediate consonant metathesis, *tabuqan > **taquban > **tauban)*]*

***katə** *PRM.* itch, feel itchy. *Doublet:* ***ŋgete.** *Etym:* *gatəl. *Pattern:* k-3. *[irr. from PRM:* *a > *e* in Rote*] [Sporadic:* *ə > *e* /σ_# in wRote (perhaps *ə > *a > *e* /_#).*]*

kete (2) na-kete (3) ma-kete (4) ma-kete-k *Termanu.* 1) biting, burning on the tongue. 2) hot, biting on the tongue; itch. 3) have an itch. 4) hot burning. (J:232f)

kete *Korbafo.*

kete *Bokai.*

kete *Bilbaa.*

ʔete *Rikou. [Form:* My consultants gave **na-ʔete** 'spicy' and **ma-ʔete** 'itchy'.*]*

kete *Ba'a.*

kete *Tii.*

(ʔ)ete *Dengka.*

ʔete *Oenale.*

ma-ʔete-ʔ *Dela.* hot (spicy).

ma|hata|ʔ *Ro'is Amarasi.* itchy.

ma|hata|ʔ *Kotos Amarasi.* itchy.

n-ma|haat *Molo.* itchy. (M:140)

ma|haat *Kusa-Manea.* itchy.

Out-comparisons:

katen *Semau Helong.* itch.

katal, katar *East Tetun.* feel itchy, itch, sting. (Mo:103)

katal *Welaun.* itchy.

akal *Kisar.* itchy.

***kati** *PRM.* call a dog. *Etym:* *kati (PCMP). *Pattern:* k-3′ (*k = *k* in Dela-Oenale; expect *k > *ʔ*).

kati *Termanu.* call a dog. (J:223)

kati *Korbafo.*

kati *Bokai.*

kati *Bilbaa.*

(ʔ)a~(ʔ)ati *Rikou.*

kati *Ba'a.*

kati *Tii.*

(ʔ)a~(ʔ)ati *Dengka.*
ka~kati *Oenale.*
kati-ʔ *Dela.* call a dog. (Theresia Tamelan pers. comm. 2017)
n-hait *Amanuban.* calls (dog). (M:135)
n-haet (2) ka= ha~hati *Molo.* 1) calls (dog). 2) in farewell poems: no longer able to be called, that is due to leaving and falling outside the reach of those who cry out. (M:135)

***kea** *PRM.* turtle. *Etym:* *keRa 'hawksbill turtle' (PCEMP). *Pattern:* k-2a. *[Sporadic:* *a > *e* /_# in wRM.*]*
kea *Termanu.* turtle. (J:225)
kea *Korbafo.*
kea *Bokai.*
kea *Bilbaa.*
kea *Landu.* (own field notes)
ʔea *Rikou.*
kea *Ba'a.*
kea *Tii.*
(ʔ)ee *Dengka.*
ʔee *Oenale.*
ʔee *Dela.* turtle.
kee *Ro'is Amarasi.* turtle, tortoise.
kee, kea *Kotos Amarasi.* turtle, tortoise.
<ke'>, <ke'a> *Molo.* turtle. *[Form:* <**ke'**> is almost certainly **kee**, but the correct interpretation of <**ke'a**> is not clear*]* (M:191)

***kees** *Morph:* ***na-kees**. *CERM.* squeeze around the waist. *Pattern:* k-1/2a.
na-kee *Termanu.* wear around the belly. (J:225)
na-kee *Korbafo.*
na-ee *Rikou.*
na-kes~kees *Kotos Amarasi.* have contractions.
na-kees *Meto.* press. (J:225)
Out-comparisons:
kees *Semau Helong.* strangle. *[Semantics:* Jonker gives the meaning for Helong **kees** as 'tie, e.g. around the belly, also: knead'.*]*

***kei** *PRM.* tickle. *Pattern:* k-3′ (*k = k in wRote and Rikou; expect *k > *ʔ*).
na-la-kei *Termanu.* touch someone softly, e.g. with a finger or stick in order to get his attention. (J:228)
na-la-kei *Korbafo.*
na-la-kei *Bokai.*
na-la-kei *Bilbaa.*
ke~kei *Rikou.*
na-la-kei *Ba'a.*
na-la-kei *Tii.* tickle. (J:710)
keis *Dengka.*
keis *Oenale.*
keis *Dela.* touch to get attention.
mahei *Kotos Amarasi.* ticklish.
mahei, mahai *Meto.* ticklish. (J:710)

***keʔe** *PnRote.* knead. *Doublet:* ***kame, *keme, *kumu₂, *ŋgumu**. *Etym:* *gəmgəm. *Pattern:* k-2/3. *[irr. from PMP:* *g > *ʔ*] [minority from PMP:* *ə > *e /_#*]*
keʔe (2) ke~keʔe *Termanu.* 1) pinch, knead, from that: squeeze out. 2) knead into a ball. (J:227)
keʔe *Bokai.*
kee *Bilbaa.*
(ʔ)ee *Rikou.*
keʔe *Ba'a.*
keʔe *Tii.*

***kela** *Rote.* leave behind. *Pattern:* k-4.
ela *Termanu.* leave over, leave behind; leave. (J:111)
ela *Korbafo.*
ela *Bokai.*
kela *Bilbaa.*
ela *Rikou.*
ela *Ba'a.*
ela *Tii.*
hela *Dengka.*
hela *Oenale.*
Out-comparisons:

hela *East Tetun.* stay, remain, reside; to abandon, to reject; *adv.* at rest, in the same state; *particle* the action is completed. *[irr. from PRM:* *k = *h* correspondence*]* (Mo:85)

kera *Hawu.* overshoot. (J:111)

***kelas** *Morph:* ***ka-kelas**. *PRM.* winter melon. Benincasa hispida. *Pattern:* k-irr. *[irr. from PRM:* *k > *ŋg in nRote; *a > *e* Meto*]* *[Form:* This is the only known form with a nRote *ŋg = wRM *h correspondence set. We could propose PRM *g to account for this correspondence, though in the absence of additional examples of this correspondence set I prefer not to posit an additional PRM proto-phoneme.*]*

ŋgelas *Termanu.* gourd, squash. (J:437)

ŋgela-ʔ *Korbafo.*

ŋela-k *Bokai.*

ŋela-k *Bilbaa.*

kelas *Rikou.*

ŋgelas *Ba'a.*

helas *Oenale.*

helas *Dela.* pumpkin.

heens *Ro'is Amarasi.* winter melon. Benincasa hispida.

ʔ|henes *Kotos Amarasi.* winter melon. Benincasa hispida.

Out-comparisons:

keliŋ *Ili'uun.* pumpkin (with red flesh and black stones). *[irr. from PRM:* *a = *i* correspondence; *s = *ŋ* correspondence*]* (dJ:121)

helas *Central Manggarai.* Benincasa hispida. (Verheijen 1984:46)

ɣelas *East Manggarai.* Benincasa hispida. (Verheijen 1984:46)

kelas *West Manggarai.* Benincasa hispida. (Verheijen 1984:46)

halaʔ *Komodo.* Benincasa hispida. (Verheijen 1984:46)

hala *Bima.* Benincasa hispida. (Verheijen 1984:46)

***kele** *CERM.* pant, breathe heavily. *Pattern:* k-3. *[Note:* Termanu and Tii have **ŋgile** 'heavy breathing like a sick person, panting' which may be related.*]*

kele~kele *Keka.* heavy coughing. **boʔo tao leo bee ndia dee lee kele~kele-ŋemi** What kind of coughing is that! You cough like you are choking. (J:710)

kele~kele *Korbafo.* heavy breathing. (J:710)

na-ʔheneʔ *Kotos Amarasi.* neigh, whinny.

<hene> *Molo.* the whinny of a mating stallion. (M:145)

***keme** *Rote.* knead. *Doublet:* ***kame, *keʔe, *kumu₂, *ŋgumu**. *Etym:* *gəmgəm. *Pattern:* k-2/3. *[minority from PMP:* *ə > *e / _#*]*

keme (2) ke~keme *Termanu.* 1) knead. 2) knead, hold tightly in the hand. (J:230)

keme *Korbafo.*

keme *Bokai.*

keme *Bilbaa.*

keme *Rikou.*

keme *Ba'a.*

keme *Tii.*

(ʔ)eme *Dengka.*

(ʔ)eme *Oenale.*

***ke(m)i** *PRM.* 2PL nominative, you all. *Etym:* *kamuyu. *Pattern:* k-4. *[Form:* The loss of medial *m in wRM, Ba'a, Tii, and Lole is parallel to the loss of medial *m in the first person plural exclusive pronoun.*]*

emi *Termanu.* 2PL. (J:113)

kemi *Korbafo.*

kemi *Bokai.*

kemi *Bilbaa.*

emi *Landu.* 2PL, you. (own field notes)

emi *Rikou.*

ei *Ba'a.*

ei *Lole.* (Zacharias et al. 2014)

ei *Tii.*

hei *Dengka.*
hei *Oenale.*
hii *Ro'is Amarasi.* 2PL.
hii (2) =kii *Kotos Amarasi.* 1) 2PL.NOM. 2) 2PL.ACC.
hii *Molo.* 2PL. (M:147)
hei *Kusa-Manea.* 2PL. *[Form:* Usually pronounced [heː] with a single mid-high vowel in isolation.*]*
Out-comparisons:
mia, mi *Semau Helong.* 2PL.
emi, imi *East Tetun.* 2PL. (Mo:29)
imi *Kemak.* 2PL.
iim *Mambae, South.* 2PL. (Grimes et al. 2014b:23)
miu, mi *Dhao.* 2PL.
muu *Hawu.* 2PL.

***keni** *Morph:* ***keni-k**. *Rote.* keel. *Pattern:* k-2/3.
keni-k *Termanu.* keel of a vessel. (J:231)
keni-ʔ *Korbafo.*
keni-k *Bokai.*
keni-ʔ *Bilbaa.*
ʔeni *Rikou.* *[Note:* The lack of any final glottal stop in Rikou, Oenale and Dengka may be due to a typographical error. Jonker (1908:231) gives 'D., On., R. **eni**'.*]*
keni-k *Ba'a.*
keni-k *Tii.*
(ʔ)eni *Dengka.*
(ʔ)eni *Oenale.*
Out-comparisons:
kəni *Hawu.* (J:231)

***kendi** *Morph:* ***ma-(sa)-kendi-k**. *nRM.* slippery, smooth. *Pattern:* k-2b. *[Form:* The Meto alternates without *s* are reflexes of ***ma-kendi-k**.*]*
masakeni *Termanu.* slippery, slick, polished, clean, shiny, glossy. (Fox 2016b:32)
masakendi-k *Tii.* clean, pure. (J:710)
maskeri|ʔ *Ro'is Amarasi.* slippery.
masʔeki|ʔ (2) maʔeki|ʔ *Kotos Amarasi.* 1) slippery. 2) fine, smooth, flat.
maʔeki|ʔ *Molo.* slippery, smooth. (M:296)

***keŋga** *Morph:* ***keŋga-k**. *PRM.* kind of sea-weed. *Pattern:* k-irr. *[irr. from PRM:* *k > Ø/ʔ /#_ in nRote (expect *k = *k* in all except Rikou)*]*
eŋa-k *Termanu.* kind of seaweed which is eaten as a vegetable. (J:114)
eŋa-ʔ *Korbafo.* *[Note:* Jonker (1908:114) gives two entries for 'T.' (Tii) but the first is surely a mistake and should be 'K.' (Korbafo).*]*
eŋa-k *Bokai.*
eŋa-ʔ *Bilbaa.*
eka-ʔ *Rikou.* *[Form:* My consultants gave vowel initial **ika doo-ʔ**. The initial part could be **ika-ʔ** 'fish'.*]*
eŋga-k *Ba'a.*
eŋga-k *Tii.*
(ʔ)eŋga-ʔ *Dengka.*
ʔeŋga-ʔ *Oenale.*
ʔeŋga-ʔ *Dela.* kind of seaweed.
keka|ʔ *Ro'is Amarasi.* seaweed.
Out-comparisons:
kəka *Hawu.* (J:114)

***kepe** *PMeto.* tick (parasite).
kepe *Ro'is Amarasi.* tick.
kepe *Kotos Amarasi.* tick.
Out-comparisons:
kepi *Central Nage.* small tick or mite that infests genital hair and embeds itself in the flesh; transferred through sexual intercourse. (Forth 2016:335)

***kera₁** *PRM.* brother-in-law. *Pattern:* k-1.
kela *Termanu.* brother-in-law (used reciprocally by men). (J:229)
kela *Korbafo.*
kela *Bokai.*
kela *Bilbaa.*
ʔera *Rikou.*
kela *Ba'a.*
kera *Tii.*
kela *Dengka.*
kera *Oenale.*

ken/baʔe *Ro'is Amarasi.* same-sex cross-cousin, person of the same gender as the speaker who is married to the speaker's opoosite sex sibling; mate, friend. *[Form:* This is a historic compound of ***kena** + **baʔe** with regular metathesis of the first element to ***keen** with subsequent reduction of the double vowel. **baʔe** is the normal term for 'same-sex cross-cousin' in other varieties of Meto.*]*

Out-comparisons:

kela *Semau Helong.* cousin, brother-in-law.

kela *Kemak.* woman's brother. *Usage:* Kutubaba dialect. *[Semantics:* Elicited from a wordlist with *saudara laki-laki dari perempuan* 'male sibling from a woman', the semantics should be properly checked.*]*

kela *Welaun.* same-sex cross-cousin.

kera *Sika.* brother-in-law. (Pareira and Lewis 1998:94)

hera *Bima.* brother-in-law. (Jonker 1893:24)

<yera> *Kambera.* brother-in-law, wife's brother. (On:558)

<wera> *Weyewa.*

kesa *Manggarai.* brother-in-law, wife's brother, sister's husband; friend, companion (of a man). (Verheijen 1967:203)

ʔedʒa, ʔedʒa kera *Ende.* man's sister's husband, wife's brother, man's male cross-cousin.

***kera2** *Morph:* ***ma-kera**. *Rote.* tickle. *Pattern:* k-1. *[History:* Blust and Trussel (ongoing) reconstruct a number of similar forms: *gidik, *giri, *kidi, and *kirik.*]*

ma-kelas (2) ma-kela *Termanu.* 1) ticklish. 2) have a ticklish feeling. (J:230)

ma-kela-ʔ *Korbafo.*

ma-kela-ʔ *Bokai.*

ma-kela-ʔ *Bilbaa.*

ma-eras *Rikou.*

ma-kelas *Ba'a.*

ma-kera-k *Tii.*

ma-kelas *Dengka.*

Out-comparisons:

kede *Semau Helong.* tickles.

kakedek, kede *East Tetun.* tickle. *Usage:* Samoro village. (Mo:95)

***kerumatu** *Morph:* ***kerumatu-k**. *Rote.* leech. *Etym:* *kalimatək 'jungle leech <u>Haemadipsa</u> species'. *Pattern:* k-2/3. *[irr. from PMP:* *ə > *u*] [Form:* Initial ***keru** in Rote may be related to the original *qali-/*kali- prefix, though this requires irregular sound changes, most problematically *l > *r, and *i > *u which are not otherwise attested.*] [History:* Osmond (2011b:414) reconstructs Proto-Polynesian *kele-mutu 'earthworm, grub' which also attests a similar initial element as well as final *ə > *u.]*

kelumatu-k *Termanu.* leech; usually refers to a small kind, but can also be used for an ordinary leech. (J:230)

kelumatu-k *Bokai.*

kelumatu-ʔ *Bilbaa.*

(ʔ)erumatu-ʔ *Rikou. [Note:* not known by my consultants.*]*

kelumatu-k *Ba'a.*

(kelumatu-k ?) *Tii.*

(ʔ)elumutu-ʔ *Dengka.*

Out-comparisons:

matak *East Tetun.* leech. (Mo:139)

makak *Ili'uun.* blood-sucker. (dJ:126)

***kesu/fani** *PRM.* sneeze. *Etym:* *bañən (Blust and Trussel (ongoing) reconstruct three similar forms: *bañən, *bañan and *bəñan.). *Pattern:* k-2b. *[Sporadic:* vowel height

harmony *e > *i* /_Cu in nRote and Ro'is Amarasi*]* *[Form:* The source of initial ***kesu** is currently unknown.*]*
kisu/fani *Termanu.* sneeze. (J:239f)
kisu/fani *Korbafo.*
kisu/fani *Bokai.*
kisu/fani *Bilbaa.*
ʔisu/fani *Rikou.*
kisu/fani *Ba'a.*
kisu/fani *Tii.*
(ʔ)esu/fani *Dengka.*
(ʔ)esu/fani *Oenale.*
ʔesu/fani *Dela.* sneeze.
n-kius/fani, n-kis/fani *Ro'is Amarasi.* sneeze.
n-ʔeus/fani *Kotos Amarasi.* sneeze.
n-ʔeus/fani *Molo.* sneeze. (M:105)
Out-comparisons:
haŋi *Semau Helong.* sneeze.
fani *Fehan Tetun.* sneeze.

ketembau** *PRM.* kind of insect. *Pattern:* k-2a. *[irr. from PRM:* *au > *u in Meto; vowel metathesis in Meto *eCu > *uCe (ketembau** > Proto-Meto ***ketepu** > **ketupe**)*]*
ketepau-ʔ *Bilbaa.*
tekepau-ʔ *Landu.* tick. *[Sporadic:* consonant metathesis *kVt > *tVk]* (own field notes)
etepau-ʔ *Rikou.*
ketempau-k *Ba'a.*
ketembau-k *Tii.*
(ʔ)etembau-ʔ *Dengka.*
ʔetembau-ʔ *Oenale.*
ʔetembau *Dela.*
ketupe *Kotos Amarasi.* kind of beetle similar to a longhorn beetle.

***ketu** *PRM.* break off, pluck off. *Etym:* *kətuq 'pick, pluck, break off' (Blust and Trussel (ongoing) also reconstruct PAN *kətun 'cut, sever' on the basis of Formosan reflexes.). *Pattern:* k-2a.
ketu *Termanu.* break off, pluck off. (J:234)
ketu *Korbafo.*
ketu *Bokai.*
ketu *Bilbaa.*
ʔetu *Rikou.*
ketu *Ba'a.*
ketu *Tii.*
(ʔ)etu *Dengka.*
ʔetu *Dela.* pick fruit or harvest beans, break (e.g. rope). *[Note:* **na-ma-ʔetu** = 'become broken (rope), stop', **na-ʔetu-ʔ** = 'break, decide'.*]*
n-ketu *Kotos Amarasi.* cut off, cut until broken.
n-ketu *Molo.* breaks off. (M:203)
Out-comparisons:
kotu *East Tetun.* break, fracture. (Mo:117)

***ketu|k** *PMeto.* bedbug. *Pattern:* k-2b.
ketuʔ *Ro'is Amarasi.* bedbug.
ʔetuʔ *Kotos Amarasi.* bedbug. Cimicidae species.
ʔetuk *Kotos Amarasi.* bedbug. *Usage:* Tais Nonof sub-dialect.
<etu> *Molo.* bedbug. (M:105)
ʔeto *Kusa-Manea.* bedbug. *[Sporadic:* vowel height harmony *i > *e* /oC_.*]*

***kənda** *PRM.* close (v.). *Pattern:* k-2b. *[Form:* *nd > *n* /ə_ in Rikou, Oepao, Landu, Lole, Tii, and wRote.*]*
kena *Termanu.* close, e.g. door. (J:231)
kena *Korbafo.*
kena *Bokai.*
kena *Bilbaa.*
(ʔ)ena *Landu.* close (door). (own field notes)
ena *Rikou.*
(ʔ)ena *Oepao.* (own field notes)
kena *Ba'a.*
kena *Lole.* close. (Zacharias et al. 2014)
kena *Tii.*
(ʔ)ena *Dengka.*
ʔena *Oenale.*
ʔena *Dela.* close.
na-kera *Ro'is Amarasi.* close.
na-ʔeka (2) n-ʔeka *Kotos Amarasi.* 1) close (transitive). 2) closed.

na-ʔeka (2) n-ʔeka *Molo.* 1) hold together. 2) close. (M:99)

***kibo** *Rote.* edible shellfish. *Etym:* *qibaw (Regarding initial PMP *q Blust and Trussel (ongoing) state: 'Wolio **hiwo** is a loan from one of the languages of the Munic group (van den Berg 1991). Although such a phonologically irregular form would not normally be cited in the main comparison, in this case it serves to disambiguate the stem-initial phoneme as *q.' The Bokai and Dengka forms provide evidence for initial *k rather than *q. However, the irregularities in the Rote forms caution against using them as deciding witnesses for initial *q or *k in PMP. It is also possible that the initial *k* in Bokai and Dengka is a reflex of the nominal *ka- prefix.). *Pattern:* k-irr. *[irr. from PMP:* *Ø > *k (accretion of nominal prefix ***ka-** ?)*]* *[irr. from PRM:* *b = *b* in Rikou and Bilbaa; *k > Ø in all nRote except Bokai (expect *k = *k* in all except Rikou), Dengka *k* Oenale *ʔ*/Ø correspondence (expect both to have *k* or *ʔ*/Ø)*]*

(ʔ)ifo(-k) *Termanu.* kind of shellfish. (J:200)

(ʔ)ifo *Korbafo.*

kifo *Bokai.*

(ʔ)ibo *Bilbaa.*

(ʔ)ibo *Rikou. [Note:* not known by my consultants.*]*

(ʔ)ifo *Ba'a.*

(ʔ)ifo *Tii.*

kifo *Dengka.*

(ʔ)ifo *Oenale.*

***kii** *PnRote.* left side or direction. *Doublet:* ***ɗii**1. *Etym:* *ka-wiRi. *Pattern:* k-1/2/3.

kii *Termanu.* left, left side, north. (J:234f)

kii *Korbafo.*

kii *Bokai.*

kii *Bilbaa.*

ʔii *Rikou.*

kii *Ba'a.*

kii *Lole.* left, north. (Zacharias et al. 2014)

kii *Tii.*

***kili** *Morph:* ***ki~kili**. *Rote.* tickle. *Etym:* *kilik. *Pattern:* k-1.

ki~kili *Termanu.* tickle. (J:237)

ki~kili *Korbafo.*

ki~kili *Bokai.*

ki~kili *Bilbaa.*

ki~kili *Ba'a.*

ki~kili *Tii.*

ki~kili *Dengka.*

ki~kili *Oenale.*

ki~kili *Dela.* tickle.

Out-comparisons:

hakili(k), kili *East Tetun.* tickle. (Mo:117)

***kilu** *Rote.* crooked, twisted. *Etym:* *kiluq 'bend, curve; bent, curved, crooked'. *Pattern:* k-1.

kilu (ka~)kaʔi (2) kilu hoʔe-k (3) kilu koʔe-k *Termanu.* 1) be or become crooked and twisted, confused. 2) crooked and bent over. 3) crooked and distorted. (J:237f)

kilu kaʔi *Korbafo.*

kilu kaʔi *Bokai.*

(ʔ)ilu ai *Rikou. [Form:* This form is given with a note ʔ**ilu-aʔi** indicating a possible alternate form with a medial glottal stop.*]*

kilu kaʔi *Ba'a.*

kilu kai *Tii.*

kilu kai *Dengka.*

kilu kai *Oenale.*

Out-comparisons:

bkilu *Helong.* crooked. (J:237)

***kima** *nRM.* giant clam. Tridacna gigas. *Etym:* *kima. *Pattern:* k-1/2a' (*k > *ʔ* in Tii, expect *k = *k*). *[Sporadic:* *k > *ʔ* /#_ in Tii.*]*

kima *Termanu.* kind of shellfish, one of the smaller kinds is used as a lamp. (J:238)

kima *Korbafo.*

kima *Bokai.*

kima *Bilbaa.*
ʔima *Rikou.*
kima *Ba'a.*
(ʔ)ima *Tii.* clam.
kimaʔ *Kotos Amarasi.* clam.
<kima> *Molo.* empty shell. (M:208)
Out-comparisons:
kima *East Tetun.* sea-shell. (Mo:107)

***kiŋgi** *Morph:* ***ki~kiŋgi**. *PRM.* cockroach. *Pattern:* k-irr. *[irr. from PRM:* *k > *h* in all nRote except Tii; *ŋg > *r* in Ro'is Amarasi*] [Form:* The Ro'is Amarasi form would be regular from earlier medial **nd. Perhaps a case of dissimilation of *ŋg > *nd /k_ in Meto. Compare #**kari** 'kidneys'. Similarly, compare ***maŋgu2** 'dry fruit skin' which shows irr. *ŋg > *nd* in wRote and Tii.*]*
hi~hiŋi *Termanu.* cockroach. (J:185)
hi~hiŋi *Korbafo.*
hi~hiŋi *Bokai.*
hi~hiŋi *Bilbaa.*
hi~hiki *Rikou.*
hi~hiŋgi *Ba'a.*
hi~hiŋgi *Lole.* cockroach. (Zacharias et al. 2014)
(ʔ)i~(ʔ)iŋgi *Tii.*
(ʔ)i~(ʔ)iŋgi *Dengka.*
ʔi~ʔiŋgi *Oenale.*
ʔi~ʔiŋgi *Dela.* cockroach.
kir~kiri *Ro'is Amarasi.* cockroach.
ik~iki *Kotos Amarasi.* cockroach.
iki *Molo.* cockroach. (M:159)

***kira1** *Rote.* hold. *Pattern:* k-2/3.
kila *Termanu.* hold, in the metaphorical sense. (J:236)
kila *Korbafo.*
kila *Bokai.*
kila *Bilbaa.*
ʔira *Rikou.* responsible for household arrangements. (J:236; own field notes)
kila *Ba'a.*
kira *Tii.*
(ʔ)ila *Dengka.*
ʔira *Oenale.*
ma-ʔira-ʔ (2) na-sa-ʔira *Dela.* 1) have an agreement. 2) chokes.
Out-comparisons:
kila *Semau Helong.* hold.

***kira2** *Rote.* stingy. *Pattern:* k-2/3′ (*k > *ʔ* in Tii; expect *k = *k*). *[Sporadic:* *k > *ʔ* /#_ in Tii.*]*
kila *Termanu.* skimp on something. (J:237)
kila *Korbafo.*
kila *Bokai.*
kila *Bilbaa.*
ʔira *Rikou.*
kila *Ba'a.*
(ʔ)ira *Tii.*
(ʔ)ila *Dengka.*
ʔira *Oenale.*
ʔira *Dela.* stingy.
Out-comparisons:
kilaʔ *Semau Helong.* stingy.

***kiri1** *Morph:* ***kiri_ei-k**. *Rote.* little bells. *Etym:* *giRiŋ 'ringing sound' (Blust and Trussel (ongoing) only give Paiwan **giriŋ** 'growl' and Batak **giriŋ** 'bell' as evidence for their reconstruction. They note that Paiwan *R > *r* is irregular.). *Pattern:* k-1/2/3′ (Dengka *ʔ* Oenale *k* correspondence; expect both to have either *ʔ* for pattern 2/3, or *k* for pattern 1). *[minority from PMP:* *R = *r (expect Ø)*] [History:* Blust and Trussel (ongoing) also reconstruct Proto-Philippine *kilíŋ 'ringing of a bell'.*] [Semantics:* The final element may be connected with Rote **ei-k** 'leg, foot' with the original meaning being 'bells on ankles' (like in Malay) with later shift to 'bells on a horse's neck'.*]*
kili_ei-k, kila_ei-k, kil/ei-k *Termanu.* little bells on the neck of a horse. (J:237)
kili_ei-k *Bokai.*
kili_ei-ʔ *Bilbaa.*
(ʔ)iri_ei-ʔ *Rikou.*
kili_ei-k *Ba'a.*

ki~kir/ei-k *Tii.*
(ʔ)i~(ʔ)ilel/ei-ʔ *Dengka.*
kiri_ei-ʔ *Oenale.*
Out-comparisons:
giriŋ~giriŋ *Malay.* bells (on anklets), bicycle bell; various plants with seeds that rattle in their shells and which can be used for green manure.

***kiri**2 *PRM.* sharpen to have a point. *Pattern:* k-2b′ (*k = *k* in Kotos Amarasi, expect *k > *ʔ*).
kili *Termanu.* sharpen to have a point. (J:237)
kili *Korbafo.*
kili *Bokai.*
kili *Bilbaa.*
kiri *Tii.*
(ʔ)ili *Dengka.*
ʔiri *Oenale.*
ʔiri *Dela.*
n-kini *Kotos Amarasi.* use a knife to remove the skin of betel nut, use a knife to sharpen to a point.
n-ʔini *Molo.* sharpen (e.g. pencil), pointing sharply. *[Form:* Given as <**anini**> and <**atini**> with the glottal stop deduced from the initial vowel before a single consonant in each form. If this were a vowel initial root I would expect <**nini**> and <**tini**>.*]* (M:160)

***kisa** *Morph:* ***kisa-k**. *CER.* single, unique. *Pattern:* k-1/2/3.
kisa-k *Termanu.* single. (J:238)
kisa-ʔ *Korbafo.*
kisa-k *Ba'a.*
Out-comparisons:
kisa *Semau Helong.* different.

***kisi** *PRM.* peel, remove skin. *Pattern:* k-irr. *[irr. from PRM:* *k > Ø in Rote except Rikou (expect other nRote *k = *k*, wRote *k > *ʔ*)*] [History:* Blust and Trussel (ongoing) reconstruct PCMP *isi 'peel, strip off' on the basis of the Termanu form and some Oceanic forms. They also list this cognate set as noise. The Ro'is (and Helong) forms indicate an initial *k, though this *k is irregularly lost in Rote.*]*
na-isi (2) nisi *Termanu.* 1) peel, e.g. onions. (J:207) 2) peel with a knife. (J:398)
na-isi (2) nisi *Korbafo.*
na-isi (2) nisi *Bokai.*
na-isi (2) nisi *Bilbaa.*
na-isi (2) nisi *Rikou.*
na-isi (2) nisi *Ba'a.*
na-isi (2) nisi *Tii.*
(na-)isi *Dengka.*
na-isi *Oenale.*
n-kisi *Ro'is Amarasi.* peel (e.g. banana).
n-ʔisi *Kotos Amarasi.* peel (e.g. banana).
<**isi**> *Molo.* peel, remove the skin of fruit. (M:162)
Out-comparisons:
kisi *Semau Helong.* nip.

***kita** *PRM.* 1PL.INCL. *Etym:* *kita1. *Pattern:* k-4.
ita *Termanu.* 1PL.INCL. (J:207)
ita *Korbafo.*
ita *Bokai.*
ita *Bilbaa.*
ita *Landu.* 1PL.INCL, we. (own field notes)
ita *Rikou.*
ita *Ba'a.*
ita *Tii.*
hita *Dengka.*
hita *Oenale.*
hiit *Ro'is Amarasi.* 1PL.INCL.
hiit, hiti, hita (2) =kiit, =kiti, =kita *Kotos Amarasi.* 1) 1PL.INCL.NOM. 2) 1PL.INCL.ACC. *[Form:* Unmetathesised forms with final /a/ are only (optionally) used before a consonant cluster. Other unmetathesised forms are used as expected (with a discourse function), with the exception that the alternation is not fully productive.*]*

hiit *Molo.* 1PL.INCL. (M:149)
hita, hiat *Kusa-Manea.* 1PL.INCL.
Out-comparisons:
kit *Semau Helong.* 1PL.INCL.
ita *East Tetun.* we, us (inclusive of the person or person spoken to). (Mo:91)

***klaha** *Morph:* ***klaha-k**. *PRM.* glowing coals. *Etym:* **klaRa (pre-RM). *Pattern:* k-1. *[irr. from PMP:* *R > *h (also in ***noh** and ***taha**)*] [Form:* regular *h > Ø /a_a in Rote, regular *kl > Rote *k* Meto *kr*/*kl.]*
haʔi_kaa-k (2) pana_kaa-k *Termanu.* 1) glowing coal. 2) dry snot. (J:209)
haʔi_kaa-ʔ (2) pana_kaa-ʔ *Korbafo.* 1) charcoal.
haʔi_kaa-k (2) pana_kaa-k *Bokai.*
ai_kaa-ʔ (2) idu_kaa-ʔ *Bilbaa.*
ai_ʔaa-ʔ (2) idu_ʔaa-ʔ *Rikou.*
haʔi_kaa-k (2) idu_kaa-k, mpinu-kaa-k *Ba'a.*
aʔi_kaa-k (2) iɗu_kaa-k *Tii.*
ai_kaa-ʔ (2) mbana_kaa-ʔ *Dengka.*
ai_kaa (2) mbana_kaa-ʔ *Oenale.*
kraha|ʔ *Ro'is Amarasi.* burning coals.
kraha|ʔ *Kotos Amarasi.* burning coals, embers; glory.
na-klaah (2) klaha|ʔ (3) a-klaha-t *Molo.* 1) emits flames. 2) flames. 3) the flaming one. (M:214)
Out-comparisons:
klaak *Fehan Tetun.* red-hot coals, red (of sunburn, coals, red hair, betel-lips).
ahi klaak *East Tetun.* ember or live coals. (Mo:108)
klara *Ili'uun.* charcoal. (dJ:121)

***kleet** *Morph:* ***na-kleet**. *CERM.* mock, tease. *Pattern:* k-1. *[Sporadic:* glottal stop insertion in Meto.*] [Form:* regular *kl > Rote *k* Meto *kr*/*kl.]*
na-ke~kee-k *Termanu.* tease someone, make someone angry, or tease a child to make it cry. *[Form:* It is unclear if the final consonant in Termanu is a suffix or not.*]* (J:225)
na-kreʔet *Kotos Amarasi.* mock.

***klou** *PRM.* bow (e.g. bow and arrow). *Pattern:* k-1. *[Form:* regular *kl > Rote *k* Meto *kr*/*kl.]*
ko~kou-k (2) kou *Termanu.* 1) shooting of a bow and arrow, bow. 2) shoot with a bow and arrow. (J:253)
ko~kou-ʔ *Korbafo.*
ko~kou-k *Bokai.*
ko~kou-ʔ *Bilbaa.*
ʔo~ʔou-ʔ *Rikou.*
ko~kou-k *Ba'a.*
ko~kou-k *Tii.*
ko~kou-ʔ *Dengka.*
ko~kou-ʔ *Oenale.*
krau-t *Kotos Amarasi.* bow.
na-klau (2) a-klau-t *Molo.* 1) shoots with a bow. 2) bow. (M:216)

***koaʔ₁** *PRM.* Friarbird. Philemon species. *Pattern:* k-1. *[Semantics:* onomatopoeia.*]*
koa, koaʔ *Termanu.* kind of bird, called *koak* or *burung siang* = 'midday bird' in Kupang. (J:241)
koa, koaʔ *Korbafo.*
koa, koaʔ *Bokai.*
koa, koaʔ *Bilbaa.*
koa, koaʔ *Rikou.* Friarbird. Philemon species. *[Form:* My consultants only gave **koaʔ**.*]* (J:241; own field notes)
koa, koaʔ *Ba'a.*
koa, koaʔ *Tii.*
koa, koaʔ *Dengka.*
koa, koaʔ *Oenale.*
koaʔ (2) koa koʔu (3) koa maat meʔe *Ro'is Amarasi.* 1) kind of bird (unsure identification). 2) Friarbird. Philemon species. 3) Green Figbird. Sphecotheres viridis.

koaʔ (2) koa kikoʔ (3) koa koʔu *Kotos Amarasi.* 1) Green Figbird. Sphecotheres viridis. 2) Timor Friarbird. Philemon inornatus. 3) Helmeted Friarbird. Philemon buceroides.

kool <koa> *Molo.* calling bird. (M:225)

Out-comparisons:

koaʔ *Semau Helong. koak* bird.

koʔak *Fehan Tetun.* bird that calls in a voice like this word. (Mo:115)

kau-koʔak *East Tetun.* bird that calls in a voice like this word. (Mo:104)

koak *Welaun.* friarbird.

***koaʔ2** *PRM.* cry out loudly. *Pattern:* k-2a′ (*k = *k* in Rikou, expect *k > *ʔ/Ø*). *[Semantics:* onomatopoeia.*]*

ko~koa *Termanu.* crowing, of a rooster. (J:242)

ko~koa *Bokai.*

ko~koa *Bilbaa.*

ko~koʔoa *Rikou.*

ko~koa *Ba'a.*

ko~koa *Tii.*

(ʔ)o~(ʔ)oa *Dengka. [Note:* On page 242, Jonker gives the Dengka form as <ooä> **ʔo~oʔa**. That this is probably a typographical error is shown by the entry on page 745 in which he gives <oöa> **ʔo~ʔoa**.*]* (J:242, 745)

na-ʔoa *Dela.* cry loudly, make **ʔoa** sound.

n-koaʔ *Kotos Amarasi.* yell out, whoop, make a loud sound without words.

n-koaʔ *Molo.* calls out loudly an announcement call. (M:225)

***koɓa** *PRM.* cover. *Pattern:* k-2a. *[irr. from PRM:* *o > *u* in Meto; *a > *o* in Rote*]*

kobo *Termanu.* hold one's hand in front of something and thereby cover it. (J:243)

kobo *Korbafo.*

kobo *Bokai.*

kobo *Bilbaa.*

ʔobo *Rikou.*

kobo *Ba'a.*

koɓo *Tii.*

(ʔ)obo *Dengka.*

ʔoɓo *Oenale.*

ʔoɓo *Dela.* cover.

n-kuba *Kotos Amarasi.* cover.

n-kuub *Molo.* cover. (M:243)

***kodo** *PRM.* bird. *Pattern:* d-2, k-1.

kolo/baʔo-k *Termanu.* kind of bird called *koro baʔok* in Kupang. (J:536)

kolo/bako-ʔ *Korbafo.*

kolo/baʔo-k *Bokai.*

kolo/bako-ʔ *Bilbaa.*

koro/bako-ʔ *Rikou.*

kolo/baʔo-k *Ba'a.*

koro/ɓako-k *Tii.*

kolo/baʔo-ʔ *Dengka.*

koro/ɓako-ʔ *Oenale.*

koro *Ro'is Amarasi.* bird.

koro *Kotos Amarasi.* bird.

kolo *Molo.* bird. (M:232)

koro *Kusa-Manea.* bird.

Out-comparisons:

koro ʃawa *Hawu.* dove.

koloŋ *Lamaholot, Ile Mandiri.* bird. *Usage:* Lewoingu dialect. *[Note:* language of east Flores ISO 639-3 [slp].*]* (Klamer 2015b)

koloŋ *Alorese.* bird. (Klamer 2011:61)

kolo/ndasi *Palu'e.* pigeon. *[Note:* language of central Flores ISO 639-3 [ple].*]* (Donohue 2003:8)

kolo *Ngadha.* dove. (Djawanai 1995:Part 2, 327)

olo *Oirata.* quail. *[Note:* non-Austronesian language of Kisar Island ISO 639-3 [oia].*]* (Nazaruddin pers. comm. May 2017)

***koɗe** *PRM.* monkey. *Pattern:* k-2a. *[irr. from PRM:* vowel metathesis in Meto *oCe > *eCo]*
kode *Termanu.* monkey. (J:243)
kode *Korbafo.*
kode *Bokai.*
kode *Bilbaa.*
kode *Landu.* monkey. (own field notes)
ʔode *Rikou.*
kode *Ba'a.*
koɗe *Tii.*
(ʔ)oɗe *Dengka.*
(ʔ)oɗe *Oenale.*
ʔoɗe *Dela.* monkey.
kero *Ro'is Amarasi.* monkey.
kero *Kotos Amarasi.* monkey.
kelo *Amanuban.* monkey. (M:196)
Out-comparisons:
kode *Manggarai.* crab-eating macaque. Macaca fascicularis. (Verheijen 1967:224)
koɗe *Ngadha.* monkey. (Djawanai 1995:Part 2, 356)

***koɗo** *PRM.* swallow. *Pattern:* k-2b. *[History:* Lynch (2001:339) reconstructs Proto-Meso-Melanesian *kodom that may be connected. This term is connected to a larger network of phonetically similar terms.*]*
kodo *Termanu.* swallow, gulp. (J:244)
kodo *Korbafo.*
kodo *Bokai.*
kodo *Bilbaa.*
ʔodo *Rikou.*
kodo *Ba'a.*
koɗo *Tii.*
(ʔ)oɗo *Dengka.*
ʔoɗo *Oenale.*
ʔoɗo *Dela.* swallow.
n-koro *Ro'is Amarasi.* swallow.
n-ʔoro *Kotos Amarasi.* swallow.
n-ʔolo *Molo.* swallows. (M:404)
Out-comparisons:
holo *Semau Helong.* swallow.
kakorok *Dadu'a.* throat. (Penn 2006:13)
koɗo *Hawu.* stay stuck in the throat. (J:244)

***koko** *Rote.* carry in hand. *Pattern:* initial k-2/3, medial k-8/9.
koʔo *Termanu.* carry on one's arm or hip, also: carry and lift something with both hands or arms. (J:250)
koʔo *Korbafo.*
koʔo *Bokai.*
koko *Bilbaa.*
(ʔ)oʔo *Rikou.*
koʔo *Ba'a.*
koʔo *Tii.*
(ʔ)oʔo *Dengka.*
ʔoʔo *Oenale.*
ʔoʔo *Dela.* carry with hands.
Out-comparisons:
koko *Semau Helong.* carry in arms.
kokkoŋ *Bugis.* carry in front of oneself, for example a child, like Jesus does, to show it to the crowd. (Mathes 1874:6)

***kola** *Morph:* ***kola-ʔ**. *PwRM.* hole. *Pattern:* k-1. *[irr. from PRM:* *a > *o* in wRote (positing irr. *a > *o* can be motivated as a sporadic case of assimilation in wRote, while alternate *o > *a* in Meto would be unmotivated)*]*
kolo-ʔ *Dengka.* hole, opening, pit. (J:712)
kolo-ʔ *Oenale.* hole, opening, pit. (J:712)
kona|ʔ *Ro'is Amarasi.* hole.
kona|ʔ *Kotos Amarasi.* hole.
kona|ʔ *Molo.* hole. (M:234)

***komba** *PwRM.* pour out. *Pattern:* k-2b. *[irr. from PRM:* *a > *o* in Dela (sporadic assimilation?)*]*
ʔombo *Dela.* pour, water (plants).
n-kopaʔ *Ro'is Amarasi.* pour out.
n-ʔopaʔ *Kotos Amarasi.* pour out.
n-ʔopan *Molo.* pours it entirely out. (M:407)

***kona** *Rote.* right (side), south. *Etym:* *kawanan 'right (side, hand, direction)'. *Pattern:* k-2/3.

kona *Termanu.* right, right-hand side; the south, south. (J:249)
kona *Korbafo.*
kona *Bokai.*
kona *Bilbaa.*
ʔona *Rikou.*
kona *Ba'a.*
kona *Tii.*
(ʔ)ona *Dengka.*
ʔona *Oenale.*
ʔona *Dela.* right, south.
Out-comparisons:
kanan *Semau Helong.* right.
kwana *Fehan Tetun.* right (hand side).
kuana *East Tetun.* right, the right side; right, of the right side. (Mo:120)
keɗana, ɗana *Hawu.* right (side). *Usage:* Dimu dialect. *[Form:* The Seba and Mehara dialects have **keɗaŋa**.*]*

***koo**1 *Morph:* ***koo-k**. *Rote.* ber tree. Ziziphus mauritiana. *Pattern:* k-2/3′ (*k = *k* in Rikou; expect *k > *ʔ/Ø*). *[Form:* Kupang Malay attests a final *m* which may have originally been present in pre-RM.*]*
koo-k *Termanu.* the ber tree, called *kom* in Kupang; specific kinds: **koo naʔu, koo sina**. (J:241)
koo-ʔ *Korbafo.*
koo-k *Bokai.*
koo-ʔ *Bilbaa.*
koo-ʔ *Rikou.*
koo-k *Ba'a.*
koo-k *Tii.*
(ʔ)oo-ʔ *Dengka.*
(ʔ)oo-ʔ *Oenale.*
Out-comparisons:
koon *Helong.* (J:241)
koo *Hawu.* thorny tree species. Can grow to a few metres tall. Parts are eaten.
kom *Kupang Malay.* ber tree. Ziziphus mauritiana.

***koo**2 *PRM.* 2SG, you. *Etym:* *kahu. *Pattern:* k-4.
oo *Termanu.* 2SG. (J:450)
koo *Korbafo.*
koo *Bokai.*
koo *Bilbaa.*
oo *Landu.* you, 2SG. (own field notes)
oo *Rikou.*
oo *Ba'a.*
oo *Lole.* (Zacharias et al. 2014)
oo *Tii.*
hoo *Dengka.*
hoo *Oenale.*
hoo *Dela.* 2SG.
hoo *Ro'is Amarasi.* 2SG.
hoo (2) =koo *Kotos Amarasi.* 1) 2SG. NOM. 2) 2SG.ACC.
hoo *Molo.* you (sg.). (M:149)
hoo *Kusa-Manea.* you (sg.).
Out-comparisons:
ku *Semau Helong.* 2SG.
oo *East Tetun.* you (sg.). (Mo:155)

***koro** *Morph:* ***ko~koro-k**. *PRM.* Rainbow Bee-eater. Merops ornatus. *Pattern:* k-1′ (*k > Ø/ʔ in Meto, expect *k = *k*). *[irr. from PRM:* wRote *k* = Meto *ʔ/Ø* correspondence*]*
ko~kolo-k *Termanu.* kingfisher. (J:248)
ko~kolo-ʔ *Korbafo.*
ko~kolo-k *Bokai.*
ko~kolo-ʔ *Bilbaa.*
ʔo~ʔoro-ʔ *Rikou.* Rainbow Bee-eater. Merops ornatus. (J:248; own field notes)
ko~kolo-k *Ba'a.*
ko~koro-k *Tii.*
ko~kolo-ʔ *Dengka.*
ko~koro-ʔ *Oenale.*
on~ono|ʔ *Ro'is Amarasi.* Rainbow Bee-eater. Merops ornatus.
on~ono|ʔ *Kotos Amarasi.* Rainbow Bee-eater. Merops ornatus.

***koru** *PRM.* strip leaves or grain from branch, harvest rice. *Pattern:* k-3.
kolu *Termanu.* strip off the rice plant culm with a closed hand. (J:248)
kolu *Korbafo.*
kolu *Bokai.*
kolu *Bilbaa.*

ʔoru *Rikou.*
kolu *Ba'a.*
koru *Tii.*
(ʔ)olu *Dengka.*
ʔoru *Oenale.*
ʔoru *Dela.* harvest rice, harvest mung beans.
n-honu (2) n-ono *Kotos Amarasi.* 1) strip leaves off a branch. 2) harvest rice.
honu *Molo.* remove paddy rice from the grain head. (M:153)
Out-comparisons:
n-ulu *Semau Helong.* strip grain off stalk with hand.

***kose** *Rote.* rub, wipe. *Pattern:* k-2/3.
ko~kose *Termanu.* rub. (J:251f)
ko~kose *Korbafo.*
ko~kose *Bokai.*
ko~kose *Bilbaa.*
ʔo~ʔose *Rikou.*
ko~kose *Ba'a.*
ko~kose *Tii.*
(ʔ)o~(ʔ)ose *Dengka.*
ʔo~ʔose *Oenale.*
ʔose *Dela.* rub.
Out-comparisons:
koos *Semau Helong.* rub, clean, wipe.
kose *East Tetun.* scrape, rub, wipe, polish. (Mo:117)
kose *Ili'uun.* whet, sharpen. (dJ:121)
kose *Dhao.* rub, wipe.

***koti** *PRM.* cut. *Etym:* *koti 'cut off' (own reconstruction) (PCEMP). *Pattern:* k-irr. *[irr. from PRM:* *k > Ø in nRote except Rikou (expect *k = *k*)*]* *[Sporadic:* vowel height harmony *i > *e* /oC_ in Meto.*]*
oti *Termanu.* chop, cut away, e.g. shrubs, brushwood. (J:459)
oti *Korbafo.*
oti *Bokai.*
oti *Bilbaa.*
oti *Rikou.*
oti *Ba'a.*
oti *Tii.*
(ʔ)oti *Dengka.*
ʔoti *Oenale.*
ʔoti *Dela.*
n-kote *Ro'is Amarasi.* cut.
n-ʔote *Kotos Amarasi.* cut.
n-ʔote *Molo.* cuts. (M:408)
ʔoet *Kusa-Manea.* cut down.
Out-comparisons:
***koti** *Proto-Oceanic.* cut off (hair, taro tops +). (Osmond 1998:130)

***k|teom** *PMeto.* sea urchin. *See:* ***tii**. *Etym:* **tayum (pre-RM). *[Form:* To account for the apparently irregular correspondence between pre-RM **tayum, PMeto ***k|teom** and Tetun **teon** we could posit vowel height harmony of *u > *o* /e_. However, this is a rare pattern of vowel height harmony.*]*
k|teom *Ro'is Amarasi.* sea urchin.
k|teom *Kotos Amarasi.* sea urchin.
Out-comparisons:
tiu/ʔoe *Semau Helong.* sea urchin. *[Form:* regular Helong mid-vowel raising before/after a high vowel; *ay > *e > *i* /_u.*]*
teo(n) *East Tetun.* sea urchin. Echinus esculenta. (Mo:184)
taʤuŋ *Komodo.* sea-urchin. Echinoidea. (Verheijen 1982:126)
taʤuŋ *Manggarai.* sea-urchin. (Verheijen 1982:126)

***kua** *Morph:* ***ku~kua-k**. *Rote.* nit. *Pattern:* k-2/3'. *[irr. from PRM:* *u > *o* in Tii and wRote*]*
ku~kua-k *Termanu.* very young lice. (J:254)
ku~kua-ʔ *Korbafo.*
ku~kua-k *Bokai.*
ku~kua-ʔ *Bilbaa.*
u~ua-ʔ *Rikou.*
ku~kua-k *Ba'a.*
ko~koa-k *Tii.*
(ʔ)o~(ʔ)oa-ʔ *Dengka.*
ʔo~ʔoa-ʔ *Oenale.*

ʔo~ʔoa-ʔ *Dela.*
Out-comparisons:
kuar *East Tetun.* nits of lice. (Mo:120)
***kue** *Rote.* civet. *Pattern:* k-2/3.
kue *Termanu.* kind of predator, civet. (J:255)
kue *Korbafo.*
kue *Bokai.*
kue *Bilbaa.*
(ʔ)ue *Rikou.*
kue *Ba'a.*
kue *Tii.*
(ʔ)ue *Dengka.*
(ʔ)ue *Oenale.*
***kuku** *PRM.* finger, toe. *Etym:* *kuhkuh 'claw, talon, fingernail'. *Pattern:* initial k-3, medial k-10.
kuʔu-k (2) kuku_haa-k, kuku_telu-k *Termanu.* 1) finger, toes. *Usage:* Normally in combination with **lima-k** ('hand, arm') or **ei-k** ('foot, leg'). (J:259) 2) two kinds of birds with four and three toes respectively, neither has a tail and both are called *bondo* in Kupang. (J:256)
kuʔu (2) kuku_haa-ʔ, kuku_telu-ʔ *Korbafo.*
kuʔu-k (2) kuku_haa-k, kuku_telu-k *Bokai.*
kuku-ʔ (2) kuku_haa-ʔ, kuku_telu-ʔ *Bilbaa.* 2) quail. (J:256; own field notes)
lima kuku-ʔ *Landu.* fingernails. (own field notes)
ʔuʔu (2) ʔuʔu_haa-ʔ, ʔuʔu_telu-ʔ *Rikou.* 2) quail. (J:256; own field notes)
kuʔu-k (2) kuku_haa-k, kuku_telu-k *Ba'a.*
kuku-k (2) kuku_haa-k, kuku_telu-k *Tii.*
(ʔ)uʔu *Dengka.*
ʔuʔu *Oenale.*
ʔuʔu-ʔ *Dela.* fingers, toes.
huku *Molo.* catch, grab. *[Form:* The existence of the alternate form **heke** 'catch' could indicate that Molo **huku** 'catch, grab' is not a reflex of ***kuku**. However, the sound changes are regular and the semantic shift from 'finger' > 'catch, grab' is a plausible semantic shift.*]* (M:155)
Out-comparisons:
kuʔu *East Tetun.* pinch, wound with the thumb-nail pressed against the forefinger; to gather with a pinching action (fruit, flowers, etc.). (Mo:122)
huʔu-t *Welaun.* fingernail, toenail.
kaba kuʔu *Dhao.* fingernail.
kolo kuʔu *Hawu.* fingertip.
***kukur** *PRM.* wallow. *Pattern:* initial k-1, medial k-5.
kuku *Termanu.* wallow in dirt or sand, said of a bird. (J:255)
kuku *Korbafo.*
kuku *Bokai.*
kuku *Bilbaa.*
ʔu~ʔuʔu *Rikou.*
kuku *Ba'a.*
kuku *Tii.*
kuku *Dengka.*
kukur *Oenale.*
n-kuku *Kotos Amarasi.* have diarrhoea without making it to the bathroom in time, wallow in the mud (e.g. of a pig or buffalo).
n-kuku *Molo.* wallows (also said of buffalo). (M:245)
***kumu₁** *PMeto.* wild pigeon, wild dove. *Etym:* **kumu (pre-RM). *Pattern:* k-1/2a. *[Semantics:* onomatopoeia.*]*
kumu *Ro'is Amarasi.* all kinds of wild pigeons and wild doves.
kumu *Kotos Amarasi.* all kinds of wild pigeons and wild doves.
umu *Amanuban.* kind of dove. (M:248, 588)

kumu (2) <umu hene> *Molo.* dove. (M:248) 1) kind of dove. 2) kind of dove. (M:588)

aʔumab *Kusa-Manea.* pigeon.

Out-comparisons:

manu_kumu, kumo *Waima'a.* wild pigeon.

***g(a)umu** *Proto-Oceanic.* Fruit Dove. Ptilinopus species. (Clark 2011:15)

***kumu2** *Morph:* ***ku~kumu**. *Rote.* make a fist. *Doublet:* ***kame, *keʔe, *keme, *ŋgumu**. *Etym:* *gəmgəm 'fist; hold in the fist'. *Pattern:* k-2/3. *[irr. from PMP:* *ə > *u (sporadic assimilation to previous velar consonant and/or following labial consonant)*] [History:* The Tii and Oenale forms additionally mean 'knead' (Jonker 1908:714).*]*

ku~kumu *Termanu.* make a fist. (J:257f)

ku~kumu *Korbafo.*

ku~kumu *Bokai.*

ku~kumu *Bilbaa.*

(ʔ)u~(ʔ)umu *Rikou. [Form:* My consultants gave **ku~kumu** and **kumu**.*]*

ku~kumu *Ba'a.*

ku~kumu *Tii.* (J:704)

(ʔ)u~(ʔ)umu *Dengka.*

ʔu~ʔumu *Oenale.*

ʔu~ʔumu *Dela.* clench one's fist.

Out-comparisons:

kumu *Helong.* (J:258)

kumu *East Tetun.* hold in the hand. (Mo:121)

akam *Kisar.* squeeze, press, flatten.

***kuna** *PwRM.* hide in folds of clothing. *Pattern:* k-1. *[Form:* The Meto unmetathesised form has not yet been attested. It could be ***kuna** or ***kunu**.*]*

ku~kuna *Dengka.* his belly has layers or folds due to its fat. (J:714)

ku~kuna *Oenale.* his belly has layers or folds due to its fat. (J:714)

na-kuun *Meto.* hides something in the folds of clothing. (J:714)

***kuni** *Morph:* ***kuni-k**. *PRM.* turmeric. *Etym:* *kunij. *Pattern:* k-4′ (*k = *k* in Termanu, Landu, Ba'a, and Lole; expect *k > Ø).

kuni-k *Termanu.* turmeric. (J:258)

kuni-ʔ *Korbafo.*

kuni-k *Bokai.*

kuni-ʔ *Bilbaa.*

kuni *Landu.* yellow. (own field notes)

uni-ʔ *Rikou.*

kuni-k *Ba'a.*

kuni-k *Lole.* turmeric, yellow. (Zacharias et al. 2014)

uni-k *Tii.*

huni-ʔ *Dengka.*

huni-ʔ *Oenale.*

hu͡ini|k *Ro'is Amarasi.* turmeric.

huni|k *Kotos Amarasi.* turmeric.

<huki> *Molo.* turmeric, dye in tissues. *[Form:* The Molo form could be related with sporadic metathesis of *nVk > **hukin and loss of final *n*. Jonker (1908:258) gives Meto **hukim** which would additionally show irr. *n > *m.]* (M:155)

Out-comparisons:

kinur *Fehan Tetun.* turmeric.

kinur (2) kinu *East Tetun.* 1) plant whose tubers are reduced to powder with the colour and taste of saffron. 2) yellow (colour). *[irr. from PMP:* vowel metathesis: *uCi > *iCu]* (Mo:107)

hinu *East Tetun.* tree from which turmeric is made. *Usage:* Samoro village. *[irr. from PMP:* vowel metathesis: *uCi > *iCu]* (Mo:86)

***kunu1** *PMeto.* breadfruit. *Etym:* *kuluR. *Pattern:* k-1/2a. *[irr. from PRM:* Ø > *m in Ro'is Amarasi*]*

kunum *Ro'is Amarasi.* breadfruit.

<**kunu**> *Molo.* Cluster fig tree. *Ficus glomerata*. *[Note:* possibly unrelated.*]* (M:251)

Out-comparisons:

kulu? (2) kulu naunu? *Funai Helong.* 1) jackfruit. 2) breadfruit.

kulu *East Tetun.* fruiting trees in various types of *Artocarpus* genus. (Mo:121)

***kunu2** *Rote.* kind of plant. *Pattern:* k-irr. *[irr. from PRM:* *k > Ø /#_ in wRote (expect *k* or *?*)*]*

kunu *Termanu.* used in a few plant names, as in: **kunu doo**, (**unu loo**); **kunu meo-?**. *[Semantics:* No other semantic details are given for this term.*]* (J:258)

kunu *Korbafo.*

kunu *Bokai.*

kunu *Bilbaa.*

kunu *Ba'a.*

kunu *Tii.*

unu *Dengka.*

unu *Oenale.*

unu hau ana? *Dela.* weed.

Out-comparisons:

kunu *Helong.* (J:258)

***kupu** *PMeto.* fog. *Pattern:* k-1/2a. *[History:* Jonker (1908:230) compares the Meto forms with Termanu, Korbafo, Bokai **kelupua** 'become murky of water', Ba'a **kelempua**, and Dengka, Oenale **elembua**, but the sound correspondences and semantics are too much of a stretch for me.*]*

kupu *Ro'is Amarasi.* fog. *[Form:* Jonker (1908:230) gives Meto **meukupa/kupa**.*]*

kupu (2) pupu *Kotos Amarasi.* 1) water vapour, like in fog. 2) fog. *[Form:* The second form possibly has sporadic assimilation of *k > *p*. Kotos Amarasi also has **nipu** 'fog'.*]*

Out-comparisons:

kuput *Funai Helong.* fog.

api kupu *Tokodede.* smoke. (Klamer 2002)

***kura** *Morph:* ***kura-k**. *Rote.* scorpion. *Etym:* **sakuraŋ (pre-RM). *Pattern:* k-2/3'. *[History:* possibly connected with PMP *qudaŋ 'shrimp, crayfish, lobster'.*]*

kula-k *Termanu.* scorpion. (J:256)

kula-? *Korbafo.*

kula-k *Bokai.*

kula-? *Bilbaa.*

kura-? *Landu.* scorpion. (own field notes)

ura-? *Rikou.*

kula-k *Ba'a.*

kura-k *Tii.*

(?)ula-? *Dengka.*

?ura-? *Oenale.*

?ura-? *Dela.* scorpion.

Out-comparisons:

khulaŋ *Funai Helong.* scorpion.

hkulaŋ *Semau Helong.* scorpion.

sakunar *East Tetun.* scorpion (poisonous insect). *[Sporadic:* consonant metathesis *rVn > *nVr.]* (Mo:165)

sa?unar *Galolen.* scorpion. *[Sporadic:* consonant metathesis *rVn > *nVr.]*

sa?uro *Waima'a.* scorpion.

sayorne *Kisar.* scorpion.

kəru *Hawu.* (J:256)

kuraŋ *Sika.* lobster. (Calon 1891:318)

***kurə** *Morph:* ***ka-kurə-k**. *PRM.* clay/ stone jar or pot. *Etym:* *kudən 'clay cooking pot'. *Pattern:* k-4.

ule-k *Termanu.* pot both for cooking and storing things. (J:665)

ule-? *Korbafo.*

ule-k *Bokai.*

kule-? *Bilbaa.*

ure-? *Rikou.* *[Form:* Whether this is vowel initial or glottal stop initial is currently unknown, but no Rikou form that fits into the first pattern for *k (pattern 1) has an initial underlying glottal stop.*]*

ule-k *Ba'a.*
ure-k *Tii.*
hula-ʔ *Dengka.*
hura-ʔ *Oenale.*
ʔ|huna|ʔ *Kotos Amarasi.* large clay or stone jar or jug.
<huun> oe *Molo.* clay pot which is filled with water as opposed to **naiʔ oe** 'iron pot' in which water is boiled. (M:156)

***kuru₁** *PRM.* call chickens, summon chickens. *Etym:* *kur(u) 'word used to call chickens, etc.'. *Pattern:* k-1. *[irr. from PRM:* *u > *o* in all Rote except Korbafo and Tii (assimilation to following ***roroo**)*] [Form:* All varieties with lowering of *u > *o* attest a second element derivable from ***roroo** except for Dengka which would require irr. *r > *ɗ.] [Semantics:* onomatopoeia.*]*
kolo/loloo *Termanu.* call chickens, summon chickens. (J:248)
kulu~kulu *Korbafo.*
kolo/loloo *Bokai.*
koro/ruruu *Rikou.*
kolo/loloo *Ba'a.*
kuru~kuru, ku~kuru *Tii.*
kolo/ɗoɗoo, ko~kolo *Dengka.*
koro/roroo *Oenale.*

***kuru₂** *Rote.* wrinkly. *Etym:* *kurut 'curly-haired' (Blust and Trussel (ongoing) also reconstruct *kulut 'curly haired' and PWMP *kərut 'shrivelled, wrinkled'.). *Pattern:* k-1/2/3. *[irr. from PRM:* *r > *nd in Tii and Ba'a*] [Form:* Tii and Ba'a attest ***kundu**, others attest ***kuru**, the Rikou alternate form with medial *l* is irregular from both these forms.*] [History:* Blust and Trussel (ongoing) reconstruct PWMP *kərut 'shrivelled, wrinkled' on the basis of Malay **kərut** and Pamona **koru**. They give an apparent doublet *kədut, for which I cannot find a main entry. Blust and Trussel (ongoing) assign the Termanu form to PMP *kuluŋ 'curl, curve' where it is one of three languages attesting this reconstruction, but this reconstruction cannot account for the reflexes in other varieties of Rote.*]*
ku~kulu (2) ku~kulu-k *Termanu.* 1) be or become wrinkly. 2) wrinkle. (J:258)
ku~kulu *Korbafo.*
ku~kulu *Bokai.*
ku~kulu *Bilbaa.*
(ʔ)u~(ʔ)uru, (ʔ)u~(ʔ)ulu *Rikou.*
ku~kunu *Ba'a.*
ku~kundu *Tii.*
ku~kulu *Dengka.*
ku~kuru *Oenale.*
Out-comparisons:
kurut *East Tetun.* wrinkled, rough, curled. (Mo:122)

***kurus** *PRM.* chilli. *Pattern:* k-2b′ (*k = *k* in Kusa-Manea; expect *k > *ʔ/Ø*).
kulus *Termanu.* chilli pepper. (J:257)
kuluʔ *Korbafo.*
kuluʔ *Bokai.*
kuluʔ *Bilbaa.*
ʔurus *Rikou.*
kulus *Ba'a.*
kurus *Tii.*
kunus *Ro'is Amarasi.* chilli.
ʔunus *Kotos Amarasi.* chilli.
kunus *Kusa-Manea.* chilli.
Out-comparisons:
kulus *Semau Helong.* chilli.
°kunus *Foho Tetun.* chilli plant. *Borrowed from:* Meto (shown by irr. *r = *n* correspondence). *[Note:* variety of Tetun spoken in the northern part of the Tetun-speaking area of central Timor ISO 693-3 [tet].*]* (van Klinken 1995)
°kunus *East Tetun.* capsicum. Capsicum annuum. *Borrowed from:* Meto (shown by irr. *r = *n* correspondence). (Mo:121)
kurus *Kupang Malay.* chilli.

uus *Welaun.* chilli. *[irr. from PRM:* *r = Ø correspondence*]* (da Silva 2012:186)
koro *Sika.* chilli. (Pareira and Lewis 1998:101)
koro *Ende.* chilli.
ŋgurus *Manggarai.* (Verheijen 1984:14)
mburus *Waerana.* *[Note:* language of central Flores ISO 639-3 [wrx].*]* (Verheijen 1984:14)

***kuta** *PnRote.* close eyes. *Pattern:* k-1/2/3.
na-kuta *Termanu.* close the eyes out of fright, for example like someone who is afraid of being hit. (J:256)
na-kuta *Korbafo.*
na-kuta *Bokai.*
(na-kuta ?) *Tii.*
Out-comparisons:
huta *Semau Helong.* close eyes. *[irr. from PRM:* *k = *h* correspondence*]*

***kutə** *Morph:* ***kutə-k**. *Rote.* brains, mantle. *Doublet:* ***kuta**. *Etym:* *hutək 'brain, marrow'. *Pattern:* k-2b′ (*k > *ʔ* in Tii, expect *k = *k*). *[irr. from PMP:* Ø > *k*]* *[irr. from PRM:* *ə > *a* in Termanu Korbafo, and Bilbaa*]* *[Form:* The initial *k may be from the nominal prefix *ka- prefix.*]* *[History:* It is possible that PMP *hutək spit into a doublet in PRM: ***kuta-k** 'mantle' and ***(k)utə-k** 'brains'.*]*
kuta-k *Termanu.* the mantle of a squid. (J:258)
kuta-ʔ *Korbafo.* the mantle of a squid. (J:258)
kuta-ʔ *Bilbaa.* the mantle of a squid. (J:258)
(ʔ)ute-k *Lole.* brains. (Zacharias et al. 2014)
(ʔ)ute-k *Tii.* brains. (J:777)
(ʔ)uta-ʔ *Dengka.* brains. (J:777)
ʔuta-ʔ *Oenale.* brains. (J:777)
ʔuta-ʔ *Dela.* brain.
Out-comparisons:
kuta *Semau Helong.* brain.
ka~kutak *East Tetun.* brains, the mind, the thinking part. (Mo:98)
gutan (2) ai gutan *Ili'uun.* 1) brains. (dJ:115) 2) heartwood. *[irr. from PMP:* *h > (*Ø) > *g* (compare *paŋdan > **keʧan**, *pusəj > **kusan**, and baqbaq > **kahan**)*]* (dJ:111)

***kutu** *PRM.* head-louse. *Etym:* *kutu. *Pattern:* k-4.
utu *Termanu.* louse. (J:672)
utu *Korbafo.*
utu *Bokai.*
utu *Bilbaa.*
utu *Landu.* louse. (own field notes)
utu *Rikou.*
utu *Ba'a.*
utu *Tii.*
hutu *Dengka.*
hutu *Oenale.*
hutu *Dela.* lice.
hutu *Ro'is Amarasi.* head-louse.
hutu *Kotos Amarasi.* head-louse.
hutu *Molo.* head-louse. (M:157)
hutu *Kusa-Manea.* head-louse.
Out-comparisons:
kutu *Semau Helong.* louse.
utu *East Tetun.* louse. (Mo:194)
uku *Kisar.* fleas.

***kutus** *PRM.* windstorm, cyclone, whirlwind. *Pattern:* k-irr. *[irr. from PRM:* *k > *n* in Meto (fossilised prefix?)*]* *[Sporadic:* diphthongisation *u > *au* in most Meto.*]* *[Form:* One way to account for the initial nasal in Meto would be to reconstruct PRM *ŋ, but this would require unexpected *ŋ > *k* in the Rote languages (expect *ŋ > *n*) and unexpected *ŋ > *n* in Kusa-Manea (expect *ŋ > *k*).*]*
kutus *Termanu.* whirlwind, tornado. (J:259)
kutu-ʔ *Korbafo.*

kutu-ʔ *Bokai.*
kutu-ʔ *Bilbaa.*
utus *Rikou.*
kutus *Ba'a.*
kutus *Tii.*
(ʔ)utus *Dengka.*
(ʔ)utus *Oenale.*
nautus *Ro'is Amarasi.* whirlwind, tornado.
ain nautus (2) nautus, autus *Kotos Amarasi.* 1) storm with strong winds, windstorm, cyclone, whirlwind, tornado. 2) beetle.
ani nautus *Molo.* storm with strong winds. (M:357)
nutus *Kusa-Manea.* whirlwind, tornado.

***kuu** *Rote.* blow the nose. *See:* ***ŋguu**. *Pattern:* k-1. *[Semantics:* onomatopoeia.*]*
na-sa-kuu (2) kuu~kuu *Termanu.* blow hard; **na-sa-kuu pana-na** he blows his nose hard, e.g. to get snot out. **anin=a na-sa-kuu koʔas=a** the strong wind blows the clouds away. (J:254) 2) blow through the nose somewhat gently. (J:253)
na-sa-kuu *Korbafo.*
na-sa-kuu *Bokai.*
na-sa-uu *Rikou.*
na-sa-kuu *Ba'a.*
na-sa-kuu *Tii.*
na-sa-kuu *Dengka.*

***kuun** *PRM.* kind of tall grass. *Pattern:* k-4′ (*k = *k* in Termanu, Ba'a, and Tii; expect *k > Ø).
ku/mea *Termanu.* kind of long grass, called *rumput kumee* in Kupang. *[Form:* The source of the second element in Rote is unknown. It could be related to ***mea** 'red'.*]* (J:257)
ku/mea *Korbafo.*
ku/mea *Bokai.*
ku/mee *Bilbaa.*
u/mee *Rikou. [Form:* Whether this is vowel initial or glottal stop initial is currently unknown, but no Rikou form which fits into this pattern for *k has an initial underlying glottal stop.*]*
ku/mea *Ba'a.*
ku/mea *Tii.*
hu/mee *Dengka.*
hu/mee *Oenale.*
huu_musuʔ *Ro'is Amarasi.* sword grass, alang-alang grass.
huun (2) huu_musuʔ *Kotos Amarasi.* 1) grass. 2) sword grass, alang-alang grass.
huun *Molo.* grass. (M:156)

ʔ - ʔ

***ʔ|fenu** *PMeto.* candlenut. *Aleurites moluccana*. *Etym:* **ka-felu (pre-Meto).
fenu *Ro'is Amarasi.* candlenut.
ʔ|fenu *Kotos Amarasi.* candlenut.
ʔ|fenu *Molo.* kind of tree. *Aleurites moluccana*. (M:116)
fenu *Kusa-Manea.* candlenut.
Out-comparisons:
<kawilu> *Kambera.* candlenut tree. *Aleurites moluccana*. (On:201)
welu *Manggarai.* candlenut. (Verheijen 1984:45)
felu *Rongga.* candlenut. *[Note:* language of central Flores ISO 639-3 [ror].*]* (Verheijen 1984:45)
felu *Ngadha.* candlenut. (Verheijen 1984:45)

***ʔ|mauka|ʔ** *PnMeto.* cuscus. *See:* ***arum**. *Etym:* *mansər (PCEMP). *[irr. from PMP:* *a > *au*] [irr. from PRM:* *a > *a ~ u*] [Form:* The best reconstruction of the vowels is unclear, whatever form is posited requires positing irregularities. The Ketun (Nai'oni') form appears to attest penultimate *a, but if this is reconstructed it requires positing otherwise unattested *a > *au* in all other lects. I thus posit that Ketun (Nai'oni') **ʔmakuʔ** attests irregular reduction of the earlier diphthong. The reconstructed diphthong *au could come from earlier *u (i.e. earlier **muka) given that diphthongisation of penultimate vowels sporadically occurs in Meto. Reconstruction of final *a can account for reflexes with final *u* by assuming irregular assimilation to previous *u* in closed syllables. Reconstruction of final *u does not seem to be able to account for reflexes with final *a.*]* *[History:* This reconstruction is possibly consistent with PCEMP *mansər given PRM *nd > PMeto *r > Proto-Nuclear Meto *k*. (Though note that Proto-Nuclear Meto *k can also be a reflex of PRM *ŋg or *k.) However, if the hypothesis that penultimate *au is from earlier *u is correct, then comparison of *mansər with ***ʔ|mauka|ʔ** would require irregular initial *a > *u.*]*

ʔmaukuʔ *Kotos Amarasi.* cuscus. *Usage:* Not known by all speakers. The usual word is **ukum**.

maukuʔ *Amanuban, South.* cuscus. *Usage:* Oebelo village, other known varieties of South Amanuban have **ukum**.

ʔmakuʔ *Ketun.* cuscus. *Usage:* Nai'oni' village.

ʔmaukaʔ *Ketun.* cuscus. *Usage:* Taloetan village.

ʔmaukaʔ *Kopas.* cuscus. *Usage:* Masikolen, Bone, Usapisonba'i, and Oben villages.

maukaʔ *Kopas.* cuscus. *Usage:* Oepaha village.

ʔmaukuʔ *Kopas.* cuscus. *Usage:* Tuale'u village.

maukuʔ, maukaʔ *Fatule'u.* cuscus.

<mauku> *Molo.* cuscus. Phalangeridae. (M:316,586)

ʔmaukuʔ *Timaus.* cuscus.

Out-comparisons:

°mauka *Funai Helong.* cuscus. *Borrowed from:* Meto.

meda *East Tetun.* small savage marsupial animal. *[irr. from PMP:* *a > *e]* (Mo:140)

k|meda *Fehan Tetun.* small savage marsupial animal. *[irr. from PMP:* *a > *e]* (Mo:112)

matʃa *Ili'uun.* cuscus. (dJ:127)

madar *Galolen.* cuscus. (Schapper 2011:264)

maat *Mambae, South.* cuscus. (Schapper 2011:264)

la/mara *Welaun.* cuscus.

mada *Kemak.* cuscus. *Usage:* Kailaku, Lemia, Atsabe, and Saneri dialects.

°meda *Kemak.* cuscus. *Usage:* Leolima, Leosibe, and Diirbati dialects. *Borrowed from:* probably Tetun (shown by irr. *a = *e* correspondence).

***ʔuta** *PwRM.* cut.

(ʔ)u~(ʔ)uta *Dengka.* cutting, usually cutting meat. (J:777)

ʔu~ʔuta *Oenale.* cutting, usually cutting meat. (J:777)

ʔuta *Dela.* cut.

<naút> *Meto.* *[Form:* This is presumably **na-ʔuut**, the metathesised form of **na-ʔuta**.*]* (J:777)

Out-comparisons:

kʾuta *Waima'a.* cut, slice meat into small mouth-sized pieces.

L - l

*laa$_1$ *Morph:* *laa-k. *PRM.* kind of tree. *[Semantics:* vague semantics.*]*
  ka/laa-k *Termanu.* kind of tree called **lalaak** in Kupang. (J:218)
  ka/laa-ʔ *Korbafo.* *[Note:* Bilbaa and Korbafo given as <**kalạ**> with only a single final vowel (rather than expected <**kalạ́**>), but this is surely a typo.*]*
  ka/laa-k *Bokai.*
  ka/laa-ʔ *Bilbaa.*
  la~laa-ʔ *Rikou.*
  ka/laa-k *Ba'a.*
  la~laa-k *Tii.*
  la~laa-ʔ *Dengka.*
  la~laa-ʔ *Oenale.*
  <naa>, <apnaa> *Molo.* kind of tree, a forest giant. *Planchonia valida, Barringtonia spicata. [Form:* **nao** is given as an alternate form of *Planchonia valida* in Middelkoop (1972:349).*]* (M:338, 26)

*laa$_2$ *PRM.* temporary hut. *[irr. from PRM:* *l > *r/l* in Meto*] [Sporadic:* *VV-k > *VVʔ > VʔV in Meto (perceptual metathesis).*]*
  laa-k *Termanu.* temporary storage hut. (J:261)
  laa-ʔ *Korbafo.*
  la~laa-k *Bokai.*
  laa-ʔ *Bilbaa.*
  laa-ʔ *Rikou.*
  la~laa-k *Ba'a.*
  laa-k *Tii.*
  la~laa-ʔ *Dengka.*
  laa-ʔ *Oenale.*
  raʔa-t (2) n-raʔan *Kotos Amarasi.* 1) temporary shelter; tent, hut. 2) reside somewhere temporarily.
  laʔa-t *Molo.* leaf-hut. (M:254)
  Out-comparisons:
    laen *Fehan Tetun.* hut in the fields, or at the beach, where the farmer/fisherman can rest. *[irr. from PRM:* *a = *e* correspondence*]*
    klaen *East Tetun.* hut on raised legs for guarding crops. *Usage:* Luka village. *[irr. from PRM:* *a = *e* correspondence*]* (Mo:108)
    salaak *East Tetun.* small hut. (Mo:108)

*laa$_3$ *Rote.* sail. *Etym:* *layaR.
  laa *Termanu.* sail. (J:260)
  laa *Korbafo.*
  laa *Bokai.*
  laa *Bilbaa.*
  laa *Rikou.*
  laa *Ba'a.*
  laa *Tii.*
  laa *Dengka.*
  laa *Oenale.*
  Out-comparisons:
    laa *Semau Helong.* sail.
    laan *East Tetun.* sails (of a boat). (Mo:98)
    walara *Kisar.* sail.

*laa$_4$ *PnRote.* fly. *Etym:* *layap.
  laa *Termanu.* flying. (J:260)
  laa *Korbafo.*
  laa *Bokai.*
  laa *Bilbaa.*
  laa *Rikou.*
  laa *Ba'a.*
  laa *Tii.* *[Note:* given as ‘also surely T’.*]*

*laa$_5$ *Morph:* *na-laa-k, *laa-k. *Rote.* open the eyes. *Etym:* *-lat ‘open the eyes wide’.
  na-laa-k mata=na (2) mata laa-k *Termanu.* 1) open the eyes. 2) someone who can see well (lit. someone whose eyes are open). (J:261)
  na-laa-ʔ *Korbafo.*
  na-laa-k *Bokai.*
  na-laa-ʔ *Rikou.*
  na-laa-k *Ba'a.*
  na-laa-k *Tii.*

na-laa-ʔ *Dengka.*
na-laa-ʔ *Oenale.*

***laɓa** *nRM.* wind around, of plants. *[irr. from PRM:* *l > *r/l* in Meto*]*

na-ka-(la~)laba *Termanu.* 1) wind all the way around something, said of plants. 2) wind around, entwine, tie around. (J:262)
na-ka-laba *Korbafo.*
na-ka-laba *Bilbaa.*
na-la~laba (2) na-laba *Rikou.*
na-ka-laba *Ba'a.*
na-ka-laɓa *Tii.*
k|raba-t *Kotos Amarasi.* obstacles, thorns. *Usage:* poetic, only in the parallel pair **kisan ma krabat** (**kisan** = 'thorny weed').
n-laba (2) okan aklab~laba (3) n-buun ma na-klaab *Molo.* 1) creeping or winding of plants. (M:254) 2) creeping cucumber. (M:254) 3) he surrounds and encloses, referring to the protective power of the chief. *Usage:* poetic. (M:91)

Out-comparisons:
raɓa *Hawu.* wind around with thorns. *[Sporadic:* *l = *r* correspondence.*]* (J:262)

***ladu** *PRM.* palm wine. *Pattern:* d-2. *[Sporadic:* consonant metathesis **lVr > *rVl* in Dela-Oenale and Rikou.*]* *[Form:* That it is Dela-Oenale and Rikou that show consonant metathesis rather than Tii, is indicated by other reconstructions with *lVr which have cognates outside of the RM languages including: ***lari** 'comb of rooster' and ***ledo** 'sun' (PMP *qaləjaw) which have undergone the same consonant metathesis *lVr > *rVl* in Dela-Oenale and Rikou.*]*

lalu *Termanu.* areng palm sap, fermented palm sap. (J:274)
lalu *Korbafo.*
lalu *Bokai.*
lalu *Bilbaa.*
ralu *Rikou.*
lalu *Ba'a.*
laru *Tii.*
lalu *Dengka.*
ralu *Oenale.*
ralu *Dela.* palm-wine.
raru *Kotos Amarasi.* palm-wine.
lalu *Molo.* lontar sap in which roots which promote fermentation have been placed. (M:260)

***lafa** *PRM.* kind of traditional cloth. *[Sporadic:* *a > *e* / _# in wRM.*]*

lafa *Termanu.* well woven piece of a sarong which is tied by men around the hips and also worn as a kind of coat. (J:267)
lafa *Korbafo.*
lafa *Bokai.*
lafa *Bilbaa.*
lafa *Rikou.*
lafa *Ba'a.*
lafa *Tii.*
lafe *Dengka.*
lafe *Oenale.*
lafe *Dela.* traditional cloth worn by men.
nafe *Kotos Amarasi.* kind of cloth worn traditionally as a belt.

Out-comparisons:
lahan *East Tetun.* thread, fibre, or filament. (Mo:123)

***lafo** *Morph:* ***ka-lafo**. *PRM.* rat, mouse. *Etym:* *balabaw. *[irr. from PRM:* initial *i ~ bi* in Molo*]*

lafo *Termanu.* rat, mouse. (J:267f)
lafo *Korbafo.*
lafo *Bokai.*
lafo *Bilbaa.*
lafo *Landu.* mouse, rat. (own field notes)
lafo *Rikou.*
lafo *Ba'a.*
lafo *Tii.*
lafo *Dengka.*
lafo *Oenale.*
k|nafo *Ro'is Amarasi.* mouse, rat.
k|nafo *Kotos Amarasi.* mouse, rat.
nafo *Amanuban/Amanatun.*

ifo, bifo *Molo.* mouse. (M:158)
nafo *Kusa-Manea.* mouse, rat.
Out-comparisons:
blaho *Semau Helong.* mouse, rat.
laho *East Tetun.* rat (rodent). (Mo:123)

***laha** *Morph:* ***na-ma-laha, *laha-s**. *CERM.* hungry. *Etym:* *lapaR. *[Form:* This is the only form in which *h /a_a is not universally lost in Rote. Instead, it follows the pattern for *h between other vowels.*]*
na-ma-laʔa (2) laʔas *Termanu.* 1) hungry. 2) hunger, famine. (J:262)
na-ma-laʔa (2) laʔa-ʔ *Korbafo.*
na-ma-laʔa (2) laʔa-ʔ *Bokai.*
na-ma-laa (2) laa-ʔ *Bilbaa.*
na-ma-laa *Landu.* hungry. (own field notes)
na-ma-laa (2) laas *Rikou.*
na-ma-laa *Oepao.* hungry. (own field notes)
na-m|naha *Ro'is Amarasi.* hungry.
na-m|naha *Kotos Amarasi.* hungry.
na-m|naha *Molo.* hunger. (M:325)
na-m|naah *Kusa-Manea.* hungry. *[Form:* metathesised form of **na-mnaha**.*]*
Out-comparisons:
halaʔa *Fehan Tetun.* hungry. *Usage:* Betun village.
hamlaha *East Tetun.* be hungry. (Mo:71)

***lai** *Rote.* run, flee; fast, quick. *Etym:* *laRiw 'run, run away, flee, escape'.
na-lai (2) lai~lai *Termanu.* 1) flee, run away. (J:270) 2) fast, quickly, speedy. (J:268)
na-lai (2) lai~lai *Korbafo.*
na-lai (2) lai~lai *Bokai.*
na-lai (2) lai~lai *Bilbaa.*
na-lai (2) lai~lai *Rikou.*
na-lai (2) lai~lai *Ba'a.*
na-lai (2) lai~lai *Tii.*
(2) lai~lai *Dengka.*
(2) lai~lai *Oenale.*
Out-comparisons:
lali *Semau Helong.* run.
lai~lais *East Tetun.* quickly, hastily, without delay. (Mo:123)

***laia** *PRM.* ginger. *Etym:* *laqia. *[Sporadic:* *a > *e* / _# in wRM (PwRM ***laie**).*] [Form:* The Rote languages have reduced this to a disyllable by deletion of the antepenultimate vowel. In Meto both initial vowels were retained with subsequent doubling of the final vowel, probably to achieve a form composed of two disyllabic feet. The Meto reflexes additionally show expected consonant insertion to break up a disallowed sequence of three vowels.*]*
lia *Termanu.* ginger. (J:310)
lia *Korbafo.*
lia *Bokai.*
lia *Bilbaa.*
lia *Rikou.*
lia *Ba'a.*
lia *Tii.*
lie *Dengka.*
naiʤee *Ro'is Amarasi.* ginger. *[History:* Expected epenthetic consonant in *VVV.*]*
naiʤeer *Kotos Amarasi.* ginger. *[History:* Final *r* indicates that this is a borrowing from a variety of Meto with word final insertion of *l* after Ve#.*]*
naiyeeʔ *Amanuban.* ginger.
naiʤee-l *Molo.* ginger. (M:342)
Out-comparisons:
°lai/ee *Semau Helong.* ginger. *Borrowed from:* Meto before *l > *n* and medial consonant insertion (shown by final *a = *e* correspondence). *[Form:* Given as **lai ee** with white space, probably indicating that this has been reanalysed as some kind of compound.*]*
ai lia *East Tetun.* ginger. *Zingibii officinale*. (Mo:2)

***lako** *PRM.* go. *Etym:* *lakaw. *Pattern:* k-8.

laʔo *Termanu.* go = break up, leave, go away (to land or over sea). (J:279f)

laʔo *Korbafo.*

laʔo *Bokai.*

lako *Bilbaa.*

laʔo *Rikou.*

laʔo *Ba'a.*

laʔo *Tii.*

lao *Dengka.*

lao *Oenale.*

n-nao *Ro'is Amarasi.* go.

n-nao *Kotos Amarasi.* go.

n-nao *Molo.* go. (M:355)

nao *Kusa-Manea.* go.

Out-comparisons:

lako *Semau Helong.* go.

laʔo *East Tetun.* walk, travel on foot, go. (Mo:127)

la *Hawu.* go, to, IRREALIS.

***laʔi** *PwRM.* male, grandfather, king. *Etym:* *laki 'male, masculine; man'.

manu_lai *Dengka.* rooster, cock. (J:716)

manu_lai *Oenale.* rooster, cock. (J:716)

naiʔi|k *Ro'is Amarasi.* grandfather.

naʔi-f (2) naiʔ (3) maun_nai (4) fe/nai (5) nai mnukiʔ *Kotos Amarasi.* 1) grandfather. *[Form:* The medial glottal stop is not deleted in Meto after suffixation, which shows that this glottal stop does not ultimately derive from the ***-k** suffix and is instead a retention of PMP *k.*]* 2) Mr. (used obligatorily before male names). *[Form:* metathesised form.*]* 3) rooster, cock. 4) wife of a dignitary. 5) royal son.

<nai> (2) <nai uuf>, <naidʒuuf> (3) <manu naif> *Molo.* 1) prince. (M:342) 2) princes, greats of the land. (M:342) 3) rooster, cock. (M:230)

naʔi *Kusa-Manea.* grandfather.

Out-comparisons:

lahi *Semau Helong.* king. *[irr. from PMP:* *k > *h] [History:* The irregular sound changes combined with the semantics indicate that this is a loan, but a precise donor cannot be confidently identified. Meto seems unlikely as this requires positing that the medial glottal stop went through intermediate *h that would be an irregular sound change for medial *k in Meto.*]*

°naʔi (2) °naʔin *Fehan Tetun.* 1) an honourable term of address for nobles, or for people much younger than the speaker (e.g. one's children). 2) noble, owner, boss, player (in a game); Can be used as title. *Borrowed from:* Meto (shown by irr. *l = *n* correspondence).

°naʔi (2) °naʔin *East Tetun.* 1) form of address always preceding the word it qualifies, not translatable to English, but can be used instead of 'Mr', 'Your Honour', 'Your Excellency'. 2) respectful title with the same meaning as **naʔi** placed before numerals and some pronouns when referring to people. (Mo:145)

***laʔus** *Morph:* ***ka-laʔus**. *PRM.* cactus.

laʔus *Termanu.* cactus. (J:286)

laʔu-ʔ *Korbafo.*

lau-ʔ *Bokai.*

lau-ʔ *Bilbaa.*

laus *Rikou.*

laʔus *Ba'a.*

laʔus *Tii.*

laus *Dengka.*

laus *Oenale.*

ʔ|naus *Molo.* cactus leaves. (M:357)

Out-comparisons:

klaus *Helong.* cactus. (J:286)

k(a)latun *East Tetun.* cactus. (Mo:98)
oplakun *Kisar.* pear cactus.

***lalu** *Morph:* ***lalu-k**. *PnRote.* cock, rooster. *Etym:* *laluŋ.
manu_lalu-k *Termanu.* rooster. (J:274)
manu_lalu-ʔ *Korbafo.*
manu_lalu-k *Bokai.*
manu_lalu-ʔ *Bilbaa.*
manu_lalu-ʔ *Rikou.*
manu_lalu-k *Ba'a.*
manu_lalu-k *Tii.*

***lamat** *Morph:* ***ka-lamat**. *PRM.* grasshopper. *[irr. from PRM:* *l = *l* in Amanuban and Kusa-Manea*] [Form:* The irregular retention of PRM *l as *l* in Amanuban may be due to early reduction of the antepenultimate syllable in ***ka-lamat** > **klamat, with subsequent loss of the initial consonant. Compare ***kalusa**, with reflexes **klusa-n**, and **knusa-n** in Amanuban from Kualiin village. Irregular initial *l* in Kusa-Manea may be due to borrowing from Kemak or antoher language with initial *l.]*
lama-k *Termanu.* grasshopper. (J:274)
lama-ʔ *Korbafo.*
lama-k *Bokai.*
lama-ʔ *Bilbaa.*
lama-ʔ *Landu.* grasshopper. (own field notes)
lama-ʔ *Rikou.*
lama-k *Ba'a.*
lama-k *Tii.*
lamat *Dengka.*
lamat *Oenale.*
k|namat *Ro'is Amarasi.* grasshopper.
k|namat *Kotos Amarasi.* grasshopper.
lamat *Amanuban.* grasshopper. *[Form:* Middelkoop (1972:196) also gives Amanuban <**nama**>.*]*
lamat *Kusa-Manea.* grasshopper.
Out-comparisons:
klamat *Funai Helong.* grasshopper.
klamat *Semau Helong.* grasshopper, locust.
lʔama *Waima'a.* grasshopper.
lamat *Kemak.* grasshopper.

***lamu** *CER.* seaweed species. *Etym:* *lamut (Blust and Trussel (ongoing) include 'Rote' **lamu** and Ngadha **lamu** form as evidence for both ***lamut** and the PMP 'disjunct' *lamu. *lamu is only otherwise supported by Malay **lamu**.). *[Note:* Helong has similar **hlamun** 'moss, lichen, algae, seaweed' which is probably a reflex of PMP *lamun 'swamp grass'.*]*
lamu_doo-k *Termanu.* kind of seaweed, kind of algae. (J:275)
Out-comparisons:
klamur *East Tetun.* seaweed. (Mo:135)

***lani** *Rote.* heaven, firmament, air. *Etym:* *laŋit 'sky'. *[irr. from PRM:* *n > Ø in all except Oenale*] [Form:* The irregular loss of medial *n in all varieties may be due to influence from semantically similar **lain** 'upper part', though this form may itself be from ***lani** with final *CV > VC metathesis. (Jonker suggests that the final *n* in **lain** is from the third person genitive enclitic =**n**). Jonker does not record Dengka as having **lain** 'upper'.*]*
la~lai *Termanu.* heaven, the firmament, air space. (J:269)
la~lai *Korbafo.*
la~lai *Bokai.*
la~lai *Bilbaa.*
la~lai *Rikou.*
la~lai *Ba'a.*
la~lai *Tii.*
la~lai *Dengka.*
la~lai (2) lani *Oenale.* 1) heaven, the firmament, air space. *Usage:* usually in the religious sense, otherwise **lani**. (J:269) 2) the firmament. (J:718)
la~lai (2) lani *Dela.* 1) sky. 2) sky.

***lanu** *Rote.* tired. *Etym:* *laŋu 'vertigo' (Blust and Trussel (ongoing) include Termanu **langu** 'langu-dizziness: expression in ritual language for serious illness' (Fox 2016b:24) as evidence for this form, but this would require irregular retention of **ŋ*.).

na-ma-lanu *Termanu.* feel uncomfortably tired. (J:279)

na-ma-lanu *Korbafo.*

na-ma-lanu *Bokai.*

na-ma-lanu *Bilbaa.*

na-ma-lanu *Tii.*

lanu~lanu *Oenale.*

Out-comparisons:

lanu (2) lanuk *East Tetun.* 1) intoxicate, inebriate, be drunk; poison. 2) intoxicated, drunk. (Mo:127)

melanu *Hawu.* dizzy. *[irr. from PMP:* *ŋ > *n]* (J:278)

***laŋga** *Morph:* ***ka-laŋga, *ka-laŋga-k**. *PRM.* head hair.

laŋa (2) laŋa-k *Termanu.* 1) head. 2) leader, village head, upper part. (J:276)

laŋa *Korbafo.*

laŋa *Bokai.*

laŋa *Bilbaa.*

laka-ʔ *Landu.* head. (own field notes)

laka *Rikou.*

laŋga *Ba'a.*

laŋga *Tii.*

laŋga-ʔ *Dengka.*

laŋga-ʔ *Oenale.*

naka-f *Ro'is Amarasi.* head, head-hair. *[Semantics:* Ambiguous between both meanings, 'head-hair' can be specified by **naak buʔu**.*]*

ʔ|naka-f *Kotos Amarasi.* head; leader, boss.

ʔ|naka-f *Molo.* head. (M:344)

Out-comparisons:

klaam/buuʔ *Funai Helong.* head-hair.

klaŋa *Semau Helong.* head-hair; prow of boat. *[Note:* **boon** = 'head'.*]*

laka/nuri (2) laka/nuri maka, nak/nuri makan (3) laka/nuri wiʔi, naknuri wiʔin *Kisar.* 1) coconut shell. *[Note:* **nor** or **noro** is the normal word for 'coconut', **nuri** could also be connected with *niuR, though the final vowel would be unexplained.*]* 2) the top half of a coconut shell, part with holes. *[Form:* **maka** = 'eye'*]* 3) the bottom half of the coconut shell without holes. *[Form:* **wiʔi** = 'butt'*]*

laga-na *Tokodede.* head, head-hair. (Lekede'e Study Group 2006:15)

gala-r *Kemak.* head. *Usage:* Diirbati dialect (Manumutin desa). *[Sporadic:* consonant metathesis *lVg > *gVl.]*

gə̆raa-ŋ *Kemak.* head. *Usage:* Kutubaba dialect.

gara-r *Kemak.* head. *Usage:* other known Kemak varieties.

***laŋge** *PRM.* stocks, block of wood placed around the head of an animal to prevent it from moving or suckling.

laŋe *Termanu.* stocks for criminals, block of wood tied around the neck of a buffalo or pig (or also a piece of bamboo on the neck of a dog, a coconut shell around the neck of a cat) to impede the movement of the animal. (J:278)

laŋe *Korbafo.*

laŋe *Bokai.*

laŋe *Bilbaa.*

lake *Rikou.*

laŋge *Ba'a.*

laŋge *Tii.*

laŋge *Dengka.*

laŋge *Oenale.*

nake *Kotos Amarasi.* wooden stocks placed around the ankles of a criminal, wooden block placed around the neck of an animal to impede its movement.

nake *Molo.* stocks that are placed around the ankles of people, also a wooden triangle placed on the head of a pig or young buffalo to prevent the piglet or calf from suckling at its mother. (M:345)

Out-comparisons:

laŋe *Semau Helong.* lashed, shackled, chain, stocks.

***lari1** *Morph:* ***lari-k**. *PRM.* comb (of rooster). *[irr. from PRM:* *i > *e* in Kusa-Manea*] [Sporadic:* consonant metathesis *lVr > *rVl* in Dela-Oenale and Rikou.*]*

lali-k *Termanu.* comb of a rooster. (J:274)

lali-ʔ *Korbafo.*

lali-k *Bokai.*

lali-ʔ *Bilbaa.*

rali-ʔ *Rikou.*

lali-k *Ba'a.*

lari-k *Tii.*

lali-ʔ *Dengka.*

rali-ʔ *Oenale.*

nane-f *Kusa-Manea.* comb of rooster. *[Note:* Jonker (1908:274) gives Meto **nani-f**.*]*

Out-comparisons:

lalit *Semau Helong.* comb.

la~larit *East Tetun.* rooster's comb, and crest of other birds. (Mo:125)

lari *Hawu.* (J:274)

laliʔ *Bugis.* chicken's comb. (Masse 2013:317)

***lari2** *PRM.* move location. *[irr. from PRM:* *r > *l* in Tii and wRote; *r > *l* ~ *r* in Oepao and Rikou*] [Sporadic:* consonant metathesis *lVr > *rVl* in Rikou.*] [History:* Possibly connected with PMP *laRiw with irregular *R > *r, but this etymon is retained regularly as ***lai** 'run, fast'.*]*

lali *Termanu.* move oneself, move something. (J:273)

lali *Korbafo.*

lali *Bokai.*

lali *Bilbaa.*

lali, na-rali *Rikou.*

lali, na-lari *Oepao.*

lali *Ba'a.*

lali *Tii.*

lali *Dengka.*

lali *Oenale.*

lali *Dela.* move.

na-naniʔ *Kotos Amarasi.* move, change.

<nani> *Molo.* move away. (M:349)

Out-comparisons:

lari *Hawu.* move location.

***larum** *Morph:* ***ka-larum**. *PRM.* variegated fig. *Ficus variegata*. *[Sporadic:* consonant metathesis *lVr > *rVl* in Dela-Oenale and Rikou.*] [Form:* That it is Dela-Oenale and Rikou which show consonant metathesis rather than Tii, is indicated by other reconstructions with *lVr that have cognates outside of the RM languages including: ***lari** 'comb of rooster' and ***ledo** 'sun' (PMP *qaləjaw) that have undergone the same consonant metathesis *lVr > *rVl* in Dela-Oenale and Rikou.*] [Semantics:* vague Rote semantics.*]*

lalu *Termanu.* kind of tree. *[Semantics:* Heyne (1950:755, cxlii) gives <**laloe loëh**> as *Peltophorum pterocarpum*.*]* (J:274)

lalu *Korbafo.*

lalu *Bokai.*

lalu *Bilbaa.*

ralu *Rikou.*

lalu *Ba'a.*

laru *Tii.*

lalu *Dengka.*

ralu *Oenale.*

ʔ|nanum *Kotos Amarasi.* kind of tree.

<nanum> *Molo.* kind of tree. *Ficus variegata*. (M:349)

***lasa** *PRM.* underlay. *[irr. from PRM:* *l > *r/l* in Meto*]*
lasa *Termanu.* anything that serves as an underlay for cutting or chopping. (J:282)
lasa *Korbafo.*
lasa *Bokai.*
lasa *Bilbaa.*
lasa *Rikou.*
lasa *Ba'a.*
lasa *Tii.*
lasa *Dengka.*
lasa *Oenale.*
rasa|k *Kotos Amarasi.* spread out leaves (with meat put on top).
n-lasan *Molo.* use as an underlay. (M:263)

***lasə** *PRM.* scrotum and testicles. *Etym:* *lasəR. *[Sporadic:* (*ə) > *a > *e* /_# in Amarasi.*]*
lase *Termanu.* scrotum. (J:283)
lase *Korbafo.*
lase *Bokai.*
lase *Bilbaa.*
lase *Rikou.*
lase *Ba'a.*
lase *Tii.*
lasa-ʔ *Dengka.*
lasa-ʔ *Oenale.*
nase-n *Ro'is Amarasi.* testicles.
nase-f *Kotos Amarasi.* testicles.
<nasa> *Molo.* scrotum. (M:351)
Out-comparisons:
lasar *Ili'uun.* penis. (dJ:123)

***lasi1** *PRM.* forest, bush. *[History:* possibly connected with PMP *alas, though this connection would require positing irr. *a > Ø and irregular final *i.]*
lasi *Termanu.* wilderness, forest. (J:283)
lasi *Korbafo.*
lasi *Bokai.*
lasi *Bilbaa.*
lasi *Rikou.*
lasi *Ba'a.*
lasi *Tii.*
lasi *Dengka.*
lasi *Oenale.*
nasi *Ro'is Amarasi.* bush, forest.
nasi *Kotos Amarasi.* bush, forest.
nasi *Molo.* bush, forest. (M:352)
nais *Kusa-Manea.* forest.

***lasi2** *Morph:* ***ma-lasi-k, *na-ma-lasi.** *PRM.* old, aged.
lasi-k (2) na-ma-lasi *Termanu.* 1) old (especially of people and animals). 2) be or become old, of people and animals. (J:283)
lasi-ʔ *Korbafo.*
lasi-k *Bokai.*
lasi-k *Bilbaa.*
lasi-ʔ *Rikou.*
lasi-k *Ba'a.*
lasi-k *Tii.*
lasi-ʔ *Dengka.*
lasi-ʔ *Oenale.*
lasi-ʔ (2) na-ma-lasi *Dela.* 1) old. 2) old.
m|nasi|ʔ *Ro'is Amarasi.* old, aged.
m|nasi|ʔ (2) na-m|mnasi *Kotos Amarasi.* 1) old, aged. 2) be or become old/aged.
m|nasi|ʔ *Molo.* old. (M:325)
m|nasi|ʔ (2) m|nasi-k *Kusa-Manea.* 1) old (of fruit). 2) old, aged (of people).

***latu1** *Morph:* ***ma-latu-k, *na-ma-latu.** *PRM.* ripe.
latu-k (2) na-ma-latu *Termanu.* 1) ripe. 2) ripen up. (J:284)
latu-ʔ *Korbafo.*
latu-k *Bokai.*
latu-k *Bilbaa.*
latu-ʔ *Rikou.*
latu-k *Ba'a.*
latu-k *Tii.*
latu-ʔ *Dengka.*
latu-ʔ *Oenale.*
m|natu|ʔ *Ro'is Amarasi.* ripe, cooked.
m|natu|ʔ *Kotos Amarasi.* ripe, cooked.
na-m|natu *Amanuban.* ripe. (M:325)
Out-comparisons:
latuʔ *Semau Helong.* ripe.
keradu *Hawu. [Sporadic:* *l = *r* correspondence.*]* (J:284)

***latu2** *Rote.* edible seaweed species. *Etym:* *latuq.
latu *Termanu.* kind of edible seaweed. (J:284)
latu *Korbafo.*
latu *Bokai.*
latu *Bilbaa.*
latu *Rikou.*
latu *Ba'a.*
latu *Tii.*
latu *Dengka.*
latu *Oenale.*

***lea** *Morph:* ***lea-k**. *PnRote.* cave, cavern. *See:* ***lua|t**. *Etym:* *liaŋ. *[irr. from PMP:* *i > *e*]*
lea-k *Termanu.* cave, cavern. (J:288)
lea-ʔ *Korbafo.*
lea-k *Bokai.*
lea-ʔ *Bilbaa.*
lea-ʔ *Rikou.*
lea-k *Ba'a. [Form:* with variant **lua-k.***]*
lea-k *Tii.*
Out-comparisons:
liaŋ *Semau Helong.* cave.

***ledo** *PRM.* sun, day. *Etym:* *qaləjaw 'day'. *[minority from PMP:* *j > *d (expect *ɗ)*] [Sporadic:* consonant metathesis *lVr > *rVl* in Dela-Oenale.*]*
ledo (2) ledo-k (3) le~ledo-k *Termanu.* 1) sun. 2) day, in certain expressions. 3) daytime, during the day. (J:290f)
ledo *Korbafo.*
ledo *Bokai.*
ledo *Bilbaa.*
ledo *Rikou.*
ledo *Ba'a.*
leɗo *Tii.*
lelo *Dengka.*
relo *Oenale.*
relo (2) re~relo-ʔ *Dela.* 1) sun. 2) daytime.
neno *Ro'is Amarasi.* day (e.g. of the week), sky.
neno *Kotos Amarasi.* day (e.g. of the week), sky. *[Semantics:* Phrases such as **neon sae-t** 'east' (**neno** + rise-NMLZ') provide internal evidence for the older meaning 'sun'.*]*
neno *Molo.* sky. (M:362)
neno *Kusa-Manea.* sun, day. *[Semantics:* **neno anan** specifies 'sky' as opposed to 'day'.*]*
Out-comparisons:
lelo *Semau Helong.* sun, day, daylight.
loro *East Tetun.* the sun. (Mo:133)
ler(e) *Kisar.* day.
loɗo *Dhao.* sun.
loɗo *Hawu.* sun, day.
leo *Ili'uun.* sun, day; time. (dJ:124)

***lee** *PRM.* river. *[irr. from PRM:* *ee > *oe* in wRM (possibly influence from ***oe** 'water')*]*
lee *Termanu.* river. (J:286)
lee *Korbafo.*
lee *Bokai.*
lee *Bilbaa.*
lee *Rikou.*
lee *Ba'a.*
lee *Tii.*
loe *Dengka.*
loe *Oenale.*
noe *Ro'is Amarasi.* river.
noe *Kotos Amarasi.* river.
noe *Molo.* river. *[Note:* Middelkoop (1972:371) includes the parallelism **noe ʔninoʔ, koe ʔninoʔ** 'the clear river'. If **koe** is related to **noe**, it would indicate PMeto ***ŋoe**. Helong has **ŋoe** 'wet', which could alternately be the source of Molo **koe**.*]* (M:377)
noa *Kusa-Manea.* river. *[Form:* regular *e > *a* /V_# in Upper Manulea.*]*

***leke** *Morph:* ***le~leke**. *PRM.* coil up. *Etym:* *ləkən 'coil' (Blust and Trussel (ongoing) only give a Cebuano and Buru form as supporting evidence.

Other semantically and formally similar forms are discussed with their entry for *reken 'coiled base on which hot cooking pots are set', which is well supported.). *Pattern:* k-5. *[minority from PMP:* *ə > *e / _# (expect *ə > *a* in wRote, possibly *ə > *a > *e)]*

le~leke *Termanu.* lay down in coils, coil up. (J:293)

le~leke *Korbafo.*

le~leke *Bokai.*

le~leke *Bilbaa.*

le~leʔe *Rikou.*

le~leke *Ba'a.*

le~leke *Tii.*

le~leke *Dengka.*

***leko** *Rote.* lure in a crafty way. *Pattern:* k-5′ (*k > Ø in Rikou; expect *ʔ* or *k*).

leko *Termanu.* lure in a crafty way. (J:293)

leko *Korbafo.*

leko *Bokai.*

leko *Bilbaa.*

leo *Rikou.*

leko *Ba'a.*

leko *Tii.*

leko *Dengka.*

leko *Oenale.*

Out-comparisons:

leko *Hawu.* (J:293)

***leku** *PRM.* winding, coiling. *Etym:* *ləkuʔ 'bend, fold, folding part of the body; curl up on the ground, of an animal'. *Pattern:* k-8/9′ (*k > Ø in Rikou; expect *k > *ʔ* or *k*). *[irr. from PRM:* *l > *r*/*l* in Meto*]*

na-le~leʔu (2) le~leʔu (3) le~leʔu-k *Termanu.* 1) with winding/coils. 2) do with twists and turns. 3) do it with winding/coils. (J:309)

na-le~leʔu *Korbafo.*

na-le~leʔu *Bokai.*

na-le~leku *Bilbaa.*

na-le~leu *Rikou.*

na-le~leʔu *Ba'a.*

na-le~leʔu *Tii.*

na-le~leʔu *Dengka.*

na-le~leʔu *Oenale.*

reuk/saen *Ro'is Amarasi.* python. *Borrowed from:* Rote for initial element **leku** or from Helong **likuŋ** before *e > *i* (shown by irr. *l = *r* correspondence). *[History:* Ultimately from ***reku** 'winding' + **sae-n** 'go up'.*]*

riuk/saen *Kotos Amarasi.* python.

liuk/saen *Molo.* python. (M:404)

lik/saan *Kusa-Manea.* python. *[Form:* regular *e > *a* /V_ in Upper Manulea.*]*

Out-comparisons:

likuŋ (2) °liuksaŋ *Semau Helong.* 1) loop around. 2) python. *Borrowed from:* Meto **liuksaen**.

°liku/saen *Fehan Tetun.* python. *Borrowed from:* probably Meto **liuksaen** without CV metathesis (shown by irr. *ə = *i* correspondence, expect *o*). *[Note:* East Tetun has **labak** and/or **foho_rai** for 'python', and Tetun Belu has **koes_ina** (Morris 1984:35, 114, 122).*]*

kaləku *Hawu.* (J:309)

***lele** *Morph:* ***lele-k**. *Rote.* time. *[Form:* Rote ***loo** 'stretch' also shows the correspondence of Helong *d* = Rote *l.]*

lele-k *Termanu.* time. (J:295)

lele-ʔ *Korbafo.*

lele-k *Bokai.*

lele-ʔ *Bilbaa.*

lele-ʔ *Rikou.*

lele-k *Ba'a.*

lele-k *Tii.*

lele-ʔ *Dengka.*

lele-ʔ *Oenale.*

Out-comparisons:

dedeŋ *Semau Helong.* night; time, moment.

***lema** *Morph:* ***ka-lema**. *PRM.* sea-snake. *[Sporadic:* *a > *e* / _# in Meto.*]*

lema-k *Termanu.* kind of ocean fish. (J:296)

lema-ʔ *Korbafo.*
lema-ʔ *Rikou.*
lema-k *Ba'a.*
lema-k *Tii.*
lema-ʔ *Dengka.*
lema-ʔ *Oenale.*
lema-ʔ *Dela.* sea-snake.
k|neme *Ro'is Amarasi.* eel, sea-snake.
k|neme *Kotos Amarasi.* eel, sea-snake. *Usage:* Tais Nonof sub-dialect.
Out-comparisons:
laleman *Galolen.* sea-snake.

***lemuk** *CER.* dolphin. *Etym:* **lemur (pre-RM). *[irr. from PMP: Ø > *k]*
lemuk *Rikou.* dolphin. (own field notes)
Out-comparisons:
lemur *Galolen.* dolphin.
lemor *Batuley.* dolphin. *[Note:* language of the Aru Islands ISO 639-3 [bay].*]* (Daigle 2015:258)

***lemba** *PRM.* carry on a shoulder pole. *Etym:* *lemba (PCMP).
lepa *Termanu.* carry, said of one or more people who are carrying a stick that has a load at each end. (J:305)
lepa *Korbafo.*
lepa *Bilbaa.*
lepa *Rikou.*
lempa *Ba'a.*
lemba *Tii.*
lemba *Dengka.*
lemba *Oenale.*
nepa-t *Kotos Amarasi.* pole for carrying.
<nepa> *Molo.* pole for carrying, bar for carrying. *[Form:* probably **ʔ-nepa-ʔ**.*]* (M:364)
Out-comparisons:
lepa *Semau Helong.* carry on shoulder with pole, one person with something on each end, or two or more people with one heavy thing in the middle.
lebo, leba *East Tetun.* carry or transport any object from the ends of a pole with the centre supported by the shoulder. (Mo:128)
ai kaleba *Welaun.* pole for carrying.

***lena** *PRM.* sesame. *Etym:* *ləŋah (Zorc 1995:1128). *[Sporadic:* *a > *e* /_# in wRM*]*
lena *Termanu.* sesame. (J:296)
lena *Korbafo.*
lena *Bokai.*
lena *Bilbaa.*
lena *Rikou.*
lena *Ba'a.*
lena *Tii.*
lene *Dengka.*
lene *Oenale.*
nene-l *Meto.* sesame. (J:296)
Out-comparisons:
°**lena** *Semau Helong.* sesame. *Borrowed from:* Rote (shown by irr. *ŋ = *n* correspondence).
leŋa *Helong.* sesame. (J:296)

***lendo** *Rote.* dance.
leno *Termanu.* perform a sword-dance, often combined with **foti** [OE: = 'jump around, dance'] to express 'dance' in general. (J:299)
leno *Korbafo.*
leno *Bokai.*
lendo *Rikou.* dance performed by women. (J:299; own field notes)
°**lendo** *Oepao. Borrowed from:* Rikou (shown by medial *nd*). (own field notes)
leno *Ba'a.*
lendo *Tii.*
lendo *Dengka.*
lendo *Oenale.*
Out-comparisons:
ledo, lendo *Hawu.* dance. Can be single or multiple. Mixed male and female.

***leŋge** *CER.* too much.
leŋe *Termanu.* oversize, too much. (J:298)

leŋe *Bokai.*
Out-comparisons:
ləŋa *Hawu.* left, gone, abandoned, no longer there; extreme, significantly beyond what is acceptable. *[Note:* Jonker (1908:298) gives Hawu from Raijua **ləŋe**.*]*

***leŋgu** *Rote.* throw. *[Note:* Meto has **na-neku** 'lose', **na-m|neku** 'lost' for which the sound correspondences with the Rote forms are perfect; however, the semantic connection is far too dubious to establish these forms as cognate.*]*
leŋu *Termanu.* throw, normally a small piece of wood; fall backwards. (J:299)
leŋu *Korbafo.*
leŋu *Bokai.*
leŋu *Bilbaa.*
leku *Rikou.*
leŋgu *Ba'a.*
leŋgu *Tii.*
leŋgu *Dengka.*
leŋgu *Oenale.*
Out-comparisons:
ligu *Hawu.* (J:299)

***leo** *Rote.* clan.
leo *Termanu.* clan, tribe. In Termanu there are nine clans: **leo dou daŋa, leo iŋu beu-k, leo iŋu naʔu, leo kiu kana-k, leo kota dea-k, leo masahuu-k, leo meno, leo ŋgofa lai-k, leo suʔi**. (J:301)
leo *Korbafo.*
leo *Bokai.*
leo *Bilbaa.*
leo *Rikou.*
leo *Ba'a.*
leo *Tii.*
leo *Dengka.*
leo *Oenale.*
Out-comparisons:
leon *Helong.* (J:301)
leo *Fehan Tetun.* hamlet.
leo *East Tetun.* the population, the total number of people in a place. (Mo:129)

***lesu₁** *PRM.* neck. *[irr. from PRM:* *s > Ø in Meto (also Helong)*]* *[Sporadic:* vowel height harmony *u > *o* /e_ in Meto.*]* *[Form:* The main difficulty in this comparison is accounting for irregular loss of medial *s in both the Meto and Helong forms. There seem to be two possible explanations: (1) This comparison combines more than one cognate set; Rote **lesu** is not cognate with the Meto forms. (2) Medial *s was irregularly lost in Meto, from which the Helong form is a borrowing. Whatever the ultimate history of these forms, it is likely that the Helong and Meto forms are a result of borrowing before Meto *l > *n*, though the direction of borrowing cannot yet be confidently determined.*]*
lesu_haʔi-k *Termanu.* neck in general, both sides of the neck. *[Form:* **lesu-k** by itself means 'the thinner portion of the arm at the wrist'.*]* (J:307)
lesu_haʔi *Korbafo.*
lesu_haʔi-k *Bokai.*
lesu_kai-ʔ *Bilbaa.*
lesu_ai-ʔ *Rikou.*
lesu_haʔi-k *Ba'a.*
lesu_haʔi *Lole.* neck. (Zacharias et al. 2014)
lesu_ai-k *Tii.* *[Form:* Grimes et al. (2014a) has **leusain** 'neck'.*]*
lesu_ai-ʔ *Dengka.*
lesu_ai-ʔ *Oenale.*
neo-f *Ro'is Amarasi.* neck.
neo-f *Kotos Amarasi.* neck.
Out-comparisons:
leo *Semau Helong.* neck.
nˀeo *Waima'a.* neck. *[Form:* Possibly a chance resemblance. Waima'a *nˀ* is not known to correspond to PRM *l. While the Waima'a form and Meto might point to pre-RM **neo 'neck', this would not account for the Helong form with initial *l*.*]*

***lesu$_2$** *Rote.* come out, take out. *Etym:* *lesu (PCMP. Blust and Trussel (ongoing) also reconstruct PWMP *ləcut 'squeeze out, slip out' which could be connected.).

lesu *Termanu.* come out, e.g. of a hole, make something come out = pull out, e.g. pull something out of a hole. (J:306)

lesu *Korbafo.*

lesu *Bokai.*

lesu *Bilbaa.*

lesu *Rikou.*

lesu *Ba'a.*

lesu *Tii.*

lesu *Dengka.*

lesu *Oenale.*

Out-comparisons:

<luhu> *Kambera.* go out. (On:246)

<lauhu> *Lewa.*

<lausu> *Anakalang.*

<lusa> *Mamboru.*

<louzo> *Weyewa.*

<loho> *Kodi.*

losa *Bima.* exit, go outside. (Jonker 1893:48)

***lete$_1$** *Morph:* ***ka-lete-k**. *PRM.* mountain, hill. *Etym:* *letay$_1$ 'above' (PCMP).

lete-k *Termanu.* mountain. (J:308)

lete-ʔ *Korbafo.*

lete-k *Bokai.*

lete-k *Bilbaa.*

lete-ʔ *Rikou.*

le~lete, lete-k *Ba'a.*

lete-k *Tii.*

lete-ʔ *Dengka.*

lete-ʔ *Oenale.*

neten *Ro'is Amarasi.* high place.

k|nete|ʔ *Kotos Amarasi.* mountain with gentle slopes on either side, hill.

<neten> *Molo.* mountain range. (M:366)

Out-comparisons:

leten *Semau Helong.* mountain.

leten *East Tetun.* above, overhead; *n.* the top, the part above. (Mo:130)

lete(n) *Ili'uun.* mountain. (dJ:124)

lede *Hawu.* mountain.

***lete$_2$** *PRM.* bridge. *Etym:* *letay$_2$ (PCMP).

le~lete *Termanu.* small bridge. (J:307)

le~lete *Korbafo.*

le~lete *Bokai.*

le~lete *Bilbaa.*

le~lete *Rikou.*

le~lete *Ba'a.*

le~lete *Tii.*

le~lete *Dengka.*

le~lete *Oenale.*

nete-ranan *Kotos Amarasi.* bridge, go-between.

<kanete> *Molo.* bridge. (M:366)

Out-comparisons:

hleten *Semau Helong.* bridge, dock.

kalete *Fehan Tetun.* intermediary, bridge (over water), go between; in traditional courtship, interpreter, mediator (in fights), anyone who carries a message for another — usually used in courtship, but not only for that.

kla~lete *East Tetun.* small bridge. (Mo:108)

***leu** *PRM.* inceptive, used to ask permission to begin an activity. *[Sporadic:* vowel height harmony *u > *o* /e_ in Dela.*]*

leu *Bilbaa.* used to ask permission to begin an activity. **lako leu** We're leaving now. (own field notes)

leu *Rikou.* used to ask permission to begin an activity. **laʔo leu** We're leaving now. (own field notes)

leo *Dela.* already, now; typically used with imperatives and invitations to indicate that the action expressed by the verb should be done now or right away.

neu *Ro'is Amarasi.* used to ask permission to begin an activity. **au ʔ-bukae neu** I'm going to start eating now

neu *Kotos Amarasi.* used to ask permission to begin an activity. *Usage:* In Kotos Amarasi **neu** is less common and considered colloquial/impolite. The more common and polite form is **nai**.

***lənde** *Morph:* ***lənde~lənde**. *PnRote.* still standing (of water). *See:* ***endən**. *[Form:* *nd > *n* /ə_ in Rikou.*]* *[History:* Jonker makes comparisons with forms in Seram, e.g. Kamarian **marene** 'calm, quiet' (van Ekris 1864:308) but I do not find this comparison convincing given the semantics. (Kamarian **marina** is given as specifically 'still [of sea]', thus indicating that **marene** probably does not also indicate 'calm of sea'). Additionally, whether *nd would correspond regularly to *n* in languages of Seram is unknown.*]*

oe=a lene~lene *Termanu.* the water is standing still, doesn't flow. (J:297)

lene~lene *Korbafo.*

lene~lene *Bokai.*

lene~lene *Rikou.*

lene~lene *Ba'a.*

lende *Tii.*

***liɓu** *CERM.* swarm, teem, abound. *Doublet:* ***rimbu**. *Etym:* *libut 'surround, encircle, as game'. *[minority from PMP:* *b > *ɓ /V_V*]*

libu *Termanu.* swarm (of fish, people), gather together. (Fox 2016b:27)

li~libu *Ba'a.* teem, abound. (J:723)

n-nibun *Kotos Amarasi.* surround.

n-nibun *Molo.* gather and meet together. (M:368)

Out-comparisons:

libur *East Tetun.* rejoin, assemble. (Mo:130)

***liɗa** *Morph:* ***liɗa-k**. *PRM.* wing. *See:* ***ɗilas**. *[irr. from PRM:* *a > *e* ~ *a* sporadically in Termanu, Ba'a and Meto (also Kemak)*]* *[Form:* regular *ɗ > **l /*l_ in Meto (and Helong).*]*

lida-k, lide-k *Termanu.* wing of a bird or insect, fin of a fish. (J:310)

lida-ʔ *Korbafo.*

lida-k *Bokai.*

lida-ʔ *Bilbaa.*

lida-k, lide-k *Ba'a.*

liɗa-k *Tii.*

liɗa-ʔ *Dengka.*

liɗa-ʔ *Oenale.*

nini-n *Ro'is Amarasi.* edge.

nine|ʔ, nini|ʔ *Kotos Amarasi.* wing, edge.

nine-n, nina-n *Molo.* wing. (M:370)

nina-f *Kusa-Manea.* wing.

Out-comparisons:

liras *East Tetun.* wing (of birds and insects). (Mo:131)

lila/faan *Welaun.* wing.

lila/paa-n *Kemak.* wing. *Usage:* Kailaku dialect.

lile/paa *Kemak.* wing. *Usage:* Diirbati dialect.

lili/paa-ŋ *Kemak.* *Usage:* Kenebibi and Leolima dialects.

lili/paa *Kemak.* wing. *Usage:* Lemia and Atsabe dialects.

lira *Mambae, South.* wing. *Usage:* Letefoho village. (Fogaça 2017:234)

lila *Mambae, South.* wing. *Usage:* Betano village and Ainaro sub-district. (Fogaça 2017:234)

lila-n *Mambae, Northwest/Central.* wing. (Fogaça 2017:234)

lilar *Tokodede.* wing. (Klamer 2002)

***liɗe** *Morph:* ***liɗe-k**. *Rote.* palm leaf nerve. *[irr. from PRM:* *e > *e* ~ *a* in Ba'a*]*

lide-k *Termanu.* nerve of a palm leaf. (J:310)

lide-ʔ *Korbafo.*
lide-k *Bokai.*
lide-ʔ *Bilbaa.*
lide-ʔ *Rikou.*
lide-k, lida-k *Ba'a.*
liɗe-k *Tii.*
liɗe-ʔ *Dengka.*
liɗe-ʔ *Oenale.*
Out-comparisons:
lidi *Malay.* ribs/veins of coconut palm fronds/leaves.

***lifu** *PRM.* body of still water; billabong, lake. *Etym:* **libun (pre-RM).
lifu *Termanu.* a) standing still, of water. b) body of water which is still, e.g. after rain: a deep gully where there is no current. (J:311f)
lifu *Korbafo.*
lifu *Bokai.*
lifu *Bilbaa.*
lifu *Rikou.*
lifu *Ba'a.*
lifu *Tii.*
lifu *Dengka.*
lifu *Oenale.*
nifu (2) nefo *Kotos Amarasi.* 1) pool, billabong. 2) lake. *[Semantics:* The two words are semantically distinct, **nifu** is smaller than **nefo**. They possibly have different etymologies.*]*
nifu *Amanuban/Amanatun.* lake.
nifu (2) nefo *Molo.* 1) pond, lake. (M:368) 2) lake. (M:359)
Out-comparisons:
lihu *Semau Helong.* depth.
lihun *East Tetun.* dam or pond, a small body of still water. (Mo:130)
welihun *Welaun.* lake.
liwu *Central Lembata.* lake. (Fricke 2015)
<kalibuku> *Kambera.* shallow hole, cavity or hollow in a stone with still water in it. (On:145)

***liha** *Morph:* ***li~liha-k**. *Rote.* centipede. *Etym:* *qalu-hipan (Blust and Trussel (ongoing) reconstruct PCEMP *qalipan.). *[irr. from PRM:* *a > *e* in Tii (sporadic assimilation)*]*
li~liʔa-k *Termanu.* kind of centipede which emits phosphoric light when rubbed (called *kalamayar* in Malay). (J:310)
li~liʔa-ʔ *Korbafo.*
li~liʔa-k *Bokai.*
li~lia-ʔ *Bilbaa.*
li~lias *Landu.* centipede. (own field notes)
li~lia-ʔ *Rikou.*
li~liʔa-k *Ba'a.*
li~liʔe-k *Tii.*
li~lia-ʔ *Dengka.*
li~lia-ʔ *Oenale.*
Out-comparisons:
la~liʔan_tali *Fehan Tetun.* centipede.

***lii1** *Morph:* ***na-lii, *lii-k**. *Rote.* sound. *Etym:* *liŋ 'sound of ringing; word, speech' (Blust and Trussel (ongoing) include Termanu **lii-k** 'sound' as evidence for three separate reconstructions: PCMP **liRi** 'sound, voice', PCEMP **liqə** 'voice', and PMP *liŋ. Of these, PCMP **liRi** is only otherwise supported by Yamdena **liri-n** 'voice; language' and **ŋé-liri** 'uproar, clamour'. Unless more cognates are forthcoming, PCMP *liRi is probably spurious.).
na-lii (2) lii-k *Termanu.* 1) make a sound. 2) sound. (J:309)
na-lii *Korbafo.*
na-lii *Bokai.*
na-lii *Bilbaa.*
na-lii *Rikou.*
na-lii *Ba'a.*
na-lii *Tii.*
na-lii *Dengka.*
na-lii *Oenale.*

Out-comparisons:

liin *Semau Helong.* sound, tune, voice.

lii *Hawu.* say, speak, tell; voice, sound.

***lii2** *Morph:* ***boto_lii-k**. *Rote.* neck. *Etym:* *liqəR. *[irr. from PMP:* *ə > *i (assimilation to previous *i)*]*

boto_lii-k *Termanu.* neck. (J:59)

boto_lii-ʔ *Korbafo.*

boto_lii-k *Bokai.*

boto_lii-ʔ *Bilbaa.*

bo/lii-ʔ *Landu.* neck. (own field notes)

bo/lii-ʔ *Rikou.*

bo/lii-ʔ *Oepao.* neck. (own field notes)

boto_lii-k *Ba'a.*

ɓoto_lii-k *Tii.*

ɓoto_lii-ʔ *Oenale.*

***lii3** *Morph:* ***ka-lii**. *PnRote.* shy, wild. *Etym:* *liaR (Dempwolff 1938:96). *[irr. from PMP:* *a > *i] [History:* Blust and Trussel (ongoing) identify several putative cognates as 'Probably a Malay loan distribution.' and this is indeed possible. However, in the case of the Rote forms, borrowing from Malay does not seem likely due to the final vowel assimilation and diphthongisation of the initial prefix. While neither process is regular in the Rote languages, they would be even more unexpected if these terms were (recently) borrowed from Malay.*]*

kai|lii, ka-lii (2) kai|liis (3) kai|li~lii *Termanu.* 1) be or become wild or shy, e.g. a horse. 2) shy, wild. 3) make shy. (J:216,310)

ka-lii (2) kai|lii-ʔ *Korbafo.*

ka-lii (2) kai|lii-k *Bokai.*

ka-lii (2) ka-lii-ʔ *Bilbaa.*

ai|lii (2) ai|liis *Rikou.*

kai|lii (2) kai|liis *Ba'a.*

(2) kaliis *Tii.*

Out-comparisons:

melei *Hawu.* (J:310)

***liku1** *Rote.* strike, knock. *Pattern:* k-8/9.

liʔu *Termanu.* hit with a stick, etc. (J:316)

liʔu *Korbafo.*

liʔu *Bokai.*

liku *Bilbaa.*

liʔu *Rikou.*

liʔu *Ba'a.*

liʔu *Tii.*

liʔu *Dengka.*

Out-comparisons:

liku *Hawu.* (J:316)

***liku2** *PRM.* back of an object. *Etym:* *likud 'back'. *Pattern:* k-9.

liʔu_dea *Termanu.* that which a weaver uses to support their back, on Rote usually a strip of goat or deer skin. (J:317)

liʔu_dea *Korbafo.*

liʔu_dea *Bokai.*

liku_dea *Bilbaa.*

liʔu_deas *Rikou.*

liʔu_dea *Ba'a.*

liʔu_ɗea *Tii.*

liʔu_ɗeat *Dengka.*

niʔu-n *Kotos Amarasi.* the back part of a blade (incl. swords, knives, machetes, etc.), which is not sharp. *[Note:* **kotif** = 'back (of person)'.*]*

niʔu-n (2) an-niʔu (3) am-koti-f =kau, am-niʔu-f =kau *Molo.* 1) back of a knife or machete. 2) hit something with the back of a knife of machete. 3) you turn your back to me. *Usage:* parallelism. (M:374)

Out-comparisons:

likun *Semau Helong.* out, outside.

liku *East Tetun.* carry on the back (a person). (Mo:131)

***lili** *Morph:* ***lili-k**. *PRM.* wax. *Etym:* *lilin 'beeswax'.

lili-k *Termanu.* wax. (J:313)

lili-ʔ *Korbafo.*

lili-k *Bokai.*

lili-ʔ *Bilbaa.*

lili-ʔ *Rikou.*

lili-k *Ba'a.*

lili-k *Tii.*

lili-ʔ *Dengka.*
lili-ʔ *Oenale.*
niin|k *Ro'is Amarasi.* wax, candle.
nini|k *Kotos Amarasi.* wax, candle.
nini|k *Molo.* beeswax. (M:371)
nini|k *Kusa-Manea.* wax, candle.
Out-comparisons:
lilin *East Tetun.* wax. (Mo:131)

***lilis** *nRM.* kind of tree. Calophyllum teysmannii. *[Semantics:* vague Rote semantics.*]*
kai/lili-k *Termanu.* kind of tree. (J:216)
kai/lili-ʔ *Korbafo.*
kai/lili-k *Bokai.*
kai-lili-ʔ *Bilbaa.*
ai_lili-ʔ *Rikou.*
ai/lili-k *Ba'a.*
(kai/lili-k ?) *Tii.*
<ninis> *Amfo'an.* kind of tree. Calophyllum teysmannii. (M:371)

***lilo** *PRM.* gold, silver. *[irr. from PRM:* vowel metathesis in Meto *iCo > *oCi]*
lilo *Termanu.* gold, silver. (J:313)
lilo *Korbafo.*
lilo *Bokai.*
lilo *Bilbaa.*
lilo *Rikou.*
lilo *Ba'a.*
lilo *Tii.*
lilo *Dengka.*
lilo *Oenale.*
noni *Kotos Amarasi.* silver; bridewealth.
noni *Molo.* silver, silver coins. (M:382)
Out-comparisons:
lila (2) lil mutiʔ (2) lil mea *Semau Helong.* 1) bridewealth. 2) silver. 3) gold.

***lima₁** *PRM.* five. *Etym:* *lima.
lima *Termanu.* five, fifth. (J:313f)
lima *Korbafo.*
lima *Bokai.*
lima *Bilbaa.*
lima *Rikou.*
lima *Ba'a.*
lima *Tii.*
lima *Dengka.*
lima *Oenale.*
nima *Ro'is Amarasi.* five.
nima *Kotos Amarasi.* five.
nima *Molo.* five. (M:370)
niam *Kusa-Manea.* five.
Out-comparisons:
lima *Semau Helong.* five.
lima *East Tetun.* five. (Mo:131)
lima *Kemak.* five.
wolima *Kisar.* five.
ləmi *Hawu.* five.

***lima₂** *Morph:* ***ka-lima-k**. *PRM.* hand/arm. *Etym:* *qa-lima.
lima-k *Termanu.* hand, arm of a person or ape, forepaws of a crocodile. (J:314)
lima-ʔ *Korbafo.*
lima-k *Bokai.*
lima-ʔ *Bilbaa.*
lima-ʔ *Landu.* hand, arm. (own field notes)
lima-ʔ *Rikou.*
lima-k *Ba'a.*
lima-k *Tii.*
lima-ʔ *Dengka.*
lima-ʔ *Oenale.*
nimi-f *Ro'is Amarasi.* arm/hand.
ʔ|nima-f *Kotos Amarasi.* arm/hand.
<nima-f> *Molo.* hand (in general). (M:370)
ʔ|nima-f *Baikeno.* arm/hand. (Charles E. Grimes pers. comm.)
nima-f *Kusa-Manea.* arm/hand.
Out-comparisons:
ima *Semau Helong.* hand, arm. *[irr. from PMP:* *l > Ø*]*
lima-(n) *East Tetun.* arm, hand. (Mo:131)
limar *Kemak.* hand, arm.
lima *Kisar.* hand, arm.

***lino** *PRM.* tree. Grewia salutaris. *Etym:* *qanilaw 'tree Grewia species'. *[Sporadic:* consonant metathesis *nVl > *lVn.*]*

lino *Termanu.* kind tree. Grewia salutaris. (J:314) (Heyne 1950:1060,cxlviii)
lino *Korbafo.*
lino *Bokai.*
lino *Bilbaa.*
lino *Rikou.*
lino *Ba'a.*
lino *Tii.*
lino *Dengka.*
lino *Oenale.*
<nino> *Amfo'an.* small crooked tree. Antidesma ghaesembilla. *[Semantics:* This may be a chance resemblance given the lack of an exact semantic match between the Meto and Rote forms.*]* (M:371)

***lise** *nRM.* shore tree with edible nuts. Terminalia catappa. *Etym:* *talisay. *[irr. from PRM:* *e > *a* in Termanu, Korbafo and Ba'a*]*
lisa, lise *Termanu.* kind of tree, the *ketapang.* Terminalia catappa. (J:315)
lisa, lise *Korbafo.*
lise *Bokai.*
lise *Bilbaa.*
lise *Rikou.*
lisa *Ba'a.*
lise *Tii.*
nisa|ʔ *Kotos Amarasi.* kind of big tree the seeds of which are medicinal. *[Note:* **ʔnisaʔ** 'gebang palm seeds (traditionally used as a kind of marble)'.*]*
<nisa> (2) ʔ|nisa|ʔ =ma ʔfenu *Molo.* 1) kind of tree. Sterculea foetidea. (M:372) 2) medicine for women especially during pregnancy and childbirth. (M:374)

***lisum** *PRM.* kind of plant with fruit. *[Semantics:* vague semantics.*]*
li~lisu-k *Termanu.* kind of plant called the *terong utan* in Kupang, that is the wild eggplant or aubergine. *[Semantics:* Heyne (1950:1345, cxlvii) gives <**lilisoe olana**> as Solanum melongena = 'eggplant'.*]* (J:315)
li~lisu-ʔ *Korbafo.*
li~lisu-k *Bokai.*
li~lisu-ʔ *Bilbaa.*
li~lisu-ʔ *Rikou.*
li~lisu-k *Ba'a.*
li~lisu-ʔ *Dengka.*
li~lisu-ʔ *Oenale.*
<nisum> (2) <nisume> *Molo.* 1) kind of tree. Ficus subglauca M.Dr. (M:372) *[Semantics:* This tree appears to have first been identified by Meijer Drees (1950).*]* 2) kind of tree. Myristica species. (M:373)

***loɓa** *PRM.* kind of bark used to make clothing.
loba *Termanu.* kind of tree bark that is used for sarongs, etc., it is supplied by foreign traders. (J:318)
loba *Korbafo.*
loba *Bokai.*
loba *Bilbaa.*
loba *Rikou.*
loba *Ba'a.*
loɓa *Tii.*
loba *Dengka.*
loɓa *Oenale.*
<noba> *Molo.* kind of dried bark used to make clothing mixed with <**baukulu**> [OE = Morinda citrifolia]. (M:376)
Out-comparisons:
luɓa *Hawu.* (J:318)
<loba> *Kambera.* kind of tree only found in the area of Parai Marapu in East Sumba. The bark and leaves are used to make a red dye for yarn and textiles. Peltophorum pterocarpum. (On:243)

***loɓo** *Rote.* tire out, hurt.
na-lobo (2) lobo *Termanu.* hurt, tire out. *[Semantics:* Both forms have the same meaning.*]* (J:319)

na-lobo *Korbafo.*
na-lobo *Bokai.*
na-lobo *Rikou.*
na-lobo *Ba'a.*
na-loɓo *Oenale.*
Out-comparisons:
loɓo *Hawu.* tire oneself out. (J:319)

***loɗe** *PRM.* stick out. *[irr. from PRM:* *e > *o* in Meto; *l = *l* in Meto (expect *n*)*]* *[Form:* regular *ɗ > **l /*l_ in Meto.*]*
maa=na lode~lode (2) lode-k maa~maa *Termanu.* 1) his tongue sticks out, hangs out (e.g. like a dog that is hot). 2) stick your tongue out. (J:319)
lode~lode *Korbafo.*
lode~lode *Bokai.*
lole~lole *Bilbaa.*
role~role *Rikou.*
lode~lode *Ba'a.*
loɗe~loɗe *Tii.*
loɗe~loɗe, lo~loɗe *Dengka.*
loɗe~loɗe *Oenale.*
n-lolok maa-f (2) mata-n na-tlolo (3) lolo-n (4) poʔa-n lolo-n *Molo.* 1) someone sticks their tongue out. (M:284) 2) he has a bulging eye-ball. (M:xlviii) 3) neck artery. (M:284) 4) cavity in the neck, or the Adam's apple. (M:284)

***loɗo** *Morph:* ***loɗo-k**. *PRM.* straight, right. *[Form:* regular *ɗ > **l /*l_ in Meto (and Helong).*]*
lo~lodo-k *Termanu.* right, without curves. (J:320)
lo~lodo-ʔ *Korbafo.*
lo~lodo-k *Bokai.*
lo~lodo-ʔ *Rikou.*
lo~lodo-k *Ba'a.*
lo~loɗo-k *Tii.*
lo~loɗo-ʔ *Dengka.*
na-m|nono, na-nono (2) m|nono|ʔ *Kotos Amarasi.* 1) straighten, correct. 2) straight, correct.
m|nono|ʔ *Molo.* agree, fair/honest. (M:327)
m|nono|ʔ *Kusa-Manea.* straight.
Out-comparisons:
lolo *Semau Helong.* straight; righteous, just, fair.
mololo *Kisar.* straight.
kelolo, lolo *Hawu.* straighten, stretch out.
kəlodo *Lamaholot, Lewotobi.* straight. *[Note:* language of east Flores ISO 639-3 [slp].*]* (Keraf 1978:296)

***loe1** *Rote.* go down.
loe *Termanu.* go down; be low. (J:320)
loe *Korbafo.*
loe *Bokai.*
loe *Bilbaa.*
loe *Rikou.*
loe *Ba'a.*
loe *Tii.*
loe *Dengka.*
Out-comparisons:
loe *Hawu.* lowness. (J:320)

***loe2** *PRM.* listless, weak.
ao=na ma-sa-loe *Ba'a.* feel tired, weak or listless. *[Form:* **ao=na** = 'body-3GEN'.*]* (J:725)
ao=na ma-sa-loe *Dengka.* feel tired, weak or listless. (J:725)
ao=na ma-sa-loe *Oenale.* feel tired, weak or listless. (J:725)
masaloe *Dela.* weak.
na-noe-b-aʔ *Kotos Amarasi.* listless, apathetic, weak.
Out-comparisons:
°noe~noe *Semau Helong.* powerless, weak, faint, soft, weak-willed, wimp. *Borrowed from:* Meto (shown by irr. *l = *n* correspondence).

***lohas** *CERM.* equipment, outfit, clothes.
loʔas *Termanu.* equipment. (J:318)
loa-ʔ *Bilbaa.*
pake_nohas *Kotos Amarasi.* clothes.
na-nohas *Molo.* equips oneself. (M:378)

Out-comparisons:
lohas *Semau Helong.* ornament, decoration.

***loke** *PRM.* hang. *Pattern:* k-8′ (*k = *k* in Dengka; expect *ʔ* or Ø).
lo~loʔe (2) loʔe~loʔe (3) beloʔe *Termanu.* 1) hang up, hang onto. 2) be hanging, be hanging up. 3) be hanging, be hanging up; for plural subjects. (J:321)
lo~loʔe *Korbafo.*
lo~loʔe *Bokai.*
lo~loke *Bilbaa.*
lo~loʔe *Rikou.*
lo~loʔe *Ba'a.*
lo~loʔe *Tii.*
lo~loke-ʔ *Dengka.*
na-k|noe *Kotos Amarasi.* hang, suspend. *[Form:* Jonker (1908:321) gives Meto **noen** 'hung up'.*]*
Out-comparisons:
loen *Semau Helong.* hanging, suspended, holding on.

***lole$_1$** *PRM.* kind of tuber. *[irr. from PRM:* *l > *r*/*l* in Meto (expect *n*); *e > *i* in most Meto*]*
lole *Termanu.* kind of tuber. (J:323)
lole *Korbafo.*
lole *Bokai.*
lole *Bilbaa.*
lole *Ba'a.*
lole *Tii.*
lole *Dengka.*
lole *Oenale.*
rauk rori *Ro'is Amarasi.* sweet potato.
rauk rori *Kotos Amarasi.* sweet potato.
lole *Fatule'u.* tuber.
loli *Molo.* sweet potato. (M:284)
Out-comparisons:
lole *Semau Helong.* taro.

***lole$_2$** *PRM.* spool.
lole *Termanu.* a) (rotating) tool used to wind up yarn; they wind yarn on the yarn winder. b) a completely different tool, a kind of frame over which the threads are stretched out in order to be divided into **boak** and on which they are tied for dyeing them according to their different patterns. (J:323)
lole *Korbafo.*
lole *Bokai.*
lole *Rikou.*
lole *Ba'a.*
lole *Tii.*
lole *Oenale.*
ʔ|none|ʔ (2) na-ʔ|none|ʔ *Kotos Amarasi.* 1) pulling device (e.g. for drawing water from a well). 2) lower down with a rope.
<an-none>(2) ʔ|none|ʔ *Molo.* 1) winds up (cotton thread). 2) spool used to wind cotton thread. (M:381)
Out-comparisons:
slale *Helong. [irr. from PRM:* *o = *a* correspondence*]* (J:323)

***lolir** *Rote.* roll, roll around, wallow. *[Note:* Jonker (1908:324) gives potential cognates in languages of South Sulawesi: Makassar **doliʔ** 'wallow', **loliʔ** 'roll (n.)', Bentong **lulir** 'roll', and Bugis **lole** 'roll up'.*]*
loli *Termanu.* wallow, roll around. (J:324)
loli *Korbafo.*
loli *Bokai.*
loli *Bilbaa.*
loli *Rikou.*
loli *Ba'a.*
loli *Tii.*
loli (2) lolil *Dengka.* 1) wallow, roll around. 2) roll, like a stone. (J:324)
loli (2) lolir *Oenale.* 1) wallow, roll around. 2) roll, like a stone. (J:324)
Out-comparisons:
lolit (2) klolit *East Tetun.* 1) roll or bowl along. (Mo:132) 2) roll. (Mo:110)

***lolo$_1$** *PRM.* liana, vine.
lolo_kode-k *Termanu.* kind of creeper. (J:326)
lolo *Dengka.* kind of winding plant. (J:726)

lolo_ne?et *Oenale.* kind of winding plant. (J:726)

nono *Kotos Amarasi.* kind of jungle rope, liana; descent group. 'lianas which encircle the clan and hence symbolize its fertility' (Schulte Nordholt 1971:116).

<nono mofa> (2) <nono panu> (3) <nono siumloli> *Molo.* 1) kind of liana. 2) kind of liana. 3) kind of liana with a white stamen the sap of which can be used successfully to quickly heal fresh wounds. (M:384)

Out-comparisons:

lolo *Helong.* (J:726)

***lolo₂** *PRM.* stretch out.

lolo *Termanu.* stretch out. (J:325)

lolo *Korbafo.*

lolo *Bokai.*

lolo *Bilbaa.*

lolo *Rikou.*

lolo *Ba'a.*

lolo *Tii.*

lolo *Dengka.*

lolo *Oenale.*

n-nono *Kotos Amarasi.* push string/thread back and forth, thread string.

n-nono *Molo.* **bifee-l an-nono mau (beti)** the woman applies striped rows along the middle part of the *ikat* woven cloth. (M:384)

Out-comparisons:

lolo *Semau Helong.* separate string. Separate the string for preparation for making a pattern for weaving cloth.

lolo *Hawu.* stretch out the yarn. (J:325)

***lolo₃** *PRM.* beam, stick.

lolo *Termanu.* the beams that lie across the **lungus**. (J:326)

lolo *Korbafo.*

lolo *Bokai.*

lolo *Bilbaa.*

lolo *Rikou.*

lolo *Ba'a.*

lolo *Tii.*

lolo *Dengka.*

nono|? *Kotos Amarasi.* stick, rod, pole; counter for long round things (e.g. cigarettes, needles).

Out-comparisons:

lolo *Semau Helong.* stick, a counter for long things like: sticks, rope, chain.

lollo *Kisar.* stalk part of a plant.

wulu lolo *Central Lembata.* long wooden stick that is part of the loom. (Hanna Fricke pers. comm.)

lolo-n *Central Lembata.* leaf. (Fricke 2015)

***lolo₄** *Morph:* ***lolo-k**. *PRM.* long impression in the ground; watercourse, valley.

oe_lolo-k (2) lolo-k *Termanu.* 1) drain, water duct. 2) path impression or groove in the ground, where the plant growth has been trodden down as the result of wildlife constantly following this path; strait. (J:326)

oe_lolo-? *Korbafo.*

oe_lolo-k *Bokai.*

oe_lolo-? *Bilbaa.*

oe_lolo-? *Rikou.*

oe_lolo-k *Ba'a.*

oe_lolo-k *Tii.*

oe_lolo-? *Dengka.*

oe_lolo-? *Oenale.*

nono-n (2) ?|nono|f *Kotos Amarasi.* 1) dry area associated with water, e.g. the beach, or a river bed. *[Note:* Jonker (1908:326) gives Meto **oe lolo?** and Amarasi **oe rorok**.*]* 2) valley.

<oe_nono> (2) <anono kekfok am anasi kekfok> *Molo.* 1) riverbed. 2) the hidden deep river valley, the dense primeval forest. (M:384)

Out-comparisons:

°oelolo, °oenonon (2) °hnono *Helong.* 1) drain, water duct. (J:326) 2) valley. *Borrowed from:* Meto.

***lombu** *Rote.* moss, algae, duckweed. *Etym:* *lumbu 'plant species' (Only supported by four putative reflexes in Blust and Trussel (ongoing).). *[irr. from PMP:* *u > *o*]*

lopu (2) lopu lee (3) lopu tasi *Termanu.* 1) moss. 2) duckweed. 3) algae. (J:328)

lopu *Korbafo.*

lopu *Bokai.*

lopu *Bilbaa.*

lopu *Rikou.*

lompu *Ba'a.*

lombu *Tii.*

lombu *Dengka.*

lombu *Oenale.*

***loo1** *Rote.* stretch. *[Form:* Rote ***lele** 'time' also shows the correspondence of Helong *d* = Rote *l.]*

loo *Termanu.* with outstretched hand to keep, reach or indicate. (J:317)

loo *Korbafo.*

loo *Bokai.*

loo *Bilbaa.*

loo *Rikou.*

loo *Ba'a.*

loo *Tii.*

loo *Dengka.*

loo *Oenale.*

Out-comparisons:

dooŋ *Semau Helong.* stretch, reach out.

lolo, kelolo *Hawu.* stretch out. *[Note:* Jonker (1908:317) includes this form preceded by the note 'compare' indicating that he does not consider it definitely cognate.*]* (J:317)

***loo2** *Rote.* household.

uma_loo (2) na-uma_na-loo *Termanu.* 1) house in more or less metaphorical senses. 2) s/he has a household; also: establish a household, marry. (J:667)

ume_loo *Dela.* household.

°looʔ *Kusa-Manea.* village. *Borrowed from:* probably Tetun.

Out-comparisons:

loʔon, loʔo *East Tetun.* holiday house, country house. (Mo:133)

loʔo (2) tuur loʔo *Fehan Tetun.* 1) a few houses together, not yet a **leo** (hamlet). 2) live separate from other people (not in a village).

***lopo** *CERM.* shelter, hut. *Etym:* *ləpaw. *[irr. from PMP:* *ə > *o; *p = p*] [irr. from PRM:* *l > Meto *r/l] [History:* The irregularities at every level indicate that this term probably spread by borrowing.*]*

lopo *Termanu.* shelter or hut made in a tree or in dry fields. (J:327)

lopo *Rikou.* small shelter made in a tree or in a field where someone can stay to protect crops. (own field notes)

ropo *Kotos Amarasi.* Timorese round social activity houses. typically with a cone shaped roof made from thatch supported on four poles and without any walls. Not commonly built in Amarasi anymore. *Borrowed from:* Rote (shown by irr. *l = *r* correspondence).

lopo *Molo.* round house without walls, especially as a storehouse with attic. (M:286)

Out-comparisons:

klobor, klobar *East Tetun.* hut with a gable roof. *[irr. from PRM: b* = *p correspondence*]* (Mo:110)

ləpo *Sika.* house. *Usage:* Hewa dialect/variety. (Fricke 2014:96)

***losa** *Rote.* arrive, reach, until, up to.

losa *Termanu.* arrive, reach, until, up to. (J:328)

losa *Korbafo.*

losa *Bokai.*

losa *Bilbaa.*

losa *Rikou.*

losa *Ba'a.*

losa *Tii.*

losa *Dengka.*
losa *Oenale.*
Out-comparisons:
lisu *Semau Helong.* arrive. *[irr. from PRM:* *o = *i* correspondence*]*
loha, lohe *Hawu.* until. (J:328)

***lua|t** *PRM.* cave, cavern. *See:* ***lea**. *Etym:* *luaŋ (Blust and Trussel (ongoing) also reconstruct formally similar PWMP *Ruqaŋ 'hole, pit' and PMP *lubaŋ 'hole, pit'.). *[Form:* Final *t in wRM could be from the nominalising suffix *t*, though why this should be attached to this form is inexplicable.*]*
lua-k *Ba'a.* hole, cave. *[Form:* with variant **lea-k**.*]* (J:727)
luat *Dengka.* hole, cave. (J:727)
luat *Oenale.* hole, cave. (J:727)
nuat *Ro'is Amarasi.* cave.
nuat *Kotos Amarasi.* cave.
nuat *Molo.* cave. (M:389)
Out-comparisons:
uee luʔa *East Tetun.* well. *[irr. from PMP: Ø > ʔ]* (Mo:134)

***lua1** *PRM.* boiling water, boil over. *Etym:* *luab 'swell up, as boiling rice; boil over'.
lua *Termanu.* 1) rise up of water when boiling, boiling, boiling over. (J:331)
lua *Korbafo.*
lua *Bokai.*
lua *Bilbaa.*
lua *Rikou.*
lua *Ba'a.*
lua *Tii.*
lua *Dengka.*
lua *Oenale.*
na-ʔnua *Kotos Amarasi.* boiling water that is bubbling away.
<na-nua> *Molo.* boils. (M:388)
Out-comparisons:
lua *Semau Helong.* boil over.

***lua2** *Morph:* ***lua-k**. *PRM.* wide, open, openness. *Etym:* *luqaR 'outside, wide open spaces; loose'. *[irr. from PRM:* *u > *o* in Rote*]*
loa-k *Termanu.* open, wide; openness, width. (J:318)
loa-ʔ *Korbafo.*
loa-k *Bokai.*
loa-ʔ *Bilbaa.*
loa-ʔ *Rikou.*
loa-k *Ba'a.*
loa-k *Tii.*
loa-ʔ *Dengka.*
loa-ʔ *Oenale.*
mai/nua|n *Ro'is Amarasi.* openness; opportunity. *[Form:* source of initial **mai** currently unknown.*]*
mai/nua|n *Kotos Amarasi.* openness; opportunity.
mai/nua|n *Molo.* wide, open. *[Form:* Middelkoop (1972:299) has a note: 'cf. **meonuan**', which presumably is an alternate form, but no separate entry is given for this form.*]* (M:299)
ma|nuʔa-k *Kusa-Manea.* outside. *[Sporadic:* *VV-k > *VVʔ > VʔV in Kusa-Manea (perceptual metathesis) followed by attachment of semi-productive **-k** suffix.*]*
Out-comparisons:
bluaŋ *Semau Helong.* wide, broad, open.
luan *East Tetun.* wide, broad; vast, extensive. (Mo:134)

***lui** *PRM.* pull off, remove.
lui *Termanu.* take off something that hangs. (J:332)
lui *Korbafo.*
lui *Bokai.*
lui *Bilbaa.*
lui *Rikou.*
lui *Ba'a.*
lui *Tii.*
lui *Dengka.*
lui *Oenale.*

n-nui *Kotos Amarasi.* take off (e.g. footwear).
n-nui *Molo.* pulls off (a horse's bridle), pulls/fetches (bark from a tree). (M:389)
Out-comparisons:
luit *East Tetun.* graze lightly, hardly touching; to remove or take out adroitly. (Mo:134)

***luku1** *PRM.* watch silently, brood. *Pattern:* k-9.
luʔu *Termanu.* brood. (J:336)
luʔu *Korbafo.*
luʔu *Bokai.*
luku *Bilbaa.*
luʔu *Rikou.*
luʔu *Ba'a.*
luʔu *Tii.*
luʔu *Dengka.*
luʔu *Oenale.*
n-nuʔu *Kotos Amarasi.* watch silently, spy.
n-nuʔu *Molo.* brood (of chicken). (M:388)
Out-comparisons:
ruku *Hawu. [Sporadic:* *l = *r* correspondence*]* (J:336)

luku2** *Rote.* bent and strengthless limb, paralysed. *Etym:* *lukut 'roll or crumple up'. *Pattern:* k-7/8′ (Dengka *k* Oenale *ʔ* correspondence, expect either *k* in both for pattern 7, or *ʔ* in both for pattern 8). *[History:* Blust and Trussel (ongoing) also reconstruct PWMP *lu(ŋ)kuq 'bend, curve' (supported by two reflexes), and POc *lukun 'bend, as an arm or leg'.*] [Semantics:* Jonker relates the first part of Termanu **luʔu_laʔa-k** with **luʔu** 'brood' (luku**), **luʔu** 'lie down (said of animals)', and **luʔu** 'kneel down'. Of these, the semantic connection between the last form and 'bent' is particularly plausible.*]*
luʔu-k, luʔu ei-k (2) luʔu_laʔa-k (3) na-ma-luʔu *Termanu.* 1) bent and strengthless, paralysed said of the arm or especially the legs. 2) = **luʔu-k**. 3) become bent and lame (of the legs), get bent and lame legs. (J:337)
luʔu-ʔ (2) luʔu_laʔa *Korbafo.*
luʔu-k (2) luku_laka-ʔ *Bokai.*
(2) luku_laka-ʔ *Rikou.*
luʔu-k (2) luʔu_laʔa-k *Ba'a.*
luʔu-k (2) luʔu_laʔa-k *Tii.*
(2) luka_laka-ʔ ? *Dengka. [Form:* Jonker explicitly states the first *a* in this form may be a spelling error instead of *u.]*
mamaluʔu *Oenale.*

***luli** *PRM.* taboo.
luli-k *Termanu.* forbidden, holy. (J:323)
luli-ʔ *Korbafo.*
luli-k *Bokai.*
luli-ʔ *Bilbaa.*
luli-ʔ *Rikou.*
luli-k *Ba'a.*
luli-k *Tii.*
luli-ʔ *Dengka.*
luli-ʔ *Oenale.*
nuni *Kotos Amarasi.* taboo.
nuni (2) na-nuni *Molo.* 1) taboo. 2) observes a taboo. (M:167)
Out-comparisons:
luli *Semau Helong.* taboo, avoided, forbidden, sacred.
luli *Kisar.* taboo.
luli, lulik *East Tetun.* prohibited, forbidden; sacred, holy. (Mo:135)
luli *Tokodede.* holy, sacred. (Schapper and Wellfelt 2018:109)

***lulun** *PRM.* roll up, as a mat. *Etym:* *lulun (Blust and Trussel (ongoing) also reconstruct PCMP *lunu 'roll up' on the basis of the Termanu form and a Kei cognate. This reconstruction is unconvincing given that most varieties of Rote have **lulu**.). *[Sporadic:* consonant metathesis *lVn > *nVl in Termanu, Bokai, and Ba'a with subsequent loss of final consonant.*]*

[Form: The hypothesis of consonant metathesis to explain the otherwise irregular medial *n* in these languages provides language internal evidence that the PRM form had a final *n.*]*
lunu *Termanu.* roll something up so it makes a roll. (J:334)
lulu *Korbafo.*
lunu *Bokai.*
lulu *Bilbaa.*
lulu *Rikou.*
lunu *Ba'a.*
lulu *Tii.*
lulu *Dengka.*
lulu *Oenale.*
n-nunu *Kotos Amarasi.* roll up.
<na-nunu> *Molo.* roll up (e.g. mat). (M:393)
Out-comparisons:
lulu *Semau Helong.* scroll, roll, waves, fold.
lulun *East Tetun.* roll up, wrap up. (Mo:135)

***lunu** *Morph:* ***ka-lunu**. *PRM.* wooden headrest, pillow. *Etym:* *qalunan. *[irr. from PMP:* *a > *u (sporadic assimilation)*]* *[Sporadic:* consonant metathesis *lVn > *nVl* in Bilbaa, Rikou, and wRote.*]* *[Form:* The initial element has apparently been reanalysed in Rote as connected with reflexes of ***kaiu** 'wood'. The out-comparisons point to pre-RM **ka(r)lun[u/i].*]*
kai/lunu *Termanu.* cushion, pillow. (J:216)
kai/lunu *Korbafo.*
kai/lunu *Bokai.*
kai/nulu *Bilbaa.*
(ʔ)ai/nulu-ʔ *Rikou.*
kai/lunu *Ba'a.*
kai/lunu *Tii.*
(ʔ)ai/nulu-ʔ *Dengka.*
ʔai/nulu-ʔ *Oenale.*
ʔai/nulu *Dela.* pillow.
aka/ʔnunuʔ *Kotos Amarasi.* pillow.
<aka/nunu>, <aika/nunu> *Molo.* pillow. (M:13)
Out-comparisons:
kluni (2) hluni *Semau Helong.* 1) pillow. 2) use pillow.
kluni, karluni *East Tetun.* pillow or cushion. (Mo:111, 102)
luni *Kisar.* pillow.
kaluni, kluni *Ili'uun.* head-rest, pillow. (dJ:120)
karaŋulu *Buru.* pillow, headrest. (Grimes and Grimes 2020:474)

***lusə** *PRM.* wrap. *[irr. from PRM:* *s > *ʔ* in Termanu, Korbafo, and Ba'a*]*
na-luʔe *Termanu.* wrap inside, cover. (J:332)
na-luʔe *Korbafo.*
na-luse *Bokai.*
na-luse *Bilbaa.*
na-luse *Rikou.*
na-luʔe *Ba'a.*
na-luse *Tii.*
na-lusa *Dengka.*
na-lusa *Oenale.*
n-tai_nusa *Kotos Amarasi.* wrap. *[Form:* **tais** = 'sarong', **na-tai** = 'clothe (v.)'.*]*
Out-comparisons:
lose *Semau Helong.* wrap, cover.

***lutə** *Morph:* ***lutə-k**. *CERM.* firebrand, burning piece of wood. *Etym:* *alutən.
haʔi_lute-k *Termanu.* burning piece of wood, a firebrand. (J:335)
haʔi_lute-ʔ *Korbafo.*
ai nuta|ʔ *Kotos Amarasi.* burning stick, firebrand.
nuta|ʔ *Molo.* glowing stumps of firewood or torch. (M:395)

***lutu**$_1$ *Morph:* ***ma-lutu-k, *na-lutu**. *PRM.* fine, delicate, tiny.
lutu-k (2) na-lutu *Termanu.* 1) delicate, small. 2) make something fine, crush, from that: make into pieces, spoil, wreck, ruin. (J:335f)
lutu-ʔ (2) na-lutu *Korbafo.*
lutu-k (2) na-lutu *Bokai.*
lutu-ʔ (2) na-lutu *Bilbaa.*
lutu-ʔ (2) na-lutu *Rikou.*
lutu-k (2) na-lutu *Ba'a.*

lutu-k (2) na-lutu *Tii.*
lutu-ʔ (2) na-lutu, na-mba-lutu-ʔ *Dengka.*
lutu-ʔ (2) na-lutu *Oenale.*
m|nutu|ʔ (2) na-nutu *Kotos Amarasi.* 1) fine, tiny. 2) slice (typically something like vegetables).
na-nutu *Molo.* cuts (meat). (M:395)
Out-comparisons:
blutuʔ (3) tai lutu-n *Semau Helong.* 1) tiny, teeny, small. 3) intestine.
lotu(k) *East Tetun.* thin, slender, dainty. (Mo:134)
blutuk *Sika.* small, short. (Pareira and Lewis 1998:24)

***lutu2** *Rote.* pile up. *Etym:* **lutuR (pre-RM). *[History:* Schapper (2020) discusses the distribution and semantics of this cognate set throughout Linguistic Wallacea in some detail.*]*
lutu_batu *Termanu.* pile up stones, especially under a tree in order to make a resting place there; piled up heap of stones. (J:335)
lutu_batu *Korbafo.*
lutu_batu *Bokai.*
lutu_batu *Bilbaa.*
lutu_mpatu *Ba'a.*
lutu_mbatu *Dengka.*
lutu_mbatu *Oenale.*
Out-comparisons:
lutaŋ *Helong.* pile up. *[irr. from PMP:* *u > *a]* (J:335)
lutu *East Tetun.* hedge, fence, enclosure, circular mud wall. (Mo:135)
lutu(r) *Ili'uun.* pile up. (dJ:125)
lukur *Kisar.* rock wall.
lotar *Central Lembata.* pile up. (Hanna Fricke pers. comm. December 2017)

***luu1** *Morph:* ***lu~luu.** *Rote.* castor-oil plant. *[Semantics:* Whether the semantic connection between 'casuarina tree' and 'castor-oil-plant' is likely or not is unclear to me as a non-botanist, but the two trees do appear to have similar seed pods. Given the existence of ***kaiou** being retained in Rote with the meaning 'casuarina tree', as well as geographically distant Helong and Dadu'a having this meaning, it seems most likely that the pre-Rote referent was casuarina tree with semantic shift in Rote.*]*
lu~luu(-k) *Termanu.* castor-oil-plant (called *damar jarak* in Kupang). Ricinus communis. *[Semantics:* Scientific identification from Heyne (1950:928).*]* (J:330)
lu~luu *Korbafo.*
lu~luu *Bokai.*
lu~luu *Bilbaa.*
lu~luu *Rikou.*
lu~luu-k *Ba'a.*
lu~luu *Tii.*
lu~luu *Dengka.*
lu~luu *Oenale.*
Out-comparisons:
luu *Funai Helong.* casuarina tree.
luu *Dadu'a.* casuarina tree. (Penn 2006:98)
<lolo> *Hawu.* castor-oil-plant. Ricinus communis. (Heyne 1950:928)

***luu2** *PRM.* tears (crying). *Etym:* *luhəq. *[irr. from PMP:* *ə > *u (sporadic assimilation)*]*
luu *Termanu.* tears. *Usage:* Normally compounded with **oe** 'water' in all Rote lects except Bilbaa. (J:330)
luu *Korbafo.*
luu *Bokai.*
luu *Bilbaa.*
luu *Rikou.*
luu *Ba'a.*
luu, luul *Dengka.*
luu *Oenale.*
nuu *Kotos Amarasi.* tears.
maat nuu *Molo.* tears. (M:387)
Out-comparisons:
luun *East Tetun.* tears. (Mo:135)

M - m

***ma** *PRM.* and. *Etym:* *mah.
ma *Termanu.* and. (J:338)
ma *Korbafo.*
ma *Bokai.*
ma *Bilbaa.*
ma *Rikou.*
ma *Ba'a.*
ma *Tii.*
ma *Dengka.*
ma *Oenale.*
=ma *Ro'is Amarasi.* and.
=ma *Kotos Amarasi.* and. *[Form:* This connector has vowel initial forms =**ama** or =**am** after consonant final roots. The final vowel is often deleted yielding =**m**.*]*
ma *Molo.* and. (M:295)

***maa** *Morph:* ***maa-k**. *PRM.* tongue. *Etym:* *maya (PCEMP).
maa-k *Termanu.* tongue. (J:338)
maa-ʔ *Korbafo.*
maa-k *Bokai.*
maa-ʔ *Bilbaa.*
maa-ʔ *Landu.* tongue. (own field notes)
maa-ʔ *Rikou.*
maa-k *Ba'a.*
maa-k *Tii.*
maa-ʔ *Dengka.*
maa-ʔ *Oenale.*
maa-f *Ro'is Amarasi.* tongue.
maa-f *Kotos Amarasi.* tongue.
maa-f *Molo.* tongue (in general). (M:373)
ma~maa-f *Kusa-Manea.* tongue.
Out-comparisons:
mee *Semau Helong.* tongue.

***maɗa** *Rote.* dry up, evaporate. *Etym:* *maja.
mada *Termanu.* dry up, dried up. (J:339)
mada *Korbafo.*
mada *Bokai.*
mada *Bilbaa.*
mada *Rikou.*
mada *Ba'a.*
maɗa *Tii.*
maɗa *Dengka.*
maɗa *Oenale.*
maɗa-ʔ *Dela.* dry.
Out-comparisons:
mara(n) *East Tetun.* dry, dried (not wet); *v.* to dry. (Mo:139)

***maɗo** *PRM.* medicinal plant. *See:* ***moɗe**. *[irr. from PRM:* *a > *o* in Rote (probably influence from ***moɗo**)*]* *[Form:* The evidence from Tetun favours reconstructing penultimate *o with an irregular sound change in Meto rather than reconstructing *a with an irregular sound change in Rote.*]*
modo *Termanu.* medicine, also magic. (J:359)
modo *Korbafo.*
modo *Bokai.*
modo *Bilbaa.*
modo *Rikou.*
modo *Ba'a.*
moɗo *Tii.*
moɗo *Dengka.*
moɗo *Oenale.*
maro *Kotos Amarasi.* tobacco.
malo *Molo.* medicine. (M:302)
Out-comparisons:
modo *East Tetun.* vegetables, leaves or fruit cooked as vegetables. *[irr. from PRM:* *a = *o* correspondence (same as Rote)*]* (Mo:142)

***mae₁** *PRM.* itchy tuber. Amorphophallus species. *Etym:* **maya (pre-RM). *[Semantics:* 'A few species [of *Amorphophallus*] are edible as 'famine foods' after careful preparation to remove irritating chemicals … These small to massive plants grow from a subterranean tuber.' ('Amorphophallus', *Wikipedia.* en.wikipedia.org/wiki/Amorphophallus. Accessed 17 September 2020).*]*

mae *Termanu.* kind of crop that causes itchiness, with thick tubers that are cooked and given to pigs as food. (J:340)
mae *Korbafo.*
mae *Bokai.*
mae *Bilbaa.*
mae *Rikou.*
mae *Ba'a.*
mae *Tii.*
mae *Dengka.*
mae *Oenale.*
mae *Kotos Amarasi.* kind of large taro which makes people itch, it can be used to feed to pigs.
lauk mae(-l) (2) ʔlali_mae *Molo.* 1) *kembang bangkai* = because the flower emits the stink of a corpse. Amorphophallus variabilis. (M:296) 2) kind of taro. (M:260)
Out-comparisons:
maek *Fehan Tetun.* short tree people used to eat when very hungry; you swell up when you eat it, it is **katar** (itchy). It must be rendered **miis** [OE = 'insipid'] before eating. It has a flowering stem about a foot long, which is red at the top, yellow in the middle and green at the bottom.
maek *East Tetun.* plant with edible tubers. (Mo:136)
mai *Tokodede.* taro (both edible and non-edible). (Klamer 2002)
madʒa *Bima.* kind of taro. *[Note:* For *y > *dʒ* compare *bayu > **mbadʒu** 'pound' and *layaR > **lodʒa** 'sail'.*]* (Ismail et al. 1985:85)

***mae₂** *PRM.* shy, ashamed, embarrassed. *Etym:* *ma-həyaq (PCEMP *mayaq).
mae *Termanu.* ashamed, embarrassed. (J:340)
mae *Korbafo.*
mae *Bokai.*
mae *Bilbaa.*
mae *Rikou.*
mae *Ba'a.*
mae *Tii.*
mae *Dengka.*
mae *Oenale.*
n-mae *Kotos Amarasi.* shy, ashamed, embarrassed.
mae *Molo.* ashamed. (M:295)
Out-comparisons:
mae *Semau Helong.* shame, ashamed, shy, embarrassed, bashful.
moe *East Tetun.* be shy, modest, demure, reserved, or coy; *n.* shyness, bashfulness, etc. *[irr. from PMP:* *a > *o]* (Mo:142)

***mafo** *PRM.* cool, shadow. *[Form:* Meto **hafoʔ** 'shadow' and Bima **hawo** 'shadow' point to earlier **kabo. The forms with initial *m* could be reflexes of **ma-kabo.*]*
ma~mafo *Termanu.* become cold, not be warm anymore, of water to the taste, etc. (J:341)
ma~mafo *Bokai.*
ma~mafo *Rikou.*
ma~mafo *Ba'a.*
ma~mafo *Tii.*
mafo~mafo (2) mafo-ʔ *Dengka.* 1) become cold, not be warm anymore, of water to the taste, etc. (J:341) 2) shadow. (J:729)
mafo (2) mafo-ʔ *Oenale.* 1) become cold, not be warm anymore, of water to the taste, etc. (J:341) 2) shadow. (J:729)
na-mafo *Ro'is Amarasi.* shelter, took shade.
mafo|ʔ, hafo|ʔ *Kotos Amarasi.* shadow.
mafo|ʔ *Molo.* shadow. (M:297)
Out-comparisons:
mahan, mahon *East Tetun.* shade, out of the sun. (Mo:136)
mavo (2) rai-mavo *Hawu.* 1) cool. 2) shadow. (J:341)
ma~maho *Dhao.* shade.

<**maü**> *Kambera.* shade, shelter, house; look for shade or shelter. (On:283)
<**mawu**> *Anakalang.*
<**mawo**> *Weyewa. [Note:* also in Mamboru.*]*
<**magho**> *Kodi.*
hau *Ende.* shade.
mawo (2) hawo *Bima.* 1) cool down, no longer hot, shady. (Ismail et al. 1985:87) 2) shadow. (Ismail et al. 1985:39)

***mafu** *PRM.* drunk. *Etym:* *ma-buhək.
mafu-k *Termanu.* drunk. (J:341)
mafu-ʔ *Korbafo.*
mafu-k *Bokai.*
mafu-ʔ *Bilbaa.*
mafu-ʔ *Rikou.*
mafu-k *Ba'a.*
mafu-k *Tii.*
mafu-ʔ *Dengka.*
mafu *Oenale.*
n-mafu *Ro'is Amarasi.* drunk.
n-mafu *Kotos Amarasi.* drunk.
n-mafu *Molo.* drunk. (M:297)
Out-comparisons:
mahu *Semau Helong.* drunk.

***mai** *nRM.* come. *Etym:* *ma(R)i.
mai *Termanu.* come, arrive. (J:341)
mai *Korbafo.*
mai *Bokai.*
mai *Bilbaa.*
mai *Rikou.*
mai *Ba'a.*
mai *Lole.* (Zacharias et al. 2014)
mai *Tii.*
Out-comparisons:
maa *Semau Helong.* come.
mai *East Tetun.* come; *prep.* to, for, here. (Mo:136)
mai *Hawu.* come.

***mali** *Morph:* ***mali-k**. *nRM.* bitter. *[irr. from PRM:* *i > *e* in Meto*]*
mali-ʔ *Rikou.*
mali-ʔ *Ba'a.* bitter. (J:730)
mali-k *Tii.*
<**an-mane**> *Molo.* brackish. *[Form:* This form may have a double final vowel; e.g. **manee**, if so it is unrelated and probably belongs under ***rekət**.*]* (M:305)
Out-comparisons:
maliʔ, madiʔ *Funai Helong.* bitter, salty.
maliʔ *Semau Helong.* bitter.

***malis** *PwRM.* laugh, smile. *Etym:* *malip (PCEMP). *[Form:* expected *p > *s* / _# (§3.5.1.3).*]*
mali *Dengka.* laugh. (J:730)
mali *Oenale.* laugh. (J:730)
n-mani (2) n-mainis *Ro'is Amarasi.* 1) laugh. 2) laugh at someone. *[Form:* As discussed in §3.5.1.3, the transitive form **n-manis** 'laugh at' appears to attest final *p > *s* /i_#. The pair **na-mtau** 'scared' and **na-mtaus** 'scared of' (see ***taku**) also has transitivity marked with final *s* and in this case the final *s* of the transitive form may also be a reflex of the final consonant of PMP *takut.*]*
n-mani (2) n-manis *Kotos Amarasi.* 1) laugh. 2) laugh at someone.
n-mani (2) n-manis *Amfo'an.* 1) laugh. 2) laugh at someone.
ma~main (2) ma~mains=aa *Kusa-Manea.* 1) laugh. 2) laugh at someone.
Out-comparisons:
mali *Semau Helong.* laugh.
mari *Dhao.* laugh at.
mari (2) mare *Hawu.* 1) laugh (pl.). 2) laugh (sg.).

***malus** *PRM.* betel-pepper. *[History:* The non-AN Timor languages have cognates of this form. Heston (2017:82) lists: Makasae **malu**, Makalero **malu**, Fataluku **maluh**, and Oirata **malu**.*]*
malu *Termanu.* betel (fruit or leaf). *Usage:* poetic. (Fox 2016b:31)
maunus *Ro'is Amarasi.* betel-pepper.
manus *Kotos Amarasi.* betel-pepper.

manus *Molo.* betel-pepper. (M:308)
manus *Kusa-Manea.* betel-pepper.
Out-comparisons:
malus *East Tetun.* betel-pepper (Piper Betel) whose leaves are used for chewing with betel nut and lime (**mama**). (Mo:138)
maul *Mambae, South.* betel, can be either the leaf of the pepper. (Grimes et al. 2014b:98)
malu *Ili'uun.* betel-pepper. (dJ:126)
maluh, malhu *Kisar.* betel vine with bean-like fruit.
malus *Welaun.* leaf of the betel vine.
malu *Central Lembata.* betel vine. (Fricke 2015)

***mama** *PRM.* chew betel nut. *Etym:* *mamaq 'chew without intending to swallow, as betel nut; premasticated food to give to an infant; premasticated food'.
mama *Termanu.* chew, especially chew betel nut. (J:344)
mama *Korbafo.*
mama *Bokai.*
mama *Bilbaa.*
mama *Rikou.*
mama *Ba'a.*
mamah *Lole.* chew betel nut. (Zacharias et al. 2014)
mama *Tii.*
mama *Dengka.*
mama *Oenale.*
mama-t *Ro'is Amarasi.* betel quid.
n-mama *Kotos Amarasi.* chew betel.
mama *Molo.* chew betel nut. (M:303)
Out-comparisons:
mama *East Tetun.* wad of **bua**, **malus**, **hoo ahu** (betel nut, betel-pepper, and lime), which is put in the mouth for chewing. (Mo:138)
mama *Kisar.* eat betel.

***mamər** *PRM.* garden, orchard. *[Sporadic:* *ə > e /σ_# in wRote (perhaps *ə > *a > e / _#).*]* *[Form:* Final *r (rather than *n) reconstructed on the basis of Kupang Malay **mamar**.*]*
mame-k *Termanu.* garden made in the bush where one plants coconuts, betel nut trees, betel pepper and so on. (J:344)
mame-ʔ *Korbafo.*
mame-k *Bokai.*
mame-ʔ *Bilbaa.*
mame-ʔ *Rikou.*
mame-k *Ba'a.*
mame-k *Tii.*
mame-ʔ *Dengka.*
mame-ʔ *Oenale.*
maman *Kusa-Manea.* grove, orchard, garden with trees (coconut, betel nut, betel-pepper, etc.).
Out-comparisons:
maman *Helong.* (J:344)
mamar *Kupang Malay.* grove, orchard; garden with trees. (own field notes)

***mamis** *Rote.* sweet. *Etym:* *ma-həmis.
mamis (2) mami *Termanu.* 1) insipid, sweetish, flavourless. 2) insipid, sweetish of taste, sweet or flavourless of water. (J:344)
mami-ʔ *Korbafo.*
mamiʔ *Bokai.*
mami-ʔ *Bilbaa.*
mamis *Rikou.*
mamis *Ba'a.*
mamis *Tii.*
mamis *Dengka.*
mamis *Oenale.*

***mana₁** *PRM.* relativiser. *[History:* Possibly connected with PMP *maRuqanay (PRM ***mane**, and ***mone**). Particularly as reflexes of *maRuqanay have the form ***mana** (as a result of antepenultimate vowel reduction) in some phrases in Rote languages (see ***mane**).*]* *[Semantics:* In the Rote languages **mana** appears to introduce relative clauses with a verb, while **foo** is used for other relative clauses.*]*

mana *Termanu.* used with verbs to form compounds with verbal meaning when the verb is used attributively or independently. (Jonker 1915:106)

mana *Rikou.* relativiser.

mana *Lole.* relativiser. (Zacharias et al. 2014)

mana *Tii.* relativiser; that, who, which. (Grimes et al. 2014a)

mana *Dela.* relativiser.

manaʔ *Ro'is Amarasi.* generic counter/classifier (occurs after the noun and before the numeral). **hiin aan-r=ini manaʔ haa**

manaʔ *Kotos Amarasi.* generic counter/classifier, less often used than in Ro'is Amarasi.

manaʔ *Molo.* counter/classifier. **bia manaʔ meseʔ** a single cow (M:304)

***mana2** *Morph:* ***mana-k**. *Rote.* place.

ma~mana-k (2) mana-k *Termanu.* 1) place in which to store something or put something in. 2) used in certain expressions for **ma~mana-k**. (J:345)

ma~mana-ʔ *Korbafo.*

ma~mana-k *Bokai.*

ma~mana-ʔ *Bilbaa.*

ma~mana-ʔ *Rikou.*

ma~mana-k *Ba'a.*

ma~mana-k *Tii.*

ma~mana-ʔ *Dengka.*

ma~mana-ʔ *Oenale.*

Out-comparisons:

mana *Semau Helong.* place.

mna [mənа] *Wersing.* village. *[Note:* non-Austronesian language of Alor ISO 639-3 [kvw].*]* (Schapper 2017:262)

maˈna: *Sawila.* village. *[Note:* non-Austronesian language of Alor ISO 639-3 [swt].*]* (Schapper 2017:262)

***ma(n)at** *PRM.* orphan.

ana_maa-k *Termanu.* orphan. (J:339)

ana_maa-ʔ *Korbafo.*

ana_maa-k *Bokai.*

ana_maa-ʔ *Bilbaa.*

ana_maa-ʔ *Rikou.*

ana_maa-k *Ba'a.*

ana_maa-k *Tii.*

ana_maa-ʔ *Dengka.*

ana_maat *Oenale.*

ana maat *Dela.* orphan.

komeʔ_manat *Kotos Amarasi.* orphan. *[Note:* Jonker (1908:339) gives Meto **aan manat**.*]*

manat (2) <hau mana> *Molo.* 1) tame. (M:305) 2) planted the, tame tree. (M:304)

***mane** *Rote.* male, man. *Doublet:* ***mone**. *Etym:* *maRuqanay. *[History:* PRM had two reflexes of *maRuqanay: ***mane** and ***mone**, both of which are attested in wRote, Ba'a, and Tii. The meaning of both forms was probably 'male, man' in PRM. Most of Rote lost ***mone**, Meto lost ***mane**, while wRote, Ba'a and Tii differentiated the semantics of the two terms.*]* *[Semantics:* That semantic expansion to include 'king' had not occurred at the level of PRM is indicated by Meto in which **mone** has no hint of this meaning. Instead, PRM ***laʔi** > **naʔi-f** has undergone a similar, though non-identical, semantic expansion. However, the wRote forms in which reflexes of *maRuqanay are combined with apparent reflexes of *Raya (that is, **manae-ʔ/monae-ʔ**, etc.) which have the meaning 'big, great' indicate that expansion to 'big, great' may have occurred, from which 'king' would be easily derived.*]*

mane-k (2) mane (3) mane feu-k *Termanu.* 1) prince, king, princely. 2) male, of animals and certain plants. (J:345) 3) son-in-law. (J:134)
mane-ʔ (2) mane(-ʔ) (3) mana_feu-ʔ *Korbafo.*
mane-k (2) mane (3) mana_feu-k *Bokai.*
mane-ʔ (2) mane (3) mana_feu-ʔ *Bilbaa.*
mane *Landu.* king. (own field notes)
mane-ʔ (2) mane (3) mana_feu-ʔ *Rikou.*
mane-k (2) mane *Ba'a.*
mane-k (2) mane *Tii.*
mane-ʔ (4) manae-ʔ (5) na-manae *Dengka.* 4) big. 5) **bisu=a na-manae** the wound is swollen up (J:735)
mane-ʔ *Oenale.*
mane-ʔ (4) manae-ʔ *Dela.* 1) king. 4) big, important. *[Form:* with variant **monae-ʔ**.*]*
Out-comparisons:
blane (2) blanen *Semau Helong.* 1) male (animal). 2) brother of a woman.
mane *East Tetun.* male, man; masculine. (Mo:139)

maneu** *Morph:* ***maneu-k, *na-maneu.** *PRM.* bright, light. *[Sporadic:* consonant metathesis *mVn > *nVm in PwRM.*] [Form:* PwRM ***nameu.]*
neu-k (2) na-neu *Termanu.* 1) bright, brightness. 2) make clear or pure. (J:394)
neu-ʔ *Korbafo.*
neu-k *Bokai.*
neu-ʔ *Bilbaa.*
neu-ʔ *Rikou.*
neu-k *Ba'a.*
neu-k *Tii.*
meu-ʔ *Dengka.*
meu-ʔ *Oenale.*
meu-ʔ *Dela.* clean.
nmeu (2) meuʔ_sineʔ *Kotos Amarasi.* 1) early morning, in two days. *[Form:* This form has possibly been re-analysed as verbal root with initial *n* interpreted as the 3SG agreement prefix. This may be the reason initial *n* does not occur on the second form.*]* 2) light (n.).
nmeu *Molo.* morning dawns. (M:322)
Out-comparisons:
mniuʔ *Funai Helong.* clean, pure, holy, undefiled.
niuʔ *Semau Helong.* clean, pure, holy, undefiled.

***manu** *PRM.* chicken. *Etym:* *manuk.
manu *Termanu.* fowl, chicken. (J:346)
manu *Korbafo.*
manu *Bokai.*
manu *Bilbaa.*
manu *Rikou.*
manu *Ba'a.*
manu *Tii.*
manu *Dengka.*
manu *Oenale.*
manu *Ro'is Amarasi.* chicken.
manu *Kotos Amarasi.* chicken.
manu *Molo.* chicken. (M:307)
manu *Kusa-Manea.* chicken.
Out-comparisons:
manu *Semau Helong.* chicken.
manu *East Tetun.* bird, a fowl (of any kind). (Mo:139)

***maŋgu₁** *Rote.* tired.
maŋu (2) sota_maŋu-k *Termanu.* 1) tired. (Jonker 1915:53) 2) tiredness. **ana ha~hae huu ana mangu-naa-n seli** s/he rested because s/he was very tired (J:730)
maŋgu *Ba'a.* tired. (J:730)
maŋgu *Tii.*
maŋgu *Dengka.*
maŋgu *Oenale.*
Out-comparisons:
<mànggilu> *Kambera.* exhausted, tired. *[Note:* also in Mangili and Lewa.*]* (On:272)
<màgilu> *Anakalang.*

<mànggula> *Mamboru.*
<manggolo> *Kodi.*

***maŋgu**$_2$ *Rote.* dry fruit skin. *Etym:* *ma-Raŋu 'dry' (*ma-Raŋu only reconstructed for PCEMP. *Raŋu reconstructed for PMP). *[minority from PMP:* *ŋ > *ŋg*] [irr. from PRM:* *m > *b* in all Rote except Korbafo, Bokai, and Bilbaa; *ŋg > *nd* in wRote and Tii*] [Sporadic:* antepenultimate vowel reduction in Termanu, Bokai, Bilbaa, Rikou, and Dengka.*] [Semantics:* Ross (2003:227) reconstructs POc *maRaŋo/*Raŋo with the meaning 'become withered (of vegetation)'.*]*
baŋa_lou-k *Termanu.* dry fruit skin; also the ash of the burnt skin of a fruit (normally the fruit of the **nitas** tress, Sterculia foetidea), which is used to make the thread for weaving a little yellow or less white. (J:29)
maŋo_lou-ʔ *Korbafo.*
maŋa_lou-k *Bokai.*
maŋa_lou-ʔ *Bilbaa.*
baka_rou-ʔ *Rikou.*
baŋgu_lou-k *Ba'a.*
ɓandu_rou-k *Tii.*
banda_lou-ʔ *Dengka.*
ɓandu_rou-ʔ *Oenale.*
Out-comparisons:
maŋu *Hawu.* be dry. (J:29)
maŋo *Bima.* dry. (Ismail et al. 1985:86)

***masi** *PRM.* salty, salt. *Etym:* *ma-qasin.
masi (2) masi-k *Termanu.* 1) salty. 2) salt. (J:347f)
masi *Korbafo.*
masi *Bokai.*
masi *Bilbaa.*
masi *Rikou.*
masi *Ba'a.*
masi *Tii.*
masi *Dengka.*
mas͡i *Oenale.*
ma͡isi|k *Ro'is Amarasi.* salt.
masi|k *Kotos Amarasi.* salt.
masi|ʔ *Molo.* salt. *[Note:* Jonker (1908:347) gives Meto **masi** = 'salty'.*]* (M:310)
Out-comparisons:
masin *Semau Helong.* insipid. *[Note:* **sila** = 'salt'.*]*
masin *East Tetun.* salt. (Mo:139)

***masu** *Morph:* ***masu-k**. *PRM.* smoke. *Etym:* *ma-qasu (PCMP).
masu-k *Termanu.* smoke of fire, (tobacco); moreover: steam of hot water, of hot viands, exhaled vapour (as visible in cold weather), vapour which rises up out of the ground, mist, also drifting dust. (J:348)
masu-ʔ *Korbafo.*
masu-k *Bokai.*
masu-ʔ *Bilbaa.*
masu-ʔ *Rikou.*
masu-k *Ba'a.*
masu-k *Tii.*
masu-ʔ *Dengka.*
masu-ʔ *Oenale.*
masu|ʔ *Ro'is Amarasi.* smoke.
masu|ʔ *Kotos Amarasi.* smoke. *[Note:* **sumaʔ** 'steam, vapour'.*]*
masu|ʔ *Molo.* smoke. (M:389)
Out-comparisons:
ai mahun *Ili'uun.* smoke. (dJ:111)
ai mahu *Kisar.* smoke.

***mata**$_1$ *Morph:* ***mata-k**. *PRM.* eye, face. *Etym:* *mata.
mata-k *Termanu.* eye, face. (J:348f)
mata-ʔ *Korbafo.*
mata-k *Bokai.*
mata-ʔ *Bilbaa.*
mata-ʔ *Landu.* eye, face. (own field notes)
mata-ʔ *Rikou.*
mata-k *Ba'a.*
mata-k *Tii.*
mata-ʔ *Dengka.*
mata-ʔ *Oenale.*
mata-f *Ro'is Amarasi.* eye.
mata-f (2) et mata-n *Kotos Amarasi.* 1) eye. 2) in front of.

mata-f *Molo.* eye (in general), a spy. (M:312)
mata-f *Kusa-Manea.* eye.
Out-comparisons:
mata *Semau Helong.* eye.
mata-n *East Tetun.* the eyes. (Mo:140)
mata *Welaun.* eye.
mada *Hawu.* eye.

***mata₂** *Morph:* ***mata-k**. *PRM.* raw, uncooked. *Etym:* *ma-hataq (Blust and Trussel (ongoing) make several reconstructions with similar forms and semantics.). *[Sporadic:* *a > *e* / _# in* wRM.*]*
mata-k *Termanu.* raw, not well-done, (rarely: not cooked). (J:350)
mata-ʔ *Korbafo.*
mata-k *Bokai.*
mata-ʔ *Bilbaa.*
ma~mata-ʔ *Rikou.*
mata-k *Ba'a.*
mata-k *Tii.*
mate-ʔ *Dengka.*
mate-ʔ *Oenale.*
nau|maet *Ro'is Amarasi.* green.
n-mate (2) ma|mateʔ *Kotos Amarasi.* 1) raw. 2) green.
mate-l *Amfo'an.* green, blue.
<mate> *Molo.* green, unripe, uncooked. (M:313)
Out-comparisons:
taa *Semau Helong.* raw, unripe, rare, crude.
matak *East Tetun.* green, still growing, immature; raw (not cooked), new, fresh (not stale); inexperienced. (Mo:140)

***mate** *PRM.* die, dead; thoroughly, extremely. *Etym:* *matay 'die; dead'.
mate (2) mate~mate *Termanu.* 1) die. 2) absolutely, thoroughly. (J:351)
mate *Korbafo.*
mate *Bokai.*
mate *Bilbaa.*
mate *Rikou.*
mate *Ba'a.*
mate *Tii.*
mate *Dengka.*
mate *Oenale.*
n-mate *Ro'is Amarasi.* die.
n-mate *Kotos Amarasi.* die, dead; extremely, very.
n-mate *Molo.* died. (M:313)
maet *Kusa-Manea.* die.
Out-comparisons:
mate *Semau Helong.* die.
mate *East Tetun.* die; to extinguish (fire); to wither, die (plants); to stop, or cease (machinery); dead, stopped. (Mo:140)
made *Hawu.* die, dead; thoroughly, forcefully.

***mau** *CERM.* kind of plant. *[Sporadic:* glottal stop insertion in Meto.*]* *[Semantics:* vague Rote semantics weakens reconstruction.*]*
mau *Termanu.* an unidentified plant or tree. *Usage:* poetic. *[Semantics:* Forms a parallel pair with **pole** (also an unidentified plant).*]* (Fox 2016b:33)
maʔu *Fatule'u.* grass.
maʔu *Molo.* grass, weed. (M:314)

***maus** *PRM.* tame, docile, domesticated. *Etym:* *maRus (own reconstruction) (PCEMP).
ka-maus (2) ka-mau (3) mata=n mau~mau *Termanu.* 1) tame, domestic. 2) be domestic. 3) he is not shy by nature (said of a person). (J:352)
ka-mau-ʔ *Korbafo.*
ka-mau-k *Bokai.*
ka-mau-ʔ *Bilbaa.*
ma~maus *Rikou.*
ka-maus *Ba'a.*
ka-mau-k *Tii.*
ma~maus *Dengka.*
ma~maus *Oenale.*
na-mausa-b (2) n-mau *Kotos Amarasi.* 1) domesticate. 2) domesticated, tame.
maus *Molo.* tame. (M:10)

Out-comparisons:

hmoa *Semau Helong.* tame, docile; tame. *[Form:* Connecting this form with *maRus requires irr. *R > Ø (expect *l*) and irr. *a > *o*. It may thus be a chance similarity.*]*

maus *Fehan Tetun.* tame (of animals, birds — not plants, people); can apply to wild animals too if they are unafraid of people (e.g. cuscus).

maus *East Tetun.* meek, mild, tame, domesticated. (Mo:140)

mhau *Waima'a.* meek, tame.

maru *Ili'uun.* tame. (dJ:127)

maru *Kisar.* tame animals.

mau *Bima.* tame, domesticated, of an animal; mild, gentle, of a person; also: accustomed to something. (Jonker 1893:51; Ismail et al. 1985:86)

maho, mahu *Buru.* tame, safe, comfortable, secure in the situation. (Grimes and Grimes 2020:578)

mamalu *Saparua.* tame, domesticated. *[Note:* language of Lease Islands ISO 639-3 [spr].*]* (van Hoëvell 1877:86, 111)

mamaru *Haruku.* tame, domesticated. (van Hoëvell 1877:86, 111)

(ma)maru *Kamarian.* soft, slow. (van Ekris 1864:306, 309)

mau *Alune. [Note:* language of west Seram, central Maluku ISO 639-3 [alp].*]* (van Ekris 1864:309)

malu *Asilulu. [Note:* also in Hatusua Kaibobo.*]* (van Ekris 1864:309)

ŋmʷa~ŋmʷaru *Mota.* docile, manageable, tame. *[Note:* language of north Vanuatu ISO 639-3 [mtt].*]* (Codrington and Palmer 1896:66)

momʷau *Lewo.* tame, quiet; heal over, of sore. *[Note:* language of south Vanuatu ISO 639-3 [lww].*]* (Malcolm Ross pers. comm. March 2017)

***mea** *PRM.* red. *Etym:* *ma-iRaq. *[Sporadic:* *a > *e* / _# in wRM; *VVʔ > VʔV in Amarasi (perceptual metathesis).*]*

mea *Termanu.* red (only used in particular expressions): **meŋe mea**, kind of reddish snake; **kuta mea**, kind of red tub; **dela mea**, kind of red fabric. *[Note:* **pilas** = 'red'.*]* (J:353)

mea *Korbafo.*

mea *Bokai.*

mea *Bilbaa.*

mea *Rikou.*

mea *Ba'a.*

mea *Tii.*

mee *Dengka.*

mee *Oenale.*

meʔe *Ro'is Amarasi.* red.

meʔe *Kotos Amarasi.* red.

meeʔ *Amanuban/Amanatun.* red.

Out-comparisons:

mea *Semau Helong.* red, brown. *[irr. from PMP:* *R > Ø (expect *l*)*]*

mean *East Tetun.* red (all shades). (Mo:140)

mea *Hawu.* red, reddish-brown.

***meɗa** *Morph:* ***na-meɗa-k**. *Rote.* wake up.

na-meda-k *Termanu.* wake up from sleep. (J:353)

na-meda-ʔ *Korbafo.*

na-meda-k *Bokai.*

na-meda-ʔ *Bilbaa.*

na-meda-ʔ *Rikou.*

na-meda-k *Ba'a.*

na-meɗa-k *Tii.*

na-meda-ʔ *Oenale.*

Out-comparisons:

melaŋ *Semau Helong.* restless, stay awake (to comfort the family of the dead).

***mee** *Morph:* ***na-ka-mee**. *PRM.* bleat. *[Semantics:* onomatopoeia.*]*
na-ka-mee *Termanu.* bleat. (J:352)
na-ka-mee *Korbafo.*
na-ka-mee *Bokai.*
na-ka-mee *Bilbaa.*
na-mee *Rikou.*
na-ka-mee *Ba'a.*
na-ka-mee *Tii.*
na-ʔa-mee *Dengka.*
na-ʔa-mee *Oenale.*
na-ʔ|mee *Ro'is Amarasi.* bleat, like a goat.
na-ʔ|meʔe *Kotos Amarasi.* bleat, like a goat.
Out-comparisons:
mee *Semau Helong.* sheep's cry.

***mehi** *Morph:* ***na-la-mehi**. *PRM.* dream. *Etym:* *ma-hipi (Blust and Trussel (ongoing) reconstruct an alternate PCEMP form *mipi, presumably from *ma-hipi with deletion of the antepenultimate vowel. The reflexes in Timor attest earlier **mepi with *ahi > *ai > *e, thus *ma-hipi > **maipi > **mepi. Blust and Trussel (ongoing) also reconstruct PAN *Səpi, with the PMP reflex *həpi. The only MP form given supporting PMP *həpi is Tetun **mehi**. However, PMP *ə > *o* is regular in Tetun, thus showing that Tetun **mehi** is from earlier **mepi < PMP *ma-hipi. Whatever the validity of PAN *Səpi, putative PMP *həpi is probably spurious.). *[Sporadic:* consonant metathesis *lm > *ml > *mn* in most Meto.*] [Form:* The source of the initial *la in the verbal forms is currently unknown. Jonker (1915:136f) gives a number of other forms with a fossilised **la-** prefix.*]*
na-la-meʔi (2) meʔi-s *Termanu.* 1) dream. 2) dream (n.). (J:354)
na-la-meʔi *Korbafo.*
na-la-meʔi *Bokai.*
na-la-mei *Bilbaa.*
na-la-mei *Landu.* dream. (own field notes)
na-la-mei *Rikou.*
na-la-meʔi *Ba'a.*
na-la-meʔi *Tii.*
na-la-meni, na-la-mein *Dengka.*
na-la-mein *Oenale.*
na-la-mei-n (2) mei-t *Dela.* 1) dream (v.). 2) dream (n.).
na-mnei *Ro'is Amarasi.* dream.
na-mnei (2) mnei-t *Kotos Amarasi.* 1) dream (v.). 2) dream (n.).
na-mnai, na-mnae *Kopas.* dream.
u-nmaiʔ *Molo.* I dream. (M:348)
na-mnei *Kusa-Manea.* dream.
Out-comparisons:
meʔi *Fehan Tetun.* dream.
mehi *East Tetun.* dream; *n.* a dream. (Mo:141)

***mela** *Morph:* ***mela-k**. *Rote.* flea. *Etym:* *qatiməla. *[Sporadic:* *a > *e* /_# in wRote.*] [Form:* compounded with **teke** in nRote.*]*
teke/mela-k *Termanu.* flea. *[Form:* Initial **teke** occurs with at least two other biting insect terms, **tekefia-k** 'tick', **tekefua-k** 'kind of wasp'. It also occurs with **tekelaba-k** 'house gecko'.*]* (J:614)
teke/mela-ʔ *Korbafo.*
teke/mela-k *Bokai.*
teke/mela-ʔ *Bilbaa.*
teke/mela-ʔ *Landu.* flea. (own field notes)
teke/mela-k *Ba'a.*
mele-ʔ *Dengka.*
mele-ʔ *Oenale.*
Out-comparisons:
kmelaʔ *Funai Helong.* flea.
hmela *Helong.* (J:614)
(k)mela *East Tetun.* flea. (Mo:112,141)
taməla *Hawu.* (J:614)

***meni₁** *PRM.* fragrant, aromatic. *Etym:* **məŋi(R) (pre-RM). *[Form:* Final pre-RM **R is attested by Dadu'a and Ende. Ende, as a member of Central Flores, has sporadic lowering of high vowels to mid before *R (Elias 2018:98f). On the other hand, Rote-Meto also should undergo *i > *e* /_*R, thus providing evidence against final pre-RM **R.*] [History:* Possibly connected with PMP *baŋəhih 'fragrant' with irr. *b > **m and sporadic antepenultimate *a > **ə. (This sporadic change is also attested in *panahik > ***hene** 'climb' and *saŋəlaR > ***seŋa** 'fry'.) If the evidence for final **R in **məŋi(R) were strengthened, then the connection with PMP *baŋəhih would become even more tenuous.*]*

meni *Termanu.* fragrant, aromatic. (J:355f)

meni *Korbafo.*

meni *Bokai.*

meni *Bilbaa.*

meni *Rikou.*

meni *Ba'a.*

meni *Tii.*

meni *Dengka.*

ma-ʔa-meni-ʔ *Oenale.*

foo meni *Kotos Amarasi.* fragrant.

foo meni *Molo.* fragrant. (M:318)

fu/miin *Kusa-Manea.* fragrant.

Out-comparisons:

miŋis *Semau Helong.* delicious, tasty, pleasant, aromatic.

meki *Mambae, South.* fragrant (of flowers, food). (Grimes et al. 2014b:32)

kai-kmeni *Waima'a.* sandalwood.

ai-kmenih *Dadu'a.* sandalwood. (Penn 2006:36)

vuməŋi *Hawu.* fragrant, aromatic.

ʔare məŋe *Ende.* kind of fragrant paddy.

***meni2** *PnMeto.* sandalwood. Sandalum album. *[Form:* Given the importance of sandalwood as an early item of trade, this could be an early loan between Meto and Tetun before Meto *l > *n.]*

meni *Kotos Amarasi.* sandalwood tree. *[Note:* The Meto term for 'fragrant' is **foo meni** the second element of which is plausibly from **meni** 'sandalwood'. There is independent evidence that Meto ***meni** is from earlier **məŋi(R).*]*

hau meni *Molo.* sandalwood. Sandalum album. (M:318)

Out-comparisons:

kameli(n) *East Tetun.* sandalwood genus. Santalum. (Mo:100)

***mendu** *PRM.* crush, grind. *[irr. from PRM:* *nd > *ŋg* in Oenale*] [Form:* An alternate solution would be to reconstruct ***meŋgu** and posit irr. *ŋg > *nd* in Rikou and Dengka. Occam's razor currently favours ***mendu** with only one irregular sound change. The Kotos Amarasi form would be regular from both ***mendu** or ***meŋgu**. A Ro'is Amarasi reflex could decide between the two alternate reconstructions as it has *nd > *r* but *ŋg > *k.]*

me~mendu *Tii.* grind the teeth. (J:732)

na-la-me~mendu *Dengka.* break into pieces by rubbing. (J:732)

me~meŋgu *Oenale.* grind the teeth. (J:732)

n-meku *Kotos Amarasi.* crush.

***meŋge** *PRM.* kind of red snake. *[Form:* Jonker (1908) connects the initial **me** with ***mea** 'red'.*]*

meŋe *Termanu.* kind of reddish snake. (J:355)

meŋe *Korbafo.*

meŋe *Bilbaa.*

meke *Landu.* snake. (own field notes)

meke *Rikou.*

meŋge *Ba'a.*

meŋge *Tii.*

meŋge *Dengka.*

meŋge *Oenale.*

uu/meke *Ro'is Amarasi.* kind of snake. *[Form:* The source of initial **uu** is currently unknown. It also is attested in Molo **uʔsao** 'viper' given in Middelkoop (1972:592), see ***sao**.]

u/meke *Kotos Amarasi.* non-poisonous grass snake, typically red in colour.

u/meke *Molo.* rat snake. (M:587)

u/meek *Kusa-Manea.* snake.

Out-comparisons:

°**mege** *Dhao.* snake (generic). *Borrowed from:* wRote **meŋge**.

***meo1** *PRM.* cat. *Etym:* **meoŋ (pre-RM). *[Semantics:* onomatopoeia.*]*

meo *Termanu.* cat. (J:356)

meo *Korbafo.*

meo *Bokai.*

meo *Bilbaa.*

meo *Rikou.*

meo *Ba'a.*

meo *Tii.*

meo *Dengka.*

meo *Oenale.*

meo *Ro'is Amarasi.* cat.

meo *Kotos Amarasi.* cat.

meo *Molo.* cat. (M:319)

Out-comparisons:

meo *Dhao.*

meo *Hawu.*

meo-ŋao *Ngadha.* cat. (Djawanai 1995:Part 2, 332)

meoŋ *Sika.* cat. (Pareira and Lewis 1998:133)

meoŋ *Manggarai.* cat. (Verheijen 1967:319)

meoŋ *Balinese.* cat. *[Note:* language of Bali ISO 639-3 [ban].*]* (Bawa and Clynes 1995:Part 2, 332)

meoŋ *Sasak.* cat. *[Note:* language of Lombok ISO 639-3 [sas].*]* (Ali 1995:Part 2, 332)

meoŋ *Bugis.* cat. (Abas 1995:Part 2, 332)

meoŋ *Coastal Konjo.* cat. *[Note:* language of South Sulawesi ISO 639-3 [kjc].*]* (Friberg 1995:Part 2, 332)

***meo2** *PnMeto.* warrior. *[History:* This term was probably spread by contact due to the cultural meaning, but the exact direction of spread cannot be confidently identified.*]*

meo *Kotos Amarasi.* warrior.

meo *Molo.* head-hunter. (M:318)

Out-comparisons:

meo *Semau Helong.* war chief; war lord.

meo *East Tetun.* desperado, thief, raiding warriors, etc. (Mo:141)

***meras** *PRM.* sick. *Etym:* *hapəjəs. *[irr. from PMP:* *ə > *a*]* *[minority from PMP:* *j > *r (expect *ɗ)*]* *[Form:* Medial *j and final *ə cannot regularly account for the Keka or Helong reflexes thus indicating irregular **ma-pəjəs > pre-RM **ma-hədas.*]*

mela_dai-k *Keka.* curse against an animal. (J:731)

mela *Dengka.* sick. (J:731)

mera *Oenale.* sick. (J:731)

meens *Ro'is Amarasi.* sickness.

menas (2) na-mena *Kotos Amarasi.* 1) sickness. 2) sick, painful. *[Form:* regular final consonant deletion to derive verb from noun.*]*

menas (2) na-mena *Molo.* 1) sickness. 2) sick. (M:318)

Out-comparisons:

heda *Semau Helong.* sick. Implies feverish or fluish. Not all diseases are **heda**.

hera *Bolok Helong.* sick.

moras *East Tetun.* sick, in poor health; ill, sick, unwell; *n.* sickness, disease, ailment. (Mo:143)

°**moras** *Mambae, South.* sick, pain, hurt. *Borrowed from:* Tetun (shown by irr. *ə = *o* correspondence). (Grimes et al. 2014b:32)

pəɗa *Hawu.* sick.

pa~pəda, papəɖa *Dhao.* sick.

***mesa** *PRM.* alone. *Etym:* *ma-əsa. *[Sporadic:* *a > *e* / _# in Meto.*]*
mesa *Termanu.* alone. (J:356)
mesa *Korbafo.*
mesa *Bokai.*
mesa *Bilbaa.*
mesa *Rikou.*
mesa *Ba'a.*
mesa *Tii.*
mesa *Dengka.*
mesa *Oenale.*
meseʔ *Ro'is Amarasi.* one.
meseʔ (2) n-mese *Kotos Amarasi.* 1) one, single. 2) be alone.
meseʔ *Molo.* one. (M:319)
meseʔ *Kusa-Manea.* one.
Out-comparisons:
mesa *Semau Helong.* one, as.
mesa(k) *East Tetun.* only, alone, solely. *[irr. from PMP:* *ə > *e* (expect *o*)*]* (Mo:141)

***metam** *PMeto.* black, civet. *Etym:* *ma-qitəm 'black; deep blue'. *[Semantics:* Balle and Cameron (2014) ascribe the etymology of Helong **maat mitaŋ** 'civet' (lit. 'black eye') to the dark fur around the eyes, its nocturnal behaviour, and ability to see at night. A similar explanation for the polysemy of Meto ***metam** is likely.*]*
meten *Ro'is Amarasi.* black; civet.
metan *Kotos Amarasi.* black; civet.
metan *Molo.* black; civet. (M:321)
metom *Kusa-Manea.* black; civet. *[Sporadic:* *a > *o* / _m (compare PRM *hendam > PMeto ***eram** > **ekam** in Upper Manulea hamlet > **ekom** is Uabau' hamlet).*]*
Out-comparisons:
mitaŋ *Funai Helong.* black. *[Note:* **maat mitaŋ** 'civet' lit. 'black eye'.*]*
mitaŋ *Semau Helong.* black. *[Note:* **maat mitaŋ** 'civet' lit. 'black eye'.*]*
metan *East Tetun.* black. *[Note:* **laku** = 'civet'.*]* (Mo:141)

***meti** *PRM.* low, of the tide. *Etym:* *ma-qəti.
meti *Termanu.* low tide, tide in general, the part of a beach that is dry at low tide. (J:357)
meti *Korbafo.*
meti *Bokai.*
meti *Bilbaa.*
meti *Rikou.*
meti *Ba'a.*
meti *Tii.*
meti *Dengka.*
meti *Oenale.*
n-meiti *Kotos Amarasi.* dry up (of water, including rivers).
n-meti *Molo.* dried up, low-tide. (M:322)
Out-comparisons:
miti *Semau Helong.* dry up, recede.
moti *East Tetun.* dry up, cease running (a current of water). (Mo:143)
meki *Kisar.* low tide.

***meto** *PwRM.* dry.
meto-ʔ *Dengka.* dry, e.g. like wood. (J:733)
meto-ʔ *Oenale.* dry, e.g. like wood. (J:733)
meto *Dela.* be(come) dry.
meto|ʔ *Ro'is Amarasi.* dry.
meto|ʔ (2) n-meto *Kotos Amarasi.* 1a) dry. 1b) indigenous, native, Meto. The second sense probably comes from phrases such as **atoin paah metoʔ** 'people of the dry land'. 2) be(come) dry.
meto|ʔ *Molo.* dry. (M:322)
ma~meto|ʔ *Kusa-Manea.* dry.

***midu** *Rote.* saliva, spit out. *Doublet:* ***ŋinu**. *Etym:* *qizuR 'saliva, spittle' (PWMP). *[irr. from PMP:* *z > *d (expect *d)*] [irr. from PRM:* vowel metathesis in nRote *iCu > *uCi] [Form:* The source of initial *m in ***midu** is not clear. It may be from the prefix *ma- though initial *maqi would regularly yield *me*. Kedang has **iyuʔ** ~ **miyuʔ** attesting an optional initial *m (Samely 1991:221), and some varieties of Lamaholot have a form attesting earlier *təmidu: e.g. Lamalera **təmiro**, Lewokukun **təmidʒu** (Keraf 1978).*]* *[History:* Rote ***midu** is cognate with PMeto ***paŋinu** and both are ultimately probably connected with *qizuR, but it is not possible to reconcile the initial *m = *paŋ correspondence and combine them into one set attesting a single PRM reconstruction.*]*

mudi *Termanu.* spit, spit out. (J:364)
mudi *Korbafo.*
mudi *Bokai.*
mudi *Bilbaa.*
mudi *Rikou.*
mudi *Ba'a.*
muɗi *Tii.*
milu *Dengka.* saliva, spit out. (J:364, 733)
miru *Oenale.* saliva, spit out. (J:364, 733)
Out-comparisons:
ilu *Hawu.* saliva, spittle.
m-miri (2) miri~miri *Onin.* 1) spit (imperative form). (Smits and Voorhoeve 1992:118) 2) saliva. *[Note:* language of the Bomberai Peninsula ISO 639-3 [oni].*]* *[Form:* regular PMP *u > *i* / _(C)#, but irregular *R > Ø (expect *R > *r*).*]* (Smits and Voorhoeve 1992:94)

***mii** *Morph:* ***ka-mii**. *PRM.* urine. *Etym:* *kəmiq. *[irr. from PRM:* *ii > *oe* in nRote (probably influence from **oe** 'water')*]*
moe *Termanu.* make water, urinate. (J:360)
moe *Korbafo.*
moe *Bokai.*
moe *Bilbaa.*
moe *Rikou.*
moe *Ba'a.*
moe *Tii.*
mii *Dengka.* piss. (J:733)
mii *Oenale.* piss. (J:733)
mii (2) miis *Dela.* 1) urinate. 2) urine.
k|mii *Ro'is Amarasi.* urine.
k|mii (2) na-k|miʔi *Kotos Amarasi.* 1) urine. 2) urinate.
mii *Amanuban/Amanatun.* urine.
mii-dʒ *Kopas.* urine.
mii-dʒ *Fatule'u.* urine.
<mi> *Molo.* urine. (M:323)
k|mii-r *Timaus.* urine.
mii (2) ma~mii-f *Kusa-Manea.* 1) urine. 2) bladder.
Out-comparisons:
mii *Semau Helong.* urine.
mii (2) mii-n *East Tetun.* 1) urinate (more polite to say **liʔur besik**). 2) urine. (Mo:142)
n-omi *Kisar.* pee.

***mina** *PRM.* delicious, comfortable, nice; fat, grease, oil. *Etym:* *miñak 'fat, grease; ointment'.
mina (2) ma-mina (3) balamina *Termanu.* 1) oil, melted fat. (J:357) 2) fatty from there = **malada** ['delicious'] (with which it is usually combined), tasty. 3) delicious. (J:358)
mina *Korbafo.*
mina *Bokai.*
mina *Bilbaa.*
mina *Rikou.*
mina *Ba'a.*
mina *Tii.*
mina *Dengka.*
mina *Oenale.*
minaʔ (2) na-mina *Kotos Amarasi.* 1) oil. 2) comfortable, nice, delicious.
minaʔ (2) na-miin *Molo.* 1) fat, oil. 2) delicious. *[Form:* metathesised form of **na-mina**.*]* (M:323)
(2) na-mian *Kusa-Manea.* delicious. *[Form:* metathesised form of **na-mina**.*]*
Out-comparisons:
mina *Semau Helong.* oil, fat.

mina *East Tetun.* oil, fat, grease. (Mo:142)

namina *Kisar.* delicious, sweet.

miina *Wetan.* sweet. *[Note:* language of southwest Maluku, member of Luang language/ dialect cluster ISO 639-3 [lex].*]* (de Josselin de Jong 1987)

***miu** *Morph:* ***na-ka-miu**. *PRM.* whistle (through the air).

na-ka-miu *Termanu.* whistle like a fired bullet. (J:358)

na-ka-miu *Korbafo.*

na-ka-miu *Bokai.*

na-ka-miu *Bilbaa.*

na-miu *Rikou.*

na-ka-muu *Ba'a.*

na-ʔa-muu *Dengka.*

na-ʔa-muu *Oenale.*

na-k|miu *Meto.* (J:358)

Out-comparisons:

<miu> (2) <kamiu> *Kambera.* whizzing sound of a thrown stone. *[Note:* also in Mangili.*]* (On: 291, 155)

<mi'u> *Lewa.*

<piu> *Weyewa.*

***m|kaka** *PnMeto.* open-mouthed, agape. *Etym:* *ŋaŋa. *[minority from PMP:* *ŋ (> *ŋ) > *k; *ŋ (> *ŋ) > *k (expect *n)*]*

na-m|kaka *Kotos Amarasi.* open-mouthed, agape, speechless, amazed.

na-m|kaka *Molo.* open the mouth, amazed. (M:324)

***mneas** *PMeto.* husked rice. *Etym:* *bəRas 'rice between harvesting and cooking; husked rice'. *[Note:* The Meto and Kemak forms both have irregular initial *b > *m* and are probably borrowed before Meto underwent *r > *l > *n*. The direction of borrowing is unclear.*]* *[minority from PMP:* *R (> *r) *n*]* *[Sporadic:* consonant metathesis *əR > *ne.*]* *[History:* Various irregularities in nearly all languages indicate that reflexes of *bəRas have spread by contact.*]*

mneas *Ro'is Amarasi.* husked rice.

mneas, mnees *Kotos Amarasi.* husked rice.

mnees *Kusa-Manea.* hulled rice.

Out-comparisons:

ael beas *Semau Helong.* uncooked rice. *[irr. from PMP:* *R > Ø (expect *l*)*]*

foos *East Tetun.* uncooked de-husked rice. *[History:* This form is mostly regular from *bəRas.*]* (Mo:36)

resa brea *Tokodede.* rice plant. (Klamer 2002)

mreas, meras *Kemak.* rice (husked, uncooked). *[irr. from PMP:* *b > *m*; *R > *r* (expect Ø)*]*

baa breas *Galolen.* rice (husked, uncooked). *[irr. from PMP:* *R > *r* (expect Ø)*]*

***moɗe** *Rote.* tobacco. *See:* ***maɗo**.

mode *Termanu.* tobacco, both the plant and readymade for use. (J:359)

mode *Korbafo.*

mode *Bokai.*

mode *Bilbaa.*

mode *Rikou.*

mode *Ba'a.*

moɗe *Tii.*

moɗe *Dengka.*

moɗe *Oenale.*

***moɗo** *Morph:* ***moɗo-k**. *PRM.* yellow, green. *Etym:* **mozo (pre-RM). *[History:* possibly connected with PMP *muda 'young (of fruits); immature; light (of colours)'.*]*

mo~modo-k *Termanu.* yellow, also: green, blue, (in this meaning not in all varieties of Rote); pale, yellowish of the face. (J:360)

mo~modo-ʔ *Korbafo.*

mo~modo-k *Bokai.*

mo~modo-ʔ *Bilbaa.*
mo~modo-ʔ *Rikou.*
mo~modo-k *Ba'a.*
mo~moɗo-k *Tii.*
mo~moɗo-ʔ *Dengka.*
mo~moɗo-ʔ *Oenale.*
moɗo-ʔ *Dela.* blue, green.
moro|ʔ *Ro'is Amarasi.* yellow.
moro|ʔ (2) k|moro-f *Kotos Amarasi.* 1) yellow. 2) egg yolk.
molo|ʔ (2) k|molo|ʔ *Molo.* 1) yellow. (M:329) 2) egg yolk. (M:222)
moroʔ *Kusa-Manea.* yellow.
Out-comparisons:
hmolo *Semau Helong.* poisonous green snake species. *[Form:* Jonker (1908:360) gives Helong **liti molo** 'brass'.*]*
modok (2) samodo *East Tetun.* 1) yellow, green (Mo:142). 2) green tree snake. (Mo:166)
mosoŋ *Ili'uun.* blue, green. (dJ:128)
mosoŋ *Perai.* green. *[Note:* language of Wetar Island ISO 639-3 [wet].*]* (Hinton 2000:122)
moso *Tugun.* green. (Hinton 2000:122)
(mo~)moti *Roma.* green. *[Form:* Taber (1993:418) has Roma [momoʧe], which would be underlying **mo~moti** + **-e** '3SG' → **momotye** according to the analysis in Steven (1991).*]* (Steven 1991:42)
mot~motni *Luang.* green. *[Note:* language of southwest Maluku ISO 639-3 [lex].*]* (Taber 1993:418)
moro *Bima.* greenish. (Jonker 1893:52)
<múru> *Kambera.* green, fresh, young. (On:295)
<moru> *Anakalang.* *[Note:* also in Mamboru.*]*
<moro> *Kodi.* *[Note:* also in Weyewa.*]*

***mofa** *PRM.* have grey hair. *Etym:* *ma-quban.
mofa *Termanu.* have grey hair or become grey. (J:360)
mofa *Korbafo.*
mofa *Bokai.*
mofa *Bilbaa.*
mofa *Rikou.*
mofa *Ba'a.*
mofa *Tii.*
mofa *Dengka.*
mofa *Oenale.*
mofaʔ *Kotos Amarasi.* grey hair, white hair.
<na-k|mofa> (2) <ʔnaak mofa> (3) <nono mofa> *Molo.* 1) greybeard. 2) kind of bird. 3) kind of liana with a white flower. (M:327)

***mofu** *PRM.* fall. *[irr. from PRM:* *f > (?*h) > *ʔ* in Rote*]*
moʔu *Termanu.* fall, fall out. (J:363)
moʔu *Ba'a.*
moʔu *Dengka.*
moʔu *Oenale.*
n-mofu *Ro'is Amarasi.* fall.
n-mofu *Kotos Amarasi.* fall.
n-mofu *Molo.* falls. (M:328)
mouf (2) mofut *Kusa-Manea.* 1) fall. 2) drop.
Out-comparisons:
mou *Mambae, South.* fall (over), fall (down), fall (off). *[irr. from PRM:* *f = Ø correspondence*]* (Grimes et al. 2014b:33)
mou *Bima.* fall. (Ismail et al. 1985:92)

***mola** *Morph:* ***mola-k**. *PRM.* node, joint. *[irr. from PRM:* *l > Ø Meto; glottal stop insertion in Amarasi*]*
mola-k *Termanu.* joint, node. (J:361)
(mole-ʔ ?) *Korbafo.*
mola-k *Bokai.*
mola-ʔ *Bilbaa.*
mola-ʔ *Rikou.*
mola-k *Ba'a.*
mola-k *Tii.*

mola-ʔ *Dengka.*
mola-ʔ *Oenale.*
moʔo|k *Kotos Amarasi.* section of something long, e.g. the section between the joints of a finger or bamboo. Usually refers to something that is a tube shape.
<moa(n)> *Molo.* joint, node. (M:527,545,586)

***mone** *PRM.* male, man. *Doublet:* ***mone**. *Etym:* *maRuqanay 'male'. *[History:* PRM had two reflexes of *maRuqanay: ***mane** and ***mone**. Both of which are attested in wRote, Ba'a and Tii. The meaning of both forms was probably 'male, man' in PRM. Most of Rote lost ***mone**, Meto lost ***mane**, while wRote, Ba'a and Tii differentiated the semantics of the two terms.*]*
mone_feu-k *Ba'a.* son-in-law. *Lit:* 'new male'. (J:134)
mone_feu-k *Tii.* son-in-law. *Lit:* 'new male'. (J:134)
mone *Dengka.* male, of animals and certain plants. (J:345, 734)
mone (2) monae-ʔ *Oenale.* 1) male, of animals and certain plants. (J:345, 734) 2) big, many. (J:735)
mone (2) monae-ʔ *Dela.* 1) male. 2) big, important. *[Form:* with variant **manae-ʔ**.*]*
mone *Ro'is Amarasi.* husband, male.
mone (2) moen feʔu *Kotos Amarasi.* 1) husband, male. 2) opposite sex sibling's son, son-in-law. *Lit:* 'new male'.
mone *Molo.* husband, male. (M:330)
mone *Kusa-Manea.* husband.
Out-comparisons:
mone *Hawu.* man, male.

***mone|ʔ** *PMeto.* outside. *Doublet:* ***muri**. *Etym:* *ma-udəhi 'behind, last' (Blust and Trussel (ongoing) reconstruct PCEMP *m-udi. A PMeto doublet with (regular) *au > *o* is required to account for the Meto forms meaning 'outside'.). *[Form:* The initial syllable and medial consonant are regular from *ma-udəhi > PRM ***more-k**. Final *əhi > *e* is possibly irregular, though the only other reflex is *binəhiq > **fini** 'seed'. There is a conceptual link in Atoni though between **moneʔ** outside and **mone** 'male' and this folk-etymology may have led to final *e* rather than *i.]*
mone|ʔ *Ro'is Amarasi.* outside.
mone|ʔ *Kotos Amarasi.* outside.
mone|ʔ *Molo.* outside. (M:330)
Out-comparisons:
molin *Fehan Tetun.* outside, excrement, urine, defecate. *[irr. from PMP:* *d > *l]*

***mono** *PnMeto.* stupid.
n-mono *Kotos Amarasi.* stupid.
mono *Molo.* dumb. (M:331)
Out-comparisons:
mono *Bolok Helong.* dumb, unable to speak.
monon *Ili'uun.* stupid. (dJ:128)

***monu** *Rote.* fall.
monu *Termanu.* fall, fall off, fall out. (J:362)
monu *Korbafo.*
monu *Bokai.*
monu *Bilbaa.*
monu *Rikou.*
monu *Ba'a.*
monu *Tii.*
monu *Dengka.*
Out-comparisons:
monu *East Tetun.* fall. (Mo:143)
monu *Waima'a.* fall.

***moo** *Morph:* ***na-ka-moo**. *PRM.* hold in lips.
na-ka-moo *Termanu.* hold or take something between one's lips or in closed mouth. (J:358)
na-ka-moo *Korbafo.*
na-ka-moo *Bokai.*
na-ka-moo *Bilbaa.*
na-moo *Rikou.*
na-ka-moo *Ba'a.*

na-ka-moo *Tii.*
na-ʔa-moo *Dengka.*
na-ʔa-moo *Oenale.*
na-ʔ|moo *Kotos Amarasi.* put in the mouth but not swallow.

***mopu** *Morph:* ***ka-mopu-k**. *PRM.* old, dead palm tree. *[irr. from PRM:* *p > Ø in Korbafo and Oenale; *m > *mb* in Oenale*] [Form:* PMP *p is usually lost in Oenale and PMP *p > *ʔ* in Korbafo. However, PRM *p is expected to be retained unchanged in both lects.*]*
mopu-k *Termanu.* an old dead and fallen down gebang or lontar palm. (J:362)
mou-ʔ *Korbafo.*
mopu-k *Tii.*
mbou-ʔ *Oenale.*
ʔ|mopu|ʔ *Kotos Amarasi.* gebang/lontar palm trunk.
ʔ|mopu|ʔ *Molo.* dead, black lontar palm or gebang palm trunk. (M:331)

***moris** *PRM.* live. *Doublet:* ***horis**. *Etym:* *ma-qudip 'living, alive'. *[Form:* expected *p > *s* / _# (§3.5.1.3).*]*
moli (2) molis *Termanu.* 1) live. 2) probably: life! health! said to a child who sneezes. (J:361)
moli *Korbafo.*
moli *Bokai.*
moli *Bilbaa.*
mori *Rikou.*
moli *Ba'a.*
mori *Tii.*
moli *Dengka.*
mori *Oenale.*
n-moni *Ro'is Amarasi.* live.
n-moni *Kotos Amarasi.* live.
n-moni *Molo.* live. (M:330)
moin *Kusa-Manea.* give birth.
Out-comparisons:
moris *Fehan Tetun.* live, be born, come about, life, lively; exist.
moris, mouris *East Tetun.* live, be alive, exist, be born. (Mo:144)
mori *Ili'uun.* live, alive, thrive, grow. (dJ:128)

***mukə** *PRM.* wild dove. *Etym:* *mukən 'omen dove'. *Pattern:* k-9. *[Sporadic:* *ə > *e* /σ_# in wRote (perhaps *ə > *a > *e* / _#).*]*
muʔe-k *Termanu.* wild dove. (J:364)
muʔe-ʔ *Korbafo.*
muke-ʔ *Rikou.* dark green doves: Asian Emerald Dove, Pacific Emerald Dove. *Chalcophaps indica*; *Chalcophaps longirostris*. (J:364; own field notes)
muʔe-k *Ba'a.*
muʔe-k *Tii.*
muʔe-ʔ *Dengka.*
muʔe-ʔ *Oenale.*
k|ma~muaʔ-r=aa *Kusa-Manea.* wild pigeon. *[Form:* metathesised form of (currently unattested) **k|ma~muʔa**.]
Out-comparisons:
hmukan *Semau Helong.* dove.
lamuka(n) *East Tetun.* dark green dove. (Mo:127)
lamukan *Welaun.* Asian Emerald Dove. *Chalcophaps indica*.

***mulu** *PRM.* crazy. *[Sporadic:* diphthongisation *u > *au* in Meto.*]*
ka-mulu-s (2) mulu-k (3) na-mulu *Termanu.* 1) crazy. 2) insanity. 3) be or become crazy. (J:366)
ka-mulu-ʔ *Korbafo.*
ka-mulu-s *Bokai.*
ka-mulu-ʔ *Bilbaa.*
ma-mulu-ʔ *Rikou.*
ka-mulu-s *Ba'a.*
ka-mulu-k *Tii.*
ma-mulu-ʔ *Dengka.*
ma-mulu-ʔ *Oenale.*
na-maunu *Kotos Amarasi.* crazy.
na-maunu *Molo.* rages, is crazy. (M:316)

***mumu₁** *Rote.* hold in the mouth and suck. *Etym:* *mulmul.
mumu *Termanu.* hold something in the mouth and suck on it, suck on a solid object. (J:366)
mumu *Korbafo.*

mumu *Bokai.*
mumu *Bilbaa.*
mumu *Rikou.*
mumu *Ba'a.*
mumu *Tii.*
mumu *Dengka.*

***mumu2** *Morph:* ***na-ka-mumu.** *Rote.* gargle, rinse the mouth. *Etym:* *muRmuR.
na-ka-mumu *Termanu.* he rinses his mouth out with water, also: he gargles. (J:366)
na-ka-mumu *Korbafo.*
na-ka-mumu *Bokai.*
na-ka-mumu *Bilbaa.*
na-mumu *Rikou.*
na-ka-mumu *Ba'a.*
na-ka-mumu *Tii.*
na-ʔa-mumu *Dengka.*
na-ʔa-mumu *Oenale.*
Out-comparisons:
mumun *Semau Helong.* gargle.

***munde** *Morph:* ***ka-munde.** *PRM.* citrus tree. *Etym:* *muntay. *[minority from PMP:* *nt > *nd (expect *t)*]*
mune *Termanu.* pomelo. (J:366)
mune *Korbafo.*
mune *Bilbaa.*
dero munde *Landu.* kind of citrus. (own field notes)
munde *Rikou.*
°munde *Oepao. Borrowed from:* Rikou **munde** (shown by irr. *nd = *nd* correspondence). (own field notes)
mune *Ba'a.*
munde *Tii.*
munde *Dengka.*
munde *Oenale.*
muri *Ro'is Amarasi.* lime (fruit).
ʔ|mukiʔ *Kotos Amarasi.* lime (fruit).
<muke> *Molo.* lime. (M:333)

***muri** *PRM.* youngest, last, west. *Doublet:* ***mone|ʔ.** *Etym:* *ma-udəhi 'behind, last' (PCEMP *m-udi).
muli-k (2) muli *Termanu.* 1) youngest child; young of people, animals, and plants. 2) west. (J:365)
muli-ʔ (2) muli *Korbafo.*
muli-k (2) muli *Bokai.*
muli-ʔ (2) muli *Bilbaa.*
muri-ʔ (2) muri *Rikou.*
muli-k (2) muli *Ba'a.*
muri-k (2) muri *Tii.*
muli-ʔ (2) muli *Dengka.*
mu̯ri-ʔ (2) muri *Oenale.*
mu͡ini|f *Ro'is Amarasi.* youngest.
muni|f (2) na-muni *Kotos Amarasi.* 1) youngest (child). 2) back, end.
muni|f (2) na-muni *Molo.* 1) young. 2) come behind. (M:330)
muni|f *Kusa-Manea.* young.
Out-comparisons:
mudi (2) hmudin *Semau Helong.* 1) follow, from behind, go along with. 2) youngest, last in a series.

***muse1** *Morph:* ***muse-ʔ.** *PwRM.* seed, pip. *Etym:* **musa (pre-RM). *[Sporadic:* vowel height harmony *e > *i* /uC_ in Ro'is Amarasi.*] [Form:* Positing earlier **musa with final *a > *e* in wRM can account for the wRM and Tetun forms based on attested sound changes. However, it cannot account regularly for the Hawu form. Earlier **muse could possible account for the Hawu form, but cannot account regularly for the Tetun form.*]*
ɓoa_muse-ʔ *Oenale.* kidney. *[Semantics:* In other Rote languages 'kidney' is most often expressed by a compound of **boa** 'fruit' with the word for 'pip, seed', e.g. in Termanu **boa deʔe-k** = 'kidney'. **muse-ʔ** is not (currently) known to have any independent meaning in Oenale and the normal word for 'pip' is **deke-ʔ**.*]* (J:683, 53)
musi|ʔ *Ro'is Amarasi.* seed, pip, stone.
Out-comparisons:
musan *East Tetun.* seed, pip, grain, etc. (Mo:144)

lamuhi *Hawu.* seed (tree). *[Note:* **vini** = 'seed (generic for seeds planted by humans)'.*]*

musi *Ngadha.* kidney. (Djawanai 1995:Part 2, 508)

***muse2** *Morph:* ***muse-k**. *CER.* white civet. *Etym:* *musaŋ 'civet cat and similar small predatory mammals of the family Viverridae'. *[irr. from PMP:* *a > *e*] [Form:* The Rote forms would be regular from **musəŋ.*]*

mu~muse-k *Termanu.* the white civet. (J:366)

mu~muse-ʔ *Korbafo.*

mu~muse-k *Ba'a.*

***musi** *PRM.* suck.

na-sa-musi (2) musi *Termanu.* 1) suck, suck up. 2) suck, suck up. (J:366)

na-sa-musi *Korbafo.*

na-sa-musi *Bokai.*

na-ka-musi *Bilbaa.*

na-sa-musi *Rikou.*

na-sa-musi *Ba'a.*

na-sa-musi *Tii.*

musi *Dengka.*

na-sa-musi *Oenale.*

musi *Dela.* suck.

n-musi *Kotos Amarasi.* suck.

n-musi *Molo.* sucks. (M:335)

***musu** *PRM.* enemy. *[History:* The Rote-Meto forms may be borrowings from Malay **musuh**. Blust and Trussel (ongoing) reconstruct *busuR that may be irregularly related.*]*

musu *Termanu.* enemy, also: personal enemy, hostile, war. (J:367)

musu *Korbafo.*

musu *Bokai.*

musu *Bilbaa.*

musu *Rikou.*

musu *Ba'a.*

musu *Tii.*

musu *Dengka.*

musu *Oenale.*

musu *Kotos Amarasi.* enemy.

musu *Molo.* enemy. (M:335)

Out-comparisons:

musu *Semau Helong.* enemy, opponent.

muhu (2) pemuhu *Hawu.* 1) enemy. 2) fight each other, war against each other, be at odds, become enemies.

***muta** *PRM.* vomit. *Etym:* *um-utaq (PCEMP *mutaq).

muta (2) muta-s *Termanu.* 1) vomit (v.). 2) vomit (n.). (J:367)

muta *Korbafo.*

muta *Bokai.*

muta *Bilbaa.*

muta *Rikou.*

muta *Ba'a.*

muta *Tii.*

muta *Dengka.*

muta *Oenale.*

n-muta *Kotos Amarasi.* throw up, said of a small child.

n-muut *Molo.* throws up (baby). **liʔanaʔ meeʔ an-muut** the baby throws up milk (M:335)

Out-comparisons:

muta *Semau Helong.* vomit.

muta *East Tetun.* vomit. (Mo:144)

madu *Hawu.* vomit.

***muti** *Morph:* ***muti-k**. *nRM.* white. *Etym:* *ma-putiq.

muti/foe-k *Ba'a.* white (albino) spot or spots on the hand or foot of a person, or on other places on an animal. (J:139)

muti/foe-k (2) kue_muti-k *Tii.* 1) white (albino) spot or spots on the hand or foot of a person, or on other places on an animal. (J:139) 2) white civet. (J:735)

muti|ʔ *Ro'is Amarasi.* white.

muti|ʔ (2) k|muti-f *Kotos Amarasi.* 1) white. 2) egg white.

muti|ʔ *Molo.* white. (M:336)

muti|ʔ *Kusa-Manea.* white.

Out-comparisons:

mutiʔ *Semau Helong.* white.

mutin, mutik *East Tetun.* white (colour). (Mo:144)

***muut** *PRM.* kind of insect. *[History:* Osmond (2011b:416) reconstructs Proto-Polynesian *mū 'flying insect', the reflexes of which designate mainly moths and dragonflies.*] [Semantics:* likely onomatopoeia, vague Rote semantics weaken reconstruction.*]*

mu~muu *Termanu.* kind of insect that appears in the fruit of the **kaa-k** (fig-tree). (J:363)

mu~muu *Korbafo.*

mu~muu *Bokai.*

mu~muu *Bilbaa.*

mu~muu *Rikou.*

mu~muu *Ba'a.*

mu~muu *Tii.*

mu~muu *Dengka.*

mu~muu *Oenale.*

muut *Ro'is Amarasi.* mosquito. *[Semantics:* Generic term for normal mosquitoes.*]*

muut *Kotos Amarasi.* kind of small white mosquito whose bite is worse than a normal mosquito.

MB - mb

***mbaa** *nRM.* meat, flesh. *[irr. from PRM:* *aa > *ee* in Fatule'u*]*

paa *Termanu.* meat, flesh. (J:459)

paa *Korbafo.*

paa *Bokai.*

paa *Bilbaa.*

paa *Landu.* meat. (own field notes)

paa *Rikou.*

paa *Oepao.* meat. (own field notes)

mpaa *Ba'a.*

mbaa *Lole.* (Zacharias et al. 2014)

mbaa *Tii.*

pee-k *Fatule'u.* meat, flesh.

<pa'> *Molo.* a piece of meat which is offered to spirits at the end of a ritual meal. *[Form:* probably [paaʔ].*]* (M:410)

Out-comparisons:

əmpaʔ *Sumbawa.* flesh, fish. *[Note:* language of Sumbawa ISO 639-3 [smw].*]* (Mbete 1990:401, 403)

əmpaʔ *Sasak.* meat, fish (as food as opposed to meat). *[Note:* language of Sasak Island ISO 639-3 [sas].*]* (Goris 1938:92)

***mbada** *Morph:* ***mbada-k**. *PRM.* short in height, squat and compact in build, of a person. *Doublet:* ***pande**. *Etym:* *pandak. *Pattern:* d-2. *[irr. from PMP:* *p > *mb, *nd = *d*]*

pala_mata-k *Termanu.* close proximity. *[Form:* The Rote forms may also connected with Meto **paumaka-ʔ, haumaka-ʔ** 'near'. The second element could be related to ***mata** 'eye' with irr. *t > *k* in Meto. (Reflexes of ***mata** also mean 'in front' in Rote and Meto.) Alternately, the second element could originally have been ***maka** with irr. *k > *t* in Rote due to influence from ***mata**.*]* (J:465f)

pala_mata-k *Bokai.*

mpala_mata-k *Ba'a.*

mbala_mata-ʔ *Dengka.*

mbara_mata-ʔ *Oenale.*

para|ʔ *Ro'is Amarasi.* short.

para|ʔ *Kotos Amarasi.* short, typically used for trees.

pala|ʔ *Molo.* short. (M:415)

pa~para|ʔ *Kusa-Manea.* short.

Out-comparisons:

kbadak *Fehan Tetun.* short (e.g. of people); width.

badak *East Tetun.* short, brief. (Mo:7)

badak *Dadu'a.* be short. (Penn 2006:85)

bada *Mambae, South.* short, low. (Grimes et al. 2014b:13)

***mbae** *Rote.* swell up, swollen. *Etym:* *baRəq 'abscess, boil, swelling on the body'. *[minority from PMP:* *b > *mb*] [Form:* regular *ə > *e* / _q#.*]*

pae *Termanu.* swell up, swollen up, only used (at least in Termanu) in combination with **peta**. (J:462)

pae *Korbafo.*

pae *Bokai.*

pae *Bilbaa.*

pae *Rikou.*

mpae *Ba'a.*

mbae *Tii.*

mbae *Dengka.*

mbae *Oenale.*

Out-comparisons:

hale *Semau Helong.* swell, swollen.

ɓai *Hawu.* (J:462)

***mbai** *CERM.* rotten. *Etym:* *baRiw 'beginning to spoil, tainted (of food left uneaten too long)' *[Form:* Jonker also gives Tii **na-sa-pai** but indicates that this is questionable. If confirmed, this would indicate nRM ***pai**.*]*

na-sa-pai *Termanu.* mouldy, bad/rotten. *[Form:* forms without initial **sa-** are currently unattested.*]* (J:463)

ma-sa-pai *Korbafo.*

ma-sa-pai *Bokai.*

na-sa-mpai, ma-sa-mpai *Ba'a.*

n-pai *Kotos Amarasi.* begin to rot.

pai *Molo.* bad/rotten. (M:412)

Out-comparisons:

(vou-)ɓai *Hawu.* mouldy. (J:463)

mbai *Bima.* rotten. (Ismail et al. 1985:87)

***mbaki** *PRM.* beetle. *Pattern:* k-9' (*k = *k* in Bokai; expect *k > *ʔ*). *[irr. from PRM:* *i > *e* in Meto*]*

paʔi *Termanu.* kind of beetle that eats coconuts. (J:463)

paʔi *Korbafo.*

paki *Bokai.*

paki *Bilbaa.*

paʔi *Rikou.* kind of grub that is found in the gebang palm or lontar palm, similar to **ba~bate-ʔ** (see ***ɓate**) but can't be eaten. (J:463; own field notes)

mpaʔi *Ba'a.*

mbaʔi *Tii.*

mbaʔi *Dengka.*

mbaʔi *Oenale.*

paʔe *Ro'is Amarasi.* beetle.

paʔe *Kotos Amarasi.* beetle. *Usage:* Tais Nonof sub-dialect.

Out-comparisons:

(mo)kebaki *Hawu.* beetle. (J:463)

***mbala** *PRM.* co-wife, concubine.

pala (2) na-pala *Termanu.* 1) co-wife; that is, the second wife of a man in comparison to the first; have or take a co-wife. 2) have concubines, said of a man. **na-pala telu lesak** he has three concubines (J:465)

pala *Korbafo.*

pala *Bokai.*

pala *Bilbaa.*

pala *Rikou.*

mpala-k *Ba'a.*

mbala *Tii.*

mbala-ʔ *Dengka.*

mbala *Oenale.*

panaʔ (2) n-panaʔ *Kotos Amarasi.* 1) co-wife, concubine. 2) be polygamous, engage in polygamy.

<in anmeu pana> *Molo.* he lives polygamously. (M:418)

panaʔ *Amfo'an.* co-wife, concubine.

***mbalu** *PRM.* cover, enclose. *Doublet:* ***balu**$_3$. *Etym:* *balun 'bind, bundle, wrap in cloth; death shroud; cloth(ing)'. *[minority from PMP:* *b > *mb*]*

palu *Termanu.* cover, enclose in a garment or similar. (J:466)

palu *Korbafo.*

palu *Bokai.*

mpalu *Ba'a.*

mbalu *Tii.*

mbalu *Dengka.*
ma-ʔa-mbalu-ʔ *Dela.* covered.
<an-pano> (2) <pan/felo> *Molo.* 1) binds closely. **anpano asu fefan** someone tightly ties up the mouth of the dog. (M:421) 2) rope around a horse's mouth. (M:420)

***mbana** *Morph:* ***mbana-k**. *PRM.* tip, end; nose.
pana-k *Termanu.* nose (of person or animal). (J:467)
pana-ʔ *Korbafo.*
pana-k *Bokai.*
pana-ʔ *Bilbaa.*
idu_pana-ʔ *Rikou.* face. (own field notes)
mpana-k *Ba'a.*
mbana-k *Tii.*
mbana-ʔ *Dengka.*
mbana-ʔ *Oenale.*
pana-f *Ro'is Amarasi.* nose.
pana-f *Kotos Amarasi.* nose; the extremity of something, e.g. point, fingertips, peninsula.
pana-f *Molo.* nose (in general), cape, promontory. (M:419)

***mbao** *Rote.* mango. *Etym:* *qambawaŋ 'large mango Mangifera odorata' (PWMP). *[irr. from PRM:* *mb > *p* in Dengka*]*
pao *Termanu.* mango tree and fruit. (J:468)
pao *Korbafo.*
pao *Bokai.*
pao *Bilbaa.*
pao *Rikou.*
mpao *Ba'a.*
mbao *Tii.*
pao *Dengka. [Note:* given as 'also D. idem'.*]*
mbao *Oenale.*

***mba|raa** *Morph:* ***mba|raa-k**. *PRM.* old (things). *Etym:* *daqan 'old, ancient'. *[Form:* The Rote languages attest an earlier element ***mba** (which is attested as semi-productive verbal prefix) while Meto attests earlier stative prefix *ma-. Furthermore, the reflexes of PMP *d are regular for medial *d, thus indicating that the initial ***mba** element was added before PRM. The best solution currently appears to be to posit PRM ***mba|raa** with irr. *mb > *m* in Meto motivated by pressure from the stative prefix *ma-, thus pre-Meto **maraa.*]*
palaa-k (2) na-palaa *Termanu.* 1) old (of things, etc.). 2) be or become old. (J:465)
palaa-ʔ *Korbafo.*
palaa-k *Bokai.*
palaa-ʔ *Bilbaa.*
paraa-ʔ *Rikou.*
mpalaa-k *Ba'a.*
mbaraa-k *Tii.*
mbalaa-ʔ *Dengka.*
mbaraa-ʔ *Oenale.*
m|naa|ʔ *Ro'is Amarasi.* old, previous, former.
m|naa|ʔ *Kotos Amarasi.* old, previous, former.
m|naʔa-k *Kusa-Manea.* old, previous former. *[Sporadic:* *VV-k > *VVʔ > VʔV in Kusa-Manea (perceptual metathesis) followed by attachment of semi-productive **-k** suffix.*]*
Out-comparisons:
blaan *Semau Helong.* old.

***mbasa** *PwRM.* slap. *Etym:* **mbasaR (pre-RM). *[History:* possibly connected with PMP *sambak with consonant metathesis, though the final consonants of the pre-RM form would also need to be accounted for.*]*
mba~mbasaʔ *Dengka.* name of a medicinal plant of which the leaf makes a noise when it is broken off. Called *daun pukul tangan* (hand hitting leaf) in Kupang. (J:750, 640)
mbasa (2) mba~mbasaʔ *Oenale.* 1) give a slap. (J:750) 2) name of a medicinal plant of which the leaf

makes a noise when it is broken off. Called *daun pukul tangan* (hand hitting leaf) in Kupang. (J:750, 640)

n-pasa *Kotos Amarasi.* slap.

n-pasa *Molo.* hit with a flat hand. (M:424)

Out-comparisons:

papas *Semau Helong.* slap. *[irr. from PRM:* initial syllable*]*

basa *East Tetun.* hit with the open hand, slap. (Mo:10)

basa, baas *Mambae, South.* slap (open hand). (Grimes et al. 2014b:12f)

paas *Ili'uun.* strike (with the hand). (dJ:132)

pahar *Kisar.* slap.

pahak *Sika.* slap. *Usage:* Hewa dialect/variety. *[irr. from PRM:* *mb = *p* correspondence (expect *b*)*]* (Klamer 2015a)

***mbau1** *Morph:* ***ka-mbau-k**. *PRM.* kind of beam. *[Sporadic:* glottal stop insertion in Amfo'an.*]*

pa~pau-k *Termanu.* kind of beam under the roof, outside the actual house. (J:471)

pa~pau-ʔ *Korbafo.*

pa~pau-k *Bokai.*

pa~pau-ʔ *Bilbaa.*

pa~pau-ʔ *Rikou.*

dii mpa~mpau-k *Ba'a.* pillar for a front gallery, the 'stup' pillar. (J:471)

mba~mbau-k *Tii.*

mba~mbau-ʔ *Dengka.*

ʔ|paʔu-f *Amfo'an.* stair joint; the place where the horizontal part meets the vertical part.

***mbau2** *PRM.* stab, prick, pound. *Etym:* *bayu 'pound rice'. *[minority from PMP:* *b > *mb*]*

pau *Termanu.* stab, prick. (J:470)

pau *Korbafo.*

pau *Bokai.*

pau *Bilbaa.*

pau *Rikou.*

mpau *Ba'a.*

mbau *Tii.*

mbau *Dengka.*

mbau *Oenale.*

na-pau *Ro'is Amarasi.* pound (rice).

na-pau *Kotos Amarasi.* pound, stab.

na-pau *Molo.* pound, stab. (M:427)

ta-pau *Kusa-Manea.* pound.

Out-comparisons:

hai *Semau Helong.* plant, stick into ground; pound, pierce, stab impale. *[History:* from *bayu.*]*

fai *East Tetun.* pound, the action for removing the husk from whole grain and polishing rice with a tapered wooden stick (**alu**) driven in and out of a tapered hole in a wooden block (**nesun**), or any similar action. *[History:* from *bayu.*]* (Mo:31)

pai *Ili'uun.* pound, thresh. *[History:* from *bayu.*]* (dJ:132)

***mbeɗa** *PRM.* put down. *[irr. from PRM:* *mb > *b* ~ *p* in Meto*]*

peda *Termanu.* set, lay, lay something down, store something in, put something in. (J:472)

peda *Korbafo.*

peda *Bokai.*

peda *Bilbaa.*

peda *Rikou.*

mpeda *Ba'a.*

mbeɗa *Tii.*

mbeɗa *Dengka.*

mbeɗa *Oenale.*

n-pera (2) na-bera *Kotos Amarasi.* 1) throw down stones. 2) put down, drop.

na-pela, na-bela *Molo.* put down. (M:56, xxxix)

***mbeʔu** *nRM.* lie down.

na-ŋa-peʔu-k *Termanu.* lie, lie down. (J:482)

na-ka-peʔu-ʔ *Korbafo.*

na-ŋa-peʔu-k *Bokai.*

na-peʔu-ʔ *Bilbaa.* *[Form:* My consultants gave **na-peu** 'lie down'.*]*

na-peʔu-ʔ *Rikou. [Form:* My consultants gave **na-peu** 'lie down'.*]*

na-ka-mpeʔu-k *Ba'a.*

na-ka-mbeʔu-k *Tii.*

peʔu-n *Kotos Amarasi.* sleepiness, typically used to refer to someone who hasn't fully woken up yet. **iin peuʔ-n=ee ka= na-mneuk =fa feʔ** s/he hasn't fully woken up yet

n-peʔu-g *Amfo'an.* sleepy.

<n-piu> (2) <masapeu> *Molo.* 1) doze. 2) nodding of the head while dozing. (M:437)

peuʔ *Kusa-Manea.* sleep. *[Form:* metathesised form of **peʔu**.*]*

***mbela** *Morph:* ***mbela-k**. *PRM.* Job's tears. *[Note:* Jonker (1912:21) gives Loura (language of Sumba, ISO 639-3 [lur]) **bəla** 'millet' (Dutch *gierst*) as cognate, but I have been unable to confirm the existence of this in the (very sparse) available sources for Loura.*] [History:* This is the only PRM crop term that does not appear reconstructible to a higher node. Given this, and the fact that both sorghum and corn (which this term designates in daughter languages) are not native to this region, this term probably originally designated a native plant with later semantic shift as new crops were assimilated to the category of old crops. The most likely candidate is Job's tears, Coix lacryma-jobi, of which a wild subspecies is present in the region. Verheijen (1984:14) states, concerning Job's tears: 'The wild native subspecies agrestis of which the stony seeds with a very tiny pip are still used as beads, greatly resembles the cultivated subspecies ma-yuen. It is very probable that the introduced edible species was named after the wild plant, which then fell into the background. I am inclined to surmise that in this way names from substratum languages were saved. That may explain the enormous diversity of names in east Indonesia and the Philippines.' PRM ***mbela** appears to be such an example of a substratum term which was retained after the shift to an Austronesian language.*]*

pela-k (2) pela hii-k *Termanu.* 1) maize (the plant and its fruit). (J:477) 2a) maize of native soil, native corn (called *jagung Rote* [OE = 'sorghum']). (J:477) 2b) sorghum, that is native maize, simply/only maize, ordinary maize. *[Form:* **hii-k** = 'simply, only'.*] [Semantics:* Fox (1991:250) states: 'At present **pela** can refer to three different plants. **pela hii-k**, 'true *pela*', refers to sorghum; **pela hii dele ŋgeo-k**, 'black-flecked *pela*' refers to Job's tears; while **pela** or **pela sina** refers to maize. On Roti [sic] it is clear that maize when it was introduced was culturally assimilated to the category of 'sorghum'. It is also conceivable that at an earlier period when sorghum was introduced, it was assimilated to the category of Job's tears. Thus this category, **pela**, may subsume three stages of an agricultural progression: **pela** [A] ('Job's tears') > **pela** [B] ('sorghum') > **pela** [C] ('maize').'*]* (J:181)

pela-ʔ (2) pela hii-ʔ *Korbafo.*

pela-k (2) pela hii-k *Bokai.*

pela-ʔ (2) pela dae-ʔ *Bilbaa. [Form:* **dae-ʔ** = 'soil, land, earth'.*]*

pela-ʔ (2) pela dae-ʔ *Rikou.*

mpela-k (2) mpela hia-k *Ba'a.*

mbela-k (2) mbela hie-k *Tii.*

mbela-ʔ (2) mbela ɗae-ʔ *Dengka. [Form:* Jonker gives the note 'Bilbaa, Dengka, Rikou have **dae-ʔ**' implying that Dengka does not have expected **mbela lae-ʔ**.*]*

mbela-ʔ (2) mbela hie-ʔ *Oenale.*
pena|ʔ *Ro'is Amarasi.* corn, maize.
pena|ʔ (2) peen minaʔ *Kotos Amarasi.* 1) corn, maize. 2) sorghum. *[Form:* The second element could be connected with **minaʔ** = 'oil' or **mina** = 'comfortable, nice, delicious'.*]*
pena|ʔ *Molo.* maize. (M:431)
pena|ʔ *Kusa-Manea.* corn, maize.

***mbena** *Rote.* fly. *Doublet:* ***kalbenu.** *Etym:* *bəRŋaw (Blust and Trussel (ongoing) reconstruct both *bəRŋaw and *baŋaw.). *[irr. from PMP:* *aw > *a*] [minority from PMP:* *b > *mb*] [Sporadic:* *a > *e* / _# in wRote*] [Form:* Helong attests earlier **mbeŋa.*]*
pena *Termanu.* fly. (J:479)
pena *Korbafo.*
pena *Bokai.*
pena *Bilbaa.*
pena-ʔ *Landu.* fly. (own field notes)
pena *Rikou.*
mpena *Ba'a.*
mbena *Tii.*
mbene *Dengka.*
mbene *Oenale.*
Out-comparisons:
lael_peŋa *Helong.* kind of fly. (J:479)

***mbesik** *PRM.* throw down. *[irr. from PRM:* *i > *e* in Meto*]*
pesi *Termanu.* throw down, fling down. (J:480)
pesi *Korbafo.*
pesi *Bokai.*
pesi *Bilbaa.*
pesi *Rikou.*
mpesi *Ba'a.*
mbesi(k) *Tii.*
mbesi-ʔ *Dengka.*
mbesi-ʔ *Oenale.*
n-pesek *Kotos Amarasi.* throw down something flat, like a playing card.
Out-comparisons:
pəhi *Hawu.* throw. *[irr. from PRM:* *mb = *p* correspondence*]* (J:480)

mbeta** *CERM.* wet. *[Form:* The Meto unmetathesised form has not yet been attested. It could be ***na-peta** or ***na-pete.]*
ma-ka-peta-k *Termanu.* still moist, not yet properly dry. (J:481)
ma-peta-ʔ *Rikou.*
ma-ka-mpeta-k *Ba'a.*
na-peet *Kotos Amarasi.* moisten, wet, satiate.
na-peet *Molo.* wet. (M:435)

***mbetak** *PRM.* swollen, sore.
peta *Termanu.* swell up, swollen. (J:481)
peta *Korbafo.*
peta *Bokai.*
peta *Bilbaa.*
peta *Rikou.*
mpeta *Ba'a.*
mbeta *Tii.*
mbeta *Dengka.*
mbeta *Oenale.*
mbeta *Dela.* ache, sore.
n-petak *Kotos Amarasi.* sore, tired, exhausted.
n-petak *Molo.* stuffed, ascites (the accumulation of fluid in the peritoneal cavity, causing abdominal swelling), swollen. (M:436)
Out-comparisons:
petaŋ *Semau Helong.* swell.
peken *Kisar.* swollen.

***mbii** *PRM.* pull taut.
na-ka-pii (2) ei_pi~pii-k *Termanu.* 1) tense, tight. 2) the Achilles tendon. (J:483)
na-ka-pii *Korbafo.*
na-ka-pii *Bokai.*
na-ka-pii *Bilbaa.*
na-pii *Rikou.*
na-ka-mpii *Ba'a.*
na-ka-mbii *Tii.*
na-ka-mbii *Dengka.*

na-ka-mbii *Oenale.*
pii_koete-f *Ro'is Amarasi.* back part of the lower leg, from the back of the knee to the Achilles' tendon.
na-ʔ-pii (2) n-pii (3) pii_ʔote-f *Kotos Amarasi.* 1) tie. 2) pull tight. 3) back part of the lower leg, from the back of the knee to the Achilles' tendon.
<na-pii> (2) <pii> (3) pii_ʔote-n (4) <pii-n enu> *Molo.* 1) tautens, pulls tight. 2) the bend of the knee. 3) because that is where the tendons of a sacrificial buffalo are severed. 4) knee nerves. (M:437)

***mbiko** *PRM.* kind of coniferous tree. Podocarpus rumphii. *Pattern:* k-6.
piko *Termanu.* a) kind of tree that yields good wood for timber. *[Semantics:* 'Podocarpus rumphii is a valuable timber tree where it attains large sizes with a clear, straight bole. Its wood is used as round wood for masts, spars, and poles, in house construction as beams, in high-grade construction for flooring, joinery and other carpentry, for furniture and cabinet work, veneer, make boxes, and for match sticks. In traditional use it was sought after for (dugout) canoes, used in coastal house construction, for household utensils, and wood carving. It is not known to be in cultivation, either as a forestry plantation tree or as an ornamental tree; the species is present in a few tropical botanic gardens and arboreta.' (Farjon 2017:920).*]* (J:484) b) kind of tree; a forest tree with thick bark and small but thick leaves. (Bark can be used for dyeing.) (Fox 2016b:46)
piko *Korbafo.*
piko *Bokai.*
piko *Bilbaa.*
piko *Rikou.*
mpiko *Ba'a.*
mbiko *Tii.*
mbiʔo *Dengka.*
<hau pio> *Miomafo.* kind of tree, rare on Ambon but occurring in the village of Ema, from which the name Lignum Emaniom comes in the high stony mountains of *Laitimor*. Also rare in Timor. Podocarpus rumphii. (M:439)

***mbila** *PRM.* blaze, emit light. *Etym:* *bilak 'shine, glitter'. *[minority from PMP:* *b > *mb*]*
pila (2) pila-s *Termanu.* 1) flaming, burning. (J:484) 2) red. (J:485)
pila (2) pila-ʔ *Korbafo.*
pila (2) pila-k *Bokai.*
pila (2) pila-ʔ *Bilbaa.*
pila (2) pilas *Rikou.*
mpila (2) mpila-s *Ba'a.*
mbila (2) mbila-s *Tii.*
mbila (2) mbila-s *Dengka.*
mbila (2) mbila-s *Oenale.*
n-pina *Ro'is Amarasi.* blaze, emit light.
n-pina *Kotos Amarasi.* blaze, emit light; be glorious.
n-pina *Molo.* flaming, shines. (M:438)
Out-comparisons:
bilan *East Tetun.* cook. (Mo:15)

***mbinu** *PRM.* snot. *[History:* possibly connected with PMP *hiŋus, though the initial *mb is unexplained. Blust and Trussel (ongoing) reconstruct *piŋus based on a comparison of Rote (presumably Termanu) **pinu** and a Cebuano form **piŋús-piŋús**. The Tii, Dengka and Oenale forms with initial *mb* in this cognate set indicate that, unless more cognates are forthcoming, the comparison of Termanu **pinu** and Cebuano **piŋús-piŋús** is sheer chance (PMP *p > *mb* is never attested in western Rote). Blust and Trussel (ongoing) *do* correctly note that the normal reflex of *p in Rote is *h*. However, in support of their etymology for Rote **pinu** from *piŋus they note that in some forms it is reflected as *p*. They give ***papan** > **papa** 'plank, board' and ***picik** > **pisi** 'to sprinkle, spray (water)' as examples. In each of these examples the cognates in *all* Rote varieties, including Tii, Dengka and Oenale have *p*, with the exception of Ba'a which has *mp*. These forms thus do not show the same sound correspondences as ***mbinu** 'snot'. Instead, both these words are loans. (*p* is often borrowed in Ba'a as *mp*.)*]*

pinu *Termanu.* snot. (J:486)
pinu *Korbafo.*
pinu *Bokai.*
pinu *Bilbaa.*
pinu *Rikou.*
mpinu *Ba'a.*
mbinu *Tii.*
mbinu *Dengka.*
mbinu *Oenale.*
pinu *Kotos Amarasi.* runny snot.
<pinu> *Amfo'an.* snivel. *Usage:* poetic. (M:439)

***mbisa** *Morph:* ***mbisa-k**. *Rote.* kind of basket made from lontar leaves.
pisa-k *Termanu.* kind of basket made from lontar leaves. (J:486)
pisa-k *Korbafo.*
pisa-k *Bokai.*
pisa-k *Bilbaa.*
pisa-ʔ *Rikou.*
mpisa-k *Ba'a.*
mbisa-ʔ *Dengka.*
mbisa-ʔ *Oenale.*
Out-comparisons:
kebiha *Hawu.* (J:486)

***mboes** *Morph:* ***ka-mboes**. *PRM.* shrimp, prawn.
poe-k *Termanu.* shrimp, lobster. (J:489)
poe-ʔ *Korbafo.*
poe-k *Bokai.*
poe-ʔ *Bilbaa.*
poe-ʔ *Landu.* shrimp, lobster. (own field notes)
poe-ʔ *Rikou.*
mpoe-k *Ba'a.*
mboe-k *Tii.*
mboe-ʔ *Dengka.*
mboe-ʔ *Oenale.*
k|poes *Ro'is Amarasi.* shrimp, prawn.
poes (2) na-k|poe *Kotos Amarasi.* 1) shrimp, prawn. 2) go shrimping, look for shrimp.
poes *Molo.* river shrimp. (M:444)
poe-k *Kusa-Manea.* shrimp.
Out-comparisons:
boek *East Tetun.* shrimp, prawns. (Mo:16)
waʔihe *Kisar.* lobster. *[irr. from PMP:* *mbo > *wa]*
voe *Hawu.* (J:489)

***mbonu** *Morph:* ***ka-mbonu-k**. *nRM.* thick hair, mane.
po~ponu-k *Termanu.* the mane of a horse, also said of a pig. (J:495)
po~ponu-ʔ *Korbafo.*
po~ponu-k *Bokai.*
po~ponu-ʔ (2) na-po~ponu *Bilbaa.* 2) the hair is luxuriant. (J:755)
po~ponu-ʔ *Rikou.*
mpo~mponu-k *Ba'a.*
mbo~mbonu-k *Tii.*
po͡unu-f *Ro'is Amarasi.* eyebrows, eyelashes, feathers.
ponu-f *Kotos Amarasi.* moustache.
ʔ|pono-f *Molo.* horse's mane, goat hair worn by a dancer around their ankles. (M:448)

***mboo** *Morph:* ***mboo-k**. *PRM.* hole, wide open. *[Sporadic:* glottal stop insertion in Meto.*]* *[History:* Blust and Trussel (ongoing) reconstruct PMP *buhaŋ 'hole, pit', which may be irregularly connected.*]*
poo~poo (2) poo-k (3) na-po~poo (4) na-poo-k *Termanu.* 1) wide open, yawning. 2) hole, cavity. 3) keep open continuously. 4) open (the mouth). (J:487)
poo~poo (2) poo-ʔ *Korbafo.*
poo~poo (2) poo-k *Bokai.*

poo~poo (2) poo-ʔ *Bilbaa.*
poo~poo (2) poo-ʔ *Rikou.*
mpoo~mpoo *Ba'a.*
mboo~mboo (2) mboo-k *Tii.*
mboo~mboo *Dengka.*
mboo~mboo *Oenale.*
poʔo (2) poʔo-f *Ro'is Amarasi.* 1) hole. 2) throat. *[Note:* Jonker (1908:487) gives Meto **puu** in the etymology notes for Termanu **poo-poo.***]*
pa~poʔo-f *Kusa-Manea.* throat.
Out-comparisons:
boo *Hawu.* hole. (J:487)

***mbori** *PRM.* pour on.
poli *Termanu.* pour, pour out, also: pour oneself out, e.g. like rain. (J:494)
poli *Korbafo.*
poli *Bokai.*
poli *Bilbaa.*
pori *Rikou.*
mpoli *Ba'a.*
mbori *Tii.*
mboli *Dengka.*
mbori *Oenale.*
n-poni *Kotos Amarasi.* pour over something, flush.
n-poni *Molo.* irrigate, water (e.g. plants). (M:448)

***mboro** *PRM.* palm leaves.
polo-k *Termanu.* palmiet, young leaves of a palmiet, young leaves of a coconut, lontar palm, etc. (J:494)
polo-ʔ *Korbafo.*
polo-k *Bokai.*
polo-ʔ *Bilbaa.*
polo-ʔ *Rikou.*
mpolo-k *Ba'a.*
mboro-k *Tii.*
mboro-ʔ *Oenale.*
pono *Ro'is Amarasi.* sugar palm leaf.
pono *Kotos Amarasi.* sugar palm leaf.
pono *Molo.* lontar palm leaves. (M:448)
Out-comparisons:
pola *Semau Helong.* palm leaves.

***mbosi** *PRM.* release, set loose. *[irr. from PRM:* *s > *ʔ* in most Rote*]*
poʔi *Termanu.* release; loosen, escape. (J:490)
poʔi *Korbafo.*
poʔi *Bokai.*
poi (2) posi *Bilbaa.* 2) slips away, becomes loose. (J:755)
poʔi *Rikou. [Form:* Jonker indicates that this could actually be **poi** without a medial glottal stop. Nako et al. (2014) give **poʔi taata** 'free, released'.*]*
mpoʔi *Ba'a.*
mboʔi *Tii.*
mboʔi *Dengka.*
mboʔi *Oenale.*
na-t|posiʔ *Kotos Amarasi.* come loose.
Out-comparisons:
°natpusi *Semau Helong. Borrowed from:* Meto. (J:490)
habusik, husik *East Tetun.* untie, loosen, leave loose. (Mo:41)
kapisu *Kamarian.* loose, loosened. *[Note:* also in some varieties of Kaibobo.*]* (van Ekris 1864:99)
pusi *Asilulu. [Note:* also in Lusa Laut.*]* (van Ekris 1864:99)
posi *Kaibobo. Usage:* Piru dialect. (van Ekris 1864:99)

***mbou** *PRM.* blanket, cloth. *[Sporadic:* *VV-k > *VVʔ > VʔV in Meto (perceptual metathesis).*]*
pou (2) pou-k *Termanu.* 1) woman's skirt, sarong. 2) the hair-like fibres between the stem and the leaf of different palm trees. (J:498)
pou (2) pau-ʔ *Korbafo.*
pou (2) pau-k *Bokai.*
pou *Bilbaa.*
pou (2) pau-ʔ *Rikou.*
mpou (2) mpou-k, mpau-k *Ba'a.*
(2) mbou-ʔ *Oenale.*
poʔu *Kotos Amarasi.* scarf.
poʔu *Molo.* blanket. (M:451)

Out-comparisons:

kaboon *Fehan Tetun.* blanket.

***mbuah** *PRM.* betel nut, areca palm. *Doublet:* ***bua**. *Etym:* *buaq 'fruit; areca palm and nut; grain; berry; seed; nut; endosperm of a sprouting coconut; kidney; heart; finger; calf of the leg; testicle; various insects; scar tissue; roe; bud; flower; blossom; bear fruit; words, speech, or songs; meaning, contents of discussion; numeral classifier for roundish objects; buttock; Adam's apple; nipple of the breast; button; marble; tattooing'. *[minority from PMP:* *q > *h; *b > *mb*] [Form:* Irregular *b > *mb is attested in many languages of the region for reflexes of ***buaq** meaning 'betel nut' and *mb can be reconstructed to proto-Timor-Babar, perhaps even to a higher node.*]*

pua *Termanu.* betel nut, areca, both the fruit and the tree. (J:499)

pua *Korbafo.*

pua *Bokai.*

pua *Bilbaa.*

pua *Landu.* betel nut. (own field notes)

pua *Rikou.*

mpua *Ba'a.*

mbua *Tii.*

mbua *Dengka.*

mbua *Oenale.*

puah *Ro'is Amarasi.* betel nut.

puah *Kotos Amarasi.* betel nut, areca palm.

puah *Molo.* both the areca palm and its fruit. Areca catecha. (M:452)

puah, puha *Kusa-Manea.* betel nut. *[Form:* The form **puha** [ˈpʊhɐ] may be due to reanalysis of **puah** as a metathesised form given that Kusa-Manea does not have assimilation of /a/ after metathesis. This is also attested in **noah**, **noha** 'coconut'.*]*

Out-comparisons:

pua *Semau Helong.* betel.

bua *East Tetun.* betel nut, areca. Areca catechu. (Mo:18)

boo *Kemak.* betel nut, areca nut.

buu *Mambae, South.* betel nut, areca nut. (Grimes et al. 2014b:14)

bua *Galolen.* betel nut.

pua *Ili'uun.* betel nut. (dJ:133)

poo *Kisar.* areca nut.

***mbuat** *PwRM.* spread out yarn. *[Form:* Final *t* could be the nominaliser **-t**.*]*

mbu~mbuat *Oenale.* the two layers of the yarn spread out in front of the weaving. (J:756)

puat *Kotos Amarasi.* round wood, over the entire length of which weft thread is rolled.

puat *Molo.* round wood, over the entire length of which weft thread is rolled. (M:452)

Out-comparisons:

pu~puat *Helong.* (J:757)

***mbui** *PRM.* quail, bird. *Etym:* *puyuq 'quail' (PWMP). *[irr. from PMP:* *p > *mb*] [Form:* Irregular *p > *mb* is also attested in Palu'e.*]*

manu_pui *Termanu.* bird, in general. (J:347)

manu_pui(-ʔ) *Korbafo.*

manu_pui *Bokai.*

manu_pui-ʔ *Bilbaa.*

man_pui-ʔ *Landu.* bird. (own field notes)

manu_pui-ʔ *Rikou.*

mpui-k *Ba'a.*

mbui-k *Lole.* (Zacharias et al. 2014)

mbui-k *Tii.*

mbui-ʔ *Dengka.*

manu_mbui-ʔ *Oenale.*

pui *Kotos Amarasi.* quail.

pui *Molo.* partridge and **meko** = kind of bird that lives in the reeds. (M:453)

Out-comparisons:

mbuu *Palu'e.* quail. *[Note:* language of central Flores ISO 639-3 [ple].*]* (Donohue 2003:12)

***mbuku**1 *PRM.* mushroom, toadstool. *Pattern:* k-6.
puku *Termanu.* mushroom. (J:501)
puku *Korbafo.*
puku *Bokai.*
puku *Bilbaa.*
puku *Rikou.*
mpuku *Ba'a.*
mbuku *Tii.*
mbuʔu *Dengka.*
mbuʔu *Oenale.*
puʔu *Kotos Amarasi.* mushroom, toadstool.
<pu'>, <a'pu'e> *Molo.* mushroom that comes up when the field is full of corn. *[Form:* The second form probably has the nominal determiner =**ee** enclitic attached.*]* (M:451)
puʔu *Kusa-Manea.* mushroom, toadstool.
Out-comparisons:
buu/manu *Semau Helong.* mushroom. *[irr. from PRM:* *mb = *b* correspondence (expect *p*); *k = Ø correspondence*]*

***mbuku**2 *Rote.* bent, hunchback. *Etym:* *bukuq 'bend, bent, bowed'. *Pattern:* k-5. *[minority from PMP:* *b > *mb*]*
puku (2) puku-k (3) (lete) pu~puku-k *Termanu.* 1) bent of back. 2) hunchbacked. 3) hill. (J:502)
puku (3) pu~puku-ʔ *Korbafo.*
puku (3) pu~puku-k *Bokai.*
puku (3) pu~puku-ʔ *Bilbaa.*
puku (3) pu~puku-ʔ *Rikou.*
mpuku (3) mpu~mpuku-k *Ba'a.*
mbuku (3) mbu~mbuku-k *Tii.*
mbuku (3) mbu~mbuku-ʔ *Dengka.*
(3) mbu~mbuku-ʔ *Oenale.*
Out-comparisons:
leten pupuku *Helong.* (J:502)
buku *Hawu.* (J:502)

***mbule** *Morph:* ***mbule-k**. *PRM.* grain head. *Etym:* *buliR '(entire) stalk of bananas; ear of grain'. *[minority from PMP:* *b > *mb*]* *[Sporadic:* *i > *e /_*R#*]* *[Form:* The Tetun, Helong and Kisar reflexes are regular from initial *b.*]*
pule-k *Termanu.* ear of grains, grasses. (J:502)
pule-ʔ *Korbafo.*
pule-k *Bokai.*
pule-ʔ *Bilbaa.*
pule-ʔ *Rikou.*
mpule-k *Ba'a.*
mbule-k *Lole.* (Zacharias et al. 2014)
mbule-k *Tii.*
mbule-ʔ *Dengka.*
mbule-ʔ *Oenale.*
pune|ʔ *Kotos Amarasi.* grain head.
pune|ʔ *Molo.* corn-cob. (M:532)
Out-comparisons:
bulin *Semau Helong.* grain head.
fulin *East Tetun.* head (of grain, rice, etc.). (Mo:37)
wurna *Kisar.* corn ears.

***mbulə** *PwRM.* wind around, twist around. *[Note:* All Rote lects (except Bilbaa) also have **pole** 'bind around, tie around, e.g. the muzzle of an animal' (Jonker 1908:493).*]* *[Sporadic:* *ə > *e* /σ_# in wRote (perhaps *ə > *a > *e* /_#).*]*
mbule *Dengka.* twist around. (J:147)
mbule *Oenale.* twist around. (J:147)
n-puna *Kotos Amarasi.* wind around.
n-puna (2) na-puun *Molo.* 1) wraps around. 2) walks around. (M:455)

***mbumbu** *Rote.* expand, swollen.
pupu *Termanu.* expand, like rice when cooked. (J:504)
pupu *Korbafo.*
mpumpu *Ba'a.*
mbumbu *Dengka.*
mbumbu *Oenale.*
Out-comparisons:
bubu *East Tetun.* swell. (Mo:18)

***mbune** *PRM.* tree with edible fruit. <u>*Antidesma bunius*</u>. *Etym:* *buRnay (PWMP). *[minority from PMP:* *b > *mb*]*

pune *Termanu.* kind of tree with small edible fruits. (J:503)
pune *Korbafo.*
pune *Bokai.*
pune *Bilbaa.*
pune *Rikou.*
mpune *Ba'a.*
mbune *Tii.*
mbune *Dengka.*
mbune *Oenale.*
<pune/klia>, <puni/klian> *Molo.* kind of plant with glossy leaves. Dillenia pentagyna. *[Note:* Middelkoop (1972:351) gives <**nasi**> as the term for Antidesma bunius.*]* (M:455)

***mbunut** *Morph:* ***ka-mbunut**. *PRM.* coconut husk, coir. *Etym:* *bunut. *[minority from PMP:* *b > *mb*]* *[Form:* The Helong, Tetun and Welaun reflexes all also attest initial *mb for pre-RM.*]*
punu-k *Termanu.* bark, fibrous husk of a coconut. (J:504)
punu-ʔ *Korbafo.*
punu-k *Bokai.*
punu-ʔ *Bilbaa.*
punu-ʔ *Landu.* hard inner shell of a coconut. (own field notes)
punu-ʔ *Rikou.*
mpunu-k *Ba'a.*
mbunu-k *Lole.* (Zacharias et al. 2014)
mbunu-k *Tii.*
mbunut *Dengka.* *[Form:* final *t* in Dengka and Oenale analysable as nominaliser **-t**.*]*
mbunut *Oenale.*
ʔ|punu-f (2) na-ʔ|punu|ʔ *Kotos Amarasi.* 1) coconut husk. 2) loud sound like 'boom, boom' this is the sound that an old coconut makes when it falls from a tree (also bombs, etc.).
a-ʔlotos na-ʔ|punu|ʔ *Molo.* the thunder rattles. (M:456)

Out-comparisons:
punut *Semau Helong.* shell, husk.
bunuk *East Tetun.* the durable external woody shell of palm trees used extensively in Timor as a building material for houses because of its strength and durability when split into long straight lengths. (Mo:19)
kabunut *Welaun.* hard inner coconut shell.
keɓunu *Hawu.* (J:504)

***mburuk** *PRM.* rotten. *Etym:* *buRuk. *[minority from PMP:* *b > *mb; *R = *r (expect Ø)*]*
pulu-k *Termanu.* old, rotten, stinking, whatever is rotten. (J:503)
pulu-ʔ *Korbafo.*
pulu-k *Bokai.*
pulu-ʔ *Bilbaa.*
puru-ʔ *Rikou.*
mpulu-k *Ba'a.*
mbulu-k *Lole.* (Zacharias et al. 2014)
mburu-k *Tii.*
mbuluk *Dengka.*
mburu-ʔ *Oenale.*
n-punu *Ro'is Amarasi.* rotten.
n-punu *Kotos Amarasi.* rot, decay, fall apart.
<punu> *Molo.* rotten, bad. (M:456)

***mbusər** *PRM.* sweat. *[Sporadic:* *ə > (*a) > *e* / _# in Meto.*]*
puse *Termanu.* sweat. (J:504)
puse *Korbafo.*
puse *Bokai.*
puse *Bilbaa.*
puse *Rikou.*
mpuse *Ba'a.*
mbuse *Tii.*
mbusa (2) na-ʔa-mbusa *Dengka.* 1) sweat. 2) stuffy. (J:757)
mbusa (2) na-ʔa-mbusa *Oenale.* 1) sweat. 2) stuffy. (J:757)
mbusar *Dela.* sweat.
puus, puse (2) n-puus *Kotos Amarasi.* 1) sweat. 2) sweating. *[Form:* The unmetathesised

form of **puus** has not yet been attested. It could be **pusa** or **pusu**. Middelkoop (1972:457) gives the Amarasi parallelism **a-n-pusun =ma maskeet** 'instils fear and fright', which indicates that the unmetathesised form is ***pusu** with final *u.]*

puus (2) n-puus *Molo.* 1) sweat. 2) sweats. *[Form:* Jonker (1908:504) gives Meto **puse-l**.*]* (M:457)

Out-comparisons:

kabβəsu *Dhao. [Form:* regular vowel metathesis in Hawu and Dhao.*]*

kebəhu *Hawu.* (J:504)

pusəʔ *Bugis.* sweat. (Masse 2013:77)

bussaŋ *Makassar.* feel stuffy due to heat. (Cense 1979:150)

***mbusu** *Morph:* ***mbusu-k**. *nRM.* thigh. *[irr. from PRM:* *s > Ø in nRote*]*

puu-k *Termanu.* thigh (of person). (J:499)

puu-ʔ *Korbafo.*

puu-k *Bokai.*

puu-ʔ *Bilbaa.*

puu-ʔ *Landu.* thigh. (own field notes)

puu-ʔ *Rikou.*

mpuu-k *Ba'a.*

mbuu-k *Tii.*

pusu-f *Ro'is Amarasi.* thigh.

pusu-f *Kotos Amarasi.* thigh.

pusu-f *Molo.* thigh. (M:458)

pusu-f *Kusa-Manea.* thigh.

***mbutu₁** *PRM.* hot, burning. *See:* ***hotu** 'burn'.

putu (2) na-putu *Termanu.* 1) burning, scorching. 2) scorch something. (J:505)

putu *Korbafo.*

putu *Bokai.*

putu *Bilbaa.*

putu *Rikou.*

mbutu *Tii.*

mbutu *Dengka.*

mbutu *Oenale.*

ma|putu|ʔ *Ro'is Amarasi.* hot.

n-putu (2) putu|ʔ (3) ma|putu|ʔ *Kotos Amarasi.* 1) burn. 2) burnt up (wood), charcoal. 3) hot.

n-putu *Molo.* is on fire, burnt off. (M:459)

puut (2) ma|putu|ʔ *Kusa-Manea.* 1) charcoal. 2) hot.

Out-comparisons:

otot *Semau Helong.* hot. *[irr. from PRM:* *u = *o* correspondences*]*

mʔutu *Waima'a.* heat, hot.

<mutuŋu> *Kambera.* burn (transitive and intransitive), on fire. *[Form:* The final vowel is epenthetic.*]* (On:295)

<mutu> *Kodi.*

poto-t *Buru.* hot. (Grimes and Grimes 2020:756)

mpoto *Kayeli.* fever. *[Note:* language of Buru Island ISO 639-3 [kzl].*]* (Charles E. Grimes pers. comm.)

pətu *Keo.* hot, cook, sick. *[Note:* language of central Flores ISO 639-3 [xxk].*]* (Baird 2002:572)

***mbutu₂** *Rote.* tie up in a bundle. *Doublet:* ***futu**. *Etym:* *butu 'group, crowd, flock, school, bunch, cluster' (PCEMP). *[minority from PMP:* *b > *mb*]*

pu~putu *Termanu.* tie up in a bundle. (J:505)

pu~putu *Korbafo.*

pu~putu *Bilbaa.*

pu~putu *Rikou.*

mpu~mputu *Ba'a.*

mbu~mbutu *Tii.*

mbu~mbutu *Dengka.*

Out-comparisons:

butuk *East Tetun.* sheaf, bundle, *v.* hang many things together. (Mo:19)

***mbuu** *PRM.* make a noise. *[irr. from PRM:* *u > *o* in Meto*] [Semantics:* onomatopoeia.*]*

puu *Termanu.* shout, make a noise. (J:498)
puu *Korbafo.*
puu *Bokai.*
puu *Bilbaa.*
puu *Rikou.*
mpuu *Ba'a.*
mbuu *Tii.*
mbuu *Dengka.*
mbuu *Oenale.*
na-poo *Kotos Amarasi.* make a sound.
na-poo *Molo.* rolls (thunder), pops (rifle). (M:442)

N - n

***naa1** *PRM.* that, there. *Etym:* *-na 'distal spatio-temporal deixis: that, there; then'.
naa (2) ana, -n *Termanu.* 1) demonstrative pronoun, that there. (J:367) 2) non-emphatic form of the third person singular pronoun. (J:12) (Jonker 1915:332ff)
naa (2) ana *Korbafo.*
naa (2) ana *Bokai.*
naa (2) ana *Bilbaa.*
naa (2) ana *Rikou.*
naa (2) ana *Ba'a.*
naa (2) ana *Tii.*
naa (2) ana *Dengka.*
naa (2) ana *Oenale.*
naa *Kotos Amarasi.* zero person demonstrative.

***naa2** *Morph:* ***naa-k**. *PRM.* woman's brother. *Etym:* *ñaRa 'brother (woman speaking)'. *[irr. from PRM:* *a > *o* in Meto*] [Sporadic:* *VV-k > *VVʔ > VʔV in Meto (perceptual metathesis).*]*
naa-k *Termanu.* brother, in relation to a sister. (J:368)
naa-ʔ *Korbafo.*
naa-k *Bokai.*
naa-ʔ *Bilbaa.*
naa-ʔ *Rikou.*
naa-k *Ba'a.*
naa-k *Tii.*
naa-ʔ *Dengka.*
naa-ʔ *Oenale.*
nao-f *Ro'is Amarasi.* brother of woman.
nao-f, naʔo *Kotos Amarasi.* brother of woman.
naʔo *Kusa-Manea.* brother.
Out-comparisons:
naan *East Tetun.* brother, cousin (only used by women to their brothers and male cousins). (Mo:145)
nara(n) *Ili'uun.* man's sister, a woman's brother. (dJ:130)

***naa3** *Rote.* Papua New Guinea rosewood. *Pterocarpus indica*. *Etym:* *naRa. *[Semantics:* Meijer Drees (1950) gives Meto <**náo**>, <**na**> and <**apnà**> as *Planchonia valida* and *Barringtonia spicata*, and <**matáni**> as *Pterocarpus indica*.*]*
naa *Termanu.* kind of tree called *kayu merah* (red wood) in Kupang. (J:368)
naa *Korbafo.*
naa *Bokai.*
naa *Bilbaa.*
naa *Rikou.*
naa *Ba'a.*
naa-k *Tii.*
naa *Dengka.*
naa *Oenale.*
Out-comparisons:
ai naa *East Tetun.* the tree that produces rosewood; rosewood tree, a good timber for furniture. *Pterocarpus indicus*. (Mo:2, 145)

***naa**4 *Morph:* ***naa-k**. *Rote.* gebang palm fibres. *Etym:* *qanahaw 'sugar palm: Arenga spp.'. *[irr. from PMP:* *aw > *a*] [Form:* The initial parts of some of the Rote terms are analysable as reflexes of ***ekut** 'palm fibres, woven ring from palm fibres'.*]*

eke_naa-k *Termanu.* the outermost hard part of a young gebang palm (called **tula pato**), which is processed (called **dusi**) and separated from the useless inner part (called **tula tei-k**) and used to make a kind of rope or string called **tali_eke/naa-k** (in Kupang called *tali heknaak*), which is used to make various things (**lapik**). (J:110)

eke_naa-ʔ *Korbafo.*

eke_naa-k *Bokai.*

heke/na-ʔ *Bilbaa.*

(henaa-ʔ ?) *Rikou.*

heke/naa-k *Ba'a.*

aki/naa-k *Tii.*

ɗaʔi/naa *Dengka.*

daʔi/naa *Oenale.*

Out-comparisons:

naa (2) naa tais *East Tetun.* 1) palm trees of various kinds. 2) thread similar to that produced by Piassava palm. (Mo:145)

***nada** *PMeto.* gums. *Doublet:* ***ŋgadas**. *Etym:* *ŋadas 'palate'. *[minority from PMP:* *d = *d (expect *d > *r > *l > *n)*]*

nara-f *Ro'is Amarasi.* gums.

nara-f *Kotos Amarasi.* gums.

nala-n *Amanuban.* palate.

<nala> *Molo.* palate, uvula. (M:342)

nara-f *Kusa-Manea.* gums.

***nade** *Morph:* ***ka-nade**. *PRM.* taro, grass. *Pattern:* d-2. *[irr. from PRM:* *e > *i* in wRM, Ba'a, Termanu and Bokai*] [History:* possibly connected with Malay *keladi*, though *l* > *n* in Rote would be unexplained.*] [Semantics:* The semantic connection between Rote and Meto is dubious.*]*

nali *Termanu.* kind of grass. (J:378)

nale *Korbafo.*

nali *Bokai.*

nale *Bilbaa.*

(nale ?) *Rikou.*

nali *Ba'a.*

nare *Tii.*

nali-ʔ *Dengka.*

nari-ʔ *Oenale.*

nari|ʔ *Ro'is Amarasi.* taro.

ʔ|nari|ʔ *Kotos Amarasi.* taro.

ʔ|lali-ʤ *Amfo'an.* taro.

ʔ|lali *Molo.* taro. Colocasia antiquorom. (M:260)

***naɗo** *Rote.* look upward. *Etym:* *ŋadaq (PWMP). *[irr. from PMP:* *a > *o (also Ende)*] [minority from PMP:* *d > *ɗ*]*

nado *Termanu.* look up, look upwards. (J:371)

nado *Bokai.*

nado *Bilbaa.*

nado *Rikou.*

nado *Ba'a.*

naɗo *Tii.*

olo/naɗo *Dengka.*

oro/naɗo *Oenale.*

Out-comparisons:

ŋada *Semau Helong.* look up, come before. *[Note:* Jonker (1908:371) gives Helong **ŋala**.*] [irr. from PMP:* *d = *d* /V_V (expect *l*)*]*

tanaat *East Tetun.* look up at (anything on a higher elevation); to look closely at someone expecting to be given something. *[Note:* Given the irregular final consonant and vowel correspondences, this may be a chance resemblance.*]* (Mo:180)

ŋaɗu, ŋaɗo *Ende.* bend oneself back.

***nadʒa** *Morph:* ***nadʒa-k**. *Rote.* name. *Etym:* *ŋajan. *[minority from PMP:* *j > *dʒ (expect *ɗ)*]* *[Sporadic:* *a > *e* /C+palatal_ in nRote.*]* *[Form:* Given that the Meto forms are not inheritances from ***nadʒa-k**, the correspondence sets are consistent with both *dʒ (see ***fudʒə** 'foam') or *d. Reconstruction of medial *d provides no explanation for the change of final *a > *e* in Nuclear Rote. By reconstructing medial *dʒ we can propose that this vowel change is due to the previous palatal consonant before the change of *dʒ > *ɗ/d*. An alternate reconstruction which can account for these reflexes would be **nadə, but this requires positing otherwise unattested final PMP *a to PRM *ə.*]*

nade-k *Termanu.* name. (J:370)

nade-ʔ *Korbafo.*

nade-k *Bokai.*

nade-ʔ *Bilbaa.*

nade=na *Landu.* name. (own field notes)

nade-ʔ *Rikou.*

nade-k *Ba'a.*

naɗe-k *Lole.* name. (Zacharias et al. 2014).*]*

naɗe-k *Tii.*

nala-ʔ *Dengka.*

nara-ʔ *Oenale.*

nara=na *Dela.* name.

°kana-f *Ro'is Amarasi.* name. *Borrowed from:* Helong **ŋala**, before *l > *n* (shown by irr. *ŋ > *k* correspondence, combined with identical semantics).

°kana-f *Kotos Amarasi.* name, clan.

°kana-f *Molo.* name. (M:178)

°kana-f *Kusa-Manea.* name.

Out-comparisons:

ŋala *Semau Helong.* name, tribe, clan, people group.

naran *East Tetun.* name. (Mo:152)

kala *Mambae, South.* name. (Grimes et al. 2014b:24)

gala-n *Kemak.* name.

nean *Ili'uun.* name, named, be named. (dJ:130)

nae** *PRM.* big, large. *Etym:* *Raya. *[irr. from PMP:* *R > *n*]* *[irr. from PRM:* *e > *i* in Kusa-Manea*]* *[Form:* One possible source of the unexpected *n in PRM is historic compounding of reflexes of *maRuqanay (mone** or ***mane**) with *Raya > **ae. Such a form is still attested in Hawu and may be the source of Dela-Oenale **monae-ʔ** (see ***mone**). The Dela-Oenale, Dengka and Meto forms without initial **mo** or **ma** could then be subsequent reanalysis of **ma** as a prefix. However, this explanation does not account for the Bima form **nae** which also has unexpected initial *n*, suggesting that the irregular appearance of this consonant is much earlier than PRM.*]*

na-ma-nae *Bilbaa.* **bisu=a na-ma-nae** the wound has swollen up (J:735)

na-anae (2) ma-nae-ʔ (3) na-ma-nae *Dengka.* 1) become big. 2) big. 3) **bisu=a na-ma-nae** the wound has swollen up (J:735)

nae (2) mo/nae-ʔ *Oenale.* 1) big, many. (J:735) 2) big. *[Form:* Historic compound of **mone** 'man' and *Raya > ***nae** (or perhaps earlier **ae.*]* (J:734)

nae-ʔ (2) mo/nae-ʔ, ma/nae-ʔ *Dela.* 1) many, much. 2) big, important.

na-ʔ|nae *Ro'is Amarasi.* grow.

na-ʔ|nae (2) ʔ|nae|k (3) ʔ|nae|f (4) kbenu_ʔ|naes *Kotos Amarasi.* 1) grow. 2) great, auspicious. 3) old man. 4) big fly.

ʔ|nae|k *Amfo'an.* big.

na-ʔ|nae *Molo.* big, eldest. (M:340)

bi/nai|ʔ *Kusa-Manea.* big. *[irr. from PRM:* *e > *i]* *[Form:* source of initial **bi** currently unknown.*]*

Out-comparisons:

mone ae *Hawu.* large, big, significant, important.

nae *Bima.* big, mature, grand. (Jonker 1893:58)

***nafu** *Rote.* to anchor. *Etym:* *nabuq 'fall'.

nafu (2) nafu-k *Termanu.* 1) anchor (v.). 2) anchor. *Usage:* used less in Termanu, used more in Ba'a. (J:373)

nafu *Korbafo.*

nafu *Bokai.*

nafu *Bilbaa.*

nafu *Rikou.*

nafu *Ba'a.*

nafu *Tii.*

nafu *Dengka.*

nafu *Oenale.*

Out-comparisons:

penavu *Hawu.* anchor.

***nafu|ʔ** *PnMeto.* body hair, feather. *Etym:* **rafu (pre-Meto).

nafuʔ *Amanuban/Amanatun.* body hair, feathers. (M:340)

nafuʔ *Amfo'an.* feathers.

nafuʔ *Kusa-Manea.* hair.

Out-comparisons:

rahun *Fehan Tetun.* feather. (Mo:158)

ravuk *Central Lembata.* body hair, feather. (Fricke 2015)

***nahe** *Morph:* ***ka-nahe-k**. *CERM.* mat. *See:* ***nehi**. *Etym:* *hapin 'liner, layer, insulation, padding; sleeping mat'. *[irr. from PMP:* *i > *e; *Ø > *n*] [irr. from PRM:* vowel metathesis in Meto *eCa > *aCe] [Form:* I have reconstructed ***nahe** with penultimate *a rather than ***neha** on the basis of the external evidence from Tetun (and PMP). While Meto has more instances of vowel metathesis than the Rote languages, it would be difficult to explain the connection between the Meto and Tetun forms as a result of borrowing due to the semantic difference. Thus, ***neha** would require two independent instances of vowel metathesis. ***nahe**, on the other hand, only requires one instance of vowel metathesis in CERM.*]*

neʔa-k *Termanu.* mat. (J:385)

neʔa-ʔ *Korbafo. [Note:* Jonker (1908:385) gives two forms marked K., but the second of these is surely a typographical error for R. = Rikou.*]*

neʔa-k *Bokai.*

nea *Bilbaa.*

nea-ʔ *Rikou.*

ʔ|nahe|k *Kotos Amarasi.* mat.

<nahe> *Molo.* mat. (M:341)

nahe *Kusa-Manea.* mat.

Out-comparisons:

kneheʔ *Funai Helong.* mat.

nehe *Semau Helong.* mat, sleeping mat.

naʔe *Fehan Tetun.* spread out.

nahe *East Tetun.* spread out, unfold (mat, towel, etc.). (Mo:146)

***nako** *Rote.* steal. *Etym:* *nakaw. *Pattern:* k-5′ (*k > *ʔ* in Tii and Dengka; expect *k = *k*).

na-ma-nako (2) nako *Termanu.* 1) steal. 2) theft. (J:374)

na-ma-nako *Bokai.*

na-ma-nako *Bilbaa.*

(2) naʔo *Rikou.* thief, burglar. *[Note:* Jonker (1908:374) gives Rikou (**na-ma-nao** ?).*]* (Nako et al. 2014)

na-ma-nako *Ba'a.*

(2) naʔo (3) nako/ɗaa *Lole.* 2) thief. 3) thief, steal. (Zacharias et al. 2014)

na-ma-naʔo *Tii.*

na-ma-naʔo *Dengka.*

na-ma-nako *Oenale.*

Out-comparisons:

nako *Semau Helong.* steal, rob.

hamnaʔo *East Tetun.* rob, steal, pilfer, plunder. (Mo:71)

menaʔo *Hawu.* steal, rob.

***nama** *PRM.* creep. *[Form:* Helong attests earlier initial *l. Initial *n in PRM could be sporadic assimilation to the following nasal.*]*

nama, nama~nama *Termanu.* creep, of a worm or insect. (J:379)

nama~nama *Korbafo.*

nama~nama *Bokai.*

nama~nama *Bilbaa.*

nama~nama *Rikou.*

nama~nama *Ba'a.*

nama~nama *Tii.*

nama~nama *Dengka.*

nama~nama *Oenale.*

<aknama> *Molo.* creeping of a plant. (M:346)

Out-comparisons:

naklama *Semau Helong.* tiptoe, sneak. *[irr. from PRM:* *n = *l* correspondence*]*

***namo**$_1$ *Morph:* ***ka-namo**. *nRM.* senna (kind of tree). Senna timoriensis.

na~namo *Termanu.* kind of healing plant called *akar pele* in Kupang. *[Semantics:* Heyne (1950:748) gives Timor Malay **kayu pelen** as Senna timoriensis.*]* (J:379)

na~namo *Korbafo.*

na~namo *Bokai.*

na~namo *Bilbaa.*

na~namo *Ba'a.*

na~namo *Tii.*

k|namo|ʔ *Kotos Amarasi.* senna. Senna timoriensis. *[Form:* Middelkoop (1972:347) gives <**tefu namo**> 'wild sugarcane' and <**namo**> 'chair of banana and sugarcane' which may be related.*]* *[Semantics:* Identification from Heyne (1950:748) who has 'Timor' <**kĕnamoh**>.*]*

***namo**$_2$ *PRM.* coast, beach. *Etym:* *namaw 'sheltered water: deep place in a river; cove, harbor, lagoon'.

namo *Termanu.* coast, beach. (J:379)

namo *Korbafo.*

namo *Bokai.*

namo *Bilbaa.*

namo *Rikou.*

namo *Ba'a.*

namo *Tii.*

namo *Dengka.*

namo *Oenale.*

namo *Molo.* area around a village. (M:347)

Out-comparisons:

namon *East Tetun.* mouth of river, port. (Mo:151)

namo(n) *Ili'uun.* earth, field, garden, place, world. (dJ:129)

***namba** *Morph:* ***ka-namba-k**. *nRM.* leaves covering fruit.

napa-k *Termanu.* the leaves which cover the fruit of palm trees. (J:380)

napa *Korbafo.*

napa-k *Bokai.*

napa *Bilbaa.*

napa *Rikou.*

namba-k *Tii.*

ma-k|napa-ʔ *Kotos Amarasi.* squeezed together, conjoined.

uki k|napa|ʔ *Molo.* the leaves of the heart-shaped banana blossom. (M:222)

***nana** *Morph:* ***nana-k**. *Rote.* pus. *Etym:* *nanaq.

nana-k *Termanu.* pus. (J:380)

nana-ʔ *Korbafo.*

nana-k *Bokai.*

nana-ʔ *Bilbaa.*

nana-ʔ *Rikou.*

nana-k *Ba'a.*

nana-k *Tii.*

nana-ʔ *Dengka.*

nana-ʔ *Oenale.*

***naŋe** *Rote.* swim. *Etym:* *naŋuy. *[irr. from PMP:* *uy > *e (expect *i)*]* *[minority from PMP:* *ŋ = *ŋ (required for Termanu and Korbafo)*]* *[irr. from PRM:* *n > Ø in most nRote (reanalysis as agreement?)*]* *[History:* The Rote forms are possible borrowings from Helong. This could explain *ŋ* in Termanu and Korbafo. Final *uy >

e would also be irregular in Helong, but proposing that the Rote forms are borrowings from Helong requires positing irregular sound changes in one less instance.*]*

(ʔ)aŋe *Termanu.* swim. (J:12)

(ʔ)aŋe *Korbafo.*

(ʔ)ane *Bokai.*

(ʔ)ane *Bilbaa.*

(ʔ)ane *Landu.* swim. (own field notes)

ʔane *Rikou. [Form:* My consultants gave **na-ʔane** 's/he swims'.*]*

(ʔ)ane *Ba'a.*

nane *Tii.*

nane *Dengka.*

nane *Oenale.*

Out-comparisons:

naŋen *Semau Helong.* swim.

nani *East Tetun.* swim; climb (of plants). (Mo:152)

***naru** *PRM.* long, length. *Doublet:* ***daru**. *Etym:* *anaduq (Reflexes of the doublet *adaduq > ***daru** are (apparently) not found in wRote. This indicates that the Meto forms are probably inheritances of *anaduq > ***naru** even though they would also be regular from *adaduq).

ma-nalu (2) nalu (3) nalu-k, ma-nalu-k *Termanu.* 1) long. 2) long. 3) length. (J:378)

ma-nalu *Korbafo.*

ma-nalu *Bokai.*

ma-nalu *Bilbaa.*

naru-ʔ *Rikou.* tall, long. (Nako et al. 2014)

ma-nalu *Ba'a.*

ma-nalu *Lole.* long. (Zacharias et al. 2014)

ma-naru *Tii.*

nalu-ʔ *Dengka.* long, tall. (J:378, 736)

naru-ʔ *Oenale.* long, tall. (J:378, 736)

naru-ʔ *Dela.* tall, long.

m|nanu|ʔ *Ro'is Amarasi.* long, length, deep, depth.

m|nanu|ʔ *Kotos Amarasi.* long, length, deep, depth.

m|nanu|ʔ *Molo.* long. *[Note:* No headword given for **mnanuʔ** but many examples of this word occur in other entries.*]* (M:583)

Out-comparisons:

naruk *East Tetun.* long, lengthy, tall, lofty. (Mo:152)

***nase** *Morph:* ***ka-nase**. *PRM.* fish, Blue-spot Mullet. <u>*Moolgarda seheli*</u>. *Etym:* *kanasay. *[Form:* The initial *ka of the PMP form was probably reanalysed as the nominal prefix in PRM.*]*

nase *Termanu.* kind of fish, the *ikan belanak*. (J:381)

nase *Korbafo.*

nase *Bokai.*

nase *Bilbaa.*

nase *Rikou.*

nase *Ba'a.*

nase *Tii.*

nase *Dengka.*

nase *Oenale.*

k|naes *Ro'is Amarasi.* mullet. *[Note:* Jonker (1908:381) gives unmetathesised Meto **knasa** which would probably attest irr. *e > *a.] [Form:* metathesised form of (currently unattested) ***knase**.*]*

Out-comparisons:

hnase *Helong.* (J:381)

knase (2) manu knase *East Tetun.* 1) fish. 2) hen or rooster whose spots are like those of the fish. (Mo:113)

***nasi** *PRM.* jackal jujube (kind of fruit tree). <u>*Ziziphus oenoplia*</u>. *[Form:* Helong attests earlier *ŋ.*]*

asi/nasi *Termanu.* kind of tree. <u>*Ziziphus oenoplia*</u>. (J:15; Heyne 1950:1003, cxv)

asi/nasi *Korbafo.*

kai_nasi *Bilbaa.*

ai_nasi *Rikou.*

asi/nasi *Ba'a.*

asi/nasi *Tii.*

ŋga/nasi *Dengka.*

ŋga/nasi *Oenale.*

<asnási> *Meto.* Ziziphus timoriensis. (Meijer Drees 1950:1)
Out-comparisons:
<kaingasi> *Helong.* Ziziphus oenoplia. (Heyne 1950:1003, cxv)
ai knase *East Tetun.* tree with sticky gum. (Mo:113)

***nasu** *PRM.* cook by boiling. *Etym:* *nasu.
nasu *Termanu.* boil. (J:381)
nasu *Korbafo.*
nasu *Bokai.*
nasu *Bilbaa.*
nasu *Rikou.*
nasu *Ba'a.*
nasu *Tii.*
nasu *Dengka.*
nasu *Oenale.*
n-nasu *Kotos Amarasi.* cook greens by boiling.
n-nasu *Molo.* cooks. **n-nasu utan** one cooks uncut greens (M:352)

***natu** *Morph:* ***natu-k**. *PRM.* ovary, gamete. *Etym:* *natuq 'ovary of an oviparous animal'.
natu-k, (2) manu natu-k, (3) manu tolo natu-k *Termanu.* 1) the pollen of flowers, etc. 2) the beginnings of an egg in the body of a chicken. 3) egg yolk. (J:382)
natu-ʔ *Korbafo.*
natu-k *Bokai.*
natu-ʔ *Bilbaa.*
natu-ʔ *Rikou.*
natu-k *Ba'a.*
natu-k *Tii.*
natu-ʔ *Dengka.*
natu-ʔ *Oenale.*
natu-f *Kotos Amarasi.* ovaries.
Out-comparisons:
natuʔ *Semau Helong.* roe.
keradu *Hawu.* egg yolk. (J:382)

***natu|n** *PRM.* hundred. *Etym:* *sa-ŋa-Ratus. *[Form:* Inherited via intermediate **ŋatus. While the final *n may be a fossilised suffix, which suffix it would be is unclear.*]*
natun *Termanu.* hundred. (J:382)
natun *Korbafo.*
natun *Bokai.*
natun *Bilbaa.*
natun *Rikou.*
natun *Ba'a.*
natun *Tii.*
natun *Dengka.*
na̯tun *Oenale.*
na͡utun *Ro'is Amarasi.* hundred.
natun *Kotos Amarasi.* hundred.
natun *Molo.* hundred. (M:355)
natun *Kusa-Manea.* hundred.
Out-comparisons:
ŋatus *Semau Helong.* hundred.
atus *East Tetun.* hundred. *[Form:* Not inherited via intermediate **ŋatus.*]* (Mo:5)
rahu *Kisar.* hundred. *[irr. from PMP:* *t > *h* (possibly via irregular medial *s)*]*
ŋasu *Dhao.* hundred.
ŋahu *Hawu.* hundred.

***nee₁** *PRM.* six. *Etym:* *ənəm. *[irr. from PMP:* *ə > Ø /#_ (or final *VC > CV metathesis)*]*
nee *Termanu.* six. (J:383)
nee *Korbafo.*
nee *Bokai.*
nee *Bilbaa.*
nee *Rikou.*
nee *Ba'a.*
nee *Tii.*
nee *Dengka.*
nee *Oenale.*
nee *Ro'is Amarasi.* six.
nee *Kotos Amarasi.* six.
<ne> *Molo.* six. (M:358)
nee *Kusa-Manea.* six.
Out-comparisons:
eneŋ *Semau Helong.* six.
neen *East Tetun.* six. *[irr. from PMP:* *ə > *e* (expect *o*)*]* (Mo:153)
neem, neme, həneem, eneem *Kemak.* six.
inam *Welaun.* six.
ineen *Galolen.* six.

ha-neen *Ili'uun.* six. (dJ:94, 130)
fa-nen *Tugun.* six. (Hinton 1991:63)
woneme *Kisar.* six.
əna *Hawu.* six.

***nee2** *PRM.* quiet, still, at rest. *Etym:* *qənəŋ. *[irr. from PMP:* *ə > Ø with doubling of the final vowel to create a disyllable, or medial VC > CV metathesis*]*
nee~nee (2) na-ma-nee *Termanu.* 1) still, quiet. 2) **ana suŋu na-ma-nee** s/he is fast asleep, s/he is deep asleep (J:384)
nee~nee (2) na-ma-nee *Korbafo.*
nee~nee (2) na-ma-nee *Bokai.*
nee~nee (2) na-ma-nee *Bilbaa.*
(2) na-ma-nee *Rikou.*
nee~nee (2) na-ma-nee *Ba'a.*
nee~nee (2) na-ma-nee *Tii.*
nee~nee (2) na-ma-nee *Dengka.*
nee~nee (2) na-ma-nee *Oenale.*
na-m|nee *Kotos Amarasi.* calm.
Out-comparisons:
hanook *East Tetun.* keep quiet, or silent, shut up. (Mo:76)

***nehi** *Rote.* mat. *See:* ***nahe**. *Etym:* **nepi (pre-RM). *[History:* Blust and Trussel (ongoing) reconstruct PMP *təpiR which is the source of Hawu **dəpi** and Dhao **ɖʐəpi**. However, initial *t cannot regularly account for initial *n* in the Rote or Bima forms.*]*
neʔi (2) ne~neʔi-k *Termanu.* 1) lie on top of something. **ana neʔi neʔa-k esa** he lies on a mat. (J:386) 2) the action of lying on something; mat, bag functioning as a pillow or mattress (Dutch *bultzak*). (J:387)
neʔi *Korbafo.*
neʔi *Bokai.*
nei *Bilbaa.*
neʔi (2) ne~neʔi-k *Ba'a.*
(2) ne~neʔi-k *Lole.* mat. (Zacharias et al. 2014)
neʔi (2) (ne~)neʔi-k *Tii.*
(2) ne~nei-ʔ *Dengka.*
(2) ne~nei-ʔ *Oenale.*
(2) ne~nei-ʔ *Dela.* mat, rug.
Out-comparisons:
nepi *Bima.* mattress, bag functioning as a pillow or mattress (Dutch *bultzak*). (Jonker 1893:60)

***neko** *Morph:* ***neko-k**. *nRM.* abomasum (the fourth and final stomach compartment in ruminants that secretes rennet). *Pattern:* k-5/6.
neko-(k) *Termanu.* one of the parts of the stomach of a ruminant, the abomasum, in Kupang *perut lingkar*. (J:387)
neko-k *Tii.*
neko-n *Meto.* (J:387)

***nembə** *Morph:* ***nembə-k**. *Rote.* hard, fixed. *Etym:* *təbəl 'thick, of objects; dense, of crowds'. *[irr. from PMP:* *t > *n; *b > *mb*] [irr. from PRM:* *n > *m* in Bilbaa and Rikou*]*
nepe-k *Termanu.* hard, fixed. (J:391)
nepe *Korbafo.*
nepe-k *Bokai.*
mepe-ʔ *Bilbaa.*
mepe-ʔ *Rikou.*
nempe-k *Ba'a.*
nemba-ʔ *Oenale.*

***nene1** *PRM.* press, push. *[irr. from PRM:* *n > *ʔ* in Rote except Bilbaa and Rikou*]*
neʔe *Termanu.* push. (J:386)
neʔe *Korbafo.*
neʔe *Bokai.*
nene *Bilbaa.*
nene *Rikou.*
neʔe *Ba'a.*
neʔe *Tii.*
neʔe *Dengka.*
n-nene *Kotos Amarasi.* press, push.
na-nene *Molo.* presses on. (M:362)

***nene2** *Rote.* hear, listen. *[History:* Perhaps connected with PMP *dəŋəR, though this requires irregular initial *d > *n and final *ə > *e (expect final *ə = *ə). Furthermore, *dəŋəR is retained regularly in Oenale and Meto (see ***rena**).*]*

na-ma-nene (2) nene~nene (3) ne~nene *Termanu.* 1) hear. 2) listen. 3) listen. (J:388)
na-ma-nene *Korbafo.*
na-ma-nene *Bokai.*
na-ma-nene *Bilbaa.*
na-ma-nene *Rikou.*
na-ma-nene *Ba'a.*
ni-mi-nene *Lole.* (J:737)
na-ma-nene, i-mi-nene *Tii.* (J:388, 705)
na-ma-nene *Dengka.*
na-ma-nene *Oenale.*

***neo** *Rote.* shy, jealous.
neo *Termanu.* shy, be scared. (J:390)
neo *Korbafo.*
neo *Bokai.*
na-neo *Bilbaa.*
neo *Rikou.*
neo *Ba'a.*
neo *Lole.* suspicious. (Zacharias et al. 2014)
neo *Tii.*
neo *Dengka.*
na-ma-neo *Oenale.*
Out-comparisons:
neo *Semau Helong.* jealous.

***neru** *Morph:* ***na-ma-neru**. *Rote.* warm oneself. *[irr. from PRM:* *e > *i* in several Rote lects (sporadic assimilation)*]* *[Form:* Reconstruction of penultimate *e requires irr. *e > *i* in at least three separate cases: West Rote (Oenale, Dengka), central Rote (Termanu, Bilbaa), and Hawu. However, this sound change can be motivated as a case of sporadic assimilation to the following high vowel and/or an earlier palatal nasal (as attested in Hawu). Reconstruction of penultimate *e would require unmotivated *i > *e* in at least two cases: eastern Rote (Korbafo, Bokai, Rikou) and Ba'a.*]*
na-ma-nilu *Termanu.* warm oneself. (J:397)
na-ma-nelu *Korbafo.*
na-ma-nelu *Bokai.*
na-ma-nilu *Bilbaa.*
na-ma-neru *Rikou.*
na-ma-nelu *Ba'a.*
na-ma-niru *Tii.*
na-ma-nilu *Dengka.*
na-mba-niru *Oenale.*
Out-comparisons:
meɲiru ai *Hawu.* warm self over fire.

***nesa** *nRM.* same, alike. *[History:* This is almost certainly connected with ***esa** 'one'.*]*
na-ka-nesak *Termanu.* compare, equate. (J:391)
na-ka-nesak *Bokai.*
na-ka-nesak *Ba'a.*
na-ka-nesak *Tii.*
na-m|nesa *Kotos Amarasi.* same.
na-nesa (2) na-m|nesa *Molo.* 1) agree with one another. 2) alike. (M:364)
Out-comparisons:
hanesa-n *East Tetun.* be the same, equal, or identical, be alike; *n.* similar; *adv.* similarly, equally, of the same type, shape, make, or size. (Mo:75)

***nesu** *Morph:* ***nesu-k**. *PRM.* mortar. *Etym:* *ləsuŋ. *[irr. from PMP:* *l > *n*]* *[irr. from PRM:* *n > Ø in most Meto (also Helong)*]* *[Form:* Out-comparisons point to pre-RM **ŋəsun, perhaps with metathesis of initial and final consonants.*]*
nesu-k *Termanu.* mortar. (J:392)
nesu-ʔ *Korbafo.*
nesu-k *Bokai.*
nesu-k *Bilbaa.*
nesu-ʔ *Rikou.*
nesu-k *Ba'a.*
nesu-k *Tii.*
nesu-ʔ *Dengka.*
n̲esu-ʔ *Oenale.*
e͡usu|k *Ro'is Amarasi.* mortar.
esu|k *Kotos Amarasi.* mortar.
esu|ʔ *Molo.* mortar. (M:104)
nesu|k *Kusa-Manea.* mortar.

Out-comparisons:

isuŋ *Helong.* mortar. (J:392)

nesun *East Tetun.* mortar, part of a tree trunk with a hollow at one end, used in conjunction with **alu** for de-husking grain; *v.* to pound or grind grain, tapioca, etc. *[irr. from PMP:* *ə > *e* (expect *o*)*]* (Mo:154)

knehun *Ili'uun.* mortar (for rice-pounding). (dJ:121)

nesug *Kemak.* mortar. *Usage:* Saneri and Leosibe dialects.

kosun *Welaun.* mortar.

ŋətʃu *Dhao.* mortar and pestle.

***neta** *Morph:* ***na-ma-neta**. *Rote.* choke. *Etym:* **ma-ŋeta (pre-RM).

na-ma-neta *Termanu.* choke, unable to take a breath. (J:392)

na-ma-neta *Ba'a.*

na-ma-neta *Tii.*

na-ma-neta *Dengka.*

na-ma-neta *Oenale.*

Out-comparisons:

meŋita *Hawu.* (J:392)

***nihe** *Morph:* ***nihe-k**. *Rote.* ant. *Etym:* *nipay 'snake'. *[irr. from PRM:* *e > *a* in Ba'a; *e > *i* in Korbafo and East Rote (sporadic assimilation?)*]*

neʔe-k *Termanu.* ant. (J:386)

niʔi-ʔ *Korbafo.*

nii-ʔ *Bilbaa.*

nii-ʔ *Landu.* (own field notes)

nii-ʔ *Rikou.*

nii-ʔ *Oepao.* (own field notes)

niʔa-k *Ba'a.*

niʔe-k *Lole.* ant. (Zacharias et al. 2014)

niʔe-k *Tii.*

nie-ʔ *Dengka.*

nie-ʔ *Oenale.*

Out-comparisons:

neʔek *Fehan Tetun.* ant.

nehek *East Tetun.* ant (of many varieties). (Mo:153)

nee *Kisar.* snake.

***nihis** *Morph:* ***ma-nihis**. *PRM.* thin. *Etym:* *nipis 'thinness (of materials)'. *[irr. from PRM:* *i > *a* in Meto; *h > *ʔ* /V_V in wRote (expect Ø)*]*

niʔis (2) na-ma-niʔi *Termanu.* 1) thin. 2) become thin. (J:396)

niʔi-ʔ *Korbafo.*

nii-ʔ *Bilbaa.*

niis *Landu.* thin. (own field notes)

niis *Rikou.*

niʔis *Ba'a.*

niʔis *Lole.* thin. (Zacharias et al. 2014)

niʔis *Tii.*

niʔis *Dengka.*

niʔis *Oenale.*

mainihas *Kotos Amarasi.* thin. *[Note:* I also have **manihis** as an alternate form in my dictionary but I don't know the source of this form and when I checked it with my main Amarasi consultant he was mystified by it.*]*

mainihas *Molo.* thin. (M:xxx)

manihis *Timaus.* thin. *[Form:* regular assimilation of *a in final closed syllables.*]*

Out-comparisons:

mnihis *Funai Helong.* thin.

nihis *Semau Helong.* thin.

niʔis *Fehan Tetun.* thin (not thick), sensitive (of a person).

mihis *East Tetun.* thin, slender (slices, etc.). (Mo:142)

***niit** *Morph:* ***ka-niit**. *PRM.* crab. *[Form:* The Tetun forms point to earlier **ka-nipis, though positing these forms as cognate requires irr. *p > (*h) > Ø in Termanu, Ba'a, Bokai, Korbafo and Tii.*]*

nii-k, iʔa nii-k *Termanu.* crab. (J:396)

nii-ʔ *Korbafo.*

nii-k *Bokai.*

nii-ʔ *Bilbaa.*

nii-ʔ *Rikou.*

nii-k *Ba'a.*

nii-k *Tii.*

niit, nii-ʔ *Dengka. [Note:* Both Dengka forms flagged as 'also surely Dengka'.*]*
niit *Oenale.*
k|niit *Ro'is Amarasi.*
k|niit *Kotos Amarasi.* crab.
k|niit *Molo.* horn (instrument). (M:223)
Out-comparisons:
kniit *Funai Helong.* crab.
hniit *Semau Helong.* crab.
niʔis *Fehan Tetun.* freshwater crab. *[irr. from PRM:* *Ø = *ʔ* correspondence; *t = *s* correspondences (perhaps influenced by **niʔis** 'thin')*]*
nihis *East Tetun.* small crab of quiet water. *Usage:* Luka and Ue Keke villages. *[irr. from PRM:* *Ø = *h* correspondence; *t = *s* correspondences (perhaps influenced by **mihis** 'thin')*]* (Mo:154)
mihis *East Tetun.* a variety of crab. *Usage:* Bubu Susu village. *[irr. from PRM:* *n = *m* correspondence*]* (Mo:154)
kaniik *Kupang Malay.* (J:396)

***nimba** *Rote.* kind of fish. *[irr. from PRM:* *a > *e* in most Rote*]*
nipa *Termanu.* kind of sea fish called *ikan nipe* in Kupang. (J:398)
nipe *Korbafo.*
nipe *Bokai.*
nipe *Bilbaa.*
nipe *Rikou.*
nimpa *Ba'a.*
nimbe *Tii.*
nimbe *Dengka.*
nimbe *Oenale.*
Out-comparisons:
nipe *Semau Helong.*(J:398)

***nini** *Morph:* ***nini-k**. *Rote.* mosquito. *Etym:* *ñikñik 'tiny biting insect: gnat, sandfly'.
nini-k *Termanu.* mosquito. (J:397)
nini-k *Korbafo.*
nini-ʔ *Bokai.*
nini-ʔ *Bilbaa.*
nini-ʔ *Landu.* mosquito. (own field notes)
nini-ʔ *Rikou.*
nini-k *Ba'a.*
nini-k *Tii.*
nini-ʔ *Dengka.*
nini-ʔ *Oenale.*
Out-comparisons:
knikiʔ *Funai Helong.* mosquito.
nikiʔ, hmiki *Semau Helong.* mosquito.
ninik *East Tetun.* small mosquito with a painful sting. (Mo:154)
nini *Hawu.* kind of small mosquito. (J:397)

***nisi** *Morph:* ***nisi-k**. *PRM.* tooth, teeth. *Etym:* *ŋis(ŋ)i(s) 'grin, show the teeth'.
nisi-k *Termanu.* tooth. (J:398)
nisi-ʔ *Korbafo.*
nisi-k *Bokai.*
nisi-ʔ *Bilbaa.*
nisi-ʔ *Landu.* (own field notes)
nisi-ʔ *Rikou.*
nisi-ʔ *Oepao.* (own field notes)
nisi-k *Ba'a.*
nisi-k *Tii.*
nisi-ʔ *Dengka.*
nisi-ʔ *Oenale.*
nisi-f *Ro'is Amarasi.* tooth.
nisi-f *Kotos Amarasi.* tooth.
nisi-k *Molo.* tooth. (M:372)
nisi-f *Kusa-Manea.* tooth.
Out-comparisons:
sii *Semau Helong.* tooth. *[irr. from PMP:* *ŋi > Ø*]*
kisaa-t *Welaun.* teeth. *[irr. from PMP:* *is > Ø, apparently from intermediate **ŋis*]*

***nitas** *PRM.* hazel sterculia tree. <u>*Sterculia foetidea*</u>.
nitas *Termanu.* kind of tree also called *nitas* in Kupang, the wood of this tree is used in carpentry, amongst other things for coffins, the fruit

of this tree (the **nita boa-k**) yields a kind of resin: **dama nitas**, the ashes of the dried husks are also used. (J:399f)

nita-ʔ *Korbafo.*

nita-ʔ *Bokai.*

nita-ʔ *Bilbaa.*

nitas *Rikou.*

nitas *Ba'a.*

nitas *Tii.*

nitas *Dengka.*

nitas *Oenale.*

<nitas> *Molo.* kind of tree. Sterculia foetidea. (M:374)

Out-comparisons:

nitas, ai knitas *East Tetun.* tree with good timber. Sterculia foetidea. (Mo:153)

nita *Sika.* Sterculia foetidea. (Verheijen 1984:67)

nitaʔ *Komodo.* Sterculia foetidea. (Verheijen 1984:67)

nintap *Manggarai.* Sterculia foetidea. (Verheijen 1984:67)

litap *East Manggarai.* Sterculia foetidea. (Verheijen 1984:67)

litat *Kepo'.* Sterculia foetidea. *[Note:* language of central Flores ISO 639-3 [kuk].*]* (Verheijen 1984:67)

litat *Rajong.* Sterculia foetidea. *[Note:* language of central Flores ISO 639-3 [rjg].*]* (Verheijen 1984:67)

***nitu** *PRM.* spirit. *Etym:* *qanitu 'ghost, ancestral spirit; nature spirit; corpse; owl; various plants'.

nitu *Termanu.* spirits of the ancestors; demon. (J:400)

nitu *Korbafo.*

nitu *Bokai.*

nitu *Bilbaa.*

nitu *Rikou.*

nitu *Ba'a.*

nitu *Tii.*

nitu *Dengka.*

nitu *Oenale.*

nitu *Kotos Amarasi.* spirit of dead person, corpse.

nitu *Molo.* corpse and spirit. (M:374)

***noɗo** *Rote.* crawl, creep. *Doublet:* ***roɗok.**

nodo~nodo *Termanu.* crawl forward, usually said of children; push forward on one's behind. (J:402)

nodo~nodo *Korbafo.*

nodo~nodo *Bokai.*

nodo~nodo *Bilbaa.*

nodo~nodo *Rikou.*

nodo~nodo *Ba'a.*

noɗo~noɗo *Tii.*

nodo~nodo used in place of **lodo** for the crawling of snakes, etc. *Dengka.*

noɗo~noɗo *Oenale.* used in place of **lodo** for the crawling of snakes, etc.

***noe** *PRM.* melt.

noe *Termanu.* melt, dissolve; melt something. (J:402)

noe *Korbafo.*

noe *Bokai.*

noe *Bilbaa.*

noe *Rikou.*

noe *Ba'a.*

noe *Tii.*

noe *Dengka.*

noe *Oenale.*

na-m|noe *Kotos Amarasi.* melt.

na-m|noe, na-t|noe (2) na-noe-b *Molo.* 1) melted. 2) someone melts something. (M:377)

Out-comparisons:

noe(m) (2) noe *Semau Helong.* 1) melt. 2) destroyed, damaged, shattered, smashed, crushed.

***noh** *PRM.* coconut. *Etym:* *niuR. *[irr. from PMP:* *i > Ø; *u > *o; *R > *h (also in ***klaha** and ***taha**)*]* *[irr. from PRM:* Ø > *a* in Meto (also Kemak)*]* *[History:* The connection between PMP *niuR and PRM ***noh** involves several irregularities. Firstly, final *h must be reconstructed to account for the Meto reflexes as Meto usually retains *h finally while it is lost in Rote (cf. ***dilah**, ***mbuah**, ***sikəh**, ***henuh**, and ***nunuh**). PRM *h could plausibly, though irregularly, be derived from *R as the change *R > *h is attested in two other forms (cf. ***klaha**, ***taha**). Secondly, the lowering of *u > *o must be accounted for. While lowering of high vowels to mid before *R is sporadically attested in the Rote-Meto languages, it is not attested in other languages of the Timor region included in the out-comparisons that also have irr. *u > *o* in this form (e.g. Ili'uun **iku** 'tail' < *ikuR, **telu** < *qatəluR 'egg'). This indicates that *u > *o* is an irregular development before the time of PRM. Thirdly, the second vowel *a* must be accounted for in Meto. This could be an irregular insertion in PMeto in order to create a disyllable, though we would probably expect that the original single vowel would have been doubled, as in the Rote languages and several other languages of the region. (Helong has **nian**, which also has irregular insertion of *a*, though the retention of *i = *i* in Helong indicates that it is not directly connected with the Meto form.) Finally, reflexes of PMP *niuR that do not attest irr. *u > *o* are also found in the greater Timor region. Examples include Tetun **nuu**, Welaun **nuu**, Leti **nura** and Dhao **ɲiu**. This indicates that the precursor to irregular ***noh** probably occurred alongside regular reflexes of PMP *niuR in this region.*]*

noo *Termanu.* coconut (tree and fruit). (J:400)

noo *Korbafo.*

noo *Bokai.*

noo *Bilbaa.*

noo *Landu.* coconut. (own field notes)

noo *Rikou.*

noo *Ba'a.*

noo *Tii.*

noo *Dengka.*

noo *Oenale.*

noah *Ro'is Amarasi.* coconut.

noah *Kotos Amarasi.* coconut.

noah *Molo.* coconut. (M:376)

noah, noha *Kusa-Manea.* coconut. *[Form:* The form **noha** [ˈnɔhɐ] may be due to reanalysis of **noah** as a metathesised form given that Kusa-Manea does not have assimilation of /a/ after metathesis. This is also attested in **puah**, **puha** 'betel nut'.*]*

Out-comparisons:

noo *Galolen.* coconut.

noo *Mambae, South.* coconut. (Grimes et al. 2014b:35)

noo *Ili'uun.* coco-tree. (dJ:130)

noor *Tugun.* coconut. (Hinton 2000:120)

nor *Kisar.* coconut.

noa *Kemak.* coconut. *Usage:* Kutubaba and Leolima dialects. *[Form:* Final *a* in Kemak may be an irregular vocalisation of earlier final *R. Compare *qauR > Kemak **oa** ~ **ua** 'bamboo'.*]*

nua *Kemak.* coconut. *Usage:* other known varieties of Kemak.

***noko** *Rote.* shake. *Pattern:* k-5. *[irr. from PRM:* *o > *u* in second sense in Korbafo, Bokai, and Bilbaa*]*

noko~noko (2) na-ka-no~noko *Termanu.* 1) shake, move in a shaking manner. 2) shake something. (J:405)

(2) na-ka-nu~nuku *Korbafo.*

noko~noko (2) na-ka-nu~nuku *Bokai.*

(2) na-ka-nu~nuku *Bilbaa.*

noko~noko *Rikou.*

noko~noko (2) na-ka-no~noko *Ba'a.*
noko~noko (2) na-ka-no~noko *Tii.*
noko~noko *Dengka.*
Out-comparisons:
ɲoko, keɲoko *Hawu.* shake. (J:405)

***nono1** *PnMeto.* sorcery. *[Form:* If these forms are indeed related, they probably point to earlier **nodo(h).*]*
<leʔu nono> *Molo.* fertility magic. (M:384)
Out-comparisons:
in nodo *Funai Helong.* sorcerer, witch.
nodoh *Semau Helong.* sorcery.

***nono2** *PnMeto.* family group.
nono (2) nono-t *Kotos Amarasi.* 1) kind of jungle rope, liana; descent group. 'lianas which encircle the clan and hence symbolize its fertility' (Schulte Nordholt 1971:116). 2) family, clan group.
nono-t *Molo.* origin group. (M:384)
Out-comparisons:
noro *Buru.* origin group, kin group, clan. (Grimes and Grimes 2020:663)

***nori** *Morph:* ***na-nori**. *PRM.* teach, learn.
na-noli *Termanu.* learn, instruct. (J:406)
na-noli *Korbafo.*
na-noli *Bokai.*
na-noli *Bilbaa.*
na-nori *Rikou.*
na-noli *Ba'a.*
na-nori *Tii.*
na-noli *Dengka.*
na-nori *Oenale.*
na-noniʔ *Ro'is Amarasi.* learn, teach.
na-noniʔ *Kotos Amarasi.* learn, teach.
na-noin-aʔ *Molo.* points out. (M:379)
Out-comparisons:
hanorin *Fehan Tetun.* teach, instruct, indoctrinate.
hanourin *East Tetun.* teach, instruct, indoctrinate. (Mo:76)
nori *Kisar.* coax, persuade, woo.
nori (2) noir *Mambae, South.* 1) teaching, lesson. 2) teach, instruct. (Grimes et al. 2014:35)
nori *Dhao.* teaching.

***noto** *Morph:* ***noto~noto**. *PRM.* slow.
noto~noto *Termanu.* slow (walking). (J:407)
noto~noto *Korbafo.*
noto~noto *Bokai.*
noto~noto *Bilbaa.*
noto~noto *Rikou.*
noto~noto *Ba'a.*
noto~noto *Tii.*
noto~noto *Dengka.*
not~notoʔ *Kotos Amarasi.* slow, taking some time; e.g. describes the situation of a person very early in the morning when they have just gotten out of bed, they are still sleepy and just sitting around without having started doing anything.
Out-comparisons:
noto~notok *Fehan Tetun.* quiet.
noto *Mambae, South.* quiet, silent. (Grimes et al. 2014b:36)

***nuɗu** *Morph:* ***nuɗu-k**. *PwRM.* outer mouth region. *Etym:* *ŋusuq 'nasal area; snout'. *[irr. from PMP:* *s > *ɗ*]* *[Sporadic:* *n > *r*/*l* in most varieties of Meto (except Ro'is Amarasi and optionally Kusa-Manea).*]* *[Form:* Irregular *s > *ɗ may have been through intermediate *z [dʒ]. Irregular *s > *z is also found in Celebic for this form, e.g. Balaesang **ŋudu**, Dampelas **ŋudʒu** (Himmelmann 2001:160f). However, while the reflexes in southwest Maluku also have irregularities in this consonant, these cannot be attributed to *z. Instead, they attest irregular *s > *d.*]*
nuɗu-ʔ *Dengka.* lip, beak of bird. (J:739)

nuɗu-ʔ *Oenale.* lip, beak of bird. (J:739)
nuru-n *Ro'is Amarasi.* lip.
ruru-f *Kotos Amarasi.* outer mouth region.
lulu-f *Molo.* lip(s). (M:292)
nuru-f, ruru-f *Kusa-Manea.* lips.
Out-comparisons:
nuru *Ili'uun.* mucus, slime. (dJ:148)
nuran (2) nuran wulla (3) nurhe *Kisar.* 1) mouth. 2) moustache. 3) snot.
nuru *Luang.* mouth. *[Note:* language of southwest Maluku ISO 639-3 [lex].*]* (Taber 1993:424)
nur-e *Central Marsela.* mouth. (Taber 1993:424)

***nuʔa** *PRM.* scabies. *Etym:* *nuka 'wound'. *[Sporadic:* *a > e / _# in Meto.*]*
nuʔa *Termanu.* scabies. (J:408)
nuʔa *Korbafo.*
nuʔa *Bokai.*
nua *Bilbaa.*
nuʔa *Rikou.*
nuʔa *Ba'a.*
nuʔa *Tii.*
nuʔa *Dengka.*
nuʔe *Amanuban.* wound. (M:389)
Out-comparisons:
nuka *East Tetun.* ulcer, atrophic sore (difficult to heal, possibly due to poor nutrition). (Mo:155)
noʔo *Kisar.* wound, sore, cut.
nua *West Damar.* wound. *[Note:* language of southwest Maluku ISO 639-3 [drn].*]* (Chlenov and Chlenova 2008:154)

***numbu** *Morph:* ***na-numbu**. *Rote.* grow, germinate, sprout. *Doublet:* ***tumbu**. *Etym:* *tu(m)buq. *[irr. from PMP:* *t > *n (also in Helong and Central Lembata)*]*
na-nupu *Termanu.* sprouting, germination of seeds, fruits. (J:409)
na-nupu *Korbafo.*
na-nupu *Bokai.*
na-nupu *Bilbaa.*
na-nupu *Rikou.*
na-numpu *Ba'a.*
na-numbu *Tii.*
na-numbu *Dengka.*
na-numbu *Oenale.*
Out-comparisons:
nupu *Semau Helong.* grow, shoot.
nubu *Central Lembata.* grow. (Fricke 2015)

***nunuh** *PRM.* banyan tree. *Etym:* *nunuk.
nunu-ʔ *Bilbaa.* banyan. (J:739)
nunu-ʔ *Rikou.*
nunu-k *Tii.*
nunu_londa-ʔ *Dengka.* aerial roots of the banyan tree. *[Note:* **liti-ʔ** = 'banyan tree'.*]* (J:739)
nunu_londa-ʔ *Oenale.* aerial roots of the banyan tree. *[Note:* **liti_bibi-ʔ** = 'banyan tree'.*]* (J:739)
nunah *Ro'is Amarasi.* banyan tree.
nunuh *Kotos Amarasi.* banyan tree.
nunuh *Molo.* banyan tree. Ficus species. (M:393)
Out-comparisons:
nunuʔ beas *Semau Helong.* banyan.

***nuŋa** *PRM.* kind of flowering tree. Cordia species. *Etym:* **nuŋan (pre-RM).
kai/nuna-k *Termanu.* kind of tree, people usually put the afterbirth in a certain kind of basket and hang it from this tree. (J:216)
kai/nuna-ʔ *Korbafo.*
kai/nuna-k *Bokai.*
kai_nuna-ʔ *Bilbaa.*
ai_nuna-ʔ *Rikou.*
ŋgai/nuna-k *Ba'a.*
nuna-k *Tii.*
nuŋga-ʔ *Dengka.*
nuŋga-ʔ *Oenale.*
nuk/baʔi *Kotos Amarasi.* kind of tree.
nun/baʔi, nuk/baʔi, kuk/baʔi (2) kuk/baiʔ tasi, nuk/baiʔ tasi (3) nuk/baiʔ <nono> (4) nun/baiʔ fui (5) ʔ|nuna fui *Molo.* 1) kind of

tree. Cordia species. *[Form:* Forms with initial and medial *k* probably show sporadic assimilation of *n > *ŋ /_Vŋ. (Compare ***ŋura** 'young' for similar assimilation.)*]* (M:390, 391, 245) 2) kind of tree. Cordia subcordata. (M:390, 245) 3) kind of tree. Cordia dichotoma. (M:390) 4) kind of tree. Cordia obliqua. (M:391) 5) kind of tree with a soft trunk. Cordia obliqua. (M:391)

Out-comparisons:

tatasi_nunaŋ *Helong.* Cordia obliqua. (Heyne 1950:1307, ccxx)

ai nunan *East Tetun.* tree with good red timber. Cordia subpubescens. (Mo:155)

***nusa** *PRM.* island, state. *Etym:* *nusa.

nusa-k *Termanu.* island; land, landscape, state; city. (J:409)

nusa-ʔ *Korbafo.*

nusa-k *Bokai.*

nusa-ʔ *Bilbaa.*

nusa-ʔ *Rikou.*

nusa-k *Ba'a.*

nusa-k *Tii.*

nusa-ʔ *Dengka.*

nusa-ʔ *Oenale.*

nusa *Timaus.* island.

nusa *Meto.* (J:409)

Out-comparisons:

nusa *Semau Hẹlong.* kingdom, nation, state, country, island.

nusa *East Tetun.* island. (Mo:155)

***nuu1** *Morph:* ***nuu-k**. *Rote.* bird's nest.

manu_nuu-k *Termanu.* kind of basket made from lontar leaves for hens to lay their eggs in. (J:408)

manu_nuu-ʔ *Korbafo.*

manu_nuu-k *Bokai.*

manu_nuu-ʔ *Bilbaa.*

manu_nuu-ʔ *Rikou.*

manu_nuu-k *Ba'a.*

manu_nuu-k *Tii.*

manu_nuu-ʔ *Dengka.*

manu_nuu-ʔ *Oenale.*

Out-comparisons:

hnoo *Semau Helong.* nest. *[irr. from PRM:* *u = *o* correspondence*]*

snoo *Bolok Helong.* nest.

knuuk *East Tetun.* nest, den, lair (of animals and birds). (Mo:114)

***nuu2** *CERM.* property, possession. *Etym:* *anu 'unnamed thing'.

nuu *Termanu.* property, possession. (J:407)

nuu *Korbafo.*

nuu *Bokai.*

nuu *Bilbaa.*

nuu *Rikou.*

=nu *Kotos Amarasi.* used to mark an otherwise unexpressed plural possessum with VV final pronouns.

***nuus** *Rote.* squid. *Etym:* *nuəs (Blust and Trussel (ongoing) comment regarding their reconstruction: 'The search for a PMP term for 'squid' is frustrating, since there are many words with this meaning that show greater than chance phonetic similarity, but few that exhibit recurrent sound correspondences, a situation that obtains even within the Oceanic group'.). *[irr. from PMP:* *ə > u (sporadic assimilation)*] [History:* Pawley (2011:200) reconstructs POc *nusa and *nus. PCEMP *nus could account for the Timor reflexes with doubling of the vowel to fulfil the disyllabic requirement for content words.*]*

(iʔa) nuus *Termanu.* squid. (J:408)

nuu-ʔ *Korbafo.*

nuu-ʔ *Bokai.*

nuu-ʔ *Bilbaa.*

nuus *Rikou.*

nuus *Ba'a.*

nuus *Tii.*

nuus *Dengka.*

nuus *Oenale.*

Out-comparisons:

nuus *Semau Helong.* squid.

ND - nd

***ndake$_1$** *PnRote.* climb, ascend. *Etym:* *dakih. *Pattern:* k-7/8/9/10. *[irr. from PMP:* *d > *nd; *i > *e (influence from *sakay > ***sake** 'go up')*]*

ndaʔe *Termanu.* climb (a mountain). (J:412)

ndaʔe *Korbafo.*

laʔe *Bokai.*

na-lake *Bilbaa.*

raʔe *Rikou.*

ndaʔe *Ba'a.*

ndaʔe *Tii.*

***ndake$_2$** *Rote.* betel leaves. *Pattern:* k-8/9′ (*k > Ø in Oepao, *k > *ʔ*, Ø in Rikou; expect only *k > *ʔ* in both). *[irr. from PRM:* *nd > *d* in Termanu, Korbafo, Bokai, Landu, and Ba'a*]* *[Form:* Assimilations of *nd > *d* in first sense are due to this term being compounded with reflexes of ***doo-k** 'leaf', compare reflexes of ***ndiki** 'ear' and ***ɓife** 'lips'.*]*

daʔe_doo-k *Termanu.* betel, betel-pepper, both the plant and the leaf. (J:69)

daʔe_doo-ʔ *Korbafo.*

daʔe_doo-k *Bokai.*

lake_doo-ʔ *Bilbaa. [Form:* My own field notes have Bilbaa **leke_doo-ʔ** '*sirih*' = 'betel leaves/pepper'.*]*

dake_doo-ʔ *Landu.* betel leaves/pepper. (own field notes)

raʔi_doo-ʔ, rai_doo-ʔ *Rikou. [Form:* Jonker (1908:69) has medial glottal stop, Nako et al. (2014) does not.*]*

rii_doo-ʔ *Oepao.* betel leaves/pepper. (own field notes)

daʔe_doo-k *Ba'a.*

ndaʔe_ɗoo-k *Lole.* betel-pepper. (Zacharias et al. 2014)

ndaʔe_ɗoo *Tii.*

ndaʔe *Dengka.*

ndaʔe *Oenale.*

ndaʔe *Dela.* betel leaves.

***ndake_ɓuʔu** *Morph:* ***ndake_ɓuʔu-k**. *Rote.* wild basil. *Pattern:* k-6′ (*k > *ʔ* in Ba'a and Tii; expect *k = *k*, *k > Ø in Rikou; expect *k > *ʔ*).

ndake_buʔu, ndaʔe_buʔu *Termanu.* wild basil, called *fleskrois* in Kupang. (J:413)

ndake_buʔu *Korbafo.*

lake_buʔu *Bokai.*

leke_buu *Bilbaa.*

(rae_buʔu ?) *Rikou.*

ndaʔe_buʔu *Ba'a.*

ndaʔe_ɓuʔu *Tii.*

ndaʔe_buu *Dengka.*

ndaʔe_ɓuu *Oenale.*

***ndaki** *Morph:* ***ka-ndaki**. *PRM.* kind of aquatic snake or leech. *Pattern:* k-5. *[irr. from PRM:* *nd > *r* in Meto (expect *k*)*]*

ndaki *Termanu.* kind of water snake called *ular ndaki* in Kupang Malay. (J:413)

ndaki *Korbafo.*

laki *Bilbaa.*

raʔi *Rikou.*

ndaki *Ba'a.*

ndaki *Tii.*

ndaki *Oenale.*

ʔ|rake|ʔ *Kotos Amarasi.* leech.

<lake> *Molo.* leech. (M:257)

ra~rake|ʔ *Kusa-Manea.* leech.

***ndaru** *PRM.* cut. *[irr. from PRM:* *r > *l* in Rikou (sporadic dissimilation?)*]*

ndalu *Termanu.* cut off, cut the end off something. (J:414)

ndalu *Korbafo.*

lalu *Bokai.*

ralu *Rikou.*

ndalu *Ba'a.*

ndaru *Tii.*

ndalu *Dengka.*

ndaru *Oenale.*

n-ranu *Ro'is Amarasi.* cut a field.

n-kanu *Kotos Amarasi.* cut a field.

<kanu> (2) <anʔote kanu> *Molo.* 1) overgrown garden. 2) he cuts down the wood in a new garden. (M:180)

***ndau** *Rote.* needle. *Etym:* *zaRum. *[minority from PMP:* *z > *nd (expect *d)*] [History:* This is probably an early loan, though the source language has not been identified.*]*

nda~ndau-k *Termanu.* needle. (J:415)

nda~ndau-ʔ *Korbafo.*

la~lau-k *Bokai.*

la~lau-ʔ *Bilbaa.*

ra~rau-ʔ *Rikou.*

nda~ndau-k *Ba'a.*

nda~ndau-k *Tii.*

nda~ndau-t *Dengka.*

nda~ndau-t *Oenale.*

Out-comparisons:

lauŋ *Semau Helong.* needle. *[irr. from PMP:* *R > Ø (expect *l*)*]*

daun *East Tetun.* needle. (Mo:23)

***ndefa** *PRM.* landslide. *See:* ***fera₂**. *[History:* Interference/collapse with ***fera₂**, which is likely related via consonant metathesis. A possible etymon for ***ndefa** is PWMP *rəbaq [ɾəbaq] 'collapse, fall down, as a house' with doublets *rəbas and *Rəbaq (Blust and Trussel ongoing).*]*

ndefa (2) na-ndefa *Termanu.* 1) landslide of earth of stones from a mountain into a chasm; collapse. 2) drop, make something fall. *[Semantics:* Both senses are verbs.*]* (J:416f)

ndefa *Korbafo.*

lefa *Bokai.*

lefa *Bilbaa.*

ndefa *Landu.* cliff, ravine, landslide. (own field notes)

refa *Rikou.*

ndefa *Ba'a.*

ndefa *Tii.*

ndefa *Dengka.*

ndefa (3) nde~ndefa-ʔ *Oenale.* 3) ravine. (J:130)

ndefa-ʔ *Dela.* push over.

refe|k (2) n-refa *Ro'is Amarasi.* 1) ravine, cliff, gap. 2) be affected or destroyed by a landslide.

kefa|n *Kotos Amarasi.* ravine, cliff, gap.

<kefa> *Molo.* gorge, steep cliff. (M:192)

***ndelat** *PRM.* lightning. *[Form:* Final *t finds external support from Ili'uun. The final *t* in Meto may have been reanalysed as a nominalising suffix.*] [History:* This could be connected with PWMP *kidəlat 'lightning' (Blust and Trussel ongoing) with irr. *d > *nd. However, the only evidence given for PWMP *kidəlat 'lightning' is Tagalog **kidlát** and Malay **kilat**. The Malay form is also given as evidence for PMP *kilat 'lightning' (from PAN *likaC) which is much better supported than putative *kidəlat.*] [Semantics:* The semantic shift from 'lightning' to 'gun' which is required for some of the forms given here is reasonable and still attested by some of the forms in Meto. The Tetun and Mambae forms could be borrowings from Meto after *nd > *r > *k* and before *l > *n*, borrowings from Malay *kilat* 'lightning', and/or inheritances of PMP *kilat 'lightning'. It has been proposed that the Atoni expansion was driven by their early acquisition of guns and maize (Fox 1988), thus Meto being the ultimate donor language is reasonable.*]*

ndela-s (2) na-ndela *Termanu.* 1) lightning. 2) lightning flashes; also glitter, sparkle, shine. (J:417)

ndela-ʔ *Korbafo.*

lela-k *Bokai.*

lela-ʔ *Bilbaa.*

ndela-s *Landu.* lightning. (own field notes)

rela-s *Rikou.*

na-rela *Oepao.* lightning. (own field notes)
ndela-s *Ba'a.*
ndela-s *Tii.*
ndela-s *Dengka.*
ndela-s *Oenale.*
renet (2) °makenet *Ro'is Amarasi.* 1) firearms, weapons. 2) be at war. *Borrowed from:* Kotos Amarasi (shown by irr. *nd = *k* correspondence, expect *r*).
kenat (2) ma-kenat (3) na-kena *Kotos Amarasi.* 1) firearms, weapons. 2) be at war. 3) thunder and lightning that is very loud and typically makes people scared. *[Note:* The normal word for 'lightning' is **rima-t** from root **rima** 'flash, shine'.*]*
kenat (2) ma-kenat (3) keen neno *Molo.* 1) firearms. 2) be at war. 3) thunderclap. *[Form:* **neno** = 'sky'.*]* (M:198)
kenat *Kusa-Manea.* firearm, gun.
Out-comparisons:
°lelat *Semau Helong.* fire-arm, weapon, gun, rifle. *Borrowed from:* probably Meto after *nd > *r and before *l > *n*.
°kilat *Fehan Tetun.* firearm of any type: gun, cannon. *Borrowed from:* perhaps pre-Meto **kelat (after *nd > *r > *k*, but before *l > *n*) perhaps also influenced by Malay *kilat*.
°kilat *East Tetun.* firearms, any type of gun. (Mo:107)
°kilat *Mambae, South.* gun. (own field notes)
ʤilat *Ili'uun.* lightning. (dJ:114)
noho t̪il~t̪ila (2) °ilak *Kisar.* 1) thunder. *[Note:* **noho** = 'island, land, earth, world, environment, weather', **noho ler~lere** = 'lightning'.*]* 2) gun.

***ndeli** *Morph:* ***ka-ndeli**. *PRM.* ring. *[irr. from PRM:* *nd > *r/l* in Nuclear Meto (expect *k*, indicates PMeto ***ka-deli**)*]*
ndeli (2) na-ka-ndeli *Termanu.* 1) ring. 2) wear a ring, have a ring. (J:417)
nde~ndeli *Keka.*
ndeli *Korbafo.*
le~leli *Bokai.*
le~leli *Bilbaa.*
nde~ndeli *Landu.* ring. (own field notes)
re~reli *Rikou.*
re~reli *Oepao.* (own field notes)
ndeli *Ba'a.*
ndeli *Tii.*
ndeli *Dengka.*
ndeli *Oenale.*
k|reni *Ro'is Amarasi.* ring.
k|reni *Kotos Amarasi.* ring.
ka|leli *Molo.* ring for finger. (M:174)
Out-comparisons:
kadeli *East Tetun.* finger ring. (Mo:93)
kadeli *Dhao.* ring.
t̪eli *Kisar.* ring.
kdyeli *Roma.* ring. (Steven 1991:37)

***ndesi** *PRM.* nettle.
ndesi *Termanu.* kind of nettle (called *daun keser* in Kupang); another kind of plant of which the crushed leaves are used as a kind of putty. (J:418)
ndesi *Korbafo.*
lesi *Bokai.*
lesi *Bilbaa.*
resi *Rikou.*
ndesi *Ba'a.*
ndesi *Tii.*
ndesi *Dengka.*
ndesi *Oenale.*
<kese> (2) <kese asu> *Molo.* 1) nettle. 2) kind of nettle that causes a severe and persistent skin condition when touched. (M:201)

***ndia** *PnRote.* third person pronoun, demonstrative pronoun. *Etym:* *si-ia '3sg. personal pronoun: he, she, it'. *[irr. from PMP:* *s > *nd (but compare Malay *dia* 'he, she, it' with irr. *s > *d)]*

ndia *Termanu.* a) demonstrative pronoun; this, that. b) third person singular pronoun; he, she, it, mainly used for emphasis (otherwise **ana**), always used as a possessive pronoun. (J:419)

ndia *Korbafo.*

lia *Bokai.*

lia *Bilbaa.* 3SG, relativiser.

ndia *Landu.* 3SG pronoun. (own field notes)

ria *Rikou.*

ria *Oepao.* 3SG pronoun. (own field notes)

ndia *Ba'a.*

ndia *Lole.* proximal, this, here, now, 3SG. (Zacharias et al. 2014)

ndia *Tii.*

***ndika** *PwRM.* stick to, cling. *Pattern:* k-7. *[irr. from PRM:* *a > *i* in some Meto (also Tetun); *nd > *r* in Kusa-Manea (expect *k)]*

ndika *Dela.* cling, stick.

na-kiʔi *Kotos Amarasi.* cling, stick.

n-kiiʔ (2) <ka na-kia fa> *Molo.* 1) stuck. 2) not stuck, not grafted. (M:205)

maʔriaʔ *Kusa-Manea.* sticky. *[Form:* metathesised form of (currently unattested) ***maʔriʔa**.*]*

Out-comparisons:

ha-kriʔit *Fehan Tetun.* stick to (e.g. prickle sticks to clothes).

kriʔik *East Tetun.* straight, stiff. (Mo:119)

***ndiki** *Morph:* ***ndiki-k**. *Rote.* ear. *Pattern:* k-7. *[Form:* Assimilations of *nd > *d* in first sense are due to this term being compounded with reflexes of ***doo-k** 'leaf', compare ***ndake_ doo-k** > **daʔe_doo-k** 'betel' and ***ɓife** > **difa_doo-k** 'lips'.*]*

ndiʔi-k (2) diʔi_doo-k *Termanu.* 1) the edges of a leaf that has small veins and is good for making a bucket, the edges are trimmed off. (J:419) 2) ear. (J:87)

ndiʔi-ʔ (2) diʔi_doo-ʔ *Korbafo.*

liʔi-k (2) diʔi_doo-k *Bokai.*

liki-ʔ (2) liki doo-ʔ *Bilbaa.*

(2) ndiki_doo-ʔ *Landu.* (own field notes)

riʔi-ʔ (2) rii_doo-ʔ *Rikou.*

(2) rii_doo-ʔ *Oepao.* (own field notes)

ndiʔi-k (2) diʔi_doo-k *Ba'a.*

(2) ndiʔi ɗoo-k *Lole.* (Zacharias et al. 2014)

ndiʔi-k (2) ndiʔi ɗoo-k *Tii.*

ndiki-ʔ (2) ndiʔi-ʔ *Dengka.* 1) edge of a palm leaf. (J:741) 2) ear.

ndiki-ʔ (2) ndiki-ʔ, ndiki roo-ʔ *Oenale.* 1) edge of a palm leaf. 2) ear. (J:741)

ndiki-ʔ *Dela.* ear.

***ndoo** *PRM.* straight, straighten.

ndoo-s (2) na-ka-ndoo (3) na-ma-ndoo *Termanu.* 1) straight, right. 2) go straight on, continue. 3) be or become straight (also in metaphorical sense), make straight. (J:420f)

ndoo-ʔ *Korbafo.*

loo-k *Bokai.*

loo-ʔ *Bilbaa.*

roo-s *Rikou.*

ndoo-s *Ba'a.*

ndoo-s *Tii.*

ndoo-s *Dengka.*

ndoo-s *Oenale.*

na-ndoo *Dela.* make straight, stretch.

na-koo *Kotos Amarasi.* stretch out (e.g. body to sleep).

na-koo *Molo.* stretches. **mu-koo nuku-m** stretch out your hand (M:225)

Out-comparisons:

loos *East Tetun.* right, correct, exact, straight, erect, vertical; truly, correctly, exactly. *[irr. from*

PRM: *nd = *l* correspondence (expect *d*)] *[Form:* Kemak has **loson** which, if connected with the Tetun form, would further indicate that this Tetun form is not (regularly) cognate with PRM ***ndoo**.*]* (Mo:133)

***ndoro** *PRM.* walk around. *[irr. from PRM:* *nd > *r* in Oenale; *nd > *n* in Meto (probably via intermediate *r, given Dela-Oenale intermediate **rolo**)*]*

ndolo *Termanu.* go around. (J:423)

ndolo *Korbafo.*

lolo *Bokai.*

lolo *Bilbaa.*

rolo *Rikou.*

roro *Oepao.* (J:423, 726)

ndolo *Ba'a.*

ndoro *Tii.*

ndolo *Dengka.*

rolo *Oenale.* (J:423, 726)

rolo *Dela.* wander, walk aimlessly.

n-non~nono *Kotos Amarasi.* walk around.

nono *Molo.* goes around. (M:384)

Out-comparisons:

loloh *Semau Helong.* walk around. only used for farms.

lodo *Hawu.* go. *[Sporadic:* consonant metathesis *dVl > *lVd.]*

ŋaro (2) rero *Bima.* 1) go back and forth, go everywhere. (Jonker 1893:66) 2) go around everywhere. (Jonker 1893:86)

reroŋ, ririŋ *Sika.* restless, go around. (Pareira and Lewis 1998:172)

***ndoto** *PRM.* hyacinth bean. <u>*Lablab purpureus*</u>. *[irr. from PRM:* *nd > *k* in Ro'is Amarasi (expect *r*)*]*

ndoto *Termanu.* 1) kind of climbing plant called *arbila* in Kupang. (J:424) 2) arbila. <u>*Dolichos lablab/ Lablab vulgaris*</u>. (Fox 1991:260)

ndoto *Korbafo.*

loto *Bokai.*

loto *Bilbaa.*

ndoto *Landu.* hyacinth bean. (own field notes)

roto(s) *Rikou.*

rotos *Oepao.* (own field notes)

ndoto *Ba'a.*

ndoto *Tii.*

ndoto *Dengka.*

ndoto *Oenale.*

koot kase *Ro'is Amarasi.* kidney beans. *Lit:* 'foreign **koto?**'.

koto? *Kotos Amarasi.* hyacinth beans.

<koto> *Molo.* kinds of beans. (M:238)

kotu-gw *Timaus.* hyacinth beans. *[Form:* vowel final root **koto**.*]*

koto *Kusa-Manea.* hyacinth beans.

Out-comparisons:

°koto *East Tetun.* variety of bean. *Borrowed from:* Meto **koto** (shown by initial *nd = *k* correspondence). (Mo:117)

°koto *Waima'a.* broad beans. *Borrowed from:* ultimately Meto **koto**, perhaps via Tetun.

°koto *Mambae, South.* bean. *Borrowed from:* ultimately Meto **koto**, perhaps via Tetun. (Fogaça 2017:236)

***ndou** *Morph:* ***ka-ndou-k**. *PRM.* nape of the neck. *[Form:* *nd develops as an initial consonant in Rote.*]*

ka|ndou-k *Termanu.* nape of the neck. (J:221)

ka|ndou-? *Korbafo.*

ka|lou-k *Bokai.*

ka|lou-? *Bilbaa.* (J:221,742)

ka|ndou-? *Landu.* nape of the neck. (own field notes)

ka|rou-? *Rikou.*

ka|rou-? *Oepao.* (own field notes)

ka|ndou-k *Ba'a.*

ka|ndou-k, ndo~ndou-k *Tii.*

ka|ndou-? *Dengka.*

ndo(u)~ndou-? *Oenale.* (J:221,742)

k|roo-n *Ro'is Amarasi.* nape of the neck.

ko/tore-f *Kotos Amarasi.* nape of the neck. *[Form:* historic compound of ***ka-ndou** + ***toɗe**.*]*

ʔ|koo-n *Amanuban.* nape of the neck.

ʔ|koo-n (2) ʔ|ko/tole-k *Molo.* 1) the nape of his neck. 2) the protuberance on the back of my head. *[Form:* historic compound of ***ndou** + ***toɗe**.*]* (M:225)

ʔ|koo-f *Timaus.* nape of the neck.

***ndui** *PRM.* draw/scoop water.

ndui *Termanu.* scoop with a pot, etc. (J:426)

ndui *Korbafo.*

lui *Bokai.*

lui *Bilbaa.*

rui *Rikou.*

ndui *Ba'a.*

ndui *Tii.*

ndui *Dengka.*

ndui *Oenale.*

n-rui *Ro'is Amarasi.* draw water.

n-kui (2) ʔ-kuʔi *Kotos Amarasi.* 1) draw water. 2) dipping bucket.

n-kui oe (2) <kui> *Molo.* 1) draw water with a container or tin. 2) water scoop. (M:245)

n-kui *Kusa-Manea.* draw water.

***nduna** *Morph:* ***ka-nduna-k**. *PRM.* nest. *[irr. from PRM:* *a > *u* in nRote (sporadic assimilation); *nd > *k* in Ro'is Amarasi (expect *r*)*]*

ndunu-k *Termanu.* nest of all sorts of animals, in compounds one normally says: **neʔe ndunu**, (**lafo ndunu**, **bafi ndunu**), ant's nest, (rat's nest, wild pig's nest). (J:427)

ndunu-ʔ *Korbafo.*

lunu-k *Bokai.*

lunu-ʔ *Bilbaa.*

ndunu-ʔ *Landu.* nest. (own field notes)

runu-ʔ *Rikou.*

runu-ʔ *Oepao.* (own field notes)

ndunu-k *Ba'a.*

ndunu-k *Tii.*

nduna-ʔ *Dengka.*

nduna-ʔ *Oenale.*

kuna|ʔ *Ro'is Amarasi.*

ʔ|kuna|ʔ *Kotos Amarasi.* nest (of bird).

ʔ|kuna|ʔ *Molo.* nest, pouch (of sarong, of marsupial). (M:249)

Ŋ - ŋ

***ŋano** *PwRM.* plait, braid. *[irr. from PRM:* *ŋ > *h* in wRote*]* *[Form:* It is not clear what initial consonant can account for wRote *h*, (most) Meto *k*, and Amanuban *n*. I have reconstructed *ŋ as this best accounts for the Meto reflexes.*]*

hano *Dengka.* plait, braid. (J:699)

hano *Oenale.* plait, braid. (J:699)

na-kano *Ro'is Amarasi.* plait.

na-kano, n-kane *Kotos Amarasi.* plait, weave. *[Form:* The form **n-kane** with final *e* may be due to influence from PRM ***ane**.*]*

na-nano *Amanuban.* plait, weave.

na-kano *Molo.* plait, braid. (M:180)

na-kaon *Kusa-Manea.* braid, plait.

Out-comparisons:

ŋana *Central Nage.* plait, weave. (Forth 2016:336)

***ŋaper** *PRM.* beckon with hand. *[irr. from PRM:* *ŋ > *k* in Ba'a (probably expect *ŋg*)*]* *[History:* Blust and Trussel (ongoing) reconstruct PWMP *ambay 'wave back and forth', PMP *kaway 'wave the hand or arms; call by waving', and PMP *kapay 'flutter the wings'. Wolff (2010:838) reconstructs PMP *abay stating: 'In S[outh] Phil[ippines] and N[orth] Sul[awesi] this form was prefixed with *ka-.'*]*

ŋgape-k *Termanu.* beckon, wave. (J:433)
ŋgape-ʔ *Korbafo.*
ŋape-k *Bokai.*
ŋape-ʔ *Bilbaa.*
kape-ʔ *Rikou.*
kape-k *Ba'a.*
ŋgape-k *Tii.*
kapel *Dengka.*
kaper *Oenale.*
kaper *Dela.* wave to get someone's attention.
n-napen *Kotos Amarasi.* beckon someone with one's hand.
n-napi, n-nape *Molo.* beckons. *[Note:* Jonker (1908:433) gives Meto **ainape**, **nape naper**.*]* (M:35)
Out-comparisons:
kahi *East Tetun.* beckon. (Mo:95)
gape *Hawu.* signal by hand, summon by hand motion.

***ŋato** *PRM.* string together, sew together.
nato *Termanu.* insert, string together. (J:381)
nato *Korbafo.*
nato *Bokai.*
nato *Bilbaa.*
nato *Rikou.*
nato *Ba'a.*
nato *Tii.*
nato *Dengka.*
nato *Oenale.*
n-katon *Kotos Amarasi.* poke and sew with a leaf stem to connect leaves or fish.
n-kato (2) <kato> *Molo.* 1) inserts. 2) fork. (M:186)
Out-comparisons:
noto *Semau Helong.* thread the needle. *[irr. from PRM:* *ŋ = *n* correspondence; *a = *o* correspondence*]*

***ŋilu** *PRM.* tamarind, sour. *Etym:* *ŋilu 'painful sensation in teeth, as from eating something sour'. *[minority from PMP:* *ŋ = *ŋ*] [irr. from PRM:* *l > Ø in all Meto except Kusa-Manea in Meto forms meaning 'tamarind'*]*
ni~nilu_naʔu (2) ni~nilu_dae_loo-k (3) ni~nilu_tasi *Termanu.* 1) tamarind. 2) star-fruit. 3) kind of seaweed called *tambrín laut* [OE = 'sea tamarind'] in Kupang. *[Semantics:* No definition given for **ninilu** when not compounded. My fieldwork on Rote consistently has **ni~nilu** as 'tamarind tree'.*]* (J:396f)
ni~nilu *Korbafo.*
ni~nilu *Bokai.*
ni~nilu *Bilbaa.*
ni~nilu *Landu.* tamarind. (own field notes)
ni~nilu *Rikou.*
ni~nilu *Ba'a.*
ni~nilu *Tii.*
ni~nilu *Dengka.*
ni~nilu *Oenale.*
niu *Ro'is Amarasi.* tamarind.
kiu (2) maiʔninuʔ *Kotos Amarasi.* 1) tamarind. 2) sour, acidic; sharp pains in the body.
kiu (2) kiu ma-tabi-ʔ (3) <maininu> *Molo.* tamarind. Tamarindus indica. (M:199) 2) star fruit. Averrhoa carambola. (M:208) 3) sour. (M:299)
ka~kinu *Kusa-Manea.* tamarind.
Out-comparisons:
ŋiduʔ, ŋiluʔ *Funai Helong.* sour.
ŋilu *Semau Helong.* sour.

***ŋinu** *PMeto.* spit out. *Doublet:* ***midu**. *Etym:* *qizuR 'saliva, spittle' (PWMP). *[minority from PMP:* *z > (*d) > *n (expect *z > *ɗ > *d)*] [Form:* The source of initial *pa* in Kusa-Manea is unclear. It may be due to historic compounding.*] [History:* PMeto ***ŋinu** is cognate with Rote ***midu** and both are ultimately probably connected with *qizuR, but it is not possible to straightforwardly reconcile the initial *m = *ŋ correspondence and combine them into one set attesting a single PRM reconstruction.*]*

na-ninu *Ro'is Amarasi.* spit.

na-kinu *Kotos Amarasi.* spit.

na-kinu, na-kinu-t *Molo.* spits. (M:210)

na-kinu *Timaus.* spit.

pakiun *Kusa-Manea.* spit.

Out-comparisons:

taniru *East Tetun.* spit. (Mo:180)

anilu *Welaun.* spit. *[irr. from PRM:* *ŋ = *n* correspondence (We expect *ŋ = *k*, thus Welaun **anilu** may be a borrowing from an unidentified source)*]*

***ŋoli** *Morph:* ***ŋoli-k**. *PRM.* canine tooth, tusk. *Etym:* **ŋəli (pre-RM).

noli(-k) *Termanu.* canine tooth, tusk. Also metaphorically: the end point, the end of a row of people. (J:405)

noli-ʔ *Korbafo.*

noli-k *Bokai.*

noli-(ʔ) *Bilbaa.*

noli-(ʔ) *Rikou.*

noli-k *Ba'a.*

noli-k *Tii.*

noli-ʔ *Dengka.*

noli-ʔ *Oenale.*

niis koni-f (2) n-koni *Kotos Amarasi.* 1) canine tooth. 2) copulate. *[Semantics:* For the semantic link between 'canine tooth' and copulate, see the Molo entry.*]*

koni-f (2) n-koni (3) ma-koni-ʔ *Molo.* 1) canine tooth, tusk, during the circumcision ritual in the phallic sense of penis. 2) have sexual intercourse. 3) unlimited sexual intercourse, practise promiscuity. (M:235)

koni-f *Kusa-Manea.* molars.

Out-comparisons:

ŋilin *Helong.* (J:405)

neli *Waima'a.* molar.

əli *Hawu.* (J:405)

<uli> *Kambera.* canine tooth. *[Note:* also in Mangili, Anakalang, and Mamboru.*]* (On:513)

<ulu> *Lewa.*

<ule> *Kodi. [Note:* also in Weyewa.*]*

neri *Kamarian.* tusks of a pig. (van Ekris 1864:315)

neri *Saparua.* tusk (of a pig). *[Note:* also in Nusa Laut language of Lease Islands ISO 639-3 [spr].*]* (van Hoëvell 1877:105)

neri-ne *Asilulu.* tusk (of a pig). *[Note:* also in Haruku.*]* (van Hoëvell 1877:105)

neli *Hitu.* tusk (of a pig). *[Note:* language of Ambon Island ISO 639-3 [htu].*]* (van Hoëvell 1877:105)

***ŋura** *PRM.* young of plants. *Etym:* *ŋuda. *[minority from PMP:* *ŋ = *ŋ*] [Sporadic:* *a > *e* / _# in wRM except for Kusa-Manea. *[Form:* The Meto reflexes are probably best explained by positing that *ŋ was retained as *ŋ into PMeto. PMeto ***ŋune** then underwent consonant metathesis to **nuŋe followed by subsequent regular PMeto *ŋ > *k*. The full hypothesised pathway is thus PMP *ŋuda > PRM ***ŋura** > PwRM ***ŋure** > **ŋule > PMeto ***ŋune** > **nuŋe > **nuke**. The Meto forms with two '*k*'s probably attest sporadic assimilation of *n > *ŋ /_Vŋ before *ŋ > *k*. Thus, **nuŋe > **ŋuŋe. (Compare ***nuŋa** '<u>*Cordia*</u> species' for similar assimilation.) The Rote forms show regular PRM *ŋ > *n.]*

nula-k (2) nula *Termanu.* 1) young, unripe fruit. (J:409) 2) woods, forest. (J:408)

nula-ʔ (2) nula *Korbafo.*

nula-k (2) nula *Bokai.*

nula-ʔ (2) nula *Bilbaa.*

(2) nura *Landu.* forest. (own field notes)
nura-ʔ (2) nura *Rikou.*
(2) nura *Oepao.* forest. (own field notes)
nula-k (2) nula *Ba'a.*
nura-k (2) nura *Tii.*
nule-ʔ *Dengka.*
nure-ʔ *Oenale.*
mai|nuki|ʔ *Ro'is Amarasi.* young (of fruit).
mai|nuke|ʔ, mai|nuki|ʔ (2) m|nuki|ʔ *Kotos Amarasi.* 1) young (of fruit). 2) young (of fruit/people). *Usage:* poetic.
mai|kuke|ʔ, ma|kuke|ʔ *Molo.* young of fruit, new moon. (M:301, xlvi)
noa ma|kuka|ʔ *Kusa-Manea.* young green coconut.
Out-comparisons:
nurak *East Tetun.* young, immature, delicate, lush (of plants). (Mo:155)

ŊG - ŋg

***ŋgadas** *PRM.* palate, gills, throat. *Doublet:* ***nada**. *Etym:* *ŋadas 'palate' (Osmond (2011a:130) reconstruct POc *gara 'gills' which could be cognate, instead of PMP *ŋadas. POc *gara would be from PMP **(g,k)a(d,r)a). *Pattern:* d-2. *[irr. from PMP: *d = *d] [minority from PMP: *ŋ > *ŋg] [Sporadic: *a > e / _# in Meto.]*
ŋgala_bote-k *Termanu.* external throat. (J:430)
ŋga~ŋgalas *Ba'a.* gills of a fish. (J:742)
ŋgara-ʔ (2) ŋgara_ɓote-ʔ *Oenale.* 1) gills of a fish. (J:742) 2) external throat. (J:742)
ŋga͡ra-ʔ *Dela.* throat.
ʔ|ka͡ere-f *Ro'is Amarasi.* palate.
ʔ|kare-f *Kotos Amarasi.* palate.
ʔ|kael uti-n *Amanuban.* uvula.
ʔ|kale-n *Molo.* fraenulum of tongue, tongue web. *[Note:* Jonker (1908:742) gives Meto **kunkalas** 'palate, gills'. The first part of this would be connected with **kun~kunu-f**, which means 'cheek' in some varieties of Meto.*]* (M:13, 174)
Out-comparisons:
hegara *Hawu.* palate, gills. (J:742)

***ŋgae** *PwRM.* cry, weep.
ŋgae *Dengka.* weep. (J:742)
ŋgae *Oenale.* weep. (J:742)
n-kae *Ro'is Amarasi.* cry, weep.
n-kae *Kotos Amarasi.* cry, weep.
n-kae *Molo.* weep, cry. (M:167)
n-kaa *Kusa-Manea.* cry. *[Form:* regular *e > *a* /V_# in Upper Manulea*]*

***ŋgaem** *PR.M.* country almond. <u>*Terminalia catappa*</u>.
ŋgae-k *Termanu.* kind of tree with edible fruit. (J:429)
ŋgae-ʔ *Korbafo.*
ŋae-k *Bokai.*
ŋae-ʔ *Bilbaa.*
kae-ʔ *Rikou.*
ŋgae-k *Ba'a.*
ŋgae-k *Tii.*
ŋgae-ʔ *Dengka.*
ŋgae-ʔ *Oenale.*
kaem *Molo.* kind of tree. <u>*Terminalia catappa*</u>. (M:167)
Out-comparisons:
kaen *Fehan Tetun.* type of big fruit tree, with big leaves, the fruit is boiled before eating.
kaen *East Tetun.* tree with edible fruit. (Mo:94)

***ŋgafat** *PRM.* light (not heavy). *[irr. from PRM:* *ŋg > *k* ~ *n* in Meto (indicates PMeto ***maʔŋafaʔ** with irr. *ŋg > *ŋ where we expect *k)*]*

ŋgafa-k *Termanu.* quick, fast at running, usually with the added meaning of: maintaining a fast pace for a long time while running; speed. (J:429)

ŋgafa-ʔ *Korbafo.*

ŋafa-k *Bokai.*

ŋafa-ʔ (2) ŋafa-ʔ *Bilbaa.* 2) light, not heavy. (J:742)

kafa-ʔ (2) kafa-ʔ *Rikou.* 2) light, not heavy. (J:742)

ŋgafa-k *Ba'a.*

ŋgafa-k *Tii.*

ŋgafa-ʔ (2) ŋgafa-ʔ *Dengka.* 2) light, not heavy. (J:742)

ŋgafa-ʔ (2) ŋgafat *Oenale.* 2) light, not heavy. (J:742)

(2) ŋgafat *Dela.* light, not heavy.

maʔ|kafa|ʔ *Ro'is Amarasi.* light, not heavy.

maʔ|kafa|ʔ *Kotos Amarasi.* light, not heavy.

<n-makafa> (2) <manafa>, <makaf> *Molo.* 1) he feels fit. (M:299) 2) light, easy. (M:299, 304)

Out-comparisons:

kahan *Semau Helong.* lightweight; easy, simple.

kawa *Kamarian.* light. *[Note:* also in Haruku and Kaibobo from Tihulale village.*]* (van Ekris 1864:100)

***ŋgafur** *PRM.* powder.

ŋgafu (2) ŋgafu~ŋgafu *Termanu.* 1) shake out, beat out (dust, etc.). 2) flutter (e.g. a sail or flag). (J:430)

ŋgafu *Korbafo.*

ŋafu *Bokai.*

ŋafu *Bilbaa.*

kafu *Rikou.*

ŋgafu *Ba'a.*

ŋgafu *Tii.*

ŋgafu *Dengka.*

ŋga~ŋgafur *Oenale.*

ŋgafur *Dela.* shake off.

kafuʔ *Kotos Amarasi.* powder or flakes which fall off something bit by bit, e.g. from the skin or a clump of something.

kafuʔ *Molo.* skin powder. (M:168)

***ŋgaha** *PwRM.* no, not. *[Form:* regular *h > Ø /a_a in Rote.*]*

ŋga *Dengka.* not. *Usage:* pre-predicate negator. (J:742)

ka= *Ro'is Amarasi.* NEGATOR. *Usage:* The normal negator in Ro'is is **maeʔ** however, **ka=** sporadically occurs as a negator, particularly in parallel pairs, and is a tag question particle in the same way as it is in Kotos Amarasi.

ka=, kahaf, kaah *Kotos Amarasi.* NEGATOR. *Usage:* The proclitic **ka=** combines with an enclitic =**fa** in (prescriptive) Kotos Amarasi.

ka= *Molo.* in denial. (M:264)

***ŋgai** *PRM.* pick at, scratch.

ŋgai *Termanu.* pick out, mainly pick one's ears. (J:431)

ŋgai *Korbafo.*

ŋai *Bokai.*

ŋai *Bilbaa.*

kai *Rikou.*

ŋgai *Ba'a.*

ŋgai *Tii.*

ŋgai *Dengka.*

ŋgai *Oenale.*

n-kai *Kotos Amarasi.* scratch.

n-kai *Molo.* one scrapes. (M:168)

***ŋgala** *Morph:* ***ŋga~ŋgala**. *PRM.* agati, vegetable hummingbird. *Sesbania grandiflora*. *[Sporadic:* *a > *e* / _# in Dela, Dengka and Meto.*]* *[History:* Blust and Trussel (ongoing) reconstruct Proto-Philippine *gala 'the almasiga tree: *Agathis celebica*' on the basis of Ilokano **gala** and Tagalog **gala-gala**. They note that the Ilokano form may be a Tagalog loan.*]*

ŋga~ŋgala *Termanu.* kind of tree called *pohon gala-gala* in Kupang. (J:430)
ŋga~ŋgala *Korbafo.*
ŋa~ŋala *Bokai.*
ŋa~ŋala *Bilbaa.*
ka~kala *Rikou.*
ŋga~ŋgala *Ba'a.*
ŋga~ŋgala *Tii.*
ŋga~ŋgale *Dengka.*
ŋga~ŋgala *Oenale.*
ŋga~ŋgale *Dela.* (Thersia Tamelan pers. comm. February 2018)
ʔ|kane *Kotos Amarasi.* vegetable hummingbird, agati. Sesbania grandiflora.
ʔ|kane *Fatule'u.* vegetable hummingbird, agati. Sesbania grandiflora.
ʔ|kane *Molo.* tree that is 5–10 metres high and has a short life-span. A beverage against thrush can be prepared from the decoction of the rough and somewhat sticky bark. Sesbania grandiflora. (M:14, 179)
Out-comparisons:
kala *East Tetun.* tree. Sesbania grandiflora. *[Note:* **ai turi** is given as identical.*]* (Mo:98)

***ŋgaŋgo** *PRM.* water spinach. Ipomoea aquatica. *[irr. from PRM:* *ŋg > Ø /#_ in Korbafo*] [History:* Ultimately a borrowing from another source, e.g. compare similar Malay *kangkung*. Blust and Trussel (ongoing) say regarding the Malay form: 'Although a precise donor language is difficult to identify, a Chinese source appears likely.'*]*
ŋgaŋo_dano *Termanu.* kind of plant, water spinach. *[Form:* **dano** = 'lake'.*]* (J:432)
aŋo_dano *Korbafo.*
ŋaŋo_dano *Bokai.*
ŋaŋo_dano *Bilbaa.*
kako_dano *Rikou.*
ŋgaŋgo_dano *Ba'a.*
ŋgaŋgo_ɗano *Tii.*
ŋgaŋgo-ʔ *Dengka.*
ŋgaŋgo-ʔ *Oenale.*
ŋgaŋgo *Dela.* water cress.
uut kako *Kotos Amarasi.* water spinach.
Out-comparisons:
hkako (2) hkako klehen *Semau Helong.* 1) kind of seaweed. 2) palm species.

***ŋgarasa** *Morph:* ***ŋgarasa-k**. *Rote.* part of the back.
karasa-ʔ *Rikou.* the part of the back behind the shoulders. (J:708)
ŋgarasa-ʔ *Oenale.* back, or part of the back. (J:743)
Out-comparisons:
keraha *Hawu.* slope, side. *[Semantics:* Jonker (1908:708) gives this as 'side of the body'.*]*
<karaha> *Kambera.* edge, side, flank. *[Note:* also in Kodi.*]* (On:183)
<karasa> *Anakalang. [Note:* also in Mamboru.*]*

***ŋgari** *PRM.* sow, scatter.
ŋgali *Termanu.* scatter, strew. (J:431)
ŋgali *Korbafo.*
ŋali *Bokai.*
ŋali *Bilbaa.*
kari *Rikou.*
ŋgali *Ba'a.*
ŋgari *Tii.*
ŋgali *Dengka.*
ŋgari *Oenale.*
n-kaniʔ (2) kan~kaniʔ, sab/kaniʔ *Kotos Amarasi.* 1) sow (seeds). 2) drizzle (rain).
kani-n *Amanatun.* outpoured portion. *Usage:* poetic. (M:179)
Out-comparisons:
kari *East Tetun.* scatter; to fling with the throwing hand. (Mo:101)
gari *Dadu'a.* sow. (Penn 2006:102)
ari *Kisar.* broadcast seed, scatter seed randomly.

***ŋgasi** *Rote.* shout, speak.

ŋgasi *Termanu.* crying, whining or howling scream. (J:433)
ŋgasi *Korbafo.*
ŋasi *Bokai.*
ŋasi *Bilbaa.*
kasi *Rikou.*
ŋgasi *Ba'a.*
ŋgasi *Tii.*
ŋgasi *Dengka.*
ŋgasi *Oenale.*
ŋgasi *Dela.* yell.
Out-comparisons:
kais *Kisar.* holler out, pig squeal.
gase *Mambae, Northwest.* speak. (Fogaça 2017:249)
kase *Mambae, South/Central.* speak. (Fogaça 2017:249)
ŋgahi *Bima.* speak, say, word, speech. *[irr. from PRM:* *s = *h* correspondence (probably expect *s*, though reflexes of intervocalic *s are somewhat unclear)*]* (Jonker 1893:67)
ŋasi *Ende.* get angry, complain. *[Note:* Jonker (1908:433) gives Ende **ŋahi** 'speak'.*]*

***ŋgeɓo** *CERM.* cut into pieces. *[irr. from PRM:* *o > *i* in Meto*] [Form:* Final *o has been tentatively reconstructed as *o > *i* in Meto can be motivated as an instance of sporadic assimilation to the previous vowel while alternate *i > *o* in nRote appears unmotivated.*]*
ŋge~ŋgebo *Termanu.* cut or chop into pieces. (J:436)
ŋge~ŋgebo *Korbafo.*
ŋe~ŋebo *Bilbaa.*
ke~kebo *Rikou.*
ŋge~ŋgebo *Ba'a.*
kebiʔ *Kotos Amarasi.* pieces of a whole.
kebiʔ *Molo.* cut into chunks. (M:192)

***ŋgeɗe** *Rote.* frog, croaking of a frog. *[Note:* With the exception of Termanu, the second forms in this entry follow the entry for Korbafo.*] [irr. from PRM:* *e > *a* in Molo; *ɗ > *l* in Termanu; *ŋg > *k* in Bokai and Dengka*] [History:* Semau Helong has **klete** which is not regularly cognate, but is phonetically similar. Funai Helong has **klatkeeʔ**.*] [Semantics:* likely onomatopoeia.*]*
ŋgede (2) lodo_ŋgele-k *Termanu.* 1) croaking of a frog, also used for the crying of a newly born child. (J:436) 2) frog. (J:320)
ŋgede (2) ŋgede oe *Korbafo.* 1) croaking of a frog, also used for the crying of a newly born child. (J:436) 2) frog. (J:743)
kede~kede *Bokai.* croaking of a frog, also used for the crying of a newly born child. (J:436)
ŋede (2) ŋede oe, ŋed/oe *Bilbaa.*
kede *Rikou.*
ŋgede (2) ŋge~ŋgede, ŋge~ŋgede oe *Ba'a.*
(2) ŋge~ŋgeɗe *Lole.* 2) frog. (Zacharias et al. 2014)
ŋgeɗe (2) ŋge~ŋgeɗe *Tii.*
keɗe~keɗe (2) ŋge~ŋgeɗe *Dengka.*
ŋgeɗe (2) ŋgeɗe *Oenale.*
(2) ŋgeɗe *Dela.* 2) frog.
kala/beʔo *Molo.* frog. *[Form:* Initial **kala** is optional, e.g. **beʔo** also occurs in isolation meaning 'frog'.*]* (M:59)
Out-comparisons:
kere *Kemak.* frog. *[irr. from PRM:* *ŋg = *k* correspondence; expect *g)]*
kere/dokon *Mambae, Northwest.* frog. *Usage:* Barzatete subdistrict. (Fogaça 2017:235)
keda/lokon *Mambae, Northwest.* frog. *Usage:* Railaco subdistrict. (Fogaça 2017:235)
kaidi/lokon *Mambae, Central.* frog. *Usage:* Laulara subdistrict. (Fogaça 2017:235)
keleʔ *Bunak.* frog. *[Note:* non-Austronesian language of central Timor ISO 639-3 [bfn].*]* (Schapper 2009:174)

***ŋgela**$_1$ *Morph:* ***ŋgela-k**. *Rote.* earwax. *Etym:* *taŋila 'ear' (Blust and Trussel (ongoing) reconstruct the doublet **taliŋa** with consonant metathesis. *taliŋa is the most common form outside of Taiwan. Nonetheless, Helong attests *taŋila, lending credibility to the notion that the Rote forms here are irregularly connected to *taŋila). *[irr. from PMP:* *i > *e*]* *[minority from PMP:* *ŋ > *ŋg*]*

diʔi_doo ŋgela-k *Termanu.* ear dirt, earwax. (J:437)

ŋgela-ʔ *Korbafo.*

ŋela-k *Bokai.*

ŋela-ʔ *Bilbaa.*

kela-ʔ *Rikou.*

ŋgela-k *Ba'a.*

ŋgela-k *Tii.*

ŋgela-ʔ *Dengka.*

ŋgela-ʔ *Oenale.*

Out-comparisons:

kŋila *Funai Helong.* ear.

hŋila *Semau Helong.* ear.

talina-r *Idate.* ear. (Klamer 2002)

liga-r *Kemak.* ear.

lika-t *Welaun.* ear.

***ŋgela**$_2$ *Morph:* ***ŋgela-k**. *Rote.* eucalyptus; gum tree.

ŋgela-k *Termanu.* kind of tree which yields good timber, called *gelang* in Kupang. (J:437)

ŋgela-ʔ *Korbafo.*

ŋela-k *Bokai.*

ŋela-ʔ *Bilbaa.*

kela-ʔ *Rikou.*

ŋgela-k *Ba'a.*

ŋgela-k *Lole.* gum tree, eucalyptus. (Zacharias et al. 2014)

ŋgela-k *Tii.*

ŋgela-ʔ *Dengka.*

ŋgela-ʔ *Oenale.*

Out-comparisons:

kelaŋ *Funai Helong.* eucalyptus.

***ŋgeŋgo** *Morph:* ***na-ŋgeŋgo**. *PRM.* shake. *Etym:* *gərgər 'shake, shiver, tremble'. *[irr. from PMP:* *ə > *o*]* *[irr. from PRM:* *o > *o* ~ *u* in Meto*]* *[Form:* Irregular final *ə > *o* is also seen in Bugis **gegoʔ** (Mathes 1874:53) and Makassar **geŋgo** (Cense 1859:68)*]*

na-ŋgeŋo *Termanu.* shake. (J:438)

na-ŋgeŋo *Korbafo.*

na-ŋeŋo *Bokai.*

na-ŋeŋo *Bilbaa.*

na-keko *Rikou.*

na-ŋgeŋgo *Ba'a.*

na-ŋgeŋgo *Tii.*

na-ŋgeŋgo *Dengka.*

na-ŋgeŋgo *Oenale.*

<na-keku>, <na-keko> (2) <anaka keku> *Molo.* 1) moves back and forth. 2) shake-head, said of someone with nervous disorder as a result of which he keeps shaking his head from front to back and from left to right. (M:194)

***ŋgeo** *Morph:* ***ŋgeo-k**. *Rote.* black.

ŋgeo-k *Termanu.* black. (J:438)

ŋgeo-ʔ *Korbafo.*

ŋeo-k *Bokai.*

ŋeo-ʔ *Bilbaa.*

keo=a *Landu.* black. (own field notes)

keo-ʔ *Rikou.*

keo-ʔ *Oepao.* black. (own field notes)

ŋgeo-k *Ba'a.*

ŋgeo-k *Tii.*

ŋgeo-ʔ *Dengka.*

ŋgeo-ʔ *Oenale.*

***ŋgete** *PRM.* pinch, nip. *Doublet:* ***katə**. *Etym:* *gətəl (Reconstructed with the doublets *getil and *ketil.). *[minority from PMP:* *ə > *e / _# (expect *ə > *a* in wRote, possibly *ə > *a > *e*)*]* *[irr. from PRM:* *t > *ʔ* /V_V in Termanu, Korbafo, Ba'a, and Tii*]*

ŋgeʔe *Termanu.* pinch, like a lobster. (J:436)

ŋgeʔe *Korbafo.*

ŋete *Bokai.*

ŋete *Bilbaa.*

ŋgeʔe *Ba'a.*

ŋgeʔe *Tii.*

ŋgete *Dengka.*

ŋgete *Oenale.*
kete, ete *Molo.* bite off. *[irr. from PRM:* *ŋg > Ø in second Molo form*]* (M:202)
***ŋgeu** *PRM.* shave. *[irr. from PRM:* *ŋg > *ŋg ~ k* in Dela-Oenale*]*
ŋgeu *Termanu.* scrape. (J:440)
ŋgeu *Korbafo.*
ŋeu *Bokai.*
ŋeu *Bilbaa.*
keu *Rikou.*
ŋgeu *Ba'a.*
ŋgeu *Tii.*
ŋgeu *Dengka.*
ʔeu *Oenale.*
ŋgeu, ʔeu *Dela.* shave.
n-keu *Ro'is Amarasi.* shave.
n-keu *Kotos Amarasi.* shave.
n-keu *Molo.* scrapes his tongue. (M:203)
keu *Kusa-Manea.* scrape, shave.
***ŋgia** *PRM.* parakeet. *[irr. from PRM:* Ø > *t* /V_V in Meto*]* *[Semantics:* onomatopoeia.*]*
ŋgia *Termanu.* turaco, lourie (kinds of parrot). *[Note:* Turacos and louries appear to be only found in Africa. This word probably designates a similar Timorese bird identified/ named thus by Jonker.*]* (J:441)
ŋgia *Korbafo.*
ŋia *Bokai.*
ŋia *Bilbaa.*
kia *Rikou.* Olive-shouldered Parrot. *Aprosmictus jonquillaceus*. *[Semantics:* My consultants gave **kia-ʔ** for a photo of an Olive-shouldered Parrot.*]*
ŋgia *Ba'a.*
ŋgia *Tii.*
ŋgia *Dengka.*
ŋgia *Oenale.*
kita *Molo.* kind of parakeet. (M:211)
Out-comparisons:
man gea *Buru.* small parrot or parakeet. (Grimes and Grimes 2020:585)

***ŋgii** *Morph:* ***ŋgii-k**. *PRM.* bunch of fruit. *[History:* Jonker (1908:440) gives Tetun Dili **kiu**, which may be cognate, but the final *u* of which would be irregular.*]*
ŋgii-k *Termanu.* blossom bunch of a palm or banana tree, bunch of coconuts of bananas. (J:440)
ŋgii-ʔ *Korbafo.*
ŋii-k *Bokai.*
ŋii-ʔ *Bilbaa.*
kii-ʔ *Rikou.*
ŋgii-k *Tii.*
ŋgii-ʔ *Dengka.*
ŋgii-ʔ *Oenale.*
<ki'> *Molo.* stem with a bunch of fruit on it (e.g. betel nut). (M:205)
Out-comparisons:
<nggai> *Kambera.* bunch. (On:353)
<nggi> *Lewa.*
<nggí> *Mamboru.*
<nggi'i> *Weyewa.*
<nggiyo> *Kodi.*
***ŋgirat** *Rote.* kind of shrub. *[Semantics:* vague semantics.*]*
ŋgila-k *Termanu.* kind of shrub. (J:441)
ŋgila-ʔ *Korbafo.*
ŋila-k *Bokai.*
ŋila-ʔ *Bilbaa.*
kira-ʔ *Rikou.*
ŋgila-k *Ba'a.*
ŋgira-k *Tii.*
ŋgilat *Dengka.*
ŋgirat *Oenale.*
***ŋgiro** *Morph:* ***ŋgi~ŋgiro**. *CERM.* lower head area. *[History:* Osmond and Ross (2016a:112) reconstruct POc *k(i,e)ju 'back of head, base of skull, occiput, nape' and Proto New Guinea Oceanic *g(i,e)ju, which are phonetically and formally similar to the PRM form. However, the final vowel correspondences are irregular and the initial PRM *ŋg = POc *k correspondence may also be irregular. Something like PCEMP **gijo may

indeed be possible, however in the absence of cognates in other areas of Wallacea, I prefer not to make such a reconstruction at this point.*]*

(lesu_haʔik) ŋgi~ŋgilo=na *Termanu.* the lower part of the neck, where it is attached to the body and on which it turns. (J:441)

ŋgi~ŋgilo=na *Korbafo.*

ŋi~ŋilo=na *Bokai.*

ki~kiro=na *Rikou.*

ŋgi~ŋgilo=na *Ba'a.*

kiunu-f *Ro'is Amarasi.* cheek.

ʔ|kinu-f *Kotos Amarasi.* cheek.

kino-n *Amanuban.* sideburns.

kino-f (2) ʔ|kinu-f (3) <kinu> *Molo.* 1) loose rope hanging down from a horse's head; also: whiskers. 2) portion of the loop of a rope around the mouth of a horse that in a tied state runs to the bottom. 2) whiskers. (M:210)

***ŋgoa** *Morph:* ***ŋgoa-k**. *Rote.* stupid.

ŋgoa-k *Termanu.* mute; dumb, foolish; muteness; stupidity, astonishment. (J:443)

ŋgoa-ʔ *Korbafo.*

ŋoa-k *Bokai.*

ŋoa-ʔ *Bilbaa.*

koa-ʔ *Rikou.*

ŋgoa-k *Ba'a.*

ŋgoa-k *Tii.*

ŋgoa-ʔ *Dengka.*

ŋgoa-ʔ *Oenale.*

Out-comparisons:

goa *Dhao.* stupid.

goa *Hawu.* stupid. *[Note:* Given with the note: 'probably borrowed' (from Rote).*]* (J:443)

***ŋgois** *PRM.* eel.

ŋgois *Termanu.* kind of ocean fish called *ikan gois* in Kupang. (J:445)

ŋgoi-ʔ *Korbafo.*

ŋoi-k *Bokai.*

ŋoi-ʔ *Bilbaa.*

kois *Rikou.* ocean eel. (J:445; own field notes)

ŋgois *Ba'a.*

ŋgois *Tii.*

ŋgois *Dengka.*

ŋgois *Oenale.*

kois *Ro'is Amarasi.* eel.

Out-comparisons:

kois *East Tetun.* water snake. (Mo:101)

kois *Galolen.* earthworm.

***ŋgoʔu** *CERM.* big, great.

leŋou *Bilbaa.* the domain of Rikou on the eastern part of Rote. (own field notes)

ri/kou, rai/kou *Rikou.* the domain of Rikou on the eastern part of Rote. *[Form:* **raikou** is reported by some of my consultants to be the original form.*] [History:* A possible etymology is ***dae** 'land' combined with an otherwise lost reflex of ***ŋgou** meaning 'big, great'. One hypothesis is that the term originally referred to the Timor mainland and later underwent semantic shift (for whatever socio-political reasons) to the eastern Rote domain of Rikou. However, in the absence of corroborating evidence this etymology is highly speculative. Note that Tetun **rai** (from PMP *daRəq) means 'earth, soil, ground; land estate, kingdom; the world'. If this is the source of the initial element, how it was borrowed into the Rote languages is unclear.*]* (own field notes)

koʔu *Ro'is Amarasi.* big, great.

koʔu *Kotos Amarasi.* big, great. *[History:* In his entry for **koʔu** Middelkoop (1972:239) has: '**Renggo'u** = **Rai nggo'u** the great prince, now a place name'. He apparently takes **rai** as meaning 'prince' by analogy with the first part of the second member of the Amarasi doublet **uis koʔu**, **naiʔ koʔu** 'the great lord'.*]*

***ŋgola** *Rote.* monitor lizard, flying lizard.
ŋgola *Termanu.* kind of flying lizard. (J:445f)
ŋgola *Korbafo.* kind of flying lizard. (J:445f)
ŋola (2) ŋala/fao *Bokai.* 1) kind of flying lizard. (J:445f) 2) kind of lizard. (J:742)
ŋala/fao *Bilbaa.* kind of lizard. (J:742)
kara/fao *Rikou.* kind of lizard. (J:742)
ŋgola *Ba'a.* monitor lizard. (J:445f)
ŋgola *Dengka.* monitor lizard. (J:445f)
Out-comparisons:
laɗura *Hawu.* monitor lizard. (J:445)
<lawora> *Kambera.* monitor lizard. Varanus salvtor. (On:236)
<laghora> *Kodi.*
ɣora *Rongga.* big lizard. *[Note:* language of central Flores ISO 639-3 [ror].*]* (Arka et al. 2007:42)

***ŋgomi** *Morph:* ***ŋgomi~ŋgomi**. *PnRote.* beard. *Etym:* *gumi(s) 'moustache, beard' (Reconstructed with the doublet *kumis.). *[irr. from PMP:* *u > *o*]*
ŋgomi~ŋgomi *Termanu.* have a thick beard or a big goatee. (J:447)
ŋomi~ŋomi *Bokai.*
komi~komi *Rikou.*
ŋgomi~ŋgomi *Tii.*

***ŋgoro** *PRM.* snout, nose, snore. *See:* ***ŋgoro₂** 'snore'. *Etym:* *ŋodok (own reconstruction) (PCEMP). *[minority from PMP:* *ŋ > *ŋg*]*
ŋgo~ŋgolo-k (2) ŋgolo_mei-k (3) ŋgolo~ŋgolo (4) na-sa-ŋgolo *Termanu.* 1) muzzle, snout of a pig, horse, buffalo, dog, etc., mouth of some fish, beak, bill of a bird; proboscis of a mosquito, etc.; also a vulgar word for the mouth of a person. 2) beard, also moustache of a person, goatee of a goat. (J:445) 3) make a snoring sound, snore. 4) make a snoring sound, snore. (J:445f)
ŋgo~ŋgolo-ʔ (2) ŋgolo_mei-ʔ (3) ŋgolo~ŋgolo *Korbafo.*
ŋo~ŋolo-k (2) ŋolo_mei-k (3) ŋolo~ŋolo *Bokai.*
(2) ŋolo_mii-ʔ (3) ŋolo~ŋolo *Bilbaa.*
(2) (koro ?) (3) koro~koro *Rikou.*
ŋgo~ŋgolo-k (2) ŋgolo_mei-k (3) ŋgolo~ŋgolo *Ba'a.*
(ŋgo)ŋgoro-k (2) ŋgoro_mei-k (3) ŋgoro~ŋgoro *Tii.*
ŋgo~ŋgolo-ʔ (2) ŋgolo_mei-ʔ (3) ŋgolo~ŋgolo *Dengka.*
(3) ŋgoro~ŋgoro *Oenale.*
(4) na-sa-ŋgoro *Dela.* snore.
kono-f (2) na-kono *Ro'is Amarasi.* 1) sideburns, beard, moustache. 2) snore.
kono-f (2) na-kono *Kotos Amarasi.* 1) beard. 2) snore.
<kono> (2) na-kono (3) <n-konolot> *Molo.* 1) beard. (M:235) 2) barks. 3) snores. (M:236)
Out-comparisons:
koon *Semau Helong.* snore.
kour *Kisar.* (dog) bark at something. *[irr. from PMP:* *o > *u]*
kagoro *Bima.* make a sound like a snoring noise. (Ismail et al. 1985:53)
***ŋoro~ŋorok (2) *ŋorok** *Proto-Oceanic.* 1) channel above upper lip. (Osmond and Ross 2016a:125) 2) snore. (Osmond et al. 2003:48)
ŋoroʔ *Malay.* snore.

***ŋgoti** *Morph:* ***ŋgoti-k**. *PRM.* back.
ŋgoti_haʔi-k *Termanu.* the lowest part of the back, the area of the tailbone. (J:448)
ŋoti_haʔi-k *Bokai.*

ŋoti-ʔ *Bilbaa.*
koti_ai-ʔ *Rikou.*
ŋgoti_haʔi-k *Ba'a.*
ŋgoti_aʔi-k, ŋgoti-k *Tii.*
ŋgoti-ʔ *Dengka.*
ŋgoti-ʔ *Oenale.*
koiti-f *Ro'is Amarasi.* back, behind.
koti-f *Kotos Amarasi.* back (body); behind (location).
koti-f (2) n-baikoti *Molo.* 1) behind. (M:174) 2) turns one's back towards someone. (M:42)
Out-comparisons:
kotuk *Fehan Tetun.* back (of person); behind.
kotuk *East Tetun.* back, loins. (Mo:117)
kodo *Hawu.* back.

***ŋgout** *PRM.* thorn. *[Note:* Ro'is and Kotos Amarasi have **kaut** 'papaya' which would be an almost perfect formal match for the first Rote forms, but the semantic connection is too far-fetched.*]*
ŋgau-k (2) ŋgou-k *Termanu.* 1) thorn on a tree, living thorn. (J:434) 2) thorn, mainly a single loose thorn. (J:448)
ŋgau-ʔ (2) ŋgou-ʔ *Korbafo.*
ŋau-k (2) ŋou-k *Bokai.*
ŋau (2) ŋou-ʔ *Bilbaa.*
kou=na *Landu.* thorn. (own field notes)
kau-ʔ (2) kou-ʔ *Rikou.*
ŋgau-k (2) ŋgou-k *Ba'a.*
ŋgau-k (2) ŋgou-k *Tii.*
ŋgaut (2) ŋgou-ʔ *Dengka.*
ŋgaut (2) ŋgou-ʔ *Oenale.*
ŋgaut (2) ma-ŋgou-ʔ *Dela.* 1) thorn. 2) thorny.
<ka'o> *Molo.* agave, aloe. Furcroea gigantea. (M:181)
Out-comparisons:
ai koon *Welaun.* thorn.
kau *Hawu.* (J:434)

***ŋgua** *Rote.* freshwater turtle. *[History:* The comparison between this form and Malay **kura-kura** 'tortoise' is striking, though the initial consonants cannot be regularly reconciled. We could posit PMP *kuRa with irr. *k > *ŋg. Dempwolff (1938:83) reconstructs *ku[l̥]aʿ (*ku(r)aq in Blust's transcription) 'milt, tortoise' giving Toba-Batak, Javanese, and Malay cognates as evidence. Blust and Trussel (ongoing) attribute these forms (and others) to being loans from Malay, noting that their explanation assumes that borrowing into Lampung and Sundanese (each with **kuya**) took place before *R > *y*. The gloss in Sundanese is 'freshwater turtle', thus matching the Rote glosses here.*]*
ŋgua_dano, ŋgua_oe *Termanu.* freshwater turtle. *[Form:* **dano** = 'lake', **oe** = 'water'.*]* (J:449)
ŋgua_dano *Korbafo.*
ŋua_dano *Bokai.*
ŋua_dano *Bilbaa.*
kua_dano *Rikou.*
ŋgua_dano *Ba'a.*
ŋgua_ɗano *Tii.*
ŋgua_ɗano *Dengka.*
ŋgua_ɗano *Oenale.*

***ŋgumu** *nRM.* make a fist. *Doublet:* ***kame, *keʔe, *keme, *kumu₂.** *Etym:* *gəmgəm 'fist; hold in the fist'. *[irr. from PMP:* *ə > *u (sporadic assimilation to previous velar consonant and following labial consonant)*]*
na-fa-ŋgumu *Termanu.* make a fist. (J:449)
na-fa-ŋumu *Bokai.*
na-fa-ŋumu *Bilbaa.*
na-la-kumu *Rikou.*
na-fa-ŋgumu *Ba'a.*
na-fa-ŋgumu, na-sa-ŋgumu *Tii.*
n-kumu *Kotos Amarasi.* squeeze, press, wring out, like getting coconut milk from a coconut.
n-kumu *Molo.* squeeze, palpate. (M:248)
kuum *Kusa-Manea.* squeeze.

***ŋguru** *PRM.* drone, growl, make a steady constant noise. *Etym:* *guru(q) 'noise, tumult'. (Both *guru and *guru(q) are reconstructed as 'disjuncts' without any difference in semantics.) *[Semantics:* onomatopoeia.*]*

ŋgulu~ŋgulu (2) na-sa-ŋgu~ŋgulu (3) na-ŋgulu *Termanu.* 1) constantly droning, grumble at someone. 2) growl, like a dog or cat. 3) thunder (of sky), roar (of sea), rumble (of stomach), also used to describe the noise that someone makes when they run fast (not everyone understands this word). (J:449)

ŋgulu~ŋgulu *Korbafo.*

ŋulu~ŋulu (3) na-ŋulu *Bokai.*

ŋulu~ŋulu *Bilbaa.*

kuru~kuru *Rikou.*

ŋgulu~ŋgulu (3) na-ŋgulu *Ba'a.*

ŋguru~ŋguru (2) na-sa-ŋgu~ŋguru *Tii.*

ŋgulu~ŋgulu *Dengka.*

ŋguru~ŋguru (2) na-sa-ŋgu~ŋguru *Oenale.*

na-kunut *Kotos Amarasi.* sigh, a sign that someone is bored or disappointed.

na-kunut *Molo.* growls (e.g. dog). (M:251)

***ŋguu** *CERM.* make a constant monotonous sound, howl (of wind), blow, drone. *See:* ***kuu**. *[Semantics:* onomatopoeia.*]*

na-ŋguu *Termanu.* howling of the wind. **hataholi=la la-ŋguu mai soo** the droning of the people comes nearer (J:448)

na-ŋguu *Korbafo.*

na-ŋuu *Bokai.*

na-ŋuu *Bilbaa.*

ku/truu *Ro'is Amarasi.* owl.

ku/truʔu *Kotos Amarasi.* owl.

<ku> (2) ku/tluu (3) ku/tlui *Molo.* 1) owl, ghost bird. (M:242) 2) owl, ghost bird. (M:242) 3) owl. (M:403)

O - o

***oe** *PRM.* water. *Etym:* *wahiR. *[Sporadic:* *i > *e / _*R#*]*

oe *Termanu.* water, fluid in general. (J:452)

oe *Korbafo.*

oe *Bokai.*

oe *Bilbaa.*

oe *Rikou.*

oe *Ba'a.*

oe *Tii.*

oe *Dengka.*

oe *Oenale.*

oe (2) oe-ʔ *Dela.* 1) water. 2) liquid.

oe *Ro'is Amarasi.* water.

oe *Kotos Amarasi.* water.

oe *Molo.* water. (M:398)

oa *Kusa-Manea.* water. *[Form:* regular *e > *a* /V_ in Upper Manulea dialect*]*

Out-comparisons:

ui *Semau Helong.* water. *[irr. from PMP:* *w > *u* (expect *p*)*]*

wee, ue *Fehan Tetun.* water.

uee (2) bee *East Tetun.* 1) water (Mo:192). 2) water. *Usage:* in the interior **uee** is more commonly used [than **bee**], but both are equally understood everywhere. (Mo:12)

bea *Kemak.* water.

eer *Mambae, South.* water, liquid. (Grimes et al. 2014b:16)

oir *Kisar.* water.

eer *Ili'uun.* water, river, place where there is water. (dJ:114)

***-oha** *Morph:* ***-oha-s**. *PnRote.* cloud. *[Form:* Medial *h is perhaps from earlier *p, e.g. **kopa. The Tii and

Landu forms with initial *s* and *si* respectively indicate some kind of historic compound. The initial *k*/*ʔ* in the other Rote forms may be from the nominal prefix ***ka-**. Reconstruction of a stem **-oha** which was combined with an initial element is supported by Tetun which appears to attest something like **kal** + **ohan**.*]* *[History:* This reconstruction is perhaps connected with PMP *awaŋ 'atmosphere, space between earth and sky' through a pathway *awan > **owan > **-oha**, as suggested by Jonker (1915:35). However, this requires otherwise unattested *w > *h, as well as initial *#aw > *o. The regular outcome of *awaŋ would be **ao(n).*]*

koʔas *Termanu.* cloud. (J:242)

koʔa *Korbafo.*

koʔa *Bokai.*

koa *Bilbaa.*

sioa-ʔ *Landu.* (own field notes)

ʔoa-ʔ *Rikou.* (J:746)

koʔas *Ba'a.*

koʔas *Lole.* cloud. (Zacharias et al. 2014)

so~soʔa-k *Tii.* cloud. (J:764)

Out-comparisons:

kaloʔan *Fehan Tetun.* cloud.

kalohan *East Tetun.* cloud. (Mo:99)

kova *Central Lembata.* cloud. *[irr. from PRM: v = h* correspondence*]* (Fricke 2015)

***ohi** *Morph:* ***n-ohi**. *nRM.* almost. *[Sporadic: Ø > h /#_V?* in Korbafo.*]* *[Form:* The initial *n* in most Rote forms is probably a historic third person prefix but has become fossilised in most varieties.*]*

noʔi *Termanu.* at the point of, almost. *[Form:* The Termanu form does not take person agreement, e.g. **au noʔi** 'I almost'.*]* (J:403)

hoʔi *Korbafo.*

noʔi *Bokai.*

noi *Bilbaa.*

ʔ-oi, n-oi *Rikou. [Form:* Given as '**oi**, **noi**, etc.' probably implying that the Rikou form takes person agreement.*]*

noʔi *Tii.*

n-oi *Kotos Amarasi.* nearly.

n-oi *Molo.* to. (M:400)

***oka**1 *Morph:* ***oka-k**. *CERM.* pen, corral. *Pattern:* k-6/9. *[Sporadic:* consonant metathesis *kVf > *ʔVf > *fVʔ* in Ro'is.*]*

oka-ʔ *Bilbaa.* pen for cattle. (J:746)

oka-ʔ *Rikou.* pen for cattle. (J:746)

oʔo|f, ofaʔ *Ro'is Amarasi.* pen corral. *Usage:* **oʔof** in Buraen, **ofaʔ** in Tunbaun.

oʔo|f *Kotos Amarasi.* pen, corral.

oʔa|f, oʔo|f *Molo.* corral, cage, jail. (M:397,406)

oʔa|f *Kusa-Manea.* pen, corral.

Out-comparisons:

okat *Semau Helong.* corral, barnyard.

oka *Dhao.* field, garden, yard; pen, corral.

<oka> *Kambera.* corral, fence. (On:383)

***oka**2 *Morph:* ***oka-k**. *Rote.* root. *Doublet:* #**baʔat**. *Etym:* *wakaR. *Pattern:* k-5.

oka-k (2) na-oka *Termanu.* 1) root. 2) have roots, rooted. (J:455)

oka-ʔ *Korbafo.*

oka-k *Bokai.*

oka-ʔ *Bilbaa.*

oka=na *Landu.* root. (own field notes)

oka-ʔ *Rikou.*

oka-k *Ba'a.*

oka-k *Tii.*

(ʔ)oka-ʔ *Dengka.*

ʔoka-ʔ *Oenale.*

ʔoka-ʔ (2) na-ʔoka *Dela.* 1) roots. 2) grow roots.

Out-comparisons:

akar *Ili'uun.* root. (dJ:112)

***oken** *Morph:* ***n-oken**. *PRM.* call someone to come here. *Pattern:* k-6.
n-oke *Termanu.* calls, requests. (J:404)
n-oke *Bokai.*
n-oke *Ba'a.*
n-oke *Tii.*
n-oʔe *Dengka.*
n-oʔe *Oenale.*
n-oʔe *Dela.* ask, call.
n-oʔen *Kotos Amarasi.* call someone to come here; to summon, beckon.
n-oʔen *Molo.* calls. (M:399)
Out-comparisons:
noken *Semau Helong.* call, refer to, greet, address.

***ombu** *PRM.* female animal.
upu-k *Termanu.* female, of very young animals. (J:670)
opu-ʔ *Korbafo.*
upu-k *Bokai.*
opu-ʔ *Bilbaa.*
opu-ʔ *Rikou.*
ompu-k *Ba'a.*
ombu-k *Tii.*
ombu-ʔ *Dengka.*
ombu-ʔ *Oenale.*
opu *Kotos Amarasi.* female animal which has not yet given birth.
<bidʒael opu> (2) <fafi opu> *Molo.* 1) buffalo cow. 2) sow. (M:407)

***oo1** *Morph:* ***n-oo**. *PRM.* with. *Etym:* **oRo (pre-RM). *[irr. from PRM: Ø > k in Meto]*
n-oo *Termanu.* s/he is with. (J:400)
n-oo *Korbafo.*
n-oo *Bokai.*
n-oo *Bilbaa.*
n-oo *Rikou.*
n-oo *Ba'a.*
n-oo *Tii.*
n-oo *Dengka.*
n-oo *Oenale.*
n-oo *Dela.* bring (someone), with.
n-ook *Ro'is Amarasi.* is with, accompanies.
n-ok, n-oka *Kotos Amarasi.* is with, accompanies (M-form, U-form).
n-ok *Molo.* come along. (M:400)
Out-comparisons:
nol *Semau Helong.* and, with.
ho *East Tetun. prep.* with; *conj.* and, also (the latter only when between two nouns). (Mo:86)
n-oro, n-or *Kisar.* with, and.

***oo2** *PRM.* bamboo (generic). *Etym:* *qauR 'type of large bamboo'. *[Sporadic: Ø > ʔ /#_ in Dela-Oenale.]*
oo *Termanu.* bamboo, also the name of a big grassy plain at Pariti (a place name). (J:450)
oo *Korbafo.*
oo *Bokai.*
oo *Bilbaa.*
oo *Landu.* bamboo. (own field notes)
oo *Rikou.*
oo *Ba'a.*
oo *Tii.*
(ʔ)oo *Dengka.*
ʔoo *Oenale.*
ʔoo *Dela.* bamboo.
oo *Ro'is Amarasi.*
oo *Kotos Amarasi.* bamboo (generic).
oo benaʔ *Kopas.* kind of bamboo. Schizostachyum blumei. *[Note:* In Kopas, Amfo'an and Fatule'u **kakaʔ** is the generic term for 'bamboo'.*]*
oo *Molo.* bamboo. (M:397)
oo *Kusa-Manea.* bamboo.
Out-comparisons:
au *East Tetun.* bamboo. (Mo:5)
oa *Kemak.* bamboo (generic).
oor *Mambae, South.* bamboo. (Grimes et al. 2014b:36)
oo *Galolen.* bamboo.
our *Kisar.* bamboo.

***osa** *PnMeto.* price, value. *See:* ***sosa** 'buy, sell'.
osa-f (2) ma-ʔosa-ʔ *Kotos Amarasi.* 1) price. 2) expensive.
osa *Molo.* price. (M:407)

Out-comparisons:

osa *Semau Helong.* value, price, worth, cost.

osan *Fehan Tetun.* money — includes old coins and modern paper money.

osan *East Tetun.* money, precious metal. (Mo:156)

osa *Ili'uun.* goods, property, cloth. (dJ:131)

osa *Kemak.* money.

***osi** *Rote.* garden in a village. *Etym:* **wasi (pre-RM).

osi *Termanu.* garden or plantation in or nearby a village. (J:458)

osi *Korbafo.*

osi *Bokai.*

osi *Bilbaa.*

osi *Ba'a.*

osi *Tii.*

osi *Dengka.*

osi *Oenale.*

Out-comparisons:

asi *Kemak.* garden.

wasi *Asilulu.* forest garden. (van Hoëvell 1877:50)

wasi *Buru.* a) grove, orchard. b) field (abandoned), garden (unused), fallow land. (M:479) *[Form:* Has the variant form **wase** with the second sense.*]* (Grimes and Grimes 2020:996)

***otas** *PRM.* kind of insect which eats thatch/string. *[irr. from PRM:* *o > *e* in Meto*]*

otas *Termanu.* kind of worm that eats the roof covering of new houses in the rainy season. (J:459)

ota-k *Bokai.*

ota-ʔ *Bilbaa.*

otas *Rikou.* *[Note:* not known by my consultants.*]*

otas *Ba'a.*

otas *Tii.*

otas *Dengka.*

otas *Oenale.*

otas *Dela.*

etas *Kotos Amarasi.* kind of louse that eats string.

P - p

***paɗo** *Rote.* octopus.

pado *Termanu.* octopus. (J:462)

pado *Korbafo.*

pado *Bokai.*

pado *Bilbaa.*

pado *Rikou.* octopus. (J:462; own field notes)

mpado *Ba'a.*

paɗo *Tii.*

paɗo *Dengka.*

paɗo *Oenale.*

paɗo *Dela.* octopus.

Out-comparisons:

kapaʄu *Dhao.* octopus.

kepaʄo *Hawu.* (J:462)

***paha** *PnMeto.* split, divide. *Doublet:* ***faka1**, ***faka2**. *Etym:* *bakaq. *[irr. from PMP:* *k > *h*] [minority from PMP:* *b > *mb *p (Tetun has regular *mb > *b*, thus attesting pre-Meto *mb)*]*

n-paha *Kotos Amarasi.* split, divide.

n-paha *Molo.* cuts. (M:411)

Out-comparisons:

baka *Fehan Tetun.*

***pande** *Rote.* short in height, squat and compact in build, of a person. *Doublet:* ***mbada**. *Etym:* *pandak. *[irr. from PMP:* *a > *e*] [minority from PMP:* *p = *p*]*

pane~pane *Termanu.* small, short in stature, kind of small. (J:467)

pane~pane *Korbafo.*

pane~pane *Bokai.*

pane~pane *Bilbaa.*
pane~pane *Ba'a.*
pande~pande *Tii.*
pande~pande *Dengka.*
pande~pande *Oenale.*

***papa** *CERM.* guard, protect. *[irr. from PRM:* *p > *f* in Meto*] [Form:* Alternately, we could reconstruct ***mbafa** with medial *f and posit irregular fortition of *f > *p* in Rote.*]*
papa *Termanu.* occasionally monitor animals that are secured in the field or bush. (J:468)
papa *Rikou.*
n-pafaʔ *Kotos Amarasi.* protect.
<n-pafa> *Molo.* takes care of. (M:410)
Out-comparisons:
papa_piara *Semau Helong.* look after, take care.

***paru** *PRM.* grate. *Etym:* *parud 'rasp, file'. *[minority from PMP:* *p = *p*]*
palu (2) pa~palu-k *Termanu.* 1) grate. 2) grating, grater. *[Semantics:* All examples in Jonker (1908) refer to coconuts.*]* (J:466)
palu *Korbafo.*
palu *Bokai.*
palu *Bilbaa.*
paru *Rikou.*
palu *Ba'a.*
paru *Tii.*
palu *Dengka.*
paru *Oenale.*
panu|ʔ *Ro'is Amarasi.* hard inner coconut shell.
ʔ|panu|ʔ *Kotos Amarasi.* hard inner coconut shell.
<panu> *Molo.* half a coconut shell. (M:421)
ʔ|panu|ʔ *Kusa-Manea.* hard inner coconut shell.

***peni** *Morph:* ***ka-peni-k**. *PRM.* underlay, saddle.
peni-k *Termanu.* native saddle made from gebang palm leaves tied onto fabric rags, used both to ride on or to put loads on. (J:480)
peni-ʔ *Korbafo.*
peni-k *Bokai.*
peni-ʔ *Bilbaa.*
peni-ʔ *Rikou.*
peni-k *Ba'a.*
peni-ʔ *Dengka.*
peni-ʔ *Oenale.*
ʔ|peni|ʔ *Kotos Amarasi.* base, pad, sandals, saddle.
<peni> *Molo.* saddle. (M:432)
Out-comparisons:
beni *Fehan Tetun.* cover; put a cloth saddle on a horse; spread dirt on a log bridge. *[irr. from PRM:* *p = *b* correspondence*]*
peni *Hawu.* (J:480)

***petun** *PnMeto.* Rough Bamboo; Giant Bamboo. Dendrocalamus species. *Etym:* *bətuŋ 'bamboo of very large diameter, probably Dendrocalamus species'. *[minority from PMP:* *b > *mb > *p*] [Form:* Initial *p in PMeto is from earlier *mb. Irregular *b > *mb is attested in many languages of the region for reflexes of *bətuŋ and *mb can be reconstructed to proto-Timor-Babar, perhaps even to a higher node.*]*
petu *Kopas.* bamboo.
petu, petun *Molo.* kind of large bamboo. Dendrocalamus asper. (M:436)
petun *Baikeno.* bamboo. (Charles E. Grimes pers. comm.)
petu *Kusa-Manea.* kind of large bamboo. Dendrocalamus asper.
Out-comparisons:
betun *East Tetun.* variety of thick bamboo. *[Form:* Tetun *mb > *b* and *b > *f* are regular, hence this form also attests initial *mb.*]* (Mo:14)
betu *Dadu'a.* bamboo. (Penn 2006:92)
petuŋ *Ili'uun.* kind of bamboo. (dJ:133)

***pio** *PnMeto.* garlic. *Etym:* **mbio (pre-Meto). *[History:* This form may have been distributed by contact, though this would have been early as the reflexes of *mb are regular.*]*

kar/peo *Kotos Amarasi.* garlic. *[Sporadic:* vowel height harmony *i > *e* /_o.*] [Form:* source of initial **kar** currently unknown.*]*

pio *Amanuban.* garlic.

peo *Molo.* onions. (M:434)

Out-comparisons:

kbiu *Foho Tetun.* garlic. *[Note:* variety of Tetun spoken in the northern part of the Tetun-speaking area of central Timor ISO 693-3 [tet].*] [Sporadic:* vowel height harmony *o > *u* /i_.*]* (own field notes)

***piru** *PRM.* sling. *[irr. from PRM:* *r > Ø ~ *n* in Meto; *p > *b* ~ *f* in Meto*]*

pilu (2) pi~pilu-k *Termanu.* 1) sling (v.). 2) throwing in a slinging manner, a sling or a piece of wood used to throw in a slinging manner. (J:485)

pi~pilu-ʔ *Korbafo.*

pi~piru-ʔ *Rikou.*

mpi~mpilu-ʔ *Ba'a.*

pi~piʔu-k *Tii.*

pi~pilut *Dengka.*

pi~pirut *Oenale.*

ʔ|fiʔu *Kotos Amarasi.* sling.

biut, fiku, finu *Molo.* sling. (M:72, 119, 120)

Out-comparisons:

tali (fa~)firun, fa~firuk *East Tetun.* sling. *[irr. from PRM:* *p = *f* correspondence*]* (Mo:30, 34)

***poka** *PRM.* swollen, paunch. *Pattern:* k-10′ (*k > *ʔ*, *k* in Termanu and Oenale; expect only *k > *ʔ*). *[irr. from PRM:* *a > *o* in first Rote forms*]*

tei_poʔo-k (2) po~poka-k *Termanu.* 1) stomach (of people and some animals). **hataholi tei_poʔo madema** someone with a 'deep stomach', a glutton (J:495) 2) **hataholi ei po~pokak** someone whose feet have swollen up due to sickness (J:492)

tei_poʔo-ʔ *Korbafo.*

tei_poʔo-k *Bokai.*

tei_poko-ʔ *Bilbaa.*

tei_poko-ʔ *Rikou.*

tei_mpoʔo-k *Ba'a.*

tei_poʔo-k *Tii.*

tei_poko-ʔ (2) po~poʔat *Oenale.* 2) kind of fish that swells up. (J:754)

n-pook *Ro'is Amarasi.* fat. *[Form:* metathesised form of **n-poka**.*]*

n-poka *Kotos Amarasi.* fat.

n-pook (2) fafi a-poka-t (3) <meen poko> *Molo.* 1) fat. 2) a fat pig. 3) kind of leprosy which causes swelling. *[Form:* **meen** metathesised from **menas** 'sickness'.*]* (M:445)

***poke** *Rote.* blind. *Pattern:* k-5.

poke (2) poke-k (3) poʔe *Termanu.* 1) be or become blind. 2) blind, a blind person. (J:492) 3) = **poke-k**, mainly as a swearword. (J:490)

poke *Korbafo.*

poke *Bokai.*

poke *Bilbaa.*

poke *Rikou.*

mpoke *Ba'a.*

poke *Tii.*

poke *Dengka.*

poke *Oenale.*

Out-comparisons:

<poki> *Kambera.* blind. *[Note:* also in Mangili, Anakalang, and Mamboru.*]* (On:418)

<poku> *Lewa.*

peke *Perai.* blind. *[Note:* language of Wetar Island ISO 639-3 [wet].*]* (Hinton 2000:125)

pok~pok *Sekar.* blind. *[Note:* language of the Bomberai Peninsula ISO 639-3 [skz].*]*

[Form: possibly a chance resemblance.*]* (Smits and Voorhoeve 1992:128)

***poko** *CER.* plop. *Pattern:* k-5/6. *[Semantics:* onomatopoeia.*]*

poko~poko *Termanu.* plop, make a plopping noise by something that falls. (J:492)

Out-comparisons:

kepoʔo *Hawu.* (J:492)

***ponia** *PwRM.* sacrifice. *[irr. from PRM:* *p > *f* in Meto*]*

ponia *Dengka.* sacrifice. (J:755)

fnia-t *Molo.* poured out sacrifice. (M:123)

***pupu** *PRM.* blowpipe blow through a blow pipe. *Etym:* *putput 'puff, blow, expel air rapidly, as in using a blowgun'. *[minority from PMP:* *p = *p; *p = *p*] [irr. from PRM:* *p > *f* in most nRote /#_*]*

fupu *Termanu.* blow through a blowpipe. (J:149)

fupu *Korbafo.*

fupu *Bokai.*

fupu *Bilbaa.*

fupu *Rikou.*

fumpu *Ba'a.*

pupu *Tii.*

pupu *Dengka.*

pupu *Oenale.*

puput *Molo.* a) bamboo from which flutes are made. (M:457) b) blowpipe. (M:479)

Out-comparisons:

pupu *Helong.* (J:149)

R - r

***raho** *nRM.* three-stone hearth, fireplace. *Etym:* *dapuR 'hearth'. *[minority from PMP:* *d > *r /#_ (expect *d)*]* *[Sporadic:* *u > *o /_*R#.*]*

laʔo *Termanu.* cooking place, the three stones on which a pot is placed to cook the food, trivet, or the space between it. Also fireplace in general. (J:279)

laʔo *Korbafo.*

laʔo *Bokai.*

lao *Bilbaa.*

rao *Rikou.*

laʔo *Ba'a.*

raʔo *Tii.*

auf_nao *Kotos Amarasi.* ash in the hearth.

nao *Kopas.* ash from the three-stone hearth.

Out-comparisons:

avu rao *Hawu.* ash.

rao *Dhao.* earth oven. Made from clay for cooking clay pots.

***raʔi** *Rote.* tie. *Etym:* *Rakit 'lay long objects side by side; raft'. *[minority from PMP:* *R = *r (expect Ø)*]*

laʔi *Termanu.* tie bamboo or betel nut together in a certain way. (J:271)

laʔi *Korbafo.*

laʔi *Bokai.*

lai *Bilbaa.*

rai *Rikou.*

laʔi *Ba'a.*

raʔi *Tii.*

lai *Dengka.*

rai *Oenale.*

Out-comparisons:

°lai *Semau Helong. Borrowed from:* Irregular reflexes of initial *R in both Rote and Helong indicates borrowing. This was probably from Rote into Helong, given initial *r* in East Rote and Dela-Oenale. *[irr. from PMP:* *R > *l* /#_*]* (J:271)

***raʔu** *PRM.* scoop up in cupped hands. *Etym:* *rakup. *[Form:* Helong attests pre-RM initial *d.*]*

laʔu *Termanu.* scoop up (e.g. sand, etc.) with cupped hands. (J:285)
laʔu *Korbafo.*
laʔu *Bokai.*
lau *Bilbaa.*
rau *Rikou.*
laʔu *Ba'a.*
raʔu *Tii.*
lau *Dengka.*
rau *Oenale.*
n-nau *Kotos Amarasi.* scoop, gouge.
Out-comparisons:
daku *Semau Helong.* scoop.

***rates** *PRM.* grave. *[irr. from PRM:* *e > *a* in Ro'is Amarasi*]*
lates *Termanu.* grave. (J:283)
late-ʔ *Korbafo.*
late-ʔ *Bokai.*
late-ʔ *Bilbaa.*
lates *Ba'a.*
rates *Tii.*
lates *Dengka.*
rates *Oenale.*
niut nata *Ro'is Amarasi.* grave.
nate *Kotos Amarasi.* grave.
naten *Molo.* cairn on grave. (M:353)
nate *Kusa-Manea.* grave.
Out-comparisons:
rate(n) *East Tetun.* grave, tomb. (Mo:159)
rata, rate *Waima'a.* cemetery, tomb.
rate *Dadu'a.* grave. (Penn 2006:13)
dare (2) rai dare *Hawu.* 1) bury, covered; establish as law, command, order, set as regulation. 2) graveyard, cemetery. *[Sporadic:* consonant metathesis *rVd > *dVr.]*
rateŋ *Sika.* grave, tomb. (Pareira and Lewis 1998:169)
<reti> *Kambera.* grave. (On:438)
<rate> *Kodi.* grave.
<rati> *Mamboru.* grave.
<ratu> *Lewa.* grave.
rade *Bima.* grave. (Jonker 1893:83)
rate *Bima.* grave. *Usage:* Kolo dialect. (Jonker 1893:83)

***ree** *Rote.* wave. *[Note:* The forms with final *ii* may be historically unrelated to those with final *ee.]*
lee-k (2) lii *Termanu.* 1) oblong tracks (e.g. of tortoise on sand, boat in water). (J:286) 2) wave, waves. (J:309)
lee-ʔ (2) lii *Korbafo.*
lee-k (2) lii *Bokai.*
lee-ʔ (2) lii *Bilbaa.*
ree *Rikou.*
lee-k (2) lii *Ba'a.*
ree-k (2) rii *Tii.*
lee *Dengka.* wave, waves. (J:309)
ree, rii *Oenale.* wave, waves. (J:309)
ree *Dela.* wave.
Out-comparisons:
leen *Semau Helong.* wave. *[Note:* Jonker (1908:286) gives Helong **lee(n)** for the second Rote meaning.*]*

***reha** *PRM.* fathom, arm span. *Etym:* *dəpa. *[minority from PMP:* *d > *r /#_ (expect *d)*] [Sporadic:* *a > *e* /_# in wRM.*]*
leʔa *Termanu.* fathom. (J:288)
leʔa *Korbafo.*
leʔa *Bokai.*
lea *Bilbaa.*
rea *Rikou.*
leʔa *Ba'a.*
reʔa *Tii.*
lee *Dengka.*
ree *Oenale.*
nehe *Kotos Amarasi.* fathom.
nehe *Molo.* an arm span. **in an-nehe nuku-n** he stretches his arms out (M:360)
Out-comparisons:
dea *Semau Helong.* fathom.
roʔa *Fehan Tetun.* unit of length, from one outstretched hand to the other (about 1.5 metres); can be measured using a **tali** (rope).

roha *East Tetun.* fathom, the length of the extended arms; *v.* to measure by fathoms. (Mo:162)
ree *Kisar.* arm width.

***rekət** *Morph:* ***ma-ka-rekət**. *PRM.* tart, brackish. *Pattern:* k-9.
ma-ka-leʔe-k *Termanu.* tart. (J:292)
ma-ka-leʔe *Korbafo.*
ma-ka-leʔe-k *Bokai.*
ma-ka-leke *Bilbaa.*
ma-reʔe *Rikou.*
ma-ka-leʔe-k *Ba'a.*
ma-ka-reʔe *Tii.*
ma-ʔa-leʔa *Dengka.*
ma-ʔa-reʔa *Oenale.*
maʔ|neʔat *Kotos Amarasi.* suffering.
maʔ|neʔat *Molo.* tart, sour; fig. trouble and sorrow, tribulation, distress. *[Note:* Jonker (1908:292) gives Meto **makneʔet**.*]* (M:305)
Out-comparisons:
mnekeŋ *Helong.* (J:292)
rəkət *Central Lembata.* (Fricke 2015)
dəkət *Lamaholot, Ile Ape. [Note:* language of Lembata Island ISO 639-3 [slp].*]* (Keraf 1978:264)
bərəkət *Lamalera. [Note:* language of Lembata Island ISO 639-3 [lmr].*]* (Keraf 1978:264)

***rena** *PwRM.* hear, listen. *Etym:* *dəŋəR.
rena *Oenale.* hear. (J:721)
rena *Dela.* hear, listen.
n-nena *Ro'is Amarasi.* hear.
n-nena *Kotos Amarasi.* hear.
n-nena *Molo.* hear. (M:361)
nean *Kusa-Manea.* hear.
Out-comparisons:
rona *East Tetun.* hear, listen, pay attention to. (Mo:162)
dene *Waima'a.* hear, believe.
ţerne *Kisar.* hear.

***reo** *PRM.* turn around.
(na)-leo *Termanu.* turning around something. (J:302)
(na)-leo *Korbafo.*
(na)-leo *Bokai.*
(na)-leo *Bilbaa.*
na-reo *Rikou.*
(na)-leo *Ba'a.*
na-reo *Tii.*
(na)-leo *Dengka.*
na-reo *Oenale.*
n-neo *Molo.* loops, winds around.
maʔu an-neo niis ane the weed loops, winds itself around the field rice, choking *[Form:* Jonker (1908:302f) gives **nero** and **neo**/**neok** = 'turn something', as well as **na-knero** and **na-kneo** = 'turn'.*]* (M:363)

***rifu|n** *PRM.* thousand. *Etym:* *Ribu. *[minority from PMP:* *R = *r (expect Ø)*] [Form:* The origin of final *n is currently unclear, though it is attested widely outside of Rote-Meto.*]*
lifun *Termanu.* thousand. (J:312)
lifun *Korbafo.*
lifun *Bokai.*
lifun *Bilbaa.*
rifun *Rikou.*
lifun *Ba'a.*
rifun *Tii.*
lifun *Dengka.*
rifun *Oenale.*
ni͡ufun *Ro'is Amarasi.* thousand.
nifun *Kotos Amarasi.* thousand.
Out-comparisons:
lihu *Semau Helong.* thousand.
rihun *East Tetun.* thousand. (Mo:161)
riwun, riwan *Kisar.* thousand.

***rimbu** *Rote.* teem, abound. *Doublet:* ***liɓu**. *Etym:* *libut 'surround, encircle, as game'. *[irr. from PMP:* *l > *r; *b > *mb*]*
ri~rimbu *Tii.* teem, abound. (J:724)
rimbu-rimbu *Oenale.* teem, abound. (J:724)

***riŋin** *Morph:* ***ma-riŋin, *ma-ka-riŋin**. *PRM.* cold. *Etym:* *diŋin. *[minority from PMP:* *d > *r #/_ (expect *d); *ŋ = *ŋ*] [Form:* Medial PRM *ŋ is required to account for Meto *k* ~ *n.] [History:* Termanu **dinis** = 'dew' (Jonker 1908:88) may be connected, as suggested by Jonker, though this would require irregular initial *d = *d*. Additionally, Tii has **denis** which would attest irr. *i > *e.]*

ma-ka-lini *Termanu.* be cold. (J:314)
ma-ka-lini *Korbafo.*
ma-ka-lini *Bokai.*
ma-ka-lini *Bilbaa.*
ma-rini *Rikou.*
ma-ka-lini *Ba'a.*
ma-ka-rini *Tii.*
ma-ʔa-lini *Dengka.*
ma-ʔa-rini *Oenale.*
mainikin *Ro'is Amarasi.* cold. *[Note:* **mainirin** was identified by my main Kotos Amarasi consultant as a Ro'is Amarasi form but was not known by any of my Ro'is consultants. If this form does exist, it would point to earlier ***madindin** and indicate that a doublet should be reconstructed to PRM.*]*
mainikin *Kotos Amarasi.* cold.
manikin, <mainini> *Amanuban/ Amanatun.* cold and coldness. *[Note:* My Amanuban and Amanatun data only has **manikin**, **mainini** is from Middelkoop (1972:298).*]* (M:298; own field notes)
<mainiki> *Molo.* cold and coldness. (M:298)
manikin *Kusa-Manea.* cold.

Out-comparisons:
bliŋin *Semau Helong.* cold, cool, chilly, fresh.
malirin *East Tetun.* cold, cool; *n.* cold; *adv.* coldly, without enthusiasm; *v.* to be cold or cool. *[irr. from PMP:* *d > (*r) > *l* (possibly sporadic dissimilation)*]* (Mo:137)
rinna *Kisar.* cold.
meriŋi *Hawu.* cold, cool.

***roɗok** *PRM.* crawl, creep. *Doublet:* ***noɗo**. *[Form:* regular *ɗ > **l /*l_ in Meto (and Helong) e.g. ***roɗok** > **loɗok > **lolok > **nonok**.*]*
lodo *Termanu.* crawl, crawl forward, like a snake. (J:319)
lodo *Korbafo.*
lodo *Bokai.*
lodo *Bilbaa.*
rodo *Rikou.*
lodo *Ba'a.*
roɗok *Tii.*
roɗoʔ *Oenale.* crawl, crawl forward, like a snake.
n-nonok *Kotos Amarasi.* slither, crawl (on chest/belly). *[History:* Both the semantics and the final *k* indicate that the Meto reflexes belong under this headword rather than similar ***noɗo**.*]*
n-nonok *Molo.* flows, crawls, leaks out. (M:384)

Out-comparisons:
lolo *Semau Helong.* crawl.
roɗo *Hawu.* (J:319)

***roko** *Morph:* ***na-ka-roko**. *Rote.* rattle. *Pattern:* k-5. *[Semantics:* onomatopoeia.*]*
na-ka-loko *Termanu.* rattling, as for instance the kernels of some fruit when shaken, also used for the sound that the contents of an old coconut makes when shaken. (J:322)
na-ka-loko *Korbafo.*
na-ka-loko *Bokai.*
na-ka-loko *Bilbaa.*
na-ro~roko *Rikou.*
na-ka-loko *Ba'a.*
na-ka-roko *Tii.*
na-ʔa-loko *Dengka.*

Out-comparisons:

kerəko *Hawu.* (J:322)

***roŋga** *Rote.* pen, corral.

loŋa *Termanu.* hutch, close in a hutch. (J:326)

loŋa *Korbafo.*

loŋa *Bokai.*

loŋa *Bilbaa.*

roka *Rikou.*

loŋga *Ba'a.*

loŋga *Lole.* corral, barn, stable, stall. (Zacharias et al. 2014)

roŋga *Tii.* caged, trapped. (Grimes et al. 2014a)

loŋga *Dengka.*

roŋga *Oenale.*

Out-comparisons:

ɗoka *Hawu.* garden, corral.

***rose** *PRM.* rub, wipe.

lose *Termanu.* rub, rub into, rub off, wipe off. (J:328)

lose *Korbafo.*

lose *Bokai.*

lose *Bilbaa.*

rose *Rikou.*

lose *Ba'a.*

rose *Tii.*

lose *Dengka.*

rose *Oenale.*

n-nose *Kotos Amarasi.* wipe away, erase.

n-nose (2) ʔ-nose-ʔ *Molo.* 1) wipe away (e.g. tears). 2) rag, handkerchief. (M:386)

Out-comparisons:

rose *Kemak.* rub.

<rúhi>, <rúhu> *Kambera.* rub, polish, clean. (On:448)

roho *Hawu.* (J:328)

blosok (2) berosok *Sika.* 1) rub. (Fricke 2014:85) 2) rub. *Usage:* Hewa dialect/variety. (Keraf 1978:292)

roso *Ende.* file.

***rou** *Morph:* ***rou-k.** *Rote.* skin. *[Note:* While the Out-comparisons are formally similar, they point to earlier **l that would not regularly develop into PRM *r. Furthermore, the semantic match between 'skin' and 'sarong', while not implausible, is also not entirely convincing. Thus, they are probably chance resemblances.*]*

lou-k *Termanu.* a) skin, hide, leather, bark, fruit peel, shell. b) anything in which things can be stored, a bag, barrel, etc. (J:329f)

lou-ʔ *Korbafo.*

lou-k *Bokai.*

lou-ʔ *Bilbaa.*

rou-ʔ *Landu.* skin. (own field notes)

rou-ʔ *Rikou.*

lou-k *Ba'a.*

lou-k *Lole.* skin. (Zacharias et al. 2014)

rou-k *Tii.*

lou-ʔ *Dengka.*

rou-ʔ *Oenale.*

Out-comparisons:

<laü> [lau] *Kambera.* skirt, sarong. (On:234)

<lawu> *Anakalang.*

<lawo> *Kodi.*

ɹawo *Ende.* female sarong.

***ruan** *PMeto.* village. *[Note:* Blust and Trussel (ongoing) reconstruct PAN *kuan on the basis of an Amis form and Meto **kuan**. Ro'is Amarasi **ruan** with initial *r* shows that this reconstruction is a result of chance similarity.*] [irr. from PRM:* *r > *l* (expect *k*) in poetic Molo form (possibly archaic retention with *r > *l* after *r > *k*)*] [Form:* perhaps from earlier **nduan.*] [History:* May be connected with Rongga, Ngadha, Lio, and Ende **nua** 'village'.*]*

ruan *Ro'is Amarasi.* village.

kuan *Kotos Amarasi.* village.

kuan (2) luan *Molo.* 1) village. (M:243) 2) village. **na-ʔuul ees Saneploon bian, hai lua ʔloo hai m-ak fauknais** literally, 'it is raining in the coastal plains below Camplong, but we in distant villages say it is the dry season', a metaphor for a complaint submitted in Kupang against a king, while in the inland people prefer stupid kings. *Word-level:* 3-rain COP Camplong side 1PL.EXCL village far 1PL.EXCL 1PL.EXCL-say drought. *Usage:* poetic.

***ruku** *Rote.* bent over. *Etym:* *duku 'bend over, stoop'. *Pattern:* k-5. *[minority from PMP:* *d > *r /#_ (expect *d)*]*

luku~luku *Termanu.* bent over, bent. (J:332)

luku~luku *Bokai.*

luku~luku *Ba'a.*

(luku~luku ?) *Tii.*

luku~luku *Dengka.*

ruku~ruku *Oenale.*

Out-comparisons:

ruʔu *Hawu.* (J:332)

***rumu** *Rote.* press. *[History:* Blust and Trussel (ongoing) identify the Termanu form as a reflex of PMP *lumu 'soft', but initial *l cannot account for Rote varieties with initial *r*, which regularly comes from *r.*]*

lumu *Termanu.* knead something softly. (J:334)

lumu *Korbafo.*

lumu *Bokai.*

lumu *Bilbaa.*

rumu *Rikou.*

lumu *Ba'a.*

rumu *Tii.*

lumu *Dengka.*

rumu *Oenale.*

Out-comparisons:

lumu *Semau Helong.* press.

***rumbi** *Rote.* mantle of a squid.

lumpi-k *Ba'a.* the mantle of a squid. (J:728f)

lumbi-ʔ *Dengka.*

rumbi-ʔ *Oenale.*

Out-comparisons:

rupu, rupe *Kisar.* huge octopus or squid that is big enough to wrap around a sailboat; also referred to as ghosts of the ocean.

***ruŋirai** *Rote.* whale. *[irr. from PRM:* *u > *o* in Rikou*] [History:* Jonker (1908:334) tentatively suggests this may be a borrowing from Hawu.*]*

luŋilai *Termanu.* whale. (J:334)

lunilai *Bokai.*

rokirai *Rikou.*

luŋgilai *Ba'a.*

ruŋgirai *Tii.*

luŋgilai *Dengka.*

ruŋgirai *Oenale.*

Out-comparisons:

luŋirai *Hawu.* whale. (J:334)

***rutus** *PRM.* rust.

na-lu~lutu (2) lu~lutu-k *Termanu.* 1) rusting. 2) rust. (J:336)

na-lu~lutu *Korbafo.*

na-lu~lutu *Bokai.*

na-lu~lutu *Bilbaa.*

na-ru~rutu *Rikou.*

na-lu~lutu *Ba'a.*

na-ru~rutu *Tii.*

na-lu~lutu *Dengka.*

na-ru~rutu *Oenale.*

nutus *Kotos Amarasi.* rust.

nutus *Molo.* rust. (M:327)

Out-comparisons:

rotus *Fehan Tetun.* rust (of iron).

rutu *Hawu.* rust.

rutu *Sika.* rusty. (Pareira and Lewis 1998:177)

S - s

***-s** *PwRM.* people group suffix.

-s *Dengka.* sometimes the same as Meto at the end of the names of people groups: **sina-sius** = **sina-siu**, Chinese. (J:757)

-s *Dela.* people group suffix. *[Note:* Examples include: **ɗela-s** = 'Dela person', **ndao-s** = 'Dhao person', **tii-s** = 'Tii person', and **sonoɓai-s** = 'Atoni'.*]*

-s, -as *Kotos Amarasi.* people group suffix. *Usage:* **-s** is used after vowel final stems and CVC# final stems (for which it replaces the final C), **-as** is used with VVC# final stems.

-s, -as *Molo.* Jonker rightly identifies the 'inorganic' final **-s** on the names of people groups that end in a vowel.When they end in a consonant they take the suffix **-as**. *[Note:* Strange as it may seem, this is the description given by Middelkoop of this suffix. He is probably referring to Jonker (1906).*]* (M:xxix)

***saa** *PwRM.* what?

saa *Dengka.* what? (J:757f)

saa *Oenale.* what? (J:757f)

saaʔn=aa *Ro'is Amarasi.* what.

saaʔ *Kotos Amarasi.* what?

<sa'> *Molo.* what. (M:462)

na-saʔa *Kusa-Manea.* why?

Out-comparisons:

saa *Semau Helong.* what.

saa *East Tetun.* what. (Mo:163)

***saɓake** *Morph:* ***saɓake-k, *na-saɓake**. *nRM.* branch. *Pattern:* k-10.

baʔe-k (2) na-baʔe *Termanu.* 1) big branch of a tree. 2) have big branches. (J:20)

baʔe *Korbafo.*

baʔe-k *Bokai.*

bake-ʔ *Bilbaa.*

bake-ʔ *Landu.* forked branch. (own field notes)

bake-ʔ *Rikou.*

baʔe-k *Ba'a.*

ɓaʔe-k *Tii.*

sbake|ʔ *Ro'is Amarasi.* forked branch.

sbake|ʔ (2) na-sbake *Kotos Amarasi.* 1) forked branches. 2) grow (forked) branches.

<sbake> *Molo.* forked branch. (M:478)

***saɓuu** *CERM.* blown up, inflated; smoke. *[irr. from PRM:* *uu > *oo* in Meto*]*

bu~buu *Termanu.* a) inflated, blown up. **suŋe=na bu~buu** his cheeks are inflated, perhaps from blowing, perhaps because he has something in his mouth **lafa=na bu~buu** his sarong is inflated (e.g. because of the wind). b) also used of the swelling up of the cheeks while smoking. **ana bu~buu modo** he smokes tobacco. (J:60)

na-sboo (2) sboo-t *Kotos Amarasi.* 1) smoke (cigarette). 2) cigarette.

***sadu** *PRM.* wig, false hair. *Pattern:* d-2.

salu *Termanu.* false hair, false plait. (J:518)

salu *Korbafo.*

salu *Bokai.*

salu *Bilbaa.*

saru *Rikou.*

salu *Ba'a.*

saru *Tii.*

salu *Dengka.*

saru *Oenale.*

saluʔ *Meto. [Note:* Jonker (1908:518) gives Amarasi **farus**.*]* (J:518)

Out-comparisons:

saluʔ *Helong.* (J:518)

ruharu *Hawu.* mane of a horse. (J:518)

***saɗa** *PRM.* cut, peel.

sa~sada *Termanu.* cut into discs. (J:507f)

sa~sada *Korbafo.*

sa~sada *Bokai.*
sa~sada *Bilbaa.*
sa~sada *Rikou.*
sa~sada *Ba'a.*
sa~saɗa *Tii.*
sa~saɗa *Dengka.*
n-sara *Kotos Amarasi.* peel fruit with a knife.
n-sala *Molo.* peels. (M:471)
Out-comparisons:
sadat *Semau Helong.* peel.

***saɗi** *Rote.* as long as.
sadi *Termanu.* only, as long as, if only, provided that. (J:508)
sadi *Korbafo.*
sadi *Bokai.*
sadi *Bilbaa.*
sadi *Rikou.*
sadi *Ba'a.*
saɗi *Tii.*
saɗi *Dengka.*
saɗi *Oenale.*
Out-comparisons:
sadi *Semau Helong.* as long as.
haɗi *Hawu.* as long as, provided that.

***saɗodo** *PRM.* slide, slip. *Pattern:* d-2. *[irr. from PRM:* *ɗ > *nd* in Oenale*]* *[Sporadic:* consonant metathesis *dVr > **rVd* in Bilbaa, Rikou and Landu; consonant metathesis *lVn > *lVn in Molo.*]*
dolo *Termanu.* slide, glide. (J:98)
dolo *Korbafo.*
dolo *Bokai.* slide, skid.
lodo *Bilbaa.* slide, skid. (J:725)
na-rodo-ʔ *Landu.* slippery. (own field notes)
rodo *Rikou.* slip, skid. (J:725)
dolo *Ba'a.*
ɗoro *Tii.*
ɗolo *Dengka.*
ndoro *Oenale.*
na-sroro *Kotos Amarasi.* slide.
<n-sikanolo>, <n-sakanolo> (2) n-sinolok *Molo.* 1) slide. (M:xliii) 2) slips, slides. (M:497)
Out-comparisons:
sarodok, sadorok *East Tetun.* slip, slide or glide. (Mo:167, 164)
heɗoɗo, heɗoɗi *Hawu.* slide. (J:98)

***safe** *CERM.* catchbirdtree, birdcatcher tree, birdlime tree. *Pisonia alba*. *[Semantics:* Hoola van Nooten et al. (1880) say of *Pisonia alba*: 'The leaves of *Pisonia sylvestris* and *P.* alba are used as a vegetable. *Pisonia alba* is known as Moluccan cabbage and is an albino form of the lettuce tree (*Pisonia grandis R.Br.*)'. Their picture is of a plant with large white (or green) leaves. This matches well the description of the plant given by Jonker (1908:511). *Pisonia sylvestris* appears to be a synonym of *Pisonia alba*.*]*
safe *Termanu.* kind of tree, called *sayur bulan* ('moon vegetable') in Kupang, the leaves are eaten as vegetables. *Pisonia alba*. (J:511; Heyne 1950:610, cxviii)
<safe> *Molo.* kind of tree the leaves of which are use at a desecration. (M:465)

***saha₁** *Morph:* ***saha-k**. *nRM.* whetstone. *Etym:* *hasaq 'whet, sharpen'. *[irr. from PMP:* *a > Ø*]* *[minority from PMP:* *q > *h*]* *[Form:* regular *h > Ø /a_a in Rote. The Waima'a out-comparison indicates earlier ***hasaq** > ****saqa**.*]*
saa-k *Termanu.* whetstone for knives and machetes. (J:507)
saa-ʔ *Korbafo.*
saa-k *Bokai.*
saa-ʔ *Bilbaa.*
saa-k *Ba'a.*
saa-k *Tii.*
saha|k *Kotos Amarasi.* large whetstone.
n-saha (2) sahan *Molo.* 1) scrapes, makes smooth. 2) large, round whetstone. (M:466)

Out-comparisons:
saʔa *Waima'a.* sharpen.

***saha2** *Morph:* ***na-saha**. *PRM.* carry on the shoulders. *Etym:* *pasaqan. *[minority from PMP:* *q > *h*] [Form:* regular *h > Ø /a_a in Rote.*]*
na-saa *Termanu.* carry on or over one's shoulder. (J:506)
na-saa *Korbafo.*
na-saa *Bokai.*
na-saa *Bilbaa.*
na-saa *Rikou.*
na-saa *Ba'a.*
na-saa *Tii.*
na-saa *Dengka.*
na-saa *Oenale.*
na-saha *Kotos Amarasi.* carry an item by placing it on one's shoulder or back.

***sai1** *nRM.* flow.
sai *Termanu.* make flow away, e.g. water that is standing still. (J:512)
sai *Korbafo.*
sai *Bokai.*
sai *Rikou.*
sai *Ba'a.*
(sai ?) *Tii.*
na-sai *Kotos Amarasi.* flow.
Out-comparisons:
sai *Funai Helong.* flow.

***sai2** *Rote.* open.
sai *Termanu.* 1) cut open the belly of a slaughtered animal. 2) open something, such as a pot or bag, and begin to use the contents, open something. (J:512)
sai *Korbafo.*
sai *Bokai.*
sai *Bilbaa.*
sii_bati (2) sai *Rikou. [Semantics:* **sii_bati** is equivalent to Termanu sense (1), **sai** is equivalent to Termanu sense (2).*]*
sai *Ba'a.*
sai *Tii.*
sai *Dengka.*
sai *Oenale.*
Out-comparisons:
sai *Semau Helong.* open, unveil, reveal.

***sai3** *Rote.* torn up.
sai~sai (2) sai *Termanu.* 1) totally torn. 2) torn. (J:513)
sai~sai *Korbafo.*
sai~sai *Bokai.*
sai~sai *Ba'a.*
sai~sai *Tii.*
sai~sai *Dengka.*
Out-comparisons:
sait *Semau Helong.* torn.

***saka** *PRM.* thigh, buttocks. *Pattern:* k-irr. *[irr. from PRM:* *a > *i* in much of Nuclear-Rote; *k > *h* /V_V in Meto*] [History:* Blust and Trussel (ongoing) reconstruct Proto-Philippine *sáka 'leg of a fowl (?)'.*]*
saki/bolo-k *Termanu.* rear haunch of an animal. (J:514)
saki/bolo-ʔ *Korbafo.*
saki/bolo-k *Bokai.*
saka/bolo-ʔ *Bilbaa.* thigh, rear haunch of an animal. (J:758)
saki/bolo-ʔ *Rikou.*
saki/bolo-k *Ba'a.*
saka_ɓolo-k *Tii.*
saka-ʔ *Dengka.* thigh of a person or animal. (J:758)
saka-ʔ *Oenale.*
saka-ʔ *Dela.* thigh.
saha-n *Amanuban.* thigh, buttocks.
saha-k *Molo.* thigh. (M:466)
Out-comparisons:
sakan *East Tetun.* hip (of people), flank (of animals). (Mo:164)
sakar *Galolen.* thigh.

***sake** *PRM.* go up, ascend, rise. *Etym:* *sakay 'climb, ascend, rise up'. *Pattern:* k-8.
saʔe *Termanu.* climbing, rising (intransitive); have gone up, is up; sit down, of birds. (J:509)
saʔe *Korbafo.*
saʔe *Bokai.*
sake *Bilbaa.*

saʔe *Rikou.*
saʔe *Ba'a.*
saʔe *Tii.*
sae *Dengka.*
sae *Oenale.*
n-sae *Ro'is Amarasi.* ascend.
n-sae *Kotos Amarasi.* go up, ascend, climb up.
n-sae *Molo.* rises, ascent. (M:464)
saa *Kusa-Manea.* go up. *[Form:* regular *e > *a* /V_# in Upper Manulea.*]*
Out-comparisons:
sake *Semau Helong.* rise, ascend.
saʔe *East Tetun.* climb on, mount; to rise up, ascend. (Mo:164)
haʔe *Hawu.* ascend, climb, go up, embark, get on.

***sakiki** *Morph:* ***na-sakiki**. *PRM.* brush teeth. *Etym:* *kiskis 'shave, scrape off' (Blust and Trussel (ongoing) also reconstruct the doublet ***gisgis** 'rub, scrape against', which is reflected as 'brush (one's teeth)' in Tausug in the Philippines). *Pattern:* initial k-2a, medial k-6.
na-sa-kiki, kiki (2) kiki-k *Termanu.* 1) brush (the teeth); rub something used as medicine on one's teeth. 2) kind of brush made from palm leaf stalks used to clean the bucket that is used for tapping palm trees. (J:236)
na-sa-kiki *Korbafo.*
na-sa-kiki *Bokai.*
na-sa-kiki *Ba'a.*
(na-sakiki ?) *Tii.*
na-sa-ʔiʔi *Oenale.*
na-sa-ʔiʔi *Dela.* use tobacco to rub one's teeth after chewing betel nut. (own field notes)
na-skiki *Ro'is Amarasi.* brush one's teeth.
na-skiki *Kotos Amarasi.* brush one's teeth.
<skiki> (2) na-skiki *Molo.* 1) toothbrush. 2) brushes (the teeth). (M:236)
ta-skiik *Kusa-Manea.* brush the teeth.
Out-comparisons:
kikin *Semau Helong.* shave (head). *[Note:* Jonker (1908:236) gives Helong **kiki**, **skiki** 'brush, sweeper'.*]*
sakiki nehan *Fehan Tetun.* brush the teeth. (Mo:165)

***sakoro** *Morph:* ***na-sakoro**. *PRM.* sip. *Pattern:* k-1. *[irr. from PRM:* *r > Ø in all Rote except Oenale*]*
na-sa-koo *Termanu.* sip, drink with sips. (J:241)
na-sa-koo *Korbafo.*
na-sa-koo *Bokai.*
na-sa-koo *Bilbaa.*
na-sa-oo *Rikou.*
na-sa-koo *Ba'a.*
na-sa-koo *Tii.*
na-sa-koo *Dengka.*
na-sa-koro *Oenale.*
na-sakono *Meto.* (J:241)

***sala** *PRM.* wrong, mistake, incorrect. *Etym:* *salaq 'wrong, in error (of behaviour); miss (a target); mistake, error, fault'.
sala *Termanu.* wrong, incorrect, mistaken. (J:514)
sala *Korbafo.*
sala *Bokai.*
sala *Bilbaa.*
sala *Rikou.*
sala *Ba'a.*
sala *Tii.*
sala *Dengka.*
sala *Oenale.*
n-sana *Kotos Amarasi.* make a mistake, be wrong.
n-sana *Molo.* is wrong. (M:473)
Out-comparisons:
sala *Semau Helong.* wrong, fault, mistake, sin.
sala *East Tetun.* err, make a mistake, be wrong, be in error, sin; *n.* error, mistake, sin, crime, blame. (Mo:165)

***sale** *nRM.* sorry, contrition.
sale *Termanu.* contrition, repentance. (J:517)
sale *Korbafo.*
sale *Bokai.*
sale *Bilbaa.*
sale *Rikou.*
sale *Ba'a.*
sale *Tii.*
sane-l=oo-n *Molo.* be sorry. (M:474)

***sali** *PnRote.* pour, fill. *Etym:* *salin 'pour from one vessel into another; translate, interpret' (PWMP. Blust and Trussel (ongoing) also reconstruct PMP *saliR 'flow, of water', which is where they place the Termanu cognate, but if this were correct we would expect the final vowel in Rote to lower before loss of final *R.).
sali *Termanu.* put a liquid somewhere, pour into. (J:517)
sali *Korbafo.*
sali *Bokai.*
sali *Bilbaa.*
sali *Rikou.*
sali *Ba'a.*
sali *Tii.*
Out-comparisons:
sali *Semau Helong.* pour, fill.
salin *East Tetun.* empty, spill out. (Mo:165)
hali *Hawu.* fill (liquid), transfer container, pour.

***salili** *Morph:* ***na-salili, *salili-k**. *PRM.* armpit. *Etym:* **salili (pre-RM).
na-sa-lili (2) lili_bolo-k *Termanu.* 1) carry something in the armpit/ under the arm while it hangs by a band from the shoulder. 2) armpit. *[Form:* The second part of the Rote nominal forms all mean 'hole'.*]* (J:313)
na-sa-lili (2) lili_poo-ʔ *Korbafo.*
na-sa-lili (2) lili_bolo-k *Bokai.*
na-sa-lili (2) lili_poo-ʔ *Bilbaa.*
na-sa-lili (2) lili_bolo-ʔ *Rikou.*
na-sa-lili (2) lili_bolo-k *Ba'a.*
na-sa-lili (2) lili_ɓolo-k *Tii.*
na-sa-lili (2) lili_kolo-ʔ *Dengka.*
na-sa-lili (2) lili_ndola-ʔ *Oenale.*
snini-f *Ro'is Amarasi.* armpits.
snini-f (2) na-snini *Kotos Amarasi.* 1) armpits. 2) carry under arm with strap around shoulder.
snini-n *Molo.* armpit. (M:507)
snini-f *Kusa-Manea.* armpit.
Out-comparisons:
slili *Helong.* armpits. (J:313)
kalili, klilin *East Tetun.* armpit. (Mo:110)
kahalilin *Ili'uun.* armpit. (dJ:119)
hililla *Kisar.* armpit.
lila-r *Kemak.* armpit.
saliri *Bima.* armpit. (Jonker 1893:91)
salili *Sumbawa.* *[Note:* language of Sumbawa ISO 639-3 [smw].*]* (J:313)

***saluku** *Morph:* ***na-saluku**. *PnRote.* gather under the wings. *Pattern:* k-5/6.
na-sa-lu~luku *Termanu.* gather under the wings. (J:332)
na-sa-lu~luku *Korbafo.*
na-sa-lu~luku *Bokai.*
na-sa-lu~luku *Bilbaa.*
na-sa-lu~luʔu *Rikou.*
na-sa-lu~luku *Ba'a.*
na-ka-lu~luʔuk *Tii.*
Out-comparisons:
herugu *Hawu.* (J:332)

***sambat** *Morph:* ***ka-sambat**. *PRM.* bucket.
samba-k *Tii.* bucket, specifically a kind of big bucket. (J:759)
sambat *Dengka.*
sambat *Oenale.*
sambat *Dela.* leaf bucket.
ʔ|sapa|ʔ *Kotos Amarasi.* leaf bucket made from lontar leaves.
Out-comparisons:
sapat *Semau Helong.* bucket. *[Note:* Jonker (1908:759) gives Helong **ksapat**.*]*

(k)naban, kanaban *East Tetun.* palm leaf basket. *[irr. from PRM:* *s = *n* correspondence*]* (Mo:165)

haba *Hawu.* pail, container made from young lontar palm leaves. *[Semantics:* Used as palm wine container, or for irrigating fields by hand.*]*

<hamba> *Kambera.* bucket made from lontar leaves. (On:60)

<saba> *Anakalang.*

<samba> *Mamboru.*

***sambi** *PRM.* remove bark.

sapi *Termanu.* cut the bark off a tree with a machete or axe, remove the bark of a tree in such a way. (J:522)

sapi *Korbafo.*

sapi *Bokai.*

sapi *Bilbaa.*

sapi *Rikou.*

sampi *Ba'a.*

sambi *Tii.*

sambi *Dengka.*

sambi *Oenale.*

sambi *Dela.* remove coconut shell.

n-sapi *Kotos Amarasi.* cut at slanted angle, cut chips off; e.g. to remove the shell of a coconut from its flesh.

n-sapi *Molo.* trims, shave off until smooth. (M:476)

Out-comparisons:

sabir *Fehan Tetun.* use knife to remove bark (from wood).

***sambudas** *PRM.* sow, scatter; scattered about; splash water on something. *Etym:* **sa(m)bura[t/s] (pre-RM). *Pattern:* d-2. *[irr. from PRM:* *mb > *p* in Oenale and Tii*] [History:* Blust and Trussel (ongoing) reconstruct a number of forms that are formally and semantically similar to the form I have placed in the etymology field: *sa(m) buR, *sabuD, *saq(ə)buR, *buras. None of these can quite account for the RM reflexes, though (of course) there are also problems with my own tentative reconstruction.*]*

na-sa-pula *Termanu.* squirt or squirt out with the mouth (stronger than **na-sa-puu**). (J:502)

na-sa-pula *Korbafo.*

na-sa-pula *Bokai.*

na-sa-pula *Bilbaa.*

na-sa-pura *Rikou.*

na-sa-mpula *Ba'a.*

na-sa-pura *Tii.*

na-sa-mbula, mbulas *Dengka.*

puras *Oenale.*

puras, purak *Dela.* spit.

na-spuraʔ, n-puran *Kotos Amarasi.* spurt water.

<na-spula> (2) <n-pula>, n-pulan (3) <Oe Pula> *Molo.* 1) bubbles up (water). 2) spits on, pushes out of the mouth. 3) source where water spurts out, the name of springs, one is at Kupang the other is at Kauniki. (M:453)

Out-comparisons:

buras *Sika.* spray/spout (medicine) from the mouth. (Pareira and Lewis 1998:30)

hura *Kamarian.* spit something out, like medicine. *[Note:* also in Haruku and Kaibobo from Tihulale.*]* (van Ekris 1864:92)

hula *Asilulu.* spit something out, like medicine. (van Ekris 1864:92)

samburat *Javanese. [Note:* language of Java ISO 639-3 [jav].*]* (J:502)

***sana|ʔ** *PMeto.* bunch of fruit. *Etym:* *saŋa 'bifurcation, fork of a branch'.

saan_oo *Ro'is Amarasi.* stick insect.

noa_sana|ʔ (2) saan_oo *Kotos Amarasi.* 1) bunch of coconuts. *[Note:* **noah** = 'coconut'.*]* 2) stick insect. *[Form:* regular final CV → VC metathesis of first element of a compound combined with **oo** = 'bamboo'.*]*

sana|ʔ *Molo.* bunch of fruit or flowers. (M:473)

Out-comparisons:
saŋa *Semau Helong.* strong forked branch.
ai sanak *East Tetun.* branch, bough, or fork of tree, a spar or pole. (Mo:166)
ʤaŋa *Hawu.* branch. *[irr. from PMP:* *s > *ʤ]*
***sanahulu** *Rote.* ten. *Etym:* *sa-ŋa-puluq. *[Sporadic:* *h > Ø in wRote.*]*
sanahulu (2) hulu *Termanu.* 1) ten. 2) multiple of ten. (J:196)
sanahulu (2) hulu *Korbafo.*
sanahulu (2) hulu *Bokai.*
sanahulu (2) hulu *Bilbaa.*
sanahulu (2) hulu *Rikou.*
salahunu (2) hulu *Ba'a. [Sporadic:* consonant metathesis *n…l > *n…l.]*
sanahulu (2) hulu *Tii.*
salahunu (2) nulu *Dengka. [Note:* Dengka **salahunu** is given as 'probably'.*] [Sporadic:* consonant metathesis *n…l > *n…l.]*
sanahulu (2) nulu *Oenale.*
Out-comparisons:
smulu *Funai Helong.* ten.
hŋulu *Semau Helong.* ten.
sŋulu *Bolok Helong.* ten.
sanulu *East Tetun.* ten. (Mo:166)
heŋuru *Hawu.* ten.
***sanasə** *PRM.* breath. *[irr. from PRM:* *ə > *u* in some Rote (probably sporadic assimilation of antepenultimate vowel to stressed vowel in some cases)*] [History:* The closest resemblance in PMP is *ŋəsŋəs.*]*
nase_buʔu-k *Termanu.* cheek of people and animals. *[Form:* **buʔu-k** = 'joint, node'.*]* (J:381)
nase_buʔu-k *Bokai.* cheek of people and animals. (J:381)
nase_buku-ʔ, nasu_bukuʔ *Bilbaa.* bump of the cheekbone, cheekbone.
nasa_buʔu-ʔ *Rikou.* cheek of people and animals. (J:381)
nasu-k *Ba'a.* cheek. (J:736)
nasu-k *Lole.* cheek. (Zacharias et al. 2014)
nasu-k *Tii.* cheek. (J:736)
nasu-ʔ *Dengka.* cheek. (J:736)
nasu-ʔ *Oenale.* cheek. (J:736)
snasa-f (2) na-snasa *Kotos Amarasi.* 1) breath. 2) take a break, rest, breathe.
snasa-f (2) na-snasa *Molo.* 1) breath in general. 2) rest. (M:505)
Out-comparisons:
na-sŋasa, na-kŋasa *Funai Helong.* breathe.
hŋasa *Semau Helong.* breath.
***sanu** *Rote.* coconut with soft flesh.
noo_sanu *Termanu.* kind of coconut of which the flesh remains soft. (J:520)
noo_sanu *Korbafo.*
noo_sanu *Bokai.*
noo_sanu *Bilbaa.*
noo_sanu *Rikou.*
noo_sanu *Ba'a.*
noo_sanu *Tii.*
noo_sanu *Dengka.*
noo_sanu *Oenale.*
Out-comparisons:
haŋo *Hawu.* (J:520)
<hangu> *Kambera.* soft, e.g. of the flesh of fruit. (On:67)
<sangu> *Anakalang. [Note:* also in Mamboru.*]*
<zangu> *Weyewa.*
***sandiit** *nRM.* an insect that makes a loud noise, either a cicada or cricket. *[irr. from PRM:* *nd > *k* in Ro'is; *nd > *r* in Kusa-Manea; *nd > *t* in Termanu and Korbafo (onomatopoeia and/or assimilation to previous *t*); *nd > *d* in East Rote*] [Form:* Onomatopoeia may be the source of some of the irregularities.*]*
toko_tii-k *Termanu.* kind of cricket. (J:640)
toko_tii *Korbafo.*
toko_lii *Bokai.*
(tee) di~dii *Landu.* kind of cricket. (own field notes)

toko/dii, di~dii *Rikou.* cricket. (own field notes)
toko_ndiʔi-k *Ba'a.*
(toko_tii-k ?) *Tii.*
skiit *Ro'is Amarasi.* cicada.
skiit *Kotos Amarasi.* cicada.
ani_kra~riit=aa *Kusa-Manea.* cicada.
Out-comparisons:
kniit *Funai Helong.* cicada. *[irr. from PRM:* *nd = *n* correspondence*]*
hnii(t) ulan *Semau Helong.* cicada. *[irr. from PRM:* *nd = *n* correspondence*]*
da~dii_derok *East Tetun.* variety of cicada. *Usage:* Luka village. (Mo:20)

***saŋgeŋger** *PRM.* surprise, startle, frighten.
ŋgeŋe (2) na-ŋgeŋe(-k) *Termanu.* 1) frighten, terrify. 2) surprise, startle. (J:437)
ŋgeŋe *Korbafo.*
ŋeŋe *Bokai.*
ŋeŋe *Bilbaa.*
keker=asa *Landu.* (own field notes)
keke *Rikou.*
ŋgeŋge *Ba'a.*
ŋgeŋger *Tii.*
ŋgeŋge *Dengka.*
ŋgeŋger *Oenale.*
ŋgeŋger (2) na-ŋgeŋge-ʔ *Dela.* 1) surprised, suddenly. 2) make surprised.
na-skeke *Ro'is Amarasi.* surprised, suddenly.
na-skeke *Kotos Amarasi.* surprised, startled, suddenly.
na-skeke *Molo.* scared, frightened. (M:501)
Out-comparisons:
°**nahkeka** *Semau Helong.* immediately, suddenly. *Borrowed from:* probably Meto **na-skeke** (shown by irr. *ŋg = *k* correspondence, expect *ŋ*).

***saŋguma** *Morph:* ***saŋguma-k**. *PRM.* hermit crab. *Etym:* *[q/k]umaŋ. *[irr. from PRM:* *ŋg > *k* in wRote*] [Form:* The source of initial ***saŋg** is currently unknown. It could be connected with Rote ***saŋga** 'look for' given that hermit crabs look for their shell, but this is highly speculative. The wRote forms probably reflect *kumaŋ without any additional element.*]*
ŋguma-k *Termanu.* kind of animal with a shell, called *bai-kumbang* [OE = 'hermit crab'] in Kupang. (J:449)
ŋguma-ʔ *Korbafo.*
ŋuma-ʔ *Bilbaa.*
kuma-ʔ *Landu.* hermit crab. (own field notes)
kuma-ʔ *Rikou.*
ŋguma-k *Ba'a.*
ŋguma-k *Tii.*
kuma-ʔ *Dengka.*
ʔuma-ʔ *Oenale.*
ʔuma-ʔ *Dela.*
skuma|ʔ *Ro'is Amarasi.* hermit crab.
skuma|ʔ *Kotos Amarasi.* hermit crab.

***sao₁** *PRM.* marry. *Etym:* *qasawa 'spouse: husband, wife'.
sao *Termanu.* marry, get married, be married, both men and women. (J:521)
sao *Korbafo.*
sao *Bokai.*
sao *Bilbaa.*
sao *Rikou.*
sao *Ba'a.*
sao *Tii.*
sao *Dengka.*
sao *Oenale.*
n-sao (2) n-mat/sao *Ro'is Amarasi.* 1) marry. 2) marry.
n-sao (2) n-mat/sao (3) mat/sao-s *Kotos Amarasi.* 1) marry, got married. 2) get married, wed. *[Semantics:* **n-matsao** focuses more on the actual wedding ceremony, while **n-sao** on the resulting state.*]* 3) wedding,

marriage. *[Form:* Initial **mat** in **matsao** could be from the reciprocal prefix **mak** with irregular assimilation of the final consonant. In modern Amarasi the normal form of the reciprocal prefix is **ma** with the form **mak** being found before some, but not all, roots that begin with /t/.*]*

n-sao (2) n-mat/sao (3) sao-m *Molo.* 1) marry. 2) wed. 3) spouse. (M:477)

Out-comparisons:

safa *Funai Helong.* spouse.

sapa (2) sapan *Semau Helong.* 1) marry, wed. 2) spouse.

***sao$_2$** *Morph:* ***kai/sao**. *PRM.* green viper. *Etym:* *sawa 'python'. *[Form:* Initial ***kai** probably from ***kaiu** 'tree, plant, wood'.*]*

kai/sao *Termanu.* kind of poisonous snake. (J:217)

kai/sao *Korbafo.*

kai/sao *Bokai.*

kai/sao *Ba'a.*

kai/sao *Tii.*

ai/sao *Dengka.*

ai/sao *Oenale.*

ai/sao *Dela.*

sao *Ro'is Amarasi.* green viper.

ʔ/sao *Kotos Amarasi.* green viper.

uʔ/sao, aʔ/sao *Molo.* poisonous green adder. *[Form:* Initial *u* is probably cognate with initial *u* in **umeke** (see ***meŋge**). Any original independent meaning of this element is unknown.*]* (M:592)

sao *Kusa-Manea.* viper.

Out-comparisons:

sa/mea *East Tetun.* the general name for all snakes. (Mo:166)

***sara** *PRM.* loose, spread out.

sala~sala *Termanu.* loose, free, not bound. (J:516)

sala~sala *Korbafo.*

sala~sala *Bokai.*

sala~sala *Bilbaa.*

sara~sara *Rikou.*

sala~sala *Ba'a.*

sara~sara *Tii.*

sala~sala *Dengka.*

sara~sara *Oenale.*

<na-siitb=oo-n =am na-saan=oo-n> *Molo.* they spread out in all directions. (M:473)

***saraa** *PRM.* light, shine. *[irr. from PRM:* *r > *l* in nRote*]*

na-sa-laa (2) bula-k na-sa-laa (3) bula ma-sa-laa-k *Termanu.* 1) shine, be light, be bright; appear, show up. 2) the moon waxes, grows. 3) waxing/growing moon. (J:261)

(2) na-sa-laa *Korbafo.*

na-sa-laa (2) na-sa-laa *Bokai.*

(2) na-sa-laa *Bilbaa.*

na-sa-laa (2) na-sa-laa *Rikou.*

na-sa-laa (2) na-sa-laa *Tii.*

(2) na-sa-la~laa *Dengka.*

na-sa-raa (2) na-sa-ra~raa *Oenale.*

snaa-f (2) snaa-t=ee n-sae *Kotos Amarasi.* 1) light, sunbeam, colour. 2) dawn from the perspective of the sun.

<snaa> (2) feʔ asnaa-t=ee *Molo.* 1) gleam, shining. 2) it begins to become light. (M:504)

***sarait** *Morph:* ***na-sarait**. *PRM.* lean.

na-sa-lai (2) (ai) la~lai-s *Termanu.* 1) lean; make something lean, lean something against something. 2) something against which a dead person leans. (J:270)

na-sa-lai *Korbafo.*

na-sa-lai *Bokai.*

na-sa-lai *Bilbaa.*

na-sa-rai *Rikou.*

na-sa-lai *Ba'a.*

na-sa-rai *Tii.*

na-sa-lai *Dengka.*

na-sa-rai *Oenale.*

na-snait *Kotos Amarasi.* lean on.

na-snait *Molo.* leans something against something. (M:505)

Out-comparisons:

nahlae *Semau Helong.* lean, hope, rely. *[irr. from PRM:* *i > *e] [Form:* Jonker (1908:270) gives Helong **naslae**.*]*

hakrai *East Tetun.* support, prop, or lean. (Mo:173)

***sarakaen** *PRM.* sand. *Pattern:* k-irr. *[irr. from PRM:* *a > *o* in most nRote; *k > Ø in Lole, Tii and Meto (expect *k = *k)] [Form:* The irregular loss of *k in Meto and (optionally) in Lole and Tii is probably due to antepenultimate vowel reduction to intermediate **sarkae with subsequent deletion medial *k to resolve the consonant cluster.*]*

solokae-k *Termanu.* sand. (J:561)

solokae-ʔ *Korbafo.*

solokae-k *Bokai.*

solokae-ʔ *Bilbaa.*

soroʔae-ʔ *Landu.* sand. (own field notes)

soroʔae-ʔ *Rikou.*

soroʔae-ʔ *Oepao.* sand. (own field notes)

solokae-k *Ba'a.*

salakae-k, salae-k *Lole.* *[Note:* **salakae-k** is the only form given by Jonker (1908:759). Zacharias et al. (2014) gives only and **salae-k**.*]*

sarakae-k, sarae-k *Tii.* *[Note:* **sarakae-k** is the only form given by Jonker (1908:561). Grimes et al. (2014a) gives both **sarakae-k** and **sarae-k**.*]*

salaʔae-ʔ *Dengka.*

saraʔae *Oenale.*

snaen *Ro'is Amarasi.* sand.

snaen *Kotos Amarasi.* sand.

snaan *Kusa-Manea.* sand. *[Form:* regular *e > *a* /V_# in Upper Manulea.*]*

Out-comparisons:

°**slaen** *Funai Helong.* sand. *Borrowed from:* PMeto ***slaen** (shown by irr. *k = Ø correspondence).

°**hlaen** *Semau Helong.* sand.

sidayik *Idate.* sand. (Klamer 2002)

sraek *Lakalei.* sand. *[Note:* language of east Timor ISO 639-3 [lka].*]* (Klamer 2002)

salae *Dhao.* beach, shore, sand, coast.

lahalae *Hawu.* sand.

sarae *Bima.* sand. (Jonker 1893:94)

siraiŋ *Kamang.* sand. *[Note:* non-Austronesian language of Alor ISO 639-3 [woi].*]* (Schapper 2010)

***sare** *Morph:* ***na-sare**. *PnRote.* facing somewhere.

na-sale *Termanu.* turn oneself to face somewhere, be located opposite something. (J:517)

na-sale *Korbafo.*

na-sale *Bokai.*

na-sale *Bilbaa.*

na-sare *Rikou.*

na-sale *Ba'a.*

na-sare *Tii.*

Out-comparisons:

salo *Semau Helong.* face, across from, front on. *[irr. from PRM:* *e = *o* correspondence*]*

***sasi** *PRM.* overflow.

sasi *Termanu.* overflow, spill over. (J:524)

sasi *Korbafo.*

sasi *Bokai.*

sasi *Bilbaa.*

sasi *Rikou.*

sasi *Ba'a.*

sasi *Tii.*

sasi *Dengka.*

sasi *Oenale.*

sasi *Meto.* (J:524)

Out-comparisons:

sasi *Helong.* (J:524)

***sau₁** *nRM.* bite.

sau *Termanu.* bite into something, bite something off. (J:524f)

sau *Korbafo.*

sau *Bokai.*

sau *Ba'a.*
sau *Tii.*
n-sau *Ro'is Amarasi.* bite.
n-sau *Kotos Amarasi.* bite.
n-sau *Molo.* bites. (M:478)
Out-comparisons:
sau *Semau Helong.* bite.

***sau**$_2$ *PRM.* pick. *[Sporadic:* *VV-ʔ > VʔV in Meto (perceptual metathesis).*]*
sau *Termanu.* pick. (J:524)
sau *Korbafo.*
sau *Bokai.*
sau *Ba'a.*
sau-ʔ *Dengka.*
n-saʔu *Molo.* strips leaves off a plant or branch. (M:477)

***sau**$_3$ *Rote.* comb. *Etym:* *sau. *[irr. from PMP:* *au = *au (expect *oo)*]*
sau-k (2) sau *Termanu.* 1) comb. 2) combing. (J:524)
sau-ʔ *Korbafo.*
sau-k *Bokai.*
sau-ʔ *Bilbaa.*
sau-ʔ *Rikou.*
sau-k *Ba'a.*
sau-k *Tii.*
sau-t *Dengka.*
sau-t *Oenale.*

***seɗa** *Rote.* kind of red coral used as bead.
(henu) seda_sada, (henu) seda_ndao (2) seɗa *Termanu.* 1) kinds of coral called *muti-salah* in Kupang. *[Note:* Jonker states that this term only occurs in certain phrases: **seda_sada** (**sada** has no independent meaning), **seda Ndao** (**Ndao** = name of an island), **seda Ndao dae huu-k** all of which can also be preceded by **henu** 'bead'. The equivalents of these phrases in other varieties of Rote are not given.*]* (J:527) 2) classifier for *muti-salah* (**henu**), hence: a *muti-salah* bead. The *muti-salah* are reddish (glass) beads of great value. (Fox 2016b:49)
seda *Korbafo.*
seda *Bokai.*
seda *Bilbaa.*
seda *Ba'a.*
seɗa *Dengka.*
Out-comparisons:
(wona) hiɗa *Hawu.* (J:527)
<hàda> *Kambera.* bead. *[Note:* also in Mangili, Lewa, and Kodi.*]* (On:38)
<sàḍa> *Anakalang.*

***seɗo** *PRM.* mix.
se~sedo-k, sedo-k *Termanu.* 1) mixing of dry things. (J:527f)
se~sedo-ʔ *Korbafo.*
se~sedo-k *Bokai.*
se~sedo-ʔ *Bilbaa.*
se~sedo-ʔ *Rikou.*
se~sedo-k *Ba'a.*
se~seɗo-k *Tii.*
se~seɗo-ʔ *Dengka.*
se~seɗo-ʔ *Oenale.*
n-seroʔ *Ro'is Amarasi.* mix.
n-seroʔ *Kotos Amarasi.* mix.
<n-selo> *Molo.* mixes. (M:483)

***see**$_1$ *PwRM.* address.
meʔu_see *Dengka.* address. (J:733)
na-see *Kotos Amarasi.* take leave, excuse one's self, warn.

***see**$_2$ *PRM.* who? *Etym:* *sai.
see *Termanu.* who? (J:525)
see *Korbafo.*
see *Bokai.*
see *Ba'a.*
see *Tii.*
see *Dengka.*
see *Oenale.*
seka *Dela.* who.
se/kau *Ro'is Amarasi.* who.
se/kau *Kotos Amarasi.* who.
se/kau *Molo.* who. (M:483)
see *Kusa-Manea.* who.
Out-comparisons:
asii, sii *Semau Helong.* who. *[irr. from PMP:* *ai > *ii]*
see *East Tetun.* who. (Mo:169)

***sefe** *Rote.* paddle. *Etym:* *bəRsay 'canoe paddle; paddle a canoe'. *[Sporadic:* consonant metathesis *fVs > *sVf.*]*
sefe *Termanu.* paddle (v. and n.). (J:529)
sefe *Korbafo.*
sefe *Bokai.*
sefe *Bilbaa.*
sefe *Rikou.*
sefe *Ba'a.*
sefe *Tii.*
sefe *Dengka.*
sefe *Oenale.*

***sefi** *PRM.* set loose, untie. *[irr. from PRM:* *f > (?*h) > *ʔ* in Termanu, Korbafo and Bokai*]*
seʔi *Termanu.* loosen that which is tied. (J:529)
seʔi *Korbafo.*
seʔi *Bokai.*
sefi *Bilbaa.*
sefi *Rikou.*
sefi *Ba'a.*
sefi *Tii.*
sefi *Dengka.*
sefi *Oenale.*
n-sefi *Kotos Amarasi.* untie.
n-sefi *Molo.* sets free (a horse). (M:480)

***seke** *PRM.* force, stuck. *Pattern:* k-10.
na-ka-seʔe, seʔe (2) seʔe~seʔe *Termanu.* 1) squeezed/stuck into something. 2) completely trapped in something; squeezed, very cramped. (J:528)
na-ka-seʔe *Korbafo.*
na-ka-seʔe *Bokai.*
na-ka-seke, seke~seke *Bilbaa.*
na-seke *Rikou.*
na-ka-seʔe *Ba'a.*
na-ka-seʔe *Tii.*
na-ʔa-seʔe *Dengka.*
na-ʔa-seʔe *Oenale.*
na-ʔ|seke|ʔ *Kotos Amarasi.* force, put pressure on, press to do.
<na-seke>, <n-seke> *Molo.* forced. (M:481)
Out-comparisons:
naseke *Helong.* forces. (J:528)

***seko** *nRM.* fish (v.). *Pattern:* k-5/6′ (*k > Ø in Rikou; expect *ʔ* or *k*).
seko *Termanu.* fish in the sea with a scoop net. (J:530)
seko *Korbafo.*
seko *Bokai.*
seko *Bilbaa.*
seo (seʔo ?) *Rikou.*
seko *Ba'a.*
seko *Tii.*
n-seko *Kotos Amarasi.* hunt.
n-seko *Timaus.* hunt.
Out-comparisons:
seko *Semau Helong.* traditional fish trap.
heko *Hawu.* small kind of net. (J:530)

***seʔi** *PRM.* roast.
seʔi *Termanu.* dry roast. (J:530)
seʔi *Bokai.*
sei *Bilbaa.*
seʔi *Rikou.*
seʔi *Ba'a.*
seʔi *Tii.*
seʔi *Dengka.*
seʔi *Oenale.*
n-seʔi *Kotos Amarasi.* smokes, roasts.
n-seʔi *Molo.* smokes (meat). (M:481)
Out-comparisons:
həŋi *Hawu.* bake. (J:530)

***sela** *Morph:* ***sela-k**. *Rote.* big, gross, coarse. *Etym:* *səlaR. *[Sporadic:* *a > *e* / _# in wRote.*]*
sela-k *Termanu.* coarse, large. (J:531)
sela-ʔ *Korbafo.*
sela-k *Bokai.*
sela-ʔ *Bilbaa.*
sela-ʔ *Rikou.*
sela-k *Ba'a.*
sela-k *Tii.*
sele-ʔ *Dengka.*
sele-ʔ *Oenale.*
Out-comparisons:
bsedaʔ *Funai Helong.* rough.

selaʔ *Semau Helong.* sore, strained, rough. *[Note:* Jonker (1908:531) gives Helong <**bsela**>.*]*

***selə** *PRM.* plant (v.).

sele *Termanu.* stick in the ground, plant. (J:581)

sele *Korbafo.*

sele *Bokai.*

sele *Bilbaa.*

sele *Rikou.*

sele *Ba'a.*

sele *Tii.*

sela *Dengka.*

sela *Oenale.*

n-sena *Kotos Amarasi.* plant.

n-seen *Molo.* plant. *[Form:* metathesised form of **n-sena**.*]* (M:483)

n-sena *Kusa-Manea.* plant.

Out-comparisons:

həle *Hawu.* plant.

***selut** *PRM.* replace, exchange. *[History:* Blust and Trussel (ongoing) reconstruct Proto-Philippine *sulit, which could be connected via vowel metathesis.*]*

selu-k (2) na-seluk *Termanu.* 1) exchange. 2) swap with someone. (J:535)

selu-ʔ *Korbafo.*

selu-k *Bokai.*

selu-ʔ *Bilbaa.*

selu-ʔ *Rikou.*

selu-k *Ba'a.*

selu-k *Tii.*

selut *Dengka.*

selut *Oenale.*

n-senu|ʔ *Kotos Amarasi.* replace.

<**n-senu**> *Molo.* reciprocates. **ina n-seun banin kau** he gives me a gift in return. (M:485)

Out-comparisons:

silu *Semau Helong.* change clothes.

haselu *East Tetun.* repay; to take revenge; to swap or exchange. (Mo:80)

selu *Ili'uun.* exchange. (dJ:136)

nʧelu (2) selu *Bima.* 1) exchange. 2) something that replaces something else, substitute. *Usage:* Kolo dialect. (Jonker 1893:121)

<**hilu**> *Kambera.* replace, reimburse. (On:91)

sulih, silih, sulur *Javanese. [Note:* language of Java ISO 639-3 [jav].*]* (J:535)

ma-silur *Balinese.* exchange, exchanged. *[Note:* language of Bali ISO 639-3 [ban].*]* (Kersten 1984:538)

sulle *Bugis.* replace. (Masse 2013:360)

***sembo** *PRM.* barter, swap, exchange.

sepo *Termanu.* go and sell or swap consumables outside the capital for salt, tobacco, etc., peddle consumables outside the capital. (J:539)

sepo *Korbafo.*

sepo *Bokai.*

sepo *Bilbaa.*

sepo *Rikou.*

sempo *Ba'a.*

sembo *Tii.*

sembo *Dengka.*

sembo *Oenale.*

na-sepo *Meto.* (J:539)

***seŋa** *PRM.* fry. *Etym:* *saŋəlaR 'stir-fry, cook in a frying pan without oil'. *[irr. from PMP:* *laR > Ø*] [minority from PMP:* *ŋ = *ŋ*] [Sporadic:* antepenultimate *a > *e.*] [Form:* Medial *ŋ is required to account for Meto *k*. Mills (2010:285) also draws attention to Leti **sekra** with irregular medial *ŋ > *k* rather than expected *n.]*

se~sena *Termanu.* fry or bake meat. (J:537)

se~sena *Korbafo.*

se~sena *Bokai.*

se~sena *Bilbaa.*

se~sena *Rikou.*

se~sena *Ba'a.*

se~sena *Tii.*
se~sena *Dengka.*
se~sena *Oenale.*
na-seka *Timaus.* fry.
ta-seek *Kusa-Manea.* fry. *[Form:* metathesised form of (currently unattested) ***ta-seke**.*]*
Out-comparisons:
neŋan *Semau Helong.* fry. *[irr. from PMP:* *s > *n]*
sona *East Tetun.* roast, fry. (Mo:173)
***seŋgi** *PRM.* snap off, harvest.
seŋi *Termanu.* break (Latin *frangi*), as a stick, etc.; break (Latin *frangere*). (J:537)
seŋi *Korbafo.*
seŋi *Bokai.*
seŋi *Bilbaa.*
seki *Rikou.*
seŋgi *Ba'a.*
seŋgi *Tii.*
seŋgi *Dengka.*
seŋgi *Oenale.*
n-seki *Kotos Amarasi.* harvest corn.
n-seki (2) na-t|seki *Molo.* 1) harvests (corn). 2) snapped off, of a branch. (M:482)
ta-seik *Kusa-Manea.* harvest corn. *[Form:* Phonetically this is a single mid-high vowel [t̪aˈseːk] in my notes.*]*
Out-comparisons:
siŋin *Semau Helong.* pick corn.
***seo** *nRM.* whisper.
na-se~seo *Termanu.* murmur, whisper. (J:538)
na-se~seo *Korbafo.*
na-se~seo *Bokai.*
na-se~seo *Bilbaa.*
na-se~seo *Rikou.*
na-se~seo *Ba'a.*
na-se~seo *Tii.*
na-ʔseʔo *Kotos Amarasi.* whisper.
<na-seo> *Molo.* whispers. (M:485)
***seru** *PRM.* weaving sword (part of the loom). *Etym:* **sədu(t).
selu *Termanu.* the sabre shaped beam of the loom. (J:535)
selu *Korbafo.*
selu *Bokai.*
selu *Bilbaa.*
seru *Rikou.*
selu *Ba'a.*
seru *Tii.*
se~seru *Oenale.*
senu *Ro'is Amarasi.* the long beam in the loom that the weaver pulls towards themself by holding on each end, it doesn't move smoothly but lurches as it is pulled.
senu *Kotos Amarasi.* the long beam in the loom that the weaver pulls towards themself by holding on each end, it doesn't move smoothly but lurches as it is pulled.
Out-comparisons:
silu *Helong.* (J:535)
souru, soru *East Tetun.* weave (cloth). (Mo:174)
seru *Waima'a.* weave.
pehəɗu *Hawu.* (J:535)
surit *Central Lembata.* weaving sword. (Hanna Fricke pers. comm.)
***sesə** *PRM.* stuff, cram in; be crowded. *Etym:* *səksək. *[Form:* The Meto unmetathesised form has not yet been attested. It could be ***na-ʔsesa** or ***na-ʔsese**.*]*
sese *Termanu.* tamp, cram, impress. (J:539)
sese *Korbafo.*
sese *Bokai.*
sese *Bilbaa.*
sese *Rikou.*
sese *Ba'a.*
sese *Tii.*
sesa *Dengka.*
sesa *Oenale.*
na-ʔsees *Kotos Amarasi.* crowded, tight.
Out-comparisons:
həhi, kehəhi *Hawu.* narrow. (J:539)

***seti** *PRM.* tight, tightly packed.
na-ka-seti *Termanu.* close together, tightly packed together, as e.g. planks. (J:541)
na-ka-seti *Korbafo.*
na-ka-seti *Bokai.*
na-ka-seti *Bilbaa.*
na-seti *Rikou.*
na-ka-seti *Ba'a.*
na-ka-seti *Tii.*
na-ʔa-seti *Dengka.*
na-ʔa-seti *Oenale.*
na-ʔ|seti|ʔ (2) n-seit=oo-n *Kotos Amarasi.* 1) force one's way (e.g. out, through). 2) involve oneself in (e.g. other people's business).
Out-comparisons:
siti *Semau Helong.* push through.
seti *East Tetun.* put a wedge or chock under. (Mo:171)

***seu** *PRM.* pick fruit.
seu *Termanu.* pick, of fruit. (J:541)
seu *Korbafo.*
seu *Bokai.*
seu *Bilbaa.*
seu *Rikou.*
seu *Ba'a.*
seu *Tii.*
seu *Dengka.*
seu *Oenale.*
n-seu *Kotos Amarasi.* pick (of fruit, etc.).
n-sio *Amanuban/Amanatun.* picks (fruit).
n-seu (2) na-t|seu *Molo.* 1) picks (fruit). 2) fallen off, of fruit. (M:488)
seu *Kusa-Manea.* pick fruit (like coconuts, mangoes).
Out-comparisons:
sikuʔ *Semau Helong.* pick, strip off.

***səru** *PRM.* meet, greet. *Etym:* **səru (pre-RM). *[irr. from PRM:* *ə > *o* in Rote*]*
na-so~solu *Termanu.* meet. (J:561)
na-so~solu *Korbafo.*
na-so~solu *Bokai.*
na-so~solu *Bilbaa.*
na-so~soru *Rikou.*
na-so~solu *Ba'a.*
na-so~soru *Tii.*
na-so~solu *Dengka.*
na-so~soru *Oenale.*
n-senu *Kotos Amarasi.* greet, meet.
n-senu *Molo.* go to meet. **too anpoi neem he nsenu usif** the people come from outside to meet the king (M:485)
Out-comparisons:
hasoru *Fehan Tetun.* meet, e.g. person in house greets a visitor, meet on the street, visitor greets a person in the house; can be meeting on the street without talking to one another.
hasouru *East Tetun.* be opposed to, go against; encounter, meet (two people meeting face to face when going in opposite directions); *prep.* against. (Mo:80)
səli *Central Lembata.* meet. *[irr. from PRM:* *u = *i* correspondence*]* (Hanna Fricke pers. comm.)

***səu** *PRM.* kind of tree. Alstonia villosa. *[irr. from PRM:* *ə > *o* in nRote*]* *[Semantics:* *'*Alstonia trees are used in traditional medicine. The bark of the Alstonia constricta and the Alstonia scholaris is a source of a remedy against malaria, toothache, rheumatism and snake bites. The latex is used in treating coughs, throat sores and fever.' ('Alstonia', *Wikipedia.* en.wikipedia.org/wiki/Alstonia. Accessed 17 September 2020).*]*
sou *Termanu.* kind of tree the bark of that is used as a healing agent. (J:565)
sou *Korbafo.*
sou *Bokai.*
sou *Bilbaa.*

sou *Rikou.*
sou *Ba'a.*
(sou ?) *Tii.*
seu-ʔ *Dengka.* (J:762)
seu-ʔ *Oenale.* (J:762)
hau seu *Molo.* kind of tree. *Alstonia villosa*. (M:488)

***siɗa** *PRM.* rip.
sida *Termanu.* rip. (J:543)
sida *Korbafo.*
sida *Bokai.*
sida *Bilbaa.*
sida *Rikou.*
sida *Ba'a.*
siɗa *Tii.*
siɗa, siɗe *Dengka.*
siɗa, siɗe *Oenale.*
<n-sila> na-klatiʔ (2) <aksil-aksila> *Molo.* 1) rips into small pieces. *[Form:* **na-klatiʔ** = 'destroy'.*]* 2) completely torn. (M:495)
Out-comparisons:
<hira> *Kambera.* rip. *[Note:* also in Mangili and Lewa.*]* (On:94)
<sira> *Anakalang. [Note:* also in Mamboru.*]*
<ira> *Weyewa.*
<hirya> *Kodi.*

***sifi** *PRM.* braid, plait.
sifi *Termanu.* the name of a particular kind of braiding. (J:544)
sifi *Korbafo.*
sifi *Bokai.*
sifi *Bilbaa.*
sifi *Rikou.*
sifi *Ba'a.*
sifi *Tii.*
sifi *Dengka.*
sifi *Oenale.*
n-sifi *Kotos Amarasi.* braiding work.
n-sifi *Molo.* inserts, braids. **bifee an-sifi <poni>** the woman repairs a basket by inserting new strips of lontar leaves (M:490)
Out-comparisons:
həɓi *Hawu.* braid (a chair). (J:544)

***sii₁** *CER.* tie up, snare. *[History:* Blust and Trussel (ongoing) reconstruct Proto-Philippine *siluq 'noose, snare; net'.*]*
sii *Termanu.* tie up a chick (or a pig) with a certain kind of noose so that its foot is not wounded. (J:542)
Out-comparisons:
hii *Hawu.* snare. (J:542)

***sii₂** *Morph:* ***sii-k.** *Rote.* shellfish. *[History:* Blust and Trussel (ongoing) reconstruct *sisi and *sisuq (with doublet *sisiq) 'small snail or periwinkle'.*]*
si~sii-k *Termanu.* normally in: **sii biʔi-k**, **sii hedu**, **sii mina**, kinds of shellfish, the general name of which is **si~sii-k**. (J:542)
si~sii-ʔ *Korbafo.*
si~sii-k *Bokai.*
si~sii-ʔ *Bilbaa.*
si~sii-ʔ *Rikou.*
si~sii-k *Ba'a.*
si~sii-k *Tii.*
laʔi_sii-ʔ *Dengka.*
lai_sii-ʔ *Oenale.*
Out-comparisons:
sii *Ili'uun.* shell-fish. *[Note:* **sii_suhun** = 'shell', **sii_ogo** = 'signalling-shell (which is blown)'.*]* (dJ:137)

***sika** *Rote.* open, uncover. *Doublet:* ***siŋga**. *Etym:* *siŋkab. *Pattern:* k-5. *[minority from PMP:* *ŋk > *k*] [Sporadic:* *a > *e* / _# in wRote.*]*
sika *Termanu.* open something wide, hold open. (J:544)
sika *Korbafo.*
sika *Bokai.*
sika *Ba'a.*
sike *Dengka.*
sike *Oenale.*

***sikəh** *PRM.* lath, rod (part of the loom). *Pattern:* k-irr. *[irr. from PRM:* *ə > *a* in Termanu and Ba'a; *k > Ø in Oenale and Meto (given other Rote *k* we expect *k > *k* or *ʔ* in both)*] [Sporadic:* *ə > *e* /σ_# in wRote (perhaps *ə > *a > *e* / _#).*]*

sika-k *Termanu.* name of part of the underside of the loom, a piece of bamboo used to make the pieces of fabric taut and to keep them apart from each other. (J:544)
si~sike-ʔ *Korbafo.*
sike-k *Bokai.*
sike-ʔ *Bilbaa.*
siʔe-ʔ *Rikou.*
sika-k *Ba'a.*
siʔe-k *Tii.*
sike-t *Dengka.*
sie-t *Oenale.*
siah *Kotos Amarasi.* name of a thin split bamboo slat used in weaving.
sia-l *Molo.* name of a thin split bamboo slat used in weaving. 'Two vertically placed laths (**sial**) behind these serve to raise the even and the odd threads in turn.' (Schulte Nordholt 1971:42). *[Note:* Jonker (1908:544) gives **siel**.*]* (M:489)
Out-comparisons:
sia *Helong.* (J:544)

***siku** *Morph:* ***siku-k**. *PRM.* elbow. *Etym:* *siku. *Pattern:* k-7. *[Sporadic:* antepenultimate vowel assimilation in wRote.*]*
siʔu-k *Termanu.* elbow. *Usage:* usually compounded with **lima** 'arm'. (J:549)
siʔu-ʔ *Korbafo.*
siʔu-k *Bokai.*
siku-ʔ *Bilbaa.*
lima siʔu-ʔ *Landu.* elbow. (own field notes)
siku-ʔ *Rikou.*
siʔu-k *Ba'a.*
siʔu-k *Tii.*
siki_buku-ʔ *Dengka.* elbow. (J:763)
siki_ɓuku-ʔ *Oenale.* elbow. (J:763)
si͡uʔu-f *Ro'is Amarasi.* elbow.
siʔu-f *Kotos Amarasi.* elbow.
siku-n *Kopas.* elbow. *Usage:* Tunfe'u hamlet, other varieties of Kopas have **siʔu-n**.
siʔu-f *Molo.* elbow. (M:500)
siʔu-f *Kusa-Manea.* elbow.
Out-comparisons:
sikun *Semau Helong.* elbow.
siku-n *East Tetun.* elbow, corner, angle. (Mo:171)

***simo** *PRM.* receive. *[irr. from PRM:* *m > *mb in Rote*]*
sipo *Termanu.* receive, accept. (J:547)
sipo *Korbafo.*
sipo *Bokai.*
sipo *Bilbaa.*
sipo *Rikou.*
simpo *Ba'a.*
simbo *Tii.*
simbo *Dengka.*
simbo *Oenale.*
n-simo, n-simu *Kotos Amarasi.* receive. *Usage:* poetic, only in the parallel pair **n-sium =ma n-toup**.
n-simo *Molo.* receives. (M:496)
siam *Kusa-Manea.* receive. *[Form:* metathesised form of (currently unattested) ***sima**. It is possible that the unmetathesised form is ***simo** and that *o* dissimilates to *a* after high vowels in Kusa-Manea, but this would go against the attested raising of final mid vowels in words such as **uim** ~ **umi** 'house' < ***ume** < ***uma**.*]*
Out-comparisons:
simu *Semau Helong.* receive, greet arrival.
simu *East Tetun.* receive, take, accept; to welcome; to respond. (Mo:172)
simu *Waima'a.* receive, accept, welcome.
sium *Mambae, South.* receive, accept, agree. (Grimes et al. 2014b:41)
həmi, həme *Hawu.* receive (sg.), receive (pl.).
səmi, həme *Dhao.* receive.
simo *Ende.* receive.
himo *Sika.* receive. (Pareira and Lewis 1998:76)

***sina** *Morph:* ***sina-k**. *PRM.* light (n.). *Etym:* *siŋaR 'ray of light; to shine'. *[Sporadic:* *a > *e* / _# in wRM.*]*

bula_sina-k *Termanu.* moonlight. (J:546)

bula_sina-k *Keka.* in bright moonlight. *[Note:* Given with a note that this form is found 'in Keka and others'.*]* (J:763)

fula sine-ʔ *Dela.* moonlight.

meuʔ_sina|ʔ *Ro'is Amarasi.* light, brightness.

meuʔ_sine|ʔ (2) sine|ʔ, sina|ʔ *Kotos Amarasi.* 1) light (n.). 2) four days from now. *[Note:* Also occurs in the parallel pair **na-toon =ma na-sineʔ** 'tell, make known'.*]*

n-sine|k (2) huma-n an-sine|k *Molo.* 1) light, not cloudy, at dawn or moonrise. 2) one looks fresh (after bathing or recovery from illness). *[Note:* **huma-n** = 'face, type'.*]* (M:497)

maʔsian *Kusa-Manea.* brightness, light.

Out-comparisons:

rai (nak)sinak *East Tetun.* return to good weather with sun shining. (Mo:172)

***sinaraʔe** *PRM.* kingfisher with white underbelly and blue back and head. There are two such species in Timor; the Sacred Kingfisher and the Collared Kingfisher. Todiramphus chloris, Todiramphus sanctus. *[irr. from PRM:* *i > u in Bilbaa; *r > *l* in Dela; *e > Ø in Dela (if the putative reflex is cognate)*]* *[Sporadic:* glottal stop insertion in Kotos Amarasi (first syllable); antepenultimate vowel reduction in all reflexes.*]* *[Form:* I have reconstructed initial *i on the basis of Rikou and Lole with *i*, as well as Amfo'an, which attests a front vowel *e*. Under this hypothesis Bilbaa has undergone irr. *i > *u* while Dela, Ro'is Amarasi, and Kotos Amarasi have reduced this vowel to the default unstressed vowel *a*. This form also has ante-penultimate vowel reduction in most lects with subsequent coalescence of the resulting consonant cluster in all lects apart from Lole.*]*

sulae *Bilbaa.* Collared Kingfisher. Todiramphus chloris. (own field notes)

sirae *Rikou.* Collared Kingfisher. Todiramphus chloris. (own field notes)

sinlaʔe *Lole.* kingfisher. (own field notes)

sanala-ʔ *Dela.* kind of small bird with blue belly and yellow neck (but not the Collared Kingfisher). *[Note:* This Dela form may not be cognate but is included here because of the phonetic and semantic similarity.*]* (Thersia Tamelan pers. comm. December 2017)

sanae *Ro'is Amarasi.* Sacred Kingfisher, Collared Kingfisher. Todiramphus chloris; Todiramphus sanctus.

saʔnaʔe|k *Kotos Amarasi.* Sacred Kingfisher, Collared Kingfisher. Todiramphus chloris; Todiramphus sanctus.

senae-l *Amfo'an.* Sacred Kingfisher, Collared Kingfisher. Todiramphus chloris; Todiramphus sanctus.

***sinor** *Rote.* maggots.

sino-k *Termanu.* maggots from fly eggs in a wound. (J:547)

sino-ʔ *Korbafo.*

sino-k *Bokai.*

sino-ʔ *Bilbaa.*

sino-ʔ *Rikou.*

sino-k *Ba'a.*

sino *Tii.*

sino-ʔ *Dengka.*

sinor *Oenale.*

Out-comparisons:

sinun *Helong.* (J:547)

***siŋga** *CER.* open, uncover. *Doublet:* ***sika**. *Etym:* *siŋkab.
siŋa *Bilbaa.* open wide. (J:763)
***siŋgadaʔ** *PwRM.* scold. *Pattern:* d-2. *[Form:* Lack of known reflexes in nRote means the medial consonant is ambiguous between *ʤ and *d-2. nRote *l/r* would support *d-2, while *d/ɗ* would support *ʤ.*]*
asiŋga~ŋgaraʔ *Dela.* scold severely.
na-skaraʔ *Kotos Amarasi.* snarl, rebuke, mad, angry, shouting mad.
***sio** *PRM.* nine. *Etym:* *siwa. *[Sporadic:* vowel height harmony *i > *e* /_o in some Meto.*]*
sio *Termanu.* nine. (J:547)
sio *Korbafo.*
sio *Bokai.*
sio *Bilbaa.*
sio *Rikou.*
sio *Ba'a.*
sio *Tii.*
sio *Dengka.*
sio *Oenale.*
seo *Ro'is Amarasi.* nine.
seo *Kotos Amarasi.* nine.
sioʔ *Amanuban/Amanatun.* nine.
seoʔ *Amfo'an.* nine.
seo, sio *Molo.* nine. (M:485)
seo *Timaus.* nine.
sio *Kusa-Manea.* nine.
Out-comparisons:
sipa *Funai Helong.* nine. *[irr. from PMP:* *w > *p* (expect *f*)*]*
sipa *Semau Helong.* nine.
siwi *Fehan Tetun.* nine.
sia *East Tetun.* nine. (Mo:171)
sibe *Kemak.* nine.
siwi *Welaun.* nine.
heo *Hawu.* nine.
***sira** *PRM.* they. *Doublet:* ***ra**. *Etym:* *si-ida.
sila *Termanu.* plural form of **ndia** [OE = 3SG]. (J:545)
sila *Korbafo.*
sila *Bokai.*
sila *Bilbaa.*
sira *Landu.* 3PL, they. (own field notes)
sira *Rikou.*
sila *Ba'a.*
sira *Tii.*
sila *Dengka.*
sira *Oenale.*
siin, sini, sina *Ro'is Amarasi.* they.
siin, sini, sina *Kotos Amarasi.* 3PL.NOM, 3PL.ACC. *[Form:* Phonetically the metathesised form **siin** almost always has a single short vowel [sin]. The unmetathesised form **sina** is only used before consonant clusters.*]*
siin *Molo.* 3PL. (M:496)
sian *Kusa-Manea.* 3PL.
Out-comparisons:
sira *East Tetun.* they; when placed after a noun indicates plural. (Mo:172)
hira *Ili'uun.* they, their, them. (dJ:118)
***sisi** *PwRM.* flesh, meat. *Etym:* *həsi. *[irr. from PMP:* Ø > *s; *ə > *i (sporadic assimilation)*]*
sisi *Dengka.* meat, flesh. (J:763)
sisi *Oenale.* meat, flesh. (J:763)
sisi-n *Ro'is Amarasi.* meat, flesh.
sisi-f *Kotos Amarasi.* meat, flesh.
sisi *Molo.* meat, flesh. (M:499)
Out-comparisons:
sisi *Semau Helong.* meat.
sisi *Idate.* meat. (Klamer 2002)
sisi *Midiki.* meat. (Dawson 2014)
°sisi *Dhao.* meat. *Borrowed from:* probably wRote **sisi** (shown by irr. *Ø = *s* and irr. *ə = *i* correspondences).
sisi *Tokodede.* meat. (Klamer 2002)
siis *Mambae, South.* meat. (Grimes et al. 2014b:41)

***soda** *Morph:* ***soda-k**. *PRM.* space. *Pattern:* d-irr. *[irr. from PRM:* *d > ɗ in wRote (expect *d > *r*/*l*)*] [Form:* Alternately, we could reconstruct ***soɗa** and posit irr. *ɗ > *n* in Meto.*]*

soda-k (2) uma=a soda=na, uma soda-k (3) dae soda-k (4) soda~soda *Termanu.* 1) space in time. 2) open space or piece of land. 3) open space of ground free from weeds; but also free unmanaged land that can be built on. (J:553f) 4) have an opportunity, have time. (J:552f)

soda-ʔ (2) soda-ʔ (4) soda~soda *Korbafo.*

soda-k (2) soda-k (4) soda~soda *Bokai.*

soda-ʔ (2) soda-ʔ (4) soda~soda *Bilbaa.*

soda-ʔ (2) soda-ʔ (4) soda~soda *Rikou.*

soda-k (2) soda-k (4) soda~soda *Ba'a.*

soɗa-k (2) soɗa-k (4) soɗa~soɗa *Tii.*

soɗa-ʔ (2) ume soɗa-ʔ, ume=a so~soɗa=na (4) soɗa~soɗa *Dengka.*

soɗa-ʔ (2) soɗa-ʔ (4) soɗa~soɗa *Oenale.*

soɗa *Dela.* yard.

sona-f (2) na-ʔsonaʔ *Kotos Amarasi.* 1) space that belongs to someone; midst, realm, by extension; kingdom, country, palace. 2) widen.

sonaʔ (2) na-ʔsonaʔ (3) sona-f *Molo.* 1) space. 2) clear (the way). 3) palace. (M:513)

***soɗa** *Rote.* sing.

soda *Termanu.* sing. (J:552)

soda *Korbafo.*

soda *Bokai.*

soda *Bilbaa.*

soda *Rikou.*

soda *Ba'a.*

soɗa *Tii.*

soɗa *Dengka.*

soɗa *Oenale.*

Out-comparisons:

hoɗa-keʄeka *Hawu.* shout praise. *[Note:* Jonker (1908:552) gives Hawu **hoɗa** 'singing on a ship'.*]*

soɗa *Ende.* singing on a vessel. (J:552)

***soe** *PRM.* disaster.

soe *Termanu.* disaster, impending disaster, compare **silaka** with which this word is often compounded: **soe silaka**. (J:554)

soe *Korbafo.*

soe *Bokai.*

soe *Bilbaa.*

soe *Rikou.*

soe *Ba'a.*

soe *Tii.*

soe *Dengka.*

soe *Oenale.*

n-soe *Kotos Amarasi.* suffer loss.

soe-l *Meto.* (J:554)

Out-comparisons:

soe *Helong.* (J:554)

***soeneru** *PRM.* leaf umbrella. *[irr. from PRM:* vowel metathesis in Meto *eCu > *uCe]*

suneru *Tii.* kind of umbrella made from a big sewn gebang-palm leaf. (J:541)

soenelu-ʔ *Dengka.*

soeneru-ʔ *Oenale.*

soeneru-ʔ *Dela.* rain cape from gebang leaves. *Usage:* archaic.

snunaʔ *Fatule'u.* umbrella made from a leaf.

snunaʔ, snuneʔ *Molo.* umbrella made from gebang palm leaves. (M:508)

Out-comparisons:

salurin *Fehan Tetun.* old-style umbrella, made of **akar** [sago palm] leaf, and held over the head.

salurik *East Tetun.* palm leaf used as an umbrella. (Mo:165)

***soi** *PRM.* open, ransom, pay off.
soi *Termanu.* 1) open (v.). 2) pay a debt, ransom. (J:556)
soi *Korbafo.*
soi *Bokai.*
soi *Bilbaa.*
soi *Rikou.*
soi *Ba'a.*
soi *Tii.*
soi *Dengka.*
soi *Oenale.*
n-soi (2) na-soitan (3) na-tsoi (4) na-soin *Kotos Amarasi.* 1) ransom, pay debt. 2) open something. 3) opened. 4) opened.
n-soi (2) na-soin (3) na-soitan *Molo.* 1) ransoms. 2) open. 3) open (the door). (M:510)
Out-comparisons:
sui *Semau Helong.* ransom, redeem, pay off.
soi *East Tetun.* redeem, pay off; to acquire, win, to possess; rich, well-to-do. (Mo:173)
soi *Waima'a.* buy.
hoʔi *Sika.* redeem. (Pareira and Lewis 1998:77)
soʔi *Ende.* buy. (J:556)

***soka** *Rote.* sack made from palm leaves. *Pattern:* k-5. *[History:* possibly connected with Dutch *zak.]*
soka *Termanu.* sack of gebang or lontar palm leaves. (J:557)
soka *Korbafo.*
soka *Bokai.*
soka *Bilbaa.*
soʔa *Rikou.*
soka *Ba'a.*
sokaʔ *Dengka.*
sokaʔ *Oenale.*
Out-comparisons:
hoka *Hawu.* (J:557)
sokal *Kupang Malay.* (J:557)
sokatol *Saparua.* kind of box (Malay *tatumbu*). *[Note:* language of Lease Islands ISO 639-3 [spr].*]* (van Hoëvell 1877:55)

***soke** *PRM.* scoop up, pick out. *Pattern:* k-8/9′ (Kotos Amarasi Ø Molo *ʔ* correspondence; expect either Ø in both for pattern 8 or *ʔ* in both for pattern 9).
soʔe *Termanu.* 1) use a coconut shell or **lalik** (kind of small basket) to scoop solids such as rice, salt, etc. 2) coconut spoon. (J:555)
soʔe *Korbafo.*
soʔe *Bokai.*
soke *Bilbaa.*
soʔe *Rikou.*
soʔe *Ba'a.*
soʔe *Tii.*
soʔe *Dengka.*
soʔe *Oenale.*
n-soe *Kotos Amarasi.* pick out, raise something up in a container.
<amso'e main le'ot> *Molo.* using the hand, scoop the finely pounded rice out of the hole in the rice pounder. (M:509)
Out-comparisons:
soke (2) soet *Semau Helong.* 1) scoop. 2) pick out.
sukit (2) sui *East Tetun.* 1) remove, extract (with any tool or implement). 2) remove, extract, withdraw. (Mo:175)
sukke *Bugis.* pry out. (Masse 2013:358)
passukkiʔ (2) anndʒukkiʔ *Makassar.* 1) bamboo stick with a hook used to remove fruit from a tree or a bucket from the well. 2) remove fruit from a tree with a stick of bamboo with a hook, use a hook to remove a bucket from a well. (Cense 1979:726)

***sokum** *PRM.* galangal. Kaempferia Galanga. *Pattern:* k-6. *[irr. from PRM:* *o > *i* in Meto*] [History:* Jonker (1908) suggests this is from Kupang Malay *koncur* (compare Malay *kencur*) with consonant metathesis, but this doesn't explain the final *m* in Meto.*]*

sokus *Termanu.* kind of medicinal root, called *kencur* in Javanese, it is offered for sale on Rote by foreigners. (J:558)
soku-ʔ *Korbafo.*
soku *Bokai.*
soku *Bilbaa.*
soʔus *Rikou.*
sokus *Ba'a.*
soku *Tii.*
soʔu *Dengka.*
soʔu *Oenale.*
sikum *Meto.* galangal. Kaempferia Galanga. (Heyne 1950:494, ccviii)
Out-comparisons:
sukuŋ *Helong.* galangal. Kaempferia Galanga. (Heyne 1950:494, ccxi)

***soʔi** *Morph:* ***soʔi-t**. *PnMeto.* comb.
soʔi-t *Kotos Amarasi.* comb (n.).
Out-comparisons:
sui (2) sa~suit *East Tetun.* 1) comb, smooth with a comb or any similar action (Mo:174). 2) comb, a hair comb for retaining the hair in place. *[Sporadic:* vowel height harmony *o > *u* / _i.*]* (Mo:168)
sui *Waima'a.* comb.

***soo** *PRM.* sew. *Etym:* **sauR (pre-RM). *[History:* Blust and Trussel (ongoing) reconstruct PCMP *sora, including Meto as one of their attestations. The cognates in Timor and Flores appear to be better explained by *sauR, with no final vowel and *R [r] instead of *r [ɾ]. The final vowel in Blust and Trussel's putative *sora would only be supported by Leti **sora**, Wetan **ora**, and Kemak **sora**. However, the Luangic languages (including Leti and Wetan) are known to added final vowels to historically consonant final stems (Blevins and Garret 1998:542f), thus rendering their evidence moot. The Kemak form provides better evidence for final *a, but this goes against the evidence of many languages in the region, including Rote-Meto, which would be expected to retain *a = *a*. Furthermore, if *R is reconstructed rather than *r, than *R > *r* is irregular in Kemak as we expect *R > Ø.*]*
soo *Termanu.* sew. In Termanu usually in a compound as **seu_soo**. (J:550)
soo *Korbafo.*
soo *Bokai.*
soo *Bilbaa.*
soo *Rikou.*
soo *Ba'a.*
soo *Tii.*
soo *Dengka.*
soo *Oenale.*
n-soo *Kotos Amarasi.* sew.
n-soo *Molo.* sews. (M:508)
Out-comparisons:
soo *Semau Helong.* sew. *Borrowed from:* probably Meto or Rote given **R > Ø (expect *R > *l*).
hour *Kisar.* sew.
sora *Kemak.* sew.
saur *Central Lembata.* sew. (Fricke 2015)
a-sor *Uruangnirin.* sew. *[Note:* language of the Bomberai Peninsula ISO 639-3 [urn].*]* (Visser 2019)

***soro** *PRM.* spoon, ladle, scoop. *Doublet:* ***suru**. *Etym:* *sudu. *[irr. from PMP:* *u > *o*] [irr. from PRM:* *r > *n* ~ *k* in Meto (compare similar ***təlo** > **tenoʔ**/ **tekoʔ** 'egg')*]*
solo *Termanu.* scoop, e.g. dirt out of water. (J:559)
solo *Korbafo.*
solo *Bokai.*
solo *Bilbaa.*
soro *Rikou.*
solo *Ba'a.*
soro *Tii.*
solo *Dengka.*
soro *Oenale.*
ʔ|sono|ʔ *Kotos Amarasi.* spoon.
<a'soko> *Molo.* spoon. (M:511)

ʔ|soko|ʔ *Timaus.* spoon.

***sosa** *PMeto.* buy. *See:* ***osa** 'price, value'.

n-sosa (2) na-ʔsosaʔ *Ro'is Amarasi.* 1) buy. 2) sell.

n-sosa (2) na-ʔsosaʔ *Kotos Amarasi.* 1) buy. 2) sell.

n-sosa (2) na-ʔsosaʔ *Molo.* 1) buy. 2) sell. (M:516)

soas *Kusa-Manea.* buy.

Out-comparisons:

sosa *Semau Helong.* buy.

sosa *East Tetun.* buy. (Mo:174)

***soso** *Rote.* peel.

soso *Termanu.* cut the meat as close as possible to the bones. (J:564)

soso *Korbafo.*

soso *Bokai.*

soso *Bilbaa.*

soso *Rikou.*

soso *Ba'a.*

soso *Tii.*

soso *Dengka.* peel. (J:564, 765)

soso *Oenale.* peel. (J:564, 765)

Out-comparisons:

soso *Bugis.* peel or de-husk with a knife. (Mathes 1874:763)

soso *Makassar.* peel, de-husk. (Mathes 1859:612)

***sua**1 *PnRote.* accuse.

sua *Termanu.* accuse someone, usually falsely accuse someone. (J:567)

sua *Korbafo.*

sua *Bokai.*

sua *Rikou.*

sua *Ba'a.*

sua *Tii.*

Out-comparisons:

suan kali *Semau Helong.* gossip, provocateur; someone who tries to find faults in others to bring them to everyone's attention.

***sua**2 *PnMeto.* rafter, roof-spar. *Etym:* *sukəd 'prop, support; to prop up or support'. *[irr. from PMP:* *k > Ø /u_*]*

sua-f *Kotos Amarasi.* roof spar. (Cunningham 1964:37, 44)

sua-f *Molo.* rafter. (M:518)

Out-comparisons:

sukan *Helong.* rafter. (J:95)

***sua**3 *Morph:* ***ka-sua-k**. *PRM.* digging stick. *Etym:* *suaR 'lift up with a lever, lever up, root up' (Blust and Trussel (ongoing) also reconstruct doublets *sual and *suat).

ai_su~sua-k *Termanu.* pointed stick used to work the ground, a kind of agricultural tool. (J:568)

ai_su~sua-ʔ *Korbafo.*

ai_su~sua-k *Bokai.*

kai_su~sua-ʔ *Bilbaa.*

ai_su~sua-ʔ *Rikou.*

ai_su~sua-k *Ba'a.*

ai_su~sua-k *Tii.*

hau_su~sua-ʔ *Dengka.*

hau_su~sua-ʔ *Oenale.*

ʔ|suak (2) na-ʔ|sua *Kotos Amarasi.* 1) digging stick. 2) dig with digging stick.

<suan> *Molo.* digging stick, plank stick. (M:519)

Out-comparisons:

ksuan *Funai Helong.* crowbar, digging stick.

suan *Semau Helong.* crowbar, digging stick.

ai suak (2) au suak besi *East Tetun.* 1) digging stick, used for weeding and digging in the garden. 2) an iron digging stick, used as above. (Mo:175)

***suɓa** *PRM.* bury. *[Semantics:* The semantic shift from 'bury' to 'engrossed' is likely (e.g. compare English phrases such as *She's buried in her book*). However, if the Dela form is cognate and its semantics are older, then the Rote forms are probably not cognate with Meto.*]*

suba *Termanu.* totally engrossed in something, so that one forgets everything else. (J:568)

suba *Korbafo.*
suba *Bokai.*
suba *Bilbaa.*
suba *Rikou.*
suba *Ba'a.*
suɓa *Tii.*
suba *Dengka.*
suɓa *Oenale.*
suɓa-k, suɓa~suɓa *Dela.* silent, idle.
n-suba *Ro'is Amarasi.* bury.
n-suba *Kotos Amarasi.* bury.
n-suba *Molo.* bury, submerge. (M:519)
suub *Kusa-Manea.* bury. *[Form:* metathesised form of (currently unattested) ***subu**.*]*
Out-comparisons:
subal, subar *East Tetun.* hide, conceal. *[Semantics:* The semantics of the Tetun form are not a very good match, and thus it may be a chance resemblance.*]* (Mo:175)

***sufu** *PRM.* cool in water. *Etym:* *səbuh 'douse a fire, extinguish a fire with water; to hiss, as water on fire'. *[irr. from PMP:* *ə > *u (sporadic assimilation)*]*
ma-ka-sufu-k (2) sufu (2) na-sufu *Termanu.* 1) cold. 2) cool down. 3) be cold. (J:571)
ma-ka-sufu-ʔ *Korbafo.*
ma-ka-sufu-k *Bokai.*
ma-ka-sufu-ʔ *Bilbaa.*
ma-sufu-ʔ *Rikou.*
ma-ka-sufu-k *Ba'a.*
ma-ka-sufu-k *Tii.*
ma-ʔa-sufu-ʔ *Dengka.*
ma-ʔa-sufu-ʔ *Oenale.*
ma-ʔa-sufu *Dela.* be cold (food).
sufuʔ *Kusa-Manea.* cool down, put out a fire.
Out-comparisons:
suhu *Semau Helong.* put out fire with water. *[Note:* Jonker (1908:571) gives Helong **suhu(n)** 'to shower'.*]*
suhu *East Tetun.* immerse in water, quench or harden (hot steel). (Mo:175)
sowo *Bima.* cool/fresh, cold. (Ismail et al. 1985:147)
həβo *Sika.* put out (fire). (Pareira and Lewis 1998:75)

***suhat** *Rote.* kind of comb. *Etym:* *suat (PRM **suhat** would be regular from PMP *supat. Blust and Trussel give the following forms as evidence for their reconstruction with no medial consonant: Binukud and Mansaka **suwat**, Blaan (Sarangani) **swat**, Manam **ruat-i**, and 'Rote' <**sua**>.).
suʔa-k *Termanu.* kind of comb worn as decoration by people from Timor, not worn by people from Rote. (J:568)
suʔa-ʔ *Korbafo.*
suʔa-k *Bokai.*
sua-ʔ *Bilbaa.*
suʔa-k *Ba'a.*
suat *Dengka.*
suat *Oenale.*

***suhu** *Morph:* ***suhu-k**. *Rote.* boundary, border. *Etym:* *supu.
suʔu-k *Termanu.* edge, side, shore. (J:578)
suʔu-ʔ *Korbafo.*
suʔu-k *Bokai.*
suu-ʔ *Bilbaa.*
suu-ʔ *Rikou.*
suʔu-k *Ba'a.*
suu-ʔ *Dengka.*
suu-ʔ *Oenale.*
Out-comparisons:
suut *Semau Helong.* edge. *[Note:* Jonker (1908:578) gives Helong **suut, ksuut**.*]*
huu *Hawu.* tip, end.

***suku** *Morph:* ***suku-k**. *Rote.* breadfruit. *Etym:* *sukun. *Pattern:* k-7.
suʔu-k *Termanu.* breadfruit tree; its fruit. (J:578)
suʔu *Korbafo.*
suʔu-k *Bokai.*

suku-ʔ *Bilbaa.*
suku-ʔ *Rikou.*
suʔu-k *Ba'a.*
suʔu-k *Tii.*
suku-ʔ *Dengka.*
suku-ʔ *Oenale.*

***sulə** *PRM.* insert, plug. *Etym:* *sulə[n/d]. *[Sporadic:* *ə > *e* /σ_# in wRote (perhaps *ə > *a > *e* / _#).*]*
sule *Termanu.* close something with a stopper, put a stopper in something to close it. (J:573)
sule *Korbafo.*
sule *Bokai.*
sule *Bilbaa.*
sule *Rikou.*
sule *Ba'a.*
sule *Tii.*
sule *Dengka.*
sule *Oenale.*
n-suun *Molo.* corks. *[Note:* Jonker (1908:573) gives unmetathesised nominalised Meto **suna-t**.*]* (M:523)

***suma** *PRM.* steam, vapour. *[History:* Blust and Trussel (ongoing) reconstruct PWMP ***s<um>ebuh** 'to hiss or steam, of water touching a fire' which is formally and semantically similar.*]*
suma *Termanu.* hold in hot steam, cook in steam, steaming. (J:574)
suma *Korbafo.*
suma *Bokai.*
suma *Bilbaa.*
suma *Rikou.*
suma *Ba'a.*
suma *Tii.*
suma *Dengka.*
sumaʔ (2) n-suma *Kotos Amarasi.* 1) steam, vapour. 2) steaming.
sumaʔ *Molo.* steam from boiling water, etc. (M:523)

***sumanə** *Morph:* ***sumanə-k**. *PRM.* soul of a living being; soul of the rice plant. *Etym:* *sumaŋəd. *[Form:* Antepenultimate *u (high back rounded vowel) is probably required to account for Landu *i* (high vowel), as well as the alternate Termanu from with antepenultimate *o* (back rounded vowel).*]*
samane-k, somane-k *Termanu.* life spirit. (J:519; Fanggidaej 1892:556)
samane-ʔ *Korbafo.*
samane-k *Bokai.*
samane-ʔ *Bilbaa.*
simane-ʔ *Landu.* (own field notes)
samane-ʔ *Rikou.*
samane-k *Ba'a.*
samane-k *Tii.*
mana-ʔ *Dengka.*
samana-ʔ *Oenale.*
smana-f *Kotos Amarasi.* spirit or soul of a person, spirit of the rice plant.
smana-f *Molo.* spirit. (M:504)
Out-comparisons:
smaŋin *Funai Helong.* spirit, soul; forehead.
hmaŋin *Semau Helong.* spirit, soul; forehead.
hemaŋa *Hawu.* spirit, soul. Spirit of both the living and the dead. What remains and continues on after the body dies.

***sunu** *Morph:* ***su~sunu**. *Rote.* kind of sea fish.
su~sunu *Termanu.* kind of sea fish. (J:576)
su~sunu *Korbafo.*
su~sunu *Bokai.*
su~sunu *Bilbaa.*
su~sunu *Rikou.*
su~sunu *Ba'a.*
su~sunu *Tii.*
su~sunu *Dengka.*
su~sunu *Oenale.*
Out-comparisons:
sunu *Kamarian.* a certain fish (*ikan papua*). *[Note:* also in Kaibobo.*]* (van Ekris 1865:118)

***suŋgə** *Morph:* ***suŋgə-k**. *PRM.* cheek hollow. *[Sporadic:* *ə > *e* /σ_# in wRote (perhaps *ə > *a > *e* / _#).*]*

[Form: The Meto unmetathesised form has not yet been attested. It could be ***suka-** or ***suku-**.*]*

suŋe-k (2) na-suŋe *Termanu.* 1) the inner part of the cheek. 2) hold something in the mouth between the cheeks. (J:575)

suŋe-ʔ *Korbafo.*

suŋe-k *Bokai.*

suŋe-k *Bilbaa.*

suke-ʔ *Landu.* cheek. (own field notes)

suke-ʔ *Oepao.* cheek. (own field notes)

suŋge-k *Tii.*

suŋge-ʔ *Dengka.*

suŋge-ʔ *Oenale.*

suk~suuk-n=aa *Ro'is Amarasi.* cheekbone. *[Note:* This form was given (unprompted) by one Ro'is consultant, but was completely unknown by all other Ro'is consultants.*]*

***sura** *Morph:* ***sura-k**. *PRM.* horn. *Doublet:* ***sure**. *Etym:* *suja 'pitfall or trail spikes made of sharpened bamboo'. *[History:* Blust and Trussel (ongoing) reconstruct both PCMP *sula and *sulan 'horn' on the basis of Termanu **sula** and Buru **sula-n**. This reconstruction is problematic as the other Rote languages clearly attest PRM *r (which also accounts regularly for Termanu *l*). Additionally, the putative Buru term **sula-n** is not found in any published sources I have access to. Instead they give **sodi-n** (Grimes and Grimes 2020:864) or **soden** (Hendriks 1897:93). Hoogervorst (2016:568) identifies Sanskrit *śūla* [ʃuːla] 'a spear or lance, an offensive weapon' as the source of putative PCMP *sula. While Sanskrit *śūla* [ʃuːla] may be the source of PRM *sura, this would not account straightforwardly for medial *r. Jonker (1908:573) compares the Rote forms to **tulane** from Asilulu in Ambon (Hoëvell 1877:69). But this form would not show regular sound correspondences. Among languages of Ambon, Stresemann (1927:37) only records *t* as a reflex of *s in Amahei, and then only before non-high vowels.*]*

su~sula-k *Termanu.* horn of a buffalo, of a deer, etc. (J:573)

su~sula-ʔ *Korbafo.*

su~sula-k *Bokai.*

su~sula-ʔ *Bilbaa.*

su~sura-ʔ *Landu.* horn. (own field notes)

su~sura-ʔ *Rikou.*

su~sula-k *Ba'a.*

su~sura-k *Tii.*

su~sula-ʔ *Dengka.*

sura-ʔ *Oenale.*

sunu-f *Ro'is Amarasi.* horn.

suna-f *Kotos Amarasi.* horn, antennae (of insects).

suna-f *Molo.* horn of livestock. (M:523)

suna-f *Kusa-Manea.* horn.

Out-comparisons:

suluʔ *Semau Helong.* horn. *[irr. from PRM:* *a = *u* correspondence*]*

***sure** *Morph:* ***sure-k**. *PRM.* pointed weapon; caltrop, sword. *Doublet:* ***sura**. *Etym:* *suja 'pitfall or trail spikes made of sharpened bamboo'. *[minority from PMP:* *j > *r (expect *d)*] [Sporadic:* *a > *e /*C+palatal_.*]*

sule-k *Termanu.* something pointed, like a thorn, which is used as a caltrop (foot-trap); place a caltrop. (J:574)

sule-ʔ *Korbafo.*

sule-k *Bokai.*

sule-ʔ *Bilbaa.*

suri-ʔ *Rikou.*

sule-k *Ba'a.*

sure-k *Tii.*

sule-ʔ *Dengka.*

sure-ʔ *Oenale.*

suni|ʔ *Kotos Amarasi.* sword, fighting sword. Particularly the long curved fighting sword found on Timor.

[Sporadic: vowel height harmony *e > *i* /uC_ in Meto.*] [Form:* Final *e > *i* on Timor mainland combined with semantic shift to 'sword' suggests diffusion/borrowing though the direction of diffusion remains to be determined.*]*

suni|ʔ *Molo.* sword. (M:524)

suni|ʔ *Kusa-Manea.* machete.

Out-comparisons:

suliʔ *Semau Helong.* sword. long thin fighting sword. May be about a metre in length, and width described as 'between 2–3 fingers'.

surik *East Tetun.* sword with a long curved sharp blade which is sheathed in a scabbard when not in use. (Mo:176)

surik *Mambae, South.* sword, long curved fighting sword found on Timor, single blade. (Grimes et al. 2014b:42)

***suru** *PRM.* spoon, ladle, scoop. *Doublet:* ***soro**. *Etym:* *sudu.

sulu (2) sulu-k *Termanu.* 1) scoop up with a spoon. (J:574) 2) spoon. (J:574)

sulu *Korbafo.*

sulu *Bokai.*

sulu *Bilbaa.*

suru *Rikou.*

sulu *Ba'a.*

suru *Tii.*

sulu *Dengka.*

suru *Oenale.*

<sunu> *Amanuban.* spoon. (M:511)

sa~sunu|ʔ *Kusa-Manea.* spoon.

Out-comparisons:

sulu *Semau Helong.* spoon, scoop.

suru *East Tetun.* extract or take out with a spoon or ladle, to perform any similar action. (Mo:175)

huru *Kisar.* spoon.

kaɓa huru *Hawu.* spoon, ladle.

***susi** *PRM.* investigate, walk around. *[irr. from PRM:* *i > *u* in Bilbaa and Rikou*] [Semantics:* The semantic connection between the Meto terms and Rote terms is unclear to me, but Jonker (1908:576) gives the Meto forms as connected and it's better to give all the (potential) data than to sweep things under the carpet.*]*

susi *Termanu.* investigate a matter, inquire into something. (J:576)

susi *Korbafo.*

susi *Bokai.*

susu *Bilbaa.*

susu *Rikou.*

susi *Ba'a.*

susi *Tii.*

susi *Oenale.*

n-susi *Kotos Amarasi.* walk around without any particular destination in mind, go to someone's house and hang out without any plan.

n-susi *Molo.* one crawls back through something. (M:525)

***susu1** *PRM.* tax. *[Semantics:* Given the semantics this may be a borrowing, though the kingdoms of Timor did have traditional systems of tribute.*]*

susu *Termanu.* apply taxes, tax. (J:577)

susu *Korbafo.*

susu *Bokai.*

susu *Bilbaa.*

susu *Rikou.*

susu *Ba'a.*

susu *Tii.*

susu *Dengka.*

nusu *Oenale.*

n-suus *Molo.* earn (money). (M:524)

Out-comparisons:

susut *Semau Helong.* tax.

***susu2** *PRM.* female breast; udder. *Etym:* *susu. *[irr. from PRM:* *s > *ʔ* in Termanu, Korbafo, Bokai and Ba'a*]*

suʔu *Termanu.* female breast. (J:577)

suʔu *Korbafo.*

suʔu *Bokai.*

susu *Bilbaa.*
susu *Rikou.*
suʔu *Ba'a.*
susu *Tii.*
susu(-ʔ) *Dengka.*
susu *Oenale.*
susu *Ro'is Amarasi.* breast.
susu-f *Kotos Amarasi.* breast.
susu *Molo.* milk, breasts (of woman). (M:525)
Out-comparisons:
susu *Semau Helong.* breast.
susu-n *East Tetun.* breast (of women), udder (of animals). (Mo:177)

***suti** *PRM.* nautilus, nautilus shell. *[Semantics:* I have reconstructed this term with the meaning 'nautilus' following the meaning in Rote rather than the meaning in Ro'is Amarasi as the people in Rote have a much stronger connection to the sea than the Atoni and it thus seems more likely that terms in Rote referring to the sea would be more conservative. This meaning is also probably partly retained in the Kotos Amarasi and Molo reflexes.*]*
suti *Termanu.* nautilus, nautilus shell. (J:577; Fox 2016b)
suti *Korbafo.*
suti *Bokai.*
suti *Bilbaa.* nautilus, nautilus shell. (J:577; own field notes)
suti *Rikou.* nautilus, nautilus shell. (J:577; own field notes)
suti *Ba'a.*
suti *Tii.*
suti *Dengka.*
suti *Oenale.*
suti *Ro'is Amarasi.* sea snails/shellfish that are oval shaped and have a wide opening, often with a distinctive lip which runs the length of the shell: conches, volutes. *[Note:* **benkae** = 'nautilus'.*]*
suti *Kotos Amarasi.* little round plate upon which the woman has the spool twirl in order to wind the cotton thread. *[Semantics:* Regarding the semantic connection between the terms in Rote and the Kotos Amarasi and Molo terms, Fox (2016a:43) states: '**Suti**, the nautilus shell, becomes the container for dye, particularly indigo dye; and **Bina**, the bailer shell, becomes the base on which the spindle for winding thread is turned. The two shells are ritual icons for the processes of preparing a cloth for weaving.'*]*
suti *Molo.* little round plate upon which the woman has the spool twirl in order to wind the cotton thread. (M:526)

***suu1** *PRM.* scrape the ground.
suu *Termanu.* dig or scoop out with the hands, also dig out in general. (J:566)
suu *Korbafo.*
suu *Bokai.*
suu *Bilbaa.*
suu *Rikou.*
suu *Ba'a.*
suu *Tii.*
suu *Dengka.*
suu *Oenale.*
na-k|suu (2) n-suu *Molo.* 1) scratches (ground), makes scratches (on the ground), scrabbles out. 2) scrabbles out. (M:518)
Out-comparisons:
suʔu *East Tetun.* mine, fossick, dig a mine shaft. (Mo:177)

***suu2** *PRM.* carry on head. *Etym:* *suqun.
suu *Termanu.* put or carry on one's head. (J:566)
suu *Korbafo.*
suu *Bokai.*
suu *Bilbaa.*
suu *Rikou.*
suu *Ba'a.*

suu *Tii.*
suu *Dengka.*
suu *Oenale.*
n-suu *Kotos Amarasi.* carry on one's head.
n-suu *Molo.* carry on one's head. (M:518)
suu *Kusa-Manea.* carry on head.

T - t

*taa1 *PRM.* track, footprint. *Etym:* *tapak 'palm of the hand, sole of the foot' (PWMP). *[irr. from PMP:* *p > Ø (*p > Ø is regular in wRote, Bilbaa, Rikou and Meto but we would expect *p > *ʔ* in the other Rote languages)*]* *[Sporadic:* *a > *e* / _# in Meto.*]*
ta~taa *Termanu.* make an impression with the hand or foot, leave tracks behind. (J:580)
ta~taa *Korbafo.*
ta~taa *Bokai.*
ta~taa *Bilbaa.*
ta~taa *Rikou.*
ta~taa *Ba'a.*
ta~taa *Tii.*
ta~taa *Dengka.*
n-tae *Kotos Amarasi.* look down.
<taè> *Molo.* look down, trace/track down. *[Form:* Jonker (1908:580) gives Meto **taʔen** with the meaning 'identical [to the Rote meaning] and: agree upon'.*]* *[Semantics:* The meaning 'trace/track down' appears to be the semantic link between 'track' and 'look down'.*]* (M:527)
Out-comparisons:
tahe *Semau Helong.* sign.

*taa2 *Rote.* unhusked rice. *See:* ***eto**. *Etym:* *qəta 'rice husk, rice bran'. *[irr. from PMP:* *ə > Ø with doubling of the final vowel to create a disyllable*]*
(hade) taa-k *Termanu.* unhusked rice grains under the husked grains. (J:581)
taa-ʔ *Korbafo.*
taa-k *Bokai.*
ka|taa-ʔ *Bilbaa.*
taa-ʔ *Rikou.*
taa-k *Ba'a.*
taa-k *Tii.*
taa-ʔ *Dengka.*
taa-ʔ *Oenale.*

*taa3 *PnRote.* negative marker: no, not. *Etym:* *taq.
taa *Termanu.* non-existent, no, not. *[Form:* Phrases such as <**ana-ták**> **ana taa-k** 'childless' provide evidence for the double vowel.*]* (J:578)
taa *Korbafo.*
taa *Bokai.*
taa *Bilbaa.*
taa *Rikou.*
taa *Ba'a.*
taa *Tii.*
Out-comparisons:
ka *Kisar.* not.

*taa4 *Morph:* ***taa-k**. *Rote.* endure. *Etym:* *taqan 'hold back, keep in reserve'. *[Form:* Final *k* cannot be straightforwardly analysed as synchronic suffix in Korbafo, Bilbaa and Dengka.*]*
na-taa-k=ana (2) na-ka-ta~taa-k *Termanu.* 1) endurance. 2) endure. (J:581)
na-taa|k=ana *Korbafo.*
na-taa-k=ana *Bokai.*
na-taa|k=ana *Bilbaa.*
na-taa-ʔ=ana *Rikou.*
na-taa-k=ana *Ba'a.*
na-taa-k=ana *Tii.*
na-taa|k=ana (2) na-ʔa-ta~taa-ʔ *Dengka.*
(2) na-ʔa-ta~taa-ʔ *Oenale.*

***taɓu** *PRM.* tread, step.
tabu *Termanu.* put the foot somewhere, step, tread. (J:582)
tabu *Korbafo.*
tabu *Bokai.*
tabu *Bilbaa.*
tabu *Rikou.*
tabu *Ba'a.*
taɓu *Tii.*
tabu *Dengka.*
taɓu *Oenale.*
tabu *Ro'is Amarasi.* time.
tabu *Kotos Amarasi.* time.
n-tabo *Amfo'an.* treads. (M:527)
tabu *Molo.* clock, hour. (M:527)
Out-comparisons:
tabu *Waima'a.* time, watch.
tabu *Galolen.* time.

***tadeŋgus** *PRM.* kind of dove, probably Rose-crowned Fruit-Dove. Ptilinopus regina. *Pattern:* d-2. *[irr. from PRM:* vowel metathesis in Kusa-Manea *eCu > *uCe > *uCi]*
rekus *Landu.* Rose-crowned Fruit-Dove. Ptilinopus regina. (own field notes)
rekus *Rikou.* Rose-crowned Fruit-Dove. Ptilinopus regina. (own field notes)
leŋgus *Dengka.* dove; in Dengka species include: **leŋgu lasi, leŋgu maʔamuu, leŋgu manu_ina.** (J:722)
reŋgus *Oenale.* dove. (J:722)
kuum_treukus *Ro'is Amarasi.* Rose-crowned Fruit-Dove. Ptilinopus regina. *[Form:* **kumu** = 'wild dove'.*]*
ra~rukis *Kusa-Manea.* wild doves. *[Sporadic:* vowel height harmony *e > *i* /uC_ (alternately *e > *i* /_Cu before vowel metathesis).*]*

***taɗu** *Morph:* ***la-taɗu-k**. *CER.* opposite.
la-tadu-k *Termanu.* sit opposite one another. (J:585)
la-tadu-k *Bokai.*
la-tadu-k *Ba'a.*
Out-comparisons:
ntando (2) satando (3) tando *Bima.* 1) facing one another. (Ismail et al. 1985:103) 2) face towards. (Ismail et al. 1985:143) 3) forward, front part; face towards. (Ismail et al. 1985:151)

***tae** *nRM.* praying mantis. *[Sporadic:* consonant metathesis *rVt > *tVr* in Nuclear Meto; glottal stop insertion in Meto*] [Form:* The source of the initial element in Meto currently unknown. This element also has irregular Ro'is *k* = Nuclear Meto *r* correspondence. This is the reverse pattern to what would be expected for PMeto *r.*]*
telu_tae *Termanu.* kind of shrimp-like creature. (Fox 2016b:13, 55)
akaʔtaʔe *Ro'is Amarasi.* praying mantis.
ataʔraʔe *Kotos Amarasi.* praying mantis.
ataʔlaʔe *Molo.* praying mantis. (M:31)
Out-comparisons:
°akatae *Semau Helong.* praying mantis. *Borrowed from:* Ro'is Amarasi.
astatae *Welaun.* praying mantis.

***tafa** *Rote.* sword, machete.
tafa *Termanu.* sabre, sword. (J:586)
tafa *Korbafo.*
tafa *Bokai.*
tafa *Bilbaa.*
tafa *Rikou.*
tafa *Ba'a.*
tafa *Tii.*
tafa-ʔ *Dengka.*
tafa-ʔ *Oenale.*
Out-comparisons:
taha *East Tetun.* machete, a jungle knife. (Mo:178)
kawa *Kisar.* machete.

***taha** *Morph:* ***na-taha**. *PRM.* answer. *Etym:* **taRa (pre-RM). *[irr. from PMP:* *R > *h (also in ***noh** and ***klaha**)*] [Form:* regular *h > Ø /a_a in Rote.*]*
na-taa *Termanu.* answer. (J:580f)
na-taa *Korbafo.*
na-taa *Bokai.*
na-taa *Bilbaa.*
na-taa *Rikou.*
na-taa *Ba'a.*
na-taa *Tii.*
na-taa *Dengka.*
na-taa *Oenale.*
na-taha *Kotos Amarasi.* answer.
ta-taah *Kusa-Manea.* answer.
Out-comparisons:
tala *Semau Helong.* answer.
hataa *Fehan Tetun.* respond, answer, give a reply to. (Mo:80)
hataan *East Tetun.* respond, answer, give a reply to. (Mo:81)

***tahi** *Rote.* winnow. *Etym:* *tapi. *[irr. from PRM:* *t > *d* in nRote*]*
daʔi *Termanu.* winnow. (J:71)
daʔi *Korbafo.*
daʔi *Bokai.*
dai *Bilbaa.*
dai *Rikou.*
daʔi *Ba'a.*
ɗaʔi *Tii.*
tai *Dengka.*
tai *Oenale.*
Out-comparisons:
tahiŋ *Semau Helong.* winnow.

***tai1** *Morph:* ***tai-k**. *PRM.* belly, stomach, guts. *Doublet:* ***tai2**. *Etym:* *taqi 'faeces, excrement'. *[irr. from PRM:* *a > *e* in Ro'is Amarasi and all Rote lects except Tii (sporadic assimilation to following *i*)*]*
tei-k *Termanu.* belly, intestines. (J:612f)
tei-ʔ *Korbafo.*
tei-k *Bokai.*
tei-ʔ *Bilbaa.*
tei-ʔ *Landu.* belly. (own field notes)
tei-ʔ *Rikou.*
tei-ʔ *Oepao.* belly. (own field notes)
tei-k *Ba'a.*
tai-k *Tii.*
tei-ʔ *Dengka.*
tei-ʔ *Oenale.*
tei *Dela.* stomach.
tei-f *Ro'is Amarasi.* belly, stomach.
tai-f *Kotos Amarasi.* belly, stomach, guts.
tai-n *Molo.* intestines. (M:623)
Out-comparisons:
tain *Semau Helong.* stomach, abdomen, belly.

***tai2** *PRM.* faeces, excrement. *Doublet:* ***tai1**. *Etym:* *taqi. *[irr. from PRM:* *a > *e* in lects except Tii (sporadic assimilation to following *i*)*]*
tei *Termanu.* faeces, excrete. (J:612f)
tei *Korbafo.*
tei *Bokai.*
tei *Bilbaa.*
tei *Landu.* faeces. (own field notes)
tei *Rikou.*
tei *Oepao.* faeces. (own field notes)
tei *Ba'a.*
tai *Tii.*
tei *Dengka.*
tei *Oenale.*
tei *Dela.* faeces.
tei *Ro'is Amarasi.* faeces.
tei (2) na-teʔi *Kotos Amarasi.* 1) faeces. 2) excrete.
tei *Molo.* faeces. (M:623)
Out-comparisons:
tai *Funai Helong.* excrement.
tai *Semau Helong.* faeces.
tee-n *East Tetun.* excrement, dregs, residue. (Mo:183)

***tai3** *Rote.* stick to.
tai *Termanu.* adhere. (J:587)
tai *Korbafo.*
tai *Bokai.*
tai *Bilbaa.*
tai *Rikou.*
tai *Ba'a.*
tai *Tii.*

tai *Dengka.*
tai *Oenale.*
Out-comparisons:
tai *Semau Helong.* hang, suspend.

***tairua** *CERM.* half. *[irr. from PRM:* *t > *h* in nRote*] [Form:* second part from *dua 'two'.*]*
hailua *Termanu.* half full. (J:155)
hailua *Korbafo.*
hailua *Bokai.*
hailua *Bilbaa.*
hairua *Rikou.*
n-tainua (2) tainua *Kotos Amarasi.* 1) halve. 2) half. *Usage:* somewhat archaic, **stenaʔ** from Malay **sətəŋa** is the usual term in my data.
Out-comparisons:
tailuaŋ *Semau Helong.* half-heartedly.

***tais** *PRM.* cloth, sarong. *Etym:* *tapis 'loincloth (?)'. *[irr. from PMP:* *p > Ø (Meto Ø could be regular from *p, but we would still expect *ʔ* in Termanu)*]*
tai_sai-k *Termanu.* cloth, a torn piece of stuff, a nappy. *Usage:* still used in Dengka and Oenale, as in Meto, in disuse elsewhere in Rote. (J:589)
tais *Dengka.* pants. (J:768)
tais *Oenale.* pants. (J:768)
tais *Ro'is Amarasi.* clothing.
tais *Kotos Amarasi.* sarong, clothes.
tais *Molo.* sarong, skirt. (M:532)
tais *Kusa-Manea.* cloth.
Out-comparisons:
tais *East Tetun.* cloth of indigenous manufacture. (Mo:178)

***taku** *PRM.* fear. *Etym:* *takut. *Pattern:* k-8.
na-ka-ta~taʔu (2) taʔu-s (3) ma-ka-ta~taʔu-k *Termanu.* 1) frighten, threaten. 2) fear. 3) someone (a person, demon, etc.) which causes fright. (J:604f)
na-ka-ta~taʔu *Korbafo.*
na-ka-ta~taʔu *Bokai.*
na-ka-ta~taku *Bilbaa.*
na-ta~taʔu *Rikou.*
na-ka-ta~taʔu *Ba'a.*
na-ka-ta~taʔu-k *Tii.*
na-ʔa-ta~taʔu-ʔ (2) na-tau-ʔ (3) na-ma-tau *Dengka.* 1) frighten, threaten. (J:604) 2) frighten. (J:769f) 3) be afraid. (J:769f)
na-ʔa-ta~taʔu-ʔ (2) na-tau-ʔ (3) na-ma-tau *Oenale.* 1) frighten, threaten. (J:604) 2) frighten. (J:769f) 3) be afraid. (J:769f)
— (2) — (3) na-ma-tau *Dela.* 3) becomes afraid, becomes worried.
na-m|tau *Ro'is Amarasi.* is scared.
na-m|tau (2) na-m|tau|s *Kotos Amarasi.* 1) scared. 2) scared of. *[Form:* The final *s* in the transitive form **na-m|taus** 'scared of' may be a reflex of the final consonant reconstructed for PMP *takut, thus *t > *s*. The nominalising suffix **-t** in Meto has the allomorph **-s** after stems which contain a *t* (Edwards 2020:455f) and thus the putative change of *t > *s* in this form may be a case of dissimilation from word initial *t. Note also that the pair **n-mani** 'laugh' and **n-manis** 'laugh at' (see ***malis**) also has transitivity marked with final *s*. In this case, the final consonant of the transitive form also appears to be a reflex of the final consonant of PMP *malip (see §3.5.1.3).*]*
na-m|tau (2) na-m|tausan (3) n-haka|tau (4) ma|taus *Molo.* 1) scared. 2) scared of. (M:332) 3) scare (someone). 4) those who are scared. (M:542)
Out-comparisons:
hataʔuk *East Tetun.* be afraid, fear, dread. (Mo:183)
-kaʔuk *Kisar.* afraid.
medaʔu *Hawu.* afraid.

***talaɗa** *PRM.* middle, centre. *[irr. from PRM:* *t > *k* in Dengka*] [Form:* regular *ɗ > **l /*l_ in Meto (and Helong).*]*

talada *Termanu.* middle. (J:590)
talada *Korbafo.*
talada *Bokai.*
talada *Bilbaa.*
talada *Rikou.*
talada *Ba'a.*
talaɗa *Tii.*
kalaɗa-ʔ *Dengka.*
talaɗa-ʔ *Oenale.*
talaɗa-ʔ *Dela.* centre.
tnana|ʔ *Ro'is Amarasi.*
tnana|ʔ, tnana-f *Kotos Amarasi.* middle, waist.
au tnana-k *Molo.* my interior. (M:561)
tnana|ʔ *Kusa-Manea.* middle.
Out-comparisons:
hlala *Semau Helong.* middle, centre.
tlala *Bolok Helong.* middle, centre.
klara-n *East Tetun.* middle, the centre. (Mo:109)
klalan *Galolen.* middle.
telora *Hawu.* middle.
ʔloraŋ *Sika.* inside, in the middle. (Pareira and Lewis 1998:124)
hatalae *Kamarian.* among, in the middle. *[Note:* also in Kaibobo and Haruku.*]* (van Ekris 1864:85)
hatarale *Kaibobo. Usage:* Piru village. (van Ekris 1864:85)
hatalea *Kaibobo. Usage:* Hatusua village. (van Ekris 1864:85)
samtarae *Alune. [Note:* language of west Seram, central Maluku ISO 639-3 [alp].*]* (van Ekris 1864:85)
hatalea, haalea *Nusa Laut. [Note:* language of Lease Islands, central Maluku ISO 639-3 [nul].*]* (van Ekris 1864:85)

***tales** *Rote.* taro. Colocasia esculenta. *Etym:* *taləs. *[minority from PMP:* *ə > *e / _# (expect *ə > *a* in wRote)*]*
tale *Termanu.* 1) kind of water plant with big leaves. (J:591) 2) taro. (Fox 1991:257)
tale *Korbafo.*
tale *Bokai.*
tale *Bilbaa.*
tale *Rikou.*
tale *Ba'a.*
ta~tale-k *Tii.*
ta~tales *Dengka.*
tale *Oenale.*
Out-comparisons:
talas *East Tetun.* an aroid plant with highly prized edible tubers. (Mo:179)

***tali** *PRM.* rope, cord, twine, string. *Etym:* *talih.
tali *Termanu.* rope. (J:591)
tali *Korbafo.*
tali *Bokai.*
tali *Bilbaa.*
tali *Rikou.*
tali *Ba'a.*
tali *Tii.*
tali-ʔ *Dengka.*
tali-ʔ *Oenale.*
tani *Ro'is Amarasi.* rope.
tani *Kotos Amarasi.* rope.
tani *Molo.* rope. (M:538)
tani *Kusa-Manea.* rope.
Out-comparisons:
tali *Semau Helong.* rope, cord, string, twine, strand.
tali(n) *East Tetun.* rope, cord, string, etc. (Mo:179)

***talin** *PRM.* money. *[History:* This could be a borrowing, but a likely source language has not been identified.*]*
tali_doi-k *Termanu.* money in general. (J:591)
tali_doi-ʔ *Korbafo.*
tali_doi-k *Bokai.*
tali_doi-k *Bilbaa.*
tali_doi-ʔ *Rikou.*
tali_doi-k *Ba'a.*
tali_ɗoi-k *Tii.*
tali_ɗoi-ʔ *Dengka.*

tali_ɗoi-ʔ *Oenale.*
tanin *Meto.* (J:591)
Out-comparisons:
talin *Helong.* (J:591)

***tama₁** *PMeto.* enter. *Etym:* *tama 'enter, penetrate; bold, of persons'.
n-tama *Ro'is Amarasi.* enter.
n-tama *Kotos Amarasi.* enter.
an-tama *Molo.* go inside. (M:536)
n-tama *Timaus.* enter.
Out-comparisons:
tama *Semau Helong.* enter, go in.
tama *East Tetun.* enter, introduce, penetrate. (Mo:179)

***tama₂** *Rote.* appropriate, suitable, right; fit together. *Etym:* *tama(q) (Blust and Trussel (ongoing) reconstruct both *tamaq and *tama as 'disjuncts' with almost identical semantics. The Termanu form is included as evidence for both.).
tama *Termanu.* fit together well. **papa-k=ala tama matalolole** the planks fit well together. (J:592)
tama *Korbafo.*
tama *Bokai.*
tama *Bilbaa.*
tama *Rikou.*
tama *Ba'a.*
tama *Tii.*
tama *Dengka.*
tama *Oenale.*

***tamae** *Rote.* bedbug. *Etym:* **tamayuŋ (pre-RM). *[Form:* I have reconstructed antepenultimate PRM *a primarily on the basis of external evidence and the fact that this is the most common antepenultimate vowel in PRM. This means proposing antepenultimate *a > *i* in Landu. This sound change finds some support from PRM **sumanə-k** 'soul' > Landu **simane-ʔ**, which also shows a shift of an antepenultimate vowel to *i*. In both words this may be sporadic assimilation to the previous apical consonant.*]*
mae-k *Termanu.* bedbug. (J:340)
mae-ʔ *Korbafo.*
mae-k *Bokai.*
mae-ʔ *Bilbaa.*
timae-ʔ *Landu.* bedbug. (own field notes)
mae-ʔ *Rikou.*
mae-k *Ba'a.*
mae-k *Tii.*
mai-ʔ *Dengka.*
mai-ʔ *Oenale.*
Out-comparisons:
kmaeŋ *Funai Helong.*
hmaeŋ bedbug. *Helong.* (J:340)
(ta)madʒuŋ *Alorese.* bedbug. (Moro 2016)
təmadʒuŋ *Central Lembata.* bedbug. (Fricke 2015)
madʒu *Central Nage.* bedbug. <u>*Cimex lectularius*</u>. (Forth 2016:335)
maiŋ *Sika.* bedbug. (Pareira and Lewis 1998:128)
madʒuŋ *Manggarai.* bedbug. <u>*Cimex rotundatus*</u>. (Verheijen 1967:304)

***tamo** *CERM.* ancestral name. *[irr. from PRM:* *o > *a* in Meto*]*
tamo-k *Termanu.* name established by divination; name of protecting ancestor. (Fox 2016b:53)
tama-f *Kotos Amarasi.* name someone after a deceased relative.
au tama-k *Molo.* the name of my grandfather after whom I must be called. (M:536)
Out-comparisons:
<tamu> *Kambera.* name, namesake. *[Note:* also in Mangili, Lewa, Anakalng and Mamboru.*]* (On:464)
<tamo> *Kodi.* *[Note:* also in Weyewa*]*
tamo *Ende.* name-sake, name-fellow.
tamo *Tolaki.* name. *[Note:* language of Southeast Sulawesi ISO 639-3 [lbw].*]* (own field notes)

san/tamo *Kulisusu.* namesake; name that two people choose in secret for each other but don't utter in public. *[Note:* language of Southeast Sulawesi ISO 639-3 [vkl]*] [Form:* initial **san-** from *isa 'one'.*]* (David Mead pers. comm. April 2016)

***tamu** *Morph:* ***na-tamu**. *PRM.* close the mouth, chew. *Etym:* *tamu (PCEMP. Blust and Trussel (ongoing) only give Motu **tamu-tamu** 'smack the lips while eating' and Uruava **tamu** 'eat' and the Termanu form as evidence for their reconstruction.).

na-tamu (2) tamu~tamu *Termanu.* 1) close the mouth suddenly. **bafi=a na-tamu bafa-n** the pig closes its mouth with a smack, **kaiboi-k kima=a na-tamu bafa-na** the clam suddenly closes itself 2) make a smacking sound while eating, like a pig. (J:593)

na-tamu *Korbafo.*

na-tamu *Bokai.*

na-tamu *Bilbaa.*

na-tamu *Rikou.*

na-tamu *Ba'a.*

na-tamu *Tii.*

na-tamu *Dengka.*

na-tamu *Oenale.*

na-tamu *Kotos Amarasi.* chew.

na-tamu *Molo.* chews. **mu-tamu koe~koe** chew your food properly (M:227)

na-tamu *Kusa-Manea.* chew.

***tamba₁** *CER.* throw.

tapa *Termanu.* throw, toss. (J:599)

tapa *Korbafo.*

tapa *Bokai.*

tapa *Bilbaa.*

tapa *Rikou.*

Out-comparisons:

taba *East Tetun.* stone, throw stones, chase away with stones; to break into fragments; grind, crush. (Mo:177)

toba *Bima.* trow, hurl, hurl at someone. (Jonker 1893:105)

taha *Kamarian.* stab, throw. *[Note:* also in Kaibobo and Nusa Laut.*]* (van Ekris 1864:119)

kaha *Haruku.* (van Ekris 1864:119)

ʧawa *Alune. [Note:* language of west Seram, central Maluku ISO 639-3 [alp].*]* (van Ekris 1864:119)

annaʔbaʔ *Makassar.* throw a small round object at something (e.g. marble or candlenut). *[Form:* root = **taʔbaʔ**.*]* (Cense 1979:744)

***tamba₂** *PRM.* mend, patch. *Etym:* *tambal (Blust and Trussel (ongoing) reconstruct a number of formally and semantically similar forms including: *tambəj 'tie up, bind tightly', and *tambəl 'patch'.).

tapa *Termanu.* stick, cleave. (J:599f)

tapa *Korbafo.*

tapa *Bokai.*

tapa *Bilbaa.*

tapa *Rikou.*

tampa *Ba'a.*

tamba *Tii.*

tamba *Dengka.*

tamba *Oenale.*

n-tapa *Molo.* binds (wound). *[Form:* Jonker (1908:600) gives Meto **na-ktapa, na-ktape**.*]* (M:539)

Out-comparisons:

tapa *Semau Helong.* connect, attach, stick to; patch.

tabar *Fehan Tetun.* join, go/be together with, mix, meet in one place from separate places; patch (clothes).

***tambele** *PRM.* suspend, hang.

pele~pele (2) pe~pele (3) pele *Termanu.* 1) to be hung up while spread out. (J:478) 2) hang something up while it is spread out. (J:478) 3) spread out, spread

(of news or rumour). In ordinary language, this has a physical sense of 'of spreading a piece of cloth, or a sail, of hanging it up'. (Fox 2016b:45)
pele~pele *Korbafo.*
pele~pele *Bokai.*
pele~pele *Bilbaa.*
pele~pele *Rikou.*
mpele~mpele *Ba'a.*
mbele~mbele *Tii.*
mbele~mbele (2) na-ta-mbele *Dengka.* 1) spread out, suspended. (J:478) 2) fly. (J:752; Fox 2016b:45)
mbele~mbele (2) na-ta-mbele *Oenale.* 1) spread out, suspended. (J:478) 2) fly. (J:752; Fox 2016b:45)
na-tpene *Ro'is Amarasi.* fly (v.).
na-kpene *Kotos Amarasi.* fly (v.).
na-tpene *Amanuban.* fly (v.).
Out-comparisons:
tabele *East Tetun.* hang, dangle; hanging, dangling. (Mo:177)

***tana|ʔ** *PnMeto.* thorn. *Etym:* **tara-k (pre-Meto).
tanaʔ *Kusa-Manea.* thorn.
Out-comparisons:
tarak, taran *East Tetun.* thorn. (Mo:180)
ai taran *Kemak.* thorn.
<tara> *Kambera.* thorns, spines; pandanus leaf. (On:482)
karna *Kisar.* cock's spur.

***tana**$_1$ *PRM.* cover.
ta~tana (2) tana *Termanu.* 1) cover something with a lid, close something. (J:593) 2) put something somewhere so that it is covered up a little. (J:593)
ta~tana *Korbafo.*
ta~tana *Bokai.*
ta~tana *Bilbaa.*
ta~tana *Rikou.*
ta~tana *Ba'a.*
ta~tana *Tii.*
ta~tana *Dengka.*
ta~tana *Oenale.*
na-taan *Meto.* (J:593)
Out-comparisons:
tuŋa *Semau Helong.* close, cover. *[irr. from PRM:* *a = *u* *correspondence]*
ketaŋa *Hawu.* lid. (J:593)
<tanga> *Kambera.* lid, cover which fits on top. (On:474)

***tana**$_2$ *Morph:* ***tana-k**. *Rote.* crispy, dried out. *Etym:* **taŋa (pre-RM).
tana-k *Termanu.* dry, snappy, crisply baked or fried. (J:593)
tana-ʔ *Korbafo.*
tana-k *Bokai.*
tana-ʔ *Bilbaa.*
tana-ʔ *Rikou.*
tana-k *Ba'a.*
tana-k *Tii.*
tana-ʔ *Dengka.*
tana-ʔ *Oenale.*
Out-comparisons:
taŋa *Semau Helong.* stiff, withered, crispy, dried out.

***tana**$_3$ *PMeto.* ask, inquire. *Doublet:* ***tane**. *Etym:* *utaña. *[History:* PRM had two reflexes of *utaña: ***tane** and ***tana**. Both are still attested in Molo.*]*
na-tana *Ro'is Amarasi.* ask.
na-tana *Kotos Amarasi.* ask.
na-tana *Molo.* queries. (M:537)

***tane**$_1$ *Rote.* mud. *Etym:* *tanəq 'earth, soil, land'. *[Form:* regular *ə > *e* /_q#.*]*
tane *Termanu.* mud. (J:594)
tane *Korbafo.*
tane *Bokai.*
tane *Bilbaa.*
tane *Rikou.*
tane *Ba'a.*
tane *Tii.*
tane *Dengka.*
tane *Oenale.*

***tane**$_2$ *Morph:* ***na-tane**. *PRM.* ask, inquire. *Doublet:* ***tana**. *Etym:* *utaña. *[Sporadic:* *a > *e /*C+palatal_.*]* *[History:* PRM had two reflexes of *utaña: ***tane** and ***tana**. Both are still attested in Molo.*]*
na-tane *Termanu.* ask, pose a question, query. (J:594)

na-tane *Korbafo.*
na-tane *Bokai.*
na-tane *Bilbaa.*
na-tane *Rikou.*
na-tane *Ba'a.*
na-tane *Tii.*
na-tane *Dengka.*
na-tane *Oenale.*
ma-tane-n *Molo.* question one-another. (M:537)

***tanee** *PRM.* contain (liquid).
na-ta-nee *Termanu.* contain something, both liquids and other things. (J:384f)
na-ta-nee *Korbafo.*
na-ta-nee *Bokai.*
na-ta-nee *Bilbaa.*
na-ta-nee *Rikou.*
na-ta-nee *Ba'a.*
na-ta-nee *Tii.*
na-ta-nee *Dengka.*
na-ta-nee *Oenale.*
na-tnee *Molo.* contains. (M:562)
Out-comparisons:
tenae *Hawu.* contain (liquid).

***tani** *PnRote.* weep, cry; mourn. *Etym:* *taŋis.
na-ma-tani *Termanu.* **manahelo=a na-ma-tani** the poet recited in a complaining tone *[Semantics:* This form is given without a definition and with a note that in (unspecified) other varieties of Rote the meaning is 'weep'.*]* (J:595)
na-ma-tani *Korbafo.*
na-ma-tani *Bokai.*
na-ma-tani *Bilbaa.*
na-ma-tani *Tii.*

***tande** *Morph:* ***ma-tande, *tande-k**. *PRM.* sharp. *Etym:* *tazəm. *[minority from PMP:* *z > *nd (expect *ɗ); *ə > *e /_# (expect *ə > *a* in wRote, possibly *ə > *a > *e)] [History:* Blust and Trussel only give cognates in Taiwan and western MP languages. This, combined, with the irregular sound changes which must be posited, may indicate that this form is not a direct inheritance from PMP, but a subsequent borrowing.*]*
ma-tane (2) tane-k (3) na-ma-tane *Termanu.* 1) sharp, pointy. 2) sharp, pointy; sharpness. 3) be or become sharp; sharpen. (J:594)
ma-tane *Korbafo.*
ma-tane *Bokai.*
ma-tane *Bilbaa.*
ma-tande *Rikou.*
ma-tane *Ba'a.*
ma-tande *Tii.*
tande-ʔ *Dengka.*
tande-ʔ *Oenale.*

***taŋga** *PRM.* jasmine tree, Indian cork tree. Millingtonia hortensis.
taŋa *Termanu.* kind of tree the leaves of which strongly resemble those leaves of the moringa tree *Moringa oleifera*. *[Semantics:* 'Kind of tree (with thick bark, fine leaves with white, sweet smelling flowers and excellent hard wood used for building)' (Fox 2016b:54).*]* (J:595)
taŋa *Korbafo.*
taŋa *Bokai.*
taŋa *Bilbaa.*
taŋga *Ba'a.*
taŋga *Tii.*
taŋga *Dengka.*
taŋga *Oenale.*
<hau taka> *Amfo'an.* kind of tree. Millingtonia hortensis. *[Note:* Middelkoop lists this form as occurring in Amfo'an, Beboki, Amarasi and Miomafo. Beboki also has the variant <**taeka**>. Middelkoop's entry is almost certainly from Meijer Drees (1950:17) who gives <(**hau**) **tàka**>.*]* (M:533)

***tao** *PRM.* put, place, do. *Etym:* *taRuq 'store, put away for safekeeping, hide valuables; to place a bet in gambling; lay an egg'. *[irr. from PMP:* *u > *o*]*

tao *Termanu.* set, lay, place, store, put in, place (a bet), etc.; do, act, make, cause. (J:595)
tao *Korbafo.*
tao *Bokai.*
tao *Bilbaa.*
tao *Rikou.*
tao *Ba'a.*
tao *Tii.*
tao *Dengka.*
tao *Oenale.*
n-tao *Ro'is Amarasi.* put.
n-tao *Kotos Amarasi.* put, do, cast a spell.
n-tao (2) tao-s *Molo.* 1) sets. 2) deeds. (M:542)
Out-comparisons:
talu *Semau Helong.* put; guarantee.
tau *East Tetun.* place, put, set. (Mo:183)

***tara** *Morph:* ***ta~tara**. *PRM.* adze. *Etym:* *taRaq 'hewing with an adze'. *[minority from PMP:* *R = *r (expect Ø)*]*
ta~tala *Termanu.* adze, that which is worked with an adze. (J:590)
ta~tala *Korbafo.*
ta~tala *Bokai.*
ta~tala *Bilbaa.*
ta~tara *Rikou.*
ta~tala *Ba'a.*
ta~tara *Tii.*
ta~talas *Dengka.*
ta~taras *Oenale.*
tan~tana *Meto.* (J:590)

***taruku** *PRM.* chiton. *Etym:* *taduku (own reconstruction) (PCEMP). *Pattern:* k-9.
luʔu *Termanu.* kind of edible mollusc without a shell that is found between rocks in seawater. (J:337)
luʔu *Korbafo.*
luku *Bilbaa.*
ruku-ʔ *Landu.* chiton. *[History:* Jonker (1908) gives Rikou **rutu** as potentially cognate, but Landu has **sarutu-ʔ** = 'sea urchin' which is a more likely cognate for this Rikou form. Thus, Rikou **rutu** and Landu **sarutu-ʔ** are probably not reflexes of ***taruku**.*]* (own field notes)
luʔu *Ba'a.*
ruʔu *Tii.*
ruʔu *Oenale.*
tnuʔu *Ro'is Amarasi.* chiton.
Out-comparisons:
kruku *Waima'a.* sticky sea creature in the rocks by the edge of the sea.
***tadruku** *Proto-East Oceanic.* chiton. (Pawley 2011:197)

***tasa** *Morph:* ***ma-tasa-k**. *PRM.* ripe, cooked. *Etym:* *tasak.
tasa-k (2) na-ma-tasa *Termanu.* 1) cooked, boiled (e.g. rice). 2) be(come) cooked. (J:601f)
tasa-ʔ *Korbafo.*
tasa-k *Bokai.*
tasa-ʔ *Bilbaa.*
tasa-ʔ *Rikou.*
tasa-k *Ba'a.*
tasa-k *Tii.*
tasa-ʔ *Dengka.*
tasa-ʔ *Oenale.*
m|tasa|ʔ (2) meʔe m|tasa|ʔ *Kotos Amarasi.* 1) cooked, ripe. 2) maroon.
a-m|tasa|ʔ *Amfo'an.* red.
m|tasa|ʔ *Molo.* red. (M:332)
Out-comparisons:
tasa *Semau Helong.* cooked.
tasak, tasan *East Tetun.* mature, ripe; edible, cooked. (Mo:181)
maɗasa *Dhao.* ripe, mature.

***tasi** *PRM.* sea, ocean. *Etym:* *tasik 'sea, saltwater'.
tasi *Termanu.* sea, ocean. (J:601)
tasi *Korbafo.*
tasi *Bokai.*
tasi *Bilbaa.*
tasi *Rikou.*
tasi *Ba'a.*
tasi *Tii.*
tasi-ʔ *Dengka.*

tasi *Oenale.*
tasi-ʔ *Dela.* sea.
tasi *Ro'is Amarasi.* sea, ocean.
tasi *Kotos Amarasi.* sea, ocean.
tasi *Molo.* sea, ocean. (M:540)
tasi *Kusa-Manea.* sea, ocean.
Out-comparisons:
tasi *Semau Helong.* sea.
tasi *East Tetun.* sea, ocean. (Mo:181)
kahi *Kisar.* salt water, sea.

***tata** *Rote.* clap, beat, hack. *Etym:* *tabtab.
tata *Termanu.* split. **tata ai** split wood, chop wood (J:602)
tata *Korbafo.*
tata *Bokai.*
tata *Bilbaa.*
tata *Rikou.*
tata *Ba'a.*
tata *Tii.*
tata *Dengka.*

***tatə** *nRM.* boy, older sibling. *[irr. from PRM:* *t > *ʔ* /V_V in most of Rote*]*
taʔe_ana-k *Termanu.* boy, youngster, of about twelve years old. (J:586)
taʔe_ana-ʔ *Korbafo.*
taʔe_ana-k *Bokai.*
tate_anaʔ (2) tate *Bilbaa.* 2) boy. (J:769)
tate_anaʔ (2) tate *Rikou.* 2) boy. (J:769)
taʔe_ana-k *Ba'a.*
taʔe_ana-k *Tii.*
tata-f *Ro'is Amarasi.* same-sex older sibling.
tata-f *Kotos Amarasi.* same-sex older sibling.
tata-f oli-f (2) an-maʔ-oil tata=n (3) tata-n *Molo.* 1) older and younger brothers. 2) younger and older brothers or younger and older sisters with respect to one another. 3) older colt or male calf in respect to a later birth. (M:541)
tata|ʔ *Kusa-Manea.* female older sibling. *[Note:* **toʔo** = 'male older sibling'.*]*
Out-comparisons:
tate, tata (2) kaka *Kisar.* 1) older sibling. *[irr. from PRM:* *t = *t* correspondence (expect *k*)*]* 2) older siblings.

***tati** *Rote.* cut, chop.
tati *Termanu.* chop with a machete, cut with a sword. (J:602)
tati *Korbafo.*
tati *Bokai.*
tati *Bilbaa.*
tati *Rikou.*
tati *Ba'a.*
tati *Tii.*
tati *Dengka.*
tati *Oenale.*
Out-comparisons:
dati *Semau Helong.* cut.

***taum** *Morph:* ***ka-taum**. *PRM.* indigo plant and dye. *Etym:* *taRum.
tau-k *Termanu.* the indigo plant, indigo; also: dark blue. (J:604)
tau-ʔ *Korbafo.*
tau-k *Bokai.*
tau-ʔ *Bilbaa.*
tau-ʔ *Rikou.*
tau-k *Ba'a.*
tau-k, tau ɗoo *Tii.*
tau-ʔ *Dengka.*
tau-ʔ *Oenale.*
ʔ|taum *Kotos Amarasi.* indigo plant, a short tree whose leaves are used to dye cloth black.
<taum> *Molo.* indigo. Indigofera spec. (M:543)
taum=aa *Kusa-Manea.* kind of plant mixed with mineral lime. **ao** to make a black dye.
Out-comparisons:
taluŋ *Helong.* indigo. Ingofera spec. (Heyne 1950:770, ccxvii)

***taun** *PRM.* year. *Etym:* *taqun 'year, season'. *[irr. from PRM:* *a > *e* in nRote*]* *[Form:* PwRM ***toon**.*]*

teu-k *Termanu.* year. (J:627)
teu-ʔ *Korbafo.*
teu-k *Bokai.*
teu-ʔ *Bilbaa.*
teu-ʔ *Rikou.*
teu-k *Ba'a.*
teu-k *Tii.*
too(-ʔ) *Dengka.*
too *Oenale.*
toon *Ro'is Amarasi.* year.
toon *Kotos Amarasi.* year.
toon *Molo.* year. (M:570)
toan *Kusa-Manea.* year. *[irr. from PRM:* *o > *a] [Form:* Kusa-Manea **toan** may not be a direct inheritance from PRM *taun. Instead, it may be a borrowing from Tetun **tonan** 'year'. If so, the form here would be the metathesised form of (currently unattested) ***tona**.*]*
Out-comparisons:
taun *Semau Helong.* year.

***tea** *PRM.* arrive, until, the point that. *[irr. from PRM:* *a > *e* in all Rote and some Meto (sporadic assimilation)*] [Form:* I have reconstructed final *a rather than *e as *a > *e* can be motivated as sporadic assimilation while the reverse sound change would be unmotivated.*]*
tee *Termanu.* come, arrive. (J:607)
teʔe *Keka.* reach. (J:770)
tee *Korbafo.*
tee *Bokai.*
tee *Bilbaa.*
tee *Rikou.*
tee *Ba'a.*
tee *Dengka.*
n-tea *Ro'is Amarasi.* arrive, until, to the point that.
n-tea, n-tee *Kotos Amarasi.* arrive, until, to the point that. *Usage:* **tea** has 36 examples in my corpus while **tee** has 29 examples.
n-tee, n-tia *Molo.* enough, arrives. (M:544, 554)
n-tee, ntea *Timaus.* arrive, until, to the point that.
tea *Kusa-Manea.* arrive.
Out-comparisons:
toʔo *East Tetun.* arrive, reach; suffice, be enough; enough, sufficient; to, until, as far as. (Mo:188)
tii *Waima'a.* until.

***teas** *PRM.* heartwood of a tree, hard, durable core of wood; ironwood tree. *Etym:* *təRas. *[Sporadic:* *a > *e* / _# in wRM.*]*
tea, teas *Termanu.* core of wood. (J:608)
tea *Korbafo.*
tea *Bokai.*
tea *Bilbaa.*
tea *Rikou.*
tea *Ba'a.*
tea *Tii.*
tee-ʔ *Dengka.*
tee-ʔ *Oenale.*
teas *Kotos Amarasi.* hard centre of tree trunk.
teas, tees *Molo.* hard core of tree-trunk. (M:544)
teas *Kusa-Manea.* hard.
Out-comparisons:
telas *Semau Helong.* beam, strong. Sense of structurally sound, not corrupted by mould or rot.
toos *East Tetun.* hard, durable; stiff, difficult to open; stubborn. (Mo:188)

***teɓes** *PRM.* true. *[irr. from PRM:* *ɓ > *ʔ* in Termanu and Bokai*]*
(teʔe~)teʔe *Termanu.* in truth, in reality, truly. (J:77)
(tebe~)tebe *Korbafo.*
(teʔe~)teʔe *Bokai.*
(tebe~)tebe, te~tebe-ʔ *Bilbaa.*
(tebe~)tebe, te~tebes=a *Rikou.*
(tebe~)tebe, te~tebes=a *Ba'a.*
(teɓe~)teɓe, te~teɓe-k *Tii.*
(tebe~)tebe, te~tebes=a *Dengka.*
(teɓe~)teɓe, te~teɓes=a *Oenale.*
te~teɓes (2) teɓe~teɓes *Dela.* 1) true. 2) truly.

tebe (2) na-ʔtebe *Kotos Amarasi.* 1) true, earnest. 2) true, earnest.

teeb (2) <nateb> *Molo.* 1) yes, it is true. 2) confirms, accords. (M:544)

Out-comparisons:

tebes *Semau Helong.* true, right.

tebes *East Tetun.* certainly, truly, in truth. (Mo:183)

***teɓi** *PRM.* break into pieces. *Etym:* *təbiq 'split off, break off a piece, as in breaking off a section of betel nut' (PWMP). *[minority from PMP:* *b > *ɓ /V_V*] [irr. from PRM:* *ɓ > *b* ~ *ʔ* in Termanu, Korbafo and Bokai*]*

tebi (2) teʔi *Termanu.* 1) chipped, crumbled at the edge. (J:608) 2) break something, break into pieces with the fingers. (J:613)

tebi (2) teʔi *Korbafo.*

tebi (2) teʔi *Bokai.*

tebi *Bilbaa.*

tebi (2) tebi *Rikou.*

tebi *Ba'a.*

teɓi *Tii.*

tebi *Dengka.*

n-tebi *Kotos Amarasi.* break up into pieces (e.g. bread).

n-tebi *Molo.* crumble into pieces. (M:544)

Out-comparisons:

teben *Semau Helong.* stubby, short, chop. *[irr. from PRM:* *i = *e* correspondence*]*

tohi(k) *East Tetun.* chip off little pieces. (Mo:187)

***teɗe** *Rote.* crush with fingernail. *Etym:* *tindəs 'crush lice with the fingernails'. *[irr. from PMP:* *nd > *ɗ; *i > *e (also in eastern varieties of Malay)*] [minority from PMP:* *ə > *e /_# (expect *ə > *a* in wRote, possibly *ə > *a > *e*)*] [Form:* Some eastern Malays (e.g. Kupang Malay, Ambon Malay) have *tendes* 'press' also with *i > *e*. Hawu also shows *i > *e.]*

tede *Termanu.* flatten, whether between the fingernails or between a fingernail and a hard object. (J:609)

tede *Korbafo.*

tede *Bokai.*

tede *Bilbaa.*

tede *Rikou.*

tede *Ba'a.*

teɗe *Tii.*

teɗe *Dengka.*

teɗe *Oenale.*

Out-comparisons:

təɗa *Hawu.* (J:609)

<tidihungu> *Kambera.* press, press down. **<tidihungu wutu>** crush lice (On:493)

<tiduhungu> *Lewa.*

<tiḍasungu> *Anakalang.*

<tede> *Weyewa.*

<katidihyo> *Kodi.*

***tee** *Rote.* spear. *Etym:* **təRə (pre-RM).

tee *Termanu.* spear. (J:605)

tee *Korbafo.*

tee *Bokai.*

tee *Bilbaa.*

tee *Rikou.*

tee *Ba'a.*

tee *Tii.*

tee *Dengka.*

tee *Oenale.*

Out-comparisons:

kere *Kisar.* spear.

tera *Wetan.* spear. *[Note:* language of southwest Maluku, member of Luang language/dialect cluster ISO 639-3 [lex.]*]* (de Josselin de Jong 1987)

too *Welaun.* spear.

***tefe** *CER.* broken, tired.

tefe *Termanu.* weary (actually: 'broken'). **tefe basa au luŋu laŋa so~solu-n** my knees and my shins are very weary (literally: broken), I'm very tired (J:612)

tefe *Korbafo.*

tefe *Bokai.*

tefe *Bilbaa.*
tefe *Rikou.* piece, broken. (J:770)
Out-comparisons:
tehen *Semau Helong.* break apart, snap.

***tefu** *PRM.* sugarcane. Saccharum officinarum. *Etym:* *təbuh.
tefu *Termanu.* sugarcane. (J:612)
tefu *Korbafo.*
tefu *Bokai.*
tefu *Bilbaa.*
tefu *Landu.* sugarcane. (own field notes)
tefu *Rikou.*
tefu *Ba'a.*
tefu *Tii.*
tefu *Dengka.*
tefu *Oenale.*
tefu *Ro'is Amarasi.* sugarcane.
tefu *Kotos Amarasi.* sugarcane.
tefu *Molo.* sugarcane. Saccharum officinarum. (M:545)
tefu *Kusa-Manea.* sugarcane.
Out-comparisons:
tihu *Semau Helong.* sugarcane.
touhu *East Tetun.* sugarcane. Saccharum officinarum. (Mo:189)
keu *Kisar.* sugarcane.

***teka** *PRM.* call, greet. *Pattern:* k-10.
na-teʔa *Termanu.* greet in passing, say goodbye. (J:608)
na-teʔa *Korbafo.*
na-teʔa *Bokai.*
na-teka *Bilbaa.*
na-teʔa *Rikou.*
na-teʔa *Ba'a.*
na-teʔa *Tii.*
na-tea *Dengka.*
na-tea *Oenale.*
n-teka *Ro'is Amarasi.* call, refer to as.
n-teka *Kotos Amarasi.* call, refer to as.
n-teka (2) <a'teka> (3) <na-teka> *Molo.* 1) names. 2) riddle. 3) someone tells a riddle. (M:546)
Out-comparisons:
teka *Semau Helong.* tell, inform.

***teke** *Morph:* ***ka-teke**. *PRM.* gecko. *Etym:* *təktək. *Pattern:* k-5. *[minority from PMP:* *ə > *e /_# (expect *ə > *a* in wRM, possibly *ə > *a > *e* in wRM)*] [Semantics:* onomatopoeia.*]*
teke *Termanu.* gecko. (J:614)
teke *Korbafo.*
teke *Bokai.*
teke *Bilbaa.*
teʔe *Rikou.*
teke *Ba'a.*
teke *Tii.*
teke *Dengka.*
teke *Oenale.*
teke *Ro'is Amarasi.*
ʔ|teke *Kotos Amarasi.* gecko.
ʔ|teke *Molo.* kind of tree lizard. (M:547)
Out-comparisons:
ktokeʔ *Funai Helong.* calling gecko. *[irr. from PMP:* *ə > *o* (expect *e*)*]*
tokeʔ *Semau Helong.* gecko.
teki *East Tetun.* gecko lizard often found living in houses. *[irr. from PMP:* *ə > *e* (expect *o*)*]* (Mo:183)

***tekə** *PRM.* staff, walking stick. *Etym:* *təkən 'downward pressure; bamboo punting pole'. *Pattern:* k-8.
te~teʔe-k (2) te~teʔe *Termanu.* 1) staff, walking stick; the use of a walking stick. (J:610f) 2) use a walking stick.
te~teʔe-ʔ *Korbafo.*
te~teʔe-k *Bokai.*
te~teke-ʔ *Bilbaa.*
te~teʔe-ʔ *Rikou.*
te~teʔe_ai-k *Ba'a.*
te~teʔe_ai *Tii.*
te~tea-s *Dengka.*
te~tea-s *Oenale.*
te~tea-s *Dela.* walking stick, staff.
tea|s *Kotos Amarasi.* walking stick, staff.
tee|s, tea|s *Molo.* staff. (M:544, 552)

Out-comparisons:
tnikan *Funai Helong.* staff.
tikan (2) hnikan *Semau Helong.* 1) support, use a walking stick. 2) staff, walking stick, rod.
ai katoʔan *Welaun.* staff, pole.

***telu** *PRM.* three. *Etym:* *təlu.
telu *Termanu.* three. (J:615)
telu *Korbafo.*
telu *Bokai.*
telu *Bilbaa.*
telu *Rikou.*
telu *Ba'a.*
telu *Tii.*
telu *Dengka.*
telu *Oenale.*
tenu *Ro'is Amarasi.* three.
tenu *Kotos Amarasi.* three.
tenu *Molo.* three. (M:550)
Out-comparisons:
tilu *Semau Helong.* three.
tolu *East Tetun.* three. (Mo:183)
telu *Waima'a.* three.
wokelu *Kisar.* three.

***tema₁** *CERM.* eagle. *[Sporadic:* *a > *e* / _# in Meto.*]*
te~tema *Termanu.* kite (bird); fly down on something like a kite. (J:617)
te~tema *Korbafo.*
te~tema *Bokai.*
te~tema *Bilbaa.*
te~tema *Rikou.*
teme *Ro'is Amarasi.* kite.
teme *Kotos Amarasi.* eagle.
teme *Molo.* hawk. (M:548)
Out-comparisons:
tem/lusi *Helong.* (J:617)

***tema₂** *Morph:* ***ka-tema-k, *teme~teme**. *PRM.* whole, entire. *[Sporadic:* *a > *e* / _# in wRM.*]*
tema~tema (2) ka-tema-k *Termanu.* 1) intact, whole, in its entirety. 2) intact, entirely. (J:616)
tema~tema (2) ka-tema-ʔ *Korbafo.*
tema~tema (2) ka-tema-k *Bokai.*
tema~tema (2) ka-tema-ʔ *Bilbaa.*
tema~tema (2) ka-tema-ʔ *Rikou.*
tema~tema (2) ka-tema-k *Ba'a.*
tema~tema (2) ka-tema-k *Tii.*
teme~teme, teme-ʔ *Dengka.*
teme~teme, teme-ʔ *Oenale.*
ʔ|teme *Kotos Amarasi.* closed, sealed; entire, whole.
<teme> *Molo.* inaccessible (forest), virgin, virginal, full (moon), receptive (heart). (M:548)
Out-comparisons:
ŋae ktemaʔ *Funai Helong.* cooked corn.
tema *Semau Helong.* whole.
naktomak *East Tetun.* be complete; completed, entire. (Mo:188)
ke~keme *Kisar.* whole.
tema *Ili'uun.* all, together, whole, complete. (dJ:138)
ketəme *Hawu.* whole. (J:616)
təmak, təmaŋ *Sika.* unbroken, whole. (Pareira and Lewis 1998:193)

***temə** *Morph:* ***na-temə**. *PRM.* accustomed to. *Etym:* *təmən. (Dempwolff 1938:135) (Reconstructed with final *a, but this seems unable to account for the reflexes of the final vowels in a number of languages. Blust and Trussel (ongoing) list cognates under their ‘noise’ section.).
na-teme *Termanu.* used to, accustomed to, usual. (J:618)
na-teme *Korbafo.*
na-teme *Bokai.*
na-teme *Bilbaa.*
na-teme *Rikou.*
na-teme *Ba'a.*
na-teme *Tii.*
na-tema *Dengka.*
na-tema *Oenale.*
na-teem *Meto.* (J:618)
Out-comparisons:
teman *Helong.* (J:618)
toman *East Tetun.* be in the habit of, accustom. (Mo:188)

tima *Hawu.* often, normally, customarily.

***temba** *Rote.* sardine. *Etym:* *tamban (PWMP). *[irr. from PMP:* *a > *e*]* *[History:* Possibly a borrowing from Malay **tembaŋ**. Jonker also gives Makassar and Bugis **tembaŋ**.*]*

iʔa tepa *Termanu.* kind of small ocean fish that is like a sardine, called *ikan tembang* in Kupang. (J:623)

tepa *Korbafo.*

tepa *Bokai.*

tepa *Bilbaa.*

tepa *Rikou.*

tempa *Ba'a.*

temba *Dengka.*

temba *Oenale.*

***tena$_1$** *PRM.* sink, submerge. *[Note:* Blust and Trussel (ongoing) reconstruct *təñəj 'sink, set (sun)' on the basis of the Termanu reflex (glossed 'sink, set (of the sun)') and a Cebuano reflex. But a regular reflex Termanu of this form would have a final *e* rather than *a.]*

tena (2) tena-k (3) te~tena-k (4) na-tena (5) na-ka-tena-k *Termanu.* 1) sinking, usually said of a ship when it is full of water; sink (transitive). 2) more definitely: drown. 3) sinking, etc.; pit, in which something has to sink, e.g. animals to catch them. 4) sink (transitive). 5) lower (something down). (J:619)

tena (2) tena-ʔ *Korbafo.*

tena (2) tena-k *Bokai.*

tena (2) tena-ʔ *Bilbaa.*

tena (2) tena-ʔ *Rikou.*

tena (2) tena-k *Ba'a.*

tena (2) tena-k *Tii.*

tena (2) tena *Dengka.*

tena *Oenale.*

n-tena *Ro'is Amarasi.* sink slowly like the sun.

n-tena *Kotos Amarasi.* sink slowly, like things in water.

Out-comparisons:

denes (2) dene *Semau Helong.* 1) submerge, drown. 2) set, go down. *[irr. from PRM:* *t = *d* correspondence; *a = *e* correspondence*]*

***tena$_2$** *PRM.* alight, land. *[irr. from PRM:* *t > *n* in Kotos Amarasi*]* *[Sporadic:* *a > *e* / _# in Meto*]*

tena *Termanu.* alight, touch the ground, land on the ground; also, be landed (of a bird). (J:619)

tena *Korbafo.*

tena *Bokai.*

tena *Bilbaa.*

tena *Rikou.*

tena *Ba'a.*

tena *Tii.*

tena *Dengka.*

n-nene *Kotos Amarasi.* press, land.

tene *Meto.* (J:619)

***tena$_3$** *PnMeto.* calm down, quieten. *Etym:* *tənəŋ 'calm, still, as the surface of water' (PWMP).

na-ʔ|tena|ʔ *Kotos Amarasi.* calm down, quieten.

<na-tena> *Molo.* become quiet. (M:548)

Out-comparisons:

tene *Semau Helong.* stop, cease.

***tene** *PRM.* kind of mangrove, with bark used for dyeing. Ceriops species. *Etym:* *təŋəR. *[irr. from PMP:* *ə > *e (expect *ə > *a* in wRM, possibly *ə > *a > *e* in wRM)*]*

tene *Termanu.* kind of tree that grows on the beach, it has good wood and yields a red dye. (J:620)

tene *Korbafo.*

tene *Bokai.*

tene *Bilbaa.*

tene *Rikou.*

tene *Ba'a.*

tene *Tii.*

tene *Dengka.*

tene *Oenale.*

tene *Molo.* small tidal forest tree. Ceriops tagal. (M:549)

***teni** *PMeto.* again.

n-teniʔ *Ro'is Amarasi.* again.

teniʔ, n-teni *Kotos Amarasi.* again.

n-teni *Molo.* again. (M:549)

Out-comparisons:

teni *East Tetun.* again, afresh. (Mo:184)

teni *Waima'a.* again.

***tenu** *PRM.* weave (cloth, baskets). *Etym:* *tənun.

tenu *Termanu.* weave. (J:623)

tenu *Korbafo.*

tenu *Bokai.*

tenu *Bilbaa.*

tenu *Rikou.*

tenu *Ba'a.*

tenu *Tii.*

tenu *Dengka.*

tenu *Oenale.*

n-tenu *Kotos Amarasi.* weave.

n-tenu *Molo.* weave. (M:550)

Out-comparisons:

tinu *Semau Helong.* weave.

kenna *Kisar.* weave (cloth).

***tendə** *Morph:* ***tendə-k**. *PRM.* ribcage, lungs.

tene-k *Termanu.* the ribcage of a pig, the ribs together. (J:621)

tene-ʔ *Korbafo.*

tene-k *Bokai.*

tene-ʔ *Bilbaa.*

tende dui-ʔ *Landu.* ribs. (own field notes)

tende-ʔ *Rikou.*

tere-ʔ *Oepao.* ribs. (own field notes)

tene-k *Ba'a.*

tende-k *Tii.*

tenda-ʔ *Dengka.* chest. (J:771)

tenda-ʔ *Oenale.* chest. (J:771)

tenda-ʔ *Dela.* chest.

tere-f *Ro'is Amarasi.* lungs.

teka-f *Kotos Amarasi.* lungs.

teek noo-n (2) teek fua-n *Amanuban.* 1) lungs. 2) heart.

teka-n *Amanatun.* heart.

teka-k *Amfo'an.* heart.

teka-n *Molo.* heart muscle. (M:546)

***teŋga** *PnRote.* hand span. *See:* ***haŋga**.

teŋa *Termanu.* span; measure with spans. (J:621)

teŋa *Korbafo.*

teŋa *Bokai.*

teŋa *Bilbaa.*

teka *Rikou.*

teŋga *Ba'a.*

teŋga *Tii.*

***teri** *Morph:* ***oo_teri-k**. *Rote.* giant bamboo. Dendrocalamus species. *Etym:* *təriŋ 'bamboo species'.

oo_teli-k *Termanu.* the biggest kind of bamboo. (J:615)

oo_teli-ʔ *Korbafo.*

oo_teli-k *Bokai.*

oo_teli-ʔ *Bilbaa.*

oo_teri-ʔ *Rikou.*

oo_teri-k *Tii.*

oo_teli-ʔ *Dengka.*

oo_teri-ʔ *Oenale.*

***tesa** *CERM.* setting (of sun/moon).

tesa *Bilbaa.* the setting of the sun or moon. (J:771)

neon n-tees *Kotos Amarasi.* west. *Lit:* 'sun sets'.

n-tesan *Molo.* decline. (M:552)

***teta** *PRM.* cut into small pieces, mince. *[Sporadic:* *a > *e* / _# in Molo.*]*

te~teta-ta~tata *Termanu.* cut into small pieces, mince. (J:625)

te~teta-ta~tata *Korbafo.*

te~teta-ta~tata *Bokai.*

te~teta-ta~tata *Bilbaa.*

te~teta-ta~tata *Rikou.*

te~teta-ta~tata *Ba'a.*

te~teta lutuʔ *Dengka.*

te~teta-ta~tata *Oenale.*

n-teta *Kotos Amarasi.* cut across something, dismantle, separate.

n-tete *Molo.* minces. (M:553)

Out-comparisons:

teta (2) tetas *Semau Helong.* 1) cut off, amputate, chop off, lop off. 2) cut.

tetak *East Tetun.* crumble into pieces; to chop at with a cutting tool. (Mo:184)

***tete** *Morph:* ***ka-tete**. *CERM.* dam, dyke. *[Semantics:* I have reconstructed the meaning 'dam, dyke' as this accounts for the semantics in both Hawu and the Rote lects. The shift to 'reef' appears to have spread by contact between Bokai, Rikou, Amarasi and Helong (with subsequent shift of 'reef' to 'ridge' in Amarasi). This scenario seems more likely than the alternate in which shift to 'dam, dyke' occurred in Hawu and other Rote lects. Note also that Jonker (1908:670) also gives **unu-k/-ʔ** as 'reef which is visible at low tide' for all Rote languages (including Oepao) except Bokai and Rikou.*]*

tete (2) na-ka-tete *Termanu.* 1) dyke, dam. 2) dam up. (J:626)

tete *Korbafo.*

— (2) — (3) tete-k *Bokai.* 3) reef that is visible at low tide. (J:772)

tete *Bilbaa.*

tete (2) — (3) tete-ʔ *Rikou.* 3) reef which is visible at low tide. (J:772)

k|tete|ʔ *Kotos Amarasi.* ridge.

Out-comparisons:

teten *Semau Helong.* reef.

titi *Hawu.* dam. (J:626)

***tetu** *PRM.* upright, midday. *[Form:* The reflexes meaning 'midday' outside of RM reflect something like **dətu or **ndətu.*]*

na-tetu (2) ledo=a na-ma-tetu (3) tetu~tetu (4) tetu-k *Termanu.* 1) upright, put upright, put something the right way up. 2) the sun stands high, it is midday. 3) completely upright. 4) in metaphorical senses: perfect, completely in order; perfection. (J:626f)

na-tetu (2) na-ma-tetu *Korbafo.*

na-tetu (2) na-ma-tetu *Bokai.*

na-tetu (2) na-ma-tetu *Bilbaa.*

na-tetu (2) na-ma-tetu *Rikou.*

na-tetu (2) na-ma-tetu *Ba'a.*

na-tetu (2) na-ma-tetu *Tii.*

na-tetu (2) na-ma-tetu *Dengka.*

na-tetu (2) na-ma-tetu *Oenale.*

na-tetu (2) na-m|tetu *Kotos Amarasi.* 1) stand upright. 2) upright.

na-tetu (2) manas na-m|tetun *Molo.* 1) is upright, stands upright. 2) the sun is in its zenith. (M:553)

Out-comparisons:

titu (2) lelo ditu *Semau Helong.* 1) straight. 2) midday.

loro natutun *East Tetun.* noon. (Mo:133)

nətu lodo *Hawu.* midday.

ləro dətu (2) dətuŋ *Sika.* 1) midday. 2) flat area. (Pareira and Lewis 1998:37)

(ɹəra) rətu (2) ndətu *Ende.* 1) midday. (J:626) 2) flat place, level ground.

***teu** *Morph:* ***ka-teu**. *PRM.* pigeon, dove. *Etym:* **lakateRu (pre-RM).

ka|teu *Termanu.* kind of pigeon, wild pigeon. (J:223)

ka|teu *Korbafo.*

ka|teu *Bokai.*

ka|teu *Bilbaa.*

ka|teu *Rikou.*

ka|teu *Ba'a.*

teu *Tii.*

teu *Dengka.*

teu *Oenale.*

too/tiu *Kotos Amarasi.* kind of bird like a White-necked Myna. *[Sporadic:* vowel height harmony *e > *i* / _u.*]*

Out-comparisons:

tiluʔ *Semau Helong.* dove, pigeon.

lakateu *East Tetun.* dove. (Mo:124)

laktyeru *Leti.* turtle-dove. *[Note:* language of southwest Maluku, member of Luang language/ dialect cluster ISO 639-3 [lti].*]* (van Engelenhoven 2004:419)

lakateun *Kamarian.* turtle-dove. *[Note:* also in Kaibobo and Haruku.*]* (van Ekris 1864:104)
rakateun *Asilulu. [Note:* also in Lusa Laut.*]* (van Ekris 1864:104)

***təlo** *Morph:* ***təlo-k**. *PRM.* egg. *Etym:* *qatəluR 'egg; testicle'. *[irr. from PRM:* *ə > *o* in nRote; *l > *n* ~ *k* in Nuclear Meto (perhaps partly via intermediate irregular PMeto *l > *r before *r > *k*)*] [Sporadic:* *u > *o /_*R#.*]*
tolo-k *Termanu.* egg. (J:641)
tolo-ʔ *Korbafo.*
tolo-k *Bokai.*
tolo-ʔ *Bilbaa.*
tolo-ʔ *Landu.* egg. (own field notes)
tolo-ʔ *Rikou.*
tolo-k *Ba'a.*
tolo-k *Lole.* egg. (Zacharias et al. 2014)
tolo-k *Tii.*
telo-ʔ *Dengka.*
telo-ʔ *Oenale.*
teno|ʔ *Ro'is Amarasi.* egg.
teno|ʔ, teko|ʔ *Kotos Amarasi.* egg.
teko|ʔ *Molo.* egg. (M:550)
teno|ʔ *Kusa-Manea.* egg.
Out-comparisons:
tilun *Semau Helong.* egg.
tolu-n (2) tolon *East Tetun.* 1) an egg. 2) the germ of seeds. (Mo:188)
thelu *Waima'a.* egg.
telon *Kemak.* egg.

***tiam** *PRM.* oyster. *Etym:* *tiRəm. *[irr. from PMP:* *ə > *a (expect *ə > *e* in nRote)*]*
ti~tia-k *Termanu.* oyster, including the creature, also **ti~tia isi-k** for the creature and also **ti~tia lou-k** for the shell. (J:629)
ti~tia-ʔ *Korbafo.*
ti~tia-k *Bokai.*
ti~tia-ʔ *Bilbaa.*
ti~tia-ʔ *Rikou.*
ti~tia-k *Ba'a.*
ti~tia-k *Tii.*
ti~tia-ʔ *Dengka.*
ti~tia-ʔ *Oenale.*
tiam *Meto.* (J:629)
Out-comparisons:
tiaŋ *Helong.* (J:629)

***tiɓa** *Morph:* ***ka-tiɓa-k**. *PRM.* bamboo container.
tiba-k *Bokai.*
tiba-k *Ba'a.* bamboo container. (J:772)
tiɓa-k *Tii.*
tiba-ʔ *Dengka.*
tiɓa-ʔ *Oenale.*
ʔ|tiba|ʔ *Kotos Amarasi.* small tube shaped container for mineral lime.

***tiɗo** *PRM.* kind of tuber.
tido (2) tido-k *Termanu.* 1) kind of plant with oblong, egg-shaped fruits. 2) **ina tei tido-k** a woman with a slim figure (J:629)
tido (2) tido-ʔ *Korbafo.*
tido (2) tido-k *Bokai.*
tido (2) tido-ʔ *Bilbaa.*
tido (2) tido-ʔ *Rikou.*
tido (2) tido-k *Ba'a.*
tiɗo (2) tiɗo-k *Tii.*
tiɗo (2) tiɗo-ʔ *Dengka.*
tiɗo (2) tiɗo-ʔ *Oenale.*
tiro|k *Kotos Amarasi.* kind of wild tuber that cannot be eaten, it causes an itch.
<tilo> *Molo.* kind of sweet potato with a stem which sticks up. (M:557)

***tii** *Morph:* ***tii-k**. *Rote.* sea urchin. *See:* ***k|teom**. *Etym:* **tiRi (pre-RM). *[Note:* Although the reflexes here are similar to those under ***k|teom** (**tayum), they cannot be straightforwardly combined as the sound correspondences are not regular and both Tetun forms **tii** and **teon** would be unexplained if this were done.*] [History:* Possibly connected with PWMP *təRi 'kind of small fish', but the semantic shift seems unlikely.*]*

tii-k *Termanu.* kind of small sea creature with long spines differentiated into **tii hade-k**, a white kind, and **tii bete-k**, a red kind. (J:628)

tii-ʔ *Korbafo.*

tii-k *Bokai.*

tii-k *Ba'a.*

tii-k *Tii.*

tii-ʔ *Dengka.*

tii-ʔ *Oenale.*

tii-ʔ *Dela.* sea urchin.

Out-comparisons:

tii *East Tetun.* sea urchin. Echinus esculenta. (Mo:185)

tiri *Fordata.* sea urchin. *[Note:* language of the Tanimbar Islands ISO 639-3 [frd].*]* (Drabbe 1932:175)

tir *Kei.* sea urchin. Echinus esculentus. *[Note:* language of the Kei Islands ISO 639-3 [kei].*]* (Geurtjens 1921)

***ti(ʔ)o** *Rote.* goatfish, family Mullidae. *Etym:* *tiqaw. *[Form:* Whether or not the Termanu form attests a medial glottal stop affects whether this should be reconstructed or not. Similarly, depending on the form of possible cognates in other Rote languages it may be possible to posit medial *h instead of *ʔ.*]*

tio (2) iʔa_tiʔo *Termanu.* 1) kind of small but ritually important fish; Bar-Tail Goat Fish. Mullidae: Upeneus tragula. (Fox 2016b:56) 2) kind of ocean fish. (J:632)

***tila** *Morph:* ***tila-k**. *PRM.* vagina. *Etym:* *tila.

tila-k *Termanu.* vagina. (J:630)

tila-ʔ *Korbafo.*

tila-k *Bokai.*

tila-ʔ *Bilbaa.*

tila-ʔ *Rikou.*

tila-k *Ba'a.*

tila-k *Tii.*

tila-ʔ *Dengka.*

tila-ʔ *Oenale.*

tini-f *Ro'is Amarasi.* vagina.

tina-f *Kotos Amarasi.* vagina.

tina|ʔ *Molo.* vagina, private parts of a woman or female animal. (M:558)

***timi** *Morph:* ***timi-k**. *PRM.* chin, jaw. *Etym:* *timid. *[irr. from PRM:* *i > *u* in Amanuban and Kusa-Manea*]*

timi-k *Termanu.* chin, jaw. (J:630)

timi-ʔ *Korbafo.*

timi-k *Bokai.*

timi-ʔ *Bilbaa.*

timi dai-ʔ *Landu.* chin. (own field notes)

timi-ʔ *Rikou.*

timi-k *Ba'a.*

timi-k *Tii.*

timi-ʔ *Dengka.*

timi-ʔ *Oenale.*

tai_timu-n *Amanuban.* chin.

tool_timi-n *Timaus.* chin.

timi-f *Meto.* (J:630)

ta~timu-f *Kusa-Manea.* chin.

Out-comparisons:

timir *East Tetun.* beard, whiskers, chin. (Mo:186)

***timu$_1$** *CER.* east wind. *Etym:* *timuR.

ani timu *Termanu.* east wind. (J:630)

***timu$_2$** *Morph:* ***ka-timu-k**. *PRM.* cucumber. Cucumis sativa L. *Etym:* *qatimun.

ti~timu-k *Termanu.* papaya (tree and fruit). (J:630)

ti~timu-ʔ *Korbafo.*

ti~timu-ʔ *Rikou.*

ti~timu-k *Ba'a.*

(ti~timu-k ?) *Tii.*

ti~timu-ʔ *Dengka.*

ook_t͡iumu|k *Ro'is Amarasi.* cucumber.

oka_ʔ|timu|k *Kotos Amarasi.* cucumber.

ook_<timo>, okan_<timo> *Molo.* watermelon. (M:401)

Out-comparisons:

saah-timun, tium-takan *Helong.* (J:630)

***tina** *Rote.* dry field which is replanted every year. *Etym:* **tiŋaR (Mills 2010:285). *[irr. from PRM:* *a > *e* in Termanu, Korbafo, Rikou, Oenale, and Dela*]*

tina, tine *Termanu.* dry field or plantation that is cleaned and replanted every year. (J:630)

tina, tine *Korbafo.*

tina *Bokai.*

tina *Bilbaa.*

tine *Rikou.*

tina *Ba'a.*

tina *Tii.*

tine *Dengka.*

tine *Oenale.*

Out-comparisons:

tinan *East Tetun.* year, the commencement of the rainy season (usually in November) to the beginning of the next rainy season. (Mo:186)

kirna *Kisar.* garden.

tiran *Roma.* garden. (Steven 1991:51)

tina *West Damar.* garden. *[Note:* language of southwest Maluku ISO 639-3 [drn].*]* (Chlenov and Chlenova 2008:145)

ti-ol *Dawera-Daweloor.* garden. *[Note:* language of the Babar Islands, southwest Maluku ISO 639-3 [ddw].*] [Form:* regular *ŋ > Ø*]* (Chlenova 2002:170)

tikan *Welaun.* year.

***tino** *PRM.* peer, mirror. *Doublet:* ***tiro**. *Etym:* *tindaw 'see in the distance'. *[Note:* I have placed the Meto forms here rather than under ***tiro** as the medial *n provides a potential motivation for irregular initial *t > *n.] [irr. from PMP:* *nd > *n*] [irr. from PRM:* *t > *n* in Meto*]*

ti~tino (2) ti~tino-k (3) ti~tino-k (4) ti~tino *Termanu.* 1) peep, peer, e.g. through a hole, but also peering in general. 2) mirror. 3) peeping, peering, peeking. 4) go see, go visit. (J:631f)

ti~tino (2) ti~tino (4) ti~tino *Korbafo.*

ti~tino (2) ti~tino-k (4) ti~tino *Bokai.*

ti~tino (2) tino_ao (4) ti~tino *Bilbaa.*

ti~tino (2) tino_ao (4) ti~tino *Rikou.*

ti~tino (2) (ti~tino-s ?) (4) ti~tino *Ba'a.*

ti~tino (4) (ti~tino ?) *Tii.*

ti~tino *Oenale.*

ʔ|ninu|ʔ *Kotos Amarasi.* glass. *[Sporadic:* vowel height harmony *o > *u* /iC_ in Amarasi.*]*

ʔninoʔ (2) noe ʔninoʔ, koe ʔninoʔ *Molo.* 1) mirror. 2) the clear river. (M:371)

***tiŋga** *Morph:* ***tiŋga-k, *na-tiŋga**. *PRM.* heel. *Etym:* *tikəd. *[irr. from PMP:* *k > *ŋg; *ə > *a*]*

ei_tiŋa-k (2) na-tiŋa (3) tiŋa *Termanu.* 1) heel. 2/3) put the heels down firmly or put them in something. *[Semantics:* The meanings for **na-tiŋa** and **tiŋa** are given as identical.*]* (J:631)

ei_tiŋa-ʔ (2) na-tiŋa *Korbafo.*

ei_tiŋa-k (2) na-tiŋa *Bokai.*

ei_tiŋa-ʔ (2) na-tiŋa *Bilbaa.*

ei_tika-ʔ (2) na-tika *Rikou.*

ei_tiŋga-k (2) na-tiŋga *Ba'a.*

ei_tiŋga-k (2) na-tiŋga *Tii.*

ei_tiŋga-ʔ (2) na-tiŋga *Dengka.* 2a) put the heels down firmly or put them in something. 2b) kick.

ei_tiŋga-ʔ (2) na-tiŋga *Oenale.* 2a) put the heels down firmly or put them in something. 2b) kick.

tiki-f *Ro'is Amarasi.* heel.

tika-f (2) na-tika *Kotos Amarasi.* 1) heel. 2) kick or stamp with the heel.

tika-n (2) <an-tika loto> (3) <bikase> na-tiik *Molo.* 1) heel. 2) tumbles over the ground. 3) the horse kicks backwards. (M:556)

***tiri** *Morph:* ***tiri~tiri**. *Rote.* drip. *Etym:* *tiRis 'drip, ooze through, leak'. *[minority from PMP:* *R = *r (expect Ø)*]*

tili~tili *Termanu.* flow by drops. (J:630)

tili~tili *Korbafo.*

tili~tili *Bokai.*

tili~tili *Bilbaa.*

tiri~tiri *Rikou.*

tili~tili *Ba'a.*

tiri~tiri *Tii.*

tili~tili *Dengka.*

tiri~tiri *Oenale.*

***tiro** *Rote.* mirror, visit. *Doublet:* ***tino**. *Etym:* *tindaw 'see in the distance'. *[irr. from PMP:* *nd > *r*]*

tiro_ao *Rikou.* mirror. (Nako et al. 2014)

ti~tilo-s *Ba'a.* mirror. (J:632)

tilo *Lole.* look in on. (Zacharias et al. 2014)

ti~tiro (2) tiro *Tii.* 1) mirror. (J:632) 2) visit. (Grimes et al. 2014a)

ti~tilo_ao *Dengka.* mirror. (J:632)

tiro_ao *Oenale.* mirror. (J:632)

***tisa** *nRM.* pour. *[irr. from PRM:* *a > *e* in Bokai, Tii and Rikou; *a > *i* in Bilbaa and Meto*]*

ti~tisa-k *Termanu.* the overhanging part of the roof from which water drips. (J:633)

ti~tisa-ʔ *Korbafo.*

ti~tise-k *Bokai.*

ti~tisi-ʔ *Bilbaa.*

ti~tise-ʔ *Rikou.*

ti~tisa-k *Ba'a.*

ti~tise-k *Tii.*

n-tisi (2) na-tisi (3) na-m|tisi *Kotos Amarasi.* 1) pour. 2) fill, complete. 3) complete.

n-tesi, n-tosi, n-tisi (2) na-m|tisi *Molo.* 1) pour. 2) complete. (M:559)

Out-comparisons:

tiis *Semau Helong.* pour.

tisi *East Tetun.* empty, spill, pour (liquids). (Mo:186)

***titi** *Rote.* drip. *Etym:* *titis 'drip, ooze'.

titi *Termanu.* drip. (J:633)

titi *Korbafo.*

titi *Bokai.*

titi *Bilbaa.*

titi *Rikou.*

titi *Ba'a.*

titi *Tii.*

titi *Dengka.*

***toɓi** *PRM.* hot, heated up. *[irr. from PRM:* *i > *e* in Meto*]*

ma-tobi-k (2) na-tobi (3) tobi *Termanu.* 1) hot. 2) be hot. 3) burn, scorch. (J:637)

ma-tobi-ʔ *Korbafo.*

ma-tobi-ʔ *Bilbaa.*

ma-tobi-ʔ *Rikou.*

ma-tobi-k *Ba'a.*

ma-toɓi-k *Tii.*

ma-tobi-ʔ *Dengka.*

ma-toɓi-ʔ *Oenale.*

na-tobe *Meto.* steam cooked. (J:637)

***toɗi** *PRM.* protuberance, stick out. *[Sporadic:* consonant metathesis *tVd > *dVt* in Ba'a for the first sense; vowel height harmony *i > *e* /oC_ for first sense in nRote and Meto.*] [Form:* The Meto forms are Historic compound of ***ka-ndou** 'nape of the neck' + ***toɗi**.*]*

tode (2) todi (3) nisi todi-k *Termanu.* 1) stick out lengthwise. 2) stick out (said of teeth). 3) tooth that sticks out. (J:637)

tode (2) todi *Bokai.* 1) stick out lengthwise. 2) stick out (said of teeth).

(2) todi *Bilbaa.*

dote (2) todi *Ba'a.* 1) stick out lengthwise. 2) stick out (said of teeth).

(2) toɗi *Tii.*

(2) toɗi *Dengka.*

ko/tore-f *Kotos Amarasi.* nape of the neck.
ʔ|ko/tole-k *Molo.* the protuberance on the back of my head. (M:225)
***tofa₁** *nRM.* weed (field).
tofa *Termanu.* weed (v.). (J:638)
tofa *Korbafo.*
tofa *Bilbaa.*
tofa *Rikou.*
tofa *Ba'a.*
tofa *Tii.*
n-tofa *Ro'is Amarasi.* weed, remove weeds.
n-tofa *Kotos Amarasi.* weed, remove weeds.
<tofa> *Molo.* weeding knife. (M:566)
Out-comparisons:
topa *Semau Helong.* weed.
***tofa₂** *PRM.* quarrel.
tofa *Tii.* quarrel. (Grimes et al. 2014a)
na-tofa *Dengka.* dispute, quarrel. (J:773)
na-tofa *Oenale.* dispute, quarrel. (J:773)
n-tofa *Kotos Amarasi.* quarrel.
n-tofan *Molo.* have a dislike of. **ho m-tofan kau** you have a dislike of me (M:566)
***toka** *Rote.* impede, against. *Pattern:* k-8/9.
toʔa *Termanu.* but up against something, rebound, be stopped, impeded, obstructed. (J:635)
toʔa *Korbafo.*
toʔa *Bokai.*
toka *Bilbaa.*
toʔa *Rikou.*
toʔa *Ba'a.*
toʔa *Tii.*
toʔa *Dengka.*
toʔa *Oenale.*
Out-comparisons:
toka *Semau Helong.* support, prop up.
toka *Hawu.* gate (of fence). *[Note:* Jonker (1908:635) gives Hawu **toka**, **toke** *'stutten'* = 'support'.*]*
tuki *Bima.* support. (Jonker 1893:107)
tuke *Sika.* support. (Pareira and Lewis 1998:201)
***toki** *PRM.* dig out. *Pattern:* k-8.
toʔi *Termanu.* bore out, chisel out. (J:639)
toʔi *Korbafo.*
toʔi *Bokai.*
toki *Bilbaa.*
toʔi *Rikou.*
toʔi *Ba'a.*
toʔi *Tii.*
toʔi *Dengka.*
n-toi *Kotos Amarasi.* dig out.
Out-comparisons:
tuki *Semau Helong.* dig out, peck, adze.
***toko** *Rote.* beat, knock. *Etym:* *tuktuk 'knock, pound, beat; crush'. *Pattern:* k-6. *[irr. from PMP:* *u > *o*]*
toko *Termanu.* beat, knock. (J:639)
toko *Korbafo.*
toko *Bokai.*
toko *Bilbaa.*
toʔo *Rikou.*
toko *Ba'a.*
toko *Tii.*
toʔo *Dengka.*
toʔo *Oenale.*
***toʔis** *CERM.* horn (instrument).
toʔi-k *Termanu.* triton shell, also a horn of a buffalo on which to blow, also a musical instrument made from lontar leaves. (J:639)
toʔi-ʔ *Korbafo.*
toʔi-k *Bokai.*
toi-ʔ *Bilbaa.*
toʔis *Rikou.*
to͡ʔi-k *Ba'a.*
toiʔis *Ro'is Amarasi.* horn.
toʔis *Kotos Amarasi.* horn (musical instrument), trumpet.
toʔis *Amanuban/Amanatun.* blow on a horn. (M:567)

toʔis *Molo.* horn (instrument). *[Semantics:* This apparently only occurs in Molo in the parallel pair **toʔis ma kniit**.*]* (M:223)

***toʔo** *PRM.* man, male. *Doublet:* ***tou**. *Etym:* *tau. *[irr. from PMP:* Ø > *ʔ*]* *[History:* The original meaning of forms combined with **huu-** (see ***huu**) 'base, source, origin, beginning' was probably 'man'. Further evidence for this comes from Oenale which has **tou huu-ʔ** 'maternal uncle' (see ***tou**) in which the first element is identical to the word for 'man'. Thus, for instance, Termanu **toʔo huu-k** was was probably originally 'man of origin'. The woman is the source of life in Timorese thinking, and thus the mother's brother has an important role as the representative of the wife-giving maternal relatives.*]*

- **toʔo-k (2) toʔo huu-k** *Termanu.* maternal uncle. *Usage:* loses the final *k* in the vocative, etc. in the same way as fv;ama-k 'father'. (J:644)
- **toʔo** *Korbafo.*
- **toʔo-k** *Bokai.*
- **too-ʔ, too huu-ʔ** *Bilbaa. [Note:* **too-ʔ** comes from my own field notes, **too huu-ʔ** from Jonker (1908:644).*]*
- **toʔo=na** *Landu.* (own field notes)
- **toʔo** *Rikou.*
- **toʔo** *Oepao.* (own field notes)
- **toʔo-k** *Ba'a.*
- **toʔo** *Lole.* (Zacharias et al. 2014)
- **toʔo-k** *Tii.*
- **too huu-ʔ** *Dengka.*
- **toʔo** *Dela.* uncle, mother's brother.
- **tooʔ** *Kusa-Manea.* male older sibling, older brother. *[Note:* **tata|ʔ** (< ***tatə**) = 'female older sibling'.*]* *[Form:* possibly the metathesised form of (currently unattested) ***toʔo**.*]*

***toŋgo** *nRM.* meet together.

- **na-toŋo** *Termanu.* meet someone or something, meet together. (J:643)
- **na-toŋo** *Bilbaa.*
- **na-toko** *Rikou.*
- **na-toŋgo** *Ba'a.*
- **na-toŋgo** *Tii.*
- **na-toko (2) noe toko-n** *Molo.* 1) meet. 2) meeting place or confluence of two rivers. (M:568)

***tou** *PRM.* person. *Doublet:* ***toʔo**. *Etym:* *tau 'person, human being'. *[irr. from PMP:* *a > *o (sporadic assimilation)*]* *[irr. from PRM:* *u > *o* in Meto (probably motivated by the rarity of the sequence *ou*)*]*

- **tou-k** *Termanu.* man (in opposition to woman). (J:645)
- **tou-ʔ** *Korbafo.*
- **tou-k** *Bokai.*
- **tou-ʔ** *Bilbaa.*
- **tou-ʔ** *Landu.* man. (own field notes)
- **tou-ʔ** *Rikou.*
- **tou-k** *Ba'a.*
- **tou-k** *Tii.*
- **tou-ʔ** *Dengka.*
- **tou-ʔ (2) tou huu-ʔ** *Oenale.* 1) man (in opposition to woman). (J:645) 2) maternal uncle. (J:644)
- **tou-ʔ** *Dela.* male (only used for humans).
- **too** *Ro'is Amarasi.* citizenry, populace.
- **too** *Kotos Amarasi.* citizenry, populace.
- **too** *Molo.* people. (M:564)
- **too** *Kusa-Manea.* citizenry, populace.

***tua₁** *Rote.* big, size. *Etym:* *tuqah 'old, of people; mature, as fruit'.

- **ma-tua (2) tua (3) na-ma-tua (4) na-ka-tu~tua (5) ma-ka-tuas** *Termanu.* 1) big, size. 2) used in place of **matua** in compounds. 3) become big. 4) (make big), from that to make arrogant, usually said of spoilt children who always get their own way. 5) finally, ultimately. (J:647f)
- **ma-tua (5) ma-ka-tua-s** *Korbafo.*
- **ma-tua (5) ma-ka-tuas** *Bokai.*
- **ma-tua (5) ma-ka-tua-s** *Bilbaa.*

ma-tua *Rikou.*
ma-tua (5) ma-ka-tuas *Ba'a.*
(5) ma-ka-tua-s *Tii.*
(5) ma-ʔa-tua *Dengka.*
(5) ma-ʔa-tua *Oenale.*
Out-comparisons:
tuan *Semau Helong.* big, large, huge.
tuan *East Tetun.* elderly, advanced age. (Mo:189)

***tua2** *PRM.* lontar palm. Borassus flabellifer. *Etym:* *tuak 'palm wine'.
tua *Termanu.* the fan palm or lontar palm; the juice of the lontar palm. (J:647)
tua *Korbafo.*
tua *Bokai.*
tua *Bilbaa.*
tua *Rikou.*
tua *Ba'a.*
tua *Tii.*
tua-ʔ *Dengka.*
tua-ʔ *Oenale.*
tua|ʔ *Kotos Amarasi.* lontar palm.
tua|ʔ *Molo.* lontar palm. Borassus flabellifer. (M:572)
Out-comparisons:
tua *Semau Helong.* lontar juice, lontar tree.
tua *East Tetun.* an alcoholic drink; a palm from which palm juice is extracted. Borassus flabellifer. (Mo:189)
due *Hawu.* lontar palm.

***tua3** *Morph:* ***tua-k**. *PRM.* lord, master. *Etym:* *qatuan. (Both Blust and Trussel (ongoing) and Wolff (2010:960) reconstruct the meaning as 'deity', but I do not consider this well supported by the non-Oceanic reflexes. Instead, 'lord' was probably the original meaning with expansion to 'deity' in POc and occasionally also in other languages. It is also unclear to me whether initial *qa is supported outside of Oceanic.)
lama/tua-k *Termanu.* lord, master, word of address for princes and officials. (J:275)
lama/tua-ʔ *Korbafo.*
lama/tua-k *Bokai.*
lama/tua-ʔ *Bilbaa.*
rama/tua-ʔ *Rikou.*
lama/tua-k *Ba'a.*
lama/tua-k *Tii.*
lama/tua-ʔ *Dengka.*
lama/tua-ʔ *Oenale.*
tua-n (2) tua|f (3) tua *Ro'is Amarasi.* 1) lord, master, owner, self. 2) individual, person. 3) sir, madam; yes, a discourse particle used to acknowledge the listener.
tua-n (2) tua|f (3) tua *Kotos Amarasi.* 1) lord, master, owner, self. 2) individual, person. 3) sir, madam; yes, a discourse particle used to acknowledge the listener.
uim_tua-f (2) ma-ʔusi-ʔ =ma ma-tua-ʔ *Molo.* 1) the owner, lord of the house. 2) have a prince and a lord. (M:573)
Out-comparisons:
lamtua *Semau Helong.* master, owner.
tuak *Fehan Tetun.* mother's brother, father's sister's husband.
am_tuak *East Tetun.* grandfather. (Mo:189)

***tudui** *nRM.* owl. *Pattern:* d-2. *[Form:* The first element in Meto reflexes is from ***ŋguu** 'howl'.*] [History:* Clark (2011:331) reconstructs POc *drudru(r,R) 'owl'.*] [Semantics:* onomatopoeia.*]*
tu~turui-ʔ *Rikou.* owl. (J:775)
tu~tului-k *Lole.* owl. (J:775)
tu~turui-k *Tii.* owl. (J:775)
ku/truu *Ro'is Amarasi.* owl.
ku/truʔu *Kotos Amarasi.* owl.
ku/tlui, ku/tluu *Molo.* owl. (M:242, 403)

***tuɗu** *PRM.* point at, point out; give directions. *Etym:* *tuzuq. *[irr. from PRM:* *t > *r* in Meto (likely sporadic assimilation; ***tuɗu** > PMeto ***dudu**)*]*

na-tudu *Termanu.* point, show, draw to someone's attention, have someone see. (J:650)

na-tudu *Korbafo.*

na-tudu *Bokai.*

na-tudu *Bilbaa.*

na-tudu *Rikou.*

na-tudu *Ba'a.*

na-tuɗu *Tii.*

na-tuɗu *Dengka.*

na-tuɗu *Oenale.*

na-ruru-ʔ (2) k|ruru-f *Ro'is Amarasi.* 1) show, point out to. 2) finger, toe.

n-ruru (2) na-ruru-ʔ (3) k|ruru-f *Kotos Amarasi.* 1) designate. 2) show, appoint, establish. 3) finger, toe.

n-lulu *Molo.* points something out with curled up lips. (M:650)

Out-comparisons:

tulu *Semau Helong.* point, show, designate.

hatudu *East Tetun.* show, indicate, point out, direct. (Mo:83)

pe-ʄuʄu *Hawu.* designated, selected, appointed (pl.).

***tufa** *PRM.* plant with roots that are pounded and put in rivers to stun fish. Derris elliptica. *Etym:* *tuba. *[Sporadic:* *a > *e* / _# in wRM.*]*

tufa *Termanu.* certain plant the roots of which are used to daze fish. (J:650)

tufa *Korbafo.*

tufa *Bokai.*

tufa *Bilbaa.*

tufa *Rikou.*

tufa *Ba'a.*

tufa *Tii.*

tufe *Oenale.*

tufe *Molo.* climbing plant the roots of which are used to daze fish. Derris elliptica. (M:573)

***tufu** *PRM.* punch. *Etym:* *tumbuk 'punch, hit, pound'. *[irr. from PMP:* *mb > (*b) > *f*] [irr. from PRM:* *u > *a* in Rote; *t > *t ~ nd* in Termanu, Ba'a and Dengka; *t > *t ~ n* in Bilbaa*]*

tufa, ndufa *Termanu.* hit with the fist, punch. (J:650, 426)

tufa *Korbafo.*

tufa *Bokai.*

tufa, nufa *Bilbaa.*

tufa *Rikou.*

tufa, ndufa *Ba'a.*

tufa *Tii.*

tufa, ndufa *Dengka.*

n-tufu *Kotos Amarasi.* punch.

n-tufu *Molo.* hit with the fist. (M:574)

Out-comparisons:

tupu *Ili'uun.* hit, strike. (dJ:140)

***tui1** *PRM.* line, carve. *[irr. from PRM:* *t > *d* in Rote*]*

dui-k *Termanu.* stripe, put stripes. (J:105)

dui-ʔ *Korbafo.*

dui-k *Bokai.*

dui-ʔ *Rikou.*

dui-k *Ba'a.*

ɗui-k *Tii.*

ɗui *Dengka.*

n-tui *Ro'is Amarasi.* write.

n-tui *Kotos Amarasi.* write, carve.

n-tui *Molo.* writes. (M:574)

Out-comparisons:

tuis *Semau Helong.* carve, chisel, sculpt; line.

tui (2) tuik *East Tetun.* 1) scratch a line; to scratch with a fingernail or any similar object. 2) line, scratch, sore, or mark; thread, yarn. (Mo:190)

***tui2** *Rote.* tui tree, mangrove trumpet tree. Dolichandrone spathacea. *Etym:* *tui.

tui *Termanu.* a) kind of tree with light wood that is used to make floating wood for fishnets. (J:652) b) kind of large tree that grows beside rivers and lakes. (Fox 2016b:58)

tui *Korbafo.*
tui *Bokai.*
tui *Bilbaa.*
tui *Rikou.*
tui *Ba'a.*
tui *Tii.*
tui *Dengka.*
tui *Oenale.*

***tuin** *CERM.* follow. *Etym:* **tuir (pre-RM).
tui *Termanu.* follow a track. (J:650f)
na-tuin *Ro'is Amarasi.* follow, because.
na-tuin *Kotos Amarasi.* follow, because of.
na-tuin *Molo.* follow. (M:575)
Out-comparisons:
tuiŋ *Helong.* follow an example. (J:650)
tuir *East Tetun.* follow, come behind; to follow, to imitate; to follow, have the same opinion as; to follow, obey the orders of…; to follow, to support. (Mo:190)
ʧoi, ʧui *Ili'uun.* follow, following, according to, because. (dJ:139)
nui *Hawu.* follow a track. (J:650)
sui *Kamarian.* follow, go along with. *[Note:* also in Alune and most varieties of Kaibobo.*]* (van Ekris 1865:117)
kui *Haruku.* (van Ekris 1865:117)

***tuka** *Morph:* ***tuka-ʔ**. *PwRM.* short, truncated. *Pattern:* k-5. *[irr. from PRM:* *a > *u* in wRote (sporadic assimilation?)*]*
tuku-ʔ *Dengka.* truncated, blunt. (J:775)
tuku-ʔ *Oenale.* truncated, blunt. (J:775)
tuka|ʔ *Kotos Amarasi.* short, cut short.
tuka|ʔ *Molo.* short. (M:575)
Out-comparisons:
tuk/leke *Semau Helong.* dwarf, stunted.

***tuke** *Morph:* ***tuke-k**. *PRM.* bamboo vessel. *Etym:* *tukil (PWMP). *Pattern:* k-5. *[Note:* Jonker (1908:652) identifies the reflexes as being borrowings from Bugis **tokka**, but it is hard to explain final RM *e* under this hypothesis.*] [irr. from PMP:* *i > *e*]*
tuke-k *Termanu.* container made from a bamboo node used to store tobacco, sugar, milk or similar things. (J:652)
tuke-ʔ *Korbafo.*
tuke-ʔ *Bilbaa.*
tuke-ʔ *Rikou.*
tuke-k *Ba'a.*
(tuke-k ?) *Tii.*
tuke-ʔ *Dengka.*
tuke-ʔ *Oenale.*
tuke|ʔ *Kotos Amarasi.* piece of bamboo used as a water container.
tuke|ʔ *Molo.* bamboo container. (M:575)
Out-comparisons:
au toka *Fehan Tetun.* bamboo container. (Mo:187)

***tuku₁** *Rote.* scull, row. *Pattern:* k-6.
tuku *Termanu.* scull, row. (J:652)
tuku *Korbafo.*
tuku *Bokai.*
tuku *Bilbaa.*
tuʔu *Rikou.*
tuku *Ba'a.*
tuku *Tii.*
tuʔu *Dengka.*
tuʔu *Oenale.*
Out-comparisons:
tuku *Semau Helong.* paddle, pole (a boat), punt (a boat), push with pole. *Usage:* archaic.
tuku *Hawu.* row.
tuku *Sika.* scull. (Pareira and Lewis 1998:201)

***tuku₂** *Rote.* throw. *Pattern:* k-8/9.
tuʔu *Termanu.* throw. (J:661)
tuʔu *Korbafo.*
(tuʔu ?) *Bokai.*
tuku *Bilbaa.*

tuʔu *Rikou.*
tuʔu *Ba'a.*
tuʔu *Tii.*
tuʔu *Dengka.*
tuʔu *Oenale.*
Out-comparisons:
tuku *Hawu.* (J:661)
<tuku> *Kambera.* toss, throw. (On:505)

***tula** *PRM.* gebang palm. Corypha utan. *[Sporadic:* *a > *e* / _# in wRM.*]*
tula *Termanu.* gebang palm. (J:652)
tula *Korbafo.*
tula *Bokai.*
tula *Bilbaa.*
tula *Rikou.*
tula *Ba'a.*
tula *Tii.*
tule *Dengka.*
tule *Oenale.*
tune, tuni *Kotos Amarasi.* gebang palm. *[Sporadic:* vowel height harmony *e > *i* /uC_.*]*
tune *Molo.* gebang palm. (M:577)
Out-comparisons:
klutiʔ *Funai Helong.* gebang palm. *[irr. from PRM:* *a > *i] [Sporadic:* consonant metathesis *lVt > *tVl.]*
klutiʔ *Semau Helong.* gebang palm.

***tuli** *Rote.* stop by to visit when travelling. *Etym:* *tuluy.
tuli *Termanu.* drop in somewhere while passing by, 'come roaring along'. (J:653)
tuli *Korbafo.*
tuli *Bokai.*
tuli *Bilbaa.*
tuli *Rikou.*
tuli *Ba'a.*
tuli *Tii.*
tuli *Dengka.*
tuli *Oenale.*
Out-comparisons:
tuli *Semau Helong.* layover, stop by.
duli *Hawu.* (J:653)

***tuma** *PRM.* clothes louse. *Etym:* *tumah. *[Sporadic:* *a > *e* / _# in wRM.*]*
tuma *Termanu.* louse, clothes louse. (J:654)
tuma *Korbafo.*
tuma *Bokai.*
tuma *Bilbaa.*
tuma *Rikou.*
tuma *Ba'a.*
tuma *Tii.*
tume *Dengka.*
tume *Oenale.*
tume *Ro'is Amarasi.*
tume *Kotos Amarasi.* clothes louse.
tume *Amanuban.* body louse.
tume *Molo.* clothes louse. (M:578)
Out-comparisons:
ktumaʔ *Funai Helong.* clothes louse.

***tumbi** *Rote.* kind of tree that has soft wood.
tupi *Termanu.* kind of tree that has soft wood. (J:657)
tupi *Korbafo.*
tupi *Bokai.*
tupi *Rikou.*
tumpi *Ba'a.*
tumbi *Tii.*
tumbi *Dengka.*
tumbi *Oenale.*
Out-comparisons:
tuwi *Bima.* kind of soft wood. (Ismail et al. 1985:158)

***tumbu** *CERM.* heap, abundant. *Doublet:* ***numbu**. *Etym:* *tu(m)buq 'grow, germinate, sprout'. *[irr. from PRM:* *mb > *p* ~ *b* in Meto (forms with medial *b* are possibly from *tubuq with irr. *b = *b*)*]*
tupu~tupu (2) tu~tupu-k *Termanu.* 1) somewhere full of it, present in abundance. 2) heap, mass. (J:657)
tupu~tupu *Korbafo.*
tupu~tupu *Bokai.*
tupu~tupu *Bilbaa.*
tumpu~tumpu *Ba'a.*

na-ʔ|tupu, na-ʔ|tubu (2) ʔ|tubu *Kotos Amarasi.* 1) heap up, pile up. 2) hill.
a-ʔ|tubu *Molo.* hill. (M:573)
ta~tubu *Kusa-Manea.* mountain.
***tuna** *PRM.* freshwater eel. *Etym:* *tuna. *[Sporadic:* *a > *e* / _# in wRM*]*
tuna *Termanu.* eel. (J:654)
tuna *Korbafo.*
tuna *Bokai.*
tuna *Bilbaa.*
tuna *Rikou.* freshwater eel. (J:654; own field notes)
tuna *Ba'a.*
tuna *Tii.*
tune *Dengka.*
tune *Oenale.*
tune, tuni *Kotos Amarasi.* eel, sea-snake. *[Sporadic:* vowel height harmony *e > *i* /uC_.*]*
tune *Molo.* eel. (M:577)
Out-comparisons:
tuna *Helong.* (J:654)
tuna *East Tetun.* conger eel. Congridae. (Mo:190)
thuno *Waima'a.* eel.
***tuni** *PRM.* press.
tuni *Termanu.* press. (J:655)
tuni *Korbafo.*
tuni *Bokai.*
tuni *Bilbaa.*
tuni *Rikou.*
tuni *Ba'a.*
tuni *Tii.*
tuni *Dengka.*
tuni *Oenale.*
tuni *Meto.* (J:655)
***tunu1** *PRM.* stumble, stub one's toe. *[irr. from PRM:* *u > *a* in Koto Amarasi; *n > *nd* in Rikou and Landu*] [Form:* The Meto forms are from ***na-sa-tunu**, while the Rote are forms from ***na-ka-tunu**.*]*
na-ka-tunu *Termanu.* bump against something with the foot, stumble. (J:656)
na-ka-tunu *Korbafo.*
na-ka-tunu *Bokai.*
na-ka-tunu *Bilbaa.*
na-tundu *Landu.* (own field notes)
na-tundu *Rikou.*
na-ka-tunu *Ba'a.*
na-ka-tunu *Tii.*
na-ʔa-tunu *Dengka.*
na-ʔa-tunu *Oenale.*
na-stunan *Kotos Amarasi.* stub one's toe.
na-stuun *Molo.* stumbles. (M:517)
Out-comparisons:
tunun *Semau Helong.* stumble.
kedune *Hawu.* (J:656)
<tunjuru> *Kambera.* stub the tow, stumble. (On:509)
<tujuru> *Anakalang.*
<katunjura> *Mamboru.*
<kantunura> *Weyewa.*
tune (2) maatune *Kamarian.* 1) step, stamp with the foot or heel. *[Note:* also in Kaibobo, Nusa Laut, and Asilulu.*]* (van Ekris 1864:127) 2) stub the toe. *[Note:* also in Haruku and some varieties of Kaibobo.*]* (van Ekris 1864:303)
tahatune *Kaibobo.* stub the toe. (van Ekris 1864:303)
***tunu2** *PRM.* roast, grill. *Etym:* *tunu.
tunu *Termanu.* fry, bake without fat. (J:656)
tunu *Korbafo.*
tunu *Bokai.*
tunu *Bilbaa.*
tunu *Rikou.*
tunu *Ba'a.*
tunu *Tii.*
tunu *Dengka.*
tunu *Oenale.*
n-tunuʔ *Kotos Amarasi.* roast, grill.
<tunu> *Molo.* roast. (M:579)
tuun *Kusa-Manea.* burn.
Out-comparisons:
tunu *Semau Helong.* burn, roast.
tunu *East Tetun.* roast, bake (in an oven or over a fire). (Mo:190)

***turis** *PRM.* pigeon pea. Cajanus cajan. *Etym:* *tuduy 'agati Sesbania glandiflora' (Fox 1991:258) (Blust and Trussel (ongoing) reconstruct *tudiq for Sesbania grandiflora, however Fox (1991) gives a number of reflexes from western languages including Sunda **turuy** and Madurese **toroy** which indicate final *uy.). *[irr. from PMP: Ø > *s] [Form:* source of final *s unclear.*] [Semantics:* The seed pods of Sesbania grandiflora are edible. This appears to be the basis for the semantic link between Sesbania grandiflora and pigeon peas.*]*

tulis *Termanu.* pigeon peas. Cajanus cajan. (J:653)
tuli-ʔ *Korbafo.*
tuli-ʔ *Bokai.*
tuli-ʔ *Bilbaa.*
turis *Landu.* pigeon peas. (own field notes)
turis *Rikou.*
tulis *Ba'a.*
turis *Tii.*
tulis *Dengka.*
tu̯ris *Oenale.*
tu͡inis *Ro'is Amarasi.* pigeon pea.
tunis *Kotos Amarasi.* pigeon pea.
tunis *Molo.* pigeon peas. Cajanus Cajan. (M:580)

Out-comparisons:
tulis *Helong.* (J:653)
turis *Fehan Tetun.* pigeon pea: bush 1–2 metres tall with yellow pea flowers, dark green beans 3' long, cooked with rice. It grows mainly in the hills.
turis, tunis *East Tetun.* bush with a fruit pod similar to pea in looks and taste when tender. (Mo:191)
turiana *Kisar.* cashews.
tori *Hawu. [irr. from PRM:* *t = *d* correspondence (expect *d*)*]* (J:653)
ulis *Welaun.* pigeon pea. *[irr. from PRM:* *t = *Ø* correspondence (expect *t*)*]*

***turu** *PRM.* overflow, leak. *Etym:* *tuduq 'leak, drip, as a leaky roof; a drop of water'. *[irr. from PRM:* *r > *r* ~ *n* in Meto*]*

tu~tulu *Termanu.* overflow, flow off around the edge while pouring. (J:653)
tu~tulu *Korbafo.*
tu~tulu *Bokai.*
tu~tulu *Bilbaa.*
tu~turu *Rikou.*
tu~tulu *Ba'a.*
tu~turu *Tii.*
tu~tulu *Dengka.*
tu~turu *Oenale.*
turu *Kotos Amarasi.* shower.
oe tunu *Amanuban.* aqueduct, that is a piece of bamboo or half a hollowed areca stem, placed in a water source on a higher level from which the water flows. (M:579)
oe tulu *Molo.* aqueduct, that is a piece of bamboo or half a hollowed areca stem, placed in a water source on a higher level from which the water flows. (M:579)
oa ta~tunu|ʔ *Kusa-Manea.* bamboo with which to shower.

Out-comparisons:
tudu *Semau Helong.* leak. *[irr. from PMP:* *d = *d* (expect *l*)*]*
turu *East Tetun.* drip, fall in drips or drops. (Mo:191)
noro *Hawu.* leak through, permeate. (J:653)

***tusi₁** *PRM.* split gebang palm leaf. *[irr. from PRM:* *t > *d* in Rote*] [Form:* Alternately we could reconstruct ***ɗusi** and propose irr. *ɗ > *t* in Meto and Helong. Under this hypothesis either the Helong or Meto form would be a borrowing.*]*

dusi *Termanu.* cut the outside part of a young gebang palm leaf off from the middle part with a knife. (J:108)
dusi *Korbafo.*
dusi *Bokai.*
dusi *Bilbaa.*
dusi *Rikou.*
dusi *Ba'a.*
ɗusi *Tii.*
ɗusi *Dengka.*
ɗusi *Oenale.*
tuis muti? (2) tuis molo? *Molo.* 1) the split pale underside of a gebang palm leaf that is used for thread in *ikat* weaving. 2) split yellowish underside of gebang palm leaf from which ropes for horses are made. the stem is **tusi** = 'divide'; which in compounds undergoes metathesis of the final syllable. (M:581)
Out-comparisons:
tusi *Helong.* (J:108)

***tusi2** *PRM.* rub.
tusi *Termanu.* rub and pinch, rub and press. (J:657)
tusi *Korbafo.*
tusi *Bokai.*
tusi *Bilbaa.*
tusi *Rikou.*
tusi *Ba'a.*
tusi *Tii.*
tusi *Dengka.*
tusi *Oenale.*
n-tuis *Kotos Amarasi.* massage, rub.
n-tusi *Molo.* rub. (M:581)
Out-comparisons:
tusi *Semau Helong.* massage.
tusi *Fehan Tetun.* rub sacred betel on someone (e.g. so he becomes a **fukun** elder).

***tute** *PRM.* join. *[irr. from PRM:* *e > *i* in Nuclear-Rote; *e > *a* in Meto (and Helong)*]*
tuti *Termanu.* join, join on, set a piece. (J:658)
tuti *Korbafo.*
tuti *Bokai.*
tuti *Bilbaa.*
tuti *Rikou.*
tuti *Ba'a.*
tuti *Tii.*
tute *Dengka.*
tute *Oenale.*
n-tuta *Kotos Amarasi.* continue, join.
Out-comparisons:
tutan *Semau Helong.* join, connect, chain, link.

***tutu** *PRM.* beat, pound. *Etym:* *tuktuk 'knock, pound, beat; crush'.
tutu *Termanu.* hitting, pounding on something with the fist or with an object. (J:659)
tutu *Korbafo.*
tutu *Bokai.*
tutu *Bilbaa.*
tutu *Rikou.*
tutu *Ba'a.*
tutu *Tii.*
tutu *Dengka.*
tutu *Oenale.*
n-tutu *Kotos Amarasi.* pound, beat.
tutu *Molo.* pounds (iron). (M:582)
Out-comparisons:
tutu *Semau Helong.* pound.
tutu (2) tuku *East Tetun.* 1) peck (birds); to prod with the end of an object (Mo:191). 2) hit, strike, hammer (with an implement). (Mo:190)

***tuu1** *Morph:* ***tuu-f.** *PMeto.* knee. *Etym:* *tuhud.
tuu-f *Ro'is Amarasi.* knee.
tuu-f *Kotos Amarasi.* knee.
<tu'> *Molo.* knee. (M:572)
tuu-f *Kusa-Manea.* knee.
Out-comparisons:
tuur *East Tetun.* knee. (Mo:191)
rutuu *Hawu.* knee.

***tuu2** *Morph:* ***tuu-k.** *PnRote.* dry. *Etym:* *tuquR 'evaporate, dry up'.
tuu-k *Termanu.* dry. (J:646)
tuu-? *Korbafo.*
tuu-k *Bokai.*

tuu-ʔ *Bilbaa.*
tuu-ʔ *Rikou.*
tuu-k *Ba'a.*
tuu-k *Tii.*
Out-comparisons:
tuu *Semau Helong.* dry. *[Note:* Jonker (1908:646) gives Helong **ptuu**.*]*
vomeduʔu *Hawu.* dry of beans. (J:646)

***tuur** *nRM.* sit. *[Form:* Reflexes of *ŋg in Rote develop as though they were word medial. Meto final *n* attests an earlier final consonant. Tetun **tuur** shows that this was *r*, with subsequent (regular) *r > *l > *n* in Meto, and loss of the final consonant in nRote.*]*
na-ŋa-tuu-k (2) na-ŋa-tuu (3) tu~tuu-s (4) tu~tuu-k *Termanu.* 1) sit oneself down, sit, sit in a physical sense. 2) sit in a figurative sense. 3) a seat of piled stones under a tree, e.g. as is used in a **huus** festival, these seats are made for the spirits of dead people. 4) seat, chair. (J:647)
na-ŋa-tuu-ʔ *Korbafo.*
na-ŋa-tuu-k *Bokai.*
na-ka-tuu-ʔ *Bilbaa.*
na-tuu-ʔ *Rikou.*
na-ŋga-tuu-k *Ba'a.*
na-ŋga-tuu-k *Tii.*
n-tuun=oo-n *Ro'is Amarasi.* sit. *Lit:* 'seat oneself'. *Usage:* poetic.
n-tuun=oo-n *Kotos Amarasi.* sit. *Usage:* poetic.
Out-comparisons:
tuur *East Tetun.* sit down; to reside, inhabit; to settle; to rest or be resting. (Mo:191)
tuur *Ili'uun.* stay, live somewhere. (dJ:140)

U - u

***uas** *PRM.* jicama. Pachyrhizus erosus. *[Sporadic:* *Ø > ʔ /#_ in Oenale.*]*
uas *Termanu.* kind of tuber also called *uas* in Kupang. (J:662)
ua-ʔ *Korbafo.*
ua-ʔ *Bokai.*
ua-ʔ *Bilbaa.*
uas *Rikou.*
uas *Ba'a.*
uas *Tii.*
(ʔ)uas *Dengka.*
ʔuas *Oenale.*
ʔuas *Dela.*
uas *Kotos Amarasi.* jicama.
uas *Molo.* kind of herb that winds to the left, the tubers are eaten peeled. Pachyrhizus erosus. (M:584)
Out-comparisons:
uas *Fehan Tetun.* edible root plant.

***uat** *PRM.* vein, tendon, muscle, palm lines. *Doublet:* ***urat**. *Etym:* *uRat 'artery, blood vessel, blood vein; muscle; nerve; sinew; tendon; fibre; vein of a leaf; grain of wood; strand (of thread, rope); fishing line; root'.
ua-k *Termanu.* vein, tendon, muscle. (J:662)
ua-ʔ *Korbafo.*
ua-k *Bokai.*
ua-ʔ *Bilbaa.*
ua-ʔ *Rikou.*
ua-k *Ba'a.*
ua-k *Tii.*
ua-ʔ *Dengka.* a) vein, tendon, muscle. (J:662) b) palm line. (J:776)
ua-ʔ *Oenale.*
ua-ʔ *Dela.* vein.
ua-n *Ro'is Amarasi.* palm lines.
ua-f (2) uat *Kotos Amarasi.* 1) the lines on the palm of one's hands. 2) blue vein, especially of an animal's liver (traditionally used in divination). *[Note:* **keo-f** = 'vein, artery, blood vessel'.*]*

ua-n (2) uat *Amanuban.* 1) the lines on the palm of one's hands. 2) veins.
<ua> *Molo.* veins in the hand; lot, age. (M:583)
Out-comparisons:
ulat, udat *Funai Helong.* veins.
ulat *Semau Helong.* strand, sinew, vein, tendon, nerve, artery; fortune, fate, luck, profit; divination, palm reading.
uan (2) uat *Fehan Tetun.* 1) fortune. 2) veins, grain of wood.
uat *East Tetun.* veins, artery, nerves, tendons. (Mo:192)
orok *Kisar.* veins.

***uɗan** *PRM.* rain. *Etym:* *quzan. *[Sporadic: Ø > ʔ /#_* in Dela-Oenale.*]*
udan (2) uda *Termanu.* 1) rain. 2) raining. (J:662)
uda *Korbafo.*
uda *Bokai.*
uda *Bilbaa.*
uda *Rikou.*
udan *Ba'a.*
uɗan *Tii.*
(ʔ)uɗan *Dengka.*
ʔuɗan *Oenale.*
ʔuɗan *Dela.* rain.
urun, uurn *Ro'is Amarasi.* rain.
uran (2) na-ʔura *Kotos Amarasi.* 1) rain. 2) rain (v.). *[Form:* automatic glottal stop insertion between CV- prefix and #V-initial stem.*]*
ulan *Molo.* rain. (M:587)
uran *Kusa-Manea.* rain.
Out-comparisons:
ulan *Semau Helong.* rain.
udan *East Tetun.* rain. (Mo:192)
usa *Kemak.* rain.
uus *Mambae, South.* rain. (Grimes et al. 2014b:46)
usan *Galolen.* rain.
usan *Ili'uun.* rain, rainy season. (dJ:141)
okon *Kisar.* rain.
əʄi *Dhao.* rain. *[irr. from PMP:* *u > *i]*
əʄi *Hawu.* rain. *[irr. from PMP:* *u > *i]*

***ue** *PRM.* rattan. Calamus species. *Etym:* *quay. *[irr. from PRM:* *e > *e ~ a* in Meto*]*
ue *Termanu.* rattan. (J:663)
ue *Korbafo.*
ue *Bokai.*
ue *Bilbaa.*
ue *Landu.* rattan. (own field notes)
ue *Rikou.*
ue *Ba'a.*
ue *Tii.*
ue *Dengka.*
ue *Oenale.*
ue *Dela.* rattan.
ue, ua *Amanuban.* rattan.
ue *Amanatun.* rattan.
ua-l *Fatule'u.* rattan.
agoe-l *Amfo'an.* rattan.
ue *Molo.* rattan. (M:574)
ua *Kusa-Manea.* rattan. *[Form:* Final *a* is also in Uabau' in which *e > *a* /V_ does not occur.*]*
Out-comparisons:
u/latu *Funai Helong.* rattan.
ui_latu *Semau Helong.* rattan.
hue *Kemak.* rattan. *[irr. from PMP: Ø > h]*
oe *Welaun.* rattan.

***ufi** *PRM.* purple yam, greater yam. Dioscorea alata. *Etym:* *qubi 'yam Dioscorea alata'.
ufi *Termanu.* tuber. (J:664)
ufi *Korbafo.*
ufi *Bokai.*
ufi *Bilbaa.*
ufi *Rikou.*
ufi *Ba'a.*
ufi *Tii.*
ufi *Dengka.*
ufi *Oenale.*
ufi *Dela.* tuber.

rauk_ufi *Ro'is Amarasi.* greater yam. Dioscorea alata.

rauk_ufi *Kotos Amarasi.* kind of long yam.

laku ufi *Amanuban.* kind of red tuber. (own field notes)

Out-comparisons:

uhi *Helong.* (J:664)

uhi *East Tetun.* creeper with a single tuber. (Mo:193)

***-uki** *PRM.* have, own, exist, wealth. *Pattern:* k-9. *[Form:* The initial consonant correspondences in Rote and Meto cannot be reconciled. The remaining three segments show regular correspondences.*]*

suʔi *Termanu.* riches, treasures; wealth. (J:571)

suʔi *Korbafo.*

suʔi *Bokai.*

suki *Bilbaa.*

suʔi *Rikou.*

suʔi *Ba'a.*

suʔi *Tii.*

suʔi *Dengka.*

suʔi *Oenale.*

n-muʔi (2) mui͡ʔi|t (3) n-maʔ|muʔi (4) n-haʔmuʔi *Ro'is Amarasi.* 1) have, own, exist. 2) domestic animal. 3) poor. 4) suffer.

n-muʔi (2) muʔi|t (3) maʔ|muʔi (4) n-haʔmuʔi *Kotos Amarasi.* 1) have, own, exist. 2) domestic animal. 3) poor. 4) torment, torture, oppress.

n-muʔi *Molo.* possess. (M:332)

Out-comparisons:

kmukit (2) muki *Funai Helong.* 1) (domestic) animal. 2) rich.

muki (2) hmuki (3) hmukit *Semau Helong.* 1) exist, is, are, have, own. 2) wealth, possessions. 3) (domestic) animal.

mukit *East Tetun.* be lacking, become poor; poor, needy, etc. (Mo:144)

mukit *Dhao.* animal. (Charles Grimes pers. comm.)

***ule** *Rote.* wring, wring out. *Etym:* *puləs 'twist, wring'. *[irr. from PMP:* *p > Ø (expect *h); *ə > *e / _# (expect *ə > *a* in wRote, possibly *ə > *a > *e)]*

ule *Termanu.* wring, wring out. (J:665)

ule *Korbafo.*

ule *Bokai.*

ule *Bilbaa.*

ule *Rikou.*

ule *Ba'a.*

ule *Tii.*

ule *Dengka.*

ule *Oenale.*

***ulə** *Morph:* ***ulə-k**. *PRM.* worm, caterpillar. *Etym:* *quləj 'maggot, caterpillar, larva of a metamorphosing insect'. *[Form:* Meto **kaunaʔ** is probably from ***ka-ulə-k** with the nominal prefix ***ka-**.*]*

ule-k *Termanu.* worm, caterpillar in general, also: intestinal worms or maggots in a wound. (J:665)

ule-ʔ *Korbafo.*

ule-k *Bokai.*

ule-ʔ *Bilbaa.*

ule-ʔ *Rikou.*

ule-k *Ba'a.*

ule-k *Tii.*

ula *Dengka.*

ula *Oenale.*

ula *Dela.* caterpillar.

ka|una|ʔ *Ro'is Amarasi.* creature; snake.

ka|una|ʔ *Kotos Amarasi.* 1) creature. **kaunaʔ** is a life form category for all creatures whose primary means of locomotion is perceived of as crawling or walking. The other life forms are **koro** 'birds' and **ikaʔ** 'fish'. 2) snake, worm.

ka|una|ʔ *Molo.* insect. (M:188)

ka|una|ʔ *Kusa-Manea.* grub, caterpillar.

Out-comparisons:

ulas *Semau Helong.* maggot, grub, caterpillar.

ular *East Tetun.* worm, caterpillar, larva. (Mo:193)
orre *Kisar.* worms, e.g. worms found in corn.
ətu *Hawu.* maggot.

***uli** *Rote.* rudder. *Etym:* *qulin 'rudder; steer (a boat)'.
uli *Termanu.* rudder of a vessel. (J:666)
uli *Korbafo.*
uli *Bokai.*
uli *Bilbaa.*
uli *Rikou.*
uli *Ba'a.*
uli *Tii.*
uli *Dengka.*
uli *Oenale.*
na-uli *Dela.* control, drive (a ship).
Out-comparisons:
ulin *Semau Helong.* rudder.

***ulu** *PRM.* front, head hair. *Doublet:* ***hulu**. *Etym:* *qulu 'head; top part; leader, chief; headwaters; handle of a bladed implement; prow of a boat; first, first-born'.
ulu-k (2) ulu *Termanu.* 1) in front. 2) head hair. (J:666)
ulu-ʔ (2) ulu *Korbafo.*
ulu-k (2) ulu *Bokai.*
ulu-ʔ (2) ulu *Bilbaa.*
ulu-ʔ (2) ulu *Rikou.*
ulu-k (2) ulu *Ba'a.*
ulu-k (2) ulu *Tii.*
ulu-ʔ (2) ulu *Dengka.*
ulu-ʔ (2) ulu *Oenale.*
unu|ʔ *Ro'is Amarasi.* at first, past time.
unu|ʔ *Kotos Amarasi.* earlier, olden days.
un~unu|ʔ *Molo.* in the beginning. (M:588)
Out-comparisons:
ulu(n) *East Tetun.* head (of anything); the upper part; a position of leadership, a leader. (Mo:193)
ulu-t *Welaun.* head.
ulu/wakun *Kisar.* head.

***uma** *PRM.* house. *Etym:* *Rumaq. *[Sporadic: *a > e / _# in wRM; vowel height harmony *e > i /uC_ in Amarasi and Kusa-Manea.]*
uma *Termanu.* house. (J:667)
uma *Korbafo.*
uma *Bokai.*
uma *Bilbaa.*
uma *Rikou.*
uma *Ba'a.*
uma *Tii.*
ume *Dengka.*
ume *Oenale.*
ume *Dela.* house, hut, building.
umi *Ro'is Amarasi.* house, building.
umi, ume *Kotos Amarasi.* house, building.
ume *Molo.* house. (M:587)
umi *Kusa-Manea.* house.
Out-comparisons:
uma *Semau Helong.* house.
uma *East Tetun.* house, dwelling place; lair (of animals); cocoon (of insects). (Mo:193)
ruma *Ili'uun.* granary. (dJ:136)
rom *Kisar.* house, clan.

***umbu** *Morph:* ***umbu-k**. *PRM.* grandchild. *Etym:* *umpu 'grandparent/grandchild (reciprocal); ancestor'.
upu-k *Termanu.* grandchild. (J:670)
upu-ʔ *Korbafo.*
upu-k *Bokai.*
upu-ʔ *Bilbaa.*
upu=na *Landu.* grandchild. (own field notes)
upu-ʔ *Rikou.*
umpu-k *Ba'a.*
umbu-k *Tii.*
umbu-ʔ *Dengka.*
umbu-ʔ *Oenale.*
umbu-ʔ *Dela.* grandchild.
upu-f *Ro'is Amarasi.* grandchild.
upu-f, upuʔ *Kotos Amarasi.* grandchild.
upu-f *Molo.* grandchild. (M:590)
upu-f *Kusa-Manea.* grandchild.

Out-comparisons:
ana-upun, upu-ana *Semau Helong.* grandchildren.
upu-n *Kisar.* grandparent, grandchild.

***unə** *Morph:* ***unə-k**. *Rote.* scale of fish or reptile. *Etym:* *quhənap 'scale of fish' (PCEMP *qunəp/*qunap).
une-k *Termanu.* scale of a fish, or of a snake; also: scale on the feet of a rooster. (J:668)
une-ʔ *Korbafo.*
une-k *Bokai.*
une-ʔ *Bilbaa.*
une-ʔ *Rikou.*
une-k *Ba'a.*
une-k *Tii.*
una-ʔ *Dengka.*
una-ʔ *Oenale.*
una-ʔ *Dela.* scales of a fish or reptile.
Out-comparisons:
unaʔ *Semau Helong.* scale.

***undu** *Rote.* bore a hole, make a hole. *[irr. from PRM:* *u > *a* in nRote*]* *[Form:* I have reconstructed final *u (rather than *a) mainly on the basis of the external evidence from Hawu.*]*
una (2) una haʔi *Termanu.* 1) hollow something out with a tool, make an opening or hole somewhere (usually with a glowing pointed piece of iron). 2) start a fire with two pieces of wood by turning one piece of wood on top of another. (J:668)
una *Korbafo.*
una *Bokai.*
una *Bilbaa.*
unda *Rikou.*
una *Ba'a.*
unda *Tii.*
undu *Dengka.*
undu *Oenale.*
Out-comparisons:
pudu *Hawu.* bore; make a fire.

***ura** *Morph:* ***ura-k**. *Rote.* palm lines, lines/sinews in the liver of a dead animal (traditionally used for divination). *Doublet:* ***uat**. *Etym:* *uRat 'artery, blood vessel, blood vein; muscle; nerve; sinew; tendon; fibre; vein of a leaf; grain of wood; strand (of thread, rope); fishing line; root'. *[minority from PMP:* *R = *r (expect Ø)*]*
ula-k *Termanu.* the lines of the hand, [...] the lines or sinews of the liver of a dead animal. (J:664f)
ula-ʔ *Korbafo.*
ula-k *Bokai.*
ula-ʔ *Bilbaa.*
ura-ʔ *Rikou.* *[Note:* not known by my consultants.*]*
ula-k *Ba'a.*
ura-k *Tii.*
ura-ʔ *Oenale.*
Out-comparisons:
urat *East Tetun.* spleen (of pigs); the word used to describe the many practices in the various customs for determining the cause of any problem, or the guilty party, or in foretelling the future. (Mo:193)

***usi1** *Rote.* pursue, chase away. *Etym:* *qusiR 'pursuit (as of enemies or game)'. *[irr. from PRM:* *Ø > *h* in Tii and Lole; *Ø > *n* in Dengka*]* *[Sporadic:* *i > *e* /_*R# in Dengka.*]*
usi *Termanu.* pursue, hunt. (J:671)
usi *Korbafo.*
usi *Bokai.*
usi *Bilbaa.*
usi *Rikou.*
usi *Ba'a.*
husi *Lole.* chase away, expel. (Zacharias et al. 2014)
husi *Tii.*
nuse *Dengka.*

***usi2** *PMeto.* king, lord. *Etym:* *usi 'relative of the third ascending or descending generation' (PCMP). *[History:* Although Middelkoop

(1972:592) makes a connection between this form and Javanese *gusti* 'lord, master', it is difficult to account for the lack of an initial consonant in Meto under a borrowing hypothesis. Furthermore, the pervasiveness of the term being used for deities that are central to the cosmology of the Atoni indicates this is unlikely to be a recently borrowed term.*]*

u͡isi-f, usiʔ (2) uis neno *Ro'is Amarasi.* 1) king. 2) God. *[History:* In traditional Atoni thought **uis neno** is the supreme god who is the source of all (see Schulte Nordholt 1972:141).*]*

usi-f, usiʔ (2) uis neno *Kotos Amarasi.* king, master, lord, custodian.

usif, usiʔ (2) usif neno *Molo.* 1) lord. 2) the lord of heaven. (M:592)

(2) uis neno (3) uis paah *Insana.* 2) the lord of heaven, the supreme god. 3) the lord of earth, the 'pendant' of **uis neno**. *[History:* 'Uis Pah [sic] is Uis Neno's pendant. They form a dual divinity, in which Uis Neno's superiority is obvious. That is not to say that Uis Pah has emanated from Uis Neno. They are two distinct entities, but are inseparable from each other — one cannot exist: without the other.' (Schulte Nordholt 1972:145)*]*

(2) usneno *Kusa-Manea.* God.

Out-comparisons:

usi *East Tetun.* title of nobility; a former manner of address to those with the rights of royalty. (Mo:194)

osi *Buru.* great-grandparent, great-grandchild. (Grimes and Grimes 2020:689)

***utan** *PRM.* vegetables. *Etym:* *qutan 'small, wild herbaceous plants; scrub-land, bush'.

uta-k, uta ai doo *Termanu.* all kinds of vegetables or herbs. (J:671)

uta ai doo *Korbafo.*

uta ai doo *Bokai.*

uta ai doo *Bilbaa.*

uta ʔai doo *Rikou.*

uta ai doo *Ba'a.*

uta-k, uta ai ɗoo *Tii.*

uta-ʔ, uta ai ɗoo *Dengka.*

uta-ʔ, uta ai ɗoo *Oenale.*

uta-ʔ *Dela.* vegetables.

utu|k, uta|k *Ro'is Amarasi.* vegetables; pumpkin, squash.

utan *Kotos Amarasi.* vegetables.

utan *Molo.* vegetables. (M:593)

Out-comparisons:

utan *Semau Helong.* vegetable.

utan *Ili'uun.* pea, bean. (dJ:141)

ʔuta *Keo.* vegetables. *[Note:* language of central Flores ISO 639-3 [xxk].*]* (Baird 2002:583)

***uti** *Morph:* ***uti-k**. *PRM.* penis. *Etym:* *qutin.

uti-k *Termanu.* penis. (J:671f)

uti-ʔ *Korbafo.*

uti-k *Bokai.*

uti-ʔ *Bilbaa.*

uti-ʔ *Rikou.*

uti-k *Ba'a.*

uti-k *Tii.*

tuti-ʔ *Dengka.*

uti-ʔ *Oenale.*

uti-ʔ *Dela.*

uti-n *Ro'is Amarasi.* penis.

uti-f *Kotos Amarasi.* penis.

<uti> *Molo.* penis. (M:594)

Out-comparisons:

uti *Semau Helong.* penis.

***uu** *Morph:* ***na-ŋga-uu**. *Rote.* oink. *Etym:* *uu 'moaning sound'. *[Semantics:* onomatopoeia.*]*

na-ŋa-uu, na-ŋa-u~uu, uu~uu *Termanu.* imitation of the sound of a pig when it wants food: **bafi=a uu~uu**; also said of people in the sense of: grunt, grumble. (J:662)

na-ka-u~uu *Korbafo.*
na-ka-uu *Rikou.*
na-ŋga-u~uu *Ba'a.*
na-ʔa-uu *Dengka.*

***uut** *nRM.* chaff. *[History:* Blust and Trussel (ongoing) reconstruct *uta on the basis of Kambera **uta** and Selaru **ut**.*]*
uu-k *Termanu.* chaff, bran. (J:662)
uu-ʔ *Korbafo.*
uu-k *Bokai.*
uu-ʔ *Bilbaa.*
uu-ʔ *Rikou.*
uu-k *Ba'a.*
uu-k *Tii.*
uut *Kotos Amarasi.* flour.
uut (2) ut~uut *Molo.* 1) corn that has been roasted and then crushed. 2) crunched to dust. (M:593)
Out-comparisons:
uut *Helong.* (J:662)
uut *East Tetun.* dust, any unwanted fine powder. (Mo:194)
huut *Sundanese.* bran. *[Note:* language of east Java ISO 639-3 [sun].*]* (Coolsma 1913: 234)
oot, uot *Balinese.* husks, thrown away with the rice stalks. *[Note:* language of Bali ISO 639-3 [ban].*]* (Kersten 1984:432)

W - w

wadi** *PRM.* same-sex younger sibling. *Etym:* *huaji 'younger sibling of the same sex; younger parallel cousin of the same sex'. *[Sporadic:* Ø > ʔ /#_ in Dela-Oenale.*]* *[Form:* PwRM ***odi**, PnRote ***fadi]*
fadi-k *Termanu.* younger brother or sister. (J:119)
fadi-ʔ *Korbafo.*
fadi-k *Bokai.*
fadi-ʔ *Bilbaa.*
fadi=na *Landu.* younger sibling. (own field notes)
fadi-ʔ *Rikou.*
fadi-k *Ba'a.*
fadi-k *Tii.*
(ʔ)odi-ʔ *Dengka.*
ʔodi-ʔ *Oenale.*
ʔodi *Dela.* younger sibling.
oriʔ *Ro'is Amarasi.* same-sex younger sibling.
ori-f *Kotos Amarasi.* same-sex younger sibling.
oli-f *Molo.* younger brother or sister. (M:403)
oriʔ *Kusa-Manea.* same-sex younger sibling.
Out-comparisons:
palin *Semau Helong.* younger brother/sister.
ali-n *East Tetun.* younger brother or sister. (Mo:3)
walin *Welaun.* younger sibling.
ali(n) *Ili'uun.* man's younger brother, father's brother's son or daughter (younger than himself), mother's sister's son or daughter (younger than himself), a woman's younger sister, father's brother's son or daughter (younger than herself), mother's sister's son or daughter (younger than herself). (dJ:112)
ari *Dhao.* younger sibling.
ari *Hawu.* younger sibling.

***wani** *PRM.* honey bee. *Etym:* *wani. *[Form:* PwRM ***oni**, PnRote ***fani**.*]*
fani *Termanu.* bee, honeybee. (J:125)
fani *Korbafo.*
fani *Bokai.*
fani *Bilbaa.*
fani *Rikou.*
fani *Ba'a.*
fani *Tii.*
oni *Dengka.*

oni *Oenale.*
oni *Dela.* bee.
oni *Ro'is Amarasi.* sugar.
oni *Kotos Amarasi.* sugar; bee.
oni *Molo.* bees. (M:405)
oni *Kusa-Manea.* bee.

Out-comparisons:
pani *Semau Helong.* bee.
wani *Fehan Tetun.* bee, wasp.
uani(n) *East Tetun.* honey bee. (Mo:192)
wani *Kisar.* bee.

#

#aɗulara *Rote.* kind of yellow wood. *Borrowed from:* Hawu **aʃu** 'wood' + **lara** 'yellow'.
adulala *Termanu.* kind of wood that yields a yellow dye which is used in weaving. Maclura cochinchinensis. (J:3; Heyne 1950:551, lvi)
adulala *Korbafo.*
adulala *Bokai.*
adulala *Bilbaa.*
adulala *Rikou.*
adulala *Ba'a.*
aɗulala *Tii.*
aɗulala *Dengka.*
aɗurala *Oenale.*
Out-comparisons:
aʃu + lara *Hawu.* wood + yellow.

#badʒu *PRM.* garment. *Borrowed from:* Malay *baju*, ultimately Persian.
badu *Termanu.* garment; wear a garment, have a garment on. (J:19)
ɓaruk *Dela.* pants.
baru *Kotos Amarasi.* shirt.

#baʔat *Morph:* **#ka-baʔat**. *PMeto.* root. *Doublet:* ***oka2**. *Etym:* *wakaR. *[irr. from PMP:* *w > *b*]* *[History:* Probably borrowing from Helong into PMeto. The opposite direction of borrowing cannot easily explain medial *k* in Helong. Note, however, that PMP *w > *b* is irregular in both Helong and Meto.*]*
ʔbaʔa-f *Kotos Amarasi.* root.
ʔbaʔat *Amfo'an.* root.
ʔbaʔat *Molo.* root of a tree or plant. (M:39)
baʔa-f *Kusa-Manea.* root.
Out-comparisons:
kbakat *Funai Helong.* root.

#baluk *Rote.* boat with one or two masts and no outrigger. *Borrowed from:* Malay *baluk*, ultimately Arabic *falawakat*. *[History:* Blust and Trussel (ongoing) make a PMP reconstruction on the basis of this Rote form and Old Javanese, though they suggest the Rote form may be a loan. The Termanu form is almost certainly a Malay loan.*]*
(ofa) balu-k *Termanu.* boat with one or two masts and no outrigger. (J:29)

#bane *PRM.* bowl. *Borrowed from:* ultimately Tamil *pāṉai* [pa:nai] 'large earthen pot or vessel' (Hoogervorst 2016).
bane *Termanu.* a kind of earthenware jug with a narrow neck and wide belly, among other things used to store dyes. (J:29)
bane *Korbafo.*
bane *Bokai.*
bane *Bilbaa.*
bane *Rikou.*
bane *Ba'a.*
ɓane *Tii.*
bane *Dengka.*
ɓane *Oenale.*
ʔ|fane|ʔ *Kotos Amarasi.* kind of bowl traditionally made from the husk of a large pumpkin and used to carry water.
ʔ|fane|ʔ *Molo.* a plate made from pumpkin skin. (M:110)

[#]**bnapa** *Morph:* [#]**bnapa-f**. *PMeto.* side, ribs. *Borrowed from:* probably Helong into Meto before *l > *n*. *bl* is a common cluster in Helong with more than 25 attestations in Balle and Cameron (2014) while *bn* is rare in Meto with only 7 attestations in my current Kotos Amarasi database.

bnapa-n *Ro'is Amarasi.* hips.

bnapa-f *Kotos Amarasi.* side, ribs; slope, incline.

bnapa-n *Molo.* side. (M:74)

Out-comparisons:

seen blapas *Funai Helong.* rib.

blapas *Semau Helong.* rib(cage); side, part; mate, partner.

[#]**[b/p]andut** *PRM.* torch. *Borrowed from:* ultimately Malay *panjut* [paɲdʒut].

banu-k *Termanu.* torch with wick, also: light. (J:30)

banu-ʔ *Korbafo.*

banu-k *Bokai.*

banu-ʔ *Bilbaa.*

bandu-ʔ *Rikou.*

baru-ʔ *Oepao.* crushed seeds of the fruit of the Ceylon Oak (*kusambi*) used to make a torch. (own field notes)

banu-k *Ba'a.*

ɓandu-k *Tii.*

bandut *Dengka.*

paru *Ro'is Amarasi.* lamp, torch.

paku *Kotos Amarasi.* lamp, torch.

paku *Molo.* lamp. (M:414)

Out-comparisons:

hadut *Semau Helong.* lamp, lantern. *[Note:* Jonker (1908:30) gives Helong **padut**.*]*

badut *East Tetun.* candles made from **kamii** [candlenut] and other plants. (Mo:8)

badu *Dadu'a.* lamp. (Penn 2006:52)

paʧu *Ili'uun.* lamp made of a fruit called **too** in Wetar and *bintanggar* in Ambon Malay. (dJ:133)

waʈu *Kisar.* lamp.

[#]**bruuk** *PMeto.* trousers. *Borrowed from:* Dutch *broek* [bru:k].

bruku *Ro'is Amarasi.* trousers. *[Form:* This form may be a result of reanalysis of **bruuk** as a metathesised form with back formation to derive an unmetathesised form.*]*

bruuk *Kotos Amarasi.* trousers.

Out-comparisons:

bduuk *Funai Helong.* trousers.

bluuk *Semau Helong.* trousers.

[#]**bukae** *PMeto.* eat, dine. *Borrowed from:* the direction of borrowing between Meto and Tetun is unclear though the wider semantic range in Meto may point to it being the donor. *Pattern:* k-6/9.

n-bukae *Ro'is Amarasi.* eat and/or drink, implies a social activity which is carried out with other people.

n-bukae *Kotos Amarasi.* eat and/or drink, implies a social activity which is carried out with other people.

n-bukae *Amfo'an.* eat. *[Semantics:* Cannot mean 'drink'.*]*

bukae|l (2) n-bukae *Molo.* 1) provisions. 2) eat. (M:88)

Out-comparisons:

bukae *East Tetun.* provisions for a trip, food taken on a journey. (Mo:18)

[#]**ɓaɓa** *PRM.* help; join with someone in doing something, do something together with someone, help someone. *Borrowed from:* ultimately a Chinese language, e.g. Hokkien 幫忙 *pang-bâng* [paŋ˥baŋ˦], Mandarin 帮帮 *bāng bāng* [baŋ˥baŋ˥] (imperative form). (J:18)

baba *Korbafo.*

baba *Bokai.*

baba *Bilbaa.*

baba *Rikou.*

baba *Ba'a.*
ɓaɓa *Tii.*
baba *Dengka.*
ɓaɓa *Oenale.*
n-baba *Kotos Amarasi.* help.
n-baba *Molo.* helps. (M:39)
Out-comparisons:
baba *Semau Helong.* follow together.

#**ɓanda** *Rote.* thing, animal. *Borrowed from:* ultimately Sanskrit *bhāṇḍa* [bʱaːɳɖa] 'goods', compare Malay *barang* 'thing'.
bana *Termanu.* animal, foremost a quadruped. (J:29)
bana *Korbafo.*
bana *Bokai.*
bana *Bilbaa.*
banda *Landu.* animal. (own field notes)
banda *Rikou.*
bara *Oepao.* (J:x)
bana *Ba'a.*
ɓanda *Tii.*
banda *Dengka.*
ɓanda *Oenale.*
bare|ʔ *Kotos Amarasi.* thing, stuff.
bale|ʔ *Amanatun.* cargo. (M:46)
bale mnasiʔ *Molo.* heirloom. (M:46)
Out-comparisons:
berai, barai, badain *Fehan Tetun.* thing.
ɓada (2) ɓara *Hawu.* 1) animal. 2) things, belongings, possessions; material; clothes.
baɖʐa *Dhao.* animal.

#**ɓasiu** *Rote.* dish. *Borrowed from:* Portuguese *bacio* [basiu].
basiu *Termanu.* kind of non-indigenous dish decorated with a flower pattern. (J:32)
basiu *Korbafo.*
basiu *Bokai.*
basiu *Bilbaa.*
basiu *Rikou.*
basiu *Ba'a.*
ɓasiu *Tii.*
basiu *Dengka.*
ɓasiu *Oenale.*
Out-comparisons:
ɓahiu *Hawu.* (J:32)

#**ɓesi** *PRM.* iron. *Borrowed from:* Malay *besi* [bəsi] ultimately from an Indic language, such as Sanskrit *vāśī* [vaːʃiː] 'sharp pointed knife or blade', as proposed by Hoogervorst (2016:566).
besi *Termanu.* iron. (J:46)
besi *Korbafo.*
besi *Bokai.*
besi *Bilbaa.*
besi *Rikou.*
besi *Ba'a.*
ɓesi *Tii.*
besi *Dengka.*
ɓesi *Oenale.*
besi *Kotos Amarasi.* knife.
besi *Molo.* iron, knife. (M:60)

#**ɓuŋga** *Rote.* decorative flower. *Doublet:* ***ɓuna**. *Borrowed from:* Malay *bunga* [buŋa].
buŋa *Termanu.* flower, in the sense of an ornamental flower. (J:64)
buŋa *Korbafo.*
buŋa *Bokai.*
buka *Rikou.*
buŋga *Ba'a.*
ɓuŋga *Tii.*
buŋga *Dengka.*

#**ɗaŋgan** *PRM.* trade, commerce. *Borrowed from:* Malay *dagang.*
daŋan *Termanu.* trading, trade. (J:75)
daŋan *Korbafo.*
daŋan *Bokai.*
daŋan *Bilbaa.*
dakan *Rikou.*
daŋgan *Ba'a.*
ɗaŋgan *Tii.*
ɗaŋgan *Dengka.*
ɗaŋgan *Oenale.*
n-rakan *Ro'is Amarasi.* trade, commerce.
n-rakan *Kotos Amarasi.* trade, commerce.
a-lakan *Molo.* trader. (M:18)

Out-comparisons:

dakaŋ *Semau Helong.* commerce.

raka *East Tetun.* buy small quantities; to buy in halves, to buy a share. (Mo:158)

ʤagan *Ili'uun.* trade. (dJ:113)

#**ɗoit** *PRM.* money. *Borrowed from:* Dutch *duit* [dœyt].

doi-k *Termanu.* money. (J:95)

ɗoi-ʔ *Dela.* money.

roit *Ro'is Amarasi.* money.

roit *Kotos Amarasi.* money.

loit moloʔ *Molo.* copper money. (M:282)

Out-comparisons:

duit *Semau Helong.* money, coin.

loit balanda *Fehan Tetun.* old Dutch money. This is more valuable, as not affected by inflation. *Borrowed from:* Meto **loit**.

doi *Hawu.* money, currency, cash, funds.

#**ʤala** *PRM.* cast net. *Borrowed from:* ultimately Sanskrit *jāla* [ʤaːla], perhaps via Malay *jala*.

dala *Termanu.* cast-net. (J:71)

dala *Korbafo.*

dala *Bokai.*

dala *Bilbaa.*

dala *Rikou.*

dala *Ba'a.*

ɗala *Tii.*

ɗala *Dengka.*

ɗala *Oenale.*

sala *Molo.* kind of net. (M:471)

Out-comparisons:

sala *Semau Helong.* cast net.

ʃala *Dhao.* cast-net.

ʃala *Hawu.* cast-net.

#**ʤinela** *nRM.* window. *Borrowed from:* Portuguese *janela* [ʒanɛla], with reported regional variant *jinela*, ultimately from Vulgar Latin *januella* diminutive of *iānua* 'door'.

dinela *Termanu.* window. (J:88)

ɗinela *Tii.* window. (Grimes et al. 2014a)

eno_sneer *Kotos Amarasi.* window. *[Form:* reanalysis as **sneer=aa** [ˈsnɛːrɐ] with the determiner =**aa** attached to a consonant final stem. **enoʔ** = 'door'.*]*

#**en** *PMeto.* similar, like; to, towards, irrealis locative indicating a location where someone will be in the future. *Borrowed from:* probably Helong into Meto before *l > *n*. *[irr. from PRM:* *e > *o* in Nuclear Meto*]*

en *Ro'is Amarasi.* a) like, similar to. b) to, towards, irrealis locative indicating a location where someone will be in the future.

on *Kotos Amarasi.* a) like, similar to. b) to, towards, irrealis locative indicating a location where someone will be in the future.

on ii *Molo.* so is it, in this way. (M:405)

on *Kusa-Manea.* like, similar to.

Out-comparisons:

el *Semau Helong.* like, similar, as; to, towards.

#**etu** *PMeto.* field. *Borrowed from:* the direction of borrowing between Meto and Tetun is unclear though the wider semantic range in Tetun indicates it is probably the donor.

etu *Kotos Amarasi.* field. *Usage:* poetic.

etu *Amfo'an.* field. *Usage:* poetic.

etu *Molo.* land for the construction of a field for the king. (M:105)

Out-comparisons:

etun (2) liman etun (3) ai tuur etun (4) manu etun *East Tetun.* 1) sustenance, nourishment, provisions. 2) the portion or share or levy of food that each person has to meet at celebrations, funerals, etc. *[Form:* **liman** = 'arm/ hand'.*]* 3) the part of the crop belonging to the king when the garden is made in another district or kingdom. *[Form:* **ai tuur** = 'tree stump'.*]* 4) the part of the crop belonging to the king when the crop is made in the proper district of the farmer. *[Form:* **manu** = 'chicken, bird'.*]* (Mo:30)

#**faɗuli** *PRM.* care for. *Borrowed from:* Arabic *faḍuli* [fadˤuli] 'curious, inquisitive', compare Malay *peduli.*

na-fa-duli *Termanu.* care for someone. (J:107)

na-fa-duli *Korbafo.*

na-fa-duli *Bokai.*

na-fa-duli *Bilbaa.*

na-fa-duli *Rikou.*

na-fa-duli *Ba'a.*

na-fa-ɗuli *Tii.*

na-fa-ɗuli *Dengka.*

na-fa-ɗuli *Oenale.*

n-fairori (2) n-pairori *Kotos Amarasi.* 1) care, pay attention to. 2) prepare; convalesce. *[Form:* Jonker (1908:107) gives Meto **filoli, firoir**.*]*

#**fei** *Rote.* file. *Borrowed from:* Dutch *vijl* [fɛil].

fei *Termanu.* file. (J:130)

fei *Korbafo.*

fei *Bokai.*

fei *Bilbaa.*

fei *Rikou.*

fei *Ba'a.*

fei *Tii.*

fei *Dengka.*

fei *Oenale.*

Out-comparisons:

vei *Hawu.* (J:130)

#**filanda** *Rote.* European person. *Borrowed from:* Malay *belanda* [bəlanda], ultimately from Dutch *Hollander* 'person from Holland'.

filana *Termanu.* Dutchmen, European in general, considered more polite than **olana**. (J:135)

fili_ana *Korbafo.*

filana *Bokai.*

fila_ana *Bilbaa.*

filanda *Rikou.*

filanda *Oepao.* (own field notes)

filana *Ba'a.*

filanda *Tii.*

filanda *Dengka.*

filanda *Oenale.*

Out-comparisons:

balanda *East Tetun.* Dutchman. (Mo:9)

walaṱe *Kisar.* Dutch, foreigner with white skin; foreign, manufactured.

#**fukar** *PMeto.* spices, seasonings. *Borrowed from:* probably Tetun into Meto given final *r*. Final *r* is rare in native Meto words (there are only about a dozen examples of final *r* in native words in my Kotos Amarasi database), but not uncommon in Tetun. The presence of this word in Galolen (whether native or borrowed) also probably indicates that Tetun is the ultimate donor. *Pattern:* k-6/9.

fukar *Kotos Amarasi.* herbs, spices, seasonings. *Usage:* archaic.

fukal *Molo.* seasonings. (M:131)

fukul *Timaus.* herbs and spices. *[Form:* regular assimilation of *a in final closed syllables.*]*

Out-comparisons:

fukar *East Tetun.* season, spice. (Mo:37)

ai fukar *Galolen.* cooking spices.

#**hada|k** *PMeto.* raised platform. *Borrowed from:* the direction of borrowing between Proto-Meto and Helong is unclear.

harak *Kotos Amarasi.* raised platform.

<hala> *Molo.* raised platform. (M:137)

Out-comparisons:

khadaŋ *Funai Helong.* platform.

hadaŋ *Semau Helong.* bed.

#hadat *PRM.* custom, tradition. *Borrowed from:* ultimately Arabic *'ādat* [ʕaːdat] 'custom, habit'.
hada-k *Termanu.* custom, morals. (J:151)
harat *Ro'is Amarasi.* custom, tradition.
harat *Kotos Amarasi.* custom, tradition.
Out-comparisons:
hadat *Semau Helong.* custom, tradition, customary law.
hadat, adat *Fehan Tetun.* usage, custom. (Mo:42)
hadʒak *Ili'uun.* custom. (dJ:155)

#horo *Rote.* saw. *Borrowed from:* ultimately probably Portuguese *corte* [kɔrtə].
holo *Termanu.* saw; cut in a sawing manner. (J:189)
holo *Korbafo.*
holo *Bokai.*
holo *Bilbaa.*
horo *Rikou.*
holo *Ba'a.*
horo *Tii.*
holo *Dengka.*
horo *Oenale.*
Out-comparisons:
holat *Semau Helong.* saw.
korat *East Tetun.* cut. (Mo:117)

#huta *Morph:* **#huta-k**. *Rote.* debt, fine. *Borrowed from:* Malay *hutang.*
huta-k *Termanu.* debt, financial debt, fine. (J:198)
huta-ʔ *Korbafo.*
huta-k *Bokai.*
huta-ʔ *Bilbaa.*
huta-ʔ *Rikou.*
huta-k *Ba'a.*
huta-k *Tii.*
huta-ʔ *Dengka.*
huta-ʔ *Oenale.*

#kaba *PRM.* copper wire. *Borrowed from:* Malay *kawat. Pattern:* k-1.
(tali) kafa *Termanu.* copper wire. (J:212)
kafa *Korbafo.*
kafa *Bokai.*
kafa *Bilbaa.*
kafa *Ba'a.*
kafa *Tii.*
kafa *Dengka.*
kafa *Oenale.*
tain kaba *Molo.* telephone wire. (M:164)
Out-comparisons:
kaba *Semau Helong.* (J:212)

#kaɓas *PRM.* cotton. *Borrowed from:* ultimately Sanskrit *kārpāsa* [kaːrpaːsa]. Reflexes of *k probably indicate this term probably dispersed after the break-up of PRM. *Pattern:* k-irr.
(ʔ)abas *Termanu.* cotton shrub; the raw material, cotton; cotton fruit; yarn, thread. (J:1f)
(ʔ)aba-ʔ *Korbafo.*
kaba-ʔ *Bilbaa.*
ʔabas *Rikou.*
(ʔ)abas *Ba'a.*
(ʔ)aɓas *Lole.* cotton. (Zacharias et al. 2014)
(ʔ)aɓas *Tii.*
(ʔ)abas *Dengka.*
ʔaɓas *Oenale.*
ʔaɓas *Dela.* thread.
kabas *Ro'is Amarasi.* cotton.
ʔabas *Kotos Amarasi.* cotton.
ʔabas *Molo.* cotton plant, also cotton thread. (M:2)
ʔabas *Kusa-Manea.* cotton.
Out-comparisons:
kabas *East Tetun.* cotton or cotton plant. (Mo:92)

#kadera *PRM.* chair. *Borrowed from:* Portuguese *cadeira* [kadeira]. *Pattern:* k-1.
kadela *Termanu.* chair. (J:211)
kaɗela *Lole.* chair. (Zacharias et al. 2014)
kaɗera *Tii.* chair. (Grimes et al. 2014a)

kanreer [kandˈrɛːr] *Ro'is Amarasi.* chair. *[Form:* reanalysis as **kanreer=aa** [ˈkandrɛːrɐ] with the determiner =**aa** attached to a consonant final stem.*]*

kanleel *Molo.* chair. (M:180)

Out-comparisons:

kdeda *Funai Helong.* chair.

dela *Semau Helong.* chair.

kader *East Tetun.* chair. (Mo:93)

#**kaɗo** *PRM.* sack. *Borrowed from:* Malay *karung/kandung. Pattern:* k-2b.

ka~kado (2) (ka~)kado-k *Termanu.* 1) carry betel (etc.) in a bag/sack formed by the fold of cloth or a sarong. 2) such a bag/sack. (J:211)

ka~kado *Korbafo.*

ka~kado *Bokai.*

na-kado *Bilbaa.*

(ʔ)a~(ʔ)ado *Rikou.*

ka~kado, kali_kado *Ba'a.*

kali_kaɗo *Tii.*

taʔi_(ʔ)aɗo *Dengka.*

(ʔ)a~(ʔ)aɗo, taʔi_(ʔ)aɗo *Oenale.*

ʔkaroʔ *Kotos Amarasi.* sack.

<kalo> *Molo.* bag, sack. (M:175)

Out-comparisons:

karon *East Tetun.* a sack made from sacking; a bale; sacking or hessian; the bag at the bottom of the casting net. (Mo:102)

kaɗo *Hawu.* (J:211)

#**kameru|ʔ** *PMeto.* rice ear bug. <u>*Leptocorisa oratorius*</u>. *Borrowed from:* Tetun into Kusa-Manea. *[Note:* While it is possible to reconstruct Proto-Flores-Lembata *kəmeruŋ which is cognate with Tetun **kamerun** (thus pointing to an earlier regional Austronesian term), the absence of this term in any Rote-Meto language apart from Kusa-Manea indicates that Kusa-Manea has borrowed this term from Tetun.*]*

kameruʔ *Kusa-Manea.* rice ear bug. <u>*Leptocorisa oratorius*</u>.

Out-comparisons:

kamerun *Fehan Tetun.* small (1/2-inch-long) bug that damages rice by sucking it, so that the grain doesn't form. <u>*Leptocorisa oratorius*</u>. *[Semantics:* Indonesian gloss given as *walang sangit* = 'rice ear bug'.*]*

kamiru *East Tetun.* beetle. *[Semantics:* This is given as identical to **diru** which is glossed as: 'beetle which attacks palm trees'.*]* (Mo:100)

kəmeruŋ *Lamaholot, Ile Mandiri.* rice ear bug. <u>*Leptocorisa oratorius*</u>. *Usage:* Lewoingu dialect. *[Note:* language of east Flores ISO 639-3 [slp].*]* (Klamer 2015b)

kəmoro(ŋ) *Central Lembata.* rice ear bug. <u>*Leptocorisa oratorius*</u>. (Fricke 2015)

kameruŋ *Alorese.* rice ear bug. <u>*Leptocorisa oratorius*</u>. *Usage:* Alor Besar village. (Moro 2016, LexiRumah)

kameliŋ *Abui.* rice ear bug. <u>*Leptocorisa oratorius*</u>. *[Note:* non-Austronesian language of Alor ISO 693-3 [abz].*]* *[Semantics:* English gloss given as 'cockroach' in Kratochvíl (2007:467).*]* (Saad 2015, LexiRumah)

#**kamba** *Rote.* buffalo. *Borrowed from:* Malay *kerbau. Pattern:* k-2/3.

kapa *Termanu.* buffalo. (J:221)

kapa *Korbafo.*

kapa *Bokai.*

kapa *Bilbaa.*

ʔapa *Landu.* buffalo. (own field notes)

ʔapa *Rikou.*

kampa *Ba'a.*

kamba *Tii.*

(ʔ)amba *Dengka.*

ʔamba *Oenale.*

ʔamba *Dela.* buffalo, water buffalo.

Out-comparisons:

kabau *Fehan Tetun.* large domestic animal – includes cow, buffalo, horse.

karau *East Tetun.* water buffalo. (Mo:102)

#**kapir** *Morph:* #**ka-kapir**. *PRM.* plaited palm leaf bag or pouch. *Borrowed from:* Malay *kampil*. *Etym:* *kampil (PWMP. Blust and Trussel (ongoing) note that the reflexes of this form may be a Malay loan distribution.). *Pattern:* k-1. *[irr. from PMP:* *mp > *p; *l > *r*]* *[irr. from PRM:* *p > *b* in Molo*]* *[Form:* Hawu also attests irregular medial *b* also found in Molo.*]* *[History:* Given the irregularities in the Rote and Meto forms, the reflexes included here were probably distributed by contact.*]*

kapi-k *Termanu.* kind of basket woven from lontar leaves. (J:222)

kapi-ʔ *Korbafo.*

kapi-k *Bokai.*

kapi-ʔ *Bilbaa.*

kapi-k *Ba'a.*

kapi-ʔ *Dengka.*

kapi-ʔ *Oenale.*

ka͡pi-ʔ *Dela.* bag from palm leaf.

ka͡ipir *Ro'is Amarasi.* braided bag typically used for holding betel nut.

ʔ|kapi|ʔ *Kotos Amarasi.* braided bag typically used for holding betel nut.

<kabi> *Molo.* four cornered betel nut basket. (M:165)

Out-comparisons:

kabir *Fehan Tetun.* container for betel nut.

kabi *Hawu.* (J:222)

#**kari** *Morph:* #**kari-f**. *PMeto.* kidneys. *Borrowed from:* probably an early borrowing from Helong into PMeto. *Pattern:* k-2b. *[Form:* The Meto cognates set indicates earlier medial **nd. While the Helong forms indicate earlier **ŋ(g). This is perhaps a case of dissimilation of *ŋg > *nd /k_ in Meto. Compare PRM ***kiŋgi** 'cockroach'.*]*

ka͡iri-f, kaer-n=aa *Ro'is Amarasi.* kidneys.

ʔaki-f *Kotos Amarasi.* kidneys.

ʔake-k *Kopas.* lungs.

ʔaki-f *Molo.* kidneys. (M:14)

Out-comparisons:

khaŋin beas *Funai Helong.* kidneys. *Usage:* obsolete. *[Form:* **beas** = 'seed'.*]*

haŋin *Semau Helong.* kidneys.

#**karu** *PRM.* cloth bag. *Borrowed from:* an early borrowing from Malay *karung* or similar. The forms collected here probably represent several independent instances of borrowing. *Pattern:* k-irr.

alu\kosu *Termanu.* bag, purse of linen or cotton. (J:9)

alu/kosu *Korbafo.*

alu/kosu *Bokai.*

alu/kosu *Bilbaa.*

alu/kosu *Rikou.*

alu/kosu *Ba'a.*

alu/kosu *Tii.*

alu/kosi *Dengka.*

a͡lu/kosi *Oenale.*

a͡uru|k *Ro'is Amarasi.* small cloth bag used for holding betel nut.

aru|k, aru|ʔ *Kotos Amarasi.* small cloth bag used for holding betel nut.

alu|ʔ, alu|k (2) <alu_kosu> *Molo.* 1) small bag for betel-nut. 2) small whey bag which can be closed up. (M:19)

ka~karu *Kusa-Manea.* betel-nut bag.

Out-comparisons:

olo\kohu *Hawu.* (J:9)

ka~kalu *Ili'uun.* a sack or bag made of imported cloth. (dJ:120)

#**kinde** *PRM.* spindle. *Borrowed from:* connected with Malay *kincir* 'spinning wheel; spool, reel'. Reflexes of *k probably indicate this term was not borrowed into PRM, but has a later dispersion. *Pattern:* k-irr.

(ʔ)ine *Termanu.* long round piece of wood which one rotates resting on the **bina** in order to spin yarn. (J:203)
(ʔ)ine *Korbafo.*
(ʔ)ine *Bokai.*
kini *Bilbaa.*
ʔindi *Landu.* spindle. (own field notes)
ʔinde *Rikou.*
ʔiri *Oepao.* (own field notes)
(ʔ)ina(_abas) *Ba'a.*
(ʔ)inda *Lole.* spinner. (Zacharias et al. 2014)
(ʔ)inde *Tii.*
(ʔ)inde *Dengka.*
(ʔ)inde *Oenale.*
kiri *Ro'is Amarasi.* spool for spinning cotton thread.
ʔike *Kotos Amarasi.* spool for spinning cotton thread.
ʔike *Molo.* spool for spinning cotton thread. (M:159)
Out-comparisons:
kida *East Tetun.* spindle (for spinning thread). (Mo:40)
kinde *Manggarai.* spindle, tools for spinning thread. (Verheijen 1967:220)
<kindi> *Kambera.* spindle. (On:211)

#k|naba|ʔ *PMeto.* spider. *Doublet:* ***lau**. *Etym:* *lawaq. *[irr. from PMP:* *wa > *ba (expect *o)*] [History:* Probably borrowing from Tetun into pre-Meto before *l > Proto-Meto *n, as *w > *b* is regular in East Tetun. Welaun has **dabadai(n)** and this may also be the source for the Meto form.*]*
k|naba|ʔ *Ro'is Amarasi.* spider.
k|naba|ʔ *Kotos Amarasi.* spider.
ʔ|nab~naba|ʔ *Molo.* spider, spider web. (M:338)
naba_k|ra~raʔi *Kusa-Manea.* spider. *[Note:* Kusa-Manea also has **labrait** which is a more recent borrowing from Tetun.*]*
Out-comparisons:
labadain *Fehan Tetun.* spider, cobweb. (Mo:122)
labadain *East Tetun.* spider. (Mo:122)

#koedʒabas *PRM.* guava. *Borrowed from:* Portuguese *goiabas* [gojaβas] (pl. of *goiaba*), ultimately Arawak *guayabo*. *Pattern:* k-1. *[Form:* In Meto the insertion of /dʒ/ can be explained as a (historic) process to break up the sequence of three vowels. All three vowels are still seen in the Baikeno form. Some varieties have subsequently undergone *dʒ > *r*, or in the case of Kusa-Manea (unexpected) *dʒ > *l*. The appearance of /dʒ/ or /d/ in Rote is not explicable in the same way and these forms may be from Meto. The Tetun form appears to result from a different borrowing event.*]*
kudʒabas, kudabas *Termanu.* in Kupang *kudʒawas* kind of edible fruit. (J:255)
kudʒawas *Lole.* guava. (Zacharias et al. 2014)
kuraibis *Ro'is Amarasi.* guava.
kudʒabis, kurabis, kurabe *Kotos Amarasi.* guava.
kudʒawas *Molo.* guava. (M:244)
koi-dʒ *Amfo'an.* guava.
kurabis *Timaus.* guava.
koedʒabis *Baikeno.* guava. (Michael Rose pers. comm.)
koelabis *Kusa-Manea.* guava.
Out-comparisons:
koiabas, goiaba *East Tetun.* guava. (Mo:116,38)
kudʒawas *Kupang Malay.* guava.

#kofa *Morph:* **#kofa-k**. *PRM.* canoe. *Borrowed from:* currently unidentified. *Pattern:* k-irr. *[Form:* Reflexes of *k indicate that this term is a borrowing after the break-up of PRM.*] [History:* May be connected (irregularly) with PMP *qabaŋ.*]*
(ʔ)ofa-k *Termanu.* vessel. (J:454)

(ʔ)ofa-ʔ *Korbafo.*
(ʔ)ofa-k *Bokai.*
kofa-ʔ *Bilbaa.*
(ʔ)ofa-ʔ *Landu.* canoe. (own field notes)
ʔofa-ʔ *Rikou.*
(ʔ)ofa-k *Ba'a.*
(ʔ)ofa-k *Tii.*
(ʔ)ofa-ʔ *Dengka.*
ʔofa-ʔ *Oenale.*
ʔofa-ʔ *Dela.* boat.
kofa|ʔ *Ro'is Amarasi.* canoe, boat.
kofa|ʔ *Kotos Amarasi.* canoe, boat.
Out-comparisons:
kova *Hawu.* boat.
kowa *Ende.* canoe with two supporting poles on each side. (McDonnell 2009:25)

#**koi** *PRM.* bed. *Borrowed from:* Dutch *kooi* [koːi], ultimately Latin *cavea. Pattern:* k-1.
koi *Rikou.* bed. (Nako et al. 2014)
koi *Lole.* bed. (Zacharias et al. 2014)
koi *Tii.* bed. (Grimes et al. 2014a)
koi *Dela.* bed.
koi *Timaus.* bed. *[Form:* Citation form with final consonant insertion is **koor**.*]*
Out-comparisons:
kui *Semau Helong.* bed.
koi *Fehan Tetun.* bed.

#**kopi** *PMeto.* knife. *See:* ***ɗombe**.
opi *Ro'is Amarasi.* knife.
Out-comparisons:
opi *Ili'uun.* sword, cutlass, chopping knife. (dJ:131, 143)
kopi *Roma.* knife.
opi-e *Central Marsela.* knife. *[Note:* language of the Babar Islands, southwest Maluku ISO 639-3 [mxz].*]* (Taber 1993:428)

#**kota** *PRM.* fortress, city. *Borrowed from:* ultimately Sanskrit *koṭa* [koʈa] 'fort', perhaps via Malay *kota. Pattern:* k-1.
kota *Termanu.* fort, fortress, in particular the fort at Kupang, also **Kota** as the Rote name for Kupang. Also: stone fence, or wall in general. (J:252)
kota *Dela.* city, city of Kupang.
koot, kota *Kotos Amarasi.* city, fort. *[Form:* The form **koot** is due to reanalysis as **koot=aa** [ˈkɔːt̪ɐ] with the determiner **=aa** attached to a consonant final stem.*]*
koot *Molo.* fort. (M:238)

#**kusapi** *PMeto.* Ceylon oak. <u>Schleichera oleosa</u>. *Borrowed from:* Hindi *kusumb. Pattern:* k-2b. *[History:* Blust and Trussel (ongoing) reconstruct PMP *kasambiʔ, but the tree is not native to this area.*]*
kusapi *Ro'is Amarasi.* Ceylon oak. <u>Schleichera oleosa</u>.
ʔusapi *Kotos Amarasi.* Ceylon oak. <u>Schleichera oleosa</u>.
ʔusapi *Molo.* kind of tree the seeds of which have oil. (M:591)
ʔusapi *Kusa-Manea.* Ceylon oak. <u>Schleichera oleosa</u>.
Out-comparisons:
sapiʔ *Semau Helong.* Ceylon oak.

#**laisona** *PRM.* shallot, eschalot, onion. <u>Allium Ascalonicum</u>. *[irr. from PRM:* *n > Ø in Meto*] [Sporadic:* glottal stop insertion in Amarasi.*] [History:* Ultimately from Sanskrit *rasuna*, perhaps via Makassar/Bugis *lasuna.]*
laisona *Termanu.* onion. (J:271)
laisona *Korbafo.*
laisona *Bokai.*
laisona *Bilbaa.*
laisona *Rikou.*
laisona *Ba'a.*
laisona *Tii.*
laisona *Dengka.*
laisona *Oenale.*
naisoʔo *Ro'is Amarasi.* eschalot, onion. <u>Allium Ascalonicum</u>.

naisoʔo *Kotos Amarasi.* eschalot, onion. Allium Ascalonicum. *[Form:* Final *ʔo* disappears in compounds e.g. **naiso noʔo** ‘spring onions, scallions’, same as **aiʤoʔo** ‘casuarina tree’.*]*

Out-comparisons:

laisʔone *Waima'a.* onion.

lahono *Kisar.* onion.

#**leko** *PMeto.* good. *Borrowed from:* probably Helong into Meto after *l > *n*. If this were from Proto-Meto ***reko**, we would not expect initial *l* in the Waima'a out-comparison. Furthermore, Kusa-Manea does not have this form and instead has **na-mria** ‘good’.

reko *Ro'is Amarasi.* good.

reko *Kotos Amarasi.* good.

leko *Molo.* be good, be healthy.

Out-comparisons:

leko *Semau Helong.* beautiful.

loko *Waima'a.* beautiful. *[irr. from PRM: e = o* correspondence*]*

#**maŋga** *Rote.* mango. *Borrowed from:* ultimately colloquial Tamil *māṅgā* [maːŋgaː] (Tamil *māṅkaṉi* [maːŋkani]), perhaps via Malay *mangga*.

(pao) maŋa *Termanu.* the name of a big kind of mango. (J:346)

maŋa *Korbafo.*

maŋa *Bokai.*

makas *Rikou.*

maŋga *Ba'a.*

maŋga *Dengka.*

maŋga *Oenale.* mango. *[Semantics:* Jonker (1908:346) states ‘Oenale has **maŋga** in place of [Termanu] **pao**’.*]*

Out-comparisons:

makas *Funai Helong.* mango.

makas *Semau Helong.* mango.

#**(m)baha** *Morph:* #**(m)baha-k**. *PRM.* fence. *Borrowed from:* ultimately Sanskrit *prākāra*. *[History:* Blust and Trussel (ongoing) reconstruct PMP *pagər, but the correspondences in the east cannot be reconciled with this reconstruction.*]*

paʔa *Termanu.* fence, wooden hedge. (J:460)

paʔa *Bokai.*

mpaʔa *Ba'a.*

mbaʔa *Lole.* fence. (Zacharias et al. 2014)

mbaʔa *Tii.*

mbaa *Dengka.*

mbaa *Oenale.*

baha|k *Ro'is Amarasi.* fence.

baha|k *Kotos Amarasi.* (wooden) fence.

bahan *Molo.* fence made from sticks. (M:41)

bahan *Kusa-Manea.* fence.

Out-comparisons:

paha *Semau Helong.* fence.

baʔa *Fehan Tetun.* fence.

baha *East Tetun.* a circle of wall, defence or enclosure (around houses). (Mo:8)

#**mei** *PRM.* table. *Borrowed from:* Portuguese *mesa* [meza]. *[Form:* In most known varieties of Meto insertion of [ʤ] occurs after /i/ before a vowel initial enclitic. Thus, Kotos Amarasi **mei** + **=aa** → **meeʤaa** [ˈmeːʤɐ] ~ [ˈmeːʒɐ] (with mid-high [eː] not mid-low [ɛː]). It would appear that the final vowel of Portuguese *mesa* [meza] was reanalysed as the determiner **=aa** (cf. ***aa**) with the previous [z] being analysed as an inserted consonant. Such an explanation is probably not possible for Rote, thus indicating that the Rote forms were borrowed from Meto. (Note further that in Baikeno and Amfo'an /ʤ/ is realised as [ʤ]~[ʒ]~[zʲ]~[z].) A similar process probably took place with cognates of #**ŋgarei** ‘church’.*]*

mei *Termanu.* table. (J:354)

mei *Korbafo.*

mei *Bokai.*

mei *Bilbaa.*
mei *Rikou.*
mei *Ba'a.*
mei *Tii.*
mei *Dengka.*
mei *Oenale.*
mei *Kotos Amarasi.* table.
mei-ʤ *Amfo'an.* table.
mei *Molo.* table. (M:394)
mei-ʤ *Baikeno.* table. (Charles E. Grimes pers. comm.)
Out-comparisons:
miʤa *Semau Helong.* table.
mesa *East Tetun.* a table. (Mo:141)

[#]**mbarani** *Rote.* brave. *Borrowed from:* Malay *berani* [bərani]. *[Form:* Either an early loan or a case of correspondence mimicry.*]*
palani *Termanu.* brave, bravery; hero. (J:466)
palani *Korbafo.*
palani *Bokai.*
palani *Bilbaa.*
parani *Rikou.*
palani *Lole.* dare, daredevil. (Zacharias et al. 2014)
parani *Tii.* hero, brave, superb. (Grimes et al. 2014a)
mbalani *Dengka.*
mbarani *Oenale.*
na-mba-rani *Dela.* brave. *[Form:* The antepenultimate syllable assimilates to the quality of the agreement prefix, thus providing evidence that it has been reanalysed as a prefix; i.e. 1SG **ʔu-mbu-rani**, 2SG **mu-mbu-rani**, 2PL/1PL. EXCL **mi-mbi-rani**, 0/obviative **ne-mbe-rani**.*]*

[#]**naka** *Rote.* anchor. *Borrowed from:* an unidentified source. Compare Persian لنگر [laŋgar], Hindi [laŋgar], Kambera <**tanangga**> (Onvlee 1984:471), Bima **maŋga** (Ismail et al. 1985:85), Balinese **maŋgar** (Kersten 1984:403), and Malay *jangkar* [ʤaŋkar]. The ending *-aŋga(r)* seems to be a kind of *Wanderwort* and may even be connected with Dutch *anker* [aŋkər], and English *anchor* [aŋkər] which are ultimately from Greek άγκυρα *ankura. Pattern:* k-5.
naka *Termanu.* anchor. (J:374)
naka *Korbafo.*
naka *Bokai.*
naka *Bilbaa.*
naʔa *Rikou.*
naka *Ba'a.*
naka *Tii.*
naka *Dengka.*
naka *Oenale.*
Out-comparisons:
tenaga *Hawu. [Form:* Grimes, Lado et. al (2008) have Seba and Raijua **penavu** and Dimu **penavo** 'anchor'.*]* (J:374)

[#]**nane** *Morph:* [#]**nane-f.** *PMeto.* daughter-in-law, opposite sex sibling's daughter. *Borrowed from:* probably Helong into Meto before *l > *n*. But note that Helong has **manhiu** 'son-in-law' which is a borrowing from another source as identified by the element **hiu**. This is ultimately from PMP *baqəRu 'new' which is otherwise retained regularly in Helong as **balu**. *[Note:* The Rote languages have phrases meaning literally 'new woman' for 'daughter-in-law', such as Termanu **feto feu-k** (Jonker 1908:134).*]*
nane-f *Kotos Amarasi.* daughter-in-law, opposite sex sibling's daughter.
nane-f *Molo.* daughter-in-law. (M:348)
Out-comparisons:
nale-n *Funai Helong.* daughter-in-law, opposite sex sibling's daughter.
nale-n *Semau Helong.* daughter-in-law.

[#]**nome** *PMeto.* Venus, morning star. *Borrowed from:* probably Helong into Meto before *l > *n. [Note:* Tetun

naroma 'light' could be connected.*]* *[Semantics:* Rikou has **ruu manalepa bafi** literally 'the star carrying a pig' for 'Venus, morning star' (Jonker 1908:722). The other Rote languages have phrases meaning 'chicken star', such as Termanu **nduu manu-k** (Jonker 1908:346).*]*

faif noem *Ro'is Amarasi.* Venus, morning star. *Lit:* 'pig **nome**'.

faif nome *Kotos Amarasi.* Venus, morning star. *Lit:* 'pig **nome**'. *[Semantics:* **nome** has no known independent meaning.*]*

faif nome (2) <nome> *Molo.* 1) the morning star. 2) a kind of plant whose leaves will gleam when the morning star shines. (M:380)

Out-comparisons:

paap lome *Semau Helong.* Venus, morning star. *Lit:* 'father **lome**'. *[Semantics:* **lome** has no known independent meaning.*]*

#**ndara** *Rote.* horse. *Borrowed from:* ultimately Javanese *jaran* [ʤaran]. *[irr. from PRM:* *nd > *d* in Rikou*]*

ndala *Termanu.* horse. (J:413)

ndala *Korbafo.*

lala *Bokai.*

lala *Bilbaa.*

ndara *Landu.*

dara *Rikou.*

rara *Oepao.*

ndala *Ba'a.*

ndala *Lole.*

ndara *Tii.*

ndala *Dengka.*

ndara *Oenale.*

ndara *Dela.* horse.

#**ŋgarei** *PRM.* church. *Borrowed from:* Portuguese *igreja* [igreʒa]. *[Note:* Jonker (1908:431) does not give the forms for each Rote language, but states: 'dialects **ŋalei**, **ŋgarei**, **karei**'.*]* *[Form:* In most known varieties of Meto insertion of [ʤ] occurs after /i/ before a vowel initial enclitic. Thus, Kotos Amarasi **krei** + **=aa** → **kreeʤaa** [ˈkreːʤɐ] ~ [ˈkreːʒɐ] (with mid-high [eː] not mid-low [ɛː]). It would appear that the final vowel of Portuguese *igreja* [igreʒa] was reanalysed as the determiner **=aa** (cf. ***aa**) with the previous [ʒ] being analysed as an inserted consonant. (A similar process probably took place with cognates of #**mei** 'table'.) Such an explanation is probably not possible for Rote, thus Meto may have been the donor for the Rote forms. However, proposing Meto as the intermediary for the Rote forms does not explain the 'regular' reflexes of *ŋg. This would appear to be a case of adaption of non-native Portuguese [g] with correspondence mimicry (Alpher and Nash 1999:14f).*]*

ŋgalei *Termanu.* church. (J:431)

ŋgalei *Korbafo.*

ŋalei *Bokai.*

ŋalei *Bilbaa.*

karei *Rikou.*

ŋgalei *Ba'a.*

ŋgalei *Lole.* church. (Zacharias et al. 2014)

ŋgarei *Tii.*

ŋgalei *Dengka.*

ŋgarei *Oenale.*

krei *Ro'is Amarasi.* church, week.

krei *Kotos Amarasi.* church, week.

klei-ʤ, klii-ʤ *Amfo'an.* church, week.

klei *Molo.* church. (M:216)

#**ŋgusi** *PRM.* water jar. *Borrowed from:* Malay *guci* [guʧi] 'earthenware jug', ultimately Chinese, e.g. Mandarin 骨瓷 *gǔ cí* [gu˨˩˦ʦʰi˧˥] 'bone china'.

ŋgusi *Termanu.* kind of jug. (J:450)

ŋgusi *Lole.* earthenware pot, clay pot. (Zacharias et al. 2014)

ŋgusi *Tii.* porcelain or earthenware jug. (Grimes et al. 2014a)

ŋgusi *Dela.* jar for water or lontar palm sugar made of clay. (Thersia Tamelan pers. comm. May 2017)

kusi *Kotos Amarasi.* water jar.
kusi *Molo.* water vessel. (M:253)
Out-comparisons:
kusi *East Tetun.* a clay jar or pot. (Mo:122)
kusi *Ili'uun.* large earthenware jar. (dJ:122)
uhi *Kisar.* water jar, earth container.

#**ŋgute** *Rote.* cut with scissors. *Borrowed from:* Malay *gunting* [guntiŋ].
ŋgute *Termanu.* cut with scissors. (J:450)
ŋgute *Korbafo.*
ŋute *Bokai.*
ŋute *Bilbaa.*
kute *Rikou.*
ŋgute *Ba'a.*
ŋgute *Tii.*
ŋgute *Dengka.*
ŋgute *Oenale.*

#**omba** *Rote.* wave, billow, swell at sea. *Borrowed from:* Malay *ombak* [ombaʔ]. *[irr. from PRM:* *mb > *m* for second sense in Termanu*]* *[History:* Blust and Trussel (ongoing) reconstruct *humbak to PWMP, but this would require irr. *u > *o* in Rote.*]*
na-o~opa (2) na-o~oma *Termanu.* 1) wave, undulate. (J:458) 2) wave, undulate. (J:457)
na-o~opa *Korbafo.*
na-o~opa *Bokai.*
na-o~opa *Rikou.*
na-o~ompa *Ba'a.*
na-o~omba *Dengka.*
na-o~omba *Oenale.*

#**oras** *PwRM.* time. *Borrowed from:* Portuguese *horas* [ɔras], plural of *hora* ‘hour, time’.
oras ia *Dela.* now.
oros *Ro'is Amarasi.* time.
oras *Kotos Amarasi.* time.
olas *Molo.* hour. (M:403)
Out-comparisons:
oras *Semau Helong.* time.
oras *East Tetun.* hour, time. (Mo:156)
ors *Kisar.* time.

#**paha** *PRM.* chisel. *Borrowed from:* Malay *pahat.*
paʔa *Termanu.* chiselling. (J:461)
paʔa *Korbafo.*
paʔa *Bokai.*
paa *Bilbaa.*
paʔa *Rikou.* chisel. (Nako et al. 2014)
mpaʔa *Ba'a.*
paʔa *Tii.*
paa *Dengka.*
paa *Oenale.*
paah *Meto.* chiselling. (J:461)
Out-comparisons:
pahat *Semau Helong.* chisel, carve.
bahat *East Tetun.* chisel. (Mo:8)

#**papan** *PRM.* plank. *Borrowed from:* Malay *papan. [History:* Blust and Trussel (ongoing) reconstruct PMP *papan, but the forms here cannot be regularly derived from this.*]*
papa-k *Termanu.* plank of ordinary wood. (J:469)
papa-ʔ *Korbafo.*
papa-k *Bokai.*
papa-ʔ *Bilbaa.*
papa-ʔ *Rikou.*
mpampa-k *Ba'a.*
papa-k *Tii.*
papa-ʔ *Dengka.*
papa-ʔ *Oenale.*
papan *Molo.* round planks or stones around the post of the **lopo** house which prevent mice from getting into the roof. (M:422)

#**paria** *Morph:* #**paria-k**. *PRM.* bitter melon. Momordica charantia. *Borrowed from:* Malay *peria* [pəria]. *[History:* An early loan as indicated by regular Meto *r > *l > *n.]*
palia-k *Termanu.* kind of bitter cucumber. (J:466)
palia-k *Bokai.*
palia-k *Ba'a.*

paria-k *Tii.*
palia *Dengka.*
paria *Oenale.*
pniaʔ *Kotos Amarasi.* bitter melon.

#**[p/b]isi** *PRM.* sprinkle. *[Form:* Meto and Helong show irregular initial consonants. The religious use of this word provides a cultural motivation for borrowing (see the note for the Hawu form).*] [History:* Blust and Trussel (ongoing) reconstruct *picik to PMP and include the Rote and Hawu forms as part of their evidence. However, (as they concede) *p > *p* would be irregular in Rote.*]*
pisi *Termanu.* sprinkle. (J:486)
pisi *Korbafo.*
pisi *Bokai.*
pisi *Bilbaa.*
mpisi *Ba'a.*
(pisi ?) *Tii.*
bisin *Kotos Amarasi.* sprinkle.
n-bisin *Molo.* sprinkles. (M:70)
Out-comparisons:
hitiʔ *Semau Helong.* splash, sprinkle, splatter.
hisik *East Tetun.* dust, shake out; to throw out. (Mo:86)
ʧebe *Dhao.* sprinkle, toss, cast, throw. *[Sporadic:* consonant metathesis: *bVʧ > *ʧVb.]*
pihi, pihe *Hawu.* sprinkle. *[Semantics:* 'In traditional Sabu culture, this act of sprinkling can be used as a ritual at any time during one's life where one feels defiled for whatever reason, and needs to be restored to a state of ritual purity. It can be done many times. It can also be done to dedicate a new house (using sugarcane juice, or coconut milk).'*]*

#**piŋga** *Morph:* #**ka-piŋga-k**. *PRM.* plate. *Borrowed from:* Malay *pinggan*, ultimately from Persian.
piŋa-k *Termanu.* dish, plate. (J:485)
piŋa-ʔ *Korbafo.*
piŋa-k *Bokai.*
piŋa-ʔ *Bilbaa.*
bika-ʔ *Rikou.*
piŋga-k *Ba'a.*
piŋga-k *Tii.*
piŋga-ʔ *Dengka.*
piŋga-ʔ *Oenale.*
ʔ|pika|ʔ *Kotos Amarasi.*
<pika> *Molo.* plate. (M:437)
Out-comparisons:
piŋas *Semau Helong.* plate.
bikan *East Tetun.* plate. (Mo:13)

#**pohat** *Morph:* #**ka-pohat**. *PMeto.* bark of tree, husk. *[History:* While borrowing between Helong and Meto is likely, the direction is unclear. Amarasi **ʔpoho-f** with medial *h* is probably a subsequent borrowing from Helong after this term had been share between these languages.*]*
pohoʔ *Ro'is Amarasi.* tree bark.
ʔ|poho-f *Kotos Amarasi.* tree bark, egg shell, book cover.
ʔ|poʔat, ʔ|poʔot *Kopas.* tree bark.
ʔ|poʔat *Molo.* shell or husk of a fruit. (M:442)
ʔ|poʔa-n *Amfo'an.* wet tree bark. *[Form:* **ʔkuit** = 'dry tree bark'.*]* (own field notes)
ʔ|poʔo-f *Timaus.* tree bark.
poʔat *Kusa-Manea.* skin, bark, fingernail, toenail.
Out-comparisons:
kpohot *Funai Helong.* bark, husk, shell.
pohot *Semau Helong.* bark.

#**pukat** *PRM.* dragnet. *Borrowed from:* Malay *pukat*. *Pattern:* k-9'.
puʔa-k *Termanu.* dragnet. (J:499f)
pua-k *Korbafo.*
puʔa-k *Bokai.*
puka-ʔ *Bilbaa.*
puka-ʔ *Rikou.*
mpuʔa-k *Ba'a.*
puʔa-k *Tii.*
puʔat *Dengka.*

puʔat *Oenale.*
puʔat *Kotos Amarasi.* dragnet. (M:453)
Out-comparisons:
pukat *Semau Helong.* dragnet.

#**puli** *Rote.* cure, heal. *Borrowed from:* Malay *pulih. [History:* While this may ultimately be connected with PMP *pa-qudip the universal *d = *l* correspondence and *aqu = *u* show that this is a borrowing.*]*
puli *Termanu.* cure someone, treat a sick person. (J:503)
puli *Korbafo.*
puli *Bokai.*
puli *Bilbaa.*
puli *Rikou.*
mpuli *Ba'a.*
puli *Tii.*
puli *Dengka.*
puli *Oenale.*

#**rapa** *Rote.* bridle. *Borrowed from:* Hawu into Rote.
lapa *Termanu.* bridle, put on a bridle. (J:281)
lapa *Korbafo.*
lapa *Bokai.*
lapa *Bilbaa.*
rapa *Rikou.*
lapa *Ba'a.*
rapa *Tii.*
la~lapa-t *Dengka.*
rapa *Oenale.*
Out-comparisons:
rapa *Hawu.* bridle. (J:281)
<rapa> *Kambera.* bridle, reins. (On:432)

#**riti** *PRM.* copper, bracelet. *Borrowed from:* ultimately Sanskrit *rīti* [riːti] 'bell-metal'. *[History:* This is an early loan, as shown by Meto *r > *l > *n.]*
liti *Termanu.* copper. (J:315)
liti *Korbafo.*
liti *Bokai.*
liti *Bilbaa.*
riti *Rikou.*
liti *Ba'a.*
riti *Tii.*
liti *Dengka.*
riti *Oenale.*
niti *Kotos Amarasi.* bracelet.
niti-ʤ *Amfo'an.* bracelet.
Out-comparisons:
li̯ti *Semau Helong.* bracelet.
riti *East Tetun.* copper, brass. (Mo:161)

#**roa** *Morph:* #**roa-k**. *CER.* room. *Borrowed from:* Malay *ruang.*
loa-k *Termanu.* room, chamber. (J:318)
loa-ʔ *Korbafo.*
loa-k *Bokai.*
loa-ʔ *Bilbaa.*
roa-ʔ *Rikou.*
Out-comparisons:
loaŋ *Helong.* (J:318)

#**rusa** *PRM.* deer. *Borrowed from:* Malay *rusa. [irr. from PRM:* *r > (*l) > *n* in Termanu, Korbafo, Bokai, and Ba'a*]*
nusa *Termanu.* deer. (J:409)
nusa *Korbafo.*
nusa *Bokai.*
lusa *Bilbaa.*
rusa *Rikou.*
nusa *Ba'a.*
rusa *Tii.*
lusa *Dengka.*
rusa *Oenale.*
ruus *Kotos Amarasi.* deer. *[Form:* reanalysis as **ruus=aa** [ˈrʊːsɐ] with the determiner =**aa** attached to a consonant final stem.*]*
luus *Molo.* deer. (M:293)
Out-comparisons:
lusa *Semau Helong.* deer.
rusa, bibi_rusa *East Tetun.* deer. (Mo:162)

#**sama** *Rote.* same. *Borrowed from:* ultimately Sanskrit *sama*, perhaps via Malay *sama.*
sama *Termanu.* be the same. (J:518)
sama *Korbafo.*
sama *Bokai.*
sama *Bilbaa.*

sama *Rikou.*
sama *Ba'a.*
sama *Tii.*
sama *Dengka.*

#**sarani** *PRM.* baptise. *Borrowed from:* Arabic *naṣrānī* [nasˤraːniː] 'Christians', compare Syriac *naṣrāyā* [nasˤraːjaː] 'Nazarene'. *[irr. from PRM:* *n = *n* /l_ in Amfo'an (expect *n > *l*)*]* *[Form:* The initial syllable was originally **na** which has been reanalysed as a third person agreement marker.*]* *[History:* This term is very old in the region. Grimes et al. (2014a) state: 'Widely used through much of eastern Indonesia in Malays and vernaculars, and its use has been established for centuries.'*]*
salani *Termanu.* make someone Christian by baptising, baptise. (J:516)
sarani *Rikou.* baptise. (Nako et al. 2014)
salani *Lole.* baptise. (Zacharias et al. 2014)
sarani *Tii.* baptise; ritual for formally initiating people as members of the Christian faith; neutral as to method (e.g. immersion or sprinkling). (Grimes et al. 2014a)
sarani *Dela.* baptise, christen.
na-srani (2) srani|ʔ *Kotos Amarasi.* 1) baptise. 2) baptism, baptismal.
na-slani (2) slaniʔ *Amfo'an.* 1) baptise. 2) baptism.
Out-comparisons:
sarani *Semau Helong.* baptise.

#**sarombo** *Rote.* pants, cover the body. *Borrowed from:* an unidentified source, possibly a language of Sulawesi give the Makassar form.
lopo (2) lopo~lopo (3) uma=a na-sa-lo~lopo *Termanu.* 1) trousers. 2) he wears his sarong hanging down to the ankles like a woman's sarong. **ana pake naa sidi=na lopo~lopo** 3) the house has a low sloping roof. (J:327)
lopo *Korbafo.* trousers. (J:327)
lopo *Bokai.* trousers. (J:327)
(2) lopo~lopo, na-sa-lo~lopo *Bilbaa.* 2) completely cover oneself or one's body. (J:727)
ropo *Rikou.* trousers. (J:327)
lompo (2) lompo~lompo *Ba'a.* 2) completely cover oneself or one's body. (J:727)
rombo (2) rombo~rombo, sa-ro~rombo *Tii.* 1) sarong. 2) completely cover oneself or one's body. (J:727)
(2) lombo~lombo, na-sa-lo~lombo *Dengka.* 2) completely cover oneself or one's body. (J:727)
Out-comparisons:
sapolo *Kisar.* trousers, pants.
robo *Hawu.* cover. (J:727)
sarombоŋ *Makassar.* pillowcase. (J:727)
sərombоŋ *Malay.* pipe, tube; hollow cylinder.

#**seŋge** *Rote.* cloves. Syzygium aromaticum. *Borrowed from:* Malay *cengkeh* [ʧeŋkeh]. *[Form:* The first element in most forms may be connected with Malay *pala* 'nutmeg'.*]*
pela/seŋe *Termanu.* cloves. (J:478)
pela/seŋe *Korbafo.*
pela/seŋe *Bokai.*
pela/seŋe *Bilbaa.*
pela/seke *Rikou.*
pela/seŋge *Ba'a.*
pele/seŋge *Tii.*
pela/seŋge *Dengka.*
seŋge *Oenale.*

#**seremere** *PRM.* Malay gooseberry. Phyllanthus acidus. *Borrowed from:* Malay *cermelek* [ʧermeleʔ].
selemele(-k), selumele-k *Termanu.* the Malay gooseberry tree, called *cermelek* in Kupang. (J:532)

sarmeri *Kotos Amarasi.* Malay Gooseberry.
salmele *Molo.* small tree the roots of which have toxic properties. Phyllantus acidus. (M:472)

#**soro** *Rote.* push forwards. *Borrowed from:* Malay *sorong. [History:* Blust and Trussel (ongoing) reconstruct PWMP *suruŋ stating: 'A number of these forms may be loans (from Malay ...), but the comparison as a whole cannot easily be dismissed as a product of borrowing.' In the case of the Rote forms Jonker (1908) suggests they are borrowings from Malay and I agree, mainly due to the identical vowels which would not be explained by inheritance from *suruŋ.*]*
solo *Termanu.* push forwards. (J:560)
solo *Korbafo.*
solo *Bokai.*
solo *Bilbaa.*
soro *Rikou.*
solo-k *Ba'a.*
soro *Tii.*
solo *Dengka.*
soro *Oenale.*

#**sumba** *PRM.* oath, pledge; curse. *Borrowed from:* Malay *sumpah.*
supa *Termanu.* oath, curse. (J:576)
supa *Korbafo.*
supa *Bokai.*
supa *Bilbaa.*
supa *Rikou.*
sumpa *Ba'a.*
sumba *Tii.*
sumba *Dengka.*
sumba *Oenale.*
n-supa *Kotos Amarasi.* swear.
Out-comparisons:
sumpa *Semau Helong.* swear, oath.

#**taɓe** *PRM.* greet. *Borrowed from:* Malay *tabek/tabik*, ultimately Sanskrit *kṣantavya* [kʂantaʋja] 'be pardoned, forgiven'.
tabe-k *Termanu.* bring greetings, greetings on arrival. (J:582)
taɓe *Dela.* shake hands.
n-tabe *Kotos Amarasi.* greet, shake hands with.
Out-comparisons:
tabe *Semau Helong.* greeting, respect. *Usage:* Archaic. Associated with pre-independence eras. A respectful greeting to a person of high status.
tabe *Fehan Tetun.* greeting. (Mo:177)

#**tai** *PRM.* weigh. *Borrowed from:* Malay *tahil* 'unit of measurement for gold'.
tai *Termanu.* weigh something. (J:586)
tai *Korbafo.*
tai *Bokai.*
tai *Bilbaa.*
tai *Rikou.*
tai *Ba'a.*
tai *Tii.*
tai *Dengka.*
tai *Oenale.*
n-tai *Kotos Amarasi.* weigh, evaluate, balance.
tai *Molo.* scales. (M:530)
Out-comparisons:
tai *Semau Helong.*

#**tanda** *PRM.* sign. *Borrowed from:* Malay *tanda* An early borrowing as indicated by the regular correspondences, particularly *nd > *r > *k* in Amarasi.
tana *Termanu.* sign. (J:293)
tana *Korbafo.*
tana *Bokai.*
tana *Bilbaa.*
tanda *Rikou.*
tana *Ba'a.*
tanda *Tii.*
tanda *Dengka.*
tanda *Oenale.*
taka *Kotos Amarasi.* sign.
Out-comparisons:
tada *Semau Helong.* sign.

ha-tada, ha-tadak, ha-tadan *East Tetun.* place a sign or mark (as a sign of ownership). (Mo:81)

#**tasu** *PRM.* fry pan. *Borrowed from:* Portuguese *tacho* [taʃu].

tasu *Termanu.* fry-pan. (J:602f)

tasu *Korbafo.*

tasu *Bokai.*

tasu *Bilbaa.*

tasu *Rikou.*

tasu *Ba'a.*

tasu *Tii.*

tasu *Dengka.*

tasu *Oenale.*

tasu *Kotos Amarasi.* wok.

Out-comparisons:

tasu *East Tetun.* small pan. (Mo:181)

#**tuhas** *Rote.* rice-cake snack cooked in a small container of woven young coconut leaves. *Borrowed from:* Malay *ketupat*. An early borrowing into Rote and Hawu as attested by the regular correspondences.

tuʔas *Ba'a.* packet of rice. (J:774)

tuʔas *Tii.*

tuʔas *Dengka.*

tuʔas *Oenale.*

Out-comparisons:

katupa, katufa, katuba *East Tetun.* rice cooked in little bags of green palm leaves. (Mo:104)

keduʔe *Hawu.* (J:774)

Total number of entries: 1,257

5

English – Rote-Meto

A - a

able	PRM. *ɓeki.
abomasum	nRM. *neko.
abound	CERM. *liɓu;
	Rote. *rimbu.
above	PRM. *ata$_1$;
	PRM. *bafo.
abundant	CERM. *tumbu.
accuse	PnRote. *sua$_1$.
accustomed	PRM. *temə.
Achilles' tendon	PRM. *mbii.
across	PRM. *ɓaat.
address	PwRM. *see$_1$.
adze	PRM. *tara.
<u>Aegle marmelos</u>	PRM. *ɗilah.
affair	nRM. *ɗasi.
afterbirth	Rote. *funi$_2$.
again	PMeto. *teni;
	PRM. *bali$_1$.
agape	PnMeto. *m|kaka.
air	Rote. *lani.
algae	CER. *lamu;
	Rote. *lombu.
alight	PRM. *tena$_2$.
almost	nRM. *ohi.
alone	PRM. *mesa.
already	PRM. *ela$_1$;
	PRM. *leu.
<u>Alstonia scholaris</u>	PMeto. *dete.
<u>Alstonia villosa</u>	PRM. *səu.
anchor	Rote. #naka
anchor (v.)	Rote. *nafu.
and	PRM. *ma.
animal	Rote. #ɓanda
answer	PRM. *taha.
ant	PRM. *ɓuit;
	Rote. *nihe.
<u>Antidesma bunius</u>	PRM. *mbune.
areca palm	PRM. *mbuah.
arm	PRM. *lima$_2$.
armpit	PRM. *salili.
aromatic	PRM. *meni$_1$.
arrive	PRM. *tea;
	Rote. *ɗai$_2$;
	Rote. *losa.
as long as	Rote. *saɗi.
ash	PRM. *afu.
ashamed	PRM. *mae$_2$.
ask	PMeto. *tana$_3$;
	PRM. *tane$_2$.
at	PRM. *ɓee.
aunt	PMeto. *baba|ʔ.
awake	PRM. *ɓeʔe.

B - b

back	PRM. *liku$_2$;
	PRM. *ŋgoti;
	Rote. *ŋgarasa.
backside	PRM. *ɓuit.
bad	PwRM. *ɗeʔu.
bag, cloth	PRM. #karu
bait	Rote. *hani$_1$.
bamboo	PRM. *oo$_2$.
bamboo container	PRM. *tiɓa;
	PRM. *tuke.
bamboo, giant <u>Dendrocalamus</u>	
	PnMeto. *petun;
	Rote. *teri.
banana	PRM. *hundi.
banyan	PRM. *nunuh.
baptise	PRM. #sarani
bark (v.)	PRM. *ŋgoro.
bark (n.)	PMeto. #pohat
bark (n.), kind	PRM. *loɓa.
barter	PRM. *sembo.
base	PRM. *peni.
basil	PRM. *ɗade.
basil, wild	Rote. *ndake_ɓuʔu.
basket	PRM. #kapir
	Rote. *hai$_1$;
	Rote. *mbisa.
bat	PRM. *ɓau.
bathe	PRM. *diu.

beach	PRM. *namo$_2$.
beads	PRM. *henuh.
beak	PwRM. *nuɗu.
beam	PRM. *lolo$_3$;
	PRM. *mbau$_1$.
bean	PRM. *fue.
bean, hyacinth	PRM. *ndoto.
beard	PnRote. *ŋgomi;
	PRM. *ŋgoro.
beat	PRM. *tutu;
	Rote. *femba;
	Rote. *toko.
beat (drum)	Rote. *ɗere.
beautiful	PMeto. #leko
beckon	PRM. *ŋaper;
	PRM. *oken.
bed	PRM. #koi
bedbug	PMeto. *ketu|k;
	Rote. *tamae.
bee	PRM. *wani.
beetle	PRM. *mbaki.
belch	PRM. *ɗoa.
bell	Rote. *kiri$_1$.
belly	PRM. *tai$_1$;
	PwRM. *kambu.
bend	CER. *felu;
	PRM. *fenu;
	Rote. *ɓeku;
	Rote. *helu.
bent	PRM. *ɓetu;
	Rote. *feɗu;
	Rote. *luku$_2$;
	Rote. *mbuku$_2$;
	Rote. *ruku.
betel leaves	Rote. *ndake$_2$.
betel nut	PRM. *mbuah.
betel-pepper	PnMeto. *funu;
	PRM. *malus.
big	CERM. *ŋgoʔu;
	PRM. *nae;
	Rote. *tua$_1$.
billabong	PRM. *lifu.
bind	PRM. *futu;
	PRM. *isa$_1$;
	Rote. *raʔi.
bird	PRM. *kodo;
	PRM. *mbui.
bird, Friarbird	PRM. *koaʔ$_1$.
bird, kind	CER. *inus.
bird, kingfisher	PRM. *sinaraʔe.
bird, Rainbow Bee-eater	PRM. *koro.
birthmark	Rote. *ila.
bite	nRM. *sau$_1$;
	PRM. *moo;
	Rote. *kaa$_1$.
bite off	PRM. *ŋgete.
bitter	nRM. *mali;
	PRM. *hedu.
bitter melon	PRM. #paria
black	PMeto. *metam;
	Rote. *ŋgeo.
blackboard tree	PMeto. *dete.
blaze	PRM. *mbila.
bleat	PRM. *mee.
blind	Rote. *poke.
blood	PRM. *daa.
blossom	PRM. *ɓuna.
blow	PRM. *buu;
	PRM. *fuu;
	PRM. *pupu;
	Rote. *kuu.
blowgun	PRM. *pupu.
blowpipe	PRM. *buu.
boat, kind of	Rote. #baluk
body	PRM. *ao.
boil	PRM. *ɓuɓu;
	PRM. *lua$_1$;
	PRM. *nasu.
bone	PRM. *dui$_1$.
bore (hole)	Rote. *undu.
bow (v.)	PRM. *ɗuɗi.
bow (arrow)	PRM. *klou.
bow, cotton	Rote. *ɓusu.
bowl	PRM. #bane
box	Rote. *ɓaraka.
boy	nRM. *tatə.
bracelet	PRM. #riti
brackish	nRM. *mali;
	PRM. *rekət.
braid	nRM. *ane;
	PRM. *sifi;
	PwRM. *ŋano.
brains	nRM. *ɗole;
	Rote. *kutə.
bran	PwRote. *eto.

branch nRM. *saɓake; PMeto. *sana|ʔ.
brave Rote. #mbarani
breadfruit PMeto. *kunu$_1$; Rote. *suku.
break PMeto. *fera$_1$; PRM. *teɓi.
break off PRM. *ketu.
breast PRM. *susu$_2$; PRM. *tendə.
breath PRM. *sanasə.
breathe CERM. *kele; PRM. *hae; PRM. *sanasə.
bride price Rote. *beli.
bridge PRM. *lete$_2$.
bridle Rote. #rapa
bright PRM. *maneu.
bring PRM. *əndi.
broken CER. *tefe; PwRM. *ɗeʔu.
brood PRM. *luku$_1$.
brother (of woman) PRM. *naa$_2$.
brother-in-law PRM. *kera$_1$.
brother, older PRM. *toʔo.
brush teeth PRM. *sakiki.
bubble PRM. *ɓuɓu.
bucket PRM. *sambat; Rote. *hai$_1$.
buffalo PMeto. *biae; Rote. #kamba
bunch, fruit PRM. *ŋgii.
bunch of fruit PMeto. *sana|ʔ.
bundle PRM. *futu.
bundle up Rote. *mbutu$_2$.
burn PRM. *hotu.
burning PRM. *mbutu$_1$.
burp PRM. *ɗoa.
bury PRM. *suɓa.
bush PRM. *lasi$_1$.
buttocks PRM. *saka.
buy PMeto. *sosa; Rote. *beli.

C - c

cactus PRM. *laʔus.
calf (of leg) PRM. *biti$_1$.
call PRM. *kati; PRM. *oken; PRM. *teka.
call chickens PRM. *kuru$_1$.
call up PRM. *hoka.
calm PnMeto. *tena$_3$; PRM. *nee$_2$.
calm down PRM. *hauk.
Calophyllum teysmannii nRM. *lilis.
caltrop PRM. *sure.
candlenut PMeto. *ʔ|fenu; Rote. *kamiri.
canine tooth PRM. *ŋoli.
canoe PRM. #kofa
capable PRM. *ɓeki.
care for PRM. #faɗuli
carry CERM. *fiti$_3$; PRM. *ɗoi; PRM. *lemba; Rote. *fua$_1$; Rote. *koko.
carry on head PRM. *suu$_2$.
carry on the shoulders PRM. *saha$_2$.
carve PRM. *ɗula; PRM. *tui$_1$.
Cassia species PRM. *ɓuni.
Casuarina species PRM. *kai/ou.
cat PRM. *meo$_1$.
catfish PRM. *etu$_1$.
cave PnRote. *lea; PRM. *lua|t.
centipede Rote. *liha.
centre PRM. *talaɗa.
Ceriops PRM. *tene.
chaff nRM. *uut.
chair PRM. #kadera
chaotic PRM. *ɗafu$_2$.
charcoal PRM. *atu; Rote. *kaɗe.

English	Rote-Meto
chase	*PMeto.* ***diʔu**;
	Rote. ***usi**$_1$.
cheek	*PRM.* ***sanasə**.
cheek hollow	*PRM.* ***suŋgə**.
chest	*nRM.* ***kara**.
chew	*PRM.* ***mama**;
	PRM. ***tamu**.
chicken	*PRM.* ***manu**.
child	*PRM.* ***anak**;
	PRM. ***ɗiki**.
chilli	*PRM.* ***kurus**.
chin	*PRM.* ***timi**.
chisel	*PRM.* **#paha**
chiton	*PRM.* ***taruku**.
choke	*Rote.* ***neta**.
choose	*PRM.* ***hiri**.
chop	*PRM.* ***huŋga**;
	Rote. ***tata**;
	Rote. ***tati**.
church	*PRM.* **#ŋgarei**
cicada	*nRM.* ***sandiit**.
citrus	*PRM.* ***ɗero**;
	PRM. ***munde**.
city	*PRM.* **#kota**
civet	*CER.* ***muse**$_2$;
	PMeto. ***metam**;
	Rote. ***kue**.
clam	*nRM.* ***kima**.
clamp	*PRM.* ***hapi**;
	PRM. ***kaɓi**.
clan	*PnMeto.* ***nono**$_2$;
	Rote. ***leo**.
claw	*PMeto.* ***kalusa**.
clean cotton	*Rote.* ***ɓusu**.
cliff	*PRM.* ***ndefa**.
climb	*PnRote.* ***ndake**$_1$;
	PRM. ***hene**.
cling	*PwRM.* ***ndika**.
close (v.)	*PRM.* ***kənda**.
close eyes	*PnRote.* ***kuta**.
close mouth	*PRM.* ***tamu**.
cloth	*PRM.* ***mbou**;
	PRM. ***tais**.
cloth, kind	*PRM.* ***lafa**.
clothes	*CERM.* ***lohas**.
cloud	*PnMeto.* ***habu**;
	PnRote. ***-oha**.
cloves	*Rote.* **#seŋge**
co-wife	*PRM.* ***mbala**.
coals	*PRM.* ***klaha**.
coarse	*Rote.* ***sela**.
coast	*PRM.* ***namo**$_2$.
cock	*PnRote.* ***lalu**.
cockatoo	*PRM.* ***kae**.
cockroach	*PRM.* ***kiŋgi**.
coconut	*PRM.* ***noh**.
coconut husk	*PRM.* ***mbunut**.
coconut, kind	*Rote.* ***sanu**.
coil	*PRM.* ***leke**;
	PRM. ***leku**.
coir	*PRM.* ***mbunut**.
cold	*PRM.* ***riŋin**.
comb	*PnMeto.* ***soʔi**;
	Rote. ***sau**$_3$;
	Rote. ***suhat**.
comb (rooster)	*PMeto.* ***dai**;
	PRM. ***lari**$_1$.
come	*nRM.* ***mai**;
	PRM. ***eti**;
	PRM. ***əmə**.
come out	*Rote.* ***lesu**$_2$.
come together	*nRM.* ***toŋgo**.
comfortable	*PRM.* ***mina**.
command	*PRM.* ***ɗenu**.
commerce	*PRM.* **#ɗaŋgan**
complain	*PnRote.* ***tani**.
completely	*PRM.* ***isa**$_2$.
conch	*PRM.* ***suti**.
concrete	*PRM.* ***ɗama**.
concubine	*PRM.* ***mbala**.
contain	*PRM.* ***tanee**.
container, coconut shell	*PRM.* ***ɓoki**.
contents	*Rote.* ***isi**.
cook	*PRM.* ***nasu**.
cooked	*PRM.* ***tasa**.
cool	*PRM.* ***mafo**.
cool (v.)	*PRM.* ***sufu**.
copper	*PRM.* **#riti**.
copulate	*PRM.* ***ŋoli**.
coral, kind	*Rote.* ***seɗa**.
<u>Cordia</u> species	*PRM.* ***nuŋa**.
corn cob	*PRM.* ***mbule**.
corpse	*PRM.* ***nitu**.

corral	CERM. *oka$_1$;
	Rote. *roŋga.
cost	Rote. *beli.
cotton	PRM. #kaɓas.
cough	PRM. *ɓoho.
count	Rote. *kahi$_2$.
country	PRM. *iŋgu.
course	PRM. *ɗalan.
cover	CER. *balu$_3$;
	PRM. *koɓa;
	PRM. *mbalu;
	PRM. *tana$_1$.
cow	PMeto. *biae.
crab	PRM. *niit.
crab, hermit	PRM. *saŋguma.
crack	Rote. *faka$_2$.
cram	PRM. *sesə.
crawl	PRM. *roɗok;
	Rote. *noɗo.
crazy	PRM. *mulu.
creature	PRM. *ulə.
creep	PRM. *nama.
cricket	nRM. *sandiit.
crisp	Rote. *tana$_2$.
croak	Rote. *ŋgeɗe.
crocodile	CER. *foe$_2$;
	PRM. *ɓeis.
crooked	Rote. *kilu.
cross	PRM. *ɗaŋga$_1$.
crossbeam	PRM. *ɓaat.
crouch	PRM. *ɗuɗi.
crow	PRM. *kaa$_2$.
crumble up	PRM. *teɓi.
crush	PRM. *mendu;
	Rote. *teɗe.
cry	PwRM. *ŋgae.
cry out	PRM. *koaʔ$_2$;
	Rote. *eki.
cucumber	PRM. *timu$_2$.
cure	Rote. #puli
current	Rote. *faa.
cuscus	PMeto. *arum;
	PnMeto. *ʔ|mauka|ʔ.
cushion	PRM. *lunu.
custom	PRM. #haɗat
cut	CERM. *ŋgeɓo;
	PRM. *fandi;
	PRM. *koti;
	PRM. *ndaru;
	PRM. *saɗa;
	PRM. *teta;
	PwRM. *ʔuta;
	Rote. *fura;
	Rote. *tati.
cut off	PRM. *ketu.
cut vegetation	Rote. *ɓeta.
cyclone	PRM. *kutus.

D - d

dam	CERM. *tete.
dance	PRM. *ɓasoko;
	PRM. *foti;
	Rote. *lendo.
dance, circle	CERM. *ɓone.
daughter-in-law	PMeto. #nane
day	PRM. *fai;
	PRM. *ledo.
day after tomorrow	PRM. *beni;
	PRM. *esak.
day before yesterday	PRM. *beni;
	PRM. *esak.
debark	PRM. *sambi.
debt, fine	Rote. #huta
decide	PMeto. *fera$_1$.
deep	PRM. *ɗəma.
deer	PRM. #rusa
delicious	PRM. *mina.
depending	nRM. *ɓoni.
Derris elliptica	PRM. *tufa.
desire	Rote. *ɗoki.
dew	CER. *ahu;
	CERM. *aŋgum.
die	PRM. *mate.

dig	PRM. *kali;
	Rote. *fuka.
dig out	PRM. *toki.
digging stick	PRM. *sua$_3$.
dip	PRM. *ɗəmbə;
	Rote. *ɗeta.
dirt	PRM. *daki.
disaster	PRM. *soe.
discussion	nRM. *ɗasi.
dish	Rote. #ɓasiu
distant	PRM. *ɗoo.
distribute	CERM. *ɓati.
divide	CERM. *ɓati;
	PnMeto. *paha;
	Rote. *faka$_1$.
do	PRM. *tao.
docile	PRM. *maus.
dog	CERM. *asu;
	Rote. *ɓusa.
Dolichandrone spathacea	Rote. *tui$_2$.
dolphin	CER. *lemuk.
domesticated	PRM. *aem;
	PRM. *maus.
door	nRM. *eno.
douse	nRM. *fui$_1$.
dove	PRM. *tadeŋgus;
	PRM. *teu;
	PRM. *mukə.
dove, wild	PMeto. *kumu$_1$.
dragnet	PRM. #pukat
draw water	PRM. *ɗolu;
	PRM. *ndui.
dream	PRM. *mehi.
dried	Rote. *tana$_2$.
dried up	PRM. *meti.
drink	PRM. *inu.
drip	Rote. *tiri;
	Rote. *titi.
drone	CERM. *ŋguu;
	PRM. *ŋguru.
drown	PRM. *ɗəma.
drunk	PRM. *mafu.
dry	PnRote. *tuu$_2$;
	PwRM. *meto;
	Rote. *maŋgu$_2$.
dry in sun	PRM. *hoi.
dry season	PRM. *fandu.
dry up	Rote. *maɗa.
duckweed	Rote. *lombu.
dugong	Rote. *dui$_2$.
dumb	PnMeto. *mono;
	Rote. *ŋgoa.
dust	PRM. *afu.
dyke	CERM. *tete.

E - e

eagle	CERM. *tema$_1$.
ear	Rote. *ndiki.
earth	PRM. *dae.
earthworm	Rote. *kalati.
earwax	Rote. *ŋgela$_1$.
eat	PMeto. #bukae
	PRM. *ha;
	PRM. *heŋgu.
edge	PRM. *liɗa;
	Rote. *suhu.
eel	PRM. *lema;
	PRM. *ŋgois.
eel, freshwater	PRM. *tuna.
egg	PRM. *təlo.
eight	PRM. *falu.
elbow	PRM. *siku.
embarrassed	PRM. *mae$_2$.
embers	PRM. *klaha.
embrace	PRM. *holu$_1$.
empty	PRM. *duman.
enclose	PRM. *mbalu.
endure	Rote. *taa$_4$.
enemy	PRM. *musu.
engrave	PRM. *ɗula.
enter	PMeto. *tama$_1$.
entire	PRM. *tema$_2$.
entwine	nRM. *laɓa.

equipment	CERM. *lohas;
	Rote. *ɓuas.
Erythrina species	PRM. *deras.
eschalot	PRM. *laisona.
ethnic group	PwRM. *-s.
eucalyptus	PnMeto. *huʔe;
	Rote. *ŋgela$_2$.
European	Rote. #filanda
evaporate	Rote. *maɗa.
exchange	PRM. *selut;
	PRM. *sembo.
excrement	PRM. *tai$_2$.
exist	PRM. *-uki.
expand	Rote. *mbumbu.
eye	PRM. *mata$_1$.
eyebrows	nRM. *mbonu.

F - f

face	PRM. *humək.
facing	PnRote. *sare.
faeces	PRM. *tai$_2$.
fall	PRM. *mofu;
	Rote. *monu.
far	PRM. *ɗoo.
fart	PnRote. *hesu.
fast	PRM. *ŋgafat;
	Rote. *lai.
fat	PRM. *mina;
	PRM. *poka.
fat-bellied	Rote. *ɓunda.
father	PRM. *ama.
fathom (n.)	PRM. *reha.
fear	PRM. *taku.
feather	PnMeto. *nafu|ʔ;
	PRM. *bulu.
feed	PRM. *hao;
	Rote. *fati.
feed (v.)	Rote. *hani$_1$.
feelings	nRM. *farəndən;
	PRM. *dalə.
female	PRM. *feto;
	Rote. *fata.
female animal	PRM. *ombu.
fence	PRM. #(m)baha
fetch	PRM. *ala.
few	PRM. *duman;
	PwRote. *hiɗa.
fibres	PRM. *ekut;
	Rote. *naa$_4$.
Ficus variegata	PRM. *larum.
field	nRM. *ɗene;
	PMeto. #etu
	Rote. *tina.
file	Rote. #fei
fill	CERM. *henu.
filth	PRM. *daki.
fin	PRM. *liɗa.
find	PRM. *hambu.
fine	PRM. *lutu$_1$.
finger	PRM. *kuku.
fingernail	PMeto. *kalusa.
finish	Rote. *həndi.
fire	PRM. *ahi$_2$.
fire, make	Rote. *ɗeu.
firebrand	CERM. *lutə.
firmament	Rote. *lani.
first	PRM. *hulu.
fish	PRM. *ika.
fish (v.)	PRM. *ɗolu.
fish, Blue-spot mullet	PRM. *nase.
fish, kind	Rote. *kahu;
	Rote. *nimba;
	Rote. *sunu.
fishing	nRM. *seko.
fist	nRM. *ŋgumu;
	Rote. *kumu$_2$.
fit together	Rote. *tama$_2$.
five	PRM. *lima$_1$.
fixed	Rote. *nembə.
flame (v.)	PRM. *mbila.
flea	Rote. *mela.
flee	PwRM. *ela$_2$;
	Rote. *lai.
flesh	nRM. *mbaa;
	PwRM. *sisi.
flesh, fruit	Rote. *isi.

flexible	PRM. *ɓetu;
	Rote. *feɗu.
floor	PRM. *afu.
flow	nRM. *sai$_1$;
	Rote. *faa.
flower	PRM. *ɓuna.
flower, decorative	Rote. #ɓuŋga
flute	PRM. *feku.
fly	PMeto. *ka|benu;
	Rote. *mbena.
fly (v.)	PnRote. *laa$_4$;
	PRM. *tambele.
flying fox	PRM. *ɓau.
foam	PRM. *fuʤə.
fog	PMeto. *kupu;
	PnMeto. *habu.
folded	PRM. *ɓetu.
follow	CERM. *tuin.
fontanelle	PMeto. *fufu$_1$;
	PRM. *ɓoto$_3$;
	PRM. *fumbu.
foot	PMeto. *hae|ʔ;
	Rote. *ei.
for	PRM. *əu.
force	PRM. *seke;
	PRM. *seti.
forehead	Rote. *dei.
foreigner	PMeto. *kase.
forest	PRM. *lasi$_1$;
	PRM. *ŋura.
fort	PRM. #kota
fortune	PRM. *uat.
four	PRM. *haa$_2$.
foxtail millet	Rote. *betə.
fragrant	PRM. *meni$_1$.
freckle	Rote. *ila.
Friarbird	PRM. *koaʔ$_1$.
frighten	PRM. *saŋgeŋger.
frizzy	nRM. *ɓuə.
frog	Rote. *ŋgeɗe.
from	PRM. *əmə.
front	PRM. *ulu.
front, be in	PRM. *hulu.
fruit	PRM. *bua.
fry	PRM. *seŋa.
fry pan	PRM. #tasu
full	CERM. *henu.
fur	PRM. *bulu.

G - g

galangal	PRM. *sokum.
gall bladder	PRM. *hedu.
gamete	PRM. *natu.
garden	nRM. *ɗene;
	PRM. *mamər;
	Rote. *osi;
	Rote. *tina.
gargle	Rote. *mumu$_2$.
garlic	PnMeto. *pio.
garment	PRM. #baʤu
<u>*Garuga floribuna*</u>	PRM. *beu$_2$.
gate	nRM. *eno.
gather	PRM. *ɓua.
gather under wings	PnRote. *saluku.
gecko	PRM. *teke.
get	PRM. *ala.
get up	PwRM. *fela$_1$;
	Rote. *foʔa.
gills	PRM. *ŋgadas.
ginger	PRM. *laia.
give	PRM. *fee$_2$.
glitter	PRM. *ɗila$_2$.
go	PRM. *eti;
	PRM. *əu;
	PRM. *lako.
go back	PRM. *bali$_1$.
go down	Rote. *loe$_1$.
go up	PRM. *sake.
goat	PRM. *ɓiɓi.
goatee	PnRote. *ŋgomi.
goatfish	Rote. *ti(ʔ)o.
gold	PRM. *lilo.
good	PMeto. #leko
gourd	PRM. *ɓoŋgo$_2$;
	PRM. *kelas.
grain, crushed	PRM. *ɗio.

grain head	PRM. *mbule.
grandchild	PRM. *umbu.
grandfather	PwRM. *laʔi;
	Rote. *ɓaʔi.
grandmother	PRM. *ɓei.
grass	CERM. *mau;
	PRM. *kuun;
	PRM. *nade.
grasshopper	PRM. *lamat.
grate	PRM. *fora;
	PRM. *paru.
grave	PRM. *rates.
great	CERM. *ŋgoʔu.
green	PRM. *mata$_2$;
	PRM. *moɗo.
greet	PRM. *səru;
	PRM. *teka;
	PRM. #taɓe
Grewia slutaris	PRM. *lino.
grey hair	PRM. *mofa.
grind	PRM. *mendu.
grope	PRM. *badoe.
ground	PRM. *afu;
	PRM. *dae.
grow	PRM. *nae;
	Rote. *numbu.
growl	PRM. *ŋguru.
grub, edible	PRM. *ɓate.
guard	CERM. *papa.
guava	PRM. #koedʒabas
gum	PRM. *ɗama;
	PRM. *ɗitə.
gum tree	Rote. *ŋgela$_2$.
gums	PMeto. *nada.
gun	PRM. *ndelat.

H - h

hair	nRM. *ɓuə;
	nRM. *mbonu;
	PRM. *bulu.
hair, body	PnMeto. *nafu|ʔ.
hair, head	PRM. *ulu.
half	CERM. *tairua.
hand	PRM. *lima$_2$.
hand span	PnRote. *teŋga;
	PwRote. *haŋga.
hang	nRM. *ɓoni;
	PRM. *heŋge;
	PRM. *loke;
	PRM. *tambele.
hang over	PRM. *ɓandae.
hard	Rote. *nembə.
harvest	PRM. *koru;
	PRM. *seŋgi.
have	PRM. *-uki;
	Rote. *ena.
he	PnRote. *ndia;
	PwRM. *eni.
head	PRM. *laŋga.
head hair	PRM. *laŋga.
head, lower	CERM. *ŋgiro.
heal	Rote. #puli
heap	CERM. *tumbu.
hear	PwRM. *rena;
	Rote. *nene$_2$.
heart	PRM. *tendə.
hearth	nRM. *raho.
heartwood	PRM. *teas.
heaven	Rote. *lani.
heavy	PRM. *berat.
heel	PRM. *tiŋga.
help	PRM. #ɓaɓa
	Rote. *fali;
	Rote. *holu$_2$.
her	PwRM. *ee.
herd (v.)	PRM. *boo$_1$.
here	PRM. *ia.
Hibiscus tiliaceus	PRM. *bau.
hide	PRM. *funi$_1$;
	PwRM. *kuna.
hill	PRM. *lete$_1$;
	Rote. *mbuku$_2$.
him	PwRM. *ee.
hit	PnMeto. *deku;
	PRM. *tufu;
	Rote. *femba;
	Rote. *liku$_1$.

hold	*Rote.* ***kira$_1$.**
hold in mouth	*PRM.* ***moo.**
hole	*PRM.* ***ɓolo$_1$**;
	PRM. ***mboo**;
	PwRM. ***kola.**
hook	*PRM.* ***kai$_2$.**
hope	*nRM.* ***farəndən**;
	PRM. ***hena.**
horn	*PRM.* ***sura.**
horn (instrument)	*CERM.* ***toʔis.**
hornet	*CERM.* ***katefuan.**
horse	*Rote.* **#ndara**
hot	*PRM.* ***hanas**;
	PRM. ***mbutu$_1$**;
	PRM. ***toɓi.**
house	*PRM.* ***uma.**
house post	*PRM.* ***dii$_2$.**
household	*Rote.* ***loo$_2$.**
hover	*PRM.* ***ɓandae.**
how much?	*PRM.* ***hida.**
howl	*CERM.* ***ŋguu.**
hug	*PRM.* ***holu$_1$.**
hundred	*PRM.* ***natu|n.**
hungry	*CERM.* ***laha.**
hunt	*nRM.* ***seko.**
hurt	*Rote.* ***loɓo.**
hut	*CERM.* ***lopo**;
	PRM. ***laa$_2$.**

I - i

I	*PRM.* ***au.**
impede	*Rote.* ***toka.**
in	*PRM.* ***ɓee**;
	PRM. ***dalə.**
incite	*CERM.* ***huti.**
indigo	*PRM.* ***taum.**
inflated	*CERM.* ***saɓuu.**
inform	*PRM.* ***faɗa.**
in-law	*PRM.* ***feu.**
insect, kind	*PRM.* ***ketembau**;
	PRM. ***muut**;
	PRM. ***otas.**
insert	*Rote.* ***ɗuŋgu.**
inside	*PRM.* ***dalə.**
insipid	*CER.* ***afa**;
	Rote. ***mamis.**
investigate	*PRM.* ***susi.**
invite	*PRM.* ***hoka.**
iron	*PRM.* **#ɓesi**
island	*PRM.* ***nusa.**
it	*PnRote.* ***ndia.**
itchy	*PRM.* ***katə.**

J - j

jar	*PRM.* ***kurə**;
	PRM. **#ŋgusi**
jealous	*Rote.* ***neo.**
jerk	*Rote.* ***biti$_2$**;
	Rote. ***fiti$_1$.**
jicama	*PRM.* ***uas.**
Job's tears	*PRM.* ***ɗele.**
join	*PRM.* ***tamba$_2$**;
	PRM. ***tute.**
joint	*PRM.* ***ɓuku**;
	PRM. ***mola.**
jump up	*Rote.* ***biti$_2$.**
just	*PRM.* ***fa.**

K - k

kapok tree	PRM. *deŋe.
keel	Rote. *keni.
kick	Rote. *fiti$_2$.
kidneys	PMeto. #kari
kill	PRM. *ɗoɗo;
	PRM. *isa$_2$.
king	PMeto. *usi$_2$;
	PwRM. *laʔi;
	Rote. *mane.
kingfisher	PRM. *sinaraʔe.
kiss	CER. *deki;
	Rote. *iɗu.
kiss (nose)	nRM. *farəndən.
Kleinhovia hospita	PRM. *ɓitinaa.
knead	PnRote. *keʔe;
	Rote. *kame;
	Rote. *keme;
	Rote. *kumu$_2$.
knee	PMeto. *tuu$_1$.
knee cavity	Rote. *ɗoka.
knife	PMeto. #kopi
	Rote. *ɗombe.
knock	PnMeto. *deku;
	Rote. *liku$_1$;
	Rote. *toko.
know	PwRM. *hine.

L - l

ladder	PRM. *eɗa.
lake	PRM. *lifu;
	Rote. *ɗano.
land	PRM. *dae;
	PRM. *iŋgu.
landslide	PRM. *ndefa;
	Rote. *fera$_2$.
lap	PRM. *ifa.
last	PRM. *muri.
lath	PRM. *sikəh.
laugh	PwRM. *malis.
leaf	PRM. *doo.
leaf, covering	nRM. *namba.
leaf, palm	PRM. *mboro.
leak	PRM. *turu.
lean	PRM. *sarait.
learn	PRM. *nori.
leave	Rote. *kela.
leech	PRM. *ndaki;
	Rote. *kerumatu.
left	PnRote. *kii.
left (side)	PwRM. *ɗii$_1$.
leg	PMeto. *hae|ʔ;
	Rote. *ei.
legume	PRM. *fue.
lemon	PRM. *ɗero.
lever	PRM. *ɗoʔi;
	PRM. *foʔi.
liana	PRM. *lolo$_1$.
lick	PRM. *damei.
lie down	nRM. *mbeʔu.
lie on	Rote. *nehi.
light (adj.)	PRM. *ŋgafat.
light (n.)	PRM. *saraa;
	PRM. *sina.
lightning	PRM. *ndelat.
like	PMeto. *domi.
lime (fruit)	PRM. *munde.
lime, mineral	PRM. *aho.
lip	PwRM. *nuɗu;
	Rote. *ɓife.
listen	Rote. *nene$_2$.
listless	PRM. *loe$_2$.
live	PRM. *moris.
liver	PRM. *ate.
living	PRM. *horis.
lizard	CER. *fae.
lizard, flying	Rote. *ŋgola.
lizard, monitor	PRM. *ɓaiafa;
	Rote. *ŋgola.
load	Rote. *fua$_1$.
lobster	CERM. *hee$_1$.
long	CER. *daru;
	PRM. *naru.
long ago	PRM. *ulu.
look	PRM. *ita.

look up Rote. *naɗo.
loom, breast beam of CERM. *atis.
loom, part PRM. *sikəh.
loom, weaving sword of PRM. *seru.
loose PRM. *sara.
loosen PRM. *hosu.
lord PMeto. *usi$_2$; PRM. *tua$_3$.
louse, clothes PRM. *tuma.
louse, head PRM. *kutu.
love nRM. *farəndən; PMeto. *domi.
low tide PRM. *meti.
lower PRM. *ɗolu.
lungs PRM. *tendə; Rote. *baa.
lure Rote. *leko.

M - m

machete PRM. *belas; Rote. *tafa.
maggots Rote. *sinor.
maize PRM. *mbela.
Malay gooseberry PRM. #seremere
male PRM. *mone; PwRM. *laʔi; Rote. *mane.
Mallotus philippensis PRM. *ɓalafo.
man PRM. *hatahori; PRM. *mone; PRM. *tou.
mane nRM. *mbonu.
mango Rote. *mbao; Rote. #maŋga
mangrove PRM. *tene.
mantis nRM. *tae.
mantle Rote. *kutə; Rote. *rumbi.
many CERM. *ɓaʔu; PRM. *nae.
marrow nRM. *ɗole.
marry PRM. *sao$_1$.
mat CERM. *nahe; Rote. *nehi.
matter nRM. *ɗasi.
meat nRM. *mbaa; PwRM. *sisi.
medicine PRM. *maɗo.
meet nRM. *toŋgo; PRM. *səru.
melon, winter PRM. *kelas.
melt PRM. *noe.
midday PRM. *fumbu; PRM. *tetu.
middle PRM. *talaɗa.
midge PMeto. *imun.
millet Rote. *betə.
Millettia pinnata PRM. *ɓoto$_2$.
Millingtonia hortensis PRM. *taŋga.
mince PRM. *teta.
mind nRM. *farəndən.
mirror PRM. *tino; Rote. *tiro.
mix PRM. *seɗo; Rote. *ɓali.
mock CERM. *kleet.
mole (skin) Rote. *ila.
money PRM. *talin; PRM. #ɗoit
monkey PRM. *koɗe.
moon PRM. *bulan.
Morinda citrifolia PRM. *baŋakuɗu.
Moringa oleifera PRM. *foo.
mortar PRM. *nesu.
mosquito PMeto. *imun; PRM. *muut; Rote. *nini.
moss Rote. *lombu.
mother PRM. *ina.
mountain PRM. *lete$_1$.
mourn PRM. *balu$_1$.
mouse PRM. *lafo.
moustache nRM. *mbonu.

mouth	PMeto. *fefa;
	PwRM. *nuɗu;
	Rote. *ɓafa$_2$.
move	PRM. *foe$_3$;
	Rote. *heo.
move location	PRM. *lari$_2$.
mud	Rote. *tane$_1$.
muscle	PRM. *uat.
mushroom	PRM. *mbuku$_1$.
mute	Rote. *ŋgoa.
mutter	CERM. *ɓoto$_1$.

N - n

nail	Rote. *faŋga.
nail, finger-/toe-	PMeto. *kalusa.
naked	PRM. *holas.
name	Rote. *naʤa.
name, ancestral	CERM. *tamo.
nautilus	PRM. *suti.
navel	PRM. *husə.
nearly	nRM. *ohi.
neck	PRM. *ɓoto$_3$;
	PRM. *lesu$_1$;
	Rote. *lii$_2$.
neck, nape	PRM. *ndou.
necklace	PRM. *heŋge.
neigh	CERM. *kele.
needle	Rote. *ndau.
nerve of palm leaf	Rote. *liɗe.
nest	PRM. *nduna;
	Rote. *nuu$_1$.
net	PRM. #ʤala
nettle	PRM. *ndesi.
new	PRM. *beu$_1$.
nice	PRM. *mina.
niece	PMeto. #nane
night	PRM. *fai.
nine	PRM. *sio.
nit	Rote. *kua.
no	PnRote. *taa$_3$;
	PRM. *fa;
	PwRM. *ŋgaha.
node	PRM. *ɓuku;
	PRM. *mola.
noise	PRM. *ɗoto;
	PRM. *mbuu.
noose	Rote. *ikə.
north	PnRote. *kii;
	PwRM. *ɗii$_1$.
nose	PRM. *mbana;
	Rote. *iɗu.
not	PnRote. *taa$_3$;
	PwRM. *ŋgaha.
now	PRM. *leu.

O - o

oakum	Rote. *ɗuɗu.
ocean	PRM. *tasi.
octopus	Rote. *paɗo.
odour	PRM. *boo$_2$.
oh!	CER. *auee.
oil	PRM. *mina.
oink	Rote. *uu.
old	PRM. *lasi$_2$;
	PRM. *mba|raa.
one	PRM. *esa.
onion	PRM. *laisona.
open	CER. *siŋga;
	PRM. *fei;
	PRM. *soi;
	Rote. *huka;
	Rote. *sai$_2$;
	Rote. *sika.
open (adj.)	PRM. *lua$_2$.
open the eyes	Rote. *ɓula;
	Rote. *laa$_5$.
open the mouth	PnMeto. *m|kaka.
opposite	CER. *taɗu.
orange (fruit)	PRM. *ɗero.

orchard	PRM. *mamər.
order	PRM. *ɗenu.
orphan	PRM. *ma(n)at.
other	Rote. *fekə.
outside	PMeto. *mone|ʔ;
	PRM. *lua$_2$.
ovary	PRM. *natu.
overflow	PRM. *sasi;
	PRM. *turu;
	Rote. *faa.
overtake	PRM. *hambu.
owl	nRM. *tudui.
owl, barn	PRM. *ɓakos.
own	PRM. *-uki;
	Rote. *ena.
owner	PRM. *tua$_3$.
oyster	PRM. *tiam.

P - p

<u>Pachyrhizus erosus</u>	PRM. *uas.
packed	PRM. *seti.
paddle	Rote. *sefe.
pain	PRM. *meras;
	Rote. *heɗis.
palate	PRM. *ŋgadas.
palm, areca	PRM. *mbuah.
palm, areng	PRM. *ɓole.
palm, dead	PRM. *mopu.
palm, gebang	PRM. *tula.
palm, lontar	PRM. *tua$_2$.
palm, trunk	PRM. *mopu.
palm leaf stem	PRM. *ɓeɓa.
palm line	PRM. *uat;
	Rote. *ura.
palm wine	PRM. *ladu.
pandanus, fragrant	CERM. *ɓona.
pandanus, wild	PRM. *hendam.
pant	CERM. *kele.
pants	Rote. #sarombo
papaya	PRM. *timu$_2$.
parakeet	PRM. *ŋgia.
paralysed	Rote. *luku$_2$.
<u>Parkia speciosa</u>	PRM. *fake.
pass	PRM. *beni.
patch	PRM. *tamba$_2$.
path	nRM. *eno;
	PRM. *ɗalan.
pattern	PRM. *ɗula.
peak	PRM. *fumbu.
peel	PRM. *kisi;
	PRM. *saɗa;
	Rote. *soso.
peer	PRM. *tino;
	Rote. *tiro.
pen	CERM. *oka$_1$;
	Rote. *roŋga.
penis	PRM. *uti.
person	PRM. *hatahori;
	PRM. *tou;
	PRM. *tua$_3$.
persuade	PRM. *fuɗi.
pestle	PRM. *halu.
pick	PRM. *sau$_2$;
	PRM. *seu.
pick at	PRM. *ŋgai.
pick out	PRM. *soke.
pierce	PnMeto. *fado.
pig	PRM. *bafi.
pigeon	PRM. *teu.
pigeon, wild	PMeto. *kumu$_1$.
pigeon pea	PRM. *turis.
pile up	Rote. *lutu$_2$.
pillar	PRM. *dii$_2$.
pillow	PRM. *lunu.
pimple	PRM. *ɓisu.
pinch	CER. *bibi;
	PRM. *ɓiti;
	PRM. *hapi;
	PRM. *kaɓi;
	PRM. *ŋgete.
pip	PwRM. *muse$_1$;
	Rote. *ɗeke.
<u>Pisonia alba</u>	CERM. *safe.
place (n.)	Rote. *mana$_2$.
place (v.)	PRM. *mbeɗa.

placenta	Rote. *funi2.
plait	PwRM. *ŋano.
plank	PRM. #papan
plant (v.)	PRM. *selə.
plant, kind	CERM. *mau;
	PRM. *lisum;
	Rote. *kunu2.
plaster	PRM. *ɗama.
plate	PRM. #piŋga
platform	PMeto. #hada|k
plop	CER. *poko.
plug	PRM. *sulə.
Podocarpus rumphii	PRM. *mbiko.
point	PRM. *tuɗu.
pole	PRM. *dii2.
pool	PRM. *lifu.
possess	Rote. *ena.
possession	CERM. *nuu2.
post	PRM. *dii2.
pot	PRM. *kurə.
pound	PRM. *mbau2;
	PRM. *tutu.
pour	nRM. *fui1;
	nRM. *tisa;
	PnRote. *sali;
	PRM. *mbori;
	PwRM. *komba.
powder	PRM. *ŋgafur.
pox	PwRM. *ɓolo2.
prawn	PRM. *mboes.
pregnant	PwRM. *kambu.
press	nRM. *ŋgumu;
	PRM. *nene1;
	PRM. *tuni;
	Rote. *hee2;
	Rote. *rumu;
	Rote. *teɗe.
price	PnMeto. *osa;
	Rote. *beli.
prick	PRM. *mbau2.
prince	Rote. *mane.
prohibit	PRM. *kahin.
protect	CERM. *papa.
protuberance	PRM. *toɗi.
provisions	PMeto. #bukae
provoke	CERM. *huti.
Pterocarpus indica	Rote. *naa3.
pull	nRM. *hela;
	PRM. *kahi1.
pull off	PRM. *lui.
pull out	PRM. *fakur;
	PRM. *hosu.
pumpkin	PRM. *ɓoŋgo2.
punch	PRM. *tufu.
pursue	Rote. *usi1.
pus	Rote. *nana.
push	PRM. *kahi1;
	PRM. *nene1;
	Rote. #soro
put	PRM. *ɗai1;
	PRM. *mbeɗa;
	PRM. *tao.

Q - q

quail	PRM. *mbui.
quarrel	PRM. *tofa2.
quick	PRM. *ŋgafat;
	Rote. *lai.
quiet	PRM. *nee2.

R - r

racing	PRM. *foti.
rafter	PnMeto. *sua2.
rain	PRM. *uɗan.
rainbow	PRM. *elus.
rainy season	PRM. *faat.
random	PRM. *ɗafu2.
ransom	PRM. *soi.
rash	PRM. *hano.
rat	PRM. *lafo.
rattan	PRM. *ue.

rattle	*Rote.* ***roko**.
ravine	*Rote.* ***fera**$_2$.
raw	*PRM.* ***mata**$_2$.
reach	*Rote.* ***ɗai**$_2$;
	Rote. ***losa**.
rear	*PRM.* ***ɓuit**.
receive	*PRM.* ***simo**.
red	*PRM.* ***mea**;
	PRM. ***mbila**.
reduce	*PwRote.* ***hiɗa**.
reef	*CERM.* ***tete**.
relativiser	*PRM.* ***mana**$_1$.
release	*PRM.* ***mbosi**.
religion, traditional	
	PMeto. ***fua**$_2$.
remember	*nRM.* ***farəndən**.
remove	*PRM.* ***lui**.
replace	*PRM.* ***selut**.
resin	*PRM.* ***ɗama**;
	PRM. ***ɗitə**.
rest	*PRM.* ***hae**.
return	*PRM.* ***bali**$_1$.
rib	*PMeto.* **#bnapa**
ribs	*PRM.* ***tendə**;
	Rote. ***kai/usu**.
rice, husked	*PMeto.* ***mneas**.
rice, paddy	*PRM.* ***hade**.
rice, unhusked	*Rote.* ***taa**$_2$.
rice ear bug	*PMeto.* **#kameru|ʔ**
rice husk	*PwRote.* ***eto**.
rice packet	*Rote.* **#tuhas**
<u>Ricinus communis</u>	*Rote.* ***luu**$_1$.
ridge	*CERM.* ***tete**.
ridgepole	*PRM.* ***fumbu**.
right	*Rote.* ***kona**.
ring	*PRM.* ***ndeli**.
ringworm	*PRM.* ***buni**.
rinse	*Rote.* ***mumu**$_2$.
rip	*PRM.* ***siɗa**.
ripe	*PRM.* ***latu**$_1$;
	PRM. ***tasa**.
rise	*PwRM.* ***fela**$_1$.
rise up	*PRM.* ***sake**.
river	*PRM.* ***lee**.
road	*nRM.* ***eno**;
	PRM. ***ɗalan**.
roast	*PRM.* ***ɗada**;
	PRM. ***seʔi**;
	PRM. ***tunu**$_2$.
rock	*PRM.* ***batu**.
rod	*PRM.* ***sikəh**.
roll	*Rote.* ***lolir**.
roll up	*PRM.* ***lulun**.
room	*CER.* **#roa**
rooster	*PnRote.* ***lalu**.
root	*PMeto.* **#baʔat**
	Rote. ***oka**$_2$.
rope	*PRM.* ***tali**.
rotten	*CERM.* ***mbai**;
	PRM. ***mburuk**.
rough	*Rote.* ***sela**.
round	*PRM.* ***ɓoŋgo**$_1$.
row	*Rote.* ***tuku**$_1$.
rub	*nRM.* ***hutu**;
	PRM. ***rose**;
	PRM. ***tusi**$_2$;
	Rote. ***kose**.
rudder	*Rote.* ***uli**.
run	*PwRM.* ***ela**$_2$;
	Rote. ***lai**.
rust	*PRM.* ***rutus**.

S - s

sack	*PRM.* **#kaɗo**
sack, kind	*Rote.* ***soka**.
sacred	*PwRM.* ***ɗeʔu**.
sacrifice	*PwRM.* ***ponia**.
saddle	*PRM.* ***peni**.
sail	*Rote.* ***laa**$_3$.
saliva	*PRM.* ***kambe**;
	Rote. ***midu**.
salty	*PRM.* ***masi**.
same	*nRM.* ***nesa**;
	Rote. **#sama**
sand	*PRM.* ***sarakaen**.
sandalwood	*PnMeto.* ***meni**$_2$;
	PnMeto. ***meni**$_2$.
sardine	*Rote.* ***temba**.
sarong	*PRM.* ***tais**.

saw (n.)	*Rote.* **#horo**
say	*PRM.* ***faɗa.**
scabies	*PRM.* ***nuʔa;**
	PwRM. ***ɓolo2.**
scale	*Rote.* ***unə.**
scared	*PRM.* ***taku.**
scatter	*PRM.* ***ŋgari.**
Schleichera oleosa	*PMeto.* **#kusapi**
scissors	*Rote.* **#ŋgute**
scold	*PwRM.* ***siŋgadaʔ.**
scoop	*CER.* ***aso;**
	PRM. ***ndui;**
	PRM. ***raʔu;**
	PRM. ***soke;**
	PRM. ***soro;**
	PRM. ***suru.**
scorpion	*PRM.* ***ɓiti;**
	Rote. ***kura.**
scour	*PRM.* ***fora.**
scrape	*PRM.* ***kao;**
	PRM. ***ŋgeu;**
	PRM. ***suu1;**
	Rote. ***karu.**
scratch	*PRM.* ***kao;**
	PRM. ***ŋgai;**
	PRM. ***suu1;**
	Rote. ***karu.**
scrotum	*PRM.* ***lasə.**
sea	*PRM.* ***tasi.**
sea cucumber	*PRM.* ***ɓanafi.**
sea snail	*PwRM.* ***ɓatus.**
sea urchin	*PMeto.* ***k|teom;**
	Rote. ***tii.**
sea-snake	*PRM.* ***lema.**
seasoning	*PMeto.* **#fukar**
seaweed	*CER.* ***lamu;**
	PRM. ***keŋga;**
	Rote. ***latu2.**
see	*PRM.* ***ita.**
seed	*PRM.* ***bini;**
	PwRM. ***muse1;**
	Rote. ***ɗeke.**
seethe	*PRM.* ***lua1.**
sell	*PMeto.* ***sosa.**
Senna timoriensis	*nRM.* ***namo1.**
separate	*Rote.* ***fekə.**
sesame	*PRM.* ***lena.**
Sesbania grandiflora	*PRM.* ***ŋgala.**
seven	*PRM.* ***hitu.**
several	*CERM.* ***ɓaʔu.**
sew	*PRM.* ***ŋato;**
	PRM. ***soo.**
shadow	*PRM.* ***mafo.**
shake	*CERM.* ***ɓeko;**
	PRM. ***ŋgeŋgo;**
	Rote. ***eko;**
	Rote. ***noko.**
shallot	*PRM.* ***laisona.**
share	*CERM.* ***ɓati.**
shark	*PRM.* ***iu.**
sharp	*PRM.* ***tande.**
sharpen	*PRM.* ***kiri2.**
shave	*PRM.* ***ŋgeu.**
she	*PnRote.* ***ndia;**
	PwRM. ***eni.**
sheep	*PRM.* ***ɓiɓi.**
shell	*PnRote.* ***hani2.**
shell, cowrie	*Rote.* ***fuli.**
shell, kind	*PRM.* ***suti;**
	Rote. ***ɓina.**
shellfish	*Rote.* ***kibo;**
	Rote. ***sii2.**
shelter	*CERM.* ***lopo.**
shine	*PRM.* ***ɗila2;**
	PRM. ***saraa.**
short	*PRM.* ***mbada;**
	PwRM. ***tuka;**
	Rote. ***pande.**
shoulder	*PRM.* ***haru.**
shout	*Rote.* ***eki;**
	Rote. ***ŋgasi.**
shrimp	*nRM.* ***tae;**
	PRM. ***mboes.**
shrub	*Rote.* ***ŋgirat.**
shy	*PnRote.* ***lii3;**
	PRM. ***mae2.**
sibling, elder	*Rote.* ***kaka.**
sibling, older	*nRM.* ***tatə.**
sibling, younger	*PRM.* ***waɗi.**
sick	*PRM.* ***meras;**
	Rote. ***heɗis.**
side	*PMeto.* **#bnapa**
sift	*Rote.* ***eko.**

English	Rote-Meto
sign	PRM. #tanda
silver	PRM. *lilo.
similar	PMeto. #en
sing	Rote. *soɗa.
sink	PRM. *tena$_1$.
sip	PRM. *sakoro.
sister	PRM. *feto.
sister-in-law	PnRote. *iha.
sit	nRM. *tuur.
six	PRM. *nee$_1$.
size	Rote. *tua$_1$.
skin	Rote. *rou.
sky	PRM. *ledo.
slant	PRM. *ɓasoko.
slap	PwRM. *mbasa.
slave	PRM. *ata$_3$.
sleep	nRM. *mbeʔu.
sleepy	nRM. *mbeʔu;
	PRM. *noto.
slide	PRM. *saɗodo.
sling	PRM. *piru.
slingshot	PRM. *biti$_3$.
slippery	nRM. *kendi.
slow	PRM. *noto.
small	PRM. *anak;
	PRM. *ɗiki;
	PRM. *lutu$_1$.
smell	PRM. *boo$_2$.
smile	PRM. *humək.
smoke	CERM. *saɓuu;
	PRM. *masu.
smooth	nRM. *kendi.
snake	PRM. *ndaki;
	PRM. *sao$_2$;
	PRM. *ulə.
snake, red	PRM. *meŋge.
snap off	PRM. *seŋgi.
snare	CER. *sii$_1$;
	CERM. *fetu;
	Rote. *ikə.
sneeze	PRM. *kesu/fani.
snore	PRM. *ŋgoro.
snot	PRM. *mbinu.
snout	PRM. *ŋgoro.
so	PRM. *ɗee.
soak	PRM. *endən.
soil	PRM. *dae.
some	PRM. *duman.
soot	PRM. *atu.
soothe	PRM. *hauk.
sorcery	PnMeto. *nono$_1$.
sorghum	PRM. *mbela.
sorry	nRM. *sale.
sound	PRM. *ɗoto;
	PRM. *hara;
	PRM. *mbuu;
	Rote. *lii$_1$.
sour	PRM. *kais;
	PRM. *ŋilu;
	PRM. *rekət.
source	PRM. *huu.
sow	PRM. *ŋgari.
space	PRM. *soda.
span	PnRote. *teŋga;
	PRM. *reha;
	PwRM. *ɗaŋga$_2$;
	PwRote. *haŋga.
speak	PRM. *faɗa;
	Rote. *ɗeha;
	Rote. *ŋgasi.
spear	Rote. *tee.
speech	nRM. *ɗasi.
spice	PMeto. #fukar
spider	PMeto. #k|naba|ʔ
	Rote. *ɓo/lau.
spindle	PRM. #kinde
spirit	PRM. *nitu;
	PRM. *sumanə.
spit out	PMeto. *ŋinu;
	Rote. *midu.
spittle	PRM. *kambe.
split	PnMeto. *paha;
	PRM. *ɓia;
	PRM. *tusi$_1$;
	Rote. *faka$_1$;
	Rote. *faka$_2$;
	Rote. *tata.
spool	PRM. *lole$_2$.
spoon	PRM. *soro;
	PRM. *suru.
spots	PRM. *foe$_1$;
	PRM. *hano.
spread out	CER. *fela$_2$;
	PRM. *ɓela;

	PRM. *sara;
	PRM. *tambele.
sprinkle	*PRM.* #[p/b]isi
sprout	*Rote.* *numbu.
spurt	*PRM.* *sambudas.
spy	*PRM.* *luku$_1$.
squash	*PRM.* *ɓoŋgo$_2$.
squeeze	*CERM.* *kees;
	nRM. *ŋgumu.
squid	*Rote.* *nuus.
stab	*PRM.* *ɗoɗo;
	PRM. *mbau$_2$.
staff	*PRM.* *tekə.
stairs	*PRM.* *eɗa.
stand	*Rote.* *dii$_1$.
stand with	*Rote.* *fali.
star	*PRM.* *fanduun.
star, morning	*PMeto.* #nome
startle	*PRM.* *saŋgeŋger.
state	*PRM.* *nusa.
steal	*Rote.* *nako.
steam	*PRM.* *masu;
	PRM. *suma.
step	*PRM.* *taɓu.
step over	*PRM.* *ɗaŋga$_1$.
<u>*Sterculia foetidea*</u>	*PRM.* *nitas.
<u>*Sterculia urceolata*</u>	*PRM.* *fuloat.
stick	*PRM.* *lolo$_3$.
stick, walking	*PRM.* *tekə.
stick out	*PRM.* *loɗe;
	PRM. *toɗi.
stick to	*PRM.* *ɗitə;
	PwRM. *ndika;
	Rote. *tai$_3$.
sticky	*PRM.* *ɗitə.
stiff	*Rote.* *kai$_1$.
still	*PRM.* *bei;
	PRM. *nee$_2$.
still (water)	*PnRote.* *lənde.
stingray	*PRM.* *hai$_2$.
stingy	*Rote.* *kira$_2$.
stink	*PRM.* *boo$_2$.
stocks	*PRM.* *laŋge.
stomach	*nRM.* *neko;
	PRM. *tai$_1$.
stone	*PRM.* *batu.
stoop	*PRM.* *ɗuɗi.
stop	*PRM.* *kahin.
stop by	*Rote.* *tuli.
storm	*PRM.* *kutus.
straight	*PRM.* *loɗo;
	PRM. *ndoo.
strait	*PRM.* *lolo$_4$.
stretch	*PRM.* *lolo$_2$;
	Rote. *loo$_1$.
strike	*PnMeto.* *deku;
	Rote. *femba;
	Rote. *liku$_1$.
strip leaves	*PRM.* *koru.
stripe	*PRM.* *tui$_1$.
strong	*PRM.* *ɓeki.
struggle	*PRM.* *foe$_3$.
stub	*PRM.* *tunu$_1$.
stuck	*PRM.* *seke.
stumble	*PRM.* *tunu$_1$.
stupid	*PnMeto.* *mono;
	Rote. *ŋgoa.
submerge	*PRM.* *tena$_1$.
suck	*PRM.* *musi;
	Rote. *mumu$_1$.
suffering	*PRM.* *rekət.
suffocate	*Rote.* *neta.
sugarcane	*PRM.* *tefu.
summon	*PRM.* *kati.
sun	*PRM.* *ledo.
sunbeam	*PRM.* *saraa.
sunset	*CERM.* *tesa.
surprise	*PRM.* *saŋgeŋger.
surround	*CERM.* *liɓu;
	Rote. *rimbu.
swallow	*PRM.* *koɗo.
swap	*PRM.* *sembo.
sway	*CERM.* *ɓeko;
	PRM. *ɓasoko.
swear	*PRM.* #sumba
sweat	*PRM.* *mbusər.
sweet	*Rote.* *mamis.
sweet potato	*PRM.* *lole$_1$.
swell	*PRM.* *mbetak;
	PRM. *poka;
	Rote. *mbae.
swim	*Rote.* *naŋe.
swollen	*Rote.* *mbumbu.
sword	*PRM.* *sure;
	Rote. *tafa.

T - t

table	*PRM.* #mei
taboo	*PRM.* *luli.
tail	*PRM.* *iko.
take	*PRM.* *ala;
	PRM. *əndi;
	Rote. *ha(ʔ)i.
tall	*PRM.* *naru.
tamarind	*PRM.* *ŋilu.
tame	*PRM.* *aem;
	PRM. *ma(n)at;
	PRM. *maus.
taro	*PRM.* *fia;
	PRM. *lole$_1$;
	PRM. *nade;
	Rote. *tales.
tart	*PRM.* *rekət.
tattoo	*PRM.* *ɗula.
tax	*PRM.* *susu$_1$.
teach	*PRM.* *nori.
tears (crying)	*PRM.* *luu$_2$.
tease	*CERM.* *kleet.
teem	*CERM.* *liɓu;
	Rote. *rimbu.
teeth	*PRM.* *nisi.
tell	*PRM.* *faɗa;
	PRM. *teka.
ten	*PMeto.* *boaʔ;
	Rote. *sanahulu.
tendon	*PRM.* *uat.
tendril	*CERM.* *ɗeli.
tense	*PRM.* *ɓetə.
<u>*Terminalia catappa*</u>	*nRM.* *lise;
	PRM. *ŋgaem.
termites	*nRM.* *daem.
testicles	*PRM.* *lasə.
that	*PnRote.* *ndia;
	PRM. *naa$_1$.
the	*PRM.* *aa.
them	*PRM.* *sira.
then	*PRM.* *ɗee.
there	*nRM.* *ele;
	PRM. *naa$_1$.
therefore	*PMeto.* *etu$_2$.
they	*PRM.* *sira;
	PwRM. *eni.
thick	*PwRM.* *faun.
thigh	*nRM.* *mbusu;
	PRM. *saka.
thin	*PRM.* *nihis.
thing	*Rote.* *ɓuas;
	Rote. #ɓanda
this	*PnRote.* *ndia;
	PRM. *ia.
thorn	*PnMeto.* *tana|ʔ;
	PRM. *ŋgout.
thorn, lontar	*CER.* *haa$_1$.
thoroughly	*PRM.* *mate.
thoughts	*nRM.* *farəndən.
thousand	*PRM.* *rifu|n.
thread	*PRM.* *lolo$_2$.
three	*PRM.* *telu.
throat	*PRM.* *ŋgadas.
throw	*CER.* *tamba$_1$;
	PRM. *mbesik;
	Rote. *leŋgu;
	Rote. *tuku$_2$.
thunder	*PRM.* *ɗoto.
tick	*PMeto.* *kepe.
tickle	*PRM.* *kei;
	Rote. *kera$_2$;
	Rote. *kili.
ticklish	*Rote.* *kera$_2$.
tie	*PRM.* *futu;
	PRM. *isa$_1$;
	Rote. *mbutu$_2$;
	Rote. *raʔi.
tie up	*CER.* *sii$_1$.
tight	*PRM.* *ɓetə;
	PRM. *mbii;
	PRM. *seti.
time	*PwRM.* #oras
	Rote. *lele.
tinder	*Rote.* *ɗuɗu.
tiny	*PRM.* *lutu$_1$.
tip	*PRM.* *mbana.
tire out	*Rote.* *loɓo.
tired	*CER.* *tefe;
	PRM. *hae;
	Rote. *lanu;
	Rote. *maŋgu$_1$.

to	_PMeto._ __#en__
	PRM. __*əu.__
tobacco	_PRM._ __*maɗo;__
	Rote. __*moɗe.__
toe	_PRM._ __*kuku.__
toenail	_PMeto._ __*kalusa.__
tomorrow, day after	_PRM._ __*beni;__
	PRM. __*esak.__
tongue	_PRM._ __*maa.__
too much	_CER._ __*leŋge.__
tooth	_PRM._ __*nisi.__
top	_PRM._ __*ata__$_1$;
	PRM. __*bafo.__
torch	_PRM._ __#[b/p]andut__
torn up	_Rote._ __*sai__$_3$.
tortoise	_PRM._ __*kea.__
touch	_PRM._ __*badoe;__
	PRM. __*kei.__
track	_PRM._ __*taa__$_1$.
trade	_PRM._ __#ɗaŋgan__
tradition	_PRM._ __#haɗat__
trample	_PRM._ __*ahi__$_1$.
trap	_CERM._ __*fetu.__
trap, fish	_PRM._ __*bufu.__
tread	_PRM._ __*ahi__$_1$;
	PRM. __*taɓu.__
tree	_PRM._ __*kaiu.__
tree, kapok	_PRM._ __*deŋe.__
tree, kind of	_PRM._ __*laa__$_1$;
	Rote. __*tumbi.__
tree trunk	_PRM._ __*huu.__
tribe	_PwRM._ __*-s.__
triton shell	_CERM._ __*toʔis.__
trousers	_PMeto._ __#bruuk__
true	_PRM._ __*teɓes.__
truncated	_PwRM._ __*tuka.__
tuber	_PRM._ __*fia;__
	PRM. __*lole__$_1$;
	PRM. __*tiɗo;__
	PRM. __*uas;__
	PRM. __*ufi.__
tuber, itchy	_PRM._ __*mae__$_1$.
turbulent	_PRM._ __*foe__$_3$.
turmeric	_PRM._ __*kuni.__
turn around	_PRM._ __*bali__$_2$;
	PRM. __*reo.__
turn back	_PRM._ __*bali__$_2$.
turtle	_PRM._ __*kea;__
	Rote. __*ŋgua.__
tusk	_PRM._ __*ŋoli.__
twist	_nRM._ __*fulə;__
	PwRM. __*mbulə.__
twisted	_Rote._ __*kilu.__
two	_PRM._ __*dua.__

U - u

ulcer	_PRM._ __*ɓisu.__
umbrella, leaf	_PRM._ __*soeneru.__
uncle	_PMeto._ __*baba|ʔ.__
uncle, maternal	_PRM._ __*toʔo.__
uncomfortable	_Rote._ __*lanu.__
underlay	_PRM._ __*lasa.__
undulate	_Rote._ __#omba__
unique	_CER._ __*kisa.__
unripe	_PRM._ __*mata__$_2$;
	PRM. __*ŋura.__
unroll	_CER._ __*fela__$_2$;
	PRM. __*ɓela.__
untie	_PRM._ __*sefi.__
until	_Rote._ __*losa.__
up	_PRM._ __*ata__$_1$.
up to	_Rote._ __*losa.__
upright	_PRM._ __*tetu.__
urine	_PRM._ __*mii.__
useless	_PRM._ __*ɗafu__$_1$.
uterus	_PwRM._ __*kambu.__

V - v

Vachellia leucophloea	*PRM.* ***ɓesa.***
vagina	*PRM.* ***tila.***
valley	*PRM.* ***lolo$_4$;***
	Rote. ***ɓafa$_1$.***
value	*PnMeto.* ***osa.***
vapour	*PRM.* ***masu;***
	PRM. ***suma.***
vegetables	*PRM.* ***utan.***
vein	*PRM.* ***uat.***
Venus	*PMeto.* **#nome**
village	*PMeto.* ***ruan;***
	PRM. ***iŋgu.***
vine	*CERM.* ***ɗeli.***
vinegar	*Rote.* ***ɗosa.***
viper	*PRM.* ***sao$_2$.***
visit	*PRM.* ***tino;***
	Rote. ***tiro.***
voice	*PRM.* ***hara.***
volute	*PRM.* ***suti.***
vomit	*PRM.* ***ɗoa;***
	PRM. ***muta.***

W - w

wake up	*Rote.* ***foʔa;***
	Rote. ***meɗa.***
walk around	*PRM.* ***ndoro;***
	PRM. ***susi.***
wall	*PnMeto.* ***dupi;***
	PRM. ***dindi.***
wallow	*PRM.* ***kukur;***
	Rote. ***lolir.***
want	*PRM.* ***hia.***
warm (v.)	*PRM.* ***ɗada.***
warm oneself	*Rote.* ***neru.***
warrior	*PnMeto.* ***meo$_2$.***
wash	*PRM.* ***fase;***
	Rote. ***fui$_3$.***
wasp	*CERM.* ***katefuan.***
watch	*PRM.* ***luku$_1$.***
water	*PRM.* ***oe.***
water spinach	*PRM.* ***ŋgaŋgo.***
watercourse	*PRM.* ***lolo$_4$.***
watermelon	*PRM.* ***timu$_2$.***
wattle (rooster)	*PMeto.* ***dai.***
wave	*Rote.* ***ree;***
	Rote. **#omba**
wax	*PRM.* ***lili.***
way	*nRM.* ***eno;***
	PRM. ***ɗalan.***
we (excl.)	*PRM.* ***ka(m)i.***
we (incl.)	*PRM.* ***kita.***
	Rote. ***ata$_2$.***
weak	*PRM.* ***loe$_2$.***
wealth	*PRM.* ***-uki.***
weave	*PRM.* ***seru;***
	PRM. ***tenu.***
weed (v.)	*nRM.* ***tofa$_1$.***
weep	*PnRote.* ***tani;***
	PwRM. ***ŋgae.***
weevil	*PRM.* ***fufu$_2$.***
weigh	*PRM.* **#tai**
weight	*PRM.* ***berat.***
west	*PRM.* ***muri.***
wet	*CERM.* ***mbeta.***
whale	*Rote.* ***ruŋirai.***
what?	*PwRM.* ***saa.***
where	*PRM.* ***ɓee.***
whetstone	*nRM.* ***saha$_1$;***
	PwRM. ***kandi.***
which	*PRM.* ***ɗee.***
while	*Rote.* ***saɗi.***
whinny	*PRM.* ***ɗii$_2$;***
	CERM. ***kele.***
whirlwind	*PRM.* ***kutus.***
whisper	*CERM.* ***ɓoto$_1$;***
	nRM. ***seo.***
whistle	*PRM.* ***miu.***
white	*nRM.* ***muti;***
	Rote. ***fula.***
who?	*PRM.* ***see$_2$.***
whole	*PRM.* ***tema$_2$.***
wide	*PRM.* ***lua$_2$.***
wide open	*PRM.* ***mboo.***

widow	*PRM.* ***balu2.**
widower	*PRM.* ***balu2.**
wife	*PMeto.* ***fee1.**
wig	*PRM.* ***sadu.**
wild	*PnRote.* ***lii3;**
	PRM. ***fui2.**
win	*PRM.* ***isa2.**
wind	*PRM.* ***anin.**
wind (v.)	*nRM.* ***laɓa;**
wind, east	*CER.* ***timu1.**
	PwRM. ***mbulə.**
winding	*PRM.* ***leku.**
window	*nRM.* **#ʤinela**
wing	*CER.* ***ɗila1;**
	PRM. ***liɗa.**
winnow	*Rote.* ***tahi.**
wipe	*PRM.* ***rose;**
	Rote. ***kose.**
wire	*PRM.* **#kaba**
with	*PRM.* ***oo1.**
woman	*PMeto.* ***fee1;**
	PRM. ***ina.**
wood	*PRM.* ***kaiu.**
wood, yellow	*Rote.* **#aɗulara**
worm	*PRM.* ***ulə;**
	Rote. ***kalati.**
wrap	*nRM.* ***fulə;**
	PRM. ***lusə.**
wrap up	*CER.* ***balu3.**
wring	*Rote.* ***ule.**
wrinkly	*Rote.* ***kuru2.**
write	*PRM.* ***tui1.**
wrong	*PRM.* ***sala.**

Y - y

yam	*PRM.* ***ufi.**
yarn, spread out	*PwRM.* ***mbuat.**
year	*PRM.* ***taun.**
yellow	*PRM.* ***moɗo.**
yesterday	*PRM.* ***afi;**
	PRM. ***beni.**
yesterday, day before	*PRM.* ***esak.**
yet	*PRM.* ***bei.**
you (pl.)	*PRM.* ***ke(m)i.**
you (sg.)	*PRM.* ***koo2.**
young	*PRM.* ***ŋura.**
youngest	*PRM.* ***muri.**

Z - z

Ziziphus mauritiana	*Rote.* ***koo1.**
Ziziphus oenoplia	*PRM.* ***nasi.**

1 - 2 - 3

1PL.EXCL	*PRM.* ***ka(m)i.**
1PL.INCL	*PRM.* ***kita;**
	Rote. ***ata2.**
1SG	*PRM.* ***au.**
2PL	*PRM.* ***ke(m)i.**
2SG	*PRM.* ***koo2.**
3PL	*PRM.* ***sira.**
3SG	*PnRote.* ***ndia.**

Total number of entries: 1,415

6

Proto-Malayo-Polynesian – Proto-Rote-Meto

A - a

*adaduq	***daru**. 'long'.
*aku	***au**. 'I, 1SG'.
*ala[q/p]	***ala**. 'fetch'.
*alutən	***lutə**. 'firebrand'.
*ama	***ama**. 'father'.
*anaduq	***naru**. 'long'.
*anak	***anak**. 'child'.
*anu	***nuu**$_2$. 'possession'.
*añam	***ane**. 'braid'.
*asu	***asu**. 'dog'.
*ata	***ata**$_2$. 'we (incl.), 1PL.INCL'.
*atas	***ata**$_1$. 'above'.

B - b

*babaq	***ɓafa**$_1$. 'valley'.
*babuy	***bafi**. 'pig'.
*bahaq	***faa**. 'current'.
*bahi	***fee**$_1$. 'woman'.
*bahuq	***boo**$_2$. 'smell'.
*bajaq	***faɗa**. 'say'.
*bakaq	***faka**$_1$. 'split'; ***faka**$_2$. 'split'; ***paha**. 'split'.
*baki	***ɓaʔi**. 'grandfather'.
*balabaw	***lafo**. 'rat'.
*balik	***bali**$_2$. 'turn back around'; ***ɓali**. 'mix'.
*baliw$_1$	***fali**. 'help with'.
*baliw$_2$	***bali**$_1$. 'go back'.
*balu	***balu**$_2$. 'widow'.
*balun	***balu**$_3$. 'cover up'; ***mbalu**. 'cover'.
*baluq	***balu**$_1$. 'mourn'.
*bañən	***kesu/fani**. 'sneeze'.
*baŋkudu	***baŋakuɗu**. '<u>*Morinda citrifolia*</u>'.
*baqbaq	***ɓafa**$_2$. 'mouth'.
*baqəRu	***beu**$_1$. 'new'; ***feu**. 'in-law'.
*baqi	***ɓei**. 'grandmother'.
*baRaq	***baa**. 'lungs'.
*baRat	***ɓaat**. 'across'.
*baRəq	***mbae**. 'swell'.
*baRu	***bau**. '<u>*Hibiscus tiliaceus*</u>'.
*basəq	***fase**. 'wash'.
**bata	***fata**. 'female'.
*batu	***batu**. 'stone'.
*ba(w)baw	***bafo**. 'top'.
*bayawak	***ɓaiafa**. 'monitor lizard'.
*bayu	***mbau**$_2$. 'stab'.
*belas	***belas**. 'machete'.
*bəkaq	***fekə**. 'separate'.
*bəkəlaj	***ɓela**. 'spread out'; ***fela**$_2$. 'spread out'.
*bəli	***beli**. 'buy price'.
*bəluk	***felu**. 'bend'; ***fenu**. 'bend'; ***helu**. 'bend'.
*bəntas	***ɓeta**. 'cut vegetation'.
*bəntəŋ	***ɓetə**. 'tense'.
*bəntuk	***ɓetu**. 'bent'; ***feɗu**. 'bent'.
*bəŋkuq	***ɓeku**. 'bend'.
*bəqbəq	***fefa**. 'mouth'.
*bəRas	***mneas**. 'husked rice'.
*bəRay	***fee**$_2$. 'give'.
*bəRəqat	***berat**. 'heavy'.
*bəRŋaw	***ka|benu**. 'fly'; ***mbena**. 'fly'.
*bəRŋi	***beni**. 'day after tomorrow, day before yesterday'.
*bəRsay	***sefe**. 'paddle'.
*bəRus	***beu**$_2$. '<u>*Garuga floribuna*</u>'.
*bəriq	***fei**. 'open'.

*bətaw	***feto**. ‘sister’.
*bətəŋ	***betə**. ‘millet’.
*bətuŋ	***petun**. ‘giant bamboo, *Dendrocalamus*’.
*bibiR	***ɓife**. ‘lip’.
*bilak	***mbila**. ‘blaze (v.)’.
*binəhiq	***bini**. ‘seed’.
*bintiq	***fiti**$_2$. ‘kick’.
*biŋaq	***ɓina**. ‘kind shell’.
*biqak	***ɓia**. ‘split’.
*biRaq	***fia**. ‘taro’.
*bisul	***ɓisu**. ‘ulcer’.
*bitbit	***bibi**. ‘pinch’; ***ɓiti**. ‘pinch’; ***fiti**$_3$. ‘carry’.
*bitiəs	***biti**$_1$. ‘calf (of leg)’.
*bitik	***biti**$_2$. ‘jerk up’; ***fiti**$_1$. ‘jerk’.
*bituqən	***fanduun**. ‘star’.
*buaq	***bua**. ‘fruit’; ***mbuah**. ‘areca palm nut’.
*buay	***fue**. ‘legume’.
*bubu	***bufu**. ‘fish trap’.
*bubuŋ	***fufu**$_1$. ‘fontanelle’; ***fumbu**. ‘fontanelle’.
*buhat	***fua**$_1$. ‘carry’.
*buhək	***ɓuə**. ‘hair’.
*bujəq	***fuʤə**. ‘foam’.
*buka	***fuka**. ‘dig’; ***huka**. ‘open’.
*bukbuk$_1$	***ɓuɓu**. ‘bubble’.
*bukbuk$_3$	***fufu**$_2$. ‘weevil’.

*bukij	***fui**$_2$. ‘wild’.
*buku	***ɓuku**. ‘node’.
*bukuq	***mbuku**$_2$. ‘bent’.
*bulan	***bulan**. ‘moon’.
*bula[n/R]	***fula**. ‘white’.
*bulat	***ɓula**. ‘open the eyes’.
*buliq	***fuli**. ‘cowrie shell’.
*buliR	***mbule**. ‘grain head cob’.
*bulu	***bulu**. ‘hair’.
*buni	***funi**$_1$. ‘hide’.
*buntər	***ɓunda**. ‘fat bellied’.
*bunut	***mbunut**. ‘coconut husk’.
*buŋa	***ɓuna**. ‘flower’.
*buqaya	***foe**$_2$. ‘crocodile’.
*buqəni	***buni**. ‘ringworm’.
*buqi	***fui**$_1$. ‘pour’.
*buRiq	***fui**$_3$. ‘wash’.
*buRit	***ɓuit**. ‘backside’.
*buRnay	***mbune**. ‘*Antidesma bunius*’.
*buRuk	***mburuk**. ‘rotten’.
*burun	***funu**. ‘betel-pepper’.
*busuR	***ɓusu**. ‘cotton bow’.
*butu	***futu**. ‘bundle’; ***mbutu**$_2$. ‘bundle up’.
*buu	***buu**. ‘blow’; ***fuu**. ‘blow’.

D - d

*dahun	***doo**. ‘leaf’.
*daki	***daki**. ‘dirt’.
*dakih	***ndake**$_1$. ‘climb’.
*daləm	***dalə**. ‘in’.
*damaR	***ɗama**. ‘resin’.
*danaw	***ɗano**. ‘lake’.
*daŋdaŋ	***ɗada**. ‘warm (v.)’.

*dapuR	***raho**. ‘hearth’.
*daqan	***mba|raa**. ‘old’.
*daqih	***dei**. ‘forehead’.
*daRaq	***daa**. ‘blood’.
*daRəq	***dae**. ‘ground’.
*dəŋəR	***rena**. ‘hear’.
*dəpa	***reha**. ‘fathom (n.)’.

*dəpdəp	*deras. 'Erythrina species'.	*ditaq	*dete. 'blackboard tree: *Alstonia scholaris*'.
*dikit	*ɗiki. 'small'.	*di-wiRi	*ɗii1. 'left (side)'.
*dilap	*ɗila2. 'shine'.	*dodok	*ɗoɗo. 'kill'.
*diŋdiŋ	*dindi. 'wall'.	*duha	*dua. 'two'.
*diŋin	*riŋin. 'cold'.	*duku	*ruku. 'bent'.
*diRi	*dii1. 'stand'.	**dumbi	*dupi. 'wall'.
*diRus	*diu. 'bathe'.	*duRi	*dui1. 'bone'.
		*duyuŋ	*dui2. 'dugong'.

Ə - ə

*əkit	*eki. 'shout out'.
*ənəm	*nee1. 'six'.
*əpat	*haa2. 'four'.
*əsa	*esa. 'one'.

F - f

**fəran	*fera2. 'landslide'.

G - g

*gatəl	*katə. 'itchy'.	*gərgər	*ŋgeŋgo. 'shake'.
*gəmgəm	*kame. 'knead'; *keʔe. 'knead'; *keme. 'knead'; *kumu2. 'fist'; *ŋgumu. 'fist, squeeze'.	*gətəl	*ŋgete. 'pinch off'.
		*giRiŋ	*kiri1. 'bell'.
		*gumi(s)	*ŋgomi. 'beard'.
		*guru(q)	*ŋguru. 'drone'.

H - h

*habaRat	*faat. 'rainy season'.	*hasaq	*saha1. 'whetstone'.
*hadiRi	*dii2. 'post'.	*hawak	*ao. 'body'.
*haŋin	*anin. 'wind'.	*həsi	*sisi. 'meat'.
*hapəjəs	*meras. 'sick'.	*hikan	*ika. 'fish'.
*hapəjis	*heɗis. 'sick'.	*hikət	*ikə. 'snare'.
*hapin	*nahe. 'mat'.	*hipaR	*iha. 'sister-in-law'.
*hapun	*ahu. 'dew'.	*huaji	*waɗi. 'younger sibling'.
*hapuy	*ahi2. 'fire'.	*hutək	*kutə. 'brains'.
*haRəzan	*eɗa. 'ladder'.		

I - i

*ia ***ia**. 'this'.
*ijuŋ ***iɗu**. 'kiss'.
*ikuR ***iko**. 'tail'.
*ina ***ina**. 'mother'.
*inum ***inu**. 'drink'.
*isiʔ ***isi**. 'contents flesh'.

K - k

*kabut ***habu**. 'cloud'.
*kaən ***ha**. 'eat'.
ka-felu ***ʔ|fenu. 'candlenut'.
*kahiw ***kaiu**. 'tree'.
*kahu ***koo$_2$**. 'you (sg.), 2SG'.
*kaka ***kaka**. 'elder sibling'.
*kakay ***hae|ʔ**. 'foot'.
*kali ***kali**. 'dig'.
*kalimatək ***kerumatu**. 'leech'.
*kali-wati ***kalati**. 'worm'.
*kambeR ***kambe**. 'saliva'.
*kambu ***kambu**. 'belly'.
*kami ***ka(m)i**. 'we (excl.), 1PL.EXCL'.
*kamiri ***kamiri**. 'candlenut'.
*kampil **#kapir**. 'basket'.
*kamuyu ***ke(m)i**. 'you (pl.)'.
*kanasay ***nase**. 'Blue-spot mullet'.
*kapit ***hapi**. 'pinch'; ***kaɓi**. 'pinch'.
*kaRat ***kaa$_1$**. 'bite'.
*kaRus ***kao**. 'scrape'.
karas ***kara. 'chest'.
*karut ***karu**. 'scratch'.
*kati ***kati**. 'call'.
*kawanan ***kona**. 'right'.
*ka-wiRi ***kii**. 'left'.
*kawit ***kai$_2$**. 'hook'.
*keRa ***kea**. 'turtle'.
*kəmiq ***mii**. 'urine'.
*kətuq ***ketu**. 'cut off'.
*kilik ***kili**. 'tickle'.
*kiluq ***kilu**. 'crooked'.
kilusa ***kalusa. 'fingernail'.
*kima ***kima**. 'clam'.
*kiskis ***sakiki**. 'brush teeth'.
*kita$_1$ ***kita**. 'we (incl.), 1PL.INCL'.
*kita$_2$ ***ita**. 'see'.
klaRa ***klaha. 'coals'.
*koti ***koti**. 'cut'.
*kudən ***kurə**. 'pot'.
*kuhkuh ***kuku**. 'finger'.
*kuluR ***kunu$_1$**. 'breadfruit'.
kumu ***kumu$_1$. 'wild pigeon'.
*kunij ***kuni**. 'turmeric'.
*kur(u) ***kuru$_1$**. 'call chickens'.
*kurut ***kuru$_2$**. 'wrinkly'.
*kutu ***kutu**. 'head louse'.

L - l

lakateRu ***teu. 'pigeon'.
*lakaw ***lako**. 'go'.
*laki ***laʔi**. 'king'.
*laluŋ ***lalu**. 'rooster'.
*lamut ***lamu**. 'seaweed'.
*laŋit ***lani**. 'heaven'.
*laŋu ***lanu**. 'uncomfortable'.
*lapaR ***laha**. 'hungry'.
*laqia ***laia**. 'ginger'.

*laRiw	*lai. 'run'.
*lasəR	*lasə. 'scrotum'.
*-lat	*laa5. 'open the eyes'.
*latuq	*latu2. 'seaweed'.
*lawaq	*ɓo/lau. 'spider'; #k|naba|ʔ. 'spider'.
*layap	*laa4. 'fly (v.)'.
*layaR	*laa3. 'sail'.
*lemba	*lemba. 'carry'.
**lemur	*lemuk. 'dolphin'.
*lesu	*lesu2. 'come out'.
*letay1	*lete1. 'mountain'.
*letay2	*lete2. 'bridge'.
*ləkən	*leke. 'coil'.
*ləkuʔ	*leku. 'winding'.
*ləŋah	*lena. 'sesame'.
*ləpaw	*lopo. 'shelter'.
*ləsuŋ	*nesu. 'mortar'.
*liaŋ	*lea. 'cave'.
*liaR	*lii3. 'shy'.
**libun	*lifu. 'billabong'.
*libut	*liɓu. 'surround'; *rimbu. 'surround'.
*likud	*liku2. 'back'.
*lilin	*lili. 'wax'.
*lima	*lima1. 'five'.
*liŋ	*lii1. 'sound'.
*liqəR	*lii2. 'neck'.
*luab	*lua1. 'boil'.
*luaŋ	*lua|t. 'cave'.
*luhəq	*luu2. 'tears (crying)'.
*lukut	*luku2. 'bent'.
*lulun	*lulun. 'roll up'.
*lumbu	*lombu. 'moss'.
*luqaR	*lua2. 'outside (adj.)'.
**lutuR	*lutu2. 'pile up'.

M - m

*ma-buhək	*mafu. 'drunk'.
*ma-əsa	*mesa. 'alone'.
*mah	*ma. 'and'.
*ma-hataq	*mata2. 'raw'.
*ma-həmis	*mamis. 'sweet'.
*ma-həyaq	*mae2. 'shy'.
*ma-hipi	*mehi. 'dream'.
*ma-iRaq	*mea. 'red'.
*maja	*maɗa. 'dry up'.
*malip	*mali2. 'laugh'.
*mamaq	*mama. 'chew'.
*mansər	*ʔ|mauka|ʔ. 'cuscus'.
*manuk	*manu. 'chicken'.
**ma-ŋeta	*neta. 'choke'.
*ma-putiq	*muti. 'white'.
*ma-qasin	*masi. 'salty'.
*ma-qasu	*masu. 'smoke'.
*ma-qəti	*meti. 'low tide up'.
*ma-qitəm	*metam. 'black'.
*ma-quban	*mofa. 'grey hair'.
*ma-qudip	*mori. 'live'.
*ma-Raŋu	*maŋgu2. 'dry'.
*ma(R)i	*mai. 'come'.
*maRuqanay	*mane. 'male'; *mone. 'male'.
*maRus	*maus. 'tame'.
*mata	*mata1. 'eye'.
*matay	*mate. 'die'.
*ma-udəhi	*mone|ʔ. 'outside'; *muri. 'last'.
*maya	*maa. 'tongue'.
**maya	*mae1. 'itchy tuber'.
**mbasaR	*mbasa. 'slap'.
**mbio	*pio. 'garlic'.
**meoŋ	*meo1. 'cat'.
**məŋi(R)	*meni1. 'fragrant'.
*miñak	*mina. 'delicious'.
**mozo	*moɗo. 'yellow'.
*mukən	*mukə. 'dove'.
*mulmul	*mumu1. 'suck'.
*muntay	*munde. 'citrus (fruit)'.
*muRmuR	*mumu2. 'gargle'.
**musa	*muse1. 'seed'.
*musaŋ	*muse2. 'civet'.

N - n

*-na	*naa$_1$. 'that'.
*nabuq	*nafu. 'anchor (v.)'.
*nakaw	*nako. 'steal'.
*namaw	*namo$_2$. 'coast'.
*nanaq	*nana. 'pus'.
*naŋuy	*naŋe. 'swim'.
**napi	*hani$_2$. 'shell'.
*naRa	*naa$_3$. '_Pterocarpus indica_'.
*nasu	*nasu. 'cook'.
*natuq	*natu. 'ovary'.
**nepi	*nehi. 'mat on'.
*nipay	*nihe. 'ant'.
*nipis	*nihis. 'thin'.
*niuR	*noh. 'coconut'.
*nuəs	*nuus. 'squid'.
*nuka	*nuʔa. 'scabies'.
*nunuk	*nunuh. 'banyan'.
**nuŋan	*nuŋa. '_Cordia_ species'.
*nusa	*nusa. 'island'.

Ñ - ñ

*ñaRa	*naa$_2$. 'brother (of woman)'.
*ñikñik	*nini. 'mosquito'.

Ŋ - ŋ

*ŋadaq	*naɗo. 'look up'.
*ŋadas	*nada. 'gums'; *ŋgadas. 'palate'.
*ŋajan	*naʤa. 'name'.
*ŋaŋa	*m|kaka. 'open the mouth'.
**ŋəli	*ŋoli. 'canine tooth'.
*ŋilu	*ŋilu. 'tamarind, sour'.
*ŋis(ŋ)i(s)	*nisi. 'tooth'.
*ŋodok	*ŋgoro. 'snout, snore'.
*ŋuda	*ŋura. 'young'.
*ŋusuq	*nuɗu. 'lip'.

O - o

**oRo	*oo$_1$. 'with'.

P - p

*pagut	*heŋgu. 'eat'.
**pai	*hai$_1$. 'bucket'.
*pajay	*hade. 'paddy rice'.
*panahik	*hene. 'climb'.
*panas	*hanas. 'hot'.
*panaw	*hano. 'spots'.
*pandak	*mbada. 'short'; *pande. 'short'.
*paniŋ	*hani$_1$. 'bait (v.)'.
**panti	*fandi. 'cut'.
**paŋga	*haŋga. 'span span'.
*paŋdan	*hendam. 'wild pandanus'.
**pao	*hao. 'feed'.
*papaq	*ɓeɓa. 'palm leaf stem'.

*paRih	***hai**$_2$. 'stingray'.
*parud	***paru**. 'grate'.
*pasaqan	***saha**$_2$. 'carry on the shoulders'.
**penuk	***henuh**. 'beads'.
*pəluk	***holu**$_1$. 'hug'.
*pənuq	***henu**. 'full'.
*pəRəq	***hee**$_2$. 'press'.
**pəsu	***hesu**. 'fart'.
*pian	***hia**. 'want'.
*pija	***hida**. 'how much?'; ***hiɗa**. 'few'.
*piliq	***hiri**. 'choose'.
*pitu	***hitu**. 'seven'.
**pue	***huʔe**. 'eucalyptus'.
*puləs	***ule**. 'wring'.
*punti	***hundi**. 'banana'.
*pu(ŋ)kaq	***huŋga**. 'chop'.
*puqun	***huu**. 'tree trunk'.
*pusəj	***husə**. 'navel'.
*putput	***pupu**. 'blow'.
*puyuq	***mbui**. 'quail'.

Q - q

*qabatəd	***ɓate**. 'edible grub'.
*qabu	***afu**. 'ash'.
*qahəlu	***halu**. 'pestle'.
*qajəŋ	***kaɗe**. 'charcoal'.
*qaləjaw	***ledo**. 'sun'.
*qa-lima	***lima**$_2$. 'hand'.
*qalu-hipan	***liha**. 'centipede'.
*qalunan	***lunu**. 'cushion'.
*qambawaŋ	***mbao**. 'mango'.
*qanahaw	***naa**$_4$. 'fibres'.
*qanilaw	***lino**. '<u>Grewia slutaris</u>'.
*qanitu	***nitu**. 'spirit'.
*qapəju	***hedu**. 'gall bladder'.
*qapuR	***aho**. 'mineral lime'.
*qaqay	***ei**. 'foot'.
*qaRta	***ata**$_3$. 'slave'.
*qaRta + *qudip	***hatahori**. 'man'.
*qaRuhu	***kai/ou**. '<u>*Casuarina*</u> species'.
*qasawa	***sao**$_1$. 'marry'.
*qasu	***aso**. 'scoop'.
*qatay	***ate**. 'liver'.
*qatəluR	***təlo**. 'egg'.
*qatiməla	***mela**. 'flea'.
*qatimun	***timu**$_2$. 'cucumber'.
*qatip	***ati|s**. 'breast beam of loom'.
*qatuan	***tua**$_3$. 'lord'.
*qaué	***auee**. 'oh!'.
*qauR	***oo**$_2$. 'bamboo'.
*qayam	***aem**. 'tame'.
*qənəŋ	***nee**$_2$. 'quiet'.
*qənuR	***eno**. 'way'.
*qəta	***taa**$_2$. 'unhusked rice'.
*qəti	***həndi**. 'finish'.
*qibaw	***kibo**. 'shellfish'.
*qihu	***iu**. 'shark'.
*qila	***ila**. 'mole (skin)'.
*qizuR	***midu**. 'saliva out'; ***ŋinu**. 'spit out'.
*[q/k]umaŋ	***saŋguma**. 'hermit crab'.
*quay	***ue**. 'rattan'.
*qubi	***ufi**. 'tuber'.
*qudip	***hori|s**. 'living'.
*quhənap	***unə**. 'scale'.
*quləj	***ulə**. 'worm'.
*qulin	***uli**. 'rudder'.
*qulu	***hulu**. 'first in front'; ***ulu**. 'front, head hair'.
*qusiR	***usi**$_1$. 'pursue'.
*qutan	***utan**. 'vegetables'.
*qutin	***uti**. 'penis'.
*quzan	***uɗan**. 'rain'.

R - R

*Rabiqi	*afi. 'yesterday'.	*Ribu	*rifu|n. 'thousand'.
*Rakit	*raʔi. 'bind'.	*Rumaq	*uma. 'house'.
*Raya	*nae. 'big'.	*Rusuk	*kai/usu. 'ribs'.
*(R)ədəm	*endən. 'soak'.		

r - r

**rafu	*nafu|ʔ. 'body hair'.
*rakup	*raʔu. 'scoop'.
*riba	*ifa. 'lap'.

S - s

*sai	*see$_2$. 'who?'.	*si-ida	*sira. 'they, 3PL'.
*sakay	*sake. 'go up'.	*siku	*siku. 'elbow'.
**sakuraŋ	*kura. 'scorpion'.	*siŋaR	*sina. 'light (n.)'.
*salaq	*sala. 'wrong'.	*siŋkab	*sika. 'open'; *siŋga. 'open'.
**salili	*salili. 'armpit'.		
*salin	*sali. 'pour'.	*siwa	*sio. 'nine'.
**sa(m)bura[t/s]	*sambudas. 'spurt'.	*suaR	*sua$_3$. 'digging stick'.
*saŋa	*sana|ʔ. 'branch of fruit'.	*suat	*suhat. 'comb'.
*sa-ŋa-puluq	*sanahulu. 'ten'.	*sudu	*soro. 'spoon'; *suru. 'spoon'.
*sa-ŋa-Ratus	*natu|n. 'hundred'.		
*saŋəlaR	*seŋa. 'fry'.	*suja	*sura. 'horn'; *sure. 'sword, caltrop'.
*sau	*sau$_3$. 'comb'.		
**sauR	*soo. 'sew'.		
*sawa	*sao$_2$. 'snake'.	*sukəd	*sua$_2$. 'rafter'.
*səbuh	*sufu. 'cool (v.)'.	*sukun	*suku. 'breadfruit'.
**sədu(t)	*seru. 'weaving sword of loom'.	*sulə[n/d]	*sulə. 'plug'.
		*sumaŋəd	*sumanə. 'spirit'.
*səksək	*sesə. 'cram'.	*supu	*suhu. 'edge'.
*səlaR	*sela. 'coarse'.	*suqun	*suu$_2$. 'carry on head'.
**səru	*səru. 'meet'.		
*si-ia	*ndia. 'she, he, it, 3SG'.	*susu	*susu$_2$. 'breast'.

T - t

*tabtab	*tata. 'split'.	*taduku	*taruku. 'chiton'.
*tabuni	*funi$_2$. 'afterbirth'.	*takut	*taku. 'fear'.
*tabuqan	*katefuan. 'wasp'.	*taləs	*tales. 'taro'.

*talih	*tali. 'rope'.
*talisay	*lise. '*Terminalia catappa*'.
*tama	*tama$_1$. 'enter'.
*tama(q)	*tama$_2$. 'fit together'.
**tamayuŋ	*tamae. 'bedbug'.
*tambal	*tamba$_2$. 'patch, join'.
*tamban	*temba. 'sardine'.
*tamu	*tamu. 'close mouth'.
*tanəq	*tane$_1$. 'mud'.
**taŋa	*tana$_2$. 'crisp'.
*taŋila	*ŋgela$_1$. 'earwax'.
*taŋis	*tani. 'complain'.
*tapak	*taa$_1$. 'track'.
*tapi	*tahi. 'winnow'.
*tapis	*tais. 'cloth'.
*taq	*taa$_3$. 'no'.
*taqan	*taa$_4$. 'endure'.
*taqi	*tai$_1$. 'belly'; *tai$_2$. 'faeces'.
*taqun	*taun. 'year'.
**taRa	*taha. 'answer'.
*taRaq	*tara. 'adze'.
*taRum	*taum. 'indigo'.
*taRuq	*tao. 'put, do'.
**tara-k	*tana|ʔ. 'thorn'.
*tasak	*tasa. 'ripe'.
*tasik	*tasi. 'sea'.
*tau	*toʔo. 'man, male'; *tou. 'man, person'.
**tayum	*k|teom. 'sea urchin'.
*tazəm	*tande. 'sharp'.
*təbəl	*nembə. 'hard'.
*təbiq	*teɓi. 'break up'.
*təbuh	*tefu. 'sugarcane'.
*təkən	*tekə. 'staff'.
*təktək	*teke. 'gecko'.
*təlu	*telu. 'three'.
*təmən	*temə. 'accustomed'.
*tənəŋ	*tena$_3$. 'calm'.
*tənun	*tenu. 'weave'.

*təŋəR	*tene. '*Ceriops*, mangrove'.
*təRas	*teas. 'heartwood'.
**təRə	*tee. 'spear'.
*təriŋ	*teri. 'giant bamboo, *Dendrocalamus*'.
*tikəd	*tiŋga. 'heel'.
*tila	*tila. 'vagina'.
*timid	*timi. 'chin'.
*timuR	*timu$_1$. 'east wind'.
*tindaw	*tino. 'peer'; *tiro. 'peer'.
*tindəs	*teɗe. 'press'.
**tiŋaR	*tina. 'field'.
*tiqaw	*ti(ʔ)o. 'goatfish, *Mullidae*'.
*tiRəm	*tiam. 'oyster'.
**tiRi	*tii. 'sea urchin'.
*tiRis	*tiri. 'drip'.
*titis	*titi. 'drip'.
*tuak	*tua$_2$. 'lontar palm'.
*tuba	*tufa. '*Derris elliptica*'.
*tuduq	*turu. 'overflow'.
*tuduy	*turis. 'pigeon pea'.
*tuhud	*tuu$_1$. 'knee'.
*tui	*tui$_2$. '*Dolichandrone spathacea*'.
**tuir	*tuin. 'follow'.
*tukil	*tuke. 'bamboo container'.
*tuktuk	*toko. 'beat'; *tutu. 'beat'.
*tuluy	*tuli. 'stop by'.
*tumah	*tuma. 'clothes louse'.
*tumbuk	*tufu. 'punch'.
*tu(m)buq	*numbu. 'grow'; *tumbu. 'heap'.
*tuna	*tuna. 'freshwater eel'.
*tunu	*tunu$_2$. 'roast'.
*tuqah	*tua$_1$. 'big'.
*tuquR	*tuu$_2$. 'dry'.
*tuzuq	*tuɗu. 'point'.

U - u

*umpu	***umbu**. 'grandchild'.
*um-utaq	***muta**. 'vomit'.
*uRat	***uat**. 'vein, palm line'; ***ura**. 'palm line'.
*usi	***usi**$_2$. 'king'.
*utaña	***tana**$_3$. 'ask'; ***tane**$_2$. 'ask'.
*uu	***uu**. 'oink'.

W - w

*wahiR	***oe**. 'water'.
*wakaR	***oka**$_2$. 'root'; #**baʔat**. 'root'.
*walu	***falu**. 'eight'.
*wani	***wani**. 'bee'.
*waRi	***fai**. 'day'; ***hoi**. 'dry in sun'.
**wasi	***osi**. 'garden'.

Z - z

*zalan	***ɗalan**. 'way'.
*zaŋkal	***ɗaŋga**$_2$. 'span'.
*zaRum	***ndau**. 'needle'.
*zauq	***ɗoo**. 'far'.
*zəlay	***ɗele**. 'Job's tears'.

Total number of entries: 558

References

Abas, Husen. 1995. Bugis wordlist. In *Comparative Austronesian dictionary: An introduction to Austronesian studies*, ed. Darrell T. Tryon, Parts 2–4. Berlin and New York: Mouton de Gruyter.

Adriani, Nicolaus. 1928. *Bare'e-Nederlandsch woordenboek: met Nederlandsch-Bare'e register.* Leiden: Brill.

Ali, Slamet Ryadi. 1995. Sasak wordlist. In *Comparative Austronesian dictionary: An introduction to Austronesian studies*, ed. Darrell T. Tryon, Parts 2–4. Berlin and New York: Mouton de Gruyter.

Alpher, Barry, and David Nash. 1999. Lexical replacement and cognate equilibrium in Australia. *Australian Journal of Linguistics* 19:5–56. doi.org/10.1080/07268609908599573

Aoki, Eriko, and Satoshi Nakagawa. 1993. *Endenese–English dictionary.* Osaka: Osaka International University.

Arka, I Wayan, Fransiscus Seda, Antonius Gelang, Yohanes Nani, and Ivan Ture. 2007. *Kamus Rongga-Indonesia dengan daftar pelacak kata Indonesia-Rongga.* Jakarta: Penerbit Universitas Atma Jaya.

Arndt, Paul. 1961. *Wörterbuch der Ngadhasprache.* Posieux, Fribourg: Studia Instituti Anthropos.

Baird, Louise. 2002. A grammar of Kéo: An Austronesian language of East Nusantara. Doctoral Thesis, The Australian National University.

Balle, Misriani, and Stuart Cameron. 2014. Helong dictionary. Unpublished Toolbox file.

Bawa, I Wayan, and Adrian Clynes. 1995. Balinese wordlist. In *Comparative Austronesian dictionary: An introduction to Austronesian studies*, ed. Darrell T. Tryon, Parts 2–4. Berlin and New York: Mouton de Gruyter.

Blevins, Juliette, and Andrew Garrett. 1998. The origins of consonant-vowel metathesis. *Language* 74:508–556. doi.org/10.1353/lan.1998.0012

Blust, Robert. 1993. Central and Central-Eastern Malayo-Polynesian. *Oceanic Linguistics* 32:241–293. doi.org/10.2307/3623195

Blust, Robert. 1999. Notes on Pazeh phonology and morphology. *Oceanic Linguistics* 38:321–365. doi.org/10.1353/ol.1999.0002

Blust, Robert. 2009a. *The Austronesian languages.* Canberra: Pacific Linguistics.

Blust, Robert. 2009b. The position of the languages of eastern Indonesia: A reply to Donohue and Grimes. *Oceanic Linguistics* 48:36–77. doi.org/10.1353/ol.0.0034

Blust, Robert, and Stephen Trussel. ongoing. The Austronesian comparative dictionary. www.trussel2.com/ACD/

Calon, L. F. 1891. Woordenlijstje bij het dialekt van Sikka (Midden-Flores). *Tijdschrift voor Indische Taal-, Land- en Volkenkunde* 34:283–363.

Cense, A. A. in collaboration with Abdoerrahim. 1979. *Makassaars-Nederlands woordenbooek met Nederlands-Makassaars register.* 's-Gravenhage: Martinus Nijhoff.

Chafe, Wallace. 1994. *Discourse, consciousness, and time: The flow and displacement of conscious experience in speaking and writing.* Chicago and London: University of Chicago Press.

Chlenov, Mikhail A., and Svetlana F. Chlenova. 2008. The Damar Batumerah (West Damar language) of south-eastern Indonesia. In *Language and text in the Austronesian world: Studies in honor of Ülo Sirk*, ed. Yury A. Lander and Alexander K. Ogloblin, 141–162. Munich: Lincom.

Chlenova, Svetlana F. 2002. Daweloor, a Southwest Moluccan language. *Малайско-индонезийские исследования [Malay-indonesian studies]* 15:145–175. Special English language edition of Малайско-индонезийские исследования ed. B. B. Parnickel.

Christensen, John. in progress. Kisar dictionary. Unpublished Toolbox file.

Christensen, John, and Sylvia Christensen. 1992. Kisar phonology. *In Phonological studies in four languages of Maluku*, ed. Donald A. Burquest and Wyn D. Laidig, 33–65. Dallas: Summer Institute of Linguistics and the University of Texas at Arlington.

Clark, Ross. 2011. Birds. In *The lexicon of Proto Oceanic: The culture and environment of ancestral Oceanic society*, ed. Malcolm Ross, Andrew Pawley, and Meredith Osmond, volume 4: Animals, 271–370. Canberra: Pacific Linguistics.

Codrington, Robert H., and Jim Palmer. 1896. *A dictionary of the language of Mota, Sugarloaf Island, Banks Islands.* London: Society for Promoting Christian Knowledge.

Coolsma, Sierk. 1913. *Soendaneesch-Hollandsch woordenboek.* Leiden: A. W. Sijthoff.

Cristo Rei, João Maria, and Mark Donohue. 2012. Galolen dictionary. MS.

Culhane, Kirsten. 2018. Consonant insertions: A synchronic and diachronic account of Amfo'an. Honours Thesis, The Australian National University. hdl.handle.net/1885/160794

Culhane, Kirsten, Laurence Jumetan, and Yedida Ora. 2018. Amfo'an dictionary. Unpublished Toolbox file.

Cunningham, Clark E. 1964. Order in the Atoni house. *Bijdragen tot de Taal-, Land- en Volkenkunde* 120:34–68. doi.org/10.1163/22134379-90002996

Daigle, Benjamin T. 2015. A grammar sketch of Batuley: an Austronesian language of Aru, eastern Indonesia. Master's Thesis, Leiden University.

da Silva, Eng. Guilherme. 2012. *Disionáriu Wekais-Tetun.* Timor-Leste: Secretaria de Estado da Cultura.

Dawson, Virginia. 2014. Manatuto survey (VD1). Digital collection managed by PARADISEC. catalog.paradisec.org.au/collections/VD1

de Josselin de Jong, J. P. B. 1947. *Studies in Indonesian culture II: The community of Erai (Wetar) (texts and notes)*. Amsterdam: Noord-Hollandsche Uitgevers-Maatschappij.

de Josselin de Jong, J. P. B. 1987. *Wetan fieldnotes: Some eastern Indonesian texts with linguistic notes and a vocabulary*. Dordrecht-Holland: Foris Publications.

Dempwolff, Otto. 1938. Vergleichende Lautlehre des austronesischen Wortschatzes, volume 3: *Austronesisches Wörterverzeichnis of Zeitschrift für Eingeborenen-sprachen.* Berlin: Dietrich Reimer. Supplement 17. doi.org/10.1017/s0041977x00135360

Djawanai, Stephanus. 1995. Ngada wordlist. In *Comparative Austronesian dictionary: An introduction to Austronesian studies*, ed. Darrell T. Tryon, Parts 2–4. Berlin and New York: Mouton de Gruyter.

Donohue, Mark. 2003. Daftar Kata Bata Lu'a [Palu'e wordlist]. MS.

Donohue, Mark, and Charles E. Grimes. 2008. Yet more on the position of the languages of eastern Indonesia and East Timor. *Oceanic Linguistics* 47:114–158. doi.org/10.1353/ol.0.0008

Drabbe, Peter. 1932. Woordenboek der Fordaatsche taal, volume 61 of *Verhandelingen van het Koninklijk Bataviaasch Genootschap van Kunsten en Wetenschappen.* Bandoeng: Nix.

Eberhard, David M., Gary F. Simons, and Charles D. Fennig. 2020. *Ethnologue: Languages of the world* (23rd ed.). Dallas, Texas: SIL International.

Edwards, Owen. 2016. Parallel sound correspondences in Uab Meto. *Oceanic Linguistics* 55:52–86. doi.org/10.1353/ol.2016.0008

Edwards, Owen. 2017. Epenthetic and contrastive glottal stops in Amarasi. *Oceanic Linguistics* 56:415–434. doi.org/10.1353/ol.2017.0020

Edwards, Owen. 2018a. Parallel histories in Rote-Meto. *Oceanic Linguistics* 57:359–409. doi.org/10.1353/ol.2018.0016

Edwards, Owen. 2018b. Preliminary report on Funai Helong. *NUSA: Linguistic studies of languages in and around Indonesia* 65:1–27. doi.org/10.15026/92897

Edwards, Owen. 2018c. Top-down historical phonology of Rote-Meto. *Journal of the Southeast Asian Linguistics Society* 11:63–90. hdl.handle.net/10524/52421

Edwards, Owen. 2019. Reintroducing Welaun. *Oceanic Linguistics* 58:31–58. hdl.handle.net/1887/79038. doi.org/10.1353/ol.2019.0002

Edwards, Owen. 2020. *Metathesis and unmetathesis in Amarasi*. Berlin: Language Science Press. doi.org/10.5281/zenodo.3700413

Elias, Alexander. 2018. Lio and the Central Flores languages. Master's Thesis, Leiden University.

Fanggidaej, J. 1892. Rottineesche spraakkunst. *Bijdragen tot de Taal-, Land- en Volkenkunde* 41:554–571. doi.org/10.1163/22134379-90000187

Farjon, Aljos. 2017. *A handbook of the world's conifers*, volume 1. (2nd ed.) Leiden-Boston: Brill.

Fogaça, Helem Andressa de Oliveira. 2017. O ecossistema fundamental da língua Mambae : aspectos endoecológicos e exoecológicos de uma língua austronésia de Timor-Leste. Doctoral dissertation, Universidade de Brasília. repositorio.unb.br/handle/10482/31396

Forth, Gregory L. 2016. *Why the porcupine is not a bird: Explorations in the folk zoology of an eastern Indonesian people*. Toronto: University of Toronto Press.

Fox, James J. 1988. The historical consequences of changing patterns of livelihood in Timor. In *Contemporary issues in development*, ed. Deborah Wade-Marshall and Peter Loveday, 259–279. Darwin: The Australian National University North Australia Research Unit.

Fox, James J. 1991. The heritage of traditional agriculture in eastern Indonesia: Lexical evidence and the indications of rituals from the outer arc of the Lesser Sundas. *Bulletin of the Indo-Pacific Prehistory Association* 10:248–262.

Fox, James J. 2016a. *Master poets, ritual masters: The art of oral composition among the Rotenese of eastern Indonesia*. Canberra: ANU Press. doi.org/10.22459/mprm.04.2016

Fox, James J. 2016b. Termanu ritual language dictionary. MS.

Fox, James J., and Charles E. Grimes. 1995. Roti. In *Comparative Austronesian dictionary: An introduction to Austronesian studies*, ed. Darrell T. Tryon, Part 1, 611–622. Berlin: Mouton de Gruyter.

Friberg, Timothy. 1995. Konjo wordlist. In *Comparative Austronesian dictionary: An introduction to Austronesian studies*, ed. Darrell T. Tryon, Parts 2–4. Berlin and New York: Mouton de Gruyter.

Fricke, Hanna. 2014. *Topics in the grammar of Hewa: A variety of Sika in Eastern Indonesia.* Munich: Lincom Europa.

Fricke, Hanna. 2015. Field notes on Lamaholot-Kalikasa. In *Lexirumah 3.0.0*, ed. Gereon A. Kaiping, Owen Edwards, and Marian Klamer. Leiden: Leiden University Centre for Linguistics. lexirumah.model-ling.eu/lexirumah/

Fricke, Hanna. 2019. Traces of language contact: the Flores-Lembata languages in eastern Indonesia. Doctoral dissertation, Leiden University. hdl.handle.net/1887/80399

Geurtjens, Hendrik. 1921. Woordenlijst der keieesche taal, volume 63 of *Verhandelingen van het Koninklijk Bataviaasch Genootschap van Kunsten en Wetenschappen.* Weltevreden: Albrecht.

Grimes, Charles E. 1991. The Buru language of eastern Indonesia. Doctoral dissertation, The Australian National University. openresearch-repository.anu.edu.au/handle/1885/10925

Grimes, Charles E. 2010. Hawu and Dhao in eastern indonesia: Revisiting their relationship. In *East Nusantara: Typological and areal analysis*, ed. Michael Ewing and Marian Klamer, 251–280. Canberra: Pacific Linguistics.

Grimes, Charles E., Bernadus Lado, Thomas Ly, and Simon Tari. 2008. *Kamus Lii Hawu (Sabu) online dictionary*. Kupang: UBB-GMIT. ubb.or.id/download/kamus-lii-hawu-lexpro/

Grimes, Charles E., Ayub Ranoh, and Helena Aplugi. 2008. *Kamus Lii Dhao (Ndao) online dictionary.* Kupang: UBB-GMIT. ubb.or.id/download/kamus-lii-dhao-lexpro/

Grimes, Charles E., Evelyn Cheng, Enna Adelaide Hayer-Pah, Jonathan Pandie, Neng Mulosing, and Johnny M. Banamtuan. 2014a. Tii dictionary. Unpublished Toolbox file.

Grimes, Charles E., Carlos Marçal, and Paolino Fereira. 2014b. *Introductory dictionary of Mambae (Same): Mambae–English, English–Mambae, Mambae–Indonesia–Tetun Dili, Indonesia–Mambae, Tetun Dili–Mambae*. Darwin: Australian Society for Indigenous Languages.

Grimes, Charles E., and Barbara Dix Grimes. 2020. *Encyclopedic dictionary of the Buru language: With English-Buru finderlist.* (3rd ed.). Kupang: Unit Bahasa & Budaya (UBB). ubb.or.id/download/kamus-buru-inggris/

Grimes, Charles E., Yanri Suana, Yedida Ora, and Kirsten Culhane, compilers. 2021. *Introductory dictionary of Amfo'an: With English-Amfo'an finderlist*. Kupang: Unit Bahasa & Budaya (UBB). ubb.or.id/bahasa/kamus/

Hammarström, Harald, Robert Forkel, Martin Haspelmath, and Sebastian Bank. 2020. Glottolog 4.3. Jena: Max Planck Institute for the Science of Human History. URL glottolog.org

Hendriks, H. 1897. *Het Burusch van Masarete*. The Hague: Martinus Nijhoff.

Heston, Tyler. 2015. The segmental and suprasegmental phonology of Fataluku. Doctoral dissertation, University of Hawai'i at Mānoa.

Heston, Tyler M. 2017. A first reconstruction of vowels in Proto-Timor-Alor-Pantar. *Oceanic Linguistics* 56:73–89. doi.org/10.1353/ol.2017.0003

Heyne, K. 1950. *De nuttige planten van Indonesië*. (3rd ed.).'s-Gravenhage and Bandung: NV Uitgeverij W van Hoeve. 2 volumes.

Himmelmann, Nikolaus P. 2001. *Sourcebook on Tomini-Tolitoli languages: General information and wordlists*. Canberra: Pacific Linguistics.

Himmelmann, Nikolaus P., John Bowden, Maurício C. A. Belo, Alex Hajek, John Tilman, and Alex Freitas. 2006. Waima'a lexical database. In DoBeS Waima'a documentation, ed. Belo Maurício C. A., John Bowden, John Hajek, Nikolaus P. Himmelmann, and Alexandre V. Tilman. DoBeS Archive MPI Nijmegen.

Hinton, Bryan. 1991. Aspects of Tugun phonology and syntax. Master's Thesis, University of Texas at Arlington.

Hinton, Bryan. 2000. The languages of Wetar: recent survey results and word lists, with notes on Tugun grammar. In *Spices from the east: Papers in languages of eastern Indonesia*, ed. Charles E. Grimes, 105–117. Canberra: Pacific Linguistics.

Hoogervorst, Tom. 2016. Problematic protoforms: Some 'hidden' Indic loans in Western Malayo-Polynesian languages. *Oceanic Linguistics* 55:561–587. doi.org/10.1353/ol.2016.0025

Hoola van Nooten, Berthe, and P. Depannemaeker. 1880. *Fleurs fruits et feuillages choisis de l'île de Java*. Bruxelles: C. Muquardt. doi.org/10.5962/bhl.title.466

Ismail, Mansyur, Muhidin Azis, M. Saleh Yakub, M. Taufik H., and M. Kasim Usman. 1985. *Kamus Bima-Indonesia*. Jakarta: Pusat Pembinaan dan Pengembangan Bahasa.

Jacob, June, and Charles Grimes. 2011. Aspect and directionality in Kupang Malay serial verb constructions: Calquing on the grammars of substrate languages. In *Creoles, their substrates, and language typology*, ed. Claire Lefebvre, 337–366. Amsterdam and Philadelphia: John Benjamins. doi.org/10.1075/tsl.95.20jac

Jonker, J. C. G. 1893. *Bimaneesch–Hollandsch woordenboek*. Batavia: Landsdrukkerij.

Jonker, J. C. G. 1906. Over de eind-medeklinkers in het Rottineesch en Timoreesch. *Bijdragen tot de Taal-, Land- en Volkenkunde van Nederlandsch-Indië* 59:263–343. doi.org/10.1163/22134379-90001964

Jonker, J. C. G. 1908. *Rottineesch–Hollandsch woordenboek*. Leiden: E. J. Brill.

Jonker, J. C. G. 1913. Bijdragen tot de kennis der Rottineesche tongvallen. *Bijdragen tot de Taal-, Land- en Volkenkunde van Nederlandsch-Indië* 68:521–622. doi.org/10.1163/22134379-90001774

Jonker, J. C. G. 1915. *Rottineesche spraakkunst*. Leiden: E. J. Brill.

Kähler, Hans. 1959. *Vergleichendes Wörterverzeichnis der Sichule-Sprache auf der Insel Simalur an der Westkuste von Sumatra*. Berlin: Dietrich Reimer Verlag.

Keraf, Gregor. 1978. Morfologi dialek Lamalera. Doctoral dissertation, Universitas Indonesia.

Kersten, J. 1984. *Bahasa Bali*. Ende: Nusa Indah.

Klamer, Marian. 2002. Timor-Leste survey word lists. In *Lexirumah 3.0.0*, ed. Gereon A. Kaiping, Owen Edwards, and Marian Klamer. Leiden: Leiden University Centre for Linguistics. lexirumah.model-ling.eu/lexirumah/

Klamer, Marian. 2011. *A short grammar of Alorese (Austronesian)*. Munich: Lincom Europa.

Klamer, Marian. 2015a. Field notes on Hewa. In *Lexirumah 3.0.0*, ed. Gereon A. Kaiping, Owen Edwards, and Marian Klamer. Leiden: Leiden University Centre for Linguistics. lexirumah.model-ling.eu/lexirumah/

Klamer, Marian. 2015b. Field notes on Lamaholot-Lewoingu. In *Lexirumah 3.0.0*, ed. Gereon A. Kaiping, Owen Edwards, and Marian Klamer. Leiden: Leiden University Centre for Linguistics. lexirumah.model-ling.eu/lexirumah/

Kratochvíl, František. 2007. A grammar of Abui: A Papuan language of Alor. Doctoral dissertation, University of Leiden.

Lambrecht, Knud. 1994. *Information structure and sentence form: Topic, focus, and the mental representations of discourse referents*. Cambridge: Cambridge University Press. doi.org/10.1017/cbo9780511620607

Lekede'e Study Group. 2006. *Disionáriu lia Tokodede - Tetun - Ingles*. Likisá: Timor Loro Sa'e – Nippon Culture Center.

Lynch, John. 2001. Too much to swallow: On terms meaning 'swallow' in Oceanic languages. *Oceanic Linguistics* 40:336–341. doi.org/10.2307/3623445

Lynch, John, Malcolm Ross, and Terry Crowley. 2002. Proto Oceanic. In *The Oceanic languages*, ed. John Lynch, Malcolm Ross, and Terry Crowley, 54–91. Richmond: Curzon. doi.org/10.4324/9780203820384

Mahdi, Waruno. 1994. Some Austronesian maverick protoforms with culture historical implications II. *Oceanic Linguistics* 30:431–490. doi.org/10.2307/3623137

Manafe, D. P. 1889. Akan bahasa Rotti. *Bijdragen tot de Taal-, Land- en Volkenkunde van Nederlandsch-Indië* 28:633–648. doi.org/10.1163/22134379-90000273

Masse, H. Abd. 2013. *Kamus bahasa Bugis-Indonesia.* Indonesia: CV. Gemilang Utama.

Mathes, B. F. 1859. *Makassaarsch-hollandsch woordenboek.* Amsterdam: Het Nederlandsch Bijbelgenootschap te Amsterdam.

Mathes, B. F. 1874. *Boegineesch-Hollandsch woordenboek.* 's-Gravenhage: M. Nijhoff.

McDonnell, Bradley. 2009. A preliminary description of Ende phonology. *Journal of the Southeast Asian Linguistics Society* 2:195–226.

Mead, David. 1998. Proto-Bungku-Tolaki: Reconstruction of its phonology and aspects of its morphosyntax. Doctoral dissertation, Rice University.

Meijer Drees, Ebertus. 1950. *Daftar nama2 pohon dan perdu, Pulau Timor = lijst van boom- en struiknamen van het eiland Timor = list of tree and shrub names from Timor.* Number 1 in Serie vegetatie-onderzoek = Seri pemeriksaan tumbuh-tumbuhan = Ecological series. Bogor: Balai Penjelidikan Kehutanan.

Middelkoop, Pieter. 1950. Proeve van een Timorese grammatica. *Bijdragen tot de Taal-, Land- en Volkenkunde* 106:375–517. doi.org/10.1163/22134379-90002474

Middelkoop, Pieter. 1972. Nederlands-Timorees woordenboek. MS.

Mills, Roger. 1991. Tanimbar-Kei: An eastern Indonesian subgroup. In *Currents in Pacific linguistics: Papers on Austronesian languages and ethnolinguistics in honour of George W. Grace*, ed. Robert Blust, 241–263. Canberra: Pacific Linguistics. C-117.

Mills, Roger. 2010. Three common misconceptions about Proto-Lettic. In *Studia anthropologica: сборник статей в честь М.А. Членова*, ed. Svetlana F. Chlenova and Artem Fedorchuk, 284–296. Moscow–Jerusalem: Gesharim.

Moro, Francesca. 2016. Field notes on Alorese-Pandai. In *Lexirumah 3.0.0*, ed. Gereon A. Kaiping, Owen Edwards, and Marian Klamer. Leiden: Leiden University Centre for Linguistics. lexirumah.model-ling.eu/lexirumah/

Morris, Cliff. 1984. *Tetun–English dictionary.* Canberra: Pacific Linguistics.

Nako, Yustin Marince, Paulus Nako, Misriani Balle, and Johnny M. Banamtuan. 2014. Rikou dictionary. Unpublished Toolbox file.

Nishiyama, Kunio, and Herman Kelen. 2007. A grammar of Lamaholot, Eastern Indonesia: The morphology and syntax of the Lewoingu dialect. Munich: Lincom.

Onvlee, Louis. 1984. *Kamberaas (Oost-Soembaas)–Nederlands woordenboek.* Dordrecht: Foris. In collaboration with OE. H. Kapita and P. J. Luijendijk.

Osmond, Meredith. 1998. Horticultural practices. In *The lexicon of Proto Oceanic: The culture and environment of ancestral Oceanic society*, ed. Malcolm Ross, Andrew Pawley, and Meredith Osmond, volume 1: Material culture, 115–142. Canberra: Pacific Linguistics.

Osmond, Meredith. 2011a. Fish. In *The lexicon of Proto Oceanic: The culture and environment of ancestral Oceanic society*, ed. Malcolm Ross, Andrew Pawley, and Meredith Osmond, volume 4: Animals, 25–136. Canberra: Pacific Linguistics.

Osmond, Meredith. 2011b. Insects and other creepy-crawlies. In *The lexicon of Proto Oceanic: The culture and environment of ancestral Oceanic society*, ed. Malcolm Ross, Andrew Pawley, and Meredith Osmond, volume 4: Animals, 371–420. Canberra: Pacific Linguistics.

Osmond, Meredith, Andrew Pawley, and Malcolm Ross. 2003. The landscape. In *The lexicon of Proto Oceanic: The culture and environment of ancestral Oceanic society*, ed. Malcolm Ross, Andrew Pawley, and Meredith Osmond, volume 2: The physical environment, 35–89. Canberra: Pacific Linguistics.

Osmond, Meredith, and Malcolm Ross. 2016a. The human body. In *The lexicon of Proto Oceanic: The culture and environment of ancestral Oceanic society*, ed. Malcolm Ross, Andrew Pawley, and Meredith Osmond, volume 5: People: body and mind, 75–208. Canberra: Asia-Pacific Linguistics.

Osmond, Meredith, and Malcolm Ross. 2016b. People: gender, age cohorts and marital status. In *The lexicon of Proto Oceanic: the culture and environment of ancestral Oceanic society*, ed. Malcolm Ross, Andrew Pawley, and Meredith Osmond, volume 5: People: body and mind, 37–74. Canberra: Asia-Pacific Linguistics.

Pareira, M. Mandalangi, and E. Douglas Lewis. 1998. *Kamus sara Sikka Bahasa Indonesia*. Ende, Indonesia: Nusa Indah.

Pawley, Andrew. 2011. Aquatic invertebrates. In *The lexicon of Proto Oceanic: the culture and environment of ancestral Oceanic society*, ed. Malcolm Ross, Andrew Pawley, and Meredith Osmond, volume 4: Animals, 161–216. Canberra: Pacific Linguistics.

Penn, David Trelly. 2006. Introducing Dadu'a: Uma língua de Timor-Leste. Honours Thesis, University of New England.

Rinnooy, N. 1886. Maleisch-Kissersch woordenlijst. *Tijdschrift voor Indische Taal-, Land- en Volkenkunde* 31:149–213.

Ross, Malcolm. 2003. Properties of inanimate objects. In *The lexicon of Proto Oceanic: The culture and environment of ancestral Oceanic society*, ed. Malcolm Ross, Andrew Pawley, and Meredith Osmond, volume 2: The physical environment, 35–89. Canberra: Pacific Linguistics.

Ross, Malcolm, and Meredith Osmond. 2016a. Bodily conditions and activities. In *The lexicon of Proto Oceanic: The culture and environment of ancestral Oceanic society*, ed. Malcolm Ross, Andrew Pawley, and Meredith Osmond, volume 5 People: body and mind, 209–333. Canberra: Asia-Pacific Linguistics.

Ross, Malcolm, and Meredith Osmond. 2016b. Cognition. In *The lexicon of Proto Oceanic: The culture and environment of ancestral Oceanic society*, ed. Malcolm Ross, Andrew Pawley, and Meredith Osmond, volume 5 People: body and mind, 535–566. Canberra: Asia-Pacific Linguistics.

Saad, George. 2015. Takalelang Abui word list. In *Lexirumah 3.0.0*, ed. Gereon A. Kaiping, Owen Edwards, and Marian Klamer. Leiden: Leiden University Centre for Linguistics. lexirumah.model-ling.eu/lexirumah/

Samely, Ursula. 1991. *Kedang (Eastern Indonesia), some aspects of its grammar*. Hamburg: Helmut Buske.

Schapper, Antoinette. 2009. Bunaq: A Papuan language of central Timor. Doctoral dissertation, The Australian National University.

Schapper, Antoinette. 2010. Field notes and dictionary on Kamang-Atoitaa. In *Lexirumah 3.0.0*, ed. Gereon A. Kaiping, Owen Edwards, and Marian Klamer. Leiden: Leiden University Centre for Linguistics. lexirumah.model-ling.eu/lexirumah/

Schapper, Antoinette. 2011. Phalanger facts: Notes on Blust's marsupial reconstructions. *Oceanic Linguistics* 50:258–272. doi.org/10.1353/ol.2011.0004

Schapper, Antoinette. 2017. Stress and gemination in Alor-Pantar languages: Revising Heston (2016). *Oceanic Linguistics* 56:257–266. doi.org/10.1353/ol.2017.0011

Schapper, Antoinette. 2020. Historical and linguistic perspectives on fortified settlements in southeastern Wallacea: Far eastern Timor in the context of southern Maluku. In *Forts and fortification in Wallacea: Archaeological and ethnohistoric investigations*, ed. Sue O'Connor and Andrew McWilliam, 221–246. Canberra: ANU Press. doi.org/10.22459/ta53.2020.10

Schapper, Antoinette, and Emilie Wellfelt. 2018. Reconstructing contact between Alor and Timor: Evidence from language and beyond. *NUSA: Linguistic studies of languages in and around Indonesia* 64:95–116.

Schulte Nordholt, H. G. 1971. *The political system of the Atoni of Timor*. The Hague: Martinus Nijhoff. Translation of Het Politieke Systeem van de Atoni van Timor (1966).

Smits, Leo, and C. L. Voorhoeve. 1992. *The J.C. Anceaux collection of wordlists of Irian Jaya languages A: Austronesian languages (part I)*. Leiden/Jakarta: DSALCUL/IRIS.

Steven, Lee Anthony. 1991. The phonology of Roma, an Austronesian language of eastern Indonesia. Master's Thesis, University of Texas at Arlington.

Stresemann, Erwin. 1927. Die Lauterscheinungen in den ambonischen Sprachen, volume 10 of *Zeitschrift für Eingeborenen-Sprachen*. Berlin: Reimer.

Taber, Mark. 1993. Toward a better understanding of the indigenous languages of southwestern Maluku. *Oceanic Linguistics* 32:389–441. doi.org/10.2307/3623199

Tamelan, Thersia. 2017. Dela dictionary. Unpublished Toolbox file.

Tamelan, Thersia. 2021. A grammar of Dela: An Austronesian language of Rote, eastern Indonesia. Doctoral dissertation, The Australian National University. hdl.handle.net/1885/250953

Therik, Tom. 2004. *Wehali: The female land. Traditions of a Timorese ritual centre.* Canberra: Pandanus Books.

Tregear, Edwards. 1891. *The Maori-Polynesian comparative dictionary.* Wellington: Lyon and Blair.

Unit Bahasa and Budaya. 2016. Manetualain Dede'a-kokolan: Hehelu-bartaa Beuk no Tutui Makasososak. Kupang: Unit Bahasa and Budaya in cooperation with Wycliffe Bible Translators.

van den Berg, René. 1991. Muna historical phonology. *NUSA: Linguistic studies of languages in and around Indonesia* 33:1–28.

van Ekris, A. 1864. Woordenlijst van eenige dialecten der landtaal op de Ambonsche eilanden. *Mededeelingen vanwege het Nederlandsch Zendelinggenootschap* 8:61–108, 301–336.

van Ekris, A. 1865. Woordenlijst van eenige dialecten der landtaal op de Ambonsche eilanden. *Mededeelingen vanwege het Nederlandsch Zendelinggenootschap* 9:109–136.

van Engelenhoven, Aone. 2004. *Leti, a language of Southwest Maluku.* Leiden: KITLV Press.

van Hoëvell, G. W. W. C. 1877. Iets over de vijf voornaamste dialekten der Ambonsche landtaal (Bahasa Tanah). *Bijdragen tot de Taal-, Land- en Volkenkunde van Nederlandsch-Indië* 25:1–136. doi.org/10.1163/22134379-90000614

van Klinken, Catharina. 1995. Tetun Fehan dictionary. Unpublished Toolbox file.

van Klinken, Catharina L. 1999. *A grammar of the Fehan dialect of Tetun: An Austronesian language of West Timor.* Canberra: Pacific Linguistics.

Verheijen, Jilis A. J. 1967. Kamus Manggarai: I Manggarai-Indonesia. 's-Gravenhage: Martinus Nijhoff.

Verheijen, Jilis A. J. 1982. Komodo: het eiland, het volk en de taal. The Hague: Martinus Nijhoff. doi.org/10.1163/9789004287273

Verheijen, Jilis A. J. 1984. *Plant names in Austronesian linguistics.* NUSA: Linguistic Studies of Indonesian and Other Languages of Indonesia.

Visser, Eline. 2019. Field notes on Uruangnirin. In *Lexirumah 3.0.0*, ed. Gereon A. Kaiping, Owen Edwards, and Marian Klamer. Leiden: Leiden University Centre for Linguistics. lexirumah.model-ling.eu/lexirumah/

Williams-van Klinken, Catharina, and Rob Williams. 2015. Mapping the mother tongue in Timor-Leste: Who spoke what where in 2010?. Dili: Dili Institute of Technology. www.tetundit.tl/Publications/Timor-Leste languages 2010.pdf

Wolff, John U. 2010. Proto-Austronesian phonology with glossary. Ithaca, NY: Cornell Southeast Asia Program Publications.

Zacharias, Albert, Adika Getroida Balukh, Misriani Balle, and Johnny M. Banamtuan. 2014. Lole dictionary. Unpublished Toolbox file.

Zorc, R. David. 1995. A glossary of Austronesian reconstructions. In *Comparative Austronesian dictionary: An introduction to Austronesian studies*, ed. Darrell T. Tryon, Part 1, 1106–1197. New York: de Gruyter. doi.org/10.1515/9783110884012.2.1105

www.ingramcontent.com/pod-product-compliance
Lightning Source LLC
Chambersburg PA
CBHW040740300426
44111CB00027B/2992

* 9 7 8 1 7 6 0 4 6 4 5 6 1 *